FOURTH EDITION

4

Series Director: **Diane Larsen-Freeman**

Grammar Dimensions

Form • Meaning • Use

Lesson Planner

Janet Gokay

THOMSON

HEINLE

Australia • Canada • Mexico • Singapore • Spain • United Kingdom • United States

Series Director: Diane Larsen-Freeman
Grammar Dimensions 4: Form, Meaning, and Use
Janet Gokay

Editorial Director: *Joe Dougherty*
Publisher: *Sherrise Roehr*
Consulting Editor: *James W. Brown*
Acquisitions Editor: *Tom Jefferies*
VP, Director of Content Development: *Anita Raducanu*
Senior Development Editor: *Michael Ryall*
Director of Product Marketing: *Amy Mabley*
Executive Marketing Manager: *Jim McDonough*
Senior Field Marketing Manager: *Donna Lee Kennedy*
Product Marketing Manager: *Katie Kelley*

Senior Production Editor: *Maryellen Eschmann-Killeen*
Senior Print Buyer: *Mary Beth Hennebury*
Development Editor: *Sarah Barnicle*
Production Project Manager: *Chrystie Hopkins*
Production Services: *Pre-Press PMG*
Interior Designer: *Lori Stuart*
Cover Designer: *Studio Montage*
Printer: *R.R. Donnelley*

Cover Image: ©Ben Hall/The Image Bank/Getty

Printed in the United States of America.
1 2 3 4 5 6 7 8 9 10 — 11 10 09 08 07

For more information contact Heinle, 25 Thomson Place, Boston, Massachusetts 02210 USA, or you can visit our Internet site at http://elt.heinle.com

Credits appear on pages C1–C4, which constitutes a continuation of the copyright page.

For permission to use material from this text or product, submit a request online at http://www.thomsonrights.com

Any additional questions about permissions can be submitted by email to thomsonrights@thomson.com

ISBN 10: 1-4240-0359-8
ISBN 13: 978-1-4240-0359-4

CONTENTS

Unit 4   Passive Verbs   60

Unit 5   Article Usage   82

Unit 6   Reference Words and Phrases   108

Unit 7   Relative Clauses Modifying Subjects   134

Opening Task   134

Unit 8   Relative Clauses Modifying Objects   148

Opening Task   148

Unit 9   Nonrestrictive Relative Clauses   164

Opening Task   164

Unit 14   Discourse Organizers   260

Unit 15   Conditionals
If, Only If, Unless, Even Though, Even If   280

Appendices   A-1

Answer Key   (Puzzles and Problems Only)   A-16

Exercises   (Second Parts)   A-17

Credits   C-1

Index   I-1

Workbook Answer Key   W-1

Audio Script   S-1

A Word from Diane Larsen-Freeman, Series Editor

Before ***Grammar Dimensions*** was published, teachers would ask me, "What is the role of grammar in a communicative approach?" These teachers recognized the importance of teaching grammar, but they associated grammar with form and communication with meaning, and thus could not see how the two easily fit together. ***Grammar Dimensions*** was created to help teachers and students appreciate the fact that grammar is not just about form. While grammar does indeed involve form, in order to communicate, language users also need to know the meaning of the forms and when to use them appropriately. In fact, it is sometimes not the form, but the *meaning* or *appropriate use* of a grammatical structure that represents the greatest long-term learning challenge for students. For instance, learning when it is appropriate to use the present perfect tense instead of the past tense, or being able to use two-word or phrasal verbs meaningfully, represent formidable challenges for English language learners.

The three dimensions of *form*, *meaning*, and *use* can be depicted in a pie chart with their interrelationship illustrated by the three arrows.

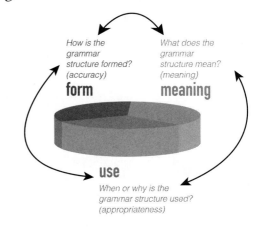

Helping students learn to use grammatical structures accurately, meaningfully, and appropriately is the fundamental goal of ***Grammar Dimensions.*** It is consistent with the goal of helping students to communicate meaningfully in English, and one that recognizes the undeniable interdependence of grammar and communication.

Enjoy the Fourth Edition of ***Grammar Dimensions***!

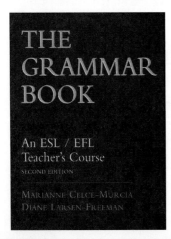

To learn more about form, meaning, and use, read ***The Grammar Book: An ESL/EFL Teacher's Course,*** Second Edition, by Marianne Celce-Murcia and Diane Larsen-Freeman. ISBN: 0-8384-4725-2.

To learn about the theory that has informed ***Grammar Dimensions,*** consult ***Teaching Language: From Grammar to Grammaring*** by Diane Larsen-Freeman. ISBN: 0-8384-6675-3.

Welcome to *Grammar Dimensions*, Fourth Edition!

The **clearest**, most **comprehensive** and **communicative** grammar series available! The fourth edition of *Grammar Dimensions* is more **user-friendly** and makes teaching grammar more **effective** than ever.

GRAMMAR DIMENSIONS IS COMPREHENSIVE AND CLEAR.

Grammar Dimensions systematically addresses the three dimensions of language—form, meaning, and use—through clear and comprehensive grammar explanations and extensive practice exercises. Each unit methodically focuses on each student's dimension and then integrates what they have learned in end-of-unit activities. In addition, grammatical structures are recycled throughout the series allowing students to practice and build upon their existing knowledge.

GRAMMAR DIMENSIONS IS COMMUNICATIVE.

Grammar Dimensions includes a large variety of lively, communicative, and personalized activities throughout each unit, eliciting self-expression and personalized practice. Interactive activities at the start of each unit serve as diagnostic tools directing student learning towards the most challenging dimensions of language structure. Integrated activities at the end of each unit include reading, writing, listening, and speaking activities allowing students to practice grammar and communication in tandem. New research activities encourage students to use authentic Internet resources and to reflect on their own learning.

GRAMMAR DIMENSIONS IS USER-FRIENDLY AND FLEXIBLE.

Grammar Dimensions has been designed to be flexible. Instructors can use the units in order or as set by their curriculum. Exercises can be used in order or as needed by the students. In addition, a tight integration between the Student Book, the Workbook, and the Lesson Planner makes teaching easier and makes the series more user-friendly.

GRAMMAR DIMENSIONS IS EFFECTIVE.

Students who learn the form, meaning, and use of each grammar structure will be able to communicate more accurately, meaningfully, and appropriately.

New to the Fourth Edition

- **NEW and revised grammar explanations** and examples help students and teachers easily understand and comprehend each language structure.

- **NEW and revised grammar charts and exercises** provide a wealth of opportunities for students to practice and master their new language.

- **NEW thematically and grammatically related Internet and *InfoTrac®College Edition*** activities in every unit of books 2, 3, and 4 develop student research using current technologies.

- **NEW Reflection activities** encourage students to create personal language goals and to develop learning strategies.

- **NEW design, art, and photos** make each activity and exercise more engaging.

- **NEW Lesson Planners** assist both beginning and experienced teachers in giving their students the practice and skills they need to communicate accurately, meaningfully, and appropriately. All activities and exercises in the Lesson Planner are organized into step-by-step lessons so that no instructor feels overwhelmed.

SEQUENCING OF *GRAMMAR DIMENSIONS*

In *Grammar Dimensions* students progress from the sentence level to the discourse level, and learn to communicate appropriately at all levels.

Grammar Dimensions Book 1	*Grammar Dimensions* Book 2	*Grammar Dimensions* Book 3	*Grammar Dimensions* Book 4

Sentence level   Discourse level

	Book 1	**Book 2**	**Book 3**	**Book 4**
Level	High-beginning	Intermediate	High-Intermediate	Advanced
Grammar level	Sentence and sub-sentence level	Sentence and sub-sentence level	Discourse level	Discourse level
Primary language and communication focus	Semantic notions such as *time* and *place*	Social functions, such as *making requests* and *seeking* permission	Cohesion and coherence at the discourse level	Academic and technical discourse
Major skill focus	Listening and speaking	Listening and speaking	Reading and writing	Reading and writing

Guided Tour of *Grammar Dimensions* 4

Unit goals **provide a roadmap** for the grammar points students will work on.

"Opening Task" can be used as a **diagnostic warm-up** exercise to explore students' knowledge of each structure.

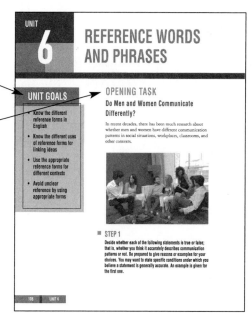

"**Focus**" sections present the **form, meaning, and/or use** of a particular structure helping students develop the skill of "**grammaring**"—the ability to use structures accurately, meaningfully, and appropriately.

Clear grammar charts present rules and explanation preceded by examples, so teachers can have students work inductively to try to discover the rule on their own.

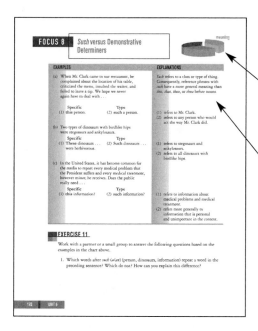

Purposeful exercises provide a wealth of opportunity for students to practice and personalize the grammar.

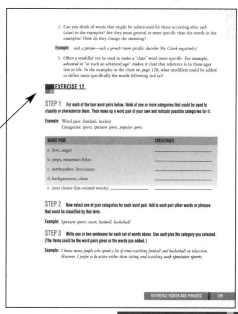

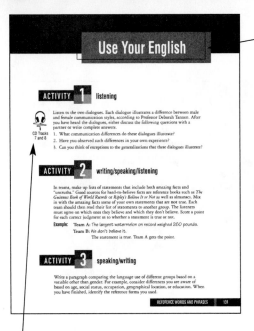

"Use Your English" section offers communicative activities that **integrate grammar with reading, writing, listening, and speaking skills.** Communicative activities consolidate grammar instruction with enjoyable and meaningful tasks.

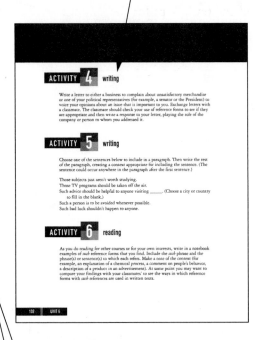

Engaging listening activities on audio cassette and audio CD further reinforce the target structure.

Research activity using *InfoTrac® College Edition* and the Internet encourages students to read articles on carefully selected topics and use this information to reflect on a theme or on information studied in each unit. *InfoTrac® College Edition*, an Online Research and Learning Center, appears in Grammar Dimensions 2, 3, and 4 and offers over 20 million full-text articles from nearly 6,000 scholarly and popular periodicals. Articles cover a broad spectrum of disciplines and topics—ideal for every type of researcher. Instructors and students can gain access to the online database 24/7 on any computer with Internet access.

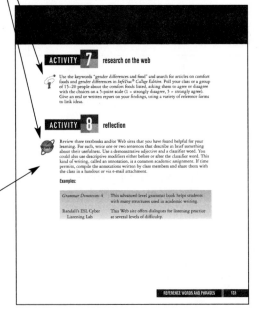

Reflection activities help students understand their learning style and create learning strategies.

Supplements

These additional components help teachers teach and students learn to use English grammar structures accurately.

The Lesson Planner

The lesson planner facilitates teaching by providing detailed lesson plans and examples, answer keys to the Student Book and Workbook, references to all of the components, and the tapescript for the audiocassette activities. The Lesson Planner minimizes teacher preparation time by providing:

- Summary of main grammar points for the teacher
- Information for the teacher on typical student errors
- Step-by-step guidelines for every focus box, exercise, and activity
- Suggested correlations between exercises and activities in the "Use Your English" pages
- Suggested timing for each exercise and each lesson
- Lead-in suggestions and examples for focus boxes
- Suggestions for expansion work follow most exercises
- Balance of cognitive and communicative activities
- Explanation for the teacher of the purpose of each activity, in order to differentiate cognitive from communicative emphasis
- Occasional methodology notes to anticipate possible procedural problems.

Assessment CD-ROM with *ExamView* Test Generator

The Assessment CD-ROM allows instructors to **create customized quizzes and tests** quickly and easily from a test bank of questions. Monitoring student understanding and progress has never been easier! The answer key appears with instructor copies of each quiz or test created.

 ## Audio Program

Audio cassettes and CDs **provide listening activities for** each unit so students can practice listening to **grammar structures.**

 ## Workbook

Workbooks **provide additional exercises** for each grammar point presented in the student text. They also offer editing practice and question types found on many language exams.

 ## Web site

Features additional grammar practice activities: elt.thomson.com/grammardimensions.

Empirical and Experiential Support for the *Grammar Dimensions* Approach

Opening Task Activities

The approach to teaching grammar used in the *Grammar Dimensions* series is well-grounded empirically and experientially. The Opening Task in each unit situates the learning challenge and allows students to participate in and learn from activity right from the beginning (Greeno 2006). In addition, students don't enter the classroom as empty vessels, waiting to be filled (Sawyer 2006). By observing how students perform on the Opening Task, teachers can analyze for themselves what students know and are able to do and what they don't know or are not able to do. Teachers can thus select from each unit what is necessary for students to build on to what they already bring with them.

Consciousness-Raising Exercises and Focus Boxes

Many of the exercises in *Grammar Dimensions* are of the consciousness-raising sort, where students are invited to make observations about some aspect of the target structure. This type of activity promotes students' noticing (Schmidt 1990), an important step in acquiring the grammar structure. The Focus Boxes further encourage this noticing, this time very explicitly. Explicit formulations of the sort found in the Focus Boxes can lead to implicit acquisition with practice (DeKeyser 1998). Moreover, certain learners (those with analytic learning styles) benefit greatly from explicit treatment of grammar structures (Larsen-Freeman and Long 1991).

Productive Practice and Communicative Activities

However, noticing by itself is insufficient. In order to be able to use the grammar structure, students need productive practice (Gatbonton and Segalowitz 1988; Larsen-Freeman 2003). Therefore, many of the exercises in **Grammar Dimensions** are of the output practice sort. Furthermore, each unit ends with communicative activities, where attention to the grammar is once again implicit, but where students can use the grammar structure in "psychologically authentic" or meaningful ways. Psychological authenticity is very important in order for students to be able to transfer what they know to new situations so that they can use it for their own purposes (Blaxton 1989) and so they are not left to contend with the "inert knowledge problem," (Whitehead 1929) where they know about the grammar, but can't use it.

The Three Dimensions of Grammar: Form, Meaning, and Use

Finally, applied linguistics research (Celce-Murcia and Larsen-Freeman 1999) supports the fundamental premise underlying **Grammar Dimensions**: that knowing a grammar structure means being able to use it accurately, meaningfully, and appropriately. Form focus or meaning focus by itself is insufficient (Larsen-Freeman 2001); all three dimensions—form, meaning, and use—need to be learned.

References

Blaxton, T. (1989). Investigating dissociations among memory measures: Support for a transfer-appropriate processing framework. *Journal of Experimental Psychology: Learning, Memory, and Cognition 15 (4): 657–668.*

Celce-Murcia, M. and D. Larsen-Freeman. (1999). *The grammar book: An ESL/EFL teacher's course.* Second Edition. Boston: Heinle & Heinle.

De Keyser, R. (1998). Beyond focus on form: Cognitive perspectives on learning and practicing second language grammar. In C. Doughty and J. Williams (eds.), *Focus on Classroom Second Language Acquisition.* Cambridge: Cambridge University Press, 42–63.

Gatbonton, E. and N. Segalowitz. (1988). Creative automatization: Principles for promoting fluency within a communicative framework. *TESOL Quarterly 22 (3):* 473–492.

Greeno, J. (2006). Learning in activity. In R. K. Sawyer (ed.), *The Cambridge handbook of learning sciences.* Cambridge: Cambridge University Press, 79–96.

Larsen-Freeman, D. (2001). Teaching grammar. In M. Celce-Murcia (ed.), *Teaching English as a Second or Foreign Language.* Third edition. Boston: Heinle & Heinle, 251–266.

Larsen-Freeman, D. (2003). *Teaching language: From grammar to grammaring.* Boston: Heinle & Heinle.

Larsen-Freeman, D. and M. Long. (1991). *An introduction to second language acquisition research.* London: Longman.

Sawyer, R. K. (2006). Introduction: The new science of learning. In R. K. Sawyer (ed.), *The Cambridge handbook of learning sciences.* Cambridge: Cambridge University Press, 1–16.

Schmidt, R. (1990). The role of consciousness in second language learning. *Applied Linguistics 11 (2), 129–158.*

Whitehead, A. N. 1929. *The aims of education.* New York: MacMillan.

Acknowledgments from the Series Director

This fourth edition would not have come about if it had not been for the enthusiastic response of teachers and students using all the previous editions. I am very grateful for the reception *Grammar Dimensions* has been given.

I am also grateful for all the authors' efforts. To be a teacher, and at the same time a writer, is a difficult balance to achieve . . . so is being an innovative creator of materials, and yet, a team player. They have met these challenges exceedingly well in my opinion. Then, too, the Thomson Heinle team has been impressive. I am grateful for the leadership exercised by Jim Brown, Sherrise Roehr, and Tom Jefferies. I also appreciate all the support from Anita Raducanu, Amy Mabley, Sarah Barnicle, Laura Needham, Chrystie Hopkins, Mary Beth Hennebury, and Crystal Parenteau of Pre-PressPMG. Deserving special mention are Amy Lawler and Yeny Kim, who never lost the vision while they attended to the detail with good humor and professionalism.

I have also benefited from the counsel of Marianne Celce-Murcia, consultant for the first edition of this project, and my friend. Finally, I wish to thank my family members, Elliott, Brent, and Gavin, for not once asking the (negative yes-no) question that must have occurred to them countless times: "Haven't you finished yet?" As we all have discovered, this project has a life of its own and is never really finished! And, for this, I am exceedingly grateful. Happy Grammaring all!

A Special Thanks

The series director, authors, and publisher would like to thank the following reviewers whose experienced observations and thoughtful suggestions have assisted us in creating and revising *Grammar Dimensions*.

Michelle Alvarez
University of Miami
Coral Gables, Florida

Edina Pingleton Bagley
Nassau Community College
Garden City, New York

Jane Berger
Solano Community College,
California

Mary Bottega
San Jose State University

Mary Brooks
Eastern Washington University

Christina Broucqsault
*California State Polytechnic
  University*

José Carmona
Hudson Community College

Susan Carnell
University of Texas at Arlington

Susana Christie
San Diego State University

Diana Christopher
Georgetown University

Gwendolyn Cooper
Rutgers University

Julia Correia
Henderson State University
Arkadelphia, Arkansas

Sue Cozzarelli
EF International, San Diego

Catherine Crystal
Laney College, California

Kevin Ccross
University of San Francisco

Julie Damron
*Interlink at Valparaiso
  University, Indiana*

Glen Deckert
Eastern Michigan University

Eric Dwyer
University of Texas at Austin

Nikki Ellman
Laney College
Oakland, California

Ann Eubank
Jefferson Community College

Alice Fine
UCLA Extension

Alicia Going
*The English Language Study
  Center, Oregon*

Molly Gould
University of Delaware

Maren M. Hargis
San Diego Mesa College

Penny Harrold
Universidad de Monterrey
Monterrey, Mexico

Robin Hendrickson
Riverside City College
Riverside, California

Mary Herbert
*University of California, Davis
  Extension*

Jane Hilbert
*ELS Language Center,
Florida International
University*

Eli Hinkel
Xavier University

Kathy Hitchcox
*International English
Institute, Fresno*

Abeer Hubi
Altarbia Alislamia Schools
Riyadh, Saudi Arabia

Joyce Hutchings
Georgetown University

Heather Jeddy
*Northern Virginia
Community College*

Judi Keen
*University of California,
Davis,* and *Sacramento
City College*

Karli Kelber
*American Language Institute,
New York University*

Anne Kornfield
*LaGuardia Community
College*

Kay Longmire
*Interlink at Valparaiso
University, Indiana*

Robin Longshaw
Rhode Island School of Design

Robert Ludwiczak
Texas A&M University
College Station, Texas

Bernadette McGlynn
*ELS Language Center, St.
Joseph's University*

Billy McGowan
Aspect International, Boston

Margaret Mehran
Queens College

Richard Moore
University of Washington

Karen Moreno
*Teikyo Post University,
Connecticut*

Gino Muzzetti
*Santa Rosa Junior College,
California*

Mary Nance-Tager
*LaGuardia Community
College, City University of
New York*

So Nguyen
Orange Coast College
Costa Mesa, California

Karen O'Neill
San Jose State University

Mary O'Neal
*Northern Virginia
Community College*

Nancy Pagliara
*Northern Virginia
Community College*

Keith Pharis
Southern Illinois University

Amy Parker
*ELS Language Center, San
Francisco*

Margene Petersen
*ELS Language Center,
Philadelphia*

Nancy Pfingstag
*University of North
Carolina, Charlotte*

Sally Prieto
*Grand Rapids Community
College*

India Plough
Michigan State University

Mostafa Rahbar
*University of Tennessee at
Knoxville*

Dudley Reynolds
Indiana University

Dzidra Rodins
DePaul University
Chicago, Illinois

Ann Salzman
*University of Illinois at
Urbana-Champaign*

Jennifer Schmidt
*San Francisco State
University*

Cynthia Schuemann
*Miami-Dade Community
College*

Jennifer Schultz
*Golden Gate University,
California*

Mary Beth Selbo
*Wright College, City Colleges
of Chicago*

Mary Selseleh
American River College
Sacramento, California

Stephen Sheeran
*Bishop's University,
Lenoxville, Quebec*

Kathy Sherak
*San Francisco State
University*

Sandra E. Sklarew
Merritt Community College
Oakland, California

Keith Smith
*ELS Language Center, San
Francisco*

Helen Solorzano
Northeastern University

Jorge Vazquez Solorzano
*Bachillerato de la Reina de
Mexico*
S. C., Mexico, D. F.,
Mexico

Christina Valdez
Pasadena City College
Pasadena, California

Danielle Valentini
Oakland Community College
Farmington Hills,
Michigan

Amelia Yongue
Howard Community College
Columbia, Maryland

Welcome to the *Grammar Dimensions* Lesson Planner

To the Teacher

This newly revised Lesson Planner for *Grammar Dimensions* (4th edition), Book 4 provides the teacher with a comprehensive guide to using the *Grammar Dimensions* student book. Its aim is to facilitate lesson planning by suggesting step-by-step guidelines for each task, focus chart, exercise, and activity. It also provides suggestions for supplementary expansion exercises and variations on the current exercises. In addition to the new guidelines, methodology, language, pronunciation, culture, and grammar notes integrated throughout the lesson plans may help to answer questions often asked by students. In addition, there are unit-by-unit examples of typical student errors for each grammar point that may be used by the teacher to predict student problems, identify areas of difficulty, and create supplementary materials.

The Lesson Planner is *not* intended as a blueprint to be followed closely in every detail. We hope that as you use *Grammar Dimensions*, you will continue to explore and discover new ways of adapting the material to suit the needs of your students, as well as your own teaching style. It is hoped, however, that by providing more detailed teachers' notes, the Lesson Planner will help guide teachers who are using *Grammar Dimensions* for the first time and provide additional ideas and activities for those have already used the book many times.

OPENING TASK

Each unit starts with an Opening Task. The aim of this task is to help you, the instructor, find out what your students know and don't know. This information will enable you to target the material in the unit. You may decide to omit sections of the unit material that are already well understood by your students. You may decide to add extra exercises to the sections that present difficulty. The best way to find out the extent to which your students are able to use a particular structure correctly is to put them into a situation or context where they need to use it. This is what the Opening Task aims to do. Each task has been constructed so that students will need to use the target structures in order to complete it.

When using these tasks, we ask you to focus students' attention on understanding and completing the task. They should not be made to feel that this is a test of their linguistic knowledge. While their attention is focused on completing the task, you will be able to listen and take note of their language use. This diagnostic approach is quite different from communicative tasks that are used to practice a given structure. The purpose here is to allow students the opportunity to make mistakes as well as to use the target structures correctly. Only by allowing them the freedom to do this, will you be able to understand which aspects of the grammar points cause difficulty and which aspects of meaning, use, and form need most attention. You may, however, decide to come back to the Opening Task, once the grammar has been studied in more detail, and use this task to practice the given structures.

The Opening Tasks are designed so that, after initially setting up the task and explaining the steps, they may be carried out by students independently in pairs or groups. This will allow you to circulate among the students with your notebook, "eavesdropping" on their conversations, and taking notes of problems in meaning, form, or use that will be useful for you later in the unit. While you are listening, try to visualize the "form, meaning, and use" pie chart in your mind and see if you can determine where they have been successful, and where they need help.

At this point, it is probably better if you avoid error correction and assistance with the grammar of the task. The tasks are designed to encourage students to work meaningfully without concern that they will be interrupted, evaluated, or corrected. The only exception might be the need to remind students to work in English if they are using another language.

In this new edition, we have recognized the importance of allowing some time for students to become familiar with the topic of the task in Step 1. Some topics may be culturally unfamiliar, for example, medical topics in Unit 5. Sometimes the vocabulary may need reviewing, for example, words for concepts of consumerism and marketing in Unit 23. In these cases, it is worth spending a little time talking around the topic in order to generate increased motivation for the task. We hope that the pictures and drawings will also help to engage students visually. (You may wish to supplement them by bringing in more pictures of your own.) In general, however, if students seem comfortable with the topic and the vocabulary, we recommend moving on to Step 2 as soon as possible.

In this new edition, we have also tried to focus more explicit attention on the target structure in the final step of the task. This final step can be used to make sure all students have recognized the link between the target language and the task. If some students have been using the target structures successfully, they can share this knowledge with the class. If no one has been able to use the structures, the teacher may use this opportunity to bridge to the first focus chart through direct instruction.

In many cases, the Opening Task is referred to at later points in the unit. If you collect examples of students' performance in the Opening Task, you may also find yourself referring back to these examples as you reach the relevant explanation or practice exercise later in the unit. For this reason, we do not recommend omitting the Opening Task. But, if you are short of time, you might want to shorten or omit either Step 1 or the final step.

FOCUS CHARTS

The focus charts present the form, meaning, and use of the target structure with examples and explanations that are appropriate for the level. Each aspect of the unit grammar is presented separately and is followed by exercises providing controlled practice. The focus charts allow students to develop step-by-step a better understanding of, and an ability to use, the structure accurately, meaningfully, and appropriately. The pie chart at the top of the focus chart indicates whether the box focuses on the form, meaning, use or combination of these to examine the target structure.

A new feature of this revised teacher's edition is the step-by-step guidelines for using the focus charts. As with all suggestions in this Lesson Planner, they are intended for guidance only. Teachers will use the focus charts in different ways depending on the needs of their students and their own teaching style.

The notes for each focus chart start with a *Lead-in* suggestion. We have tried to include a variety of presentation styles in the Lead-in, such as using student examples, using diagrams or pictures, creating information gaps, and other ideas that may help to vary the presentation format of the chart. We hope that you will experiment with different ideas and find the best way to present each grammar point, noting only that any student (and teacher) may get tired of repeatedly using the same presentation format.

In some cases, we have suggested asking students to look at the examples and try to work out the rules. You may find this takes longer, but the increased engagement of the learner and the greater time investment involved may result in greater retention. If you prefer a more deductive approach, you may ask students to read the information in the chart and come up with further examples of their own. A variation on this is to ask students individually or in pairs to present the information in a focus chart to another pair of students, or even to the whole class, adding a few new examples of their own. Teaching something to others is a great way to learn, helping students to understand if they truly understand a point!

Another possible way of using the focus charts is not to present them at all, but rather to assign students the exercises that go along with them. The focus charts can be used for reference purposes as the students work their way through the exercises. In this way, the material becomes more meaningful to students because they will need to understand it in order to complete the exercise.

EXERCISES

At least one exercise follows each focus. There is a wide variety of exercises in *Grammar Dimensions*. Comprehension exercises work on students' awareness and understanding. Production exercises develop students' skill in using the structures. The step-by-step teacher's notes for each exercise begin with an introductory sentence explaining which grammar point is being practiced and whether the purpose is to practice the form or use of the target structure.

Some exercises continue the theme of the Opening Task and some introduce students to new themes and vocabulary in order to provide variety and to foster students' ability to transfer their learning to new contexts. There are also many personalized exercises, in which students use their own background knowledge or opinions to answer questions.

As with the focus charts, there is a variety of different ways in which you may decide to use the exercises. Depending on your class length, you may decide to assign some exercises for homework and go over the answers in class. You may do the exercises in class using pairs or groups, perhaps assigning one section of the exercise to one set of groups and pairs, and another section of the exercise to the others. You may do the exercise orally in class and ask students to write the answers for homework.

Reviewing Exercises

There are also many options for how exercise answers can be checked. For example:

1. You can circulate while students are doing an exercise in class and spot-check.
2. You can go over the exercise afterwards as a whole class with each student being called on to supply an answer.
3. Exercises can be done individually and then pairs of students can get together to check their answers with each other. Where a difference of opinion occurs, you (or another pair of students) can act as a referee.

4. Different students, pairs, or groups of students can be assigned different parts of an exercise. For example, the first group does 1–5, the second group does 6–10, etc. The groups post their answers on newsprint or butcher block paper and everyone circulates at the end noting the answers and asking questions.

5. A variation of number 4 is to have one student from each group present to the other students the exercise answers that his or her group came up with.

6. You can prepare a handout with the answers, and each student corrects his or her answers individually.

7. You can collect the written work, and make a list of common errors. You can put the errors on an overhead transparency and show it to the students during the next class and have them correct the errors together.

Many exercises require students not only to choose the best answer, but also to explain the reasons for their choices. We believe that this ability to justify and explain the reasons for grammatical choices will enhance students' ability to use grammar accurately, meaningfully, and appropriately.

TIMING AND LESSON PLANS

In this new edition, we have made suggestions for the estimated time needed to complete each unit as well as timing for each exercise and activity. Most of the units are divided into two distinct lessons of 90 minutes each. A few units are not long enough for two 90 minute lessons, but they always contain at least an hour's worth of work. The length of a lesson will vary depending on the degree of difficulty your students have with this structure, whether they have previewed the exercise for homework, and other factors such as the size of your class. The time length given for exercises and activities is only a rough estimate of the minimum time needed to complete the exercise in class.

WORKBOOK

All lesson plans have been correlated with the additional exercises provided in the *Grammar Dimensions 4* Workbook. The workbook provides extra practice with each grammar point and its form, meaning, or use designation. Every three units, the workbook examines the grammar points covered as well as editing skills gained through a summarizing quiz.

ASSESSMENT

For further pre-assessment, unit assessment, and end of semester assessment of student skills, the instructor is reminded at the end of each unit to use the *Grammar Dimensions 4 ExamView* which provides a bank of relevant grammar questions that can be modified or grouped with questions from other units. These quizzes developed may be saved for future use and individualized per class need.

USE YOUR ENGLISH ACTIVITIES

The Use Your English activities section at the end of each unit offer a range of activities where students can apply the language discussed in the unit to wider contexts and integrate it with the language they already know. Many activities give students more freedom than the exercises do and offer them more opportunities to express their own points of view across a range of topics. Most of the activities lend themselves to being done with structures covered in the unit, but they do not absolutely require their use.

The activities section is also designed to give instructors a variety of options. As you will probably not have time to do all the activities, you might select the ones you think would be most beneficial, or ask your students to choose ones that they would prefer. Perhaps different groups of students could do different activities and then report on their experience to the whole class. We suggest that the activities should be interspersed throughout the unit (as well as at the end of the unit) in order to provide variety and also to allow you to assess students' ability to use the target structures in natural contexts. In the Lesson Plans, therefore, we have suggested correlations between the exercises and the activities, keeping in mind that these are entirely optional. Also, it may be useful to go back to a previous unit and do an activity for review purposes. This is especially useful at the beginning of a new, but related, unit.

Skills

You will notice that the activities section provides activities in the four major skill areas (reading, writing, listening, speaking), some skills in combination and some skills practiced exclusively. In addition to these four cornerstone language skills, students will have the opportunity to practice research on the Internet and through InfoTrac (See more on these sections below.). Students are also guided to reflect on the learning process by examining the why's and how's of their own language learning experience.

If you are teaching in a skill-based program, you might want to collaborate with your colleagues and distribute the activities among yourselves. For example, the writing teacher could assign the activities that involve a written report, the teacher of listening could work on the listening activities during his or her class periods, or the teacher of speaking could work with students on activities where students are supposed to make an oral presentation.

The activities are an integral part of each unit because they not only provide students with opportunities to stretch their language use, but, as with the opening task, they also provide you with the opportunity to observe your students' language use in action. In this way, activities can be informal holistic assessment measures encouraging students to show you how well they can use the target structures communicatively. Any problems that still exist at this point can be noted for follow-up at a later time when students are more ready to deal with them.

Internet and InfoTrac® Activities

 This new edition includes a "research on the Web" activity at the end of each unit. The purpose of this Internet search activity is to provide a natural context for using the target grammar. An additional purpose is to encourage students to share strategies for finding information on the Internet. Internet search engines are suggested, but instructors are encouraged to assist students in looking for information in a discriminating manner.

 In some cases, the research activity is based on using *InfoTrac® College Edition,* a resource of over 20 million articles accessed online by means of an individual password bound into each student book. Once the students establish a link to InfoTrac they are able to access over 6,000 academic journals and newspapers. It is highly recommended for *Grammar Dimensions* Book 4 users that instructors initially provide a suggested list of sources to read through in *InfoTrac* or provide specific keywords to assist students in finding level-appropriate articles.

Reflection Activities

Also new to this edition is the addition of a *reflection* activity towards the end of each unit. These activities provide an opportunity for students to use the target structures of the unit while reflecting on their language learning. Many of these activities can be done as pair or group activities in class. Others can also be assigned for homework. In this case, you may consider it a good idea to ask students to keep a learning journal. As well as providing you with firsthand feedback on your students' progress, it is also a good way to encourage reflection and self-evaluation that can facilitate language learning. In addition to the reflection activities, here are some suggested topics to include in a learning journal:

- Which grammar points do you find difficult, confusing, or easy—and why?

- Which grammar points are similar to or different from your native language?

- Which learning activities did you enjoy most in this unit and why?

- Which learning activities would you like to do more of or less of?

- What aspect of your learning did you feel most proud of when doing this unit?

Other Features

 • Correlations to Audio CD tracks are noted in the student books as well as in the lesson plans. (Audiotape cassettes are also available.) In the Appendix of this Lesson Planner are the printed audio scripts, which instructors might wish to read through prior to the lesson or to photocopy for student use and review if needed.

• An Answer Key for the *Grammar Dimensions 4* Workbook exercises is provided in the Appendix.

As you can see, *Grammar Dimensions* is meant to provide you with a great deal of flexibility so that you can provide quality instruction appropriate for your class. We encourage you to experiment with different aspects of the material in order to best meet the needs of your unique group of students.

VERB TENSES IN WRITTEN AND SPOKEN COMMUNICATION

UNIT GOALS

- **Use verb tenses correctly to describe events and situations**
- **Use verb tenses consistently**
- **Understand why tense and time frames may change**

OPENING TASK
Describing In-Groups

■ **STEP 1**

Read the following information about *in-groups* and find the definition of this term.

Gordon Allport, a Harvard psychologist, used the term *in-groups* to describe the groups that individuals are part of at one time or another. We are born into some in-groups, such as our ethnic groups, our hometowns, and our nationalities. We join other in-groups through our activities, such as going to school, making friends, entering a profession, or getting married. Some in-groups, such as ethnic groups, are permanent, but others change as our activities, beliefs, and loyalties change.

■ **STEP 2**

Read the list of in-group memberships that Kay, a Thai-American woman in her mid-thirties, currently belongs to or has belonged to in the past.

the family she grew up in
her own family (husband Mark
   and child Hanna)
Thai people (her ethnic group)
residents of Bangkok (where she was born)
residents of Chicago (where she lived
   from ages 8 to 18)
residents of Palo Alto, California
   (the city she lives in now)
her girlhood group of friends
the Girl Scouts (as a child)

students from her elementary and
   secondary school
Princeton University students
Stanford Medical School students
physicians (her profession)
Buddhists (her religion)
National Organization for Women
   members
her neighborhood volleyball team
Sierra Club members
residents of the United States

■ **STEP 3**

Make a list of some in-groups to which you belonged as a child (pick an age between 5 and 12 years old). Some of these groups might be the same as present ones. Next, make a list of in-groups that you belong to now. Finally, create a third list which consists of your present in-groups that you believe will remain important groups for you ten years from now.

■ **STEP 4**

Compare your lists with another class member. Discuss which groups on your childhood lists have changed and which have remained important groups to you at the present time.

■ **STEP 5**

As an out-of-class assignment, write three paragraphs. For the first paragraph, describe a childhood in-group that was especially important to you. For the second paragraph, write about your current involvement in an in-group. In the third paragraph, speculate about what might be some new in-groups for you in the future—for example, a new school, a profession, your own family (as contrasted to your family of origin)—and when you think some of them might become a part of your life. Save your paragraphs for Exercise 2.

UNIT OVERVIEW

The first two units of *Grammar Dimensions 4* provide a detailed review of how verb tenses are used in English to describe events and situations. Unit 1 gives students valuable tools to choose verb tenses correctly and consistently. It explains how two main factors determine choice of verb tense: time frame, or when an event or situation occurs (past, present, future), and aspect, or whether an action or state is completed or ongoing (simple, progressive, perfect, perfect progressive). The unit also explores how and why verb tenses within a given time frame are consistent, and how they shift as the time frame shifts.

The exercises in the unit provide a series of meaningful contexts within which students can explore and practice tense usage. They can see and understand how tense usage affects and expresses meaning, rather than simply concentrating on the forms.

METHODOLOGY NOTE

The ability to consistently choose the correct verb tense in spoken and written communication is one of the hallmarks of an accomplished language learner. Even the most advanced students can be expected to have difficulties with certain tenses, such as the perfect tenses, and will benefit from this systematic review.

UNIT GOALS

Some instructors may want to review the goals listed on Student Book (SB) page 0 after completing the Opening Task so that students understand what they should know by the end of the unit. These goals can also be reviewed at the end of the unit when students are more familiar with the grammar terminology.

OPENING TASK [30 minutes]

The purpose of the Opening Task is to provide a compelling context in which students can review how different verb tenses are used in English to describe different time frames. Students generate lists of "in-groups" to which they belonged as children and to which they now belong. The problem-solving format is designed to show the teacher how well the students can produce the target structures implicitly and spontaneously when they are engaged in a communicative task. For a more complete discussion of the purpose of the Opening Task, see To the Teacher, Lesson Planner (LP) page xxii.

Setting Up the Task

1. Ask students to describe the two pictures on SB page 0. Do the people in each photo belong to a group? What might that group be? Do the members of each group appear to share any visible similarities, such as similarities in age or appearance?

2. Point to the title of the Opening Task: *Describing In-Groups.* Write *in-group* on the board, and ask students what that term might mean. Some students will probably suggest the colloquial usage ("a popular group"). If they do, acknowledge that this is one meaning of the term, but that the author of this selection has a different definition, which they will now learn about.

Conducting the Task

■ STEP 1

Read the introduction to the task and Allport's definition of in-groups with your students.

■ STEP 2

1. Read the list of in-groups.

2. Explain that *Thai* describes someone or something from Thailand. Elicit that Chicago and Palo Alto are cities in the United States, and that the *Sierra Club* is an environmental conservation organization in the United States.

3. Respond to any other vocabulary questions.

■ STEPS 3 AND 4

1. Divide students into pairs or groups of three. Have them create three lists of in-groups (past, present, and future), and then share these with their groups.

2. While students are creating and sharing their lists, you may want to walk around the room to offer assistance and observe their production of the different verb tenses.

Closing the Task

1. Ask volunteers from several groups to share their lists with the class.

2. You might like to conduct a poll—or have a volunteer conduct one—of the in-groups students belonged to during one time frame, such as the past. You could then analyze and discuss similarities and differences. Don't worry about accuracy at this point, although you may want to take notes of errors in meaning, form, or use in order to focus on those problems later.

■ STEP 5

1. Read this step with your students and answer any questions they might have about this three paragraph homework assignment.

2. It might be helpful to outline the paragraph assignments on the board.

Note: Students will use the resulting paragraphs they write in Step 5 when they do Exercise 2. Please find a list of typical student errors in the Grammar Note box on LP page 3.

FOCUS 1 | The English Verb System: Overview

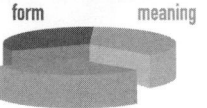

Verbs in English express how events take place in time. The verb tenses give two main kinds of information:

Time Frame When the event takes place: now, at some time in the past, or at some time in the future.

Aspect The way we look at an action or state: whether it occurs at a certain point in time (for example, *stop*) or lasts for period of time (for example, *study*). (See Unit 2 for more detail on verb aspect.)

Time frame and **aspect** combine in twelve different ways in English.

ASPECT	PRESENT	PAST	FUTURE*
Simple (at that point in time)	*stop/stops* *study/studies* (simple present)	*stopped* *studied* (simple past)	*will stop* *will study* (simple future)
Progressive (in progress at that point in time)	*am/is/are stopping* *am/is/are studying* (present progressive)	*was/were stopping* *was/were studying* (past progressive)	*will be stopping* *will be studying* (future progressive)
Perfect (before that time)	*has/have stopped* *has/have studied* (present perfect)	*had stopped* *had studied* (past perfect)	*will have stopped* *will have studied* (future perfect)
Perfect Progressive (in progress during and before that time)	*has/have been stopping* *has/have been studying* (present perfect progressive)	*had been stopping* *had been studying* (past perfect progressive)	*will have been stopping* *will have been studying* (future perfect progressive)

*Please note that there are many ways to express the future time frame in English. The chart above gives examples of the future using *will* only. See Focus 7 in Unit 2 for other ways.

EXERCISE 1

In *The Story of My Life,* high school student Farah Ahmedi tells about growing up in Kabul, Afghanistan, during the war between the mujahideen and the Soviets, her life as a refugee in Pakistan, and her immigration to the United States along with her mother, the only other surviving member of her family. The following passages are from her book. Underline the verbs of main clauses in each sentence. Then identify the time frame for each passage: present, past, or future. Circle any words and phrases that help to signal the time frame. The first one has been done as an example.

Example:

1. (a) Our caseworker, Zainab, <u>came</u> from Sudan. (b) (Years ago) she <u>had been</u> a refugee like us. (c) World Relief <u>had brought</u> her to America. (d) She <u>had found</u> her footing here, <u>gone</u> to school, <u>gotten</u> her degree, and now she <u>worked</u> for the organization. Time frame: *past*

2. (a) You <u>have</u> to realize how vastly this world differed from the one we left behind. (b) Everything <u>moves</u> quickly in America. (c) You <u>notice</u> the difference sharply if you have come from a slow-paced land like Pakistan. (d) Here in America events <u>unfold</u> in a flash. (e) Outside your window the traffic never <u>stops</u> zooming. (f) On the street no one <u>has</u> time to answer your questions. Time frame: present

3. (a) Alyce <u>invited</u> us to her house for Thanksgiving (that first year.) (b) We <u>had</u> never <u>seen</u> a turkey before and didn't know what it was. (c) We never <u>imagined</u> a bird could grow so big. (d) My mother <u>didn't eat</u> any of it. Time frame: past

4. (a) My mother (now) <u>has</u> a bit of a social life of her own. (b) She <u>has gotten</u> to know some other Afghan women in the neighborhood. (c) (On warm days) they all <u>walk</u> to the park <u>together</u> with their thermoses. (d) They <u>sit</u> on the grass and chat and <u>have</u> tea. (e) (In the last couple of months) my mother <u>has</u> even <u>started</u> going to school. (f) She <u>is going</u> to an English-language course three times a week. Time frame: present

5. (a) In my ESL classes I <u>got</u> to know an Indian girl named Apanza. (b) I <u>met</u> two Afghan girls as well. (c) They <u>had come</u> to America (one year earlier) than I and <u>had</u> therefore <u>gone</u> to American schools one year longer, but we <u>were</u> all in the same class. (d) In any case, I <u>had</u> companions now. Time frame: past

6. (a) (Next year) I'<u>ll be</u> out of ESL altogether. (b) Even my English class <u>will be</u> mainstream. (c) Officially, at least, I'<u>ll be</u> caught up. Time frame: future

FOCUS 1 [15 minutes]

This focus explains that verbs give two kinds of information: (1) the **time frame** (past, present, or future), and (2) the **aspect**, or whether an action or state is completed or ongoing (the simple, progressive, perfect, and perfect progressive forms).

1. **Lead-in:** Guide students through a review of the tenses by asking them questions about their lives. Ask a volunteer to write responses on the board. Proceed through the different aspects, asking questions of the whole class or individual students. For example, you might ask:

   What's your favorite food these days?
   What was your favorite food a year ago?
   What do you think your favorite food will be a year from now?
   What are you wearing today? etc.

2. Have students look at the organization of the focus chart. Elicit that the left column contains information about aspect, and the right three columns contain information about time frame.

3. Read the left-hand column with the class and answer any questions they might have about aspect.

4. Then, read the examples and the explanations in the other three columns.

5. You might like to review how the perfect forms are generally used to describe something that has happened up to a specific point in time, whether recently completed or right until the present moment.

LANGUAGE NOTE

One stumbling block for many students is the fact that, in English, a tense is not necessarily equivalent to a time. Many students will, for example, use past tenses only to express things that existed in the past, but exist no longer. This can lead to errors such as: *She was my babysitter when I was young.* * *She is very nice* (rather than *was very nice*). The speaker uses the

present tense because the babysitter (in this case) still is nice today—the situation has not ceased to exist.

Explain to students that, in English, the past tenses are often used to describe a condition that existed at some time in the past. Using the past tense does not mean that these conditions are no longer true.

EXERCISE 1 [10 minutes]

In this controlled exercise students read passages about growing up in Kabul, Afghanistan, during a time of war. They first identify the main verbs, then the time frame for each passage, and then the expressions that signal those time frames.

1. Students could complete this exercise independently or in pairs.

2. Make sure students understand what a *main clause* is (that it contains a subject and a verb and expresses a complete thought). Read—or have a volunteer read—the example sentence. Elicit which are the verbs and what is the time frame (past). Could the expression *years ago* be used for any other time frame?

3. Have students complete the exercise.

4. Review answers as a class. See answers on LP page 2.

For more practice, use *Grammar Dimensions 4* Workbook page 1, Exercise 1.

EXPANSION [15 minutes]

You can use the following exercise to provide further practice with identifying verbs and their time frames.

1. On the board write these phrases that identify time frames:

   As a child . . .
   For the time being . . .
   Someday . . .

2. Have students work in pairs.

3. Ask them to write at least six sentences about their lives, using the phrases on the board.

4. Have them exchange papers, read their partner's sentences, and discuss the similarities and differences between their experiences.

GRAMMAR NOTE

Typical student errors (form)

- Errors in third-person singular:—e.g., * *She were watching TV.* * *They was listening to music.*

- Using past participle instead of present participle:—e.g., * *I was lived in Japan for one year.* (See Focus 1.)

- Using moment of focus:—e.g., * *My sister has been in California three years ago.* (See Focus 2.)

- Inconsistency in tense usage: —e.g., *I know him.* * *He was my friend. He is a good guy;* and *He is studying economics.* * *He had studied economics for three years.*

- Problems with auxiliary verb sequences, especially involving tense agreement: —e.g., * *He should have talk to her.* (See Focus 3.)

- Time-frame shifts: —e.g., *The company is doing very well.* * *Last year profits increase by 40 percent.* (See Focus 4.)

Typical student errors (use)

- Using past progressive with verbs of perception:—e.g., * *She was hearing a loud noise.*

- Using simple past for temporary or uncompleted events in the past:—e.g., * *When she left, the children played next door.* (See Focus 1.)

- Incorrect sequence of tenses:—e.g., * *When I was cooking dinner, I was talking on the phone.* * *When they watched TV, they heard the baby cry.* (See Focus 3.)

EXERCISE 2

Exchange the paragraphs you wrote for the Opening Task with those of a classmate. After reading the paragraphs, write one or two questions that you have about your classmate's in-groups and ask him or her to respond to them. Then decide whether there is a consistent time frame used for each paragraph. If so, identify the time frames and underline any time indicators. Check with your classmate to see if he or she agrees with your analysis. Discuss any changes you think should be made.

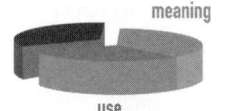

meaning

use

FOCUS 2 | Moment of Focus

Verbs can describe events that happen at a point in time (for example, *last night, three weeks ago*) or an event that lasts a period of time (for example, *all night long, three weeks*). We call this the **moment of focus**.

The moment of focus will help you to decide whether to use the verb's present, past, or future tense. Here are examples of moment of focus for each of the three time frames:

	POINT OF TIME	PERIOD OF TIME
Present	(a) Her son *is* 4 years old today.	(b) Her son *listens* to music for hours at a time.
Past	(c) The tornado *touched* down just before dawn.	(d) During the early nineteenth century, millions of Italians *immigrated* to the United States.
Future	(e) On Saturday morning, they *will leave* for their trip.	(f) In the decades to come, computer technology *will continue* to change our lives.

The moment of focus may be stated explicitly or it may be implied in the context.

Present	(g) I can't talk now; I'm trying to study.	(h) Her son goes to a private school. (Implied: now)
Past	(i) Until the end of the Cretaceous period, dinosaurs roamed the earth	(j) Dinosaurs evolved into two distinct groups. (Implied: during a period of time in the past)
Future	(k) After you finish that chapter, I'll give you a ride to school.	(l) The weather will continue to be warm and sunny. (Implied: for a future period of time)

In written and spoken communication, the moment of focus may be the same for a number of sentences or it may change from sentence to sentence:

SAME POINT OF FOCUS	CHANGING POINT/PERIOD OF FOCUS
(m) When Kay first moved to Chicago from Bangkok, she had a hard time adjusting to her new life. She didn't like the food at school. Other children seldom talked to her and she had no one to play with.	(n) Kay met Mark the summer after she graduated from college. They dated for two years. When they got married, it was on the same date, July 15th, that they had first met. This year they celebrated their fifteenth anniversary.

EXERCISE 3

The following passages are from Studs Terkel's book *The Great Divide*, in which Americans talk about their lives, the lives of their families, and their thoughts on changes in the United States. With a partner or in a small group, do the following: (1) Identify the moment or moments of focus for each passage. (2) State whether the moment of focus is (a) past or (b) present. (3) Determine whether each moment of focus is (a) a point of time or (b) a period of time. (4) State whether the moment of focus is (a) explicitly stated or (b) implied.

1. (a) Right now, he's working the night shift at a twenty-four hour service station, with ten or twelve pumps. (b) He pumps the cash register. (c) His goals are very short-term, to get through the day.

2. (a) I grew up in an environment where my parents sacrificed their lives for their children. (b) They came here as immigrants, circumscribed in opportunity, to a country that allowed freedom. (c) Whether I became a carpenter like my father or a professor was irrelevant as long as I strove and availed myself of what this country offered.

3. (a) In the last five years, there's been much more discussion of ethics on the campuses. (b) Remember, many of the young people of the sixties are the professors of today and they haven't changed their basic beliefs.

4. (a) A friend of mine, who is 40 had been a stock analyst on Wall Street fifteen years ago. (b) She married, had babies, raised her children, and now wanted to go back. (c) They said, "It doesn't matter what you did before."

5. (a) I would like to be chief of police. (b) I'll probably apply for jobs. (c) If nothing happens, I'll go to Cape Cod, build a house, and look at the waves.

6. (a) [My students] have learned how to take college tests. (b) They score high, especially in math. (c) They are quite verbal. (d) They give the impression of being bright. (d) Encouraged by their families, they come with the conviction that education is something they want, something they need. (e) But their definition of education is something else.

ANSWER KEY

Exercise 3 1. present; period of time; explicit 2. past; period of time; implicit 3. present; period of time; explicit 4. past; period of time; explicit (**Note:** The use of *now* in (b) is colloquial English; the time period is still past.) 5. future; period of time; implicit 6. present; period of time; implicit

EXERCISE 2 [10 minutes]

This exercise gives students a chance to review the homework assignment they did in Step 5 of the Opening Task.

1. Have students work in pairs.
2. Ask students to read the directions, and answer any questions they might have.
3. Set a time limit for discussion, such as 5 minutes. As students work, observe their progress and assist as needed.
4. Ask volunteers to share one or two sentences from their partner's paper, identifying the time frames and time indicators in each sentence.

For more practice, use *Grammar Dimensions 4* Workbook page 2, Exercise 2.

EXPANSION 1 [20 minutes]

This exercise returns to the Opening Task and focuses on actively considering time frames and verb tenses.

1. Have students work in pairs or groups of three.
2. Ask them to think about what in-groups they might have/could have belonged to had they been born 100 years earlier.
3. Have them write the same three lists as they did in the Opening Task (in-groups as a child, at present, and in the future), assuming they lived 100 years ago.
4. Ask them to exchange and discuss those lists. What has changed in 100 years?

EXPANSION 2 [30 minutes per activity]

You may wish to use Activities 5 (research on the web) and/or 6 (reflection/speaking) on SB page 11 for additional research and writing practice in using a range of tenses.

FOCUS 2 [15 minutes]

This focus chart defines the **moment of focus** of a verb—whether the verb describes an event or a condition that occurred at a point in time or one that existed for a period of time.

1. **Lead-in:** Read the introduction to the first focus chart and discuss the concepts of *point in time* and *period of time*. Model the two concepts by making statements about your life, such as *I ate a cheese sandwich for lunch yesterday. I've been eating cheese sandwiches for lunch since I was 10 years old.* Elicit that the first sentence refers to an action (eating) that happened at a point in time (lunch), and the second refers to a recurring action (eating) that occurred over a period of time (since I was 10 years old).
2. Read the first two examples of the present tense in the first focus chart. Elicit that the first sentence—*Her son is 4 years old today*—describes a state. The word *today* indicates that the state is occurring in the present. The second example—*Her son listens to music for hours at a time*—describes an action (listens to music) in the present that endures for a period of time (for hours at a time).
3. Continue this analysis with the remaining four examples.
4. Before reading the second chart, make sure students understand the terms *explicit* and *implied*. Tell students that when the period of time is implied rather than explicitly stated, the tense of the verb indicates the time period.
5. Read the next two charts, or ask volunteers to read them (the third chart is on SB page 5).

EXPANSION [20 minutes]

In this exercise students practice identifying the moment of focus (past, present, future) of verb tenses.

1. Ask students to work in groups of three.
2. Have each write at least four sentences describing life in the past and in the present in the United States or their home country. Tell them to explicitly express both the point of time and the period of time in each sentence.
3. Have them exchange papers and mark (underline or circle) the verbs and time frames in the sentences.
4. Ask each group to write a list of at least three predictions about the future. If time permits, ask volunteers to share these predictions with the class.

EXERCISE 3 [10 minutes]

Students identify the moment of focus in these passages from Studs Terkel's book, *The Great Divide.*

1. Have students work in small groups.
2. Read the directions as a class and answer any questions students might have.
3. To model, do the first passage as a class.
4. Review answers as a class. See answers on LP page 4.

For more practice, use *Grammar Dimensions 4* Workbook page 3, Exercise 3.

EXPANSION [20 minutes]

This expansion activity can function as a preview of the next focus, Consistency in Tense Usage.

1. Have students work in pairs.
2. Have them each create a chart similar to the first chart in Focus 2, listing their answers to the questions in Exercise 3.
3. Have them identify any explicit expressions of the moment of focus.
4. Ask them to analyze whether the author changed the time frame within any passage.
5. Ask volunteers to share their charts and answers with the class.

FOCUS 3 | Consistency in Tense Usage

use

Being consistent in tense means keeping verbs in the same time frame.

EXAMPLES	EXPLANATIONS
PRESENT TIME FRAME	
(a) Self-help groups have become very common all over America.	The tense may change within a time frame. For example, the tense may change from present perfect to simple present, as in sentences (a) and (b), but the time frame remains in the present.
(b) These groups assist people with everything from weight problems to developing confidence.	
PAST TIME FRAME	
(c) Vera graduated from college last June.	Sometimes, however, it is necessary to change from one time frame to another, for example from past to present. A time-frame shift is usually signaled by a time marker (for example, *last week, currently, next year*.)
PRESENT TIME FRAME	
(d) She now works for a law firm.	In example (d) *now* signals a shift from past to present time. Example (e) shifts to the present perfect, but remains in the present time frame.
(e) She has worked there for a month.	
PAST TIME FRAME	
(f) NOT: She had worked there for a month.	If (e) had a past-time reference, as in (f), the verb would be ungrammatical because there is no explicit time marker to signal a time-frame shift. Nor is there any reason to depart from the present time frame, which has been established in (d).

EXERCISE 4

Each of the following passages has one sentence with an inappropriate verb tense. (1) Identify the time frame of the passage. (2) Identify the sentence that has the error and correct it. You may want to consult the time-frame chart in Focus 1 for reference. Correction may involve changing the verb tense or using an explicit time marker to signal the shift in time frame. More than one verb tense can be correct in some cases.

Example: (a) I am taking this coat back to the store. (b) Someone had burned a hole in it. (c) One button is missing too.

Time Frame: *Present*; Error: (*b*)

Possible Corrections: *Someone **has burned** a hole in it.*

OR *Someone **had burned** a hole in it **before I bought it**.*

1. (a) My music class is interesting. (b) We have been studying the history of American jazz. (c) I will have been taking this course for six weeks.

2. (a) Sula's in-groups include her softball team. (b) She had belonged to this team for three years. (c) Last year she played second base, but this year she is playing first base.

3. (a) Internet social Web sites are becoming increasingly popular, especially with high school and college students, as ways to meet people. (b) These Web sites offered users their own personalized Web page for posting photos, messages, music and video. (c) Millions of users subscribe to the Web sites to make friends and get information about popular culture.

4. (a) One user of MySpace.com, a social Web site started in 2003, told a reporter he started using MySpace to keep track of his high school classmates. (b) Another user tells the reporter that the site allowed her to get to know people in different ways. (c) But some people expressed negative opinions about Web sites that allow anyone to see your personal information.

ANSWER KEY

Exercise 4 1. Present; Error: (c); change will have been taking TO have taken (or add a time reference such as as of next week)   2. Present; Error: (b); change had belonged TO has belonged
3. Present; Error: (b); change offered TO offers   4. Past; Error: (b); change tells TO told

FOCUS 3 [15 minutes]

This focus clarifies one source of confusion for many English language learners: consistency in tense usage. Further discussion is provided in Focus 4 on SB page 8.

1. **Lead-in:** Many students incorrectly believe that it is not permissible to change verb tenses within paragraphs in English. It is important to help students understand that consistency in tense means keeping verbs in the same time frame—not in the same tense. Ask a volunteer to read aloud examples (a) and (b) in the focus chart. Elicit the time frame (present) and the tenses (present perfect, simple present). Explain that these two sentences would be perfectly acceptable in one paragraph, since the actual time frame does not shift.

2. Explain that shifts in time frame are fine as long as they are signaled by a time marker, such as *now, last year, currently.*

3. Ask individual students to read aloud examples (c), (d), and (e). Guide students in identifying the time markers.

EXERCISE 4 [10 minutes]

In this exercise, students identify the time frame of each passage, find the sentence with an error in verb tense, and correct it. Students may find it helpful to refer to the time frame chart in Focus 1 on SB page 2 as they do this exercise.

1. Write the example sentences (a–c) on the board. Ask students to identify the time frame for each, and say whether that time frame is explicit or implicit.

2. Ask students to identify the sentence with an error in it. Ask a volunteer to write the correction on the board.

3. Have students work in pairs to complete the exercise.

4. Have them compare answers with another pair. See answers on LP page 6.

 For more practice, use *Grammar Dimensions 4* Workbook pages 3–4, Exercise 4.

EXPANSION 1 [15 minutes]

This exercise gives students extra practice in using time frame expressions.

1. Have students work in pairs.

2. Ask them to each choose two passages from Exercise 4 and rewrite them, adding at least one time frame expression to each passage.

3. Model an example, using item 1:

   (a) My music class is interesting.

       *The music class **I'm taking now** is interesting.*

4. Ask students to exchange papers and identify the time expressions they have added.

EXPANSION 2 [30 minutes per activity]

Activitiy 1 (listening/speaking) and Activity 2 (reading) on SB page 10 and Activity 3 (reading) on SB page 11 provide additional practice in identifying changes in time-frame and tenses.

FOCUS 4 — Time-Frame Shifts in Written and Spoken Communication

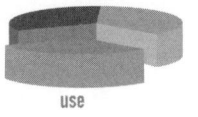

Time-frame shifts, such as from present to past, can occur in both written and spoken communication. These shifts will often be necessary when you move from statements that introduce a topic to ones that provide further information about the topic. There may or may not be explicit markers to signal time shifts.

Below are some reasons why you might change from one time frame to another, with examples given for each.

EXAMPLES	EXPLANATIONS	
	TYPE OF TIME-FRAME SHIFT	REASON FOR SHIFT
(a) The city of Wichita Falls has an interesting history. It *became* a town over a hundred years ago when the railroad started a route through that area. The land that was to become Wichita Falls *was* a prize in a poker game.	Present → Past	To explain or support a general statement with past description or elaboration on a topic.
(b) Our school is helping to conserve natural resources. We *recycled* tons of aluminum last year. We *started* using paper cups instead of Styrofoam ones.	Present → Past	To support a claim about the present with examples from the past.
(c) The social connections of Americans have changed during the last century. In the past, individuals *depended* on their extended families and neighborhoods for social activities. Today many Americans live far from their extended families and often do not know many of their neighbors.	Present → Past	To support a general statement about change by comparing present and past situations.
(d) Last year our city witnessed an increase in the number of people who volunteered time for organizations helping those in need. Donations to these organizations also increased. We *need* to continue this assistance to others less fortunate than we are.	Past → Present	To express a comment or an opinion about a topic.

NOTE: The simple present and present perfect tenses often "frame" topics. We frequently use them to introduce topics, to make topic shifts, and to end discussion of a topic. These tenses often express general statements that the speaker believes to be true at the present time.

EXERCISE 5

Below are more passages from Farah Ahmedi's *Story of My Life* about her experience as a newcomer to the United States, living in Chicago, Illinois. Discuss the reasons for the verb tense shifts in each passage. Which passages change tenses within a time frame (e.g., two different tenses within the past frame)? Which passages change time frames (e.g., a change from past time to present time)? Which verb tense is used to introduce the topic in each of these passages?

Example: (a) Every time my mother and I left the house, we felt like hares venturing out of our holes. (b) We were panting with nervous dread. (c) Everybody enjoys reading an adventure story or seeing and adventure movie, but a real life adventure is hard to enjoy because you don't know how it will end. (d) I always felt the blood pounding in my wrists when I walked out the doors of our apartment building.

Reason for verb tense shift: The verb tense shifts from past tense to present tense in (c) to add a general comment related to the situation that Farah was describing. This passage changes time frames in (c) but returns to the past time frame in (d).

Introducing the topic: The past tense is used to introduce the topic.

1. World Relief tried to connect us up with other Afghans in the area, but the other Afghans led busy lives of their own. (b) Many of them had to work two jobs just to survive. (c) They had no time for us. (d) Two people don't automatically become friends just because they come from the same country. (e) And we didn't know any Americans, either, so we lived an empty life, homesick by day for a world we never wanted to see again, a world we visited too often in our nightmares.

2. (a) With most people, I have never been much of a talker. (b) Conversation does not come easily to me. (c) In a group I often feel shy and keep my thoughts to myself. (d) But Alyce* brought the stories, questions and confidences pouring out of me! (e) As soon as she walked into our house, her eyes had such a sparkle and her face wore such a flock of smiles that my heart opened wide.

3. (a) When you are trying to master a new language, you learn quicker if you have a chance to speak without hesitation or fear. (b) In class I didn't have the chance to speak much. (c) I had to spend most of my time listening to the teacher. (d) When I was called upon to say something, it was a public situation and a performance. (e) People were looking at me, and even as I tried to shape a thought, I worried that I might make a mistake and that the class might laugh at me. . .

4. (a) When I first came to America, I wanted to forget the past. (b) I wanted to take a big eraser and rub out every memory I had. (c) I wanted to become totally American through and through as quickly as I could. (d) But time passed, and I began to think about it. (e) I realized that it's good to remember my own customs and traditions. (f) Now I don't want to erase, or forget, or destroy any part of myself. (g) I want to love myself and keep adding to who I am.

*Alyce was Farah's English tutor, mentor, and very special friend from the World Relief Organization.

Exercise 5 1. Time frame shift: past (a)–(c), (e) to present (d). Reason: to express an opinion about the topic. Introducing the topic: present 2. Tense shift within present time frame: present perfect (a) to present (b). Reason: to support a general satement with elaboration. Introducing the topic: present 3. Time frame shift: present (a) to past (b)–(e). Reason: to support a general statement with description from the past. Introducing the topic: present perfect 4. Time frame shift: past (a)–(e) to present (f)–(g); tense = present perfect (a)–(d). Reason: to support a statement about change by comparing past and present situations. Introducing the topic: present perfect

FOCUS 4 [10 minutes]

1. **Lead-in:** Explain that changes in verb tense are used to define relationships between events and states in time.

2. Remind students that Focus 3 concentrated on the importance of maintaining consistency in tense usage within a time frame. Explain that when the time frame shifts, however, the tense used must shift also. This focus will explain reasons why such shifts occur.

3. Tell students that, in general, writers express their main idea with one tense—usually either simple present, simple past, or present perfect. They then indicate shifts in time frame by changing tense. Remind students that a shift in tense can be explicit or implicit.

4. Read the examples and explanations in the focus chart.

EXERCISE 5 [20 minutes]

Students read further passages from Ahmedi's *Story of My Life* about her experience as a newcomer to the United States, which they first encountered in Exercise 1.

1. (Optional) Use a visual or graphic organizer such as a chart to help students identify, visualize, and understand the time-frame shifts through verb tense shifts in these passages. Write on the board (and have students copy) a chart with these five column headings: (1) passage number; (2) shifts in tense; (3) reasons for shifts; (4) shifts in time-frame; (5) tense used to introduce topic.

2. Read the instructions and do the example with the class. Make sure students refer to specific lettered sentences in each passage. Have a volunteer fill out the chart on the board with information for the example.

3. Answer any questions students may have.

4. Set a time limit for students to work individually or in pairs to complete the exercise.

5. Review and discuss answers as a class. See answers on LP page 8.

For more practice, use *Grammar Dimensions 4* Workbook pages 4–6, Exercise 5; page 6, Exercise 6; and page 7, Exercise 7.

EXPANSION [15 minutes]

Activity 4 (reading) on SB page 11 offers excellent additional practice in identifying time-frame and tense shifts. You can assign this activity for homework or use it as a class activity.

UNIT GOAL REVIEW [5 minutes]

Ask students to look at the goals on the opening page of the unit again. Refer to the pages of the unit where information on each goal can be found.

For assessment of Unit 1, use *Grammar Dimensions 4 ExamView®*.

ACTIVITY 1 listening/speaking

CD1 Tracks 1, 2

You will hear two passages from the autobiography *I, Rigoberta Menchu*. Rigoberta Menchu is a young Guatemalan peasant woman who won the Nobel Peace Prize in 1992 for her work to ensure human rights and justice for Indian communities in Guatemala. These passages describe her peasant life in Guatemala. In each passage, there is one or more sentences that shift to a different time frame from the main time frame of the passage (for example, from the past to the present).

■ **STEP 1** Listen to each passage once for content and note the main time frame: present, past, or future.

■ **STEP 2** Listen to each passage again and write down the verbs that represent time-frame shifts and as much of the sentences they are in as you can recall.

■ **STEP 3** Explain the reason for each time-frame shift, with reference to Focus 4 for the possible different reasons. Here is some vocabulary from the passage that will be helpful to know while listening:

finca—a Guatemalan farm or plantation where the Indian peasants are contracted to work by the landowners. Crops such as coffee, cotton, and sugar are grown.
lorry—a truck that transports people from their villages to the finca
Altiplano—a high plateau in a mountainous region.

ACTIVITY 2 reading

Scan some comic strips in the newspaper to find ones that use a variety of verb tenses. In groups, discuss what the time frames are for each, and why tense changes occur. As a variation of this activity, cover up or blacken the verbs in comic strips. Then give another classmate the base forms of the verbs (the verb that comes after *to* in *to* + verb) and see if he or she fills in the same tenses as the original. Discuss any differences in choices.

ACTIVITY 3 reading

Select several paragraphs of something you find interesting from a textbook (for example, history, literature, or psychology) or some other book. Analyze the verb tense use in the paragraphs. What types of verb-tense shifts or time-frame shifts occur? Analyze the reasons for tense- or time-frame shifts.

ACTIVITY 4 reading

Look at a piece of writing you or a classmate has done recently, such as an essay or other type of paper. Analyze the types of verb-tense shifts you see, such as shifting from the present tense to the past tense. Describe why the verb tenses shifted. Underline any verb tenses that you think might not be correct and discuss them with your classmates or instructor.

ACTIVITY 5 research on the web

Millions of young people spend hours every day on social Web sites such as MySpace and Facebook, posting pictures and blogs about themselves and looking at Web pages of others. Although these social Web sites are among the most popular sites on the Internet, the media have warned that there are some problems associated with these sites. Research the topic of problems associated with social Web sites using keywords on a search engine such as Google® or Yahoo®, including the names of the Web sites. Write a summary of what you discovered, using appropriate verb tenses.

ACTIVITY 6 reflection/speaking

Consider an in-group, as defined by Gordon Allport, that has been helpful to your learning of English. The in-group could be friends, relatives, or classmates. Or it could be a particular school or program in which you were a student. Write an essay explaining the ways in which belonging to this group has contributed to your language development in the past and or present. Share with your class.

ANSWER KEY

Activity 1   Passage 1: Past; time frame shift to present: *The lorry holds about 40 people, but in with the people go the animals (dogs, cats, chickens) which the people from Altiplano take with them while they are in the finca.*
Reason for time frame shift: To provide a description of the lorry trucks that Rigoberta and her family rode to get to the finca. (Note: This use in Focus 4 shows a shift from present to past, but this shift can also be from past to present for this use.)

Passage 2: Present; time frame shift to past: *We were poor and had neither money to buy cane leaves nor anyone to go and get them.*
Reason for time frame shift: To explain why Rigoberta's family could not make their houses from cane leaves (elaborating a statement through explanation about the past).

USE YOUR ENGLISH

The Use Your English activities at the end of the unit contain situations that should naturally elicit the structures covered in the unit. For a more complete discussion of how to use the Use Your English activities, see To the Teacher, LP page xxvi.

ACTIVITY 1
listening/speaking
[30 minutes]

You may want to use this activity after Exercise 4 on SB page 7. Students listen to an audio excerpt from Rigoberta Menchu's autobiography and identify the time-frame shifts. The audio script for this listening appears on LP page S-1.

CD1 Tracks 1,2

1. Make sure students understand the meaning of essential vocabulary from the passages before they listen to it. The vocabulary is defined in Step 3.

2. Ask students to work independently for Steps 1 and 2, in which they listen to the passage and note the time-frame shifts.

3. Have students work with a partner or small group for Step 3, in which they explain the reason for each time-frame shift.

4. As a class, discuss which passages were the easiest and which the hardest to understand. See answers on LP page 10.

ACTIVITY 2
reading
[homework/30 minutes]

You may want to use this activity after Exercise 4 on SB page 7.

1. In preparation for this activity, encourage students to make copies of comic strips in which the time frame and/or verb tenses change.

2. Distribute your comic strips and the students' comic strips back to students for discussion of time frames and tense changes.

3. Students in groups discuss the changes in time-frame and tense in a series of comic panels.

4. Have some comic strips prepared with blacked out verbs and/or have students use markers or liquid paper to create blanks where verbs appear. Students will particularly enjoy this variation, in which they change some of the verbs in their comic strips, and then exchange their results with other students, taking turns supplying the answers.

5. Discuss any successful or amusing results of changing the verb tenses.

ACTIVITY 3
reading
[30 minutes]

This activity could be assigned after Exercise 4 on SB page 7 for reading and speaking practice in analyzing tense shifts.

1. Ask students to choose a passage to read from a book that interests them.

2. Have them write down any changes in tense and in time frame within the passage.

3. Have them choose a partner and take turns identifying the changes and explaining why each occurs.

4. Walk around the class while students are discussing the passages in order to observe their facility with the language and the concepts.

ACTIVITY 4
reading
[30 minutes]

Use this activity after Exercise 5 on SB page 9 to give students extra reading and speaking practice in analyzing tense shifts.

1. Have students work in pairs and exchange a piece of writing they have done recently, such as an essay.

2. Ask them to circle any shifts in tense, and underline any tenses they think may be incorrect.

3. Have them revisit the focus charts to find reasons to support their corrections.

4. Ask them to discuss their findings.

ACTIVITY 5
research on the web
[30 minutes/homework]

This activity offers students extra research, reading, and writing practice with a range of verb tenses. You may want to assign this activity as homework after Exercise 2 on SB page 4.

1. Ask a volunteer to read the activity text on SB page 11.

2. Discuss students' knowledge of and personal experience with Web sites that encourage friendship or dating connections.

3. Discuss what might be some problems associated with the different sites.

4. Students could research the problems independently or in pairs. Have students brainstorm keywords to find criticism of the online social sites.

5. Ask students to write a summary of their findings and share this with the class.

ACTIVITY 6
reflection/speaking
[30 minutes]

This activity returns to the topic of in-groups and is a good follow-up to Exercise 2 on SB page 4. Students use past, present, and present perfect in an essay about an in-group that has helped them learn English.

1. Brainstorm a list of in-groups students have belonged to that have helped them learn English, and write these on the board.

2. Ask students to choose an in-group and write an essay about how that group has contributed to their language development in the past or present.

3. Set a time limit for writing.

4. Ask students to work in pairs. Have them exchange papers, read them, and discuss.

5. Ask a few volunteers to read their partners' papers aloud to the class.

VERBS
Aspect and Time Frames

- Use simple verb tenses correctly
- Use progressive verb forms correctly
- Use perfect verb forms correctly
- Understand verb-tense meanings and uses in present, past, and future time frames

OPENING TASK

Insiders and Outsiders

In Unit 1, the Opening Task asked you to consider the in-groups to which you belong. At times the process of joining a new group can be uncomfortable. Most of us have experienced the sense of not belonging, of feeling somewhat like an "outsider," when first joining a new group. This often happens when people move to a new place, begin attending a new school, or start a new job.

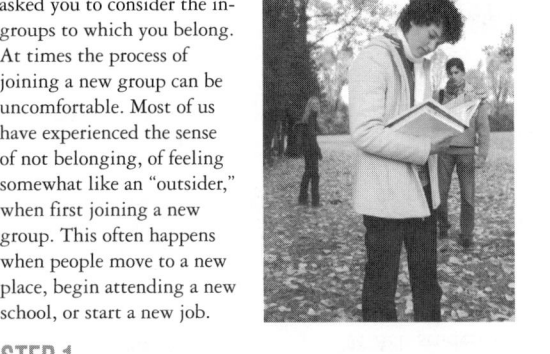

◼ STEP 1

Read the passages below and on the next page about experiences of feeling like an outsider.

In the first passage, Farah Ahmedi, whose life story you read about in Unit 1, describes her difficulties as an Afghan refugee trying to make friends with Americans while attending high school in Chicago, Illinois.

> I have no American friends my age. I guess it's partly because the American kids grew up here and found their friends long ago. They don't need more friends, now, so they ignore anyone they don't already know. If you say hi, they say hi back, but it doesn't lead to conversation.

From Farah Ahmedi with Tamim Ansary (2005). *The Story of My Life: An Afghan Girl on the Other Side of the Sky*. New York: Simon & Schuster.

The next passage describes the sense of not belonging and confusion that many students experience when entering college, especially when they find themselves in large lecture classes, where they do not have much direct contact with a teacher.

> People are taking notes and you are taking notes. You are taking notes on a lecture you don't understand. You get a phrase, a sentence, then the next loses you. It's as though you're hearing a conversation in a crowd or from another room—out of phase, muted. The man on the stage concludes his lecture and everyone rustles and you close your notebook and prepare to leave. You feel a little strange. Maybe tomorrow this stuff will clear up. Maybe by tomorrow this will be easier. But by the time you're in the hallway, you don't think it will be easier at all.

From Mike Rose (2005). *Lives on the Boundary*. New York: Penguin Books.

◼ STEP 2

For fifteen minutes, write your thoughts in response to the passages. You could discuss one of the passages, or you might want to describe a situation from your own experience, from a movie or TV show you have seen, or from something you have read that relates to the idea of being an outsider in a new place or with a new group. In small groups, take turns reading your responses aloud.

UNIT OVERVIEW

Unit 2 continues the review begun in Unit 1 of verb tense usage in English. Unit 2 focuses on the meanings and uses of the simple, progressive, and perfect tenses, provides guided practice in selecting appropriate forms in context, and gives students opportunities for using verb tenses appropriately in communicative contexts.

Please note that because this is a longer unit, it is divided into three lesson plans. For a faster review of the unit, review each focus box and complete only one exercise that follows each.

METHODOLOGY NOTE

Although most students will be familiar by now with the forms of these tenses, many will still be unclear about when to use a particular tense and how to sequence tenses in speech and writing. You can use these reviews to explore any difficulties students might have with tenses.

UNIT GOALS

Some instructors may want to review the goals listed on Student Book (SB) page 12 after completing the Opening Task so that students understand what they should know by the end of the unit. These goals can also be reviewed at the end of the unit when students are more familiar with the grammar terminology.

OPENING TASK [30 minutes]

The purpose of this task is to provide a compelling context in which students can review how different verb tenses are used in English to describe different time frames. The theme of the task—insiders and outsiders—expands on the topic of in-groups that students explored in Unit 1. In this opening task, students read two passages about feelings of not belonging to a group. Then write and discuss the

topic. The problem-solving format is designed to show the teacher how well the students can produce the target structures implicitly and spontaneously when they are engaged in a communicative task. For a more complete discussion of the purpose of the Opening Task, see To the Teacher, Lesson Planner (LP) page xxii.

Setting Up the Task

1. Write *insider* and *outsider* on the board, and define these terms. Ask students to study and comment on the photo. Does the photo show an insider or an outsider?

2. Read, or ask a volunteer to read the paragraph entitled *Insiders and Outsiders.*

3. Ask students to describe situations from their childhoods in which they felt like outsiders.

4. Ask them to comment on current situations in which people might feel like outsiders, such as arriving in a new country.

Conducting the Task

■ STEP 1

Have students read the two passages.

■ STEP 2

Ask students to write down their thoughts in response to the passages, and set a time limit of 15 minutes. While students are writing, you may want to walk around the room to offer assistance and observe how well they use different verb tenses.

Closing the Task

1. Assign students to small groups.
2. Have them take turns reading what they have written to the rest of their group.
3. Encourage them to discuss the similarities and differences between their thoughts.

GRAMMAR NOTE

Typical student errors (form)

- Using the simple present to describe a situation in the past that remains true today: —e.g., *She was my third grade teacher. * She is a good teacher.* (See Focus 1.)

- Omitting the auxiliary with the present progressive, or omitting the *-ing* ending: —e.g., * *She running now. * She is run now.* (See Focus 2.)

- Conjugating *to be* rather than *to have* as the auxiliary: —e.g., * *Phyllis was lived with her parents for 20 years.* (See Focus 3.)

- Omitting the auxiliary: —e.g., * *The man been to Chicago twice.* (See Focus 3.)

- Using the simple past to express actions that have not been completed at the moment of focus: —e.g., * *Tam listened to the news when the explosion occurred.* (See Focus 4.)

Typical student errors (use)

- Using the present progressive with verbs of perception: —e.g., * *I'm believing you.* (See Focus 2.)

- Using the present progressive to express the future with inanimate objects: —e.g., * *The red car is belonging to me tomorrow. * That tree is falling tomorrow.* (See Focus 2.)

- Using the present perfect to express a complete action in the past: —e.g., * *William has bought it last Saturday.* (See Focus 3.)

FOCUS 1   Review of Simple Tenses

use

Simple tenses include the simple present, simple past, and simple future. They have the following uses:

TIME FRAME	EXAMPLES	USE
Present	(a) Our in-groups **help** to define our values.	To express general ideas, relationships, and truths.
Past	(b) Immigrants to America in the mid-nineteenth century **included** large numbers of Chinese.	
Future	(c) Families **will** always **be** important to most of us.	
Present	(d) Our family **visits** my grandparents after church every Sunday.	To describe habitual actions.
Past	(e) Almost every year we **celebrated** my great aunt's birthday with a family picnic.	
Future	(f) The club **will collect** dues once a month.	
Present	(g) Kay **thinks** she has chosen the right profession.	To describe mental perceptions or emotions.
Past	(h) People once **believed** the earth was flat.	
Future	(i) You **will love** our new puppy.	
Present	(j) Mark **has** three brothers.	To express possession or personal relationships.
Past	(k) We **owned** an SUV, but we traded it in for a hybrid car.	
Future	(l) By next month, Hannah **will have** a new computer.	
Present	(m) The environmental agency **reports** that new evidence has been gathered about global warming.	To establish the time frame and the moment of focus.
Past	(n) When the United States **passed** the Chinese Exclusion Act in 1882, 100,000 Chinese were living in the United States.	
Future	(o) Phyllis **will call** you Thursday morning; I hope you will not have left for Omaha by then.	

EXERCISE 1

The sentences below tell about James McBride, a writer and jazz musician, and his mother Ruth McBride Jordan, whose life story he describes in *The Color of Water: A Black Man's Tribute to his White Mother*. For each sentence, do the following: (1) Identify the tense of the underlined verb. (2) Decide which of the five uses in Focus 1 (listed below) each verb represents and write the appropriate letter from the list in the blank before the sentence. The first one has been done for you.

a. Expresses a general idea, relationship or truth
b. Describes an habitual action
c. Describes a mental perception or an emotion
d. Expresses possession or a personal relationship
e. Establishes the time frame or a moment of focus

<u>Past</u>   <u>a</u>   1. James McBride <u>grew up</u> in an all-black housing project in Brooklyn, New York.

<u>Past</u>   <u>a</u>   2. His father <u>was</u> a black minister, but James was raised by his mother and a stepfather as his father had died before James was born.

<u>Past</u>   <u>d</u>   3. James <u>had</u> eleven brothers and sisters, all of whom, like him, went to college, partly as a result of his mother's strong desire for her children to be educated.

<u>Past</u>   <u>c</u>   4. As a child, James <u>felt</u> that his mother was strange because she didn't look or act like the other mothers he knew in his neighborhood.

<u>Past</u>   <u>b</u>   5. Ruth McBride Jordan, James's mother, always <u>refused</u> to tell her children about her past life before she moved to New York and married James's father.

<u>Present</u>   <u>a</u>   6. In *The Color of Water*, James <u>describes</u> a discussion with his mother about God.

<u>Past</u>   <u>e</u>   7. When James's mother told him God was a spirit, James <u>asked</u> her what color God's spirit is.

<u>Present</u>   <u>d</u>   8. His mother responded that God is the color of water and that water doesn't <u>have</u> a color.

<u>Past</u>   <u>e</u>   9. James <u>spent</u> 14 years researching and writing *The Color of Water*.

<u>Past</u>   <u>c</u>   10. Through his interviews with his mother and others who knew her, James <u>understood</u> why his mother, the daughter of Jewish immigrants from Poland, left her family and became part of a black community.

<u>Past</u>   <u>e</u>   11. In 1986, at the age of 65, Ruth <u>graduated</u> from Temple University with a degree in social work.

<u>Present</u>   <u>b</u>   12. Today, Ruth <u>works</u> as a volunteer in a shelter for homeless teenage mothers, <u>runs</u> a reading club, and <u>travels</u> regularly to Europe.

FOCUS 1 [10 minutes]

Emphasize that this focus is not simply a review of the forms of these tenses, but an exploration of how each is used.

1. First, read the third column, *Use*.

2. Ask different volunteers to read the first two columns, *Time Frame* and *Examples*.

3. Guide students in discussing how each example expresses the specified time frame and the specified use.

4. Explain that the last *Use* category—establishing the time frame and the moment of focus—simply means that the speaker or writer uses a particular verb tense to tell a listener or reader whether an event is past, present, or future, as well as whether it happened at a specific point of time (*Jean went to church on Sunday.*) or during a period of time (*Jean lived in Atlanta for many years.*).

EXERCISE 1 [5 minutes]

In this structured exercise students read a passage by James McBride, identify the tense of each underlined verb, and then select the use that each represents, as described in Focus 1, from the list a–e.

1. Have students work in pairs.

2. Each student should complete the exercise independently. Then compare and discuss their answers with other students.

3. Review answers as a class. See answers on LP page 14.

 For more practice, use *Grammar Dimensions 4* Workbook page 8, Exercise 1.

EXPANSION [15 minutes]

You can use the following exercise to provide further practice with identifying verbs and their time frames.

1. Write these phrases that identify time frames on the board:

> *As a child . . .*
> *For the time being . . .*
> *Someday . . .*

2. Have students work in pairs.

3. Ask them to write sentences about their lives, using the phrases on the board.

4. Have them exchange papers, read their partner's sentences, and discuss the similarities and differences between their experiences.

Below are two more passages related to the themes in the Opening Task (pages 12–13): forming friendships and entering college. The first passage, from James McBride's *The Color of Water*, describes an incident from his mother's girlhood, when her Jewish immigrant family was living in rural Virginia in the 1930s. The second passage is from sports journalist Mitch Albom's book *Tuesdays with Morrie*, about Albom's college sociology professor who became his good friend. Identify the tense of each underlined verb. Then choose any five of the underlined verbs from the two passages and state the use or uses of each. The first has been done as an example.

Example: (1) Verb: liked

Tense: *past*

Use: *describes mental perceptions or emotions*

A. (1) Nobody <u>liked</u> me. (2) That's how I <u>felt</u> as a child. (3) I know what it feels like when people <u>laugh</u> at you walking down the street, or snicker when they hear you speaking Yiddish,* or just look at you with hate in their eyes. (4) When I was in the fourth grade, a girl came up to me in the schoolyard during recess and said, "You <u>have</u> the prettiest hair." (5) "<u>Let's</u> be friends." (6) I <u>said</u>, "Okay." (7) Heck, I was glad someone <u>wanted</u> to be my friend. (8) Her name <u>was</u> Frances. (9) I'<u>ll</u> never <u>forget</u> Frances as long as I live. (10) She <u>was</u> thin, with light brown hair and blue eyes. (11) She <u>was</u> a quiet gentle person.

* Yiddish is the language that Jews all over the world speak. It derived from German dialects spoken by Jews in central Europe.
From: James McBride, *The Color of Water: A Black Man's Tribute to His White Mother*. New York: Penguin, 2006, pp. 80–81.

B. (1) It <u>is</u> our first class together, in the spring of 1976. (2) I <u>enter</u> Morrie's large office and notice the seemingly countless books that line the wall, shelf after shelf. (3) There is a large rug on the hardwood floor and a window that <u>looks out</u> on the campus walk. (4) Only a dozen or so students <u>are</u> there, fumbling with notebooks and syllabi. (5) I tell myself it <u>will</u> not <u>be</u> easy to cut a class this small. (6) Maybe I shouldn't take it.

From: Mitch Albom, *Tuesdays with Morrie: An Old Man, A Young Man and Life's Greatest Lesson*. New York: Doubleday, 1997, p. 80.

STEP 1 Write a paragraph summarizing how the experience of James McBride's mother in Passage A of Exercise 2 contrasts with Farah Ahmedi's passage in the Opening Task.

STEP 2 Write a paragraph summarizing how Mitch Albom's experience in Passage B of Exercise 2 contrasts with that described in Mike Rose's passage in the Opening Task.

STEP 3 Go back to the paragraphs you've written and underline the verbs you used. Then state what the verb tenses and uses are.

Underline the verbs in these sentences from Unit 1, Exercise 1 in the first column. Then write the letter for the verb tense and use that matches each one from the second column. The first one has been done as an example.

_b_	1. Everything <u>moves</u> quickly in America.	a. Past: Describes mental perception
_e_	2. Outside your window the traffic never <u>stops</u> zooming.	b. Present: Expresses general idea or truth
_d_	3. Alyce <u>invited</u> us to her house for Thanksgiving that first year.	c. Future: Describes general idea of truth
_a_	4. We never <u>imagined</u> a bird could grow so big.	d. Past: Establishes time frame or moment of focus
_f_	5. In any case, I <u>had</u> companions now.	e. Present: Describes habitual actions
_e_	6. Next year I'<u>ll be</u> out of ESL altogether.	f. Past: Describes possession or personal relationships

ANSWER KEY

Exercise 2 **Note:** Not all numbers are listed below as only some verbs are underlined. Answers will vary depending on which five individuals choose from the ten underlined verbs other than the one in A (1).
A: (2) felt, past, describes mental perception/emotion (3) laugh, present, expresses general idea (4) have, past, describes possession (5) let, present, to express general idea (6) said, past, to express general idea (7) wanted, past, describes mental perception/emotion (8) was,

(10) was, past, expresses general idea or truth (11) was, past, expresses general idea or truth
B: (1) is, present, established time frame (2) enter, present, establishes a moment of focus (3) looks, present, expresses a general idea (4) are, present, establishes time frame and moment of focus (5) will be, future, expresses a general idea (6) (not simple tense).
Exercise 3 Answers will vary.

EXERCISE 2 [10 minutes]

This exercise builds on the skills utilized in Exercise 1. Students read two passages and identify the tense of the underlined verbs. They then state the use or uses of five of these.

1. Read the example, identifying the verb (likes), the tense (past), and the use (to describe mental perceptions or emotion).
2. Have students work in pairs.
3. Ask them to take turns identifying the tense of the underlined verbs.
4. Have each choose five verbs, and then take turns stating the use(s) of these. See answers on LP page 16.

 For more practice, use *Grammar Dimensions 4* Workbook page 8, Exercise 2.

EXERCISE 3 [10 minutes]

Students first write a paragraph in which they compare and contrast the readings from the Opening Task and Exercise 2. Then they underline the verbs they used in their paragraphs and identify their tenses and use(s).

1. Have students write their paragraphs and then choose a partner.
2. Give them a specific amount of time in which to share their paragraphs and their analysis of the verbs used.
3. Ask several volunteers to share their partners' paragraphs with the class. As a class, identify the verb tenses and use(s).

EXERCISE 4 (OPTIONAL) [10 minutes]

In Exercise 4, students reread sentences from Unit 1, Exercise 1, this time identifying the tense and use(s) of each verb.

1. Do the first sentence as a class.
2. Have students complete the next five sentences on their own.
3. Review answers as a class. Encourage students to ask questions about any answers they do not understand. See answers on LP page 16.

FOCUS 2 — Review of Progressive Verbs

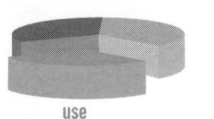

use

Progressive verbs include a form of *be* + a present participle (verb + *-ing*).

EXAMPLES	USES
(a) When Mark gets home from work, Hannah **is** often **studying**.	To describe actions already in progress at the moment of focus.
(b) I **was driving** to the restaurant when I saw the meteor shower.	
(c) Bob **will be working** the night shift when Roberta gets home.	
(d) Eric usually goes out to eat on Fridays. This Friday, however, he **is cooking** at home.	To describe actions at the moment of focus in contrast to habitual actions.
(e) The robins usually took up residence every spring in our old apple trees. One summer, though, they **were building** nests in some of the taller trees.	
(f) Most winters we spend our Christmas vacation at home. But this year we **will be going** to Vermont.	
(g) She **is** constantly **reminding** me to water the plants.	To express repeated actions.
(h) As a young boy, my brother **was** always **getting** into trouble.	
(i) Our math teacher **will be checking** our assignments each morning when class starts.	
(j) Kendra works in the principal's office, but she **is helping** the new school nurse this week.	To describe temporary situations in contrast to permanent states.
(k) My father lived in Chile most of his life, except for two years when he **was living** in Argentina.	
(l) We'll live in a new home after the winter. Until then, we'll **be renting** an apartment in the city.	
(m) The final paper is due soon. **I'm finishing** it as fast as I can.	To describe periods of time in contrast to points of time.
(n) Yesterday the students discussed the projects they **were working** on this semester.	
(o) When they finish their projects, they **will be evaluating** each other's work for several days.	
(p) Sara **is doing** volunteer work for the homeless this summer.	To express uncompleted actions.
(q) When I last saw Ali, he **was** still **planting** his vegetable garden.	
(r) I bet the baby **will** still **be sleeping** when we get home.	

EXERCISE 5

Underline the progressive verbs in the passage below. State what additional information the progressive aspect expresses for each verb. (Refer to the uses presented in Focus 2.)

Example: (a) progressive verb: *am sitting*

additional information expressed: *to describe action in progress at the moment of focus*

> (a) I <u>am sitting</u> under a sycamore by Tinker Creek. (b) I am really here, alive on the intricate earth under trees . . . (c) What else <u>is going</u> on right this minute while groundwater creeps under my feet? (d) The galaxy <u>is careening</u> in a slow, muffled widening. (e) If a million solar systems are born every hour, then surely hundreds burst into being as I shift my weight to the other elbow. (f) The sun's surface <u>is</u> now <u>exploding</u>; other stars implode and vanish, heavy and black, out of sight. (g) Meteorites <u>are arcing</u> to earth invisibly all day long. (h) On the planet the winds <u>are blowing</u>: the polar easterlies, the westerlies, the northeast and southeast trades.
>
> From Annie Dillard, *Pilgrim at Tinker Creek*. New York: Bantam, 1974.

EXERCISE 6

Decide whether a simple tense or progressive tense is appropriate for each blank and give the correct form(s) of the verb in parentheses. The first one has been done for you.

1. Andre (a) ____comes____ (come) from Brazil and (b) ____is____ (be) a native speaker of Portuguese. Currently he (c) __is studying__ (study) English at the University of Colorado. He (d) __is taking__ (take) two courses: composition and American culture.

2. One of my most important in-groups (a) ____is____ (be) my church group. Right now we (b) __are providing__ (provide) lunches for homeless people in the city park. Also, some of us (c) __are tutoring__ (tutor) junior high students in math and English for the summer. Others in my group (d) __are spending__ (spend) part of the summer doing volunteer work at senior citizen centers. We all (e) ____feel____ (feel) that we (f) __are gaining__ (gain) a great deal ourselves by participating in these activities.

(Exercise 6 is continued on LP page 20.)

ANSWER KEY

Exercise 5 The underlined progressive verbs are shown above. Answers may vary for meanings expressed; possible answers are: incomplete action (c), (d), (f), (g), and (h) show progressive forms that inquire about and then describe action already in progress.

Note: Other meanings, such as uncompleted actions, are also relevant. You might point out that "action already in progress" relates most specifically to the question raised in (c).

Exercise 6 Answers will vary. Possible answers are given above.

FOCUS 2 [20 minutes]

Even advanced students may still use the progressive tenses inappropriately. This focus chart will help clarify the different uses of the progressive tenses.

1. **Lead-in:** Before reading the chart with students, remind students that the progressive tenses are only used with action verbs and verbs of perception. Give an example: *I am talking to you now.* NOT * *I am believing you now.* But: *I am feeling sick* or *We're listening to the program* are appropriate, since they refer to perceptions.

2. Review the concept of **moment of focus** from Unit 1: the moment of focus is either a point in time, or a period of time. Speakers choose different verb tenses depending on the moment of focus and the time frame of the action or state they are describing.

3. Write *be* + verb + *-ing* on the board. Model the past, present, and future progressive in sentences, and write these on the board.

4. Read examples (a)–(c) aloud and elicit the time frame of each (past, present, future). Then, ask a volunteer to read the use, and guide students in analyzing the first three examples in terms of that use.

5. Continue this procedure with the remaining examples.

6. Ask volunteers to create sentences exemplifying the six uses, and write these on the board.

7. Encourage students to ask questions about anything they do not understand.

LANGUAGE NOTE

Many students have difficulty grasping the progressive verbs. For many, the simple present or past tenses are as valid a means of describing an action as are the progressive forms. You may want to explain that the progressive forms are often used to express a relationship between two actions or states: *I was watching TV when . . . Until then, we'll be working on . . .* Point out that the progressive forms are accompanied by a time expression, which can be explicit or implied.

EXERCISE 5 [10 minutes]

Students underline the progressive verbs in this passage from Annie Dillard's book, *Pilgrim at Tinker Creek.* They then refer to Focus 2 to identify the use of each verb.

1. Read and discuss the first example with the class.

2. Have students work in pairs to complete the exercise. They should take turns identifying the uses of each verb.

3. Review answers as a class.

EXPANSION [30 minutes/homework]

You may wish to use Activity 2 (writing) on SB page 35 after Exercise 5. In this activity, students spend 15–20 minutes observing nature or people and recording their observations. Later, they share them with a small group or the class, and their classmates guess the place described. You can assign the observation and writing activities as homework, and complete the in-class activities during your next class.

EXERCISE 6 (OPTIONAL) [10 minutes]

Students complete the sentences by writing either the simple tense or progressive tense of the verbs in parentheses. Exercise 6 is continued on SB page 20.

1. This exercise can also be used as a homework assignment.

2. Have students work independently.

3. Review answers as a class, or have students work in pairs to review their answers. Ask them to identify the use of each verb. Encourage them to refer to Focus 2 as needed. See answers on LP pages 18 and 20.

For more practice, use *Grammar Dimensions 4* Workbook pages 9–10, Exercise 3.

3. Next summer our family (a) __is having__ (have) a reunion during the July 4th holiday weekend. My uncle from Finland (b) __is trying__ (try) to come, but he (c) __is starting__ (start) a new business this year so it (d) __is__ (be) difficult for him to get away. Another uncle (e) __is spending__ (spend) the whole summer with us. He (f) __is working__ (work) at my mother's travel agency from June through August.

4. For many immigrants to the United States, their ethnic associations (a) __remain__ (remain) important in-groups long after they have left their home countries. Even while they (b) __are learning__ (learn) a new language, many (c) __look to__ (look to) speakers of their native language as an in-group that (d) __understands__ (understand) their struggles to adapt to a new way of life.

■ EXERCISE 7

Ask another classmate to tell you five things he or she does now as a result of in-group associations. Write a sentence for each, using present-time reference verbs, and report several of the ones you find most interesting to the rest of the class.

Example: *Marco hikes every week with the Sierra Club. As a student at Northwestern, he is majoring in environmental sciences.*

FOCUS 3	Review of Perfect Verbs

Perfect verbs are formed by *have* (*has, have, had, will have*) + a past participle (verb *-ed* or irregular form).

EXAMPLES	USES
(a) *To date*, Mark **has taken** five days off from work for vacation.	To describe events that happen before the moment of focus.
(b) *When I last spoke to my mother*, she **had sent** me a letter, so she didn't want to repeat her news over the phone.	The time phrases and clauses in italics signal the moment of focus.
(c) *By this time tomorrow*, even more acres of the rain forest **will have been destroyed**.	

Present Perfect (Continuing to present)	Simple Past (Completed)	To describe events that started in the past and continue to be true in the present. This contrasts with the use of simple past for completed events.
(d) My parents **have lived** in their house for 40 years; this year they are remodeling the kitchen.	(e) My grandparents **lived** in their house on Tower Avenue until 1996.	

		To describe events that the speaker believes are relevant to the moment of focus. In (f), the moment of focus is the present; in (g), it is the past. (f) and (g) contrast with (h), which has a simple past verb. And in (i), it is the future.
(f) I **have finished** that chapter, so I can help you answer the questions. (My finishing the chapter is relevant to my ability to help now.)		
(g) I **had finished** the chapter before the soccer match started, so I was able to watch the whole match. (My finishing the chapter is relevant to having watched the match.)	(h) I **finished** the chapter. Then I played video games. (Finishing the chapter and playing games are related only sequentially.)	
(i) I **will have taken** my last exam on the day you arrive here. (My completion of exams is relevant to your arrival date.)		

ANSWER KEY

Exercise 7 Answers will vary.

EXERCISE 7 (OPTIONAL) [10 minutes]

This exercise recycles the theme of in-groups from Unit 1. Students interview each other about what they do now as a result of in-group associations, write sentences, and report to the class.

1. Have students work in pairs and take turns interviewing each other.
2. Ask volunteers to share what they have learned about each other with the class.

Suggestion: Collect students' papers. Then read them aloud and ask the class to guess the person described in each.

LESSON PLAN 2

FOCUS 3 [15 minutes]

This focus reviews the perfective verbs and their uses. These tenses may continue to challenge even advanced students.

1. **Lead-in:** Point out that the essential meaning of the perfect is "prior" or "before." The perfect verbs are used to describe an event that happens before, or prior to, another.
2. Draw a simple time line on the board with two divisions: *before* and *next.*
3. Read the first section of the chart. Ask students to analyze each example and say which action happened before, and which next. Write these on the board.
4. Continue this process with the remaining examples.
5. Encourage students to ask questions about anything they do not understand.

GRAMMAR NOTE

There are really only two tenses in English that are expressed by the verb alone: the present and the past. The many other tenses in English are expressed by adding one or more auxiliaries to the past participle of a verb.

The perfect tenses often present a special hurdle for many students. In particular, many students find it difficult to correctly sequence the perfect tenses in speech and writing.

LANGUAGE NOTE

Point out that the present and past perfect are much more frequently used in writing than in speech in the U.S. English. In fact, most Americans avoid the perfect tenses when speaking. For example, in discourse, the common response to the question *Are you hungry?* is *No, I already ate* rather than the more technically correct *No, I have already eaten.*

Underline the present perfect and past perfect verbs in the following passages. Explain what information is expressed by the perfect aspect for these verbs. Decide which of the uses listed in Focus 3 is expressed. (A perfect verb can convey more than one kind of information.) The first has been done as an example.

Example: 1. (d) <u>had seen, heard, learned</u>—past perfect

Information: *describe events that happen before the moment of focus (Fatt Hing at the age of 19) and that are relevant to the moment of focus.*

1. (a) By 1851, in a matter of three years, there were 25,000 Chinese in California. (b) Fatt Hing was one of these 25,000. (c) His story is typical of the pioneer Chinese, many who came with him and many who came after him. (d) As a lad of 19, Fatt Hing <u>had already seen</u> and <u>heard</u> and <u>learned</u> more about the world than most of the men in his village, who <u>had</u> seldom <u>set foot</u> beyond the nearest town square. (e) For Fatt Hing was a fish peddler who went frequently from Toishan to Kwanghai on the coast to buy his fish to sell at the market. (f) Down by the wharves, where the fishing boats came in, Fatt Hing <u>had</u> often <u>seen</u> foreign ships with their sails fluttering in the wind. (g) He <u>had seen</u> hairy white men on the decks, and he <u>had</u> often <u>wondered</u> and <u>dreamed</u> about the land they came from.

2. (a) The dog <u>has got</u> more fun out of Man than Man <u>has got</u> out of the dog, for the clearly demonstrable reason that Man is the more laughable of the two animals. (b) The dog <u>has</u> long <u>been bemused</u> by the singular activities and the curious practices of men, cocking his head inquiringly to one side, intently watching and listening to the strangest goings-on in the world. (c) He <u>has seen</u> men sing together and fight one another in the same evening. (d) He <u>has watched</u> them go to bed when it is time to get up, and get up when it is time to go to bed. (e) He <u>has observed</u> them destroying the soil in vast areas, and nurturing it in small patches. (f) He <u>has stood by</u> while men built strong and solid houses for rest and quiet, and then filled them with lights and bells and machinery.

From James Thurber, *Thurber's Dogs, A Collection of the Master's Dogs, Written and Drawn, Real and Imaginary, Living and Long Ago.* New York: Simon and Schuster, 1955.

Decide whether a simple form (present, past) or present perfect should be used for each verb in parentheses. The first has been done for you.

The Hotter'n Hell Hundred

Near the Texas-Oklahoma border, where the wind never (1) ____seems____ (seem) to stop, where the sun (2) ____broils____ (broil) the blacktop and (3) ____saps____ (sap) the strength, the cyclists (4) ____come____ (come) each year. They (5) ____come____ (come) to Wichita Falls, Texas, by the thousands to ride in what (6) __has become__ (become) the largest one-hundred-mile bicycle race in the world—the Hotter'n Hell Hundred. The race (7) ____takes____ (take) place on Labor Day weekend at the beginning of September, when temperatures regularly (8) ____soar____ (soar) past 100 degrees.

The oddity of this race is that, with each passing year, it (9) __has become__ (become) more and more a symbol of Wichita Falls, a city that, until recently, (10) __has hardly been__ (be, hardly) a cycling bastion. In days past, the sight of a bicyclist (11) ____caused____ (cause) heads to turn in the pickup truck. Tornadoes (12) ____were____ (be) once more numerous than bicyclists in Wichita Falls.

The Hotter'n Hell Hundred (13) ____started____ (start) in 1982 when a postal worker (14) ____suggested____ (suggest) a one-hundred-mile bike ride in 100-degree heat to celebrate Wichita Falls' one-hundredth birthday. Today, the race (15) ____commands____ (command) the attention of almost the whole city as race weekend (16) ____approaches____ (approach).

Adapted with permission from J. Michael Kennedy, "It's the Hottest Little Ol' Race in Texas," *Los Angeles Times*, September 2, 1991.

Decide whether a simple future or future perfect verb should be used for each verb in parentheses. The first one has been done for you.

Our class has been discussing which in-groups we think (1) ____will____ (be) or (2) __will not be__ (be, not) important to us ten years from now. Hua says she knows her family (3) __will remain__ (remain) an important in-group forever. However, she thinks her associations with some campus groups, such as the French Club, (4) __will have ended__ (end) by the time she graduates.

Kazuhiko thinks that he (5) __will have been__ (be) married for several years by that time. He hopes he (6) ____will have____ (have) a few children of his own. He believes his family (7) __will represent__ (represent) his most important in-group in the future. Jose predicts that he (8) __will have become__ (become) a famous physicist by that time and that one of his important in-groups (9) ____will be____ (be) other Nobel Prize winners.

ANSWER KEY

Exercise 8   The verbs are underlined above. The explanations are: 1. Past perfect describes events that happened before the moment of focus.   2. Present perfect describes events that happened before the moment of focus.

EXERCISE 8 [15 minutes]

Students read two passages, underline the present perfect and past perfect verbs, and explain the uses of each, referring back to Focus 3.

1. Read and discuss the first example with the class.
2. Have students underline the verbs, and then work in pairs to identify the uses of each verb.
3. Review answers as a class. See answers on LP page 22.

 For more practice, use *Grammar Dimensions 4* Workbook pages 10–11, Exercise 4.

EXPANSION [30 minutes]

You may want to use Activity 4 (writing) on SB page 36 as an expansion or homework activity. In Activity 4, students write a commentary on humankind modeled on Thurber's commentary in Exercise 8, but from the point of view of a different animal.

EXERCISE 9 [10 minutes]

Students write either the simple and the present perfect form of the verbs in parentheses to complete the sentences.

1. Have students work independently.
2. Ask volunteers to read their paragraphs to the class. Guide the class in making any necessary corrections and identifying the uses of the verbs. See answers on LP page 22.

 For more practice, use *Grammar Dimensions 4* Workbook page 12, Exercise 5.

EXERCISE 10 [5 minutes]

Students complete the sentences with either the simple future or future perfect form of the verbs in parentheses.

1. Have students work independently.
2. Ask them to work in pairs to check their answers, or review answers as a class. See answers on LP page 22.

 For more practice, use *Grammar Dimensions 4* Workbook pages 12–13, Exercise 6.

EXPANSION [30 minutes]

You may wish to assign Activity 5 (speaking/writing) on SB page 36 after this exercise. In this activity, students explore Gordon Allport's theory of out-groups. Working in small groups, they generate a list of out-groups that, they feel, discriminate against them. They then write a short essay about one of the out-groups in which they will use past, present, and future tenses.

EXERCISE 11

With a partner, take the roles of Person A and Person B below. Each person should write five questions to ask the other person in an interview, based on the information given. In your questions, use present, past, and future perfect verb forms. Use them in your responses when appropriate. Here are some patterns that may be useful for your questions:

Have you ever (done X)?

Had you (done X) before (Y)?

Do you think you will have (done X) before (Y)?

Example: Person A: *So you've taken piano lessons. Have you ever studied any other musical instruments?*

Person B: *Actually, yes. Before I took piano lessons, I had studied the violin for a year, but my playing was terrible!*

Person B: *I see you've lived in two other countries besides the United States. Which one did you live in first, and how long did you live in each one?*

Person A: *Well, I had lived in Peru for 15 years before I moved to Madrid. I lived in Madrid for a little over three years.*

PERSON A	PERSON B
was on the track team in high school	took piano lessons as a child
lived in Peru	grew up in Korea
lived in Madrid	moved to the United States in 1998
traveled in Egypt and Africa	attended the University of Florida
parents live in New Mexico	attended Penn State
enrolled at the University of Texas	currently lives in New York
belongs to a health club	likes to watch basketball
loves old movies	loves to go to music concerts
is a sophomore	works at a television station
will graduate from college in three years	plans to move to Tokyo
plans to do a bicycle tour of Vietnam	will get a degree in broadcast journalism

FOCUS 4 — Review of Perfect Progressive Verbs

use

Perfect progressive verbs include present perfect progressive, past perfect progressive, and future perfect progressive. They are formed by *have* (*has, have, had, will have*) + *been* + a past participle (verb + *-ing*).

EXAMPLES		USE
Incomplete: Progressive	**Complete: Nonprogressive**	
(a) The jurors **have been discussing** the evidence. They still haven't reported their verdict.	(b) The jurors **have discussed** the evidence for a week. They are ready to report their verdict.	To express actions that have not been completed at the moment of focus, in contrast to actions that have been completed.
(c) Tam **had been listening** to the news when the explosion occurred.	(d) Tam **had listened** to the news before she left for work.	
(e) Jochen **will have been working** on his Master's degree for two years at the end of this month. He expects to finish in six months.	(f) Jochen **will have worked** at the bank for five years when he leaves for his new job in Quebec.	

EXERCISE 12

For each blank below, choose a simple past, present perfect, or present perfect progressive verb. The first one has been done for you.

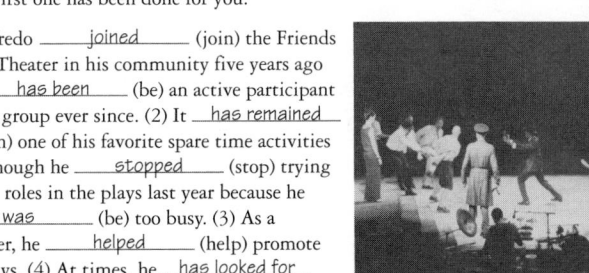

(1) Alfredo ____joined____ (join) the Friends of the Theater in his community five years ago and ___has been___ (be) an active participant in this group ever since. (2) It __has remained__ (remain) one of his favorite spare time activities even though he ____stopped____ (stop) trying out for roles in the plays last year because he ____was____ (be) too busy. (3) As a member, he ____helped____ (help) promote the plays. (4) At times, he __has looked for__ (look for) costumes for the actors. (5) For last month's play, he ____worked____ (work) with the props crew to get furniture and other props for the stage sets. (6) He ____found____ (find) an antique desk to use for one of the sets, and he also ____made____ (make) a fireplace facade. (7) Most recently, he ____has tried____ (try) to get more businesses to advertise in the playbills.

ANSWER KEY

Exercise 11 Answers will vary.

EXERCISE 11 [20 minutes]

This exercise prompts students to use present, past, and future perfect verb forms.

1. Have students work in pairs.
2. Ask them to choose a role (Person A or B). Explain that each student will interview the other.
3. Ask two volunteers to role-play the example.
4. Have another two volunteers practice using different question formats.
5. Give students a few minutes to develop their lists of five questions.
6. Set time limits for the interviews.
7. Ask volunteers to role-play their interviews for the class.

FOCUS 4 [15 minutes]

1. **Lead-in:** Draw a time line on the board to help students visualize the contrasts between actions that have been completed at the moment of focus and those that have not been completed.
2. Read the first two examples (a and b), have a volunteer add them to the time line on the board, and discuss them as a class.
3. Continue with the remaining examples and discuss any student questions together.

EXERCISE 12 [10 minutes]

This controlled exercise give students practice in writing the simple past, present perfect, or present perfect progressive form of the verbs in parentheses to complete the sentences.

1. Read and discuss the first example with the class. Ask students to identify the use of the simple past in the example.
2. Have students work independently or in pairs to complete the exercise.
3. Review answers as a class. See answers on LP page 24.

 For more practice, use *Grammar Dimensions 4* Workbook page 13, Exercise 7.

Write five sentences that express activities you have been doing for six months or more. For each sentence state how long you have been doing the activity and for what purpose.

Examples: *I have been taking yoga classes for two years in order to improve my flexibility.*

I have been working at the bookstore since the beginning of October so that I can pay my tuition.

1. _____
   _____

2. _____
   _____

3. _____
   _____

4. _____
   _____

5. _____
   _____

EXERCISE 14

Write down three things that you are doing right now and plan to continue doing for at least a month. Then, with a classmate, share the information you wrote. For each statement, ask each other how long you will have been doing the activity by the end of a certain time period within the next month (e.g. by a certain date, by the end of the month). Since this is oral English communication, you can use contractions in your responses.

Example: A: I've been taking a global studies course.
B: Oh really? How long will you have been taking that course by the end of this week?
A: Let's see . . . by the end of this week, I'll have been taking it for eight weeks.

form   meaning

use

FOCUS 5	Summary: Present Time Frame

FORMS	EXAMPLES	USES	MEANINGS
SIMPLE PRESENT base form of verb or base form of verb + -s	(a) Children **need** social interaction to develop language.	timeless truths	now
	(b) Kay **plays** on a volleyball team once a week.	habitual actions	
	(c) Kay **considers** her Thai heritage an important in-group.	mental perceptions and emotions	
	(d) Hannah **has** a red bicycle.	possession	
PRESENT PROGRESSIVE *am/is/are* + present participle (verb + -*ing*)	(e) I **am completing** my Bachelor's degree in Spanish.	actions in progress	in progress now
	(f) Hannah **is writing** an essay.	duration	
	(g) Someone **is knocking** at the door.	repetition	
	(h) Kay's brother **is staying** with her this summer.	temporary activities	
	(i) Mark **is making** dinner.	uncompleted actions	
PRESENT PERFECT *have/has* + past participle (verb + -*ed* or irregular form)	(j) Kay **has belonged** to the Sierra Club for four years.	situations that began in the past, continue to the present	in the past but related to now in some way
	(k) Kay **has applied** to several hospitals for positions; she is waiting to hear from them.	actions completed in the past but related to the present	
	(l) Hannah **has** just **finished** junior high school.	actions recently completed	
PRESENT PERFECT PROGRESSIVE *have/has* + present participle (verb + -*ing*)	(m) Both Kay and Mark **have been playing** volleyball since they were teenagers.	continuous or repeated actions that are incomplete	up until and including now
	(n) This weekend Mark **has been competing** in a tournament that ends tomorrow.		

ANSWER KEY

Exercise 13   Answers will vary.

Exercise 14   Answers will vary.

EXERCISE 13 (OPTIONAL) [15 minutes]

1. Ask a volunteer to read the directions and examples aloud.
2. Elicit that the examples use the present perfect, and discuss why (because the activities were begun in the past and are continuing in the present).
3. Have students work in pairs to share their sentences. Ask them to check that each sentence describes an action and the reason for that action.

EXERCISE 14 (OPTIONAL) [15 minutes]

1. Ask a volunteer to read the directions and examples aloud.
2. Elicit that the examples use the present perfect progressive, and discuss why (because the activities have not been completed).
3. Have students work in pairs to share their sentences and ask each other questions about the duration of each activity.
4. Ask volunteers to share some sample sentences with the class.

EXPANSION [30 minutes/homework]

You may wish to use Activity 7 (reflection) on SB page 37 after completing these exercises. This activity asks students to write and share strategies for communicating with ease and effectiveness in social situations.

LESSON PLAN 3

FOCUS 5 [15 minutes]

Focuses 5, 6, and 7 summarize the forms, meanings, and uses of the present, past, and future time frames, respectively. These focus charts can serve as reference charts for work throughout *Grammar Dimensions 4*. The information in these focus charts is repeated in Appendix 1, LP pages A-1–A-4, using different example sentences.

1. **Lead-in:** Have students look at the structure of the chart, and read the column headings.
2. Read, or ask volunteers to read, the examples for the simple present. Discuss the use and meaning of each.
3. Repeat this procedure with the remaining three forms: present progressive, present perfect, and present perfect progressive.
4. If time permits, ask volunteers to give other examples of each use (and meaning).
5. Discuss which uses and meanings are most problematic for students.

Choose simple present, present progressive, present perfect, or present perfect progressive for each blank. More than one answer could be correct; be prepared to explain your choices. The first one has been done for you.

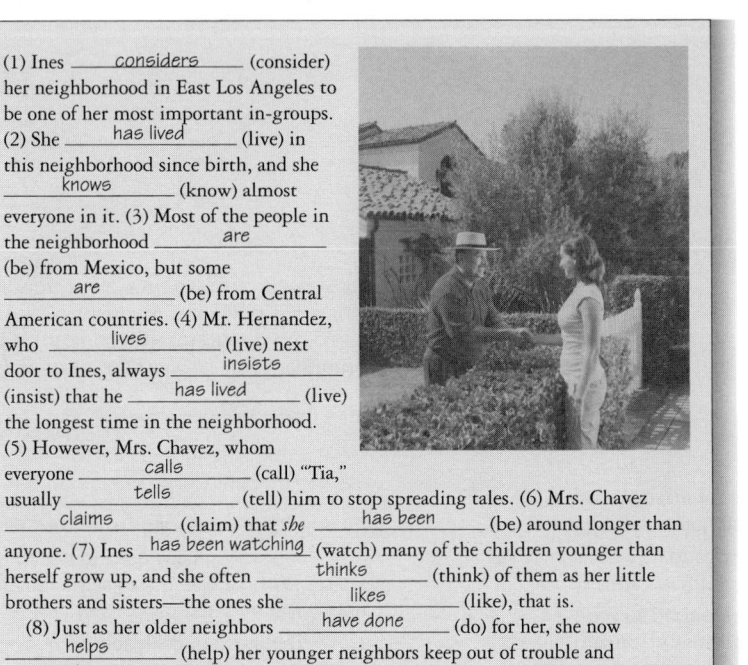

(1) Ines __considers__ (consider) her neighborhood in East Los Angeles to be one of her most important in-groups. (2) She __has lived__ (live) in this neighborhood since birth, and she __knows__ (know) almost everyone in it. (3) Most of the people in the neighborhood __are__ (be) from Mexico, but some __are__ (be) from Central American countries. (4) Mr. Hernandez, who __lives__ (live) next door to Ines, always __insists__ (insist) that he __has lived__ (live) the longest time in the neighborhood. (5) However, Mrs. Chavez, whom everyone __calls__ (call) "Tia," usually __tells__ (tell) him to stop spreading tales. (6) Mrs. Chavez __claims__ (claim) that she __has been__ (be) around longer than anyone. (7) Ines __has been watching__ (watch) many of the children younger than herself grow up, and she often __thinks__ (think) of them as her little brothers and sisters—the ones she __likes__ (like), that is. (8) Just as her older neighbors __have done__ (do) for her, she now __helps__ (help) her younger neighbors keep out of trouble and __gives__ (give) them advice.

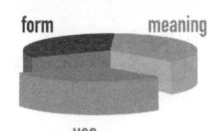

form · meaning · use

| FOCUS 6 | Summary: Past Time Frame |

FORMS	EXAMPLES	USES	MEANINGS
SIMPLE PRESENT	(a) So on Friday, Terry **calls** Lila and **tells** her to be ready for a surprise.	past event in informal narrative	at a certain time in the past
SIMPLE PAST verb + *-ed* or irregular past form	(b) Kay **joined** the Girl Scouts when she **was** 8.	events that took place at a definite time in the past	at a certain time in the past
	(c) Mark **attended** Columbia University for two years as an undergraduate.	events that lasted for a time in the past	
	(d) Kay **went** to Girl Scout camp every summer until she entered high school.	habitual or repeated actions in the past	
	(e) Kay always **knew** that she wanted to be a doctor.	past mental perceptions and emotions	
	(f) Although she **didn't have** a car in college, Kay **owned** a motorbike.	past possessions	
PAST PROGRESSIVE *was/were* + present participle (verb + *-ing*)	(g) At midnight last night, Kay **was** still **making** her rounds.	events in progress at a specific time in the past	in progress at a time in the past
	(h) Kay **was talking** to one of the nurses when Mark called.	interrupted actions	
	(i) Hannah **was acting** in a community theater play for a month last year.	repeated actions and actions over time	
PAST PERFECT *had* + past participle (verb + *-ed* or irregular form)	(j) Before starting medical school, Kay **had taken** a long vacation.	actions or states that took place before another time in the past	before a certain time in the past
PAST PERFECT PROGRESSIVE *had* + *been* + present participle (verb + *-ing*)	(k) Hannah **had been studying** for two hours when her grandmother arrived to take her to the circus.	incomplete events taking place before other past events	up until a certain time in the past
	(l) Mark **had been working** at his computer when the power went out.	incomplete events interrupted by other past events	

ANSWER KEY

Exercise 15 Answers will vary. Possible answers written above.

EXERCISE 15 [5 minutes]

Students complete the sentences with the simple present, present progressive, present perfect, or present perfect progressive form of the verbs in parentheses.

1. Have students work independently.

2. Ask volunteers to share what they wrote for each blank and say why they chose a particular verb form. Discuss the answers with the class: more than one answer can be correct in many instances. See possible answers on LP page 28.

 For more practice, use *Grammar Dimensions 4* Workbook page 14, Exercise 8 and page 15, Exercise 9.

FOCUS 6 [20 minutes]

This focus chart gives a summary of the forms, uses, and meanings of past-reference verbs.

1. **Lead-in:** Call attention to the first form in the chart in which speakers express past events using the simple present. Explain that this use is almost exclusively restricted to informal speech—students will rarely encounter it in writing.

2. Explain that the present progressive can also be used in informal speech to express past events: *Well, last night I'm sitting in my living room and I'm watching TV when I hear a strange sound . . .*

3. As you did with Focus 5, read, or ask volunteers to read, the examples in each row and discuss the use and meaning of each.

4. If time permits, ask volunteers to give other examples of each use.

5. Discuss which uses and meanings are most problematic for students. Answer any questions they might have.

VARIATION

You could review these past forms by having students watch a video (a movie or TV program) that contains a lot of action. Then ask them to describe what happened. Have a volunteer record their accounts on the board. After that, discuss the forms, meanings, and uses, referring to the focus chart.

EXERCISE 16

The comic strip below uses the following tenses: simple present, present progressive, simple past, past progressive, and past perfect. Find an example of each of these tenses in the comic strip. Then identify one verb phrase from the strip that expresses each of the following meanings:

1. event in progress
2. present situation
3. event completed in the past before another event
4. action completed at a definite point in the past
5. event in progress at a specific time in the past

Reprinted by permission of the U.F.S. Inc.

EXERCISE 17

The following passage tells the story of the mythological character Dryope. For each blank, choose a simple past, past progressive, past perfect, or past perfect progressive form of the verb in parentheses. More than one choice could be possible. Be prepared to explain your choices. The first one has been done for you.

(1) One day Dryope, with her sister Iole, _____went_____ (go) to a pool in the forest. (2) She _____was carrying_____ (carry) her baby son. (3) She _____planned_____ (plan) to make flower garlands near the pool for the nymphs, those female goddesses of the woodlands and waters. (4) When Dryope _____saw_____ (see) a lotus tree full of beautiful blossoms near the water, she _____plucked_____ (pluck) some of them for her baby.

(5) To her horror, drops of blood _____flowed_____ (flow) from the stem; the tree _____was_____ (be) actually the nymph Lotis. (6) Lotis _____had fled_____ (flee) from a pursuer and _____had taken_____ (take) refuge in the form of a tree. (7) When the terrified Dryope _____tried_____ (try) to run away, she _____found_____ (find) that her feet would not move; they _____were rooted_____ (root) in the ground. (8) Iole _____watched_____ (watch) helplessly as tree bark _____grew_____ (grow) upward and _____covered_____ (cover) Dryope's body. (9) By the time Dryope's husband _____came_____ (come) to the spot with her father, the bark _____had reached_____ (reach) Dryope's face. (10) They _____rushed_____ (rush) to the tree, _____embraced_____ (embrace) it, and _____watered_____ (water) it with their tears. (11) Dryope _____had_____ (have) time only to tell them that she _____had done_____ (do) no wrong intentionally. (12) She _____begged_____ (beg) them to bring the child often to the tree to play in its shade. (13) She also _____told_____ (tell) them to remind her child never to pluck flowers and to consider that every tree and bush may be a goddess in disguise.

From Edith Hamilton, *Mythology*. Copyright 1942 by Edith Hamilton. Copyright renewed 1969 by Dorian Fielding Reid and Doris Fielding Reid. By permission of Little, Brown and Company.

EXERCISE 18

Retell Dryope's story in Exercise 17 in an informal narrative style. Use present tense verbs instead of past tense verbs.

Example: *One day this woman named Dryope and her sister Iole go to a pool in the woods. Dryope's carrying her baby son with her. . . .*

ANSWER KEY

Exercise 16 Answers will vary. Examples of each tense include: Simple present: 'm, are, is Present progressive: 's happening   Simple past: were, came, saw   Past progressive: were erupting, were melting   Past perfect: had come   1. event in progress: 's happening (5th panel)   2. present situation: am (awake) (4th panel)   3. event completed in the past before another event: had come (10th panel)   4. action completed at a definite point in the past: came (6th panel)   5. event in progress at a specific time in the past: were melting (7th panel)

Exercise 18 Answers may vary. Possible answers include: 1. goes   2. is carrying   3. plans   4. sees; plucks   5. flow; is   6. flees; takes   7. tries; finds; are rooted   8. watches; grows; covers   9. comes; has reached   10. rush; embrace; water   11. has; has done   11. begs   12. tells

EXERCISE 16 [15 minutes]

1. Have students work in pairs or small groups.
2. Review answers as a class. See possible answers on LP page 30.
3. Ask a volunteer to poll the answers: How many students chose the same example for each of the verb uses?

EXPANSION [30 minutes]

Use Activity 6 (research on the web) on SB page 37 to give students additional practice with a range of tenses.

EXERCISE 17 [20 minutes]

Students complete the sentences by writing the simple past, past progressive, past perfect, or past perfect progressive form of the verb in parentheses. As in Exercise 15, there can be more than one correct answer.

1. Have students work independently.
2. Ask volunteers to share what they wrote for each blank and give the reason for each choice. Discuss that choice with the class, and ask students to suggest other answers that could also be correct. See possible answers on LP page 30.

 For more practice, use *Grammar Dimensions 4* Workbook pages 15–16, Exercise 10.

EXERCISE 18 (OPTIONAL) [20 minutes]

Students retell the story in Exercise 17, using present rather than past tense forms.

1. Read and discuss the first example with the class. Ask students to look back at the original passage in Exercise 17 and identify the past tense verbs that are changed to present tense in the example.
2. Have students work independently or in pairs to complete the exercise.
3. Ask volunteers to read their passages to the class. Which style do students prefer, the more formal, or less formal? See possible answers on LP page 30.

EXPANSION [30 minutes]

Use Activity 1 (listening/speaking/writing) on SB page 35 to give students practice with past-reference tenses.

FORMS	EXAMPLES	USES	MEANINGS
SIMPLE PRESENT	(a) Kay **completes** her residency next May. (b) After Kay **finishes** her residency, she will take a vacation.	definite future plans or schedules events with future time adverbials in dependent clauses	already planned or expected in the future
PRESENT PROGRESSIVE	(c) I **am leaving** at 7:00 AM tomorrow. (d) The family **is spending** the Christmas holidays in Boston.	future intentions scheduled events that last for a period of time	already planned or expected in the future
BE GOING TO FUTURE *am/is/are going to* + base verb	(e) The movie **is going to start** in a few minutes. (f) I **am going to finish** this no matter what! (g) When you get older, you**'re going to wish** that you had saved more money. (h) They **are going to travel** in India next summer.	probable and immediate future events strong intentions predictions about future situations future plans	at a certain time in the future
SIMPLE FUTURE *will* + base verb	(i) We **will** most likely **stay** at our beach cottage next summer. (j) I **will help** you with your homework this evening. (k) She**'ll be** very successful.	probable future events willingness/ promises predictions about future situations	
FUTURE PROGRESSIVE *will* + *be* + present participle (verb + *-ing*)	(l) Kay's parents **will be driving** from Chicago to Palo Alto next week. (m) Kay's family **will be living** in Palo Alto until she finishes her residency.	events that will be in progress in the near future future events that will last for a period of time	in progress at a certain time in the future

FORMS	EXAMPLES	USES	MEANINGS
FUTURE PERFECT *will* + *have* + past participle (verb + *-ed*)	(n) Kay's parents **will have left** Palo Alto before Hannah starts school.	before a certain time in the future	future events happening before other future events
FUTURE PERFECT PROGRESSIVE *will* + *have* + *been* present participle (verb + *-ing*)	(o) By the end of the year, Kay **will have been living** in California for four years.	up until a certain time in the future	continuous and/or repeated actions continuing into the future

EXERCISE 19

Choose an appropriate future-reference verb tense—simple present, present progressive, *be going to*, simple future, future progressive, or future perfect—to complete the dialogue below between Justin and his friend Patty. More than one verb tense might be appropriate for some blanks. Read the dialogue with a classmate. Discuss any differences in the choices you made. The first exchange has been done for you.

Justin: My brother (1) ___is leaving___ (leave) tomorrow for his third trip to Europe this year!

Patty: What time (2) _does he go/is he going_ (he, go)?

Justin: His plane (3) ___takes off___ (take off) really early—at 6 AM, I think—so he (4) ___needs___ (need) to get out of here by 4 AM or so. I (5) ___am driving___ (drive) him to the airport.

Patty: So why (6) ___is he going___ (he, go) to Europe again?

Justin: It's for his job. He (7) ___is meeting___ (meet) his company's executives in Germany and then he (8) ___is spending___ (spend) a few days in Denmark. You know something? When I (9) ___finish___ (finish) school and (10) ___get___ (get) a job, I (11) _am going to have_ (have) an exciting lifestyle too!

Patty: Oh, really? And what (12) ___will you do___ (you, do), if you don't mind my asking.

(Exercise 19 is continued on LP page 34.)

ANSWER KEY

Exercise 19   Answers may vary. Example answers above.

FOCUS 7 [15 minutes]

This focus chart summarizes the forms, uses, and meanings of future time frame verbs.

1. **Lead-in:** For additional examples, use the sentences in the Appendix 1C chart on LP pages A-3–A-4 to review forms, uses, and meanings of these forms.
2. Write examples from Appendix 1 in random order on the board.
3. Ask students to first identify the forms (e.g., simple present, present progressive), referring to the first column in Focus 7.
4. Then ask them to identify which use is expressed (e.g., future intentions, predictions about future situations), and the meaning of each.

EXERCISE 19 [20 minutes]

Students choose a future-reference verb tense to complete the dialogue. Exercise 19 continues on SB page 34.

1. Read and discuss the first exchange with the class. What other tenses might also be appropriate here?
2. Have students work independently to fill in the blanks.
3. Ask them to work in pairs and take turns reading their dialogues to each other.
4. Ask them to discuss the choices they have made. Which choices were the same, and which different? How do different choices change the meaning of the dialogue? See the answers on LP pages 32 and 34.

work book For more practice, use *Grammar Dimensions 4* Workbook page 17, Exercise 11.

EXPANSION [30 minutes]

You may wish to use Activity 3 (writing/speaking) on SB page 36 to expand on Exercise 19.

(Exercise 19 is continued from LP page 32.)

Justin: Not at all. Next summer, of course, after I (13) _____graduate_____ (graduate), I (14) _____will look_____ (look) for a job for a while. With a little effort, I'm sure I (15) _____will find_____ (find) a very challenging and lucrative position in my field. Five years or so from now I (16) _____will have saved_____ (save) enough money to put a down payment on a penthouse condominium. By that time, I (17) _____will have made_____ (make) enough to buy a flashy little sports car. I (18) _____will have put_____ (put) away enough money by then to rent a beach vacation home every summer.

Patty: It sounds as if you (19) _____will be living_____ (live) the good life!

Justin: Well, I just said I (20) _____will have_____ (have) enough money to live like that. That doesn't mean I (21) _____will do_____ (do) it. Actually, now that I think about it, I (22) _____am not going to get_____ (not, get) any of those things. At the end of the five years I (23) _____will take_____ (take) all that money I saved and (24) _____buy_____ (buy) the largest sailboat I can afford. I (25) _____am going to quit_____ (quit) my job and sail around the world! Care to join the crew?

Use Your English

CD1 Track 3

ACTIVITY 1 listening/speaking/writing

In *The Man Who Mistook His Wife for a Hat*, Dr. Oliver Sacks writes about his experiences treating unusual neurological disorders. You will hear a passage summarizing part of Dr. Sacks's true story of Dr. P., the man he refers to in the title.

■ **STEP 1** Listen to the passage once for overall meaning.

■ **STEP 2** On a separate piece of paper, make a chart like the one below.

■ **STEP 3** Listen to the passage again. In the left-hand column of your chart, write down the past events that occurred before other past events. The first one has been done for you.

EARLIER PAST EVENT	PAST EVENT
1. He had been a singer.	1. Later he became a teacher at the local school of music.

■ **STEP 4** Listen to the whole passage one more time. In the right-hand column of your chart, write the past event that the earlier past event precedes, as in the example.

■ **STEP 5** Compare your chart with a partner's and discuss the verb forms used in the column.

ACTIVITY 2 writing

Find a place that you think would be interesting to observe nature or people: a quiet place outdoors, a school cafeteria, an airport, or a busy restaurant, for example. Spend 15 or 20 minutes in this place with a notebook to record observations of interesting sights and sounds. You might want to reread Annie Dillard's observations in Exercise 3. Read your observations to the rest of the class or in a small group without telling them where you were. Have your classmates guess the place you are describing.

UNIT GOAL REVIEW [5 minutes]

Ask students to look at the goals on the opening page of the unit again. Refer to the pages of the unit where information on each goal can be found.

ExamView *Test Generator* For assessment of Unit 2, use *Grammar Dimensions 4 ExamView®*.

USE YOUR ENGLISH

The Use Your English activities at the end of the unit contain situations that should naturally elicit the structures covered in the unit. For a more complete discussion of how to use the Use Your English Activities see To the Teacher, LP page xxvi. While students are doing these activities in class, you can circulate and listen to see if they are using the structures accurately. Errors can be corrected after the activity has finished.

ACTIVITY 1 listening/speaking/writing [30 minutes]

You may want to use this activity after Exercise 18 on SB page 31. Students listen to an audio passage from Oliver Sacks's book, *The Man Who Mistook His Wife for a Hat*. They chart the events, indicating the order in which they took place, and then share their charts with a partner.

CD1 Track 3

1. Tell students that they are going to listen to an audio passage from Oliver Sacks's book, *The Man Who Mistook His Wife for a Hat*. Elicit what students may know about the book and about Sacks's work in treating unusual neurological disorders. Some students may have seen the movie about Sacks's work, *Awakenings*, with Robin Williams.

2. Explain that students are going to chart the actions they hear about. Reproduce the sample chart from SB page 35 on the board.

3. Ask volunteers to give sample sentences describing events from their own lives, and add these to the chart on the board.

4. Follow Steps 1 through 5 in the student book.

ACTIVITY 2 writing [30 minutes/homework]

You may want to use this activity after Exercise 5 on SB page 19.

1. Tell students that you would like them to observe nature or people and record their observations, much as Anne Dillard did in the excerpt from *Pilgrim at Tinker Creek* that they read in Exercise 3.

2. You may want to discuss places students might like to go to observe nature or people, such as a park or a mall. Tell students that they should spend at least 15 minutes observing and writing down their observations, but not mention the place where all these activities are happening.

3. During the next class session, have students meet in small groups and read their observations. Ask the others in the group to take turns guessing what place is being described.

4. Ask volunteers to share. Did many students correctly guess the place that was described?

 **ACTIVITY 3** writing/speaking

Choose one person in the class. Describe what you think that person will be doing and how he or she will change in the next ten years or so. Read your descriptions to the class or in a small group to see if your classmates can identify the person.

 **ACTIVITY 4** writing

Reread the passage by James Thurber in Exercise 8. Think of another animal that might have some opinions about the human race that are very different from those humans tend to have about themselves. The animal could be a house pet, such as a canary; another domestic animal, such as a pig; or a wild animal, such as a wolf. Write a description of how this animal has probably regarded the human race.

 **ACTIVITY 5** speaking/writing

Gordon Allport used concepts of in-groups and out-groups to develop a theory about how prejudices are formed. The very nature of in-groups means that other groups are "out-groups." For example, if someone is Christian, then non-Christians would be "out-groups." Not all "out-groups" are at odds with each other. However, Allport believed that sometimes people treat certain out-groups as "the enemy" or as inferior to their group. As a result, prejudices towards those of other religions, races, or nationalities may form. Do you see evidence, in your school, community, or a larger context, of "out-groups" who are victims of prejudice? Working in groups, list some of the out-groups you think are discriminated against. Then describe the situation affecting one of these out-groups in an essay. State whether the situation has improved or gotten worse over time and whether you think it will have improved by the end of the next decade or so.

 **ACTIVITY 6** research on the web

 Since 2002, Beloit College in Wisconsin has released an annual "Mindset List" for its entering freshmen class. This list is meant to reflect the worldview of its new students. For example, here are a few of the seventy-five "Mindset" items for students in the Class of 2009, most of whom were born around 1987:

- Voicemail has always been available.
- They may have fallen asleep playing their Gameboys in the crib.
- Scientists have always been able to see supernovas.

Look up the Mindset List for one of the Beloit freshman classes (go to www.beloit.edu and use Mindset in your search). Report back on five of the most interesting or humorous items you found. There are many references to American culture (e.g., television personalities and shows) in the lists, so you may need to do more research to learn about the references or ask someone familiar with American culture to explain them to you. As a follow-up, you and your classmates may want to compose your own Mindset List.

 **ACTIVITY 7** reflection

Learners of a second or foreign language may sometimes feel like outsiders in situations where many people around them are native speakers of that language. For example, they may feel a lack of confidence when they attend social situations such as a party or when they are asked to participate in classroom discussions. Consider strategies you have used in the past to build confidence when communicating in situations with English speakers, strategies you are using now, and strategies that you could use in the future. Here are a few examples:

I have learned some questions that are good to start conversation with people when I go to parties, such as "What did you do over the summer?" or "Do you have any recommendations for places to visit during the spring break?" I am practicing some "starter phrases" to express opinions in class discussions, such as "I agree with what you said, and I also think that . . ." or "That's a good point; however, I feel that . . ." I am going to ask one of my dormitory roommates who is a native speaker of English to explain some of the slang expressions I hear other students using a lot.

Individually or in small groups, write down three to five examples of strategies you have used in the past, are using now, or plan to use, and share your strategies with others in the class.

USE YOUR ENGLISH

ACTIVITY 3 writing/speaking
[30 minutes]

You could use this activity after Exercise 19 on SB page 33 to give additional writing and reading practice with future-reference verbs.

1. Have students choose one student and write a prediction of what that person will be doing and how she/he will change in the next ten years or so.
2. Model some predictions by asking students to say what they will be doing in five years, and write responses on the board. For example, say: *In five years, I will have won the lottery, and I will be living in a huge house in the south of France.*
3. Have volunteers identify the verbs and their uses in the sentences on the board.
4. Have students work independently to write their predictions. Tell students not to name the person.
5. Assign students to small groups. Ask them to read their predictions aloud, and ask the other students to guess who the person is.
6. Ask volunteers to share their predictions with the class, and have the class guess the person described.

ACTIVITY 4 writing
[30 minutes]

You may want to use this activity after Exercise 8 on SB page 22.

1. Ask students to work in pairs or small groups.
2. Have them reread Thurber's passage on SB page 22.
3. Have students take turns reading and discussing their commentaries.

ACTIVITY 5 speaking/writing
[30 minutes]

You may want to use this activity after Exercise 10 on SB page 23.

1. Ask students to reread the information about Gordon Allport and in-groups from the Opening Task of Unit 1 on page 0.
2. Write *in-group, friends,* and *out-groups/enemies* in three columns on the board.
3. Tell students that Allport thought that people not only have in-groups, they also have *out-groups*, or groups to which they do not belong.
4. On the board, write a short list of in-groups for a hypothetical person, such as *male, American, swimmer, Republican, cook.*
5. Elicit what out-groups this person might have, and write these on the board.
6. Tell students that Allport believed that people have strong feelings about some out-groups, but not all. A swimmer, for example, might not care whether someone else is a swimmer, or not. Allport did think that people can have negative feelings about some out-groups.
7. Read the description of Allport's theory.
8. Ask students to revisit the list of in-groups and out-groups on the board. Which might elicit strong feelings, and which probably would not?
9. Have students work in small groups to list some out-groups they think discriminate against them.

ACTIVITY 6 research on the web
[30 minutes]

You may want to use this activity after Exercise 16 on SB page 30.

1. Tell students that the URL in the text (www.beloit.edu) will take them to the home page of Beloit College. They will then need to click the Search button on the left-hand side of the page and type in *mindset.*
2. Have students work in pairs and write down five of the most interesting or humorous items they find on the lists.
3. Have them work with another pair and take turns reading their lists.
4. Ask volunteers to share their lists, and write these on the board. Ask students to identify the verbs and their uses, and then discuss the content of what they have found.

ACTIVITY 7 reflection
[30 minutes/homework]

You may want to use this activity after Exercise 14 on SB page 26.

1. Discuss how learners of a second or foreign language may sometimes feel like outsiders in situations where many people around them are native speakers of that language. Ask students to brainstorm other places or contexts where communication can be difficult.
2. As a class, analyze the reasons why communication is difficult in specific circumstances. Is it always a language problem? Could it be a problem of the context itself? Noise? Cultural issues? Body language? Tone of voice?
3. Elicit strategies for both enhancing language strategies and for adapting to or coping with various contexts (phone, parties, offices, appointments, conversation with strangers). Briefly elicit other strategies students have used in the past to build their confidence in various situations, and write these on the board.
4. Give groups or pairs a specific context for which they should develop strategies.
5. Ask them to write down three to five examples of strategies they a) have used in the past, b) are using now, and c) plan to use in the future.
6. Ask students to share their best strategies with the class.

SUBJECT-VERB AGREEMENT

- **Identify the head noun in a subject**
- **Use correct verb forms for subjects with correlative conjunctions**
- **Know which kinds of nouns take singular or plural verbs**
- **Know how subject-verb agreement forms vary in formal and informal English**

OPENING TASK
Reading Habits

For over five decades, the Gallup News Service, which examines national trends in the United States, has been surveying Americans' reading habits. They have asked people how often they read, what kinds of reading they do, and how reading compares with other leisure activities, such as going to movies or using the Internet.

■ STEP 1

Read the results on the next page from a 2005 Gallup Poll about reading habits. Then write a paragraph summary of the poll. In your summary, include the following information:

- The number of adults responding to the survey questions
- The percentage of American adults reading books at that time
- What the first question shows about Americans reading in 2005 compared to the poll in 1990
- What the first question shows about which groups are reading more
- What the second question reveals about the number of books that the respondents have read during the year the poll was taken
- What the third question indicates about the effect of the Internet on reading habits

Gallup Poll on Americans' Reading Habits

May, 2005   Based on telephone interviews with 1,006 adults

Question 1. Do you happen to be reading any books or novels at the present?

	YES %
2005 May 20–22	47
1990 Dec 13–16	37
1957 Mar 15–20	23

WHO IS READING A BOOK?		YES %
Overall		47
Gender		
	Male	42
	Female	53
Age		
	18–29	40
	30–49	47
	50–64	51
	65+	47
Education		
	High school or less	33
	Some college	46
	College grad	63
	Postgraduate	74

Question 2. During the past year, about how many books, either hardcover or paperback, did you read either all or part of the way through?

NONE	1 to 5	6 to 10	11 to 50	51+	NO ANSWER
16%	38%	14%	25%	6%	1%

Question 3. What best describes the effect that the Internet has had on the amount of time that you, personally, spend reading books?

READING MORE BOOKS	NOT AFFECTED	READING FEWER BOOKS	NO OPINION
6%	73%	16%	5%

From *Gallup New Service* June 3, 2005.

UNIT OVERVIEW

This unit offers instruction and practice in subject-verb agreement in a variety of challenging situations. Students learn a number of useful grammar skills, such as how to identify the head nouns in subjects with long modifying phrases or clauses—that is, the noun with which a verb must agree in number. The unit also covers structures that pose the greatest challenges in mastering subject-verb agreement rules in English.

Please note that this lesson has been divided into 4 lesson plans due to its length.

GRAMMAR NOTE

The English verb system that can be a problem area even for native speakers of English: subject-verb agreement. Contrary to popular belief, identifying and using correct subject-verb agreement in writing is not always easy, nor is it always completely agreed upon by instructors. Spoken English provides even more problems as a variety of subject-verb agreement combinations are tolerated by the general public and may even be heard on newscasts and read in the newspaper. Not all advanced level learners possess the specific knowledge required to make informed decisions about these grammar points.

UNIT GOALS

Some instructors may want to review the goals listed on Student Book (SB) page 38 after completing the Opening Task so that students understand what they should know by the end of the unit. These goals can also be reviewed at the end of the unit when students are more familiar with the grammar terminology.

OPENING TASK [20 minutes]

The purpose of this task is to create a realistic and engaging context in which students write and talk about their reading habits and preferences using a variety of head nouns: quantifiers (*many, most, some,* etc.), percentages, and gerund phrases (e.g., *reading books*). The problem-solving format is designed to show the teacher how well the students can produce the target structures implicitly and spontaneously when they are engaged in a communicative task. For a more complete discussion of the purpose of the Opening Task, see To the Teacher, Lesson Planner (LP) page xxii.

Setting Up the Task

1. Ask students to comment on the photo. Where is this person? What is he doing?
2. Discuss students' experiences with polls: Do they find polls interesting? Do they think polls are a good source of information?
3. Discuss reading: How many students read books on a regular basis? How does the Internet affect their reading habits: do they read more, or less, now than when they did not have access to the Internet?
4. Read the opening paragraph about the Gallup Poll, or ask a volunteer to read it aloud.

Conducting the Task

Divide students into pairs and have them read the results of the Gallup Poll and then write a paragraph summarizing it.

1. Ask students to exchange their papers with their partners and to check that all the information outlined in the six bullets is included in the paragraph. Then, give them some time to discuss the poll.

2. You may want to walk around and listen in order to diagnose students' facility with subject-verb agreement.

Closing the Task

Discuss the poll as a class. Were any of the results surprising? Were any not surprising?

Ask students how the Internet has affected their reading habits and those of people they know.

Don't worry about accuracy at this point, though you may want to take notes of errors in meaning, form, or use in order to focus on those problems later.

GRAMMAR NOTE

Typical student errors (form)

- Omitting the third person singular inflection: —e.g., * *She live in Los Angeles.* * *John say he will come.* (See Focus 1.)
- Errors in subject-verb agreement when the verb has more than one part: —e.g., * *One of the novels that **have** been published . . .* (See Focus 2.)
- Using a singular verb when two subjects are connected by *both . . . and:* —e.g., * *Both Ana and Liz is coming to our house.* (See Focus 3.)
- Using a plural verb with money: —e.g., * *Fifty dollars are too much to pay for that.* (See Focus 5.)
- Using a plural verb with *every one of:* —e.g., * *Every one of the boys are going to the game.* (See Focus 6.)

Typical student errors (use)

- Using the wrong form of *be*: —e.g., * *You is late. We was on time.* (See Focus 1.)
- Using *do* rather than *be*: —e.g., * *Do they be happy? We don't be students.* (See Focus 1.)

FOCUS 1 — Overview of Subject-Verb Agreement

EXAMPLES	EXPLANATIONS
(a) I **am** you/we/they **are** he/she/it **is**	In English, all verbs in the present tense must agree in number with the subjects of sentences. • Present tense *be* has three forms.
(b) I/you/we/they **have** he/she/it **has**	• Present tense *have* changes to *has* with third-person singular subjects.
(c) I/you/we/they **work** He/she/it **works**	• Other present tense verbs add an *–s* or *–es* at the end for third-person singular subjects.
(d) I/you/we/they **pass** He/she it **passes**	
(e) I/he/she/it **was** we/you/they **were**	• Past tense *be* has two forms.
(f) This book **has** been a bestseller for a year.	If the verb is complex, the first part or auxiliary agrees with the subject.
(g) **Science fiction** and **mysteries are** two of my favorite kinds of summer reading.	If the subject has more than one part (two or more noun phases), the verb is plural.
(h) There **is** one book I especially like.	In formal English, when the grammatical subject is *there*, the verb agrees with the logical subject, the noun phrase that follows the verb.
(i) There **are** two books I need to buy.	Choosing the correct verb form is not always easy, even for native speakers of English. Some reasons for difficulties are the following:
Head Noun (j) (The main **reason** we decided to take a trip to the Rocky Mountains) **is** to learn geological history. (k) (That **novel** about alien invasions in several South American countries) **has** been made into a TV film.	• subjects with long modifying phrases following the main noun requiring agreement, as in (j) and (k). This noun is often called the **head noun.**
(l) The **pair of scissors** you bought **is** really dull now. (m) **Every book** in the library **has** been entered in the new computer system.	• nouns and pronoun phrases whose number (singular/plural) may be confusing, as in (l) and (m).
Plural Noun (n) Those comic **books** make me laugh. **Singular Verb** (o) That comic book **makes** me laugh.	• the *–s* ending in English as both a plural marker for nouns and a singular marker for third-person present-tense verbs, as in (n), which has a plural noun, and (o), which has a 3rd person singular verb.

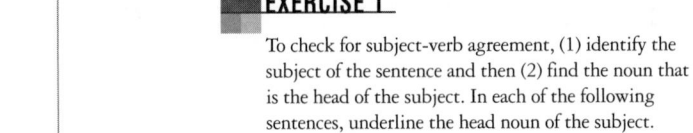

EXERCISE 1

To check for subject-verb agreement, (1) identify the subject of the sentence and then (2) find the noun that is the head of the subject. In each of the following sentences, underline the head noun of the subject. Then circle the correct form of the verb in parentheses.

Example: *Book clubs (is/are) very popular social activities.*

1. The popularity of book clubs (seem/seems) to be increasing throughout the world.

2. Organizing a successful book club (involve/involves) a number of considerations.

3. Some of the many considerations (is/are) are how often to meet and whether the members (want/wants) to conduct serious discussions or just have social chats about books.

4. A book club organizer also (has/have) to think about how large the group should be.

5. Other questions to consider (concern/concerns) where the book club will meet, such as in the members' homes or in a public place like a bookstore, and who will be responsible for structuring each meeting.

6. Once the book club (is/are) formed, the members (need/needs) to agree on how they will select the books; sometimes, each member (suggest/suggests) a number of books and then the members (vote/votes) on them.

7. During the book club discussions, an individual who (is/are) critical of a book that other members (like/likes) (has/have) to be careful not to hurt anyone's feelings.

8. There (is/are) now hundreds of virtual book clubs online.

9. These online book clubs, which (connect/connects) readers around the world, (has/have) helped to promote interesting discussions about books from multicultural perspectives.

10. Another advantage of online book clubs (is/are) that they can link groups of friends who (want/wants) to discuss books but who (do/does) not live near each other.

EXERCISE 2

Write three questions about the Gallup reading habits poll results shown in the Opening Task. Check to make sure that your verbs agree with their subject. With a classmate, take turns asking and responding to the questions.

Examples: *What percentage of Americans say they have not read any books during the past year?*
Which group has more people reading a book: males or females?

ANSWER KEY

Exercise 1   The head nouns are underlined and the correct verbs circled above; the subjects are as follows: 1. The popularity of book clubs   2. Organizing a successful book club   3. Some of the many considerations   4. A book club organizer   5. Other questions to consider   6. the book club   7. an individual who is critical of a book that other members like   8. hundreds of virtual book clubs   9. These online book clubs   10. Another advantage of online book clubs
Exercise 2   Answers will vary.

FOCUS 1 [10 minutes]

Focus 1 gives examples of several tricky situations: noun-verb agreement with compound verbs, head noun-verb agreement in sentences with long modifying phrases, verb agreement with noun and pronoun phrases, and the -s ending as both a plural marker for nouns and a singular marker for third-person present-tense verbs.

1. **Lead-in:** Tell students that subject-verb agreement presents problems even for native speakers of English. Discuss how many languages do not inflect verb for number. Review the terminology associated with subject-verb agreement, such as *number, agree, head noun, modifying phrase, singular* and *plural marker*.

2. Read the examples and the explanations in the first row of the focus chart.

3. Write *Head Noun* on the board and explain that a *head noun* is a noun that is modified by a phrase. Write example (j) from the focus chart on the board. Ask students to find the head noun and the phrase that modifies it. Circle the head noun and underline the modifying phrase.

4. Read the remaining examples in the focus chart, guiding students in identifying the head noun and modifying phrase in each.

5. Ask volunteers to choose one of the examples and read the sentence, omitting the modifying phrase, as in (j): *The main reason is to learn geological history.*

6. To give students some extra practice, write a cloze version of (n) and (o) on the board: *Those _____ make me laugh. That _____ makes me laugh.* Ask volunteers to complete the sentences.

LANGUAGE NOTE

The verb *be* is one of the most irregular verbs in English. Many languages have no equivalent, and so some students, translating from their first language, will make these kinds of errors: * *John engineer. John in next room. He tall.* Guide students in recognizing that *be* reflects person, number, and tense.

The -s ending as both a plural marker for nouns and a singular marker for verbs causes confusion for many people, as does knowing which kinds of nouns take singular or plural verbs. Watch for errors in these areas and offer extra support and practice, as needed.

EXERCISE 1 [10 minutes]

In this exercise students practice identifying the subject of the sentence and the noun that is the head of the subject, and then practice choosing the verb form with which it agrees. This focus on recognition prepares students for more communicative work later on in the lesson.

1. This activity can be done individually, in pairs, or as a class.

2. Have students identify the subject of a sentence, the head noun of the subject, and the correct form of the verb in the parentheses with which it agrees. See answers on LP page 40.

3. Have volunteers identify the modifying clauses in the sentences.

4. Ask others to read the sentence, omitting the modifying clauses. Is it easier for them to identify the subject and verb without those clauses?

For more practice, use *Grammar Dimensions 4* Workbook page 18, Exercise 1.

EXPANSION [30 minutes]

The following exercise can be used in class or assigned as homework to provide further practice of subject-verb agreement.

1. Have students work in pairs.

2. Ask them to research book clubs online and write two or three-sentence descriptions of at least three book clubs. One sentence should begin with *There. . .* and one with *Every . . .*

3. Have each pair exchange sentences with another pair and read and discuss their findings.

4. Ask volunteers to share interesting information they have learned.

EXERCISE 2 [15 minutes]

In this exercise students continue practicing subject-verb agreement by writing, asking, and answering three questions about the Gallup Poll results from the Opening Task.

1. Have students work in pairs.

2. As a class, read the example question and answer and identify the head noun, modifying phrase, and verb in each.

3. Ask volunteers to share their sentences—or their partner's sentences—with the class.

EXPANSION [30 minutes]

In Activity 3 (research/speaking/writing) on SB page 58 students conduct a survey on their classmates' reading habits, using the questions from the Gallup Poll in the Opening Task. Then have them report their findings, using a variety of subjects and verb tenses.

FOCUS 2 — Identifying Head Nouns in Long Subjects

EXAMPLES	EXPLANATIONS
(a) That **novel** about alien invasions in several southwestern states **has** recently been made into a TV movie. (b) All of the **characters** in that story written by our teacher **were** very believable. (c) One **poll** of Americans' reading and attitudes **was taken** in 2004.	When the subject head noun and the verb are separated from each other, it is harder to check for agreement. It can be especially troublesome when the head noun is singular but nouns in a modifying phrase are plural or vice versa. Here are strategies to find the head nouns: • First, find the verb for the clause or sentence. This will help you determine what the subject is.
Head Noun before Prepositional Phrase (d) Another **poll** of Americans' reading and attitudes **was taken** in 2005.	• If the subject has a prepositional phrase, locate the head noun to the left of the first preposition (for example, *of*).
Head Noun before Compound Preposition (e) The **library**, { together with / along with / as well as } bookstores, **provides** reading materials.	• Use the same strategy with subjects followed by compound prepositions, such as *together with, along with,* and *as well as.* Look for the head noun to the left of these phrases.
Head Noun with *Not* + Noun Phrase (f) The **child**, not her parents, **was** an avid reader.	• Locate the head noun before *not* + a noun phrase.
Relative Clause (g) A **child** who likes to read **books** and whose parents encourage reading **does** better in school.	• Similarly, look to the left of relative clauses (*who, which, that, whose* clauses) to identify the head noun.

EXERCISE 3

For each of the following sentences, put brackets {} around any modifying phrases or clauses following the head noun of the main clause. Underline the head nouns of main clauses and subordinate clauses. Then circle the appropriate verb from the choices given in parentheses.

Example: *The* <u>library</u>, *{along with bookstores},* ((provides)/provide) *reading materials.*

1. About <u>one</u> {in every two Americans} ((was)/were) reading some type of book, according to a recent Gallup poll.
2. People {who usually ((follow)/follows)} current events (is/(are)) also likely to read books.
3. A high <u>frequency</u> {of movie attendance} (do/(does)) not seem to decrease book reading.
4. Tom Clancy, {along with John Grisham and Louis L'Amour,} (rank/(ranks)) very high in popularity among contemporary authors.
5. Horror story writer <u>Stephen King</u>, {as well as romance novelist Danielle Steele,} (remain/(remains)) extremely popular with readers.
6. A <u>person</u> {who (belong/(belongs)) to one of the higher income groups} ((tends)/tend) to read more.
7. While the leisure <u>activity</u> {of reading books} (seem/(seems)) to be thriving, as indicated by polls and other sources, some <u>researchers</u> {in universities and public agencies} ((express)/expresses) concern about the kinds of material that <u>people</u> ((report)/reports) reading.
8. In Great Britain, a <u>study</u> {of people's diaries about reading habits} (reveal/(reveals)) that although most people reported <u>they</u> (was/(were)) reading a book at some point during a three-month period, many of them only consulted a reference book on gardening or cooking.
9. In other words, a <u>reference book</u>, {and not literature or serious nonfiction,} ((was)/were) the only kind of book read.
10. A recent <u>survey</u> {of literary reading in America by the National Endowment for the Arts} (conclude/(concludes)) that literary <u>reading</u> {among almost all groups of Americans} ((is)/are) declining.

Information from: *Gallup News Service* June 3, 2005 and July 21, 1999 www.gallup.com; *The Bookseller,* April 11, 2003 p27(3). Source: *InfoTrac® College Edition.*

EXERCISE 4

Edit the following paragraph to correct errors in subject-verb agreement.

(1) Comics and comic books are very popular kinds of reading for young people throughout the world. (2) Some of the most well-known characters from American comics ~~is~~ [are] Charlie Brown and Snoopy, his beagle dog, from the comic *Peanuts*. (3) The comic book super heroes, such as Superman, ~~has~~ [have] also been very popular. (4) Of course some of these heroes are also featured in movies as well as reading

(Exercise 4 is continued on LP page 44.)

FOCUS 2 [20 minutes]

Focus 2 concentrates on a major source of confusion for many students: how to identify head nouns in long subjects.

1. **Lead-in:** Write some sample sentences on the board about the Gallup Poll survey from the Opening Task. Separate the head noun from the verb by a modifying phrase in these sentences. For example, you could write: *The Gallup Poll survey about reading habits in the United States has shown that more people are reading novels now.* Guide students in identifying the head noun, modifying phrase, and verb in each sentence.

2. Read the examples in the focus chart and guide students in identifying the head noun, modifying phrase, and verb in each sentence. Write some of the examples on the board, and ask a volunteer to underline the head noun, circle the verb, and place the modifying phrase in brackets.

LANGUAGE NOTE

Many students are not able to identify the word that is the head noun of a long subject. The following exercises will help them develop this skill. Be ready to offer help in identifying head nouns as students work.

EXERCISE 3 [15 minutes]

In this exercise students continue reading results from the Gallup Poll and gain further practice in identifying head nouns, modifying phrases, and verbs.

1. Read the example sentence as a class. Discuss why the head noun is *library*, and not *library and bookstores*.

2. Students could do this exercise independently or in pairs.

3. Review answers as a class. Which sentences were particularly difficult? Encourage students to ask questions if they do not understand something, such as how to identify the head noun. See answers on LP page 42.

4. Ask students to locate the reason(s) for their choices in the Focus 2 chart on SB page 42.

 For more practice, use *Grammar Dimensions 4* Workbook page 19, Exercise 2.

EXPANSION [30 minutes]

For an expansion of Exercise 3, use Activity 2 (speaking) on SB page 57. This speaking practice might be a welcome change from the previous writing exercises.

EXERCISE 4 [20 minutes]

Students are asked to edit subject-verb agreement errors in a paragraph about comics and comic books in the United States, Japan, and Korea. Exercise 4 continues on SB page 44.

1. Have students work in pairs or small groups.

2. Discuss some popular comics and comic books. Who are some popular heroes? Ask students to share what comics and comic books are popular in their home countries.

3. Review answers as a class. Ask students to support their answers by identifying head nouns, modifying phrases, and verbs. See answers on LP pages 42 and 44.

4. Discuss students' reactions to statements (9) and (10) at the end of the paragraph.

materials. (5) In Korea and Japan, students like to read comic books called *manga* to pass the time. (6) The United States ~~are~~ [is] now publishing manga for American readers. (7) Meanwhile, in Japan, two American English teachers ~~has~~ [have] conducted a study on reading of manga. (8) They found that many of the most popular manga for college students ~~is~~ [are] about school life. (9) Although many young people enjoy comic books as an escape from everyday life, parents and teachers often disapprove of this kind of reading. (10) They believe that such reading ~~are~~ [is] not productive and that students may become lazy readers.

Information adapted from "Manga Literacy: Popular Culture and the Reading Habits of Japanese College Students," Kate Allen and John Ingulsrud, *Journal of Adolescent & Adult Literacy*, May 2003, v46, i8 p674 (10). *InfoTrac College Edition*®.

| FOCUS 3 | Agreement in Sentences with Correlative Conjunctions: *Both . . . and; Either . . . or; Neither . . . nor* | form |

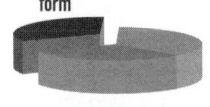

EXAMPLES	EXPLANATIONS
(a) Both J. K. Rowling and J. R. R. Tolkien were named as favorite authors by Britons in recent polls.	**Both . . . and** When two subjects are connected by *both . . . and*, use a plural verb.
(b) Either the library or **bookstores have** current magazines. (c) Either bookstores or the **library has** current magazines. (d) Neither the book nor the **magazines discuss** this issue. (e) Neither the magazines nor the **book discusses** this issue.	**Either . . . or; Neither . . . nor** The traditional rule is that the verb should agree with the head noun after *or* or *nor*.
(f) Either Kay or **I am** going to the library this afternoon. (g) Neither the twins nor **he is** planning to go to the library. (h) Obviously, neither she nor **they are** interested in that topic.	This agreement rule also determines verb form when one or more of the subjects is a pronoun.

Select the appropriate verb form and, in some cases, the correct noun phrase after the verb, for each sentence. In cases of *either . . . or* or *neither . . . nor*, use the rule in Focus 3 to select the verb.

Example: *Neither the books nor the bookshelf ((is)/are) mine.*

1. Either books or a magazine subscription (makes a nice gift/make nice gifts) for someone.
2. For a less expensive gift, both bookplates and a bookmark (is a good choice/(are good) (choices)).
3. Neither the Russian novelist Leo Tolstoy nor the Irish writer James Joyce (was)/were) known to more than 50 percent of American respondents in one Gallup Poll.
4. She said that either the reserved book librarian or the librarians at the main checkout desk (has/(have)) the information you need.
5. Both reading and writing (is/(are)) what we consider literacy skills.
6. Either you or I ((am)/are) going to present the first report.
7. In my opinion, neither the front page of the newspaper nor the sports pages (is/(are)) as much fun to read as the comics.
8. ((Does)/do) either the lifestyle section of the newspaper or the business section interest you?
9. I can see that neither you nor he ((is)/are) finished with your sections yet.
10. Both my brother and my parents (is/(are)) reading that new book about Bill Gates. Neither he nor they (has/(have)) read more than a few chapters, though.

In groups of three, ask and answer questions about the kinds of reading you like to do. Make up five statements summarizing the responses of your group using *both . . . and* or *neither . . . nor*. Report your findings to another group.

Examples: *Neither Mohammed nor Juanita likes to read novels.*
Both Tomoyo and Wanbo enjoy reading sports magazines.

ANSWER KEY

Exercise 6 Answers will vary.

FOCUS 3 [20 minutes]

1. **Lead-in:** Tell students that even native speakers have trouble applying the rules about subject-verb agreement in sentences containing *both . . . and*, *either . . . or*, and *neither . . . nor*. Point out that in informal contexts, such as conversation, many native speakers often do not observe the traditional rules. For example, a native English speaker might say, "* *I don't think either my brothers or my sister are going to be able to come to the picnic this afternoon.*" Some exceptions to traditional agreement rules are presented in Focus 7 on SB page 55.

2. Remind students that it is best to use the traditional rules for formal writing. Encourage them to use the focus charts as reference tools and to refresh their memories.

3. Read the examples in the focus chart. Ask students to point to *or* or *nor* and the verb that follows each in sentences (b) through (h).

EXERCISE 5 [15 minutes]

Students read a series of sentence containing correlative conjunctions, select the correct verb form and, in some cases, the correct noun phrase after the verb.

1. Write the example sentence on the board. Ask a volunteer to underline the word *nor* and the head noun that follows it. Is the head noun plural, or singular? Then ask students to chose one of the verbs in parentheses to complete the sentence.

2. Students could do this exercise independently or in pairs.

3. Review answers as a class. Ask students to point to the word *both, or,* or *nor* in each sentence,

identify the head noun that follows it, and say whether that noun is singular or plural. See answers on LP page 44.

4. Ask students to find the reason(s) for their answers in the Focus 3 chart on SB page 44.

For more practice, use *Grammar Dimensions 4* Workbook page 20, Exercise 3.

EXPANSION 1 [30 minutes]

This activity will give students further practice with correlative conjunctions.

1. Have students work in groups of four.

2. Ask them to each create a "mini-survey" with four or five questions relating to gifts and where people might buy them. Each sentence should contain a correlative conjunction.

3. Have them take turns conducting their surveys with their groups. They should write down the responses they gather.

4. Ask each student to create a chart in which they poll the responses to their survey. They could summarize results using percentages, fractions, or other quantifiers, such as *most of . . . some of . . . none of . . .*

5. Have them share those results with their groups.

EXPANSION 2 [45 minutes/homework]

You might like to assign Activity 4 (research/speaking/writing) on SB page 58 as homework to give students practice in generating sentences with *either of* + plural noun.

EXERCISE 6 [20 minutes]

In this exercise students ask and answer questions about the kinds of reading they like to do and report the results to another group, using correlative conjunctions.

1. Have students work in groups of three.

2. Give students a set amount of time, such as 2–3 minutes, to ask their questions.

3. Ask them to write a short summary of their results using sentences with correlative conjunctions. As a class, review the example sentences.

4. Ask them to share their results with another group.

EXPANSION [20 minutes]

You might like to assign Activity 6 (reflection) on SB page 59 to pairs of students as a continuation of the discussion begun in Exercise 6. It might be helpful to combine lists of the qualities of a good reader into a poster to display. If the class is using a journal, this might be a good topic for a journal entry.

FOCUS 4 — Agreement with Noncount Nouns, Collective Nouns, and Nouns Derived from Adjectives

EXAMPLES	EXPLANATIONS
	Noncount Nouns
(a) The new gym **equipment has** just been delivered.	Noncount nouns in English include mass nouns and abstract nouns. These nouns take a singular verb.
(b) That **information is** very helpful.	

	Mass Nouns	**Abstract Nouns**
(c) My English **vocabulary has** increased.	*equipment*	*advice*
(d) Your **advice is** always appreciated.	*furniture*	*behavior*
	grass	*education*
	homework	*information*
	machinery	*knowledge*
	money	*research*
	traffic	*transportation*
	vocabulary	*violence*

EXAMPLES	EXPLANATIONS
	Collective Nouns
(e) The **audience is** waiting patiently for the performance to begin.	Some collective nouns define groups of people, animals, or things:
(f) A **flock** of geese **is** flying overhead.	

	audience	*group*
	class	*herd*
	committee	*the public*
	family	*swarm*
	flock	*team*

EXAMPLES	EXPLANATIONS
(g) The **class is** going on a field trip.	If the group is considered as a whole, use a singular verb. In most cases, collective nouns take singular verbs.
(h) The **team has** been practicing all week.	Note: In American English, a later pronoun reference to a collective noun can use a plural pronoun and plural verb, as in (i).
(i) The **committee** is meeting tomorrow. **They** will choose a new Chairperson.	
(j) A **variety** of art books **has** been added to the library.	Some collective nouns also can refer to things as well as to people and animals. These include *assortment, collection, variety.*
(k) A **collection** of old coins **remains** one of my grandfather's most cherished possessions.	
	Nouns Derived from Adjectives
(l) **The young want** to grow up fast and **the old wish** to be younger.	Noun phrases derived from adjectives that describe people, such as *the young, the rich,* and *the homeless,* take plural verbs.
(m) Is it true that **the rich are** getting richer and **the poor are** getting poorer?	

Take turns giving oral responses (between one and five sentences) to the following questions. Use the noun or nouns in bold print as the subject in at least one sentence for each response. The first one is done as an example.

1. What kind of **transportation** do you prefer for getting to school?
   *Well, the **transportation** I prefer is driving my own car. But finding a parking space is difficult, so I take the bus most of the time. Once in a while my friend gives me a ride.*

2. What is some good **advice** you've gotten during the past year from a friend, a relative, or something you read?

3. What is some useful **information** you've learned in your English class?

4. What computer **equipment** do you think is the most helpful for you as a student?

5. Do you think **violence** is ever justified? Explain your opinion.

6. How would you describe your **knowledge** of sports? (Good? Fair? Poor? Does it vary according to particular sports?)

7. Do you think **the homeless** are being neglected in our society? What evidence do you have for your opinion?

8. Do you believe that **a college education** is necessary for everyone in our society? Who might not need a college education?

■ **EXERCISE 8**

Write an answer for each question using the noun phrase in parentheses as the subject of your sentence.

Example: What is going on outside the courthouse? (group of protesters)

A group of protesters seems to be gathering on the street.

1. Were there a lot of people at the political rally? (the audience)

2. What did that restaurant offer for dessert? (an assortment of sweets)

3. How do you celebrate birthdays in your family? (my family)

4. What did the city government decide to do about the rise in crime? (the government)

5. What is that nest-like thing under the roof of the house? (a swarm of bees)

6. Do you think the city you live in getting bigger or smaller? (the population of [CITY'S NAME])

7. What do you like best about shopping in that store? (the variety of [PRODUCT NAME])

8. Do young people have much influence on fashion trends? (the young)

ANSWER KEY

Exercise 7   Answers will vary. Possible answers are: 2. Some good advice I've gotten is . . .
3. Some useful information I've learned is . . .   4. Some home office equipment I think is most helpful is . . .   5. Violence is/is not ever justified because . . .   6. My knowledge of sports is good/poor/so-so . . .   7. The homeless are/are not . . .   8. A college education is not necessary for everyone since . . .

Exercise 8   Answers will vary. Possible answers are: 1. The audience was . . .   2. An assortment of sweets was offered.   3. My family has a special birthday dinner.   4. The government is planning employment opportunities for teens to reduce crime.   5. A swarm of bees has built a nest there.
6. The population of Phoenix is growing.   7. The variety of vegetables is amazing!   8. The young are very influential in setting the trends for casual clothes.

FOCUS 4 [20 minutes]

1. **Lead-in:** Write the name of a well-known sports team on the board, such as the New York Yankees. Elicit the names of some players, and write these on the board, as well. Then ask questions about the players and about the team: *Is _____ a good player? Are _____ and _____ good batters? Is the team doing well?*

2. Discuss which of the nouns listed in the right-hand column for (c) and (d) are most problematic for them. Ask them to add any other nouns they can think of to the two categories.

3. For examples (k) and (l), remind students that although these nouns take plural verbs, the nouns themselves cannot have plural markers—that is, we do not use *the youngs, the elderlies, the poors*, etc., to refer to groups of people.

METHODOLOGY NOTE

In reviewing material presented in this focus, pay particular attention to the mass nouns and abstract nouns, since these typically cause the most problems for students, partly because they occur more frequently in English than do collective nouns.

EXERCISE 7 [20 minutes]

Students take turns giving responses to a series of questions.

1. Have students work in pairs.

2. Read the example sentence as a class.

3. Tell students that they should use the noun or nouns in bold print as the subject in at least one sentence for each response.

4. Ask volunteers to share their answers with the class, and discuss these answers. See possible answers on LP page 46.

 For more practice, use *Grammar Dimensions 4* Workbook page 21, Exercise 4.

EXERCISE 8 [15 minutes]

Students respond in writing to questions, using the noun phrase in parentheses as the subject of each sentence.

1. Have students work independently to respond to these sentences.

2. Read the example sentence as a class. Point out the head noun (*group*). Ask students what the verb would be if the subject of the sentence were *the protesters*.

3. Have students choose a partner and take turns reading their sentences.

4. Ask volunteers to share their sentences with the class. See possible answers on LP page 46.

5. Discuss students' experiences in relation to several of the questions, such as how they celebrate birthdays in their families.

FOCUS 5 | Subjects Requiring Singular Verbs

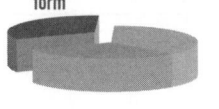

Some types of subjects always take singular verbs.

EXAMPLES	EXPLANATIONS
(a) **Mathematics is** my favorite subject. Others: *physics, economics*	**Some common or proper singular nouns that end in -s:** • courses
(b) **Measles is** no fun to have! Others: *mumps, arthritis*	• diseases
(c) **Leeds is** where my aunt was born.	• place names
(d) **The news** from home **was** very encouraging.	• news
(e) *Tracks* **was** written by Louise Erdrich.	• book and film titles
(f) *Dances with Wolves* **was** awarded an Oscar for the best movie.	
(g) **Six hundred miles is** too far to drive in one day.	**Plural unit words of distance, time, and money:** • distance
(h) **Two weeks goes** fast when you're on vacation.	• time
(i) **Fifty dollars is** a good price for that painting.	• money
(j) **Seven plus three equals** ten; **seven minus three equals** four.	**Arithmetical operations (addition, subtraction, multiplication, division):** • addition, subtraction
(k) **Four times two equals** eight; **four divided by two equals** two.	• multiplication, division

EXAMPLES	EXPLANATIONS
(l) My **pair** of scissors **is** lost. BUT	**Items that have two parts when you use the noun *pair*** In (l) and (n), the head noun *pair* takes a singular subject. Note, however, that you would use the plural verb as in (m) and (o) if the noun *pair* is absent.
(m) My **scissors are** lost.	
(n) A pair of plaid shorts **was** on the dresser. BUT	
(o) Those plaid shorts **were** on the dresser.	
Subject (p) [What we need] **is** more reference books.	**Clause subjects:** Clause subjects have a subject and a verb embedded within them. These subjects may begin with noun clause markers such as *what* or *that*. The verb is singular even when the nouns referred to are plural.
(q) [That languages have many differences] **is** obvious.	
(r) [Reading books and magazines] **is** one of my favorite ways to spend free time.	Gerund (verb + *-ing*) and infinitive (*to* + verb) clauses also take singular verbs.
(s) [To pass all my exams] **is** my next goal.	

EXERCISE 9

Imagine that you are competing on a quiz show. For each definition below, you will be given three words, phrases, or numbers. You must choose the correct match and state the answer in a complete sentence.

Example: a film set in California (*Badlands, Down and Out in Beverly Hills, Star Wars*)

Answer: ***Down and Out in Beverly Hills*** *is a film set in California.*

1. the number of days in a leap year (364, 365, 366)

2. a disease that makes you look like a chipmunk (shingles, mumps, warts)

3. four (54 divided by 9, 100 divided by 20, 200 divided by 50)

4. a poem written by Geoffrey Chaucer (*The Canterbury Tales, Great Expectations, Guys and Dolls*)

(*Continued on next page*)

ANSWER KEY

Exercise 9 1. Three hundred sixty-six is . . . 2. Mumps is . . . 3. Two hundred divided by 50 is . . . 4. The Canterbury Tales is . . .

FOCUS 5 [20 minutes]

1. **Lead-in:** Read the first row of the focus chart, and then rephrase the first three statements as questions: *What is your favorite subject? What disease is no fun to have? What is the name of the place you were born?*

2. Read, or have volunteers read, the remaining rows of the chart. Encourage students to ask questions about anything that confuses them.

3. If time allows, have students work in pairs and generate new variations of the sample sentences.

METHODOLOGY NOTE

Many students may be unfamiliar with the rules governing clause subjects as illustrated in examples (p–s). Explain that the subject in these sentences is one idea, such as *reading books and magazines*, and so the verb is singular, as well.

EXERCISE 9 [15 minutes]

For practice with subjects requiring singular verbs, students can work in teams to complete this exercise.

1. Have students quietly work in two teams to discuss and then practice the correct answer to items 1 through 10. Answers **must** be in complete sentence form with correct grammar.

2. Read the topic aloud and call on the first team to raise their hands when you finish reading the question, including the three possible answers. Do not call on groups who raise their hands before you are finished reading.

3. Ask the class to judge the answers, correcting them, as necessary. Award two points to the team that gets both the answer and grammar correct; award one point if only the answer is correct, but the response is incomplete grammatically.

Exercise 9, items 5 through 10 continue on SB page 50.

For more practice, use *Grammar Dimensions 4* Workbook pages 21–22, Exercise 5.

EXPANSION [30 minutes]

For further entertaining practice with subjects requiring singular verbs, have students do this expansion activity.

1. Have students work in teams of three or four and create a list of five to ten factual questions with three answer choices for each, similar to those in Exercise 9.

2. Act as moderator and have teams compete in a "quiz show" before the class, answering the other team's questions.

3. Ask the class to judge the answers, correcting them, as necessary.

4. If time permits, have a play-off between winning teams.

5. a common plumber's tool (a pair of scissors, a pair of pliers, a pair of flamingoes)

6. a city in Venezuela (Buenos Aires, Caracas, Athens)

7. what you most often find on the front page of a newspaper (sports news, political news, entertainment news)

8. the study of moral principles (ethics, physics, stylistics)

9. the number of years in a score (ten, twenty, thirty)

10. a course that would discuss supply and demand (mathematics, economics, physics)

EXERCISE 10

What are your opinions and attitudes about each of the following topics? State at least two things that could complete each of the sentences below. Share some of your answers with the class. The first one has been done as an example.

1. What my country needs is health insurance for everyone and better jobs _____ .

2. What my country needs _____

3. What I would like to have in five years _____

4. Having a job while going to school _____

5. That energy costs are rising _____

6. What really irritates me _____

7. What I find most enjoyable about being in school _____

8. Learning the rules of subject-verb agreement in English _____ .

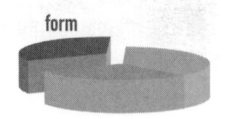

With fractions, percentages, and quantifiers *all (of)* and *a lot of*, agreement depends on the noun or clause after these phrases.

EXAMPLES	EXPLANATIONS
(a) Fifty percent of the **book is** about poetry.	Use a singular verb when the subject is: • a singular noun
(b) Half of **what he says is** not true.	
(c) All (of) our **information is** up-to-date.	• a noun clause
(d) One-fourth of the **students have** computers.	• a noncount noun
(e) All (of) the **computers need** to be checked.	With plural nouns, use a plural verb.
(f) One-sixth of our **Spanish club has** relatives in Mexico. (g) A lot of my **family live** in Pennsylvania.	With collective nouns after percentages and fractions, the singular verb is usually used in American English. However, a plural verb is used when the collective noun follows quantifiers such as *a lot of* or *many*.
(h) Each **book has** a code number. (i) Every one of the **students is** on time.	With quantifiers *each, every*, and *every one*, use a singular verb, whether the noun is singular or plural.
(j) A number of **students are** taking the TOEFL® Test today. (k) The number of **students** taking the exam **is** 175.	With *a number of*, use a plural verb since the noun it modifies is always plural. *The number of*, however, takes a singular verb.
(l) None of the **advice was** very helpful. (m) None of the **magazines** I wanted **is** here.	With *none of*, use a singular verb in formal written English.

*TOEFL is a registered trademark of the Educational Testing Service (ETS). This publication is not endorsed or approved by ETS.

(Focus 6 is continued on Student Book page 52.)

ANSWER KEY

(Continued from LP page 48)

Exercise 9   5. A pair of pliers is . . .   6. Caracas is . . .   7. Political news is . . .   8. Ethics is . . .
9. Twenty . . . 10. Economics is . . .

Exercise 10   Answers will vary.

EXERCISE 10 [15 minutes]

Students complete sentences about different topics, stating their opinions and attitudes in two different ways.

1. Read the example sentence. Ask students to give different endings to the sentence, expressing different attitudes.
2. Have students work in pairs or small groups.
3. Have them take turns completing each sentence once, and then repeat the same sentence, expressing a different opinion.
4. Ask volunteers to share sentences with the class.

EXPANSION [15 minutes]

You could extend the work students did in Exercise 10 with this activity.

1. Have students, in pairs, each write a list of three to five sentences about topics of general interest, such as those in Exercise 10.
2. Have them exchange papers and give two ways to complete each sentence.
3. Have them share results with the class.

FOCUS 6 [20 minutes]

The chart in Focus 6 contains two main sections: (1) agreement with fractions, percentages, and quantifiers (SB page 51) and (2) a summary of the verb form following traditional agreement rules (SB page 52). Remind students that charts such as these make excellent reference tools. Tell them that this chart is particularly useful when summarizing statistical information in academic writing.

1. **Lead-in:** Review language used to express these quantities, such as fifty percent of, half of, all of, one-fourth of, a lot of, each, every one of, a number of, and none of.
2. Ask students to identify the complete subjects in sentences (e.g., fifty percent of the book).
3. Point out the bolded head noun (word or phrase) that requires agreement. Note that for phrases with fractions, percentages and some quantifiers, the head noun is the object of a preposition (of the book, etc.), contrary to other agreement rules in which head nouns are located outside prepositional phrases, as in Focus 2 examples (a) and (c).
4. Ask students to identify what kind of noun each is: singular, noncount, plural, or collective.
5. Ask them to then identify whether the verb is singular or plural.

GRAMMAR/METHODOLOGY NOTE

Pay special attention to example (h): *Each book has a code number. Each* is a frequently used quantifier that is often the source of errors in agreement: students often use a plural or base form verb (e.g., *have* instead of *has*) with *each*.

On the board or an overhead transparency, write a few verb phrases with base forms expressing facts that would be true for most of the students in the class, such as *eat at least one meal a day* and *read books in English*. Ask them to form sentences using these phrases with *each student*, supplying the correct singular verb form—for example, *Each student eats at least one meal a day*.

Summary: Form of the Verb Following Traditional Agreement Rules

	SINGULAR NOUN	NONCOUNT NOUN	PLURAL NOUN	COLLECTIVE NOUN
percentages	singular	singular	plural	singular/plural
fractions	singular	singular	plural	singular/plural
all (of)	singular	singular	plural	singular/plural
a lot of	singular	singular	plural	singular/plural
each, every	singular	singular	singular	
a number of			plural	
the number of			singular	
none of	singular	singular	singular	singular

EXERCISE 11

Circle the correct verb in parentheses, using the traditional agreement rules presented in Focus 6.

Example: *Almost three-fourths of the respondents (believe/believes) they spend too little time reading books for pleasure.*

1. Forty-two percent of Americans (claim/claims) they have a favorite author.

2. Forty-nine percent of the population surveyed in a recent poll (consider/considers) Ernest Hemingway to be the greatest author of all time.

3. However, almost none of the respondents (mention/mentions) Hemingway as their favorite author.

4. Although half of Americans polled (say/says) that they have read a book by Ernest Hemingway, less than a third of the respondents (was/were) able to recognize him as the author of one of his most famous novels, *The Old Man and the Sea.*

5. All of the information for the Gallup Poll (was/were) obtained through telephone interviews.

6. A number of Gallup Polls (is/are) now being conducted in countries other than the United States, such as China and India.

Information from *Gallup News Service* June 3, 2005 and July 21, 1999 www.gallup.com.

EXERCISE 12

The National Endowment of the Arts conducted a survey to see how literary reading compared to other leisure activities. Summarize the information below from the survey by writing five sentences about some of the findings, using present tense verbs. To refer to the participants in this study, you could use any of the following or others: U.S. adults, the population, the respondents. Use a variety of phrases to refer to the participants.

Examples: *Almost half of the population does some kind of gardening.*

The majority of the respondents do some kind of exercise.

U.S. Adults' Participation in Cultural, Sports, and Leisure Activities in a 12-Month Period

	% OF POPULATION
Watch at least one hour of TV per day (on average)	95.7
Go out to movies	60.0
Jog, lift weights, walk or follow other exercise program	55.1
Work with indoor plants or do any gardening	47.2
Read literature	46.7
Watch three or more hours of TV per day (on average)	46.2
Go to amusement/theme park or carnival	35.0
Visit historic park or monument	31.6
Do outdoor activities such as camping, hiking, or canoeing	30.9
Visit art museum or gallery	26.5

Adapted from *Reading At Risk: A Survey of Literary Reading in America June.* 2004, National Endowment of the Arts.

ANSWER KEY

Exercise 12   Answers will vary.

EXERCISE 11 [15 minutes]

Students complete sentences by choosing the correct verb form in parentheses, following the traditional agreement rules.

1. Read the example sentence with the class, and have a volunteer give the answer. Ask students to identify the noun and say what kind of noun it is: singular, noncount, plural, or collective.
2. Ask them to identify the verb and say whether it is singular or plural.
3. Have students work independently to complete the sentences. Remind them to refer to the traditional agreement rules presented in Focus 6 as they work.
4. Have students compare their answers in pairs. See answers on LP page 52.

 For more practice, use *Grammar Dimensions 4* Workbook pages 22–23, Exercise 6.

EXPANSION [30 minutes]

Activity 1 (listening) on SB page 57 offers an excellent follow-up to Exercise 11. Students listen to statistics on American culture and then listen to eight statements based on those statements. Students must declare either orally or in writing whether the statements are true or false.

EXERCISE 12 [15 minutes]

Students write a five-sentence summary of the results of a survey about adult participation in cultural, sports, and leisure activities using a variety of quantifying phrases.

1. Give students some time to glance at the survey results.
2. Go over the first example with the class. Have students identify the subject in each sentence and say what kind of noun each is.
3. Ask them to identify the verb in each and say whether it is singular or plural.
4. Ask students to write their summaries, and then share them with a partner.
5. Ask volunteers to share their summaries with the class, and discuss them.

 For more practice, use *Grammar Dimensions 4* Workbook pages 23–24, Exercise 7.

EXPANSION 1 [15 minutes]

For an expansion activity after Exercise 12, have students respond to the survey questions, and then discuss their responses in small groups.

EXPANSION 2 [45 minutes]

 Use Activity 5 (research on the web) on SB page 59 as a homework assignment for additional practice with agreement with fractions, percentages, and quantifiers. Students use InfoTrac® to research reading surveys anywhere in the world, write a summary, and compare their findings to the survey in the Opening Task.

EXERCISE 13

Write three sentences that are true and three that are false about the members of your class, using the words in parentheses as the subjects. Read your sentences aloud to a classmate. Your classmate should decide which are true and which are false and should orally correct each false statement.

Example: *The number of female students in our class is 12.*

Response: *False. The number of female students in our class is 14.*

1. (The number of) _____ .
2. (Each) _____ .
3. (None) _____ .
4. (All) _____ .
5. (A lot of) _____ .
6. (A number of) _____ .

EXERCISE 14

Fill in each blank of the following radio news report with a *be* verb form that would be appropriate for formal English use.

Example: *A number of reporters from other states <u>are</u> in town to cover news about the earthquake.*

Here is the latest report on the aftermath of the earthquake. As most of you know, the earthquake has caused a great deal of damage and disruption to our area. A lot of the houses near the epicenter of the quake (1) <u>were/have been</u> badly damaged. A number of trees (2) <u>were/have been</u> uprooted in that area also, so be careful if you are driving. All the electricity (3) <u>is/has been</u> shut off for the time being. Water (4) <u>is/has been</u> turned off also. None of the freeways in the vicinity (5) <u>are</u> currently open to traffic. Almost every side street (6) <u>is</u> jammed with drivers trying to get back home. The police (7) <u>are</u> directing traffic at major intersections. To date, the number of deaths resulting from the earthquake (8) <u>is</u> two. All people (9) <u>are</u> urged to stay at home if at all possible.

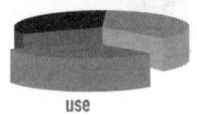

| **FOCUS 7** | **Exceptions to Traditional Agreement Rules** |

use

Some of the agreement rules presented in this unit are observed mainly in formal English contexts, especially in formal written English. The following are cases where native speakers of English frequently do not follow the formal (traditional) rules, especially in spoken and less formal written English:

EXAMPLES		EXPLANATIONS
		Either/Neither of the **+ Noun Phrase** Formal rule: use a singular verb with *either* or *neither*.
(a)	Either of the outfits **is** appropriate.	Formal
(b)	Either of the outfits **are** appropriate.	Informal
(c)	Neither of the choices **is** desirable.	Formal
(d)	Neither of the choices **are** desirable.	Informal
		Either . . . or / Neither . . . nor Formal rule: the verb agrees with the closest subject noun.
(e)	Either my parents or John **has** the car.	Formal
(f)	Either my parents or John **have** the car.	Informal
(g)	Neither you nor I **am** convinced.	Formal
(h)	Neither you nor I **are** convinced.	Informal
		None **+ Prepositional Phrase** Formal rule: use a singular verb.
(i)	None of the magazines **is** here.	Formal
(j)	None of the magazines **are** here.	Informal
		There **+ Be (present tense) + Plural Noun** Formal rule: use *are* with plural nouns.
(k)	There **are** three books here you might like.	Formal
(l)	There's three books here you might like.	Informal

Note: Many informal forms are becoming more common in all but the most formal written English contexts. *There are* is usually used with plural noun phrases in written English, however.

(Focus 7 is continued on Student Book page 56.)

ANSWER KEY

Exercise 13 Answers will vary.

EXERCISE 13 [15 minutes]

In this exercise students write six sentences—three true, and three false—about their classmates, using the quantifiers in parentheses.

1. Read the example sentence. Ask students to identify the quantifier (*the number of*) and to say whether this is singular or plural (*singular*).
2. Ask whether the verb is singular or plural.
3. Repeat with the response.
4. Ask a volunteer to respond to the statement.
5. Have students complete the statements, and then read them aloud to a partner. The partner should correct each false statement.
6. Ask students to share some true and some false statements with the class, and ask the class to respond.

EXERCISE 14 [10 minutes]

Students complete sentences in a news report with the correct *be* verb form.

1. Read and discuss the example sentence with the class.
2. Have students complete the exercise.
3. Check answers with the class. Ask students to identify full subjects and head nouns in the sentences. See answers on LP page 54.
4. If time permits, ask students to describe experiences they may have had with earthquakes.

FOCUS 7 [20 minutes]

1. **Lead-in:** Explain to students that native English speakers tend to bend the rules of agreement in informal speech and certain types of informal writing. Explain that they will always be correct if they follow the rules for formal expression.
2. Start discussion of this focus by reading examples (a) and (b) to give students a general idea of the types of exceptions dealt with in this chart. Note that a focus summary of agreement rules in formal and informal usage appears on SB page 56.
3. Ask students if they have heard native speakers using the less formal forms or if they have read them in less formal forms of writing, such as blogs. Have them give examples, and write these on the board.
4. Remind students that they can use this chart—and particularly the summary portion on SB page 56—as a reference tool.

Summary: Form of the Verb in Formal versus Informal Usage

	FORMAL	INFORMAL
Either of the + (plural noun)	singular verb	singular or plural verb
Neither of the + (plural noun)	singular verb	singular or plural verb
Neither (noun) *nor* (singular noun)	singular verb	singular or plural verb
None of the + (plural noun)	singular verb	singular or plural verb
There + singular logical subject	singular verb	singular verb
There + plural logical subject	plural verb	singular or plural verb

EXERCISE 15

Decide which of the underlined verbs would be appropriate for formal written contexts and which would be acceptable in spoken English. Write "formal" or "informal" to indicate the usage.

Examples: *Either of these economics courses <u>are</u> useful for my major.*

     Informal

1. Neither of those political surveys <u>are</u> valid because the population sample was not random.

2. I am sure that either Professor Tori or Professor Kline <u>have</u> already addressed the issues you mention.

3. As far as we know, none of the experiment's results <u>has</u> been duplicated to date.

4. There <u>are</u> some results that will surprise you.

5. Neither Dr. Gonzalez nor Dr. Vuong <u>are</u> presenting the findings of their studies until the results are checked again.

6. In conclusion, either of the textbooks I have reviewed <u>is</u> an excellent choice for an introductory chemistry course.

7. We have reviewed the report. None of the figures <u>seem</u> correct; they should be checked again.

8. Either of the reports submitted <u>are</u> useful for further study of this environmental problem.

9. Neither the campus medical center nor the library <u>is</u> safe should a strong earthquake occur.

10. Either you or I <u>are</u> responsible for this month's financial report; please let me know if I should submit it.

11. Neither of the claims Senator Holmes presented <u>is</u> justified.

12. There<u>'s</u> a number of errors in this report.

Use Your English

You will hear a summary of information from another Gallup survey. This one asked people questions about raising children.

CD1 Track 4

■ **STEP 1**   As you listen to the summary, take notes on the information you hear.

■ **STEP 2**   At the end of the summary, you will hear eight statements based on the information in the survey. Listen to all the statements and decide whether each statement is true or false.

■ **STEP 3**   Listen to the statements again, pausing after each one. On a separate piece of paper, write T or F after you hear each statement. If a statement is false, write a correction using a complete sentence.

■ **STEP 4**   Listen to the summary again to check your answers and corrections.

ACTIVITY **2** speaking

Below are some examples of spoken and written English that were found in a newspaper. Discuss the traditional rules of subject-verb agreement that have not been observed. How do they illustrate some of the troublesome cases of subject-verb agreement? (Why do you think the speaker or writer used a singular or plural verb in each situation?)

1. "I have decided that everyone in these type of stories are rich." (Quoted statement by an actress in reference to a TV movie she appeared in)

2. "Her expertise in the water as a lifeguard and her understanding of ocean currents, coupled with the fact that she is a strong swimmer, makes her a strong competitor." (Quoted comment about a champion swimmer)

ANSWER KEY

Exercise 15   1. informal   2. informal   3. formal   4. informal   5. formal   6. formal   7. informal   8. informal   9. formal   10. informal   11. formal   12. informal

▪ EXERCISE 15 [15 minutes]

Students identify whether the usage of the verbs in sentences is formal or informal. Read the example sentence.

1. Ask students to identify the subject and verb, and the number of each (singular or plural).
2. Ask a volunteer to say why this usage is considered informal.
3. Have students work in pairs to complete the exercise.
4. Review answers as a class, answering any questions students might have. See answers on LP page 56.

 For more practice, use *Grammar Dimensions 4* Workbook page 24, Exercise 8.

EXPANSION 1 [20 minutes]

To give students additional practice in generating and identifying formal and informal usage, have them complete this activity.

1. Have students work in pairs.
2. Ask each pair to write two sentences—one formal, the other informal—for each of the four categories in Focus 7.
3. Have each pair work with another pair and take turns reading their sentences aloud. The other pair should say whether the use is formal or informal.
4. Ask volunteers to share sentences with the class.

EXPANSION 2 [30 minutes]

Activity 2 (speaking) on SB page 57 offers an excellent follow-up to Exercise 15. Students read and discuss a series of examples of informal spoken and written English.

UNIT GOAL REVIEW [5 minutes]

Ask students to look at the goals on the opening page of the unit again. Refer to the pages of the unit where information on each goal can be found.

 For a grammar quiz review of Units 1–3, refer students to pages 25–27 in the *Grammar Dimension 4* Workbook.

 For assessment of Unit 3, use *Grammar Dimensions 4 ExamView®*.

USE YOUR ENGLISH

The Use Your English activities at the end of the unit contain situations that should naturally elicit the structures covered in the unit. For a more complete discussion of how to use the Use Your English Activities see To the Teacher, LP page xxv. While students are doing these activities in class, you can circulate and listen to see if they are using the structures accurately. Errors can be corrected after the activity has finished.

ACTIVITY 1 listening [30 minutes]

CD1 Track 4

Review the audio script before asking students to do the exercise. If you decide that the exercise might prove difficult for some of your students, preview the content of the survey by asking students to respond to some of the questions. Students could also work in pairs to gather information.

▪ STEP 1

1. Tell students that they are going to listen to a summary of another Gallup Poll. Explain that this poll asked people questions about raising

children. Tell them that they will hear the summary and then a series of eight statements based on the survey.
2. Tell students to take notes as they listen to the summary, and then listen to the series of statements. Have them listen to all eight statements once.

▪ STEP 2
Replay or have the students replay the statements individually and note whether each one is true or false. If they hear a false statement, they should write a correction using a complete sentence.

▪ STEPS 3 AND 4

1. Have students compare answers with a partner.
2. Finally, have students listen to the summary one final time and check and correct their answers.

ACTIVITY 2 speaking [30 minutes]

You may wish to use this activity after Exercise 15 on SB page 56.

1. Have students work in small groups for this exercise. The quotes continue onto SB page 58.
2. Ask them to read each sentence, identify the subject and the number of the subject (singular or plural), and identify the verb and number of the verb.
3. Have them rewrite—or say—the sentence, following traditional rules of agreement.
4. Have them discuss why the speaker/writer may have used a singular or plural verb in each situation.
5. Ask volunteers to share their answers with the class.

Suggestion: Statements such as the ones in this activity abound in newspapers and magazines. You may want to start a "data file" of such examples and ask students to read and analyze them throughout your course. Ask students to contribute to the file if they come across any examples in their reading.

3. "I know there is going to be a major hassle with certain smokers, plus there is going to be a lot of attempts to bypass the regulation." (From a letter to the editor about no-smoking regulations)

4. ". . . the chances of him coming back in the next eight years was very unlikely." (Quoted comment about a politician who ran for President)

5. "In the Jewelry Center, All That Glitter Sure Is Gold" (Headline for a feature article)

 **research/speaking/writing**

Conduct a poll within your class using the three questions in the reading habits survey from the Opening Task on page 39. Tally the results and write a survey report comparing them to the Gallup Poll results.

 **research/speaking/writing**

Usage surveys have suggested that native speakers of English often use plural verbs with *either of* + plural noun, such as in sentences like this: "*Either of those times are okay with me for a meeting.*" Which verb do you think native speakers would use in the following question form: "*Are / Is either of those times okay with you?*"

■ **STEP 1**   In groups or with a partner, create a set of five questions with *either + of + plural noun* to test what verbs native speakers would choose. Here are some examples:

Examples: *1. Do/does either of you boys have a match?*

2. Is/are either of you going to come with us to the movies?

3. Has/have either of your parents ever worked in a restaurant?

■ **STEP 2**   Conduct a survey by giving your set of questions to at least ten native speakers of English. Ask them to choose the verb they would use.

■ **STEP 3**   Write a report of your results or give an oral report to the class.

 **research on the web**

 Using *InfoTrac® College Edition*, research the topic of reading surveys. The survey could be one conducted anywhere in the world. Write a summary of your results using the present tense and, if possible, compare some of the findings to the Gallup Poll survey in the Opening Task.

 **reflection**

Most students have to do a great deal of reading for their academic courses. What are some of the skills and strategies that a good reader uses? With a partner, brainstorm a list of all the things you can think of that a good reader does.

Example: *A good reader previews a textbook or chapter before starting to read.*

USE YOUR ENGLISH

ACTIVITY 3 research/speaking/writing
[30 minutes]

You may wish to assign this activity after Exercise 2 on SB page 41 to give students practice with subject-verb agreement.

1. Have students work in pairs.
2. Ask them to write down the three questions from the Gallup Poll survey on SB page 39.
3. Have pairs move around the room, asking the survey questions and recording responses.
4. Ask pairs to tally the results and write a survey report in which they compare their results to the Gallup Poll results.
5. Ask volunteers to share their results with the class.

ACTIVITY 4 research/speaking/writing
[45 minutes]

In this activity, students survey native speakers of English to find out whether they tend to use singular or plural verbs with *either of* + plural noun. You can use this activity after Exercise 6 on SB page 45.

■ STEP 1

1. Read the introductory paragraph as a class, and discuss.
2. Ask students to identify the plural count nouns in the example sentences.
3. Elicit answers to the example sentences.
4. Ask students to think of at least two additional examples, and write these on the board. Discuss possible answers.
5. Assign students to small groups.
6. Have them write five questions with *either of* + plural noun.

■ STEP 2 Have them conduct a survey in which they ask at least ten native speakers of English to answer their questions. Tell them to record all responses.

■ STEP 3

1. Ask students to write a report about their findings.
2. Have volunteers present their reports to the class.

ACTIVITY 5 research on the web
[45 minutes]

You may wish to use this activity as a homework assignment after Exercise 12 on SB page 53. Students use InfoTrac® to research reading surveys anywhere in the world, write a summary using the present tense, and compare their findings to the survey in the Opening Task. For more information on InfoTrac, read To the Teacher, page xxvi and the InfoTrac information and password postcard in each student book.

1. Read the instructions with the class.
2. Review the results of the Gallup Poll survey in the Opening Task on SB pages 38–39.
3. Guide students in making statements summarizing the Gallup Poll results using the present tense and fractions, percentages, and quantifiers, such as *Forty-seven percent of the respondents say they are reading a book.*
4. Have students work on their own to research the topic and write a summary. Tell them to include percentages, fractions, and quantifiers in their summaries.
5. Ask volunteers to share their results with the class, and discuss their findings.

ACTIVITY 6 reflection
[20 minutes]

In this activity students work with a partner to brainstorm a list of the skills and strategies a good reader uses.

1. Read the instructions and the example with the class.
2. Elicit other skills and strategies a good reader uses, and write these on the board.
3. Ask whether the subject and the verb are singular or plural.
4. Have students work in pairs to complete the activity. Have pairs exchange lists and then discuss them.

PASSIVE VERBS

- Know when to use passive verbs rather than active verbs

- Use correct forms of *be* and *get* passives

- Know the correct form and use of passives in descriptions

- Use passives correctly after *that* clauses and infinitive clauses

- Use passives to create connections in discourse

OPENING TASK

A Short-Term Memory Experiment

Short-term memory describes the brain function in which information is retained temporarily, somewhere between 30 seconds and a few minutes. Numerous experiments have been conducted to test the recall of information stored in short-term memory, resulting in various theories about memory. One phenomenon believed to characterize short-term memory is called the *serial position effect*. In this task, you will be testing this effect. (You will find out later exactly what it means.)

■ STEP 1

Work with a partner. One person will be the researcher; the other will be the subject. Have a blank piece of paper and a pen ready. The subject's book should be closed.

■ STEP 2

Researcher: Show the list of words on page A-17 to your partner. Ask your partner to study the list of words for one minute. After one minute has passed, close the book.

■ STEP 3

Subject: Immediately write down on the blank sheet of paper as many words as you can recall for one minute. You can write the words in any order. Then give the list to the researcher. Note: It is important that you start writing immediately after the study time is up.

■ STEP 4

Read the explanation of the serial position effect on page A-17. Do the results of your experiment support or contradict this belief about short-term memory?

■ STEP 5

Write a brief report of the experiment, using the written list of words as your data. Assume that your reader has no previous information about your experiment. Describe the procedures and summarize the results. Use the model below to start the report. Save the report for exercises later in the unit.

> **Memory Experiment**
>
> This experiment was conducted to test the serial position effect on recalling information. One subject participated in the experiment. The subject was shown a list of 30 common words . . .

UNIT OVERVIEW

This unit explores passive verbs in all their forms, contrasts the uses of stative and dynamic passives, and explains complex passives and their uses in discourse and writing. Note: Because of its length, this unit has been divided into four lesson plans. If a quick review of the topic is necessary, read each focus box with students and complete only the first exercise for each.

UNIT GOALS

Some instructors may want to review the goals listed on Student Book (SB) page 60 after completing the Opening Task so that students understand what they should know by the end of the unit. These goals can also be reviewed at the end of the unit when students are more familiar with the grammar terminology.

OPENING TASK [20 minutes]

The purpose of this task is to provide a writing context—a report on an experiment—in which writers commonly use passive verbs to describe procedures. The problem-solving format is designed to show the teacher how well the students can produce the target structures implicitly and spontaneously when they are engaged in a communicative task. For a more complete discussion of the purpose of the Opening Task, see To the Teacher, Lesson Planner (LP) page xxii.

Setting Up the Task

1. Ask students to comment on the photo. Are these people in an informal situation or a more formal one, such as work ? Do students think they are probably discussing facts or opinions?

2. Write *short-term memory* on the board, and read the first sentence of the opening paragraph of the task, in which short-term memory is defined. Contrast the term with *long-term memory*, or memory of people and events from long ago.

3. Discuss the topic of short-term memory: Does short-term memory become stronger or weaker with age? Do students think their short-term memories are good, adequate, or not-so-good?

4. Read the opening paragraph, or ask a volunteer to read it aloud.

Conducting the Task

■ STEP 1

Divide students into pairs. One student will act as the researcher, and the other as the subject in this experiment. Tell students to close their books and to have a blank piece of paper and a pen ready.

■ STEPS 2 AND 3

The subject studies a list of words for 1 minute, then writes down as many as he or she can remember in 1 minute. Tell students that it is critical that they begin writing immediately after reading the list of words. You might want to act as time keeper, calling out start and finish times.

■ STEP 4

Have them read and perform the material on SB page A-17, in which they read about the *serial position effect* and evaluate it, based on their experiment.

■ STEP 5

Have them write a report summarizing the results of their experiment using passive verbs. Tell students to follow the style of the "Memory Experiment" text when writing their reports.

You may want to walk around and observe in order to diagnose students' facility with using passive verbs.

Closing the Task

1. Tell students to keep their reports: they will use them again later in the lesson.

2. Ask volunteers to describe the serial position effect.

3. Discuss students' experiences with the experiment: Were they able to remember many of the words? Did their experiments support the hypothesis of the serial position effect, or not?

4. To model and elicit passive verb use in an oral context, pose hypothetical questions about the experiment. For example, ask a student who played the role of "subject": *Tam, if you had been shown only 20 words instead of 30, do you think you would have recalled all of them?"*

5. Don't worry about accuracy at this point, though you may want to take notes of errors in meaning, form, or use in order to focus on those problems later.

GRAMMAR NOTE

Typical student errors (form)

- Mixing tenses and auxiliaries improperly: —e.g., * *Kim will be had tested on her English proficiency.* (See Focus 1.)

- Omitting *be* in forming passives: —e.g., * *He born in Seoul in 1985.* (See Focus 2.)

- Replacing *be*-passives with *get*-passives when using nondynamic verbs: —e.g., * *This bed has not got slept in.* * *Her son hasn't got seen for days now.* (See Focus 2.)

- Omitting the past participle endings on stative verbs: —e.g., * *He is call "Pepe" by his friends.* (See Focus 4.)

- Confusion of tense when using complex passives: —e.g., * *It is being said that the price of oil will rise.* (See Focus 5.)

Typical student errors (use)

- Using passive verbs when active verbs are appropriate: —e.g., * *The accident was happened yesterday.* (See Focus 1.)

- Using a stative passive to describe an activity: —e.g., * *The goal is scored by the opposing team.* (See Focus 3.)

Overview of Passive versus Active Verb Use

use

EXAMPLES		EXPLANATIONS
ACTIVE VERBS	**PASSIVE VERBS**	We often use passive instead of active in the following contexts:
(Agent) (a) The brain **retains** (Recipient) information temporarily in short-term memory.	(Recipient) (b) Information **is retained** (Agent) temporarily by the brain in short-term memory.	• when we want to focus on the receiver of an action (recipient) rather than the performer (agent) of the action. We do this by making the recipient the grammatical subject. We may express the agent in a *by*-phrase following the verb.
(c) I **asked** the subject to look at the word list for one minute.	(d) The subject **was asked** to look at the word list for one minute.	• when the agent is less important than the recipient of an action. In reporting research procedures, for example, we do not need to refer to the researcher.
(e) The subject wrote down all the words she could remember. She **recalled** a total of 13 words.	(f) The subject wrote down all the words she could remember. A total of thirteen words **were** **recalled.**	• when the agent is obvious from the context.
(g) It appears that something **is altering** the rats' brain cells.	(h) It appears that the rats' brain cells **are** **being altered.**	• when the agent is unknown.
(i) The researchers who did this study **have** **made several major** errors in analyzing the data.	(j) Several major errors **have been made** in analyzing the data.	• when we want to avoid mentioning the agent. For example, we may not want to say who is responsible for some wrongdoing or mistake.

Provide a likely reason for each of the italicized passive verbs in the sentences below. Refer to the explanations in Focus 1.

Example: Two masterpieces of sixteenth-century painting *were taken* from the museum. *The agent is unknown.*

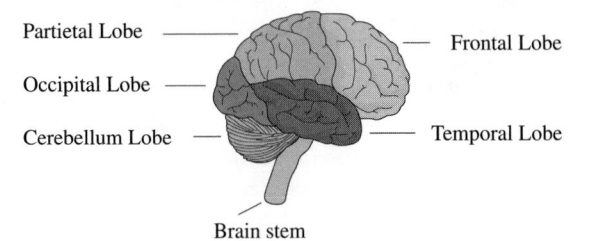

Partietal Lobe — Frontal Lobe

Occipital Lobe —

Cerebellum Lobe — Temporal Lobe

Brain stem

1. One method that is *used by* psychologists in research on memory is the relearning method.

2. In the relearning method, people have to relearn information that *was learned* earlier.

3. Sometimes when you *are introduced* to another person, you forget the person's name a few minutes later.

4. It seems that some misleading statements *were made* in advertising your auto repair services.

5. We have just received reports that a bomb *was set off* in the airport terminal shortly before midnight.

6. Construction of the Leaning Tower of Pisa *was begun* by Bonanno Pisano in 1173.

7. Small bits of information *are* often *remembered* by grouping the information into larger units, known as chunks.

8. Short-term memory *has been called* "a leaky bucket."

EXERCISE 2

Reread the first paragraph of the Opening Task on pages 60–61. Identify the passive verbs and state why they are used.

EXERCISE 3

With your partner for the Opening Task, identify any passive verbs you used in your report, and state why they are used. If you didn't use any passive verbs, find one or two sentences that you might change from active to passive based on the information in Focus 1. State what use each would reflect.

ANSWER KEY

Exercise 1 Answers may vary. Possible answers include: 1. The writer wants to focus on "method."
2. The agent is obvious from the context.   3. The agent is less important than the recipient.
4. The writer may want to avoid directly blaming the agent; also, the actual writer of the ad is unknown.   5. The agent is unknown; the speaker wants to put focus on the bomb.   6. The writer wants to focus on the building, not the builder.   7. The agent is obvious from the context (people in general).   8. The agent is either unknown or considered less important than the recipient.

Exercise 2 Note: The following list of passive doesn't include reduced participle clauses such as believed to characterize.
. . . information is retained (focus on recipient, agent obvious from context)
. . . experiments have been conducted (agent less important than recipient)
one phenomenon . . . is called (focus on recipient)
Exercise 3 Answers will depend on what students wrote in the Opening Task.

FOCUS 1 [20 minutes]

This unit begins with the uses of passive verbs rather than with its forms in order to underscore the reasons why people choose to use them in speech and writing. The contrast with active verbs should help students understand the different functions passive and active forms serve.

1. **Lead-in:** Write the terminology used in this focus chart on the board: *agent, recipient.* Define *agent* (the performer of an action) and *recipient* (the receiver of the action).

2. Read the first row (examples a and b and explanation) with the class. Discuss how passive construction places the focus on the recipient, rather than the agent. Examine the sentence structure of the passive example and how the recipient is the grammatical subject.

3. Read, or have volunteers read, the remaining examples in the chart, analyzing each in terms of the agent, recipient, and sentence structure.

Suggestion: Supplement the sentences in the focus chart with examples from a newspaper or magazine.

4. After reading the last example, (i), ask students if they can think of other contexts in real life in which passive is used to avoid saying who is responsible for some wrongdoing or mistake. Give an example: *A company has to issue a statement about a product it has been forced to recall. How might the company word that announcement?*

LANGUAGE NOTE

Learning when to use passive verbs presents a challenge for many students, who will tend to follow the patterns of their native languages and therefore overuse or underuse passive verbs.

Many advanced students may have learned and practiced the forms of passive verbs, most will have received little instruction on how to use these verbs. Also, a number of students will have been told in composition classes that they should avoid using passive verbs, and use active verbs instead.

EXERCISE 1 [10 minutes]

In this exercise students find reasons for the italicized passive verbs in the sentences, referring to Focus 1.

1. This activity can be done individually, in pairs, or as a class.

2. Read the example as a class, and ask students to find the reason for the verb (*were taken*) in Focus 1.

3. Have students work in pairs and compare answers.

4. Ask volunteers to share their answers with the class, and discuss them. See possible answers on LP page 62.

EXERCISE 2 [10 minutes]

In this exercise students reread the first paragraph of the Opening Task, identify the passive verbs, and say why each was used.

1. You may want to read the first sentence of the paragraph and analyze the verb as a class.

2. Have students work in pairs. Remind them to refer to Focus 1 to find the reason why the passive form of each verb was used.

3. Review answers with the class. See answers on LP page 62.

work book For more practice, use *Grammar Dimensions 4* Workbook page 28, Exercise 1.

EXPANSION [20 minutes]

Have students read an excerpt from a factual text, identify the passives, and state the reason for using each.

1. Have students choose a paragraph from a scientific or technical text. Ask them to list all the passive verbs, and write the reason why each was used, referring to Focus 1.

2. Have students work in pairs to share and discuss their lists.

EXERCISE 3 [10 minutes]

Students review the reports they wrote for the Opening Task and either identify passives they used, or rewrite some sentences to include passive verbs.

1. Have students work in pairs. Ask them to reread the reports they wrote for the Opening Task, identify any passive verbs they used, and state why they used them.

2. If they did not use any passives in their reports, ask them to rewrite one or two sentences using passive verbs.

3. Ask them to explain the use of all passives, referring to Focus 1 and share their findings with the class.

EXPANSION [20 minutes]

Students conduct their own short-term memory experiments and summarize the passive results using passive verbs.

1. Have students work in groups of five. Four students will actively participate in the "experiment," and the fifth will be the reporter.

2. Have three of the students, in turn, state what they ate for breakfast today. The reporter should write this information down.

3. The fourth student should then repeat what each student had for breakfast.

4. The reporter should then say whether the fourth students remembered the details accurately, or not.

5. Repeat, starting with the next student in the group, and having the four students report on what two movies or TV shows they have seen in the past week.

6. Students can then choose the next two topics, and repeat the procedure.

7. Have the group write a short report in which they evaluate their short-term memories, which kinds of information were most easily retained, and which proved the most difficult to remember.

8. Have representatives of each group share their report with the class.

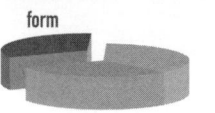

FOCUS 2 Review of Passive Verb Forms

All passive verbs are formed with *be* or *get* + past participle.

EXAMPLES	EXPLANATIONS
(a) I **am called** by telemarketers more than I would like. (b) The garbage **gets picked up** once a week.	**SIMPLE PRESENT** *am/is/are* (or *get*) + past participle
(c) The possibility of life on Mars **is being explored.** (d) We **are getting asked** to do too much!	**PRESENT PROGRESSIVE** *am/is/are* + *being* (or *getting*) + past participle
(e) The butterflies **were observed** for five days. (f) Many homes **got destroyed** during the fire.	**SIMPLE PAST** *was/were* (or *got*) + past participle
(g) The Olympics **were being broadcast** worldwide. (h) She **was getting beaten** in the final trials.	**PAST PROGRESSIVE** *was/were* + *being* (or *getting*) + past participle
(i) Short-term memory also holds information that **has been retrieved** from long-term memory. (j) Did you hear he's **gotten fired** from his job?	**PRESENT PERFECT** *has/have* + *been* (or *gotten*) + past participle The passive with a form of GET instead of BE is common in spoken English.
(k) This store **has been being remodeled** for six months now! I wonder if they'll ever finish. (l) Our computer system **has been getting threatened** by viruses a lot this year.	**PRESENT PERFECT PROGRESSIVE*** *has* + *been* + *being* (or *getting*) + past participle
(m) The National Anthem **had** already **been sung** when we entered the baseball stadium. (n) He was disappointed to learn that the project **hadn't gotten completed** in his absence.	**PAST PERFECT** *had* + *been* (or *gotten*) + past participle
(o) The horse races **will be finished** in an hour. (p) The rest of the corn **will get harvested** this week.	**SIMPLE FUTURE** *will* + *be* (or *get*) + past participle

EXAMPLES	EXPLANATIONS
(q) I bet most of the food **will have been eaten** by the time we get to the party. (r) The unsold books **will have gotten sent back** to the publishers by now.	**FUTURE PERFECT** *will* + *have* + *been* (or *gotten*) + past participle
(s) The election results **will have been getting tallied** by the time we reach the headquarters	**FUTURE PERFECT PROGRESSIVE*** *will* + *have* + *been* + *being* (or *getting*) + past participle
(t) A different chemical **could be substituted** in this experiment. (u) Don't stay outside too long. You **may get burned** by the blazing afternoon sun.	**MODAL VERBS (Present Time Frame)** modal (*can, may, should,* etc.) + *be* (or *get*) + past participle
(v) All of our rock specimens **should have been identified**, since the lab report is due. (w) The file **might have gotten erased** through a computer error.	**MODAL VERBS (Past Time Frame)** modal (*can, may, should,* etc.) + *have* + *been* (or *gotten*) + past participle

*Note: The *be* form of these passive tenses is quite rare. Even the get form is not very common.

EXERCISE 4

Rewrite each sentence below to put focus on the recipients of action rather than on the performers (agents) of the action. Delete the agent if you do not think it needs to be mentioned. In some cases, you may want to restate the agent in a prepositional phrase beginning with *in* rather than with *by*.

Example: The brain stores information.
Information is stored in the brain.

1. A bundle of millions of fibers connects the brain cells.
2. In visual processing, the right hemisphere of the brain registers unfamiliar faces; the left hemisphere registers familiar ones.
3. The memory does not store an exact replica of experience.
4. The brain alters, organizes, and transfers information into one or more memory stores.
5. The multistore model of memory cannot explain some facts about processing information.

(Continued on next page)

ANSWER KEY

Exercise 4 1. The brain cells are connected by a bundle of millions of fibers. 2. In visual processing, unfamiliar faces are registered by the right hemisphere of the brain; familiar ones are registered by the left hemisphere. 3. An exact replica of experience is not stored in memory. 4. Information is altered, organized, and transferred into one or more memory stores. 5. Certain facts that the multistore model cannot explain have been discovered (by psychologists). (Agent might be deleted if obvious from the context.)

6. Other ways in which we organize information in long-term memory are now being investigated.

7. The difference between recognition and recall has been demonstrated in numerous experiments.

8. Case studies of stroke victims were used to learn more about information storage.

FOCUS 2 [25 minutes]

Focus 2 makes an excellent reference tool for students. The chart continues on SB page 65.

1. **Lead-in:** Write the formula for forming passive verbs on the board: *be* or *get* + past participle. Write the first two examples on the board, elicit the tense (simple present), and ask students to identify the forms of *be* or *get* and the past participles.
2. Ask students to identify the agent and recipient in the examples. Point out that the agent is often not mentioned.
3. Repeat this procedure for the remaining examples in the chart.
4. Encourage students to use this chart as a reference tool throughout their work in this course.

Suggestion: Ask students to review the forms of passive verbs for homework.

LANGUAGE NOTE

Students need to understand the differences in usage between *be*-passives and *get*-passives. The *get*-passive is very common in informal discourse and certain types of informal writing. Point out that *get* does not function as a true auxiliary in questions and negatives, as does *be*. Rather, native speakers use *do* in questions and negatives: *Did the garbage get picked up? No, the garbage didn't get picked up.*

EXERCISE 4 [15 minutes]

In this exercise students rewrite eight sentences using passive constructions and deleting the agent if it does not need to be mentioned. Exercise 4 continues on SB page 66.

1. Before students do this exercise, review the reasons for deleting agents when transforming a sentence from active to passive.
2. Review the example with the class.
3. Have students work in pairs.
4. Review and discuss answers as a class. Were students able to delete or restate agents? See answers on LP page 64.

EXPANSION [25 minutes]

Activity 8 (reflection) on page 81 is a good follow-up to Exercise 4. Students reflect and write sentences about the activities and strategies of good language learners using passive verbs, then discuss them with a partner.

6. Researchers are now investigating other ways in which we organize information in long-term memory.
7. Scientists have demonstrated the difference between recognition and recall in numerous experiments.
8. The researchers used case studies of stroke victims to learn more about information storage.

▮EXERCISE 5

Rewrite the underlined sentences or clauses in the following research report, changing the verbs to passives. Delete the agent if it is not needed.

Example: Researchers gave students a questionnaire about food likes and dislikes.

Students were given a questionnaire about food likes and dislikes.

(1) Psychologist Elizabeth Loftus and a team of researchers have been exploring a new method of weight control that involves manipulating subjects' memories about certain kinds of food. (2) <u>In a series of experiments, the research team convinced university students</u> that certain foods made them sick when they were children. (3) The scientists said they also successfully implanted positive memories about nutritious fruits and vegetables. (4) In one experiment involving attitudes toward strawberry ice cream, <u>the researchers asked 131 students to complete forms in which they described food experiences, likes and dislikes.</u> (5) <u>The researchers then gave the subjects a computer analysis of their responses.</u> (6) <u>The analysis inaccurately told some students</u> that strawberry ice cream had made them sick as children. (7) Later, almost 20 percent of these students agreed on a questionnaire that <u>this kind of ice cream had sickened them</u> and that they planned not to eat it in the future. (8) In a second experiment, <u>the researchers encouraged students to detail the imaginary ice cream episode.</u> (9) At the end of this experiment, an even greater percentage of the students believed the false information. (10) Although the scientists have been able to plant false memories about strawberry ice cream,

they have not been able to implant false memories about two popular snack foods: chocolate chip cookies and potato chips. (11) Loftus believes that <u>researchers could resolve this problem of limited influence</u> by additional feedback and drills. (12) Meanwhile, Stephen Behnke, ethics director of the American Psychological Association is concerned about the ethics of such research. (13) He comments that <u>the deliberate implanting of false memories raises serious ethical questions.</u> (14) Loftus acknowledges that <u>scientists need to discuss ethical issues,</u> but she notes that <u>parents often tell their children things that aren't true.</u>

Information summarized and adapted from "Swallowing a Lie May Aid in Weight Loss, Research Suggests," Rosie Mestel, *Los Angeles Times*, August 2, 2005.

FOCUS 3 | Stative Passives in Contrast to Dynamic Passives

use

EXAMPLES		EXPLANATIONS
DYNAMIC PASSIVES	**STATIVE PASSIVES**	
(a) The missing library book **was found** in the parking lot by a custodian.	(b) A map of Miami **can be found** on the Internet.	Many verbs can be either dynamic or stative depending on their meaning. *Dynamic* passive verbs describe activities. *Stative* passive verbs do not report activities; they express states or conditions. Stative passive verbs do not have agents. (More about stative verbs in Focus 4.)
(c) Our telephone line **is** finally **being connected** tomorrow.	(d) The transmission of a car **is connected** to the gearshift.	
(e) Stella **was called** for a job interview yesterday.	(f) The biological rhythm with a period of about 24 hours **is called** a circadian rhythm.	

Exercise 5   2. In a series of experiments, university students were convinced that certain foods made them sick when they were children. (Note: Some students might include the agent *by the research team*. This would be acceptable also.)   4. In one experiment . . . strawberry ice cream, 131 students were asked to complete forms . . . (Note: for this sentence, the agent should be omitted since by this point it is obvious.)   5. The subjects were then given a computer analysis of their responses.   6. Some students were inaccurately told that strawberry ice cream had made them sick as children. (Agent unnecessary.)   7. . . . that they had been sickened by this kind of ice cream . . .   8. . . . students were encouraged to detail the imaginary ice cream episode.
11. . . . that this problem of limited influence could be resolved by additional feedback and drills.
13. . . . serious ethical question are raised by the deliberate implanting of false memories.
14. . . . that serious ethical issues need to be discussed (by scientists), but she notes that children are often told things that aren't true by their parents. (Note: *scientists* would be an optional agent; *parents* would be needed to make meaning clear.)

EXERCISE 5 (OPTIONAL) [15 minutes/homework]

In this exercise students rewrite sentences and clauses in a research report, changing the verbs to passives and deleting the agent, where appropriate.

1. Have students work in pairs or small groups initally and then complete the rest for homework.
2. Review the example with the class. Have students identify the agent and recipient in the first sentence. Is the agent stated in the second sentence?
3. Have students work independently to rewrite the sentences, and then compare answers with a partner. See answers on LP page 66.
4. Discuss the topic of the report with students. Are the results of the experiment hard to believe?

 For more practice, use *Grammar Dimensions 4* Workbook page 28, Exercise 2.

EXPANSION [20 minutes]

Students practice writing general warnings using passive modal verbs.

1. Write the formula for passive modal verbs on the board: modal (*can, may, should*, etc.) + *be* (or *get*) + past participle.
2. Write the example sentence from Focus 1 on the board: *Don't stay outside too long. You **may get burned** by the blazing afternoon sun.*
3. Ask volunteers to suggest other sentences that warn people about dangers, and write these on the board.
4. Have students work in pairs to create a list of four or five general warnings for people.
5. Have volunteers share their lists with the class.

LESSON PLAN 3

FOCUS 3 [10 minutes]

Many students either may not have studied stative passives or may not have learned the distinction between stative and dynamic passives.

1. **Lead-in:** Write *dynamic* and *stative* on the board and define the terms (dynamic verbs describe actions, accomplishments, or achievements; stative verbs describe states of being that do not involve change).
2. Read the explanation in the left-hand column of the focus chart. Re-emphasize that dynamic passives describe actions, and stative passives describe states or conditions.
3. Read the first two examples (a and b), and ask students to say whether an action or a state is described in each.
4. Point out that stative passive verbs do not have agents. Reread the first two examples and ask students to identify any agents.
5. Repeat this process for the remaining four example sentences.
6. Encourage students to ask questions about anything they do not grasp.

LANGUAGE NOTE

The concept of stative verbs can be a very challenging one for many students. Explain that stative verbs include verbs of emotion and perception, such as *love* and *smell*, and verbs of measurement, such as *weigh, equal*. Tell students that Focus 4 will explore many of the uses of stative passive verbs.

EXERCISE 6

Each of the famous monuments or group of buildings below can be matched to two descriptions in a–j. (1) Match each landmark to the appropriate descriptions. (2) Rewrite each description as a sentence with a passive verb (or verbs) to put focus on the monuments and buildings as the main topics. (3) Delete the agents if they do not add much to the meaning or if they can be inferred from the context. (4) Make any other necessary changes.

Example: *The Parthenon is considered to represent the peak of Greek architectural achievement.*

MONUMENTS AND BUILDINGS

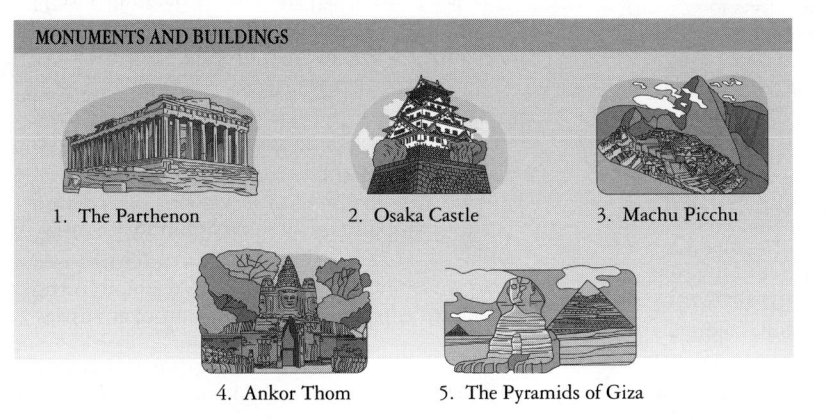

1. The Parthenon   2. Osaka Castle   3. Machu Picchu

4. Ankor Thom   5. The Pyramids of Giza

DESCRIPTIONS

a. Some call this Peruvian ruin the "Lost City of the Incas."

b. The Cambodian god-king Suryavarman II intended it to be a funerary monument for himself.

c. Unlike in Europe, where builders used stone for castles, builders made this of wood.

d. People believe that workers constructed them using mounds or ramps to position the stone blocks.

e. Many consider it the peak of Greek architectural achievement.

f. In ancient times, a large complex of buildings surrounded them.

g. Located south of the Cambodian capital of Ankor Thom, people built it in the twelfth century.

h. Pericles had it built to celebrate Athens' victory over the Persians.

i. You can find this fifteenth-century ruin on a high mountain ridge above the Urubama Valley in Peru.

j. Historians regard it as the most formidable stronghold in Japan before people destroyed it in the early seventeenth century.

FOCUS 4   Uses of Stative Passive Verbs

use

Stative passive verbs have a number of descriptive uses in discourse. Note that many of the stative passives in the examples below are followed by prepositions such as *in, with, by,* or *for.*

EXAMPLES	USES
(a) The Amazon River **is located** in Brazil. (b) The ratel, a fearless animal, **is found** in Africa and India. (c) The Secret Service agents **were positioned** near the President.	• To describe location or position *Located* is often used in geographical description. *Found* typically describes plant and animal habitats. *Positioned* often suggests placement. Other verbs: *placed, situated, bordered (by), surrounded (by)*
(d) *The Daily Scandal* **is filled** with untrue stories. (e) The sea horse's body **is covered** with small bony plates.	• To describe characteristics or qualities This type of description is common in science.
(f) Temperature **is measured** in degrees. (g) The elements **are listed** according to weight.	• To describe manner or method This use is common in science and mathematics.
(h) France **is divided** into regions. (i) Geology **is made up** of many subfields, such as seismology and petrology.	• To describe part-whole relationships Other verbs: *composed (of), organized into*
(j) The Geiger counter **is used** for detecting radiation. (k) Greetings such as "How are you?" **are intended** to promote communication, not to get information.	• To describe purpose These verbs may be followed by *for* + gerund (verb + *-ing*) or an infinitive (*to* + verb). Other verbs: *designed, meant*

ANSWER KEY

Exercise 6 Answers may vary. Possible answers include: 1. (e/h) The Parthenon is considered the peak of Greek architectural achievement. It was built to celebrate Athens' victory over the Persians. 2. (c/j) Unlike in Europe where stone was used for castles, Osaka Castle is made of wood. Before it was destroyed in the early seventeenth century, Osaka Castle was regarded by historians as the most formidable stronghold in Japan.   3. (a/i) The Peruvian ruin Machu Pichu is called the "Lost City of the Incas" by some. It is found on a high mountain ridge above the Urubama Valley in Peru.

4. (b/g) Ankor Thom was intended by the Cambodian god-king Suryavarman to be a funerary monument for himself. Located south of the Cambodian capital of the same name, Ankor Thom was built in the twelfth century.   5. (d/f) The Pyramids of Giza were constructed using mounds or ramps to position the stone blocks. In ancient times, the Pyramids of Giza were surrounded by a large complex of buildings.

EXERCISE 6 [20 minutes]

Students match landmarks with their descriptions, and then rewrite the sentences with passive verbs.

1. Ask students which of the monuments and buildings pictured are familiar to them. Can they say where each is located? (1. *Greece;* 2. *Japan;* 3. *Peru;* 4. *Cambodia;* 5. *Egypt*)

2. Read the example sentence as a class. Ask students whether the passive *is considered* is stative or dynamic (stative). Elicit what is being described (a state—*the peak of achievement*).

3. Students could complete this exercise independently, or work with a partner.

4. Ask volunteers to read their sentences to the class. In how many of the sentences were students able to delete the agent? See answers on LP page 68.

 For more practice, use *Grammar Dimensions 4* Workbook pages 29–30, Exercise 3.

EXPANSION [20 minutes]

Use Activity 2 (reading) on SB page 79 to give students additional practice in analyzing whether a verb is dynamic or stative. In this activity, students analyze ten verbs from a text of their choice in terms of whether each is stative or dynamic, and they identify the writer's reason for using each.

FOCUS 4 [15 minutes]

Focus 4 gives students a comprehensive overview of the uses of stative passive verbs. Encourage them to use this focus chart as a resource tool. Focus 4 continues on SB page 70.

1. **Lead-in:** Remind students that stative verbs are used to describe states or conditions that do not change. Write the prepositions on the board: *in, with, by, for, near.*

2. Read the first three examples (a–c), then have a volunteer read their uses. Ask students to say whether an action or a state is described in each.

3. Ask students to identify any prepositions in the sample sentences.

4. Repeat this procedure with the remaining examples in the chart.

Suggestion: Textbooks, newspapers, and magazines are good sources of examples of the uses of stative passive verbs. Bring sample materials to class and ask students to identify the stative passives and their uses.

EXAMPLES	USES
(l) Do you know the old song that begins: "The knee bone's **connected** to the thigh bone"? (m) The two buildings **are joined** by an elevated walkway.	• To describe physical connection Other verbs: *attached (to), accompanied (by), separated (by, from)*
(n) El Greco **is** best **known** for his religious paintings. (o) Nagoya Castle **is considered** one of the greatest fortresses in the history of Japan.	• To describe reputation or association Other verbs: *regarded (as), thought to be, viewed (as); linked to; associated with*
(p) The ratel **is** also **known** as "the honey badger." (q) Pants having legs that flare out at the bottom **are called** bellbottoms.	• To define or name Other verbs: *labeled, named, termed*

EXERCISE 7

Identify the stative passive verbs in the following passage and state the use of each, based on the categories in Focus 4.

Example: The answer can be found deep inside the brain.

Stative passive: *can be found*　　Use: *to describe location*

(1) What makes people engage in the activities they do, whether running marathons, solving crossword puzzles, or playing a musical instrument? (2) Gregory Burns, a neuroscientist and psychiatrist, says that the answer can be found deep inside the brain. (3) In his book, *Satisfaction: The Science of Finding True Fulfillment*, Burns claims that explanations for the activities people pursue are connected not with pleasure and happiness but rather with satisfaction. (4) While pleasure and happiness may be regarded as passive emotions, satisfaction, according to Burns, is a much more active component. (5) Satisfaction, in turn, is made up of two essential ingredients that humans, by nature, desire: novelty and challenge. (6) Burns has identified the neurotransmitter dopamine, a structure that has long been associated with happiness and well-being, as a key element in the biology of satisfaction. (7) In adolescence, a time of life that is known for impulsive behavior and great enthusiasm, our brains are rich with dopamine. (8) As people grow older, they need a greater stimulus to trigger the flow of dopamine. (9) The hormone cortisol has also been linked to feelings of satisfaction. (10) Although cortisol is known mainly as a stress hormone, the level of this hormone rises during vigorous exercise and thus can elevate mood and even help to improve memory. (11) According to Burns, this is why even physical activities that cause pain can be regarded as satisfying. (12) This area of psychology has been called "positive psychology" because it focuses on positive emotions rather than psychological problems.

Information from "For True Fulfillment, Seek Satisfaction, Not Happiness," Marianne Szedgedy-Maszak, *Los Angeles Times*, September 5, 2005.

EXERCISE 8

1. Match each numbered word or phrase in column A to the appropriate phrase in column B.
2. Write a sentence for each, using a stative passive.
3. Add other words or change word forms as necessary.

Examples: 1, c. Language **may be defined** as the spoken or written means by which people express themselves and communicate with others. The spoken or written means by which people express themselves and communicate with others **is called** language.

A	B
1. language	a. the part of consciousness that involves feeling or sentiment
2. challenge	b. usually a negative condition to be avoided
3. emotions	c. the spoken or written means by which people express themselves and communicate with others
4. stress	d. a key component of human satisfaction

EXERCISE 9

With a partner, take turns asking and responding to the questions below. Use a stative verb in your responses.

Example:　**Question:** Where is the city or town in which you were born?
　　　　　　　Answer: *It's located in the southern part of China.*

1. Where is the city or town in which you were born?
2. What is your hometown (or the place you live now) best known for?
3. How is the country you were either born in or live in now divided geographically (such as states, provinces etc.) and how many divisions are there?
4. Do your friends or family call you by any special nicknames?
5. What are you considered good at doing?
6. What do you think the following cities in the United States are often associated with?
   a. Las Vegas, Nevada
   b. New York, New York
   c. Los Angeles, California
   d. Orlando, Florida

ANSWER KEY

Exercise 7 2. (Answer given in example.) 3. are connected: describes connection 4. may be regarded: describes reputation 5. is made up of: describes part-whole relationship 6. has been associated: describes association 7. is known: describes reputation 9. has been linked: describes association 10. is known: to define or name 11. can be regarded: describes reputation 12. has been called: to define or name

Exercise 8 Forms of some sentences may vary. 2. d. can be considered 3. a. can be defined as (Note: This sentence would be more difficult to process if the definition were used as the subject of the sentence). 4. b. is usually regarded as (Note: In most cases, usually will need to be moved, either between the two parts of the stative passive or placed at the beginning of the sentence.)
Exercise 9 Answers will vary.

EXERCISE 7 [15 minutes]

Students read a passage on the work of a neuroscientist and identify the stative passive verbs and their uses, referring to Focus 4.

1. Write two key vocabulary words from this passage on the board and define them: *neuroscientist* (a scientist who studies the anatomy and chemistry of the nervous system, especially in relation to behavior and learning), and *neurotransmitter* (a chemical substance that transmits nerve impulses). Tell students that they are going to read a passage about the work of a neuroscientist who has researched the chemical reasons for why people do things.

2. Have students work independently to find and label the verbs, then compare answers with a partner. See answers on LP page 70.

3. Discuss the topic of the reading with students. Were they more impulsive as teenagers than they are now? Do they agree with the statement that most people crave novelty and change?

EXPANSION [30 minutes]

You might use Activity 3 (writing/speaking) on SB page 79 as an expansion activity after Exercise 7. Students, in small groups, create sentences using stative passive verbs to describe people, places, or things. Their classmates then guess what they are describing.

EXERCISE 8 [10 minutes]

In exercise 8 students match the language in the two columns, then write sentences for each using stative passives.

1. Review the example as a class. Ask students to state the use of the stative passive. Encourage them to refer to Focus 4 for reasons.

2. Have students work independently to rewrite the sentences, then compare answers with a partner.

3. Review answers as a class. What words did they change? See answers on LP page 70.

 For more practice, use *Grammar Dimensions 4* Workbook page 31, Exercise 4.

EXERCISE 9 [15 minutes]

Students take turns asking and answering questions about their lives using stative passives.

1. Review the example as a class. Ask students to state the use of the stative passive in the example (to describe location), referring, as needed, to Focus 4.

2. Have students work in pairs. Have them alternate asking and answering all six questions.

3. Ask volunteers to report on what they've learned about their partners.

EXPANSION [25 minutes]

Assign Activity 4 (writing) on SB page 80 as an expansion activity in class or as homework. In this activity, students draw and label a map and then describe the contents using stative passives.

FOCUS 5 | Complex Passives

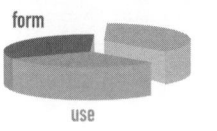

form

use

Complex passives are passive constructions followed by *that* clauses or infinitive clauses (*to* + verb).

EXAMPLES	EXPLANATIONS
(a) It **is believed** that primates first appeared on the earth about sixty-nine million years ago. (b) It **is said** that the number 13 is bad luck. (c) It **was reported** that a man suspected of burning an abandoned building was arrested this morning.	**Form:** Introductory *it* + passive verb + *that* clause **Use:** This form often serves to introduce a topic, since the new information comes at the end of the sentence.
(d) The topic of today's lecture is early primates. Primates **are believed** to have appeared on the earth about sixty-nine million years ago. (e) Many numbers are associated with superstitious beliefs. For example, thirteen **is said** to be an unlucky number. (f) Police arrested a man suspected of burning an old factory building. The suspect **was reported to have been** near the building when the fire started.	**Form:** Subject (other than introductory *it*) + passive verb + *to* infinitive The infinitive may often be a perfect form: *to* + *have* + past participle as in (d) and (f) **Use:** This form could also be used to introduce topics, but it is especially appropriate after a topic has been introduced because the topic can then be put in the subject position.

EXERCISE 10

For each of the following numbered sentence groups, choose the wording or sentence that best fits the context, using the principles of introducing or continuing topics as discussed in Focus 5. Consider each numbered group to be the beginning of a written article or spoken announcement.

1. Some people believe that opening an umbrella in the house will bring bad luck. In parts of Asia, as early as the eleventh century,
   a. it was considered to be an insult to open an umbrella inside a building.
   (b.) opening an umbrella inside a building was considered to be an insult.

2. a. It has been alleged that an employee of the museum is responsible for the theft of dozens of paintings.
   (b.) An employee of the museum is alleged to be responsible for the theft of dozens of paintings. Police are currently investigating the claim.

3. (a.) It was reported this morning that a Pacific blacktip shark gave birth to three healthy pups at Sea World.
   b. A Pacific blacktip shark was reported to have given birth to three healthy pups at Sea World this morning. Officials commented that this marks the first documented birth of the species in captivity.

4. Of the comets that have been recorded, the least frequently returning one is Delavan's Comet, which appeared in 1914.
   (a.) This comet is not expected to return for twenty-four million years.
   b. It is not expected that this comet will return for twenty-four million years.

EXERCISE 11

What will happen if you step on a spider? Walk under a ladder? Every culture has superstitions describing good or bad things that may result from something else happening. In small groups, discuss some of the superstitions that you have heard or read about. Write down four or five of the superstitions, using a complex passive structure.

Example: *It is said that if you break a mirror, you will have seven years of bad luck.*

OR *Breaking a mirror is believed to result in seven years of bad luck.*

ANSWER KEY

Exercise 11 Answers will vary.

FOCUS 5 [20 minutes]

Focus 5 explains the different uses of the two complex passive forms (passive constructions followed by *that* or infinitive clauses) depending on whether a topic is newly introduced or has already been mentioned.

1. **Lead-in:** Write example (a) on the board. Circle *that* to highlight the beginning of the subordinate clause.
2. Have students note that the new information is contained in the *that*-clause.
3. Ask students to substitute other verbs for *is believed*, giving them base forms (e.g., *know, assume, say*).
4. Follow this procedure with the next two examples in this first row.
5. Write example (d) on the board. Put a slash between *believed* and *to have appeared* to show the structure of the sentence. Circle the two instances of *primates* in the two sentences to highlight the explanatory point about information already introduced to the reader or listener. Note that examples (d), (e), and (f) are variations of the information in (a), (b), and (c).

METHODOLOGY NOTE

As noted previously, it is likely that many students will not have studied complex passives, although they should be familiar with them from their reading or from listening to instances of formal speech, such as radio or television newscasts.

EXERCISE 10 [15 minutes]

Students choose the sentences that best fit the context of introducing or continuing a topic. Exercise 10 continues on SB page 73.

1. Read the first sentence as a class to clarify the relationship between the different complex passive forms illustrated in Focus 5 and to analyze why writers or speakers would choose one over the other.
2. Have students work in pairs.
3. Encourage them to discuss the principles explained in Focus 5.
4. Ask volunteers to share their answers with the class, and discuss the reasons for their choices. See answers on LP page 72.

 For more practice, use *Grammar Dimensions 4* Workbook page 31, Exercise 5, and page 33, Exercise 6.

EXPANSION [30 minutes]

Activity 5 (writing) on SB page 80 is an excellent follow-up to Focus 5 and Exercise 10. Students write a memo from a boss about employees' inappropriate behavior. To make the memo sound impersonal, students use complex passives.

EXERCISE 11 [20 minutes]

Students discuss superstitions in small groups and then write down four or five of them using complex passives.

1. Read the instructions and example as a class. Elicit any other superstitions students are aware of concerning mirrors. Ask students to use complex passives in their descriptions.
2. Divide students into small groups of three or four. Have them discuss superstitions for 5 minutes, then write descriptions of four or five of these using complex passives.
3. Have students share their sentences with the class, and discuss the superstitions.

 For more practice, use *Grammar Dimensions 4* Workbook pages 33–34, Exercise 7.

EXPANSION [15 minutes]

1. Ask students to work in small groups and create three or four additional sentences describing other superstitions they know. Remind them to use complex passives in their descriptions.
2. Have groups read their sentences to the rest of the class. Are the superstitions only believed by the people in one country or area of the world, or many?

FOCUS 6 — Contexts for the Use of Complex Passives

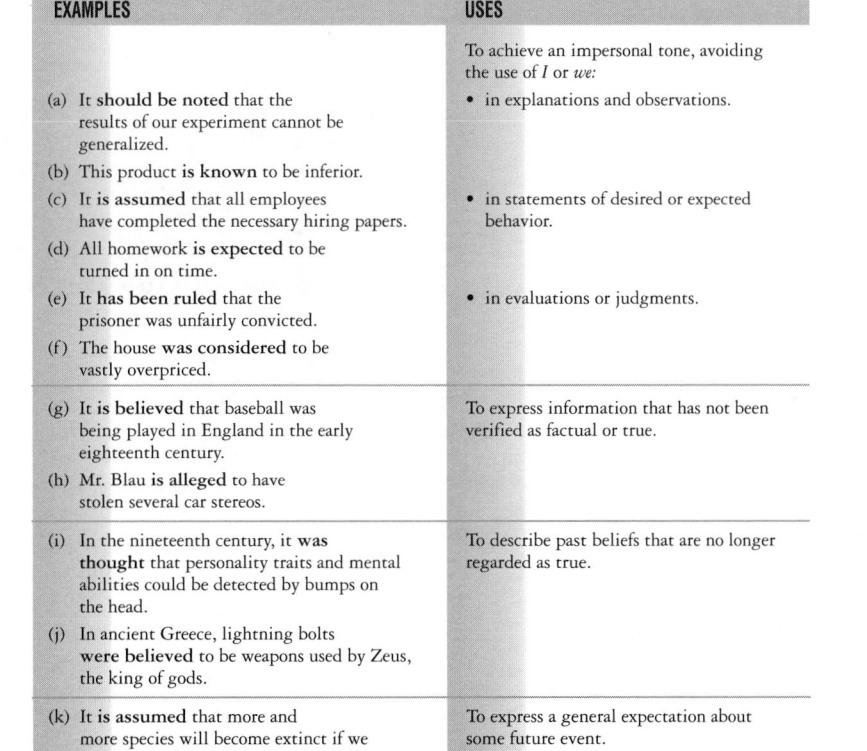

use

Complex passives are often used in journalism, in business, and in academic writing. Although not commonly used in informal spoken English, complex passives are frequent in formal spoken English (for example, news reports, speeches). Some of the most common uses follow.

EXAMPLES	USES
	To achieve an impersonal tone, avoiding the use of *I* or *we:*
(a) It **should be noted** that the results of our experiment cannot be generalized.	• in explanations and observations.
(b) This product **is known** to be inferior.	
(c) It **is assumed** that all employees have completed the necessary hiring papers.	• in statements of desired or expected behavior.
(d) All homework **is expected** to be turned in on time.	
(e) It **has been ruled** that the prisoner was unfairly convicted.	• in evaluations or judgments.
(f) The house **was considered** to be vastly overpriced.	
(g) It **is believed** that baseball was being played in England in the early eighteenth century.	To express information that has not been verified as factual or true.
(h) Mr. Blau **is alleged** to have stolen several car stereos.	
(i) In the nineteenth century, it **was thought** that personality traits and mental abilities could be detected by bumps on the head.	To describe past beliefs that are no longer regarded as true.
(j) In ancient Greece, lightning bolts **were believed** to be weapons used by Zeus, the king of gods.	
(k) It **is assumed** that more and more species will become extinct if we continue to destroy the world's rain forests.	To express a general expectation about some future event.
(l) The weather **is expected** to be warm and sunny all weekend.	

The *Guinness Book of World Records* presents hundreds of fascinating facts about the natural world, human feats, and other topics. Rewrite the following facts in complete sentences. Use the passive form of the verb given in parentheses. Change the phrasing of information and add words as needed. The first has been done as an example. Note that if an activity happened in the past (as in 1b), an infinitive verb expressing it must be perfective: *to + have + past participle.*

1. a. longest living individual fish: European eel (think)
        The longest living fish is thought to be the European eel.
        OR *It is thought that the longest living fish is the European eel.*

    b. life span of one specimen of European eel: 88 years (report)
        It was reported that one specimen lived for 88 years.
        OR *One specimen was reported to have lived for 88 years.*

2. animal with the highest frequency hearing: the bat (believe)

3. longest sneezing bout of a human: 978 days (record)

4. the deepest and oldest freshwater lake in the world: Lake Baikal in Siberia, Russia (know)

5. the greediest living animal: larva of the polyphemus moth, which consumes an amount equal to 86,000 times its own body weight (consider)

6. coldest place in the universe: The Boomerang Nebula, 5,000 light years from earth (think)

7. Sirius A, the Dog Star: brightest of the 5776 stars we are able to see (presume)

8. fastest text message typed on a cell phone: 43.2 seconds for a 160-character text by a Korean woman (allege) (Hint: use *a Korean woman* for the subject.)

ANSWER KEY

Exercise 12 Some answers may vary.   2. The animal with the highest frequency hearing is believed to be the . . .   3. The longest sneezing bout of a human was recorded as (or to be) 978 days.   4. The deepest and oldest freshwater lake in the world is known to be . . .   5. The greediest living animal is considered to be the . . .   6. It is thought that the coldest place in the universe is . . .   7. It is presumed that Sirius . . . is the brightest of the 5,776 stars.   8. A Korean woman is alleged to have typed the fast message on a cell phone: . . .

FOCUS 6 [25 minutes]

This focus summarizes some of the most common reasons complex passive verbs are used in communicative contexts. Both types of complex passives presented in Focus 5 are shown in the examples.

1. **Lead-in:** Read the introduction to the chart, then the list of uses for the first row of examples. Ask a volunteer to read the first example. Ask students to analyze it: is the sentence an observation? (yes)

2. Repeat this procedure with the remaining examples in the focus chart.

3. Answer any questions they might have.

4. Discuss contexts in which students have heard or read complex passives used, such as formal speeches, news reports, and scientific texts.

5. Encourage students to use this chart as a reference tool.

LANGUAGE NOTE

Emphasize that complex passives in English are considered somewhat formal, and so are not normally used in everyday speech. They are, however, commonly used in formal speeches, such as political addresses, and in writing, particularly factual writing.

EXERCISE 12 [20 minutes]

Students use information from the *Guinness Book of World Records* to write sentences using passive verbs.

1. Review example 1. a as a class. Which sentence contains a complex passive? (*It is thought that . . .*).

2. Repeat with example 1. b.

3. Have students work independently to write their sentences.

4. Have them exchange papers with a partner and make corrections and comments.

5. Ask volunteers to share the sentences they wrote that contain complex passives. See answers on LP page 74.

For more practice, use *Grammar Dimensions 4* Workbook page 34, Exercise 8; page 35, Exercise 9; page 36, Exercise 10; and page 37, Exercise 11.

EXPANSION 1 [45 minutes]

Activity 6 (speaking/listening/writing) on SB page 80 can be used for further practice with complex passives. Students interview a classmate about family or hometown history and write a report using complex passives.

EXPANSION 2 [45 minutes]

Use Activity 7 (research on the web) on page 81 after Exercise 12. Students research more interesting facts on the Guinness Book of World Records Web site, then report on them using complex passives.

FOCUS 7 — Using the Passive to Create Cohesion in Discourse

use

EXAMPLES	EXPLANATIONS
(a) For the first time, researchers have found **the remains of a mammal that has been entombed in amber. The remains,** including a backbone and ribs, **are estimated** to be eighteen million to twenty-nine million years old. Discovered in the West Indies, **these remains are believed** to be those of a tiny insect-eating mammal.	As explained in Focus 1, we put focus on a topic in English by making it the grammatical subject. Often a new topic is introduced at the end of a sentence. This topic then becomes the subject of the next sentence. As a result, a passive verb may be needed. Putting the topic in the subject position helps to create cohesion, making it easier for the reader or listener to understand the main ideas.
(b) Biologists have recently determined that **even the tiny brains of bees can recognize and interpret patterns. This feat was** once **thought** possible only through reason. In an experiment, bees learned to look for food only near **certain symmetrical or asymmetrical patterns. These patterns are reflected** in nature, such as blossoms of plants.	Often a synonym for the topic or a shortened form of the topic is used as the subject with a passive verb. (See Unit 6, Focus 2 for more information about these forms of reference.) This also helps to create cohesion. In some cases, it allows the writer or speaker to avoid using a subject with a long modifying phrase.
(c) Most theories of long-term memory **distinguish** skills or habits ("knowing how") from abstract or representational knowledge ("knowing that"). **This distinction is supported** by recent evidence that skill learning and the acquisition of knowledge are handled by different areas of the brain.	The subject of a passive verb may also be derived from the verb of a previous sentence.

EXERCISE 13

Circle the passive verbs in the following passages. Then explain why each passive verb is used.

Example: One of the world's largest pharmaceutical companies has recently fired its chairperson. The chairperson (was suspected) of unethical accounting practices. Explanation: *The passive verb "was suspected" is used in the second sentence to put focus on the topic, "the chairperson."*

1. Researchers in Hungary have been studying the cognitive and communication skills of dogs. In numerous experiments, dogs (were found) to be very sensitive to cues produced by humans and performed some tasks better than humans' closest relative, the chimpanzee.

2. The ability of electric currents to float through certain materials completely untouched, without energy loss, (is called) superconductivity. This phenomenon (was explained) in a theory developed in 1972, an accomplishment that won the Nobel Prize. Superconductivity (was thought) to exist only at extremely cold temperatures, but in 1986 a scientist in Germany discovered a high-temperature superconductor.

3. The repeated eruptions of Mexico's Popocatepetl volcano have resulted in the growth of a lava dome to within 50 feet of the rim of the volcano. The dome (is being fed) by 20,000 cubic feet of fresh lava daily. If the lava overtops the rim, it could melt glaciers on the side of the mountain and create life-threatening mudflows.

4. In experiments to examine the ways in which infants form attachments to mothers or other caretakers, researchers separated infant chimpanzees from their mothers. Extended separations (were found) to result in abnormal social development.

5. A team of scientists have decoded the 1700 genes of a microbe living on the ocean floor. This microbe belongs to a class called arachae, a different class from the two most common branches of life—bacteria and eukaryotes, which include plants, animals, and humans. The existence of archaea (was) first (proposed) by Carl Woese and Ralph Wolfe at the University of Illinois. Archaea has some characteristics of other life forms but functions differently. About five hundred species of archaea (have been) identified. The life form is thought to produce about 30 percent of the biomass on earth.

Adapted from "Decoding of Microbe's Genes Sheds Light on Odd Form of Life," *Los Angeles Times*, August 8, 1996.

ANSWER KEY

Exercise 13   The verbs are circled above. The uses are: 1. To create cohesion and to put focus on dogs as a topic.   2. is called: To focus on the topic being defined; was explained: To create cohesion and to put focus on the topic of superconductivity; was thought: To create cohesion and to put focus on the topic superconductivity.   3. To create cohesion and to put focus on the topic of the lava dome.   4. To create cohesion and to put focus on the topic of the separation of chimpanzees from their mothers. 5. was proposed: To create cohesion and to put focus on the topic of arachae microbes; have been.

FOCUS 7 [20 minutes]

Focus 7 explores the role of the passive in creating cohesion in discourse.

1. **Lead-in:** Read the first row of examples and explanations. Then, to illustrate the ways in which grammatical subjects put focus on topics, rewrite example (a) with *researchers* as the subject of the last two sentences (e.g., *Researchers estimate the remains. . . . to be . . .* etc.).

2. Ask students to tell you the topic that these rewritten sentences focus on (*researchers*). Ask them to compare this to the sentences in example (a) in the focus chart, in which the topics are boldfaced.

3. If necessary, repeat this process with example (b), asking students to express the second sentence with a noun that would be the agent of *thought*.

4. To help students understand the derivation of subjects from verbs as shown in example (c), give them other verbs and have them come up with the abstract noun forms (e.g., *distinguish–distinction; estimate–estimation; behave–behavior*).

LANGUAGE NOTE

Using passive verbs to achieve cohesion in writing is an important skill for advanced learners to develop. Students' writing will greatly improve once they have mastered how to focus on a topic by making it the grammatical subject of a sentence.

EXERCISE 13 [15 minutes]

In this exercise students circle the passive verbs in reading passages and explain their uses.

1. Read the example as a class. What is the topic of the sentence?

2. Have students work in pairs. Tell them to circle the passive verbs in the passages.

3. Have them take turns identifying the topic of each sentence and explaining the use of each passive verb.

4. Ask volunteers to share their answers with the class, and discuss the reasons for their choices. See answers on LP page 76.

EXPANSION [20 minutes]

For additional practice in identifying and analyzing the use of passives, ask students to analyze a passage from a scientific text as a homework assignment.

1. Tell students to choose a scientific text from the library or on the Internet. They should read at least one page of the text.

2. Ask them to write down all the passive verbs they find in the text, and list the reason each was used.

3. Have students exchange papers with a partner and review their work.

4. Ask volunteers to share their lists with the class.

After each sentence or group of sentences, add a sentence with a passive verb to create cohesion, using the information given in parentheses.

Example: Any substance that is toxic to insects is known as an insecticide. (We use insecticides to control insects in situations where they cause economic damage or endanger health.)

Insecticides are used to control insects in situations where they cause economic damage or endanger health.

1. The ancient city of Troy was the setting of the legendary Greek siege described in *The Iliad*. (An earthquake destroyed the city around 1300 BCE)

2. There are three types of muscle in humans and other vertebrates. One type is skeletal muscle. (Under a microscope, we see that this muscle is striped or striated.)

3. Most people associate the phrase "Survival of the fittest" with Darwin's Theory of Evolution. (However, a British philosopher, Herbert Spencer, first used the phrase, and Darwin later adopted it.)

4. The Great Wall of China served as a defensive wall between the old Chinese border with Manchuria and Mongolia. The first section was completed in the third century BCE. (The Chinese later extended it until it was 1400 miles long.)

5. Although the idea of submarines is an old one, the first submarine, made of wood and covered with greased leather, was not built until 1620. David Bushnell invented the first submarine used in warfare in 1776.

Use Your English

 **ACTIVITY 1** listening/writing/speaking

CD1 Track 5

A famous psychology laboratory experiment conducted by Stanley Milgram tested subjects' willingness to obey authority even when they believed they would be required to administer painful electric shocks to other subjects. Listen to the audio recording, in which you will hear a description of the procedures and the results of this experiment. Take notes on the information you hear. With a partner, compare notes to get information you may have missed. Then write a summary of the experiment, using passive verbs where appropriate to put focus on recipients of action and to achieve coherence.

 **ACTIVITY 2** reading

Find a text that has a number of passive verbs. (Science texts, instruction manuals, and texts that define or classify are good sources). Analyze ten passives that you find. Are they dynamic passives or stative passives? Why do you think the writer used them?

ACTIVITY 3 writing/speaking

In small groups, make up five sentences describing people, places, or things, but don't reveal who/what they are. In each sentence, use a stative passive verb. See if other groups can guess who or what you are describing. Here are some examples. Can you guess the answers?

Examples: 1. *It is divided into nine innings.*

2. *It can be found in tacos, spaghetti sauce, and ceviche.*

3. *This famous British dramatist is known as the Bard of Avon.*

4. *They are also called twisters.*

5. *This country is bordered by Italy, Austria, Germany, and France.*

ANSWER KEY

Exercise 14   Answers will vary. Possible answers include: 1. The city was destroyed by . . .
2. Under a microscope, this muscle is seen . . .   3. However, the phrase was first used by a British philosopher . . .   4. It was later extended until . . .   5. The first submarine used in warfare was invented in 1776 by David Bushnell.

Activity 3   1. Baseball is divided into nine innings.   2. Tomatoes can be found in those foods.
3. Shakespeare is known as the Bard of Avon.   4. Tornadoes are also called twisters.
5. Switzerland is bordered by those four countries.

EXERCISE 14 [15 minutes]

Students rewrite the sentences in parentheses with passive verbs in order to create cohesion within short passages.

1. Read the example as a class. What is the passive verb in the example?
2. Have students work independently. Tell them to rewrite the information in parentheses using passive verbs.
3. Ask volunteers to share their answers with the class. For each answer, ask students for other ways in which they phrased the information. See answers on LP page 78.

EXPANSION [30 minutes]

Activity 1 (listening/writing/speaking) on SB page 79 gives students practice in using the passive to achieve cohesion.

UNIT GOAL REVIEW [10 minutes]

Ask students to look at the goals on the opening page of the unit again. Refer to the pages of the unit where information on each goal can be found.

 **ExamView** Test Generator For assessment of Unit 4, use *Grammar Dimensions 4 ExamView®*.

USE YOUR ENGLISH

The Use Your English activities at the end of the unit contain situations that should naturally elicit the structures covered in the unit. For a more complete discussion of how to use the Use Your English Activities see To the Teacher, LP page xxvi. While students are doing these activities in class,

you can circulate and listen to see if they are using the structures accurately. Errors can be corrected after the activity has finished.

ACTIVITY 1 listening/writing/speaking [30 minutes]

CD 1 Track 5

Activity 1 provides an excellent expansion or follow-up to Exercise 14 on SB page 78. This activity gives students practice in using the passive to achieve cohesion.

1. Review the audio script on LP page S-2 before assigning this activity. If you think your students may need a brief overview of the topic or key vocabulary before listening to the tape, provide them with this information.
2. Tell students that they are going to listen to a description of a famous experiment that tested people's willingness to obey authority. Ask your students if they have heard of this experiment by Stanley Milgram and/or similar experiments and briefly discuss them.
3. Have students listen to the audio and take notes on the information they hear.
4. Have students work with a partner to compare notes and add any information they may have missed.
5. Ask the pairs to write a summary of the experiment, using passive verbs where appropriate to put focus on recipients of action and to achieve coherence.
6. Ask volunteers to read their summaries to the class, and discuss how the use of passives creates cohesion in their accounts.

ACTIVITY 2 reading [30 minutes]

Use this activity after Exercise 6 on SB page 68. In this activity students analyze ten verbs from a text of their choice in terms of whether each is stative or dynamic, and they identify the writer's reason for using each.

1. Have students chose a text. Suggest that they chose a science text or instruction manual, since these tend to use a number of passives.
2. Ask them to list ten verbs from the text.
3. Have them identify whether each verb is stative or passive.
4. Have them write the author's reason for using each verb.
5. Ask volunteers to share their lists and analyses with the class, and discuss.

ACTIVITY 3 [30 minutes]

Activity 3 is a good follow-up to Exercise 7 on SB page 70. Students, in small groups, create sentences using stative passive verbs to describe people, places, or things. Their classmates then guess what they are describing.

1. Divide students into groups of three or four.
2. Tell them that they are to write five sentences in which they describe people, places, or things—but do not name them. They are to use a stative passive verb in each sentence.
3. Read the example sentences as a class and have students guess what is being described in each.
4. Have each group get together with another group. Have the groups take turns reading their descriptions and guessing what is being described.
5. Ask a volunteer from each group to share two of the group's best sentences with the class.

 **ACTIVITY 4** writing

Draw a diagram or map of one of the following:

- an area (your room, apartment or house, a neighborhood, or commercial district, for example)
- a machine or device
- an invention of your own creation (a machine that writes your papers for you? a device that gets you out of bed in the morning?)

In your diagram/map, label at least four or five objects, parts, buildings, or whatever would be found there. Then write a paragraph describing the locations of objects or the ways in which you have divided your diagram/map into parts. Use stative passives in your descriptions. (As reviewed in Focus 4 on page 69.)

ACTIVITY 5 writing

As the manager of a large office-supply store, you have observed repeated inappropriate behavior among some of the employees. This behavior includes the following:

- showing up late for work and leaving early
- taking breaks longer than the 15 minutes allowed
- eating snacks at the service counter
- talking to other employees while customers are waiting for service.

Write a memo to the employees to let them know what kind of behavior is expected of them while they are at work. Since you want to assume an impersonal tone, use complex passives.

 **ACTIVITY 6** speaking/listening/writing

Interview a classmate about family or hometown history. Ask him or her to tell you about some events that are thought to be true but are not documented. The events might concern some long-ago period (for example, "Juan's great-grandfather was believed to have been born in Guatemala. The family is thought to have moved to Mexico in the early 1900s."). They could also include information about your classmate's youth as reported by his or her parents (for example, "Sonia is said to have been very good-natured as a baby."). Take notes during the interview. Then write up a report from your notes, using complex passives where appropriate to express some of the information. If time permits, present your report orally to the class.

 **ACTIVITY 7** research on the web

 Read more interesting facts and world records on the Guinness Book of World Records Web site: www.guinnessworldrecords.com. Divide the class into groups, with each group finding five interesting facts from one of the following categories: Human Body, Amazing Feats, Natural World, Science and Technology, Arts & Media, Sports and Games. Write down the facts using complex passives as was done in Exercise 12.

 **ACTIVITY 8** reflection

How can good language learners be described by the kinds of activities they engage in and strategies they practice? Make a list of qualities by completing the statement "A good language learner can be defined as someone who . . ." in five ways on a piece of paper. Then compare your definitions with a partner to see if you had any in common.

Example: *A good language learner can be defined as someone who is willing to make mistakes.*

ACTIVITY 4 · writing
[25 minutes]

In this activity, students draw and label a map and then describe the contents using stative passives. Use Activity 4 after Exercise 9 on SB page 71.

1. Read the directions with the class, then have them work independently to draw their diagrams and write a descriptive paragraph about the contents of these using stative passives.

2. Have students exchange diagrams and paragraphs with a partner and discuss.

VARIATION

1. Have students create two separate documents: a diagram or map, and a descriptive passage. Tell them not to write their names on either paper.

2. Post the diagrams/maps (or some of them, depending on the size of your class) on the classroom wall. Label them with numbers or letters (1, 2, 3; A, B, C, etc.).

3. Have students read their descriptions aloud to the class.

4. Have the class identify the diagram or map described.

ACTIVITY 5
[30 minutes]

Use this activity after Exercise 10 on SB page 72 for additional work with complex passives. Students write a memo from a boss about employees' inappropriate behavior. To make the memo sound impersonal, students use complex passives.

1. Read the activity text with the class and discuss what students think of the employees' behavior. Elicit suggestions about what the manager

could do to let the employees know what kind of behavior is expected of them while they are at work.

2. Have students work independently to write the memo from the boss, using complex passives.

3. Have students form small groups and share their memos.

4. Ask volunteers to share their memos with the class. How did they use complex passives?

ACTIVITY 6
[45 minutes]

Use this activity after Exercise 12 on SB page 75. Students interview a classmate about family or hometown history and write a report using complex passives.

1. Read and discuss the directions with the class. Write on the board: *events that are thought to be true but are not documented.* Have volunteers write the examples from the text on the board. Ask students to give other examples, and write these on the board as well.

2. Have students work independently to interview a classmate about family or hometown history. Tell them to elicit some statements about events that are thought to be true but are not documented. Remind them to take notes as they interview.

3. Ask students to write a report about the information they learned using their interview notes. They should use complex passives where appropriate to express some of the information.

4. Ask volunteers to present their reports orally to the class.

ACTIVITY 7 · research on the web
[45 minutes]

Use this activity after Exercise 12 on page 75. Students research more interesting facts on the Guinness Book of World Records Web site, then report on them using complex passives.

1. Read the directions with the class.

2. Divide the class into groups of 3–4.

3. Have each group choose one of the categories and find at least five facts about that category on the Guinness Book of World Records website.

4. Ask them to summarize those facts using complex passives.

5. Write the five categories on the board. Ask a representative from each group to write the facts the group found on the board.

6. Discuss the findings as a class.

ACTIVITY 8 · reflection
[25 minutes]

This activity is a good follow-up to Exercise 4 on page 65. Students reflect and write sentences about the activities and strategies of good language learners using passive verbs.

1. Read the directions with the class. Ask a volunteer to read the example aloud.

2. Have students work independently to write at least five answers to the question, "A good language learner can be defined as someone who . . ."

3. Have them work in pairs, exchange papers, and discuss their answers.

4. Ask volunteers to share answers with the class.

Suggestion: You may want to conduct a poll of students' answers, and guide them in noting similarities and differences.

UNIT GOALS

- Distinguish classification from identification meaning in articles

- Use definite, indefinite, and zero articles appropriately

- Distinguish particular from general (generic) reference in articles

- Distinguish abstract generic from concrete generic meaning in articles

- Use the article in definitions of generic nouns

- Use the appropriate articles to correspond to body parts and illnesses

OPENING TASK

■ STEP 1

Read the list of current or possible practices in the medical profession on the next page. Check whether you believe they are ethical or not ethical.

ETHICAL?

Yes	No	
❏	❏	a. Researchers using animals (mice, cats, cows, etc.) to test the poison level of drugs or the effect of artificial organs that might be implanted into a human being.
❏	❏	b. Doctors refusing to accept calls from patients who do not have medical insurance.
❏	❏	c. Drug companies bribing doctors with vacations and other perquisites ("perks") to prescribe new but less well-known drugs to their patients.
❏	❏	d. Using doctors to torture accused terrorists in prison.
❏	❏	e. Machines keeping alive severely injured people who are in a vegetative state.
❏	❏	f. Childless couples using surrogate (substitute) mothers to bear children.
❏	❏	g. Engineering genetic changes in embryos to prevent birth defects or diseases.
❏	❏	h. Medical students practicing techniques on patients who are technically still alive but beyond the help of extraordinary life-saving measures.
❏	❏	i. Forcing birth control on a population that for religious or cultural reasons does not desire it.
❏	❏	j. Parents conceiving a child in order to obtain a matching organ or tissue to save the life of another one of their children.
❏	❏	k. Poor people selling their own organs in order to make a living.
❏	❏	l. Requiring doctors to reveal the results if they have a positive AIDS test and to quit their active medical practices.

■ STEP 2

In small groups, discuss the pros and cons of several of these practices based on information you have heard or read about. Choose one member of your group (the Recorder) to take notes on the discussion.

■ STEP 3

(Recorder) Summarize your group's discussion for the rest of the class. Which topics were the most controversial? Which opinions did your group agree on?

UNIT OVERVIEW

Unit 5 tackles what many teachers have found to be their greatest challenge: the English article system. All nine focuses in this unit explore a different facet of the article system. The detailed explanations and sample exercises in the unit will help students grasp and apply the form, use, and meaning of articles. Note: Because of its length, this unit has been divided into five lesson plans. If a quick review of the topic is necessary, read each focus box with students and have them complete only the first exercise for each.

LANGUAGE NOTE

The definite article is the most frequently used word in the English language, yet understanding the article system in English can be particularly challenging, even for advanced students. As you teach this unit, it is helpful to bear in mind that many languages—most Asian and Slavic, and many African languages—do not have articles. Many other languages—including Spanish, French, Farsi, Scandinavian, and Semitic languages—have articles, but sometimes use them differently. Many of the common errors with article usage reflect the speaker's native language patterns.

UNIT GOALS

Some instructors may want to review the goals listed on Student Book (SB) page 82 after completing the Opening Task so that students understand what they should know by the end of the unit. These goals can also be reviewed at the end of the unit when students are more familiar with the grammar terminology.

OPENING TASK [30 minutes]

The purpose of this task is to engage students in a discussion about current medical topics and, in the process, to use a number of articles with a variety of nouns. In the course of the discussion, they will talk about practices associated with medical and research procedures, diseases, body parts, and the like, all of which require a fairly sophisticated knowledge of the English article system. If your class has students from a number of different countries, the discussion can become quite lively, as certain practices may be more common in certain countries than others. The problem-solving format is designed to show the teacher how well the students can think about and produce the target structures implicitly and spontaneously when they are engaged in a communicative task. For a more complete discussion of the purpose of the Opening Task, see To the Teacher, Lesson Planner (LP) page xxii.

Setting Up the Task

■ STEP 1

1. Tell students that they are going to read a list of current or possible medical practices and say whether they think each is ethical, or not.
2. Read the first question (a) as a class. Ask students whether they think the practice is ethical, or not. Ask several students to give reasons to support their opinions.

Conducting the Task

■ STEP 2

1. Divide students into groups of four. Assign one student the role of note taker.
2. Draw a three-column chart with the headings *Practice/Ethical/Not Ethical* on the board, and ask the note taker in each group to copy it.
3. Have the groups answer the questions in Step 1, and have the note taker record their answers in the appropriate columns in the chart. (Refer to SB page 83.)
4. Have the groups do Step 2 on SB page 83, in which they discuss the pros and cons of these

practices. Tell the note taker to record their comments on a separate piece of paper.

Closing the Task

■ STEP 3

Have the note taker summarize the group's discussion and present it to the class. Ask the note taker to identify which topics were the most controversial, and which opinions the group agreed with. Don't worry about accuracy at this point, though you may want to take notes of errors in meaning, form, or use in order to focus on those problems later.

GRAMMAR NOTE

Typical student errors (form)

- Using an indefinite rather than the definite article with a single unit: —e.g., * *A bacon fell on the floor.* (See Focuses 2, 4, 6.)
- Using an article with a noncount noun: —e.g., * *She has a coffee on her dress.* (See Focus 1.)
- Omitting the definite article when making abstract generic references: —e.g., * *These days, personal computer is not a luxury.* (See Focus 6.)
- Including a definite article when making concrete generic references: —e.g., * *She loves writing the poetry.* (See Focus 6.)

Typical student errors (use)

- Using an article with certain nouns of time: —e.g., * *She studied until the midnight.* (See Focus 3.)
- Omitting the definite article when making a general reference to plural nouns: —e.g., * *The Sierra Club works to save wolves.* (See Focus 5.)
- Omitting an article with names of illnesses: —e.g., * *I have bad cold. She has sore throat.* (See Focus 9.)

FOCUS 1 — Classification versus Identification*
Meaning of Articles

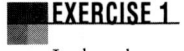

form | meaning

EXAMPLES	EXPLANATIONS
	An indefinite article (*a/an* or Ø) classifies a noun and shows that it represents or reflects a type, group, or a class distinct from some other type, group or class.
(a) What did you see yesterday? I saw a horror movie last week.	
(b) An earthquake (a natural disaster) struck at 7:10 AM.	• singular nouns (*a/an*)
(c) A gas (a type of gas) that can be deadly is carbon monoxide.	
(d) Ø Stars (celestial bodies) shine brightly.	• plural nouns (Ø)
(e) We expect Ø complications (additional problematic conditions) while she is sick.	
(f) Have you ever seen Ø traffic (passage of vehicles) like this?	• noncount nouns (Ø)
(g) Ø Mango juice (tropical fruit juice) can be made from Ø syrup (thick sweet liquid).	
	The definite article (*the*) can *identify* a noun and show that it has been singled out in some way. Generally, the speaker or writer knows the listener or reader is aware of the noun because it was previously mentioned or he or she can see it, has heard of it, has experienced it, has read about it, etc.
(h) **The** movie (you heard about it) featured Dracula.	• singular nouns (*the*)
(i) **The** earthquake (you know about it) destroyed many buildings.	
(j) **The** gas (you smell it) can be harmful.	
(k) **The** stars (we read about them) were discovered in 1952.	• plural nouns (*the*)
(l) **The** medical complications (you experienced them) were unexpected.	

*Adapted from P. Master, *Systems in English Grammar*. Englewood Cliffs, New Jersey: Prentice-Hall Regents, 1996.

EXAMPLES	EXPLANATIONS
(m) **The** traffic (we are riding in it) is dangerous.	• noncount nouns (*the*)
(n) Could you pass the maple syrup (you are near it)?	

■ EXERCISE 1

Look at the use of *a, an,* or *the* in each of the following cartoons.

STEP 1 Describe what is happening in each cartoon.

STEP 2 Discuss how the article classifies or identifies its corresponding noun.

Example: *Two children are pretending to be a doctor and a nurse to a teddy bear mother. The doctor is announcing the gender of a stuffed animal.*

• "A" is used to classify the newborn as a male.

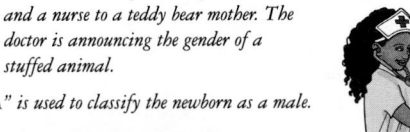

It's a boy!

1.

Do you think Bob minds sitting in the back row?

2.

A bone doesn't seem to satisfy his appetite anymore!

3.

I beat the eggs. Now what?

ANSWER KEY

Exercise 1 Answers will vary. Possible answers are: **Step 1:** (1) Three friends: a man and two women went to a movie. All the seats were filled except two in the front row and one in the back row. Two found seats in the front row. Bob found a seat in the back row between two attractive women. (2) A dog is eating human style food at the table in a human manner: using a bib and utensils. The humor in the caption is that the dog's owners have clearly spoiled the dog by feeding him human food too often instead of typical dog food such as a bone. (3) An inexperienced cook is following a recipe that includes eggs. The man is hitting the eggs with a bat. The humor in the caption is the double meaning of the word beat, which can signify hitting an object strongly with a bat or similar weapon, or it can mean breaking eggs with a whisk in a bowl. **Step 2:** (1) **The** is used to identify the exact location of the seats (i.e., the very last row in the theater). (2) **A** refers to a type of dog food that most dogs usually receive (3) **The** is used to identify the eggs that the listener is aware of, as it is probably mentioned in the specific recipe the man is using or in the directions he was given.

FOCUS 1 [10 minutes]

Focus 1 explains the meaning of articles according to whether they are used to classify or identify a noun.

1. **Lead-in:** Explain the concepts of *classification* and *identification* before reading the focus chart. Explain that a *class* is a group, and that *classification* is the act of assigning something to a group. Explain that we use indefinite articles to classify nouns: *a boy, an idea.* Then explain that when we *identify* a noun, we are distinguishing it from others, and use the definite article: *That is the book I've been looking for!*

2. Review the concept of a zero article (∅). Remind students that no article—definite, or indefinite— is needed when referring to a nonspecific noun or noun phrase: *Doctors save lives.*

3. Read the explanations column on the right, and then read the first three examples with the class. Ask students to say whether each noun is a type, group, or a class distinct from some other type, group, or class.

4. Review that *a* precedes indefinite noun phrases that begin with consonant sounds and *an* precedes indefinite noun phrases that begin with vowel sounds. Emphasize that it is the sound, not the letter, that determines which indefinite article is required: *an hour* (following sound is a silent consonant + vowel); *a union* (following sound is the semivowel *y*).

5. Read through the remaining sections of the chart: first read the explanation, next the examples, and then ask students to analyze the examples.

METHODOLOGY NOTE

Students may be helped by knowing the history of definite and indefinite articles: *the* began as *that,* and *a* began as *one.* If they mentally substitute *that* and *one* for *the* and *a*, it may make the distinction between the definite and indefinite article clearer for them.

PRONUNCIATION NOTE

You may want to review the four different pronunciations of the definite article: (1) before consonant sounds (*the book, the song*); (2) before vowel sounds (*the apple, the orange*); and (3, 4) the stressed versions of these (*The word* the *can be pronounced four ways. I saw THE designer shoes you love at the department store today.*)

EXERCISE 1 [10 minutes]

In this exercise students describe the use of definite and indefinite articles in a series of cartoons.

1. Read the example with the class and discuss the use of *a* in the cartoon.

2. This activity can be done individually, in pairs, or as a class.

3. Tell students to be aware of the use of *a/an* for classification and *the* for identification as they respond.

4. Review answers as a class. See answers on LP page 84.

EXERCISE 2

Answer the following questions with noun phrases. Use *a/an, the,* or Ø to show that the noun is classified (shows kind, type, class, etc.) or identified (shows specific feature, aspect, characteristic, etc.).

Examples: What part of a holiday dinner do you enjoy the most? *The stuffed turkey* (*identified*)

What kind of meat do you like the most? *Beef, a hot dog (classified)*

1. What kind of movie is most exciting?
2. What feature of your classroom is unusual?
3. What kind of person would make a good roommate?
4. What type of vegetables do you dislike the most?
5. What aspect of your English class was most interesting this week?
6. What type of clothing is usually made of wool?
7. What characteristic of the weather is most frustrating where you live?
8. What class of animal gives birth to live young?
9. What part of the day is your most effective work time?
10. What aspect of your home or your friend's home is unusual?

EXERCISE 3

Fill in the following blanks with *a/an, the,* or Ø. In which blanks did you use *the* to refer to identifiable nouns?

On (1) __the__ night of January 11, 1983, Nancy Cruzan, (2) __a__ healthy, 25-year-old woman, lost control of her car while driving in Jasper County, Missouri. As (3) __the__ car overturned, Nancy was thrown into (4) __a__ ditch. When the ambulance reached (5) __the__ ditch, (6) __the__ paramedics found her with no (7) __Ø__ detectable breathing or (8) __Ø__ heartbeat. For seven years, Nancy lay in (9) __a__ Missouri state hospital, in what was described all too neatly as (10) __a__ "persistent vegetative state." In reality, she lay in (11) __a__ bed in (12) __the__ hospital, horribly contorted with (13) __Ø__ irreversible muscular and (14) __Ø__ tendon damage. She was fed through (15) __a__ tube in her side. (16) __The__ Cruzan family were hopeful that Nancy would recover. However, after five years they fought and lost (17) __the__ battle in court to euthanize her. This case brought (18) __the__ question of the morality of an individual's right to die to (19) __Ø__ national attention.

EXERCISE 4

Fill in the following blanks with *the* or Ø. In which blanks, did you use the Ø to refer to classifiable nouns?

(1) __The__ students entering our medical schools have (2) __Ø__ outstanding grade-point averages, and (3) __Ø__ impressive scores on (4) __the__ Medical College Admissions Test, and (5) __Ø__ glowing recommendations. There's no doubt that they have (6) __the__ capability to become (7) __Ø__ good scientists and (8) __Ø__ good science doctors. But do they have (9) __the__ makings of humanists with (10) __the__ commitment to treat everything from (11) __Ø__ broken bones to (12) __Ø__ broken hearts? It is this delicate balance between (13) __Ø__ science and (14) __Ø__ wisdom that makes (15) __Ø__ great physicians— (16) __the__ ability to know what to do with what has been learned.

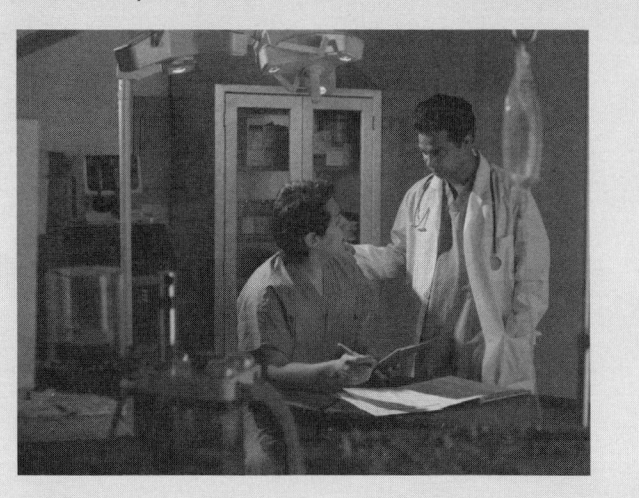

ANSWER KEY

Exercise 2 Answers will vary. Possible answers include: 1. a detective movie 2. the large orange clock on the wall 3. a person with an enthusiastic personality 4. green vegetables such as broccoli 5. the lesson on adjectives 6. a coat 7. the heat 8. a mammal 9. the morning 10. the leather seats

EXERCISE 2 [15 minutes]

In this exercise students answer questions with noun phrases and definite or indefinite articles.

1. As a class, read the two examples.
2. Have students work in pairs.
3. Ask students to pay attention to the noun following *what* in each question. Remind them that a kind, type, or class of something indicates a classification. More specific details in the question, such as a feature, aspect, or characteristic, calls for identification.
4. Ask volunteers to share their sentences—or their partner's sentences—with the class. See possible answers on LP page 86.

EXERCISE 3 [10 minutes]

Students fill in the blanks in a news account of an accident using definite and indefinite articles.

1. As a class, read the first sentence. Ask students to say what article belongs in the second blank.
2. Have students work independently to complete the exercise.
3. Review answers as a class. Ask students to identify where they used *the* to refer to identifiable nouns. See answers on LP page 86.

EXERCISE 4 [15 minutes]

In this exercise students complete a reading passage by supplying the definite or the zero article.

1. Remind students that classifiable noncount and plural noun phrases are preceded by Ø article, and identifiable noun phrases require *the*.
2. As a class, read the example. Ask students to explain why *the* is used here.
3. Have students work independently to complete the exercise.

4. Review answers as a class. Ask students to point out where they used the zero article to refer to classifiable nouns.

 For more practice, use *Grammar Dimensions 4* Workbook page 38, Exercise 1.

EXPANSION [40 minutes]

Activity 6 (reflection) on SB page 107 can be used after these first exercises for additional practice using a range of articles.

FOCUS 2 — Special Uses of the Definite Article

use

EXAMPLES	EXPLANATIONS
(a) **The sun** is very bright.	Use *the*: • with unique nouns
(b) **The most significant effect** occurred in June.	• before superlatives
(c) **The third component** was missing.	• before ordinals (*first, second, third,* etc.)
(d) **The main operator** was not on duty.	• before modifiers that make the noun that follows specific (*same, sole, chief, only, single, solitary, main,* etc.)
(e) **Each of the experiments** was successful.	• in phrases that refer to a specific part of a whole group
(f) Half of **the population** suffered greatly.	
(g) **The effect** of an earthquake can be felt for miles.	• with identifiable nouns that are followed by a modifying *of*-phrase
(h) We were uncertain about **the cause** of the fire.	
(i) **The beginning** of the movie was frightening.	
(j) A major urban problem is caring for **the poor** (people).	• before adjectives that represent groups of people
(k) "Heartbreak" is a song on **the radio**.	• with certain nouns, such as mechanical inventions and devices, to refer to a general example of something rather than a specific object the speaker/writer has in mind
(l) She got here fast because she took **the train**.	
(m) I went to **the barber** after classes.	• before locations associated with certain typical or habitual activities. The listener/reader may have no idea of the exact location to which the speaker/writer is referring.
(n) Have you been to **the beach** this summer?	
(o) She needs to pick up a few things at **the store**.	

For each of the following sentences, circle the correct article in parentheses. Explain your choices to a partner.

Example: (A/**The**) sun is very bright today. I need to buy (**a**/the) cap at (a/**the**) store.

The sun is very bright today. I need to buy a cap at the store.
Sun *is a unique noun; therefore,* **the** *is used.* **A cap** *is used because it refers to a type of hat, not to a particular one.* **The store** *is used because a location referring to a specific habitual activity (shopping) is being referred to.*

1. All civilizations of (a/**the**) world are enriched by trade and (a/**the**) stimulating impact of other cultures.

2. There are two main precursors to skin cancer. (A/**the**) first indication is spontaneous bleeding on some part of (a/**the**) skin. (A/**the**) second is the enlargement of a freckle or mole.

3. I'll be late for (a/**the**) meeting because I have to make (**a/the**) deposit at (a/**the**) bank.

4. (A/**the**) most significant effect of (an/**the**) earthquake was (a/**the**) destruction of many homes.

5. I read (**a**/the) wonderful story yesterday. (A/**the**) beginning of the story takes place in Vienna about (a/**the**) turn of (a/**the**) century.

6. In (a/**the**) past, (a/**the**) most important factor determining world power was (**a**/the) navy that could navigate (a/**the**) Mediterranean.

7. There were many reasons for (a/**the**) success of (a/**the**) project. (A/**the**) main reason was that at least half of (a/**the**) workgroup had PhDs from around (a/**the**) globe.

8. (A/**the**) radio described several ways in which (an/**the**) elderly could obtain (a/**the**) best medical help.

9. In (a/**the**) next year, (an/**the**) exact mechanism by which cell receptors work will be better understood.

10. (A/**the**) last decade has been marked by (**a**/the) large increase in violence.

Exercise 5   1. the: world is a unique noun; the: before identifiable noun followed by modifying *of*-phrase.   2. the: before ordinals; the: phrase that refers to a specific part of a whole; the: before ordinals.   3. the: meeting is identifiable to both listener and speaker; a/the: depends on whether the listener is familiar or unfamiliar with what deposit is being made; the: bank is a location associated with a typical or habitual activity; is   4. The: before superlatives/with identifiable nouns that are followed by a modifying *of*-phrase; the: in phrases that refer to a specific part of a whole; the: with identifiable nouns that are followed by a modifying *of*-phrase.   5. a: before modifiers that make the noun that follows specific; The: with identifiable nouns that are followed by a modifying *of*-phrase;

the: with identifiable nouns that are followed by a modifying *of*-phrase; the: in phrases that refer to a specific part of the whole group.   6. the: before ordinals; the: before superlatives; a: represent a distinct group; the: a specific place.   7. the: with identifiable nouns that are followed by a modifying *of*-phrase; the: known to the speaker; The: before modifiers that make the noun that follows specific; the: refers to a specific part of the whole group; the: before a unique noun.   8. The: refers to a general example of something; the: before adjectives that represent groups of people; the: before superlatives.   9. the: before ordinals; the: before modifiers that make the noun that follows specific.   10. The: before ordinals; a: represents a class distinct from another.

FOCUS 2 [15 minutes]

Since most students will have studied the uses of the definite article already, this focus should serve as a review.

1. **Lead-in:** Tell students that they are going to review special uses of the definite article, and that they can use this focus chart as a reference tool.

2. Read the first four examples and explanations, and discuss.

3. Ask volunteers to give an example of each instance.

4. Read the remaining examples and explanations, asking students to give other examples.

EXERCISE 5 [10 minutes]

Students circle the correct article in parentheses and explain their choices to a partner.

1. Ask volunteers to read the two example sentences and explanations.

2. Have students work in pairs. Tell them to complete the sentences by circling the correct article in parentheses.

3. Have them review and explain their choices with their partner. Encourage them to refer back to Focuses 1 and 2 to remind themselves of the rules and to locate reasons for their choices. See answers on LP page 88.

EXPANSION [25 minutes]

Use Activity 2 (reading/speaking) on SB page 105 after Exercise 5 to give students an opportunity to analyze uses of the definite article.

FOCUS 3 Review and Special Uses of Ø (Zero Article)

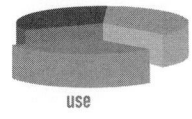

use

EXAMPLES	EXPLANATIONS
	Ø is used when the following noun is nonspecific. Use Ø with:
(a) Ø Flowers should be watered regularly.	• nouns that have general or generic reference (see Focus 4)
(b) I need to get Ø gas before we start for Seattle.	• nonspecific nouns that do not refer to a specific quantity or amount
	Also use Ø with:
(c) The children ran directly Ø home.	• certain nouns associated with familiar destinations
(d) They went Ø downtown after supper.	
(e) My grandmother walked to Ø school everyday.	
(f) He worked until Ø midnight.	• certain nouns of time (*night, dusk, noon, midday, midnight*, etc.)
(g) Ø Spring is a wonderful time of year.	• names of seasons (*spring, summer, fall, winter*)
(h) We had Ø lunch at a very good restaurant.	• names of meals (*breakfast, brunch, lunch, dinner*, etc.)
(i) The group arrived by Ø car.	• means of transportation (*by boat, by plane, on foot*, etc.)
(j) They came on Ø foot from the meeting.	
(k) We were informed by Ø mail that our subscription had been canceled.	• means of communication (*by phone, by mail, by telegram*, etc.)
	Certain idioms use Ø:
(l) They walked Ø arm in Ø arm down the aisle.	• phrases joined with *by, in,* or *and* (*day by day, week by week, side by side, arm in arm, neck and neck*, etc.)
(m) The ship was lost at Ø sea.	• participle + preposition + noncount noun (*wounded in action, lost at sea, missing in action, cash on delivery*, etc.)
(n) He put his heart and Ø soul into the project.	• phrases joined by *and* (*heart and soul, bread and butter, husband and wife*, etc.)
(o) Peter took Ø care of the details.	• verb + objects + preposition (*shake hands with, take care of, take advantage of, take part in, take notice of, take pride in*, etc.)

EXERCISE 6

Fill in the following blanks with *a/an, the,* or Ø. More than one answer may be appropriate depending on the meaning you want to convey.

It was (1) _____Ø_____ spring and (2) _____a_____ young GI, returning (3) _____Ø_____ home from (4) _____Ø/the_____ war, called his parents from (5) _____a_____ phone booth in (6) _____the/a_____ bus station. His parents had waited for a message by (7) _____Ø_____ mail or (8) _____Ø/a_____ telegram, but he had not gotten around to writing. On (9) _____the_____ phone, he told his parents that he would be coming by (10) _____Ø_____ bus and that he would be (11) _____Ø_____ home by 5:00 that evening. But he hesitated (12) _____a_____ moment and then added that he was bringing (13) _____Ø_____ home (14) _____a_____ friend, and he hoped that it would be okay with them because his friend was handicapped. He had been wounded in (15) _____Ø_____ action and had no legs. He asked his parents' permission. They told him that they felt very sorry for (16) _____the_____ friend but they were not really set up to cook (17) _____Ø_____ breakfast, (18) _____Ø_____ lunch, and (19) _____Ø_____ dinner for him—this was not (20) _____a_____ good time for him to come. The mother worked; there were two floors in (21) _____the_____ house; she would have to run up and down; (22) _____the/Ø_____ money was tight, etc., etc. As it turned out, (23) _____the_____ young man did not get off (24) _____the_____ bus that night, because he was (25) _____the_____ handicapped soldier. It was their son who had been wounded in (26) _____Ø_____ action. The parents never saw him again.

FOCUS 3 [20 minutes]

Focus 3 provides a review and explains some special uses of the zero (Ø) article, including several idiomatic usages.

1. **Lead-in:** Read the first two examples and explanations. Ask students how the meaning of the first sentence would change if the definite article was used: *The flowers should be watered regularly.* Ask students if the nouns *flowers* and *gas* in the two example sentences refer to specific quantities or amounts.

2. Follow this procedure with the remaining examples in the chart.

3. Encourage students to ask questions about anything they do not understand.

 For more practice, use *Grammar Dimensions 4* Workbook page 39, Exercise 2.

EXERCISE 6 [15 minutes]

In Exercise 6 students fill in the blanks of a passage with definite and indefinite articles, or Ø article.

1. Tell students that they are going to read a passage about a young soldier returning from war.

2. Have students work independently to complete the exercise, filling in the blanks with *a/an, the,* or Ø.

3. Ask volunteers to share their answers with the class, and discuss their article choices. In some cases, more than one answer could be correct. See answers on LP page 90.

4. If time permits, ask students to express their reactions to the passage without referring to the text. Take note of their use of articles as they speak.

 For more practice, use *Grammar Dimensions 4* Workbook page 39, Exercise 3.

Particular versus Generic Reference of Articles

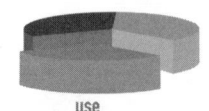
use

Generic reference relates to the general rather than the particular nature of something. Particular reference indicates one member of a class; generic reference indicates all or representative members of a class. Note in the following examples the particular and generalized meanings of *laser* in different contexts.

EXAMPLES	EXPLANATIONS
(a) Her doctor used a laser to treat her varicose veins.	• particular reference
(b) The laser cured Paul's cataract problem.	• particular reference
(c) The laser has been used in medicine since the 1960s.	• generic reference
(d) A laser can cut through soft tissue with a searing light.	• generic reference
(e) Lasers reduce the recovery period needed for ordinary operations.	• generic reference

EXERCISE 7

For each of the following pairs of sentences, circle the option that makes a general rather than a particular reference about the italicized noun phrase. Note that different references are not always marked by different articles.

Example: (a.) An *immunity* is a resistance to infection.

b. I have an *immunity* to small pox.

1. a. You should take *the vitamins* on the counter.
   (b.) You should take *vitamins* in order to stay healthy.

2. a. A *cholera epidemic* was started by contaminated food and water.
   (b.) *Cholera epidemics* kill many people every year.

3. a. A *doctor* claimed to have discovered a miracle burn ointment.
   (b.) A *doctor* is trained to treat burns.

4. (a.) *The motion picture industry* has created many movie idols.
   b. She is working for *the motion picture industry* in Los Angeles.

5. (a.) There is no cure for *a cold*.
   b. I have had *a cold* for four weeks.

6. a. *The mouse* used in the experiment was injected with morphine.
   (b.) *The mouse* is an excellent research animal.

7. a. The patient will sit in *the wheelchair* until her daughter arrives.
   (b.) *The wheelchair* has improved the lives of the handicapped.

8. (a.) Angela has been playing *the saxophone* for three years.
   b. Angela has been playing *the saxophone* that was in the corner.

9. a. *Some people* have been sitting in the waiting room since 11:00 AM.
   (b.) *People* kept alive only by machines should be allowed to die.

10. (a.) *Water* from springs contains minerals.
    b. *The water* from the spring cured my illness.

FOCUS 5

The + Plural Nouns for General Reference

use

EXAMPLES	EXPLANATIONS
(a) The Sierra Club is intent on saving **the redwoods**.	Sometimes, *the* may be combined with plural nouns when referring generally to:
(b) We went to a fund-raising benefit for **the whales**.	• plant and animal groups that are the target of special attention.
(c) **(The) Neo-Nazis** propagate discrimination and hate.	• social, political, religious, and national groups. (Note that *the* is optional here.) The names of some nationalities do not allow plural endings and require *the: the Swedish, the Danish, the Finnish, the Polish, the Swiss, the English, the French, the Dutch, the Irish, the Welsh, the British, the Chinese, the Japanese*, etc.).
(d) **(The) Republicans** have conservative values.	
(e) **(The) Jews** celebrate Passover.	
(f) **The Dutch** are very good at learning languages.	

FOCUS 4 [15 minutes]

Focus 4 contrasts the use of articles when making particular or generic references.

1. **Lead-in:** Read the introductory paragraph in the focus chart so that students understand the meanings of *particular reference* and *generic reference*.
2. Ask five different students to read the five example sentences and their explanations.
3. After reading example (e), ask students to look back at example (a) in Focus 3. Ask if that sentence contains a particular or generic reference (generic).
4. Ask volunteers to create other sentences for each example.

EXERCISE 7 [15 minutes]

Students identify general references to noun phrases in this exercise.

1. Read the example as a class.
2. Have students work independently to complete the exercise.
3. Review answers as a class. Ask students to say whether each generic reference indicates all members of a class or representative members. See answers on LP page 92.

 For more practice, use *Grammar Dimensions 4* Workbook page 40, Exercise 4.

EXPANSION [30 minutes]

For additional practice, have the class do Activity 1 (listening/writing) on SB page 105, in which students listen to a short lecture on computers and then write about what they learned.

LESSON PLAN 3

FOCUS 5 [15 minutes]

Focus 5 explains when *the* may be used with plural nouns for general references.

1. **Lead-in:** Read the first two examples and the explanation. Ask students to create sentences about other plant and animal groups that are the target of special attention, and write these on the board.
2. Read the remaining examples and explanations, and ask volunteers to create sentences about social, political, religious, and national groups, and write these on the board.

   Suggestion: Bring in a *National Geographic* or a *Sierra Club* magazine with pictures of different endangered wildlife and/or different groups of people around the world. Flip to one or more pages and ask students what they know about some of these groups—for example, the redwoods, the Tahitians, or the Amish.

Match up the following associations with the corresponding types of people. (Some associations may apply to more than one group.) Select five of them and write about them in complete sentences below.

Example: *(The) Italians eat a lot of pasta.*
            Criminals commit serious crimes.

Association	**People**
1. face racial discrimination j.	a. Swiss
2. want equality in marriage h.	b. Muslim
3. know many languages a.	c. professor
4. like to dance f.	d. racist
5. eat a lot of pasta k.	e. politician
6. like to loan money at high interest l.	f. Brazilian
7. discriminate against different races d.	g. criminal
8. must "publish or perish" c.	h. feminist
9. forget campaign promises e.	i. laborer
10. pray to Allah b.	j. African American
11. want more than the minimum wage i.	k. Italian
12. commit serious crimes g.	l. banker

1. _____
   _____

2. _____
   _____

3. _____
   _____

4. _____
   _____

5. _____
   _____

Abstract Generic versus Concrete Generic

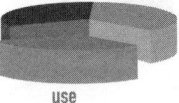

use

EXAMPLES	**EXPLANATIONS**
definite article = the laser indefinite article = a laser zero article = Ø lasers = Ø blood	The most common way to signal general reference in English is: • *the* + singular count nouns • *a/an* + singular count nouns • Ø + plural count nouns • Ø + noncount nouns

(a) **The dermatologist** specializes in skin care.
(b) **The platypus** is an unusual creature.
(c) The heaviest organ is **the skin.**
(d) **The eucalyptus** is native to Australia.
(e) What has revolutionized the workplace is **the computer.**
(f) It is difficult to play **the harp.**
(g) NOT: The towel absorbs water.
(h) **The/A dermatologist** uses a **special solution** to remove warts.
(i) **The/A kangaroo** carries **its young** in a pouch.
(j) NOT: An elephant is in danger of becoming extinct.
	There are two types of generic reference[*]:
	• *Abstract* generic reference uses *the* with singular countable nouns and noncount nouns to refer to certain well-defined, entire classes of entities. These entities are humans, animals, organs of the body, plants, complex inventions, and devices that can often serve as agents of change. They are not simple inanimate objects.
	
	• Abstract generic nouns can also be preceded by *a(n)* if there are subsequent references which relate to the human, animal, organ of the body, etc. noun one member at a time.
	
	• *Concrete* generic reference pertains to each or all of the representatives of a class rather than to the whole class. It uses a greater variety of forms than abstract generic reference does.
	   a(n) + singular count noun
	   Ø + plural noun
	   Ø + noncount noun

(k) **An operation** is stressful to one's body. (l) Ø **Carriers** may pass infections on to others. (m) Ø **Ultrasound** can detect the sex of an unborn baby.	
(n) **A police officer carries a gun.** (o) **A laser** directs **a beam of light** to make an incision.	*Singular concrete* generic nouns with *a(n)* describe generalized instances of something. This means that the noun class is being referred to one member at a time and there may be references to other singular count nouns in the sentence.

[*]P. Master, "Teaching the English Article System, Part II: Generic versus Specific." *English Teaching Forum*. July 1988.

ANSWER KEY

Exercise 8   Answers may vary. Possible answers are listed above.

EXERCISE 8 [20 minutes]

In this exercise students match associations with people, and then write five complete sentences about them.

1. Read the example as a class. Why is it correct to use either the definite article or no article with *Italians* in the first sentence? Why would it be incorrect to use the definite article in the second sentence? (Remind students that certain nouns are common nouns that do not correspond to social, political, religious, and national groups (e.g., *criminal*) and, therefore, are not preceded by *the*.)

2. Have students work in pairs.

3. Ask volunteers to share their sentences—or their partner's sentences—with the class. Is more than one answer possible?

 For more practice, use *Grammar Dimensions 4* Workbook page 40, Exercise 5.

EXPANSION [45 minutes]

Have students do Activity 4 (speaking) on SB page 106 after they have completed Exercise 8. In this activity, students use *the* + plural nouns while discussing how different groups might respond to various medical practices outlined in the Opening Task of this unit.

FOCUS 6 [25 minutes]

Focus 6 contrasts the use of articles with abstract generic references versus concrete generic references.

1. **Lead-in:** Create a six-column chart on the board with these headings: *humans, animals, organs of the body, plants, complex inventions*, and *devices*. Title the chart "The Special 6."

2. Ask volunteers to supply words for each of the six columns—e.g., *doctor, bears, liver, fern, computer*, etc.

3. Emphasize that "The Special 6" are the only types of words that can be referred to generically using the definite article *the*.

4. Tell students that all other words can be referred to generically with a wider variety of predeterminers: *a, an*, and Ø.

5. Read examples and explanations (a) through (j) in the focus chart.

6. Read examples (k) through (o) and explain that the set of words listed on the board will sometimes be referred to generically with *a, an*, or Ø when there is another singular count noun reference in a sentence—e.g., *A politician is a master of deceit* (preferred). *The politician is a master of deceit* (but also acceptable). Both sentences refer to politicians (people) in a general way.

In each set, select one noun phrase that we can refer to with abstract generic *the*. Then, use that noun phrase in a general sentence. Note that descriptive words before and after nouns do not affect the use of generic *the*.

Example: tattered flag/California redwood/stepbrother
The California redwood is older than other trees.
Correct answer: The redwood is a well-defined class of plants and can be preceded by abstract generic "the". "Tattered flag" and "stepbrother" do not refer to well-defined classes of entities.

1. lining of the coat/apartment made of brick/African elephant
2. dust on the moon/illustration of the month/telephone for emergency communication
3. barbecue/artificial heart/Persian rug
4. free love/fin of a fish/French marigold
5. Hungarian embroidery/American automobile/Spanish tile
6. locksmith/key/door
7. accurate diagnosis/radiation/family-practice physician
8. bottom layer/Golden Delicious apple/proteins
9. automatic dishwasher/detergent/waste paper
10. bold pattern/air bag/lunch menu

EXERCISE 10

Check the sentences in which *the* could be substituted for *a(n)* to make a generic reference. Then explain why.

Example: A transistor is used in computers.
*Because the transistor is a complex device, the use of **the** is possible.*

✓ 1. An X-ray machine is used in radiotherapy. The X-ray machine (complex device)
___ 2. A solar eclipse lasts about 7.5 minutes.
✓ 3. An octopus has eight legs. The octopus (animal)
___ 4. A sprain is suffered when an ankle is wrenched.
✓ 5. A piano has 52 white keys. The piano (instrument)
___ 6. A road is wider than an alley.
✓ 7. A human brain is larger than a bird brain. The human brain (body part)
✓ 8. A governor of a state (in the United States) has limited power. The governor of a state (human)
___ 9. A headache is a common physical complaint.
___ 10. A polygraph detects if a person is telling a lie.
___ 11. A deodorant can help eliminate odor.
___ 12. A kangaroo guards its young within a frontal pouch.

EXERCISE 11

Read the following sentences that use *the* for abstract generic reference of a noun. Replace *the* with *a/an* and add singular noun phrases within a new sentence to show that you are talking about generalized instances of something.

Example: <u>The dog</u> is man's best friend. *A dog needs its owner's attention every day.*

1. <u>The store manager</u> needs good organizational skills.
   <u>A store manaer needs good organizational skills.</u>
2. One of the slowest animals is <u>the snail</u>.
   <u>One of the slowest animals is a snail.</u>
3. <u>The cactus</u> grows in warm climates.
   <u>A cactus grows in warm climates.</u>
4. <u>The piano</u> is commonly found in American homes.
   <u>A piano is commonly found in American homes.</u>
5. <u>The stomach</u> is essential for digestion.
   <u>A stomach is essential for digestion.</u>
6. <u>The ophthalmologist</u> examines eyes.
   <u>An opthalmologist examines eyes.</u>
7. <u>The printing press</u> was essential to mass communication.
   <u>A printing press was essential to mass communication.</u>

EXERCISE 12

Describe a usual or general tendency by completing the sentences below.

Example: A chocolate chip cookie is made of <u>sugar, flour, butter, and chocolate chips.</u>

1. A good party consists of <u>good company and a lot of food.</u>
2. The Internet has changed <u>the way people obtain information.</u>
3. A healthy life includes <u>intellectual and social stimulation.</u>
4. Builders name streets after <u>names of trees.</u>
5. The police are needed for <u>executing the law.</u>
6. Amnesia causes <u>someone to forget who and where they are.</u>
7. Skillful architects create <u>magnificent buildings.</u>
8. A valuable education includes <u>instruction in various areas.</u>
9. Ladies' shoes come in all varieties including <u>sneakers and sandals.</u>
10. The digital camera allows <u>people to take many pictures.</u>

ANSWER KEY

Exercise 9 Sentences will vary. Possible answers include: 1. The African elephant is a magnificent beast. 2. The telephone for emergency communication has become a useful accessory in modern life. 3. The artificial heart has allowed many people to live who otherwise would have died. 4. The French marigold is a popular variety. 5. The American automobile used to be revered all over the world. 6. The locksmith can assist people in making keys or unlocking doors. 7. The family-practice physician keeps track of childhood diseases and immunizations. 8. The Golden Delicious apple is a sweet, yellow apple used in salads and applesauce. 9. The automatic dishwasher freed generations of women from after-dinner drudgery. 10. The air bag has saved countless victims of automobile accidents.

Exercise 11 Answers will vary. Possible answers are listed above.

Exercise 12 Answers will vary. Possible answers are listed above.

EXERCISE 9 [20 minutes]

Students choose noun phrases that can be referred to with the abstract generic *the* and use them in sentences.

1. Read the example as a class. Point out that an adjective before a noun does not affect article choice—i.e., *the* is used with *redwood* because *redwood* is a plant. Adding the adjective *California* does not affect the class of the noun.

2. Have students work in pairs.

3. Tell students to refer to the categories of nouns listed in Focus 6 to help them make their choices of noun phrases.

4. Ask volunteers to share their sentences—or their partner's sentences—with the class. Ask others to share alternative sentences they created, as well. See possible answers on LP page 96.

 For more practice, use *Grammar Dimensions 4* Workbook page 41, Exercise 6.

EXERCISE 10 [15 minutes]

In Exercise 10 students indicate in which sentences *the* could be substituted for *a(n)* to make a generic reference, and give reasons why.

1. Read the example as a class. Ask a volunteer to substitute the name of another complex device and restate the sentence.

2. Have students work independently to complete the exercise.

3. Have them check their answers with a partner, and discuss the reasons for their choices. Tell them to refer to Focus 6 for assistance.

4. Review answers as a class, discussing reasons. See possible answers on LP page 96.

 For more practice, use *Grammar Dimensions 4* Workbook page 42, Exercise 7.

LESSON PLAN 4

EXERCISE 11 [15 minutes]

Students replace abstract generic references in sentences with concrete generic references.

1. Read the example as a class. This exercise may be challenging for students. Remind them to include words like *its* _____ and *a(n)* _____, after the verb—e.g., A dog is **an** *excellent* pet.

2. Have students work in pairs.

3. Ask students to analyze the difference between each abstract and concrete generic reference by referring to Focus 6.

4. Review answers with the class. See answers on LP page 96.

EXERCISE 12 [15 minutes]

Students complete sentences to describe general tendencies.

1. Read the example as a class. Ask a volunteer to give a similar example using another food item.

2. Have students work independently to complete the exercise.

3. Have them share their answers with a partner. Encourage them to be creative. Tell them that the longer the sentence, the more opportunity they will have to use multiple count and noncount nouns. See answers on LP page 96.

EXPANSION [30 minutes]

Have students do Activity 3 (reading/writing) on SB page 106 for additional practice with abstract and concrete generic references.

FOCUS 7 — Definitions of Common Nouns

form   meaning
use

Standard definitions of generic nouns follow the pattern below. Generic nouns appear in the subject position of these definitions.

GENERIC NOUN	+ *BE*	+ CLASSIFYING NOUN*	+ RELATIVE PRONOUN	+ VERB PHRASE
(a) **The dinosaur**	is	a prehistoric animal	that	scientists discovered through excavations.
(b) **A dinosaur**	is	a prehistoric animal	that	is now extinct.
(c) **Dinosaurs**	are	prehistoric animals	that	roamed the earth during the Mesozoic Age.

(d) **The chicken** is an animal that lays eggs.	Abstract generic nouns emphasize: • a class
(e) **A chicken** is an animal that lays eggs.	Concrete generic nouns emphasize:
(f) **Chickens** are animals that lay eggs.	• an example, any members
(g) **Chicken** is a meat that is very moist.	• a group, all members • all/any of something
	Definitions can include:
(h) **The platypus** is a mammal that lays eggs.	• classifications
(i) **A duck** is a bird that has webbed feet.	• attributes
(j) **Vultures** are birds that are larger than rats.	• comparisons

*See Focus 1.

EXERCISE 13

Write incorrect definitions for the words provided below. Then, in pairs, take turns reading and correcting each other's definitions.

Examples: bicycle
A bicycle is a four-wheeled vehicle that you can sit on.
No, a bicycle is a two-wheeled vehicle that you can sit on.

1. stethoscope	4. spatula	7. nail	10. violin
2. koala bears	5. palm tree	8. movie stars	11. patient
3. liver	6. eye	9. honey	12. straw

EXERCISE 14

Find the incorrect article (*a/an*, *the*, Ø) in the following definitions. Then, correct the error.

Example: $\overset{The}{\wedge}$ Universe is a system of galaxies that was created 10,000 million years ago.

1. The fashion design is a major that requires artistic talent.
2. A radio telescope is telescope that collects long-wavelength radiation.
3. Astronaut is a person who travels in space.
4. A neurosis is mental disorder that is relatively minor.
5. Dirge is a musical piece played at a funeral.
6. In many homes, prayers are said before meal.
7. The somnambulism is a word for a condition called sleepwalking.
8. The mercury is a white metallic element, which is liquid at atmospheric temperature.
9. Vaporization is the conversion of liquid into a vapor.
10. The blackboard is a surface that is used for writing.

FOCUS 8 — Articles with Names of Body Parts

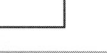
form

EXAMPLES	EXPLANATIONS
	When generally referring to names of organs, parts of the body, or body fluids, we can use *the* for:
(a) **The heart** can be transplanted.	
(b) Cancer of **the bladder** has been linked to cigarette smoking.	• singular body parts (*the* + noun)
(c) **(The) blood** carries nutrients to body tissues.	• massive areas or fluids of the body (*the* + noncount noun)
(d) **(The) skin** is sensitive to ultra-violet rays.	
(e) Excessive smoke inhalation damages the **lungs**.	• plural or paired body parts (*the* + noun + plural)
(f) Regular exams of **the teeth** will prevent serious dental problems.	
(g) **The veins** carry blood throughout the body.	

Exercise 13 Answers will vary. Examples of incorrect definitions include: 1. A stethoscope is an instrument that a dentist uses to examine your teeth. 2. Koala bears are animals that live in the woods of North America. 3. The liver is a type of flower that blooms at night. 4. A spatula is an implement that is used to stir oatmeal. 5. A palm tree is a type of tree that grows in frigid zones. 6. An eye is a part of the body that allows someone to smell. 7. A nail is a type of song that is popular with teenagers. 8. Movie stars are marketing executives who sell trips to the moon. 9. Honey is a substance that gardeners sprinkle on the ground to make flowers grow. 10. The violin is a tool similar to a hammer. 11. A patient is child that attends elementary school. 12. A straw is a piece of silverware that is used to eat hot soup.

Exercise 14 1. Fashion design is a . . . 2. A radio telescope is a telescope that collects . . . 3. The/An astronaut is . . . 4. A neurosis is a mental . . . 5. A dirge is a musical . . . 6. . . . are said before a meal. 7. Somnambulism is a word . . . 8. Mercury is a white . . . 9. . . . of a liquid into a vapor. 10. A blackboard is . . .

FOCUS 7 [15 minutes]

Focus 7 gives standard definitions of generic nouns. This focus chart is an excellent reference tool for students to use.

1. **Lead-in:** Remind students that, as they learned in Focus 1, a *classifying noun* is one that represents a type, group, or class distinct from some other type, group, or class.
2. Ask different volunteers to read the examples, and discuss these with students.

METHODOLOGY NOTE

This focus will help students to write grammatically correct definitions. Remind them to refer to the principles detailed in Focus 6 as they create definitions for certain words. Also remind them that humans, animals, organs of the body, plants, and complex inventions/devices may be preceded by *the*.

EXERCISE 13 [15 minutes]

In Exercise 13 students write incorrect definitions for 12 nouns, and then work with a partner to share and correct these.

1. Read the example as a class. Could you also say *the* bicycle? Why, or why not?
2. Have students work independently to write inaccurate definitions of the twelve nouns.
3. Have them work in pairs and take turns reading their definitions to each other and correcting them.
4. Have volunteers share some of their most outrageous definitions and corrections with the class. See possible answers on LP page 98.

 For more practice, use *Grammar Dimensions 4* Workbook page 42, Exercise 8.

EXPANSION [15 minutes]

Give students extra practice in defining nouns with this expansion activity.

1. Have students, in pairs, each write a list of ten generic nouns.
2. Have them exchange their lists, and write incorrect definitions for half of them, and correct definitions for the other half.
3. Have them exchange their definitions, and take turns reading each aloud. They should state whether each definition is correct or not, and correct the inaccurate ones.
4. Ask volunteers to share some of their definitions and corrections with the class. See possible answers on LP page 98.

EXERCISE 14 [15 minutes]

Students find and correct the incorrect articles in the ten sentences.

1. Read the example sentence as a class.
2. Have students work in pairs to complete the exercise.
3. Remind students to look carefully at each noun to determine whether it is one of the "Special 5" types of nouns that takes *the* or whether it is another type of count or noncount noun that will require *a, an*, or Ø.
4. Ask volunteers to share their answers with the class, and discuss these answers. See answers on LP page 98.

FOCUS 8 [10 minutes]

1. **Lead-in:** Read the examples in this focus chart as a class.
2. Point out that *the* is generally used with the names of body parts, unless the body parts are noncount nouns, in which case *the* is optional.
3. Ask volunteers to create other sentences using the names of organs, parts of the body, or body fluids.

EXERCISE 15

Study the following diagram and write sentences describing the location or function of at least eight of the following body parts.

Examples: *The diaphragm is below the lungs.*

The brain controls all muscular movements of the body.

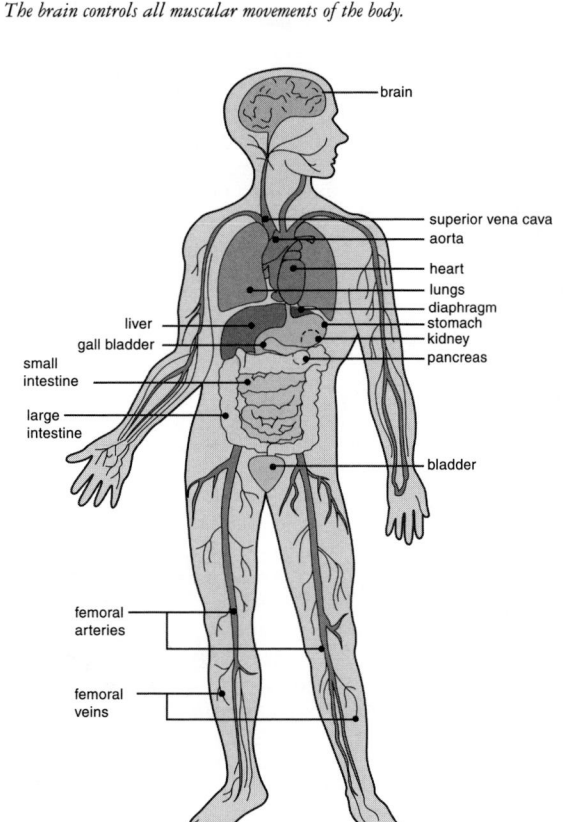

- brain
- superior vena cava
- aorta
- heart
- lungs
- diaphragm
- stomach
- kidney
- pancreas
- liver
- gall bladder
- small intestine
- large intestine
- bladder
- femoral arteries
- femoral veins

FOCUS 9   Articles with Names of Illnesses

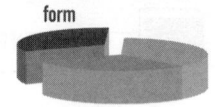

The names of illnesses follow a range of noun patterns:

THE + NOUN	*A/AN* + NOUN		*(THE)* + NOUN + PLURAL
the flu	a cold	an ulcer	(the) mumps
the gout	a hernia	a stroke	(the) measles
the plague	a headache	an earache	(the) hiccups
	a heart attack	a sore throat	

Ø + NONCOUNT NOUN		*Ø* + NOUN (WITH FINAL *-S*)
influenza	leukemia	diabetes
pneumonia	diarrhea	rabies
malaria	mononucleosis	herpes
arthritis	cardiovascular disease	AIDS
cancer	tuberculosis	

EXERCISE 16

Work with a partner. Fill in a correct disease/illness that matches the information in the following blanks.

Example: _AIDS_ is caused by a blood-borne virus (HIV, Human Immunodeficiency Virus).

1. _____The plague_____ is a disease that ravaged Europe between 1347 and 1351.

2. _____A hernia_____ is the bulging out of a part of any of the internal organs through a muscular wall.

3. _____(The) measles_____ is a contagious disease that causes red spots to appear on the skin.

4. _____Malaria_____ is caused by a parasite, which is transmitted by a female mosquito.

5. _____Leukemia_____ is a form of cancer that is marked by an increase in white blood cells.

6. _____Tuberculosis_____ is an inflammation of the lungs caused by bacteria or viruses.

(Exercise 16 is continued on LP page 102.)

ANSWER KEY

Exercise 15   Answers will vary. Possible answer are: 1. The diaphragm is used in the production of speech.   2. The kidney excretes urine.   3. The pancreas is the digestive gland behind the stomach. 4. The femoral arteries carry blood from the heart.   5. The lungs are used to breathe.

■ EXERCISE 15 [15 minutes]

Students write at least eight sentences describing the location or function of the body parts shown in the diagram.

1. Read the two example sentences as a class.
2. Ask volunteers to create two other example sentences using *diaphragm* and *brain*.
3. Have students work independently to write their sentences.
4. Have them share and review their sentences with a partner.
5. Ask volunteers to share their sentences with the class. See possible answers on LP page 100.

 For more practice, use *Grammar Dimensions 4* Workbook page 43, Exercise 9, and page 44, Exercise 10.

LESSON PLAN 5

FOCUS 9 [20 minutes]

Focus 9 lists the complex array of articles used with the names of various illnesses.

1. **Lead-in:** Write a three-column chart on the board with these headings: *common ailments / common illnesses / serious illnesses.* Brainstorm entries for each column, such as *headache, cold, AIDS,* and add these to the chart.
2. Have students look at the focus chart and see if they can find any of the nouns on the board. Ask them to identify the article that is used with each.
3. Read the examples in the chart.
4. Encourage students to ask questions about anything they do not understand.

METHODOLOGY NOTE

Most of these uses will simply have to be memorized. Encourage students to use this focus chart as a reference tool. You could assign the focus as homework, and review the material during the next class.

■ EXERCISE 16 [10 minutes]

Students complete the sentences with the name of the appropriate illness. This exercise continues on SB page 102.

1. Read the example sentence as a class.
2. Have students work independently to complete the exercise.
3. Tell them to refer to Focus 9 for the names of illnesses.
4. Review answers as a class. See answers on LP pages 100 and 102.

 For more practice, use *Grammar Dimensions 4* Workbook page 44, Exercise 11, and page 45, Exercise 12.

EXPANSION [20 minutes]

This expansion activity gives students extra practice with using articles with the names of illnesses.

1. Divide students into groups of three.
2. Have one student in each group create a tic-tac-toe grid with the name of different illnesses in each square. That student will act as referee during the game.
3. Have one of the other two students in each group select a square and say what article goes with that illness.

4. The referee should refer to Focus 9 to judge.
5. For every correct answer, students mark an X in the appropriate box. If the answer is incorrect, the other student takes a turn.
6. The game continues until one student gets all Xs or all Os horizontally, vertically, or diagonally.

7. _____(The) bends_____ is a decompression sickness experienced in the air or the water.

8. _____Herpes_____ consists of sores on the skin or internal parts of the body and is often caused by stress.

9. _____A stroke_____ is a common name for a cerebral hemorrhage.

10. _____(The) hiccups_____ is a sound caused by contractions of the diaphragm.

EXERCISE 17

Make a "Health Log" which lists the illnesses that you (or other family members) have had as far back as you can remember. Indicate the name of the disease, the kind of doctor that cared for you, and the remedies or medicines that helped you get better. Then, share some or all of this information with a partner. If you are not comfortable sharing this information, make up fictional information to discuss with your partner.

Example: *A general practitioner recommended aspirin, tea with lemon, and bed rest for my cold.*

FAMILY MEMBER	DISEASE	DOCTOR (IF ANY)	REMEDY OR MEDICINE
Self	a cold	general practitioner	an aspirin, tea with lemon, bed rest
Mother	tonsillitis	an ear, nose, and throat doctor	tonsil surgery
Brother	cancer	oncologist	radiation, chemotherapy

EXERCISE 18

Review all of the rules in this unit. Place *a/an, the,* or Ø in the following paragraph. The first one has been done for you.

(1) The gap between the^ rich and the poor, among countries and within countries, is widening. (2) Most of world's AIDS cases and HIV-infected people are in the developing countries. (3) Yet drug and hospitalization costs mean that "early intervention" is still meaningless concept in these countries. (4) Drug AZT remains too expensive for most of people who need it. (5) The industrialized world's total annual contributions to the AIDS in the developing world is estimated at $200 million or less. (6) The last year, the total expenditure for AIDS prevention and care in New York state alone was five times greater. (7) Total budget of the average national AIDS program in the developing world today is less than medical cost of caring for only fifteen people with AIDS in United States.

Adapted from J. Mann, "Global AIDS: Revolution, Paradigm, Solidarity." In O. Peterson, ed., *Representative American Speeches*, New York: The H.W. Wilson Co., 1991.

EXERCISE 19

Review all of the rules in Unit 5. Place *a/an, the,* or Ø in each of the following blanks. Explain your choices to a partner.

(1) ___Ø___ insulin functions as (2) ___an___ indispensable middleman in (3) ___Ø___ metabolism. When we eat (4) ___Ø___ carbohydrate foods such as (5) ___Ø___ bread, (6) ___Ø___ vegetables, or (7) ___Ø___ fruit, (8) ___the___ simple sugar called (9) ___Ø___ glucose is usually (10) ___the___ end product of (11) ___Ø___ digestion, and this sugar provides (12) ___Ø___ energy to each living cell; (13) ___Ø/the___ insulin, in its turn, functions as (14) ___a___ doorman to these cells, controlling (15) ___Ø/the___ access of (16) ___Ø___ glucose molecules and other food sources such as (17) ___Ø___ protein and (18) ___Ø___ fat across (19) ___the___ cell membrane and into each cell's interior. With (20) ___Ø/the___ insulin, (21) ___Ø___ metabolism is (22) ___a___ finely tuned feedback mechanism. Without it, only (23) ___a___ trickle of (24) ___Ø___ fuel leaks into (25) ___the___ cells, hardly enough to stoke (26) ___the___ great human metabolic furnace.

Adapted from S. Hall, *Invisible Frontiers*, New York: The Atlantic Monthly Press, 1987.

ANSWER KEY

Exercise 17 Answers will vary.

Exercise 18 The corrections are: 2. Most of the world's AIDS cases and HIV-infected people are in Ø developing countries. 3. . . . is still a meaningless concept . . . 4. The drug AZT. . . for most of the people . . . 5. . . . contributions to AIDS in the developing world . . . 6. Ø Last year, . . . 7. The total budget . . . is less than the medical cost . . . with AIDS in the United States.

EXERCISE 17 [20 minutes]

In this exercise students create a "Health Log" in which they list illnesses they and their families have had, the kind of doctor who was consulted for each, and the remedies employed. Please keep in mind that this exercise requests personal information that students might prefer to keep private. Suggest that students can create both fictional family members and fictional illnesses so they get the practice working on the assignment, but don't reveal anything about which they might be embarrassed.

1. Read the directions with the class, and go over the first example. Ask volunteers to read the other two entries in the chart.
2. Walk volunteers through naming two or three other conditions. Ask them for the family member name, the name of the disease, the type of doctor consulted, and what was done for each.
3. Have students work independently to complete their charts.
4. Ask them to work in pairs to talk about the illnesses, using the information they have written in their charts.
5. Ask volunteers to share some of their information with the class. Discuss if other students (or their family members) have experienced those same illnesses, and what they did for them.

EXERCISE 18 [15 minutes]

Students find ten article errors in a paragraph about AIDS.

1. Read and discuss the example sentence as a class.
2. Have students work independently to complete the exercise. Tell them to refer to the nine focuses in Unit 5 to find reasons to support their choices.

3. Review answers as a class. See answers on LP page 102.
4. If time permits, discuss the topic of AIDS treatment in developing countries.

EXERCISE 19 [15 minutes]

This exercise continues the review of article rules begun in Exercise 18.

1. Read and discuss the first example as a class. Why would it be incorrect to use a definite or indefinite article here?
2. Have students work independently to complete the exercise. Tell them to refer to the nine focus charts in Unit 5 to find reasons to support their choices.
3. Have students work in pairs to review their answers.
4. If time permits, discuss students' knowledge of diabetes and how that disease affects the way the body produces and processes insulin.

EXERCISE 20

Look at the underlined articles and nouns in the following paragraph. Explain the choice of article in each case. Refer to rules throughout this unit.

Example: the Monterey pine *abstract generic noun requires "the"*

> (1) <u>The Monterey pine</u> may bring tidings of (2) <u>Ø joy</u> to many a household during (3) <u>the holiday season</u>, but its own fate is less cheery. Although (4) <u>Ø researchers</u> are cautiously optimistic that (5) <u>the species</u> may survive in (6) <u>the wild</u>, it faces (7) <u>an uphill battle</u> in its native habitat as a result of (8) <u>Ø human interference</u>.
>
> (9) <u>Ø Monterey pine (Pinus radiata)</u> has various personalities—that of (10) <u>a Christmas tree</u> and (11) <u>Ø landscaping enhancement</u>, especially on (12) <u>the West Coast</u>, and that of (13) <u>a hard-working timber producer</u> in plantations in (14) <u>the southern hemisphere</u>.
>
> (15) <u>Ø Refinements</u> of (16) <u>the original California stock</u> have enabled (17) <u>Ø forestry experts</u> in (18) <u>Ø Australia</u>, (19) <u>Ø Chile</u>, (20) <u>Ø New Zealand</u>, and (21) <u>Ø Spain</u> to produce (22) <u>Ø straight-trunked "workhorse" trees</u> much sought after by (23) <u>the lumber industry</u>. More than 10 million acres of domesticated Monterey pine are grown in (24) <u>plantations</u> worldwide.
>
> Adapted from "Monterey Pine Struggles to Survive." In *UC MexUS News*, University of California Institute for Mexico and the United States (UC MEXUS), UC Riverside, Number 43, Spring 2006, p. 19.

EXERCISE 21

Imagine that you have just taken notes on a lecture about the medical field. Rewrite your notes (given below) in a paragraph, inserting articles where necessary.

Example: medical field changed rapidly last century
The medical field has changed rapidly in the last century . . .

1. in past, family practitioner responded to all of family's medical needs (childbirths, surgeries, diseases, etc.)

2. doctor relied on natural remedies to alleviate pain

3. doctor's role was more of onlooker as "nature took its course"

4. today, doctors play more active role in healing

5. with their more specialized training, they are able to prescribe wonder drugs and perform surgeries on patients

6. prolonging life has always been ideal goal

7. sometimes lifesaving/enhancing procedures come in conflict with well-established social, religious, and moral values

8. thus, there is need for medical ethics

9. this is field that considers ethical implications of medical procedures and argues reasonable rights and limits doctors should have in making decisions about improving, prolonging, or saving lives

Use Your English

ACTIVITY 1 listening/writing

Listen to the mini-lecture about computers.

CD1 Track 6

- **STEP 1** Take notes about the following items in the grid below.

- **STEP 2** Extend your notes to make as many sentences as you can, using the principles about article selection that you have learned in this unit.

Example: abacus
An abacus was the earliest computing device used by the ancient Greeks and Romans.

1. use of the slide rule	
2. type of machine Gottfried Liebniz built	
3. invention of Charles Babbage	
4. mathematical theory of Alan Turing	
5. CPU	
6. memory	
7. VDU	
8. four ways computers can function	

ACTIVITY 2 reading/speaking

Select an 800 to 1000- word article from your local newspaper. Underline all instances of nouns preceded by *the*. With a partner, discuss why *the* was chosen instead of *a/an* or *Ø* articles.

Example: *Ernesto Sanchez grabbed his wife's hand when <u>the ground</u> reared up beneath them, cracking roads and collapsing nearby buildings in seconds.*

The is chosen in this example because it describes a location associated with typical, daily activities but no specific idea of the exact location is provided.

ANSWER KEY

Exercise 20 2. Ø joy—idiom: verb+ object +preposition: tidings of joy   3. the holiday season—*modifier makes noun specific*   4. Ø researchers—*plural noun*   5. the species—*generic count noun*   6. the wild—*unique noun* 7. an uphill battle—*single noun; represents a type of battle;*   8. Ø human interference—*noncount noun*   9. Ø Monterey pine (pinus radiata)—*Concrete noncount noun pertaining to all the representatives of a class*   10. a Christmas tree—*single noun; represents a type of tree;*   11. Ø landscaping enhancement—*abstract noncount noun*   12. the West Coast—*section of a country*   13. a hard-working timber producer—*single noun; represents a type distinct from another type*   14. the southern hemisphere—*section of the Earth*   15. Ø Refinements

of—*plural noun*   16. the original California stock—*modifier makes noun specific*   17. Ø forestry experts—*plural noun representing a group*   18. Ø Australia—*place name; phrases joined by in*   19. Ø Chile—*place name; phrases joined by in*   20. Ø New Zealand—*place name; phrases joined by in*   21. Ø Spain—*place name; phrases joined by in*   22. Ø straight-trunked "workhorse" trees—*plural noun representing a group*   23. the lumber industry—*modifier makes noun specific*   24. plantations—*plural count noun*

Exercise 21 The answer key is provided at the foot of SB pages 106–107.

Activity 1 The answer key is provided at the foot of SB pages 106–107.

EXERCISE 20 [15 minutes]

Students read a paragraph about the Monterey pine and analyze the use of articles.

1. Read and discuss the first example as a class. Ask students to name a few other abstract generic nouns, and write these on the board.
2. Have students work independently to complete the exercise. Encourage them to refer to the rules in Unit 5 to support their choices.
3. Have students work in pairs to review their answers. See answers on LP page 104.

EXERCISE 21 [15 minutes]

Students rewrite notes from a lecture on the medical field in paragraph form, using articles as appropriate.

1. Read and discuss the example sentence as a class. Why is *the* appropriate in this instance?
2. Have students work independently to write their paragraphs. Tell them to refer to the nine focuses in Unit 5 to check their choices.
3. Have students exchange papers with a partner and discuss each other's work. See the paragraph on LP page 106.
4. If time permits, discuss how the medical field has changed in the past few decades, in this country and in other countries.

EXPANSION [60 minutes]

Activity 5 (research on the web/writing) on SB page 106 offers additional practice using a range of articles. In this activity students learn about the field of medicine in other parts of the world using the Internet and/or interviewing other students. Then have them write a short paper on one aspect of medical practice that interests them.

UNIT GOAL REVIEW [10 minutes]

Ask students to look at the goals on the opening page of the unit again. Refer to the pages of the unit where information on each goal can be found.

 For assessment of Unit 5, use *Grammar Dimensions 4 ExamView®*.

USE YOUR ENGLISH

The Use Your English activities at the end of the unit contain situations that should naturally elicit the structures covered in the unit. For a more complete discussion of how to use the Use Your English Activities see To the Teacher, LP page xxvi. While students are doing these activities in class, you can circulate and listen to see if they are using the structures accurately. Errors can be corrected after the activity has finished.

 **listening/writing [30 minutes]**

CD1
Track 6

This activity, in which students listen to a short lecture on computers and then write about what they learned, is an excellent follow-up to Exercise 7 on SB page 92.

■ STEP 1

1. Tell students that they are going to listen to a mini-lecture about computers and take notes about certain information they hear.
2. Review the example and the eight items in the first column of the grid.
3. Have students listen to the audio once without taking notes.

4. Have them listen a second time, taking notes about the eight items in the grid. (The audio script for this listening appears on LP page S-3.) Tell them to replay the audio as many times as necessary for them to record all the information about the items.

■ STEP 2

1. Encourage them to write as many sentences about the items as they can, using the principles of article selection they learned in this unit.
2. Ask volunteers to share sentences about each item with the class. See answers on LP page 106.

ACTIVITY 2 reading/speaking [25 minutes]

Use this activity after Exercise 5 on SB page 89. This activity gives students an opportunity to analyze the use of articles in extended text.

1. Read the example as a class. Discuss why the definite article was chosen, rather than an indefinite or zero article.
2. Have students work in pairs to underline all instances of nouns preceded by *the*, and discuss why the definite article was chosen in each instance.
3. Review answers as a class.

ACTIVITY 3 reading/writing

Locate one chapter in an introductory science textbook (physics, chemistry, biology, etc.) that talks about general principles in that field. With a partner, read the first five paragraphs of the chapter. Make a list of abstract generic and concrete generic articles. Which type seems to be more frequent in this type of writing?

ACTIVITY 4 speaking

Discuss which types of political, social, or religious groups would disagree most with each of the medical practices mentioned in the Opening Task on page 83. For example, would (the) Catholics be in favor of birth control? Would doctors be in favor of declaring positive AIDS tests results for themselves?

ACTIVITY 5 research on the web/writing

The field of medicine can vary in different cultures. Do research on the Internet and conduct interviews with other students to learn about the practice of medicine in a place you are not familiar with. What are the medical training, medicine, and techniques associated with synthetic drugs, surgical technology, CAT scans, natural herbal drugs, acupuncture, homeopathy, massage, osteopathy, etc.? From your Web research and interviewing, select one aspect of medical practice that interests you and write a short paper, incorporating correct use of the generic article.

ACTIVITY 6 reflection

Think of a difficult school-based problem you would like to solve.

■ **STEP 1**   Try to state the problem in the form of a question.

Example: *How can I write a research paper on a current events topic?*

■ **STEP 2**   List the steps you will need to follow to complete your goal.

Example: 1. Develop a working hypothesis.

2. Conduct interviews with experts and take notes.

3. Find sources in the library or on the Internet.

4. Read sources and take notes.

5. Create an outline.

6. Write a rough draft.

7. Obtain peer and teacher feedback.

8. Revise and edit the final paper.

■ **STEP 3**   Discuss your plan with a classmate, elaborating on each step.

Example: *First, I plan to develop a working hypothesis like "Genetic engineering can alleviate many serious illnesses today." Then, I plan to interview one or two professors in the Biology Department to try to refine my hypothesis. Next . . .*

Page 104, Exercise 21   1. In the past, the family practitioner responded to all of the family's medical needs (e.g., childbirths, surgeries, diseases, etc.).   2. The doctor relied on natural remedies to alleviate pain.   3. The doctor's role was more of an onlooker as nature took its course.   4. Today, doctors play a more active role in healing. 5. With their more specialized training, they are able to prescribe wonder drugs and perform surgeries on patients. 6. Prolonging life has been the ideal goal.   7. Sometimes lifesaving/enhancing procedures come in conflict with well-established social, religious, and moral values.   8. Thus, there is a need for medical ethics.   9. This is a field that considers the ethical implications of medical procedures and argues the reasonable rights and limits doctors should have in making decisions about improving, prolonging, or saving lives.

Activity 1   Answers will vary. Possible answers include: 1. The slide rule was used for various kinds of navigational calculation.   2. Gottfried Liebniz built a machine that could perform multiplication.   3. Charles Babbage designed the first mechanical computer.   4. Alan Turing developed the mathematical theory of computation.   5. The CPU is the central processing unit.   6. Memory holds the current program and data.   7. The VDU is a screen used for user input and output.   8. The four ways that a computer can function are: input/output operations, arithmetical operation, logic and comparison operations, and movement of data to, from, and within the central memory of the computer.

USE YOUR ENGLISH

ACTIVITY 3 reading/writing [30 minutes]

Use this activity after Exercise 12 on SB page 97.

1. Have students work in pairs. Have them choose an introductory science textbook and find a chapter that discusses general principles in that scientific field.
2. Tell them to read the first five paragraphs of the chapter, and make a list of all the abstract generic and concrete generic articles they find.
3. Remind students to review Focus 6 if they cannot recall the difference between abstract generic and concrete generic articles. They should be able to find several examples of abstract generic use, particularly in the first paragraphs of a chapter.
4. Have pairs determine which type of generic articles—abstract or concrete—is most prevalent in this type of writing.
5. Discuss findings with the class.

ACTIVITY 4 speaking [45 minutes]

In this activity, students use *the* + plural nouns while discussing how different groups might respond to various medical practices. Use Activity 4 after Exercise 8 on SB page 94.

1. Divide students into groups of four or five.
2. Have them reread the text in the Opening Task of this unit and list all the medical practices mentioned there.
3. Give them a specific amount of time, such as 20 minutes, to discuss which types of political, social, or religious groups would disagree most with each of the medical practices mentioned in the Opening Task.

4. Elicit examples of groups, such as: the Moslems, the Christians, the Jews, the Arabs, the Chinese, the Israelis, the feminists, surgeons, nurse', right to life proponents, and Planned Parenthood employees.
5. Give an example: *Would (the) Catholics be in favor of birth control?*
6. Discuss results with the class.

ACTIVITY 5 research on the web/ writing [60 minutes]

Use this activity as a homework assignment after Exercise 21 on SB page 104. Students learn about the field of medicine in other parts of the world using the Internet and/or interviewing other students, and then write a short paper on one aspect of medical practice that interests them.

1. Read the activity text with the class.
2. Briefly discuss what areas of medicine most interest students, and write some of these on the board.
3. Have students work independently to research medicine in other parts of the world. You could ask them to use the Internet, the library, and/or interview classmates to find information.
4. Ask them to choose one aspect of medicine in another country that particularly fascinates them, and write a short paper about it.
5. Encourage them to check their work by referring to the focus charts in Unit 5.
6. Have students form small groups of three or four and discuss their findings.

VARIATION

1. Pair up students from different countries. Ask them to take turns describing remedies or treatments used in their home countries.

2. Ask students to write a paragraph describing some of these remedies or treatments. Circulate around the room and select one or two examples of paragraphs that are particularly interesting and informative.
3. Ask the authors of those paragraphs to read them to the class.
4. Collect the paragraphs students wrote and grade them only on article usage.

ACTIVITY 6 reflection [40 minutes]

In this final activity students reflect on how they might solve a particularly difficult school-based problem, and then share their strategies with a partner. You could assign this activity after Exercise 4 on SB page 87 for additional work with a range of articles.

Ask the class to brainstorm a list of school-based problems they find particularly challenging, and write these on the board.

■ STEP 1

1. Read the example as a class.
2. Ask students to state some of the problems on the board in the form of questions, and write these on the board.

■ STEPS 2 AND 3

1. Have students list the steps they will need to follow to complete their goal and then discuss their plan with a classmate, elaborating on each step.
2. Have a volunteer poll the class on the problems they chose to discuss. Were any very common? Were there any similarities between strategies?

REFERENCE WORDS AND PHRASES

- Know the different reference forms in English

- Know the different uses of reference forms for linking ideas

- Use the appropriate reference forms for different contexts

- Avoid unclear reference by using appropriate forms

OPENING TASK

Do Men and Women Communicate Differently?

In recent decades, there has been much research about whether men and women have different communication patterns in social situations, workplaces, classrooms, and other contexts.

■ STEP 1

Decide whether each of the following statements is true or false; that is, whether you think it accurately describes communication patterns or not. Be prepared to give reasons or examples for your choices. You may want to state specific conditions under which you believe a statement is generally accurate. An example is given for the first one.

1. Women talk more than men.

   This statement may be true if we compare two women talking together with two men talking together. But I don't think it's the case when women and men are together at a social event or in classroom discussions. In those situations, I think men do more of the talking. So overall, I'd say the statement is false.

2. Men are more likely to interrupt women than to interrupt other men.

3. Female speakers are more animated in their communication style than are males; for example, they gesture more than men do.

4. In business situations, female managers communicate with more emotional openness than male managers do.

5. During conversations, women spend more time looking at their partner than men do.

6. Women are more likely to answer questions that are not addressed to them.

7. In general, men smile more often than women.

8. Women are more likely to disclose information about intimate personal concerns than men are.

■ STEP 2

Discuss your answers and explanations with a partner.

■ STEP 3

Turn to page A-16 to see answers and explanations based on research about the ways in which American men and women communicate. Match each with one of the eight statements above. Check your answers with classmates.

UNIT OVERVIEW

This unit helps students to understand the reference system in English, including personal pronouns, demonstrative pronouns, and determiners, *the* + noun phrase and *such* + noun phrase. Along with a review of forms, this unit explains the contexts and motivations for choosing reference words and phrases in communicative contexts, both spoken and written. Note: Because of its length, this unit has been divided into three lesson plans. If a quick review of the topic is necessary, read each focus box with students and complete only the first exercise of each.

GRAMMAR NOTE

Students at this level should be familiar with all of these forms, but many will still have difficulty choosing between them when referring to previously stated information.

UNIT GOALS

Some instructors may want to review the goals listed on Student Book (SB) page 108 after completing the Opening Task so that students understand what they should know by the end of the unit. These goals can also be reviewed at the end of the unit when students are more familiar with the grammar terminology.

OPENING TASK [20 minutes]

The purpose of this task is to create a compelling context in which students can exhibit their command of various reference forms. Here, students engage in reading and discussing whether men and women have different communication patterns. The problem-solving format is designed to show the teacher how well the students can produce the target structures implicitly and spontaneously when they are engaged in a communicative task. For a more complete discussion of the purpose of the Opening Task, see To the Teacher, Lesson Planner (LP) page xxii.

Setting Up the Task

1. Ask students to comment on the photo. Are there any apparent differences in the way the men and women seem to be communicating? Ask them to describe the body language of the people in the photo.
2. Ask students if they think there are significant differences in the way men and women communicate. Draw a three-column chart on the board with the headings *Situation/Men/Women*. Guide students in brainstorming different situations, such as social situations, work, school, recreational, and write these on the board.
3. Ask students to comment on the similarities and differences in the ways men and women communicate in a social situation, such as a party, and write their responses in the chart.

Conducting the Task

■ STEP 1

1. Divide students into pairs.
2. Read the directions and example as a class. Point out that the example differentiates between situations.
3. Have them read the series of statements, decide whether each is true or false, and discuss them, giving reasons to support their decisions.

■ STEP 2

Have them discuss their answers with a partner. You may want to walk around and listen in order to diagnose students' facility with subject-verb agreement.

■ STEP 3

Have them read SB page A-16 and match research-based explanations with the statements they read in Step 1.

Closing the Task

1. Review answers to Step 3 as a class. How many students agreed with the explanations? How many disagreed? Ask students to support their opinions with examples. Which results were the most surprising?
2. Don't worry about accuracy at this point, although you may want to take notes of errors in meaning, form, or use in order to focus on those problems later.

GRAMMAR NOTE

Typical student errors (form)

- Using *this* or *that* with plural nouns:—e.g.,* *We drove that cars for 12 hours.* (See Focus 1.)
- Repeating descriptive modifiers:—e.g.,* *I bought a new red car last week. * I drove the new red car to the city two days ago.* (See Focus 2.)
- Using an article after *such* before a noncount noun:—e.g.,* *The leaders met for two hours yesterday. One such a leader was Harold Warner.* (See Focus 7.)

Typical student errors (use)

- Repeating nouns in a second mention rather than using pronouns when there is only one possible referent:—e.g., * *I like that movie. That movie is a great movie.* (See Focus 3.)
- Using the wrong demonstrative determiner to refer to nearby objects:—e.g.,* *This speed sign says 35 mph. * I'd like to see this movie again.* (See Focus 4.)
- Placing incorrect emphasis on the referent:—e.g., * *I listened to this president's speech.* (See Focus 6.)

FOCUS 1 — Review of Reference Forms

EXAMPLES

	Referent
(a)	Ruth enjoys talking about [gender-based language differences]. She finds **the topic** an interesting one.

(b) Alma agrees that [men and women communicate differently in our society]. She believes **the observation** is true based on her personal experience.

(c) **Lin:** Do you know much about [language variation]?
Yumi: Not a lot, but I did read a little about **it** in my introductory linguistics course.

(d) [Phonology and semantics] are areas of linguistics. **They** are concerned with language sounds and meanings, respectively. I studied **them** a few years ago.

(e) Our sociology professor says that [male students tend to be criticized more than female students in classroom situations].
My experience supports { **this.** / **this claim.** }

(f) **Fred:** Do you think [men tend to interrupt more than women do]?
Yani: I would agree with { **that.** / **that generalization.** }

(g) [Two of the gender differences] seem especially true to me.
{ **These** / **These differences** } will be the topic of my paper.

(h) **George:** I know [people who constantly interrupt other people].
Lily: { **Those** / **Those people** } are the ones that I avoid!

(i) I read several studies about how [young boys are often encouraged to be aggressive and competitive]. I think **such an upbringing** would influence a boy's behavior when he gets older.

(j) I've never thought much about how [age, social status, and gender] influence the way we use language. However, I agree that **such factors** probably do affect greatly the ways in which we communicate.

EXPLANATIONS

Words and phrases that refer to information previously stated are called *reference forms*. The information that you are referring to is called a *referent*. The referents are here indicated by brackets.

Reference Forms
- *the* + noun phrase

- Pronouns:
  it

  they, them

- Demonstrative pronouns and determiners:
  this; this + singular/noncount noun

- *that; that* + singular/noncount noun

  these; these + plural noun

  those; those + plural noun

- Reference forms with *such a/an* + singular noun. The reference form *such* will be covered in greater detail in Focus 7 of this unit.
- *such* + plural or noncount noun

EXERCISE 1

Find five different types of reference forms in the sentences giving answers for the quiz in the Opening Task on pages 108–109. In the first column write the number of the item and the reference form. In the second column, write what the form refers to (the referent). You can paraphrase the referent. An example is given to start you off.

Example: **Reference Form:** this

Referent: that women look at their partners more than men do

REFERENCE FORM	REFERENT
1.	
2.	
3.	
4.	
5.	

EXERCISE 2

Underline the reference forms (*the* + noun, *it, this*, etc.) in the second sentence of each problem that refer to information in the previous sentence. Put brackets around the referents. There may be more than one reference form in a sentence.

Example: Our group discussed [the responses to Situation 1].
We didn't always agree that <u>such responses</u> were typical.

1. According to our psychology professor, for women, talk is important for creating [connections between people] For men <u>these connections</u> tend to be formed more through activities than talk.

2. Men and women sometimes experience[frustration]with each other because of their different communication styles. <u>The frustration</u> may be especially great between men and women who spend a great deal of time together.

3. Our professor notes that women have[a tendency to make suggestions rather than give commands when they want something done.] She thinks <u>this tendency</u> may reflect women's sense that they lack authority in certain situations.

4. Speakers use language differently depending on[differences in age, education, social status, and gender.] <u>Such differences</u> are of interest to linguists.

5. [Pitch and volume]are two aspects of speech. The way we use <u>them</u> in speech may affect how we are perceived by others in communication situations.

6. Women have[higher-pitched voices]than men do. <u>This</u> can be a disadvantage when they are trying to assert authority.

(Continued)

ANSWER KEY

Exercise 1 Answers will vary.

FOCUS 1 [20 minutes]

Focus 1 provides an overview of reference forms in English.

1. **Lead-in:** Emphasize how reference forms in English form a bridge between sentences that links ideas. To illustrate this, write two sentences on the board with a noun phrase subject repeated in the second sentence. Underline the repeated noun phrase. Example: *The Opening Task is concerned with communication differences between men and women. The Opening Task describes three communicative situations.* (A nonhuman subject is best since it offers a greater variety of reference forms.)

   a. Ask students to substitute reference forms for the repeated noun phase. (Elicit forms such as *it, this task, the task.*) Suggest others that they don't come up with, such as *this activity.* Tell students that these substitutions make comprehension easier for listeners and readers than repeating the noun phrase.

2. Ask volunteers to read the examples and explanations for (a) through (h). Ask others to identify the reference forms in each example.

3. To clarify *such* reference in examples (i) and (j), write two sentences on the board that contain ideas that could be summarized with a classifying word. For example, you could write two maxims: *A bird in the hand is worth two in the bush; A stitch in time saves nine.*

4. Write a third sentence using *such* followed by a blank. Ask students to supply the classifying word—e.g., *Most cultures have such _____.* For this example, students might supply *phrases, sayings, proverbs,* etc. Elicit that the *such* reference refers to previous information and indicates members of a group or class.

METHODOLOGY NOTE

Although most advanced students will be familiar with these forms, many may not have studied them as part of a reference system. Ask students to study the content of this focus chart as homework.

EXERCISE 1 [10 minutes]

In Exercise 1 students analyze the sentences in Step 3 of the Opening Task, writing the reference forms and referents they find in each sentence in a chart.

1. This activity can be done individually, in pairs, or as a class.

2. Read the directions and example as a class. Elicit that *that* refers to *this* in the phrase *One reason for this.* Point out that the referent acts like a bridge between the two phrases, linking an idea.

3. Review answers as a class.

work book For more practice, use *Grammar Dimensions 4* Workbook page 46, Exercise 1.

EXERCISE 2 [10 minutes]

In this exercise students identify the reference forms and referents in a series of ten statements. The exercise is intended to help students become more familiar with the range of reference forms in English and with the kinds of grammatical constructions to which the forms can refer. The most challenging part of the exercise is identifying the referents in the first sentences, especially clause referents. Exercise 2 continues on SB page 112.

1. As a class, read the directions and example.

2. Have students work in pairs to complete the exercise.

3. Ask volunteers to share their answers with the class. See answers on LP pages 110 and 112.

EXPANSION [40 minutes]

Show a scene from a movie or TV show that illustrates a difference in communication styles. The difference could be based on gender, age, or ethnic background. Have students discuss the differences in small groups.

7. In some business contexts, women may regard [personal questions,] such as how a fellow worker spent the weekend, as a way of showing friendliness. Men may consider <u>the questions</u> inappropriate in these contexts.

8. Some studies show that [men tend to dominate conversation in groups] including males and females. Based on your experience, do you agree with <u>that?</u>

9. I agree with [the idea that men and women should try to understand each other's different communication styles.] <u>It</u> makes sense to me.

10. [We could accept the communication differences we have with the "other gender," or we could try to negotiate different ways of communicating that would be more productive and less frustrating.] <u>These</u> are two possible approaches to our differences in communication styles.

EXERCISE 3

In the book *You Just Don't Understand: Women and Men in Conversation*, sociolinguistics professor Deborah Tannen describes a number of situations in which men and women have different communication styles. Choose one of the two situations summarized below and write a paragraph in response to the two questions that follow. Exchange your paragraph with a classmate. Underline the reference forms in your classmate's paragraph.

Situation 1: Talking About Troubles

Someone (male or female) has a personal problem. He or she is very upset and tells a friend about the problem.

If the friend is female: She empathizes by telling the person that she knows how it feels to have the problem. She may provide an example of the same problem or a similar one from her own experience (e.g.,"I know what you mean. Something like that happened to me too!")

If the friend is male: He offers advice about how to solve the problem (e.g., "Well, why don't you stop seeing your friend if her behavior bothers you?")

Situation 2: Expressing Troubles

Someone expresses an opinion about a topic or presents his or her ideas on a topic.

If the listener is female: She expresses agreement with the speaker or, if she disagrees, asks for clarification or further explanation.

If the listener is male: He challenges the speaker's views and explores possible flaws in the argument or idea.

Questions

1. Do you agree that such responses are typical of men and women in the situations described? Why or why not?

2. Do you think the gender-based communication differences described are common in cultures other than American culture?

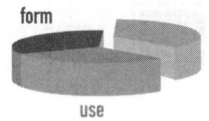

form

use

| FOCUS 2 | Reference Forms with *the* and Demonstrative Determiners |

EXAMPLES	EXPLANATIONS
(a) I liked [the novels] very much. I might even reread some of them. I would recommend **the novels** to anyone who wants to know more about Chinese history.	**Complete Repetition** Reference forms may repeat all of the referent. We use this form more often as a later mention than as a second mention.
(b) Oh, look at [this book] in the children's section! My sisters and I must have read it a hundred times when we were young.	**Partial Repetition** Some reference forms repeat only part of the referent. We do not usually repeat a demonstrative determiner (*this, that, these, those*) + noun. Instead, we tend to us *it, them* or *the* + (noun phrase).
(c) I read [two interesting studies about language variation between different age groups]. I have summarized { the two studies / these two studies } in the introduction of my paper.	We do not usually repeat descriptive modifiers. In (c), only *two* and *studies* have been repeated for both example reference forms.
(d) I read [one study about language differences based on educational levels]. I did not, however, use { the article / that article } in my paper.	**Synonym** A reference form can be a synonym of the referent. In (d), *article* is used as a synonym for *study* and the modifiers are not repeated.
(e) We went to see [*Hamlet*]. **The play** was performed outdoors at the city center. (f) I would like to take [South American literature and the history of jazz] next quarter. Several of my friends recommended **those courses**.	**Classifier** A reference form can also be a classifier of the referent. A classifier word or phrase describes a class or group that could include the referent. In (e), *Hamlet* can be classified as a play. In (f), *courses* classifies the two courses mentioned.

ANSWER KEY

Exercise 3   *Responses will vary.*

EXERCISE 3 [20 minutes]

In this exercise students choose one of two excerpts from a book about differences in communication styles between men and women, write a paragraph in response to questions, and identify reference forms in their partner's paper.

1. Read the directions as a class.
2. Have students work in pairs.
3. Tell them to read both excerpts and the two questions that follow each and chose one to respond to.
4. Ask them to write a paragraph responding to the questions.
5. Have them exchange papers and underline the reference forms in their partner's paper.
6. Have them review and discuss their papers.
7. Ask volunteers to share some examples with the class.

EXPANSION [30 minutes]

Activity 1 (listening) on page 131 is an excellent follow-up to these first exercises. In it students listen to two dialogues about the difference between male and female communication styles and then respond orally and/or in writing to questions about them, using a variety of reference forms.

FOCUS 2 [20 minutes]

This focus chart explains the different ways in which reference forms with *the* and demonstrative determiners are used. Focus 2 continues on SB page 114.

1. **Lead-in:** Write the first example sentence on the board. Ask a volunteer to bracket the referent and the reference form.
2. Write the three terms used in the explanations on the board—*synonym, classifier, paraphrase*—and discuss their meaning: *synonym* (a word with a similar meaning); *classifier* (a general word that describes members of a set or group); *paraphrase* (writing or saying something in your own words rather than repeating what you have read or heard).
3. Read the examples and explanations as a class. Ask students to analyze each example in terms of the explanation given, identifying the reference forms with *the* and the demonstrative determiners.

METHODOLOGY NOTE

Ask students to pay attention in their reading to the ways in which these reference forms are used. Tell them that paying deliberate attention to forms when reading is an excellent way for to gain mastery over grammatical systems, whether verbs, article usage, reference forms, or other structures. As they read they should ask themselves why writers use particular forms in the contexts in which they occur.

EXAMPLES	EXPLANATIONS
	Paraphrase
(g) Over the weekend [you should revise your essay and type it]. **The revised paper** should be turned in on Monday.	A reference form can also paraphrase a clause or sentence. We commonly use this form to refer to activities and the results of them:
	Activity: You revise an essay.
	Result: The revised paper
(h) [The aerosol is sprayed into the chamber where the water vaporizes.] **This vaporization process** is repeated.	Paraphrases also refer to processes, as in (h). The reference form may repeat part of the referent as in (g) (*revise*), or it may include a word that classifies or describes, such as process, effects, or *results* as in (h).

EXERCISE 4

STEP 1 Underline reference forms with *the* and demonstrative adjectives in the second sentence of each sentence pair.

STEP 2 Bracket the referents in the first sentence.

STEP 3 State what type of reference is used: (1) complete repetition of the referent, (2) partial repetition, (3) synonym, (4) classifier, or (5) paraphrase.

As a class, you may want to discuss why the various forms are used.

Example: Psychologists have distinguished [three dimensions of emotions]. These dimensions can be used to characterize differences in the ways cultures recognize and express emotions.

partial repetition: It is not necessary to repeat the entire referent. We do not usually use complete repetition when there are modifiers.

1. One dimension distinguishes between what are called[the primary emotions]and what are termed the secondary emotions. The primary emotions are considered universal by some psychologists.

2. [The primary emotions]are also considered to be biologically based. These feelings include anger, grief, joy, and disgust.

3. [The secondary emotions]are blends of the primary emotions. These emotions, such as contempt (a blend of anger and disgust), are not universal.

4. Another dimension of emotions distinguishes[pleasant feelings]from unpleasant ones. The positive emotions are ones such as love and joy, whereas the negative emotions are ones such as sorrow and shame.

5. [The last dimension classifies emotions based on intensity.]This classification of feelings can distinguish worry from terror and sadness from depression.

6. All societies have what are called[display rules]regarding emotions. These rules dictate how and when people may express certain emotions.

7. For example, in some cultures, people would express grief by[crying.]In other cultures, this emotion might be expressed by silence.

EXERCISE 5

Make up a sentence using *the* reference or demonstrative reference to elaborate on ideas in each of the sentences below. The referent is underlined. Try to use a variety of the reference types discussed in the chart on pages 113–114.

Example: *Anger* is a primary emotion.
This emotion is biologically based.

1. Everyone has negative feelings.
2. Psychologists note that the smile does not have universal meaning.
3. Facial expressions are important signals of emotion.
4. Fury is a very intense emotion.
5. Nonverbal signals such as posture, gestures, and eye contact also express emotions.

ANSWER KEY

Exercise 4 Step 3: Answers may vary. Possible answers include: 1. repetition of entire referent: necessary to repeat the entire referent 2. synonym: emotions=feelings 3. partial repetition: emotions=feelings 4. synonym: pleasant feelings=positive emotions; unpleasant ones= negative emotions 5. paraphrase: referring to the result of the activity classifies 6. partial repetition: descriptive modifiers do no have to be repeated 7. classifier: grief can be classified as an emotion.

Exercise 5 Answers will vary. Possible answers include: 1. However, in some cultures, it is considered polite not to express these emotions. 2. In other words, this facial expression does not always mean a person is happy. 3. We should be aware of such displays of feeling if we want to be effective communicators. 4. This feeling can sometimes cause people to do things they wouldn't normally do. 5. Such expressions are just as important as words in communicating feelings.

EXERCISE 4 [20 minutes]

In this exercise students identify the referents and reference forms in sentences and state what type of reference is used in each.

This is a very challenging exercise. As a class, read the directions and example. You may also want to do the first sentence with the class, to make sure students understand the exercise.

1. Have students work in pairs to identify the reference forms. (STEP 1)

2. Have them bracket the referents. (STEP 2)

3. Have them identify the types of references. (STEP 3)

4. Review answers with the class. Discuss other answers students came up with and their reasons for them. Refer back to Focus 2 as needed to explain the correct answers. See answers on LP page 114.

For more practice, use *Grammar Dimensions 4* Workbook page 47, Exercise 2, and page 48, Exercise 3.

EXPANSION [45 minutes]

You may wish to use Activity 7 (research on the web) on SB page 133 for additional practice in using a variety of reference forms in speaking and writing. This activity may be done in class if students have access to *InfoTrac® College Edition,* or assigned as homework.

EXERCISE 5 [10 minutes]

A follow-up to the work in Exercise 4, this exercise gives students guided practice in creating their own sentences that refer to previous text.

1. As a class, read the directions and example.

2. Have students work in pairs. Encourage them to refer to Focus 2 for a variety of the reference types.

3. Ask volunteers to share their answers with the class. Could other reference forms also be correct in each instance? See possible answers on LP page 114.

EXPANSION [30 minutes]

Use Activity 3 (speaking/writing) on SB page 131 as a follow-up to Exercise 5 for additional practice in using and identifying reference forms in writing.

Using Personal Pronouns versus *The* Noun Phrases

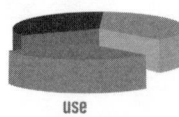

use

EXAMPLES	EXPLANATIONS
(a) I like [that book] a lot. I read **it** last year. (b) Kip is taking [math and English]. **They** are his most challenging subjects, and he has homework for both of **them** almost every day.	Use the personal pronouns *it, they, them* when there is only one possible referent.
(c) **Toni:** There is some evidence that [women are likely to worry more than men.] **Ricardo:** I believe it. (d) **Rita:** [Men tend to apologize less than women do.] **Lee:** I don't doubt **it**.	Use *it*: • when the one possible referent is a clause. • when the one possible referent is a sentence.
(e) I read [the book *The Bee Season*] before I saw the movie. I thought **the book** was very interesting. (f) To Whom It May Concern: I am returning [the enclosed MP3 player]. The volume control does not work. Also, the sound quality does not seem very good. **The player** came with a one-year warranty. (g) [Violence] is increasing in our society. **The problem** cannot be ignored. (h) This medicine should not be taken when you are driving because [it can make you sleepy or it may affect your vision]. **The adverse effects** are only temporary, but nevertheless, you need to be cautious.	Use *the* + noun phrase: • when there is more than one possible referent. In (e), *the book* and *the movie* would be possible referents if you used it. • when the referent might not be clear unless a noun phrase rather than a pronoun is used. In written English, this is often the case when the referent is more than one sentence before the reference form. • when you want to replace the referent with a classifier, a synonym, or a paraphrase. Sometimes you may want to replace a referent with a paraphrase because you cannot repeat the whole referent, and a pronoun reference would not be clear. In (h), the referent is an entire clause. Using *they* for reference would be too vague.

Decide whether *it, they, them*, or *the* + noun phrase is appropriate for each item below.

1. Identify the referent and bracket it.

2. If *the* + noun phrase should be used, choose a noun phrase that fits the context.

Example: Have you read [the book *Men Are from Mars, Women Are from Venus*]? It also discusses communication differences between men and women.
(Only one possible referent, so *it* is appropriate.)

1. I have to write a paper for my sociology class about the 1960s. I can't decide whether to write my paper about the Civil Rights marches in the early '60s or about the women's movement in the late '60s. (a) The Civil Rights marches appeals to me because I'd like to find out more about the history of segregation in the South. (b) _____They_____ are both interesting topics, however.

2. **Felix:** Do you think it's true that men tend to be more direct about what they want than women do?
   Alicia: Oh yes, I'm convinced of _____it_____.

3. I am not surprised by the research finding that boys get reprimanded in school more than girls. It (or The finding) corresponds with my own experience.

4. Neurologists at Stanford University have been studying differences in how men and women react to humor. In their experiments, they studied brain responses when men and women looked at a series of cartoons. They discovered that women and men used different parts of their brains in reacting. They also found that women reacted more intensely when they viewed ____the cartoons____ .

5. Scientists believe that there are more than five senses. The organ for the sense of hearing is, of course, the ear. However, in addition, _____it_____ has receptors that help us to create a sense of balance.

FOCUS 3 [20 minutes]

Focus 3 enumerates the contexts in which we use personal pronouns and those in which *the* + noun phrase is needed for clarity.

1. **Lead-in:** To help students relate the explanations to the examples and get more familiar with terminology, read the first section of the chart and ask students to tell you what the "one possible referent" is for examples (a) and (b).

2. Ask volunteers to read the dialogues in (c) and (d). Ask students what the "clause referent" is in (c). Ask what the sentence referent is in (d). (They should identify the text in brackets.)

3. Help students fully grasp the explanations in the last section of the chart by replacing the *the* reference forms with pronouns. In examples (e) and (f), replace the *the* reference forms with *it*. In example (h), replace *the adverse effects* with *they*.

4. Ask students to explain why these pronoun referents might be confusing to a listener or reader. Elicit that other nouns could be considered possible referents, such as *the movie* in (e); or that the referent is far away, as in (f); or that pronoun reference would be unclear, as in (h).

EXERCISE 6 [10 minutes]

In this exercise students complete sentences with the appropriate *the* noun phrase or personal pronoun and identify the referent.

1. As a class, read the directions and example.

2. Have students work independently to complete the exercise.

3. Have them exchange papers with a partner, review each other's answers, and discuss them. See answers on LP page 116.

For more practice, use *Grammar Dimensions 4* Workbook page 48, Exercise 4.

Demonstrative Determiners and Pronouns

meaning

use

The forms of demonstrative pronouns and determiners *this, that, these,* and *those* tell the reader/listener whether a referent is singular or plural and whether the speaker/writer regards the referent as near or far.

	SINGULAR	PLURAL
Near	this	these
Far	that	those

EXAMPLES	EXPLANATIONS
	The concept of distance (near or far) may involve the following:
	Space
(a) Take **this chair** right here.	• Near: The speaker regards something as physically nearby.
(b) I'll get two of **these**, please. And one melon.	• Far: The speaker regards something as physically distant.
(c) Can you see **that** tall **tower** in the distance?	
(d) **Those buildings** next to the tower are part of the new arts center.	
(e) Let's finish watching **this movie**. It's almost over.	**Time**
	• Near: There is a link to present time.
(f) **These** are difficult times because of the economy.	
(g) I'd like to see **that** again. It was one of my favorite musicals.	• Far: Reference is to a time in the past not regarded as close to the present.
(h) **Those** were called the golden years because prosperity was widespread.	
(i) [Age] is another factor affecting language use. **This influence** can be seen in the use of slang.	**Discourse Distance**
	• Near: The referent is close to the reference form in the text.
(j) [The introduction to my thesis] provided background on my topic. It offered several hypotheses about language differences. **That section** also presented an outline of my thesis.	• Far: The speaker or writer views the referent as distant. In (j), the writer regards the introduction as distant from the part being written.

EXAMPLES	EXPLANATIONS
	Psychological Distance
(k) I believe [gun control laws are needed]. I feel very strongly about **this**.	• Near: The referent is mentioned by the speaker herself or himself; and is something she believes.
(l) **Hal:** I think [gun control laws are needed]. **Tori:** I don't agree with **that**.	• Far: The referent is mentioned by another speaker. Tori disagrees with Hal's position.
(m) When Wilhelm Roentgen discovered the X-ray in 1895, he did not completely understand the nature of these new rays. He called them X-rays because the letter x stands for an unknown quantity in mathematics. **That** is how the X-ray came to be named.	Finally, we often use the demonstrative pronoun *that* in concluding statements to refer to an explanation or description we have given.

EXERCISE 7

Put an appropriate demonstrative form (*this, that, these,* or *those*) in each blank. If you think more than one might be appropriate, discuss the contexts (including speaker attitude) in which each might be used.

Example: In ancient Greece, the great classical philosophers, such as Aristotle and Plato, developed theories about emotions. At ____that____ time, they were especially interested in the effect of poetry and drama on the emotions. (In referring to ancient Greece, *that* indicates distance in terms of time.)

1. The ancient philosopher Aristotle wrote that it was easy to become angry; however, to become angry with the right person to the right degree at the right time and for the right purpose was not so easy. I think ____that____ was a very wise reflection about the emotion of anger.

2. New theories about intelligence include emotional intelligence. As defined by psychologist Daniel Goleman, (a) ____this____ type of intelligence refers to the capacity to recognize our own feelings and (b) ____those____ of others.

3. **Erin:** Did you know that scientists are using neuroimaging to see how the human brain responds to emotions such as fear?
   Victor: No, I hadn't heard about ____that____.

(Exercise 7 is continued on LP page 120.)

FOCUS 4 [20 minutes]

Focus 4 explains the role of the demonstrative determiners *this, that, these,* and *those* in communicating whether a referent is singular or plural, and whether the speaker/writer regards the referent as being near or far.

1. **Lead-in:** Tell students that the demonstrative determiners *this, that, these,* and *those* are used to indicate distance. Write on the board the four kinds of distance shown in bold in the Explanations column of the chart: *space, time, discourse distance,* and *psychological distance*.

2. Ask volunteers to read the first four examples and explanations in the first row (examples a through d) of the chart. Ask students to say how each sentence expresses physical distance.

3. Repeat this procedure with the second row (examples e–h). Ask volunteers to give examples of sentences that express distance in time, using the different demonstrative determiners.

4. Have volunteers read the remaining examples and explanations.

5. Answer any questions students may have.

METHODOLOGY NOTE

Advanced students should be familiar with using demonstrative determiners and pronouns to express distinctions between near and far in space and time. For many students, though, the contrasts associated with *discourse distance* and *psychological distance* may be new.

Emphasize that the concepts of "near" and "far" are determined by speakers and writers—that is, they reflect how speakers and writers view a thing, an event, or a situation. Consequently, different people could choose different references, depending on their perspectives. For example, in example (m), it is possible to replace *that* with *this*. Remind students that the explanations reflect general principles, not absolute rules.

In summary, it is important to help students understand that there are indeed principles governing the choice of these forms; on the other hand, they shouldn't get frustrated if they find exceptions to these principles in the language use they encounter in communicative situations.

EXERCISE 7 [20 minutes]

In this exercise students complete sentences with demonstrative determiners, and then discuss the possible choices in small groups. Exercise 5 continues on SB page 120.

1. As a class, read the directions and example. What does *that* indicate in the example? What other demonstrative determiners could be used, and what would each communicate?

2. Have students work independently to complete the exercise.

3. Have them work in small groups to discuss their choices and explore other possible choices for those contexts.

4. Ask volunteers to share their answers with the class. For each answer, ask students what other choices they made. Discuss what each expresses. See answers on LP pages 118 and 120.

 For more practice, use *Grammar Dimensions 4 Workbook* page 49, Exercise 5.

EXPANSION [45 minutes]

Activity 4 (writing) on page 132 will give students additional practice with demonstrative determiners and pronouns.

4. Have you ever wondered how the brain processes fear? (a) _____This_____ emotion relies on pathways deep in a part of the brain called the amygdala. Research shows that (b) _____the_____ pathways will be activated by frightening stimuli such as loud buzzing or fearful faces. The brain can also store information about signals that suggest danger. (c) _____That_____ is, in brief, what happens.

5. **Eduardo:** I think I'm going to watch a program about emotional intelligence on the science channel tonight. Do you want to come over?

   Soo: Do you really like (a) _____those_____ science shows? I think I'd rather stay home and watch some videos. Take a look at (b) _____these_____ movies I just picked up. Maybe you'll change your mind.

6. Dear Senator Gilman: I am writing (a) _____this_____ letter to urge you to do something about improving services for our homeless people who have severe emotional problems. (b) Right now _____the_____ situation is disgraceful; some people in our community have suggested asking the homeless people to move to a larger city where there are more services, but (c) _____that_____ is certainly not the answer to (d) _____this_____ problem.

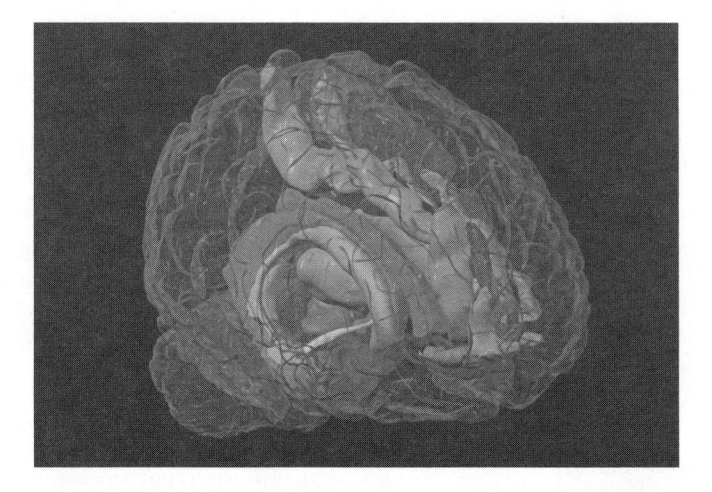

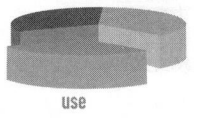

FOCUS 5 | Using Demonstrative Determiner + Noun Phrase for Clear Reference

use

EXAMPLES	EXPLANATIONS
(a) When you do strenuous exercise, you should wear proper clothing and [you should warm up first]. **This warm-up** will help prevent injuries.	Sometimes we need to use a demonstrative determiner + a noun phrase for clear reference.
(b) NOT: **This** will help prevent injuries.	In (b), *this* does not clearly signal the referent. *This* could be interpreted as both wearing proper clothing and warming up.
(c) Before writing your essay, you should try to [brainstorm some ideas and then put your ideas into categories]. **These prewriting techniques** can help you get started on your paper.	Like *the* + noun phrase reference, demonstrative determiner + noun phrase reference can help to describe or classify the referent.

EXERCISE 8

Use a demonstrative determiner and a classifying or descriptive noun from the list below to complete each of the blanks. Change the noun to plural where needed. The reference forms should refer to the words that are in brackets, [. . .]. There may be more than one possible answer.

Example: [Research indicates that men tend to tell jokes more than women do]. <u>This tendency</u> has been observed among Americans.

difference	idea	response	trait
expression	issue	result	
factor	pattern	tendency	

1. Psychology researchers at the University of Wisconsin examined differences between men and women based on [120 different aspects of human behavior], including personality, communication skills, and leadership potential. They found significant differences in only 22 percent of _____the traits_____.

(Continued)

ANSWER KEY

Exercise 8 Answers will vary. Possible answers are given above and on LP page 122.

FOCUS 5 [10 minutes]

Focus 5 explains how a demonstrative determiner + a noun phrase can be used to make a reference clearer.

1. **Lead-in:** Read the first example and explanation, and ask students why simply using *this* rather than *this warm-up* could cause confusion. Then read the second explanation in the chart, which gives the answer.

2. Read example (c) and the explanation. Why wouldn't *these* be just as appropriate as *these prewriting techniques?*

3. Ask volunteers to create a few other example sentences, and discuss these with the class.

EXERCISE 8 [20 minutes]

In this exercise students complete the sentences with a demonstrative determiner and a classifying or descriptive noun from a list, making the nouns plural, as needed. Exercise 8 continues on SB page 122.

1. As a class, read the directions and example, and discuss why *this tendency* is a better choice than *this*.

2. Have students work independently to complete the exercise.

3. Have them exchange papers with a partner, review each other's answers, and discuss them.

For more practice, use *Grammar Dimensions 4 Workbook* page 50, Exercise 6.

EXPANSION [30 minutes]

You may wish to assign Activity 8 (reflection) on SB page 133 for extra practice with demonstrative determiners.

2. In Canada and the United States, brain research has indicated that [men and women appear to use different parts of the brain for different purposes, such as storing memories, solving problems and sensing emotions; some research shows that men's and women's brains are constructed differently]. The implications of these results (or effects) have been hotly debated by other researchers and scholars.

3. Some scholars argue that [brain research showing male and female differences could lead to discrimination]; others point out that [physical differences in men's and women's brains may be the results of conditioning that starts in infancy and lifelong mental processes]. _____These issues_____ and others will be debated for years to come.

4. [Smiles, frowns, raised eyebrows, and shrugs of the shoulder] all convey emotions. These expressions (or gestures) may have different meanings in different cultures, though.

5. [Women] sometimes [think men are being unsympathetic] when they give advice about a problem rather than share troubles. This tendency (or reaction) stems from a difference between men and women in what they think is an appropriate reaction to such a situation.

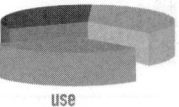
use

FOCUS 6 — Demonstrative Forms versus *The* and *It/Them* References

EXAMPLES	EXPLANATIONS
(a) Oh, I've heard { that joke. / the joke before. / it.	In many contexts, you can use demonstrative, *the*, or *pronoun* reference forms. All would be acceptable.
(b) Norm told us { the jokes. / those jokes. / them.	The choice often depends on (1) the speaker's or writer's intentions, or (2) what the speaker/writer thinks the listener/reader knows.
	Emphasizing the Referent Use demonstrative determiners or pronouns when you want to emphasize the referent.
(c) More emphasis: I heard [a speaker] on campus this afternoon. **This speaker** was the best I've heard on the topic of workplace communication.	Demonstrative adjective *this* in the second sentence of (c) emphasizes the referent "a speaker" more.
(d) Less emphasis: I heard [a speaker] on campus this afternoon. **The speaker/she** was talking about communicating effectively in the workplace.	The reference forms in the second sentence of (d) do not emphasize the referent "a speaker."
(e) Less emphasis: I'm not sure if I'll [type my paper myself]. If I do, **it** will probably take me all day!	In (e), *it* puts less emphasis on the referent, focusing on new information (the result of having to type without help). In example (f) placing *that* at the end of the sentence puts more emphasis on the referent *type my paper*.
(f) More emphasis: I'm not sure if I'll [type my paper myself]. I have more important things to do than **that**!	
	Avoiding Unnecessary Repetition Use a demonstrative pronoun to avoid unnecessary repetition.
(g) I asked my instructor if I needed [to include a bibliography with my draft]. She told me **that** would not be necessary.	
(h) Repetitious: She told me [including **the bibliography**] would not be necessary.	In example (h), the paraphrase with *the* + noun phrase gives too much information. We often use demonstrative pronouns when the referent is a clause or a sentence.
(i) [This paper] is one of the best I've written. I'm sure my classmates will enjoy **it**.	As mentioned in Focus 2, we do not usually repeat demonstrative phrases in second mention. We use some other reference form such as *it* or *the*.
(j) NOT: I'm sure my classmates will enjoy **this paper**.	

ANSWER KEY

Exercise 8 is continued from LP page 120.

FOCUS 6 [10 minutes]

This focus box outlines reasons a speaker/writer may have for choosing demonstrative forms as opposed to *the* and *it/them* reference forms.

1. **Lead-in:** Review (a) and (b) and then read examples (c) and (d) with the class. Ask students to state what the referent is (*a speaker*) and bring attention to the difference in the two forms in (c) and (d).

2. Repeat this process for examples (e) through (h), in which the referents are *type my paper myself* and *include a bibliography*.

3. Ask volunteers to read examples (i) and (j) and the explanations. Discuss how the demonstrative pronoun avoids unnecessary repetition in each instance.

Put an appropriate reference form in each blank. The referent is in brackets. Use one of the following forms: (1) *it*, (2) *the* + noun phrase, (3) demonstrative determiner (*this, that, these,* or *those*) + noun phrase, (4) demonstrative pronoun (*this, that, these,* or *those*). Use the notes in parentheses to guide your choice. For some blanks, more than one choice might be possible.

Example: An article I read claims that [hot water freezes faster than cold water]. Were you aware of _____that_____? (Also possible: *that fact*)

1. I read [an article reporting on a survey about Americans' ideas of comfort foods]. _____The article_____ discusses how women tend to prefer snack-related comfort food like candy and chocolates while men prefer meal-related comfort foods such as pasta or casseroles. (Put focus on the new information in the second sentence, not the referent.)

2. The article stated that men may be conditioned from upbringing to prefer hot, labor-intensive meals, while women like comfort foods that require less preparation. _____This_____ was an interesting explanation of the survey results. (Put focus on the subject of the second sentence.)

3. I just found out that [Einstein's brain actually weighed less than the average man's brain]. I didn't know _____that_____ before.

4. The ancient Egyptians believed that the heart, rather than the brain, was the source of all human wisdom. In fact, they believed the brain's only function was to pass fluids to the nose. _____This_____ and other beliefs were, of course, discarded as science developed.

5. One theory of the origin of language is closely related to emotions. _____This theory (or It)_____ maintains that speech started when people made instinctive sounds caused by emotions.

6. Some studies have suggested that women tend to speak less assertively than men. [When they do so], _____it_____ may cause others to doubt their authority or credibility. (Emphasize the result.)

7. Whether true or not, it is commonly believed that [men will not ask for directions when they are lost]. _____This trait_____ has been a topic of many jokes and cartoons in American culture. (Emphasize the referent.)

"WE'RE NOT *LOST*, AND I'M **NOT** STOPPING TO ASK FOR DIRECTIONS!"

---

form   meaning

FOCUS 7 Reference Forms with *Such*

EXAMPLES	EXPLANATIONS
(a) We need [a strong and honest leader]. **Such a person** is Mario Baretta.	The meaning of *such*, when referring to previous information, is similar to "like that" or "of that type of thing." In (a) *such a person* refers to a person belonging to the type "a strong and honest leader." In (b), *such responses* refer to responses that can be classified as "different for the same situation." With plural nouns, *such* phrases often follow a list or series of things as in (c).
(b) Men and women often have [different responses to the same situations]. **Such responses** may result from the ways they have been brought up.	
(c) You should try to eat more [fruits, vegetables, and whole grains]. **Such foods** are important for good health.	
(d) The police thoroughly investigated [the burglary]. They concluded that only experienced thieves could have accomplished **such a crime.**	**Structure forms with *such*:** • *Such* + singular noun Use *a* or *an* after *such*.
(e) Did you hear [what he said]? I've never heard of **such an idea** before.	
(f) [Impatiens and fuchsia plants] need little sun. **Such plants** are good for shady areas of your garden.	• *Such* + Plural Noun
(g) I can't believe [the things] they told us about their neighbors. In my opinion, they shouldn't repeat **such personal information**.	• *Such* + Noncount Noun No article is used after *such* before a noncount noun.
(h) [Several students] have demonstrated superior performance in the field of mathematics. **One such student** is Ruby Pereda.	• (Number) + *Such* + Singular or Plural Noun Note that no article is used before *student* in (h).
(i) Now more than ever we need reform-minded candidates for our city council. **Two such candidates** are Ben Ho and Ulla Teppo.	
(j) I admire **your attitude**. Such an attitude shows great respect for others.	**Referents of *such* phrases** The information that references with *such* refer to may be: • a phrase
(k) They said that **women should stay at home.** Such an attitude does not reflect the feelings of most Americans.	• a clause

---

ANSWER KEY

Exercise 9 Answers may vary. Possible answers are listed above.

EXERCISE 9 [10 minutes]

In this exercise students complete the sentences with the appropriate reference forms.

1. As a class, read the directions and example. Discuss the possible reasons for using *that* and *that fact*.
2. Have students work in pairs to complete the sentences. Tell them that, in some cases, more than one answer will be correct.
3. Ask volunteers to share their answers with the class. For each answer, ask students what other choices they made.
4. Discuss the various motivations for different choices so that students understand why more than one answer is possible. See possible answers on LP page 124.

work book For more practice, use *Grammar Dimensions 4* Workbook page 51, Exercise 7 and Exercise 8.

EXPANSION [45 minutes]

Activity 2 (writing/speaking/listening) on SB page 131 will give students extra practice with the demonstrative forms versus *the* and *it/them* references. In this activity students, working in teams, create lists of true and false "facts," and then read them to another team, which tries to identify which are true and which are false.

FOCUS 7 [10 minutes]

Focus 7 concentrates on the form and meaning of reference forms with *such*. This focus chart is an excellent reference tool for students to use throughout the course. It continues on SB page 126.

1. **Lead-in:** Read the first three examples and explanations. Ask volunteers to give another example of each use, and have others identify the meaning of each use of *such*.
2. Follow this procedure for the remainder of the examples and explanations.
3. Call students' attention to the ways in which the same *such* reference phrase can refer to different grammatical structures, as shown in examples (j) through (m), where *such an attitude* refers to several different constructions.

METHODOLOY NOTE

Although reference forms with *such* are common in writing and formal speech, many students may not have studied their various uses in depth. Many students will need practice with these forms, and will need to be reminded to use articles *a* or *an* with singular nouns after *such* and to add *-s* plural endings to count nouns that occur after *such*.

EXAMPLES	EXPLANATIONS
(l) "The world owes me a living." Such an attitude will not get you very far, my father always tells me.	• a sentence
(m) **Girls should do all the housework. Women should serve the men in the family.** Such an attitude about the role of women is common in some cultures, but it seems to be changing.	• more than one sentence

■ EXERCISE 10

Underline the *such* reference in each of the following groups of sentences or dialogues. Then state what the referent is. If you wish, you may paraphrase the referent.

Example: Men tend to view conversation as a way to assert status and to impart information. <u>Such attitudes</u> are not as common with women.
Referent: <u>Men's attitudes that conversation is for asserting status and imparting information.</u>

1. The Italian composer Guiseppe Verdi wrote one of his greatest operas, *Falstaff*, when he was 80. To have created this brilliant musical work at <u>such an advanced age</u> is truly remarkable.
Referent: <u>eighty</u>

2. In the early decades of American filmmaking, Asians were often portrayed as servants, launderers, cooks, gardeners, and waiters. <u>Such stereotypes</u> denied the many achievements of Asian-Americans at that time.
Referent: <u>Asian servants, launderers, cooks, gardeners, and waiters</u>

3. Lightning never strikes in the same place twice. Rattlesnakes intentionally give warnings to their victims by rattling their tails. The sap of a tree rises in the spring. <u>Such beliefs,</u> although common, are not supported by scientific evidence.
Referent: <u>the first three sentences</u>

4. Some people who pursue physical fitness with a passion fill up their homes with stationary bicycles, rowing machines, and stair climbers. Each time a new exercise machine appears on the market, they rush to their local sporting goods stores. However, <u>such equipment</u> is not needed to become physically fit.
Referent: <u>stationary bicycles, rowing machines, stair climbers (new exercise machines)</u>

5. We are now faced with a number of serious problems in our metropolitan areas. <u>One such problem</u> is how to best help the thousands of homeless people.
Referent: <u>a number of serious problems in our metropolitan areas</u>

6. When you have just met someone, what types of personal questions should you avoid asking? The answer depends on what culture you are in. For example, in some cultures it might be acceptable to ask a woman how old she is, how much money she makes, or even how much she weighs, but in many cultures <u>such questions</u> are considered impolite.
Referent: <u>asking how old a woman is, how much money she makes, or how much she weighs</u>

EXERCISE 10 [10 minutes]

In this exercise students identify the *such* reference and the referent in sentences. As a class, read the example. Ask a volunteer to paraphrase the referent.

1. Have students work independently to complete the exercise.
2. Have them share and discuss their answers with a partner.
3. Ask volunteers to share their answers with the class. See answers on LP page 126.

For more practice, use *Grammar Dimensions 4* Workbook page 52, Exercise 9.

EXPANSION 1 [10 minutes]

For additional practice with reference forms with *such*, have students paraphrase the referent in each sentence in Exercise 10 by transforming the sentences into complex noun phrases.

Have them take turns reading their sentences to a partner, and discussing them.

EXPANSION 2 [30 minutes]

You may wish to assign Activity 6 (reading) on SB page 132 as homework for additional work with *such* references.

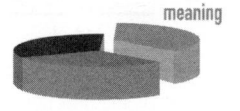

FOCUS 8 — *Such* versus Demonstrative Determiners

EXAMPLES	EXPLANATIONS

(a) When Mr. Clark came to our restaurant, he complained about the location of his table, criticized the menu, insulted the waiter, and failed to leave a tip. We hope we never again have to deal with . . .
 	
  Specific **Type**
  (1) **this** person. (2) **such** a person.
	Such refers to a class or type of thing. Consequently, reference phrases with *such* have a more general meaning than *this, that, these,* or *those* before nouns.
	
	(1) refers to Mr. Clark.
	(2) refers to any person who would act the way Mr. Clark did.

(b) Two types of dinosaurs with birdlike hips were stegosaurs and ankylosaurs.
  Specific **Type**
  (1) **These** dinosaurs . . . (2) **Such** dinosaurs . . .
  were herbivorous.
	(1) refers to stegosaurs and ankylosaurs.
	(2) refers to all dinosaurs with birdlike hips.

(c) In the United States, it has become common for the media to report every medical problem that the President suffers and every medical treatment, however minor, he receives. Does the public really need . . .
  Specific **Type**
  (1) **this** information? (2) **such** information?
	(1) refers to information about medical problems and medical treatment.
	(2) refers more generally to information that is personal and unimportant in the context.

EXERCISE 11

Work with a partner or a small group to answer the following questions based on the examples in the chart above.

1. Which words after *such (a/an)* (person, dinosaurs, information) repeat a word in the preceding sentence? Which do not? How can you explain this difference?

2. Can you think of words that might be substituted for those occurring after *such (a/an)* in the examples? Are they more general or more specific than the words in the examples? How do they change the meaning?

   Example: *such a person—such a grouch (more specific; describes Mr. Clark negatively)*

3. Often a modifier can be used to make a "class" word more specific. For example, *advanced* in "at such an advanced age" makes it clear that reference is to those ages late in life. In the examples in the chart on page 128, what modifiers could be added to define more specifically the words following *such (a)*?

EXERCISE 12

STEP 1 For each of the four word pairs below, think of one or more categories that could be used to classify or characterize them. Then make up a word pair of your own and indicate possible categories for it.

Example: Word pair: football, hockey
  Categories: *sports, spectator sports, popular sports*

WORD PAIR	CATEGORIES
a. love, anger	_____
b. jeeps, mountain bikes	_____
c. earthquakes, hurricanes	_____
d. backgammon, chess	_____
e. your choice (list-related words): _____	_____

STEP 2 Now select one of your categories for each word pair. Add to each pair other words or phrases that could be classified by this term.

Example: *Spectator sports: soccer, baseball, basketball*

STEP 3 Write one or two sentences for each set of words above. Use *such* plus the category you selected. (The items could be the word pairs given or the words you added.)

Example: *I know many people who spend a lot of time watching football and basketball on television. However, I prefer to be active rather than sitting and watching **such spectator sports**.*

(Exercise 12 continued on page 130)

Exercise 11 Answers will vary for some. 1. Ones that repeat: dinosaurs. Ones that do not: person, information. Dinosaurs is a class; thus it can be used to characterize the individual members. Person is needed as a classifier of Mr. Clark. Information is needed to characterize the result of the media's reporting. 2. dinosaurs: creatures, animals (more general), person: grouch (more specific), man (specific); information: news (more general); details (same). Meaning changes may involve negative or positive connotations. They may widen or narrow the scope of the set of things that would be included in the classifier (e.g., such animals would refer to all animals, not just the subclass of dinosaurs). 3. Person: such a rude (uncivilized) person; dinosaurs: such birdlike dinosaurs; information: such unimportant (irrelevant) information

Exercise 12 Answers may vary for all parts. **Step 1:** (a) emotions, feelings; (b) vehicles; (c) natural disasters, catastrophes; (d) games, pastimes; (e) (student's choice) **Step 2:** (a) hate, fear, joy; (b) motorcycles, SUVs; (c) tornadoes, floods; (d) checkers, Go **Step 3:** (a) Everyone is familiar with the emotions of love, hate, anger, fear, and joy. Such emotions are, however, expressed differently in different cultures. (b) Motorcycles, jeeps, and mountain bikes are all popular with young people. Such vehicles are popular for recreational activities. (c) Every year, earthquakes, hurricanes, and floods cause enormous damage. Unfortunately, we seldom have much time to prepare for such natural disasters. (d) Chess and Go are challenging games; such strategy games are not only fun but exercise your mind.

FOCUS 8 [10 minutes]

Focus 8 explains the difference in meaning between *such* and demonstrative determiners.

1. **Lead-in:** Read the examples and explanations with the class. Discuss the differences in meaning between using *such* or a demonstrative determiner in each instance.
2. Write two sentences on the board with a *such* reference in the second sentence, e.g., *Rosa spends three hours doing her homework every night. Such behavior characterizes a conscientious student.*
3. Elicit other examples of sentences that use a *such* phrase. In this example, you could ask, *"What other types of behavior characterize a conscientious student?"*
4. Replace *such behavior* with the demonstrative phrase *this behavior*. Ask students to explain the difference in meaning between *such behavior and this behavior*.

EXERCISE 11 [10 minutes]

In Exercise 11 students answer a series of questions based on the examples they just read in Focus 8.

1. Have students work in small groups. Ask one member of each group to be the note taker and record the answers the group comes up with.
2. Ask various volunteers to share their answers with the class. Review and discuss all answers with the class. Encourage students to share any alternative wordings they came up with. See possible answers on LP page 128.

EXERCISE 12 [15 minutes]

In this exercise students think of categories that could be used to classify or characterize a series of word pairs. Step 4 for this exercise appears on SB page 130.

STEP 1

1. Read the example as a class.
2. Have students individually think of any other words to describe these categories.
3. Write responses on the board.

STEP 2

1. Read the example aloud. Point out that *spectator sports* is one of the categories listed in the example in Step 1.
2. Have students work in small groups and choose one category to add words to. Each group should choose a different category.
3. Ask a representative from each group to share their group's answers with the class.

STEP 3

1. Have students return to groups to write one or two sentences based on their categories.
2. Have representatives from each group write their sentences on the board or on an overhead projector.

STEP 4 (This step begins on SB page 130.)

1. Have students return to groups to discuss the replacement of *such* with a demonstrative determiner.
2. Have students present the results to the class and explain.

EXPANSION [25 minutes]

For additional practice with *such*, have students complete this activity.

1. Have students work in pairs.
2. Have them create a list of at least five categories, such as *scary movies, great Internet sites, bad music groups.*
3. Have them exchange their papers with another pair.
4. Ask them to write statements about each category in which they give one or two examples of the category. Give an example: *I think children should not be allowed to see scary movies such as* **Halloween** *and* **Saw.**
5. Ask various volunteers to share some sentences with the class.

STEP 4 Discuss the difference in meaning that would result if you replaced *such* in each statement with a demonstrative determiner (*this, that, these, those*).

Example: *However, I don't enjoy **those** spectator sports.*
*"**Such** spectator sports" refers to any sports that people watch; "**those** spectator sports" refers only to football and baseball.*

EXERCISE 13

Correct the inappropriate or repetitive reference forms in each of the following sentences. There may be more than one way to correct errors.

Examples: My friend suggested that I drop out of school and work for a while. I'm not sure what I think about such an advice.
Correction: *I'm not sure what I think about **such advice**. (Advice is a noncount noun, so no article is used.)*

1. In my paper, I plan to discuss two emotions that all cultures share. The two emotions that all cultures share are joy and grief.

2. In ancient times, people thought that fear was a result of the brain overheating and that anxiety arose from the brain cooling off. I may use those information in the introduction to my paper.

3. This year I took both an English course and a Spanish course. It was quite easy for me because French is my native language and the two languages are similar.

4. Our math teacher gave us a surprise quiz. Can you believe he would be this unkind man?

5. I have a friend who likes to wear only two colors of clothing: blue and purple. She dresses in such colors every day.

6. One study says that male children do not pay as much attention to female children as they do to other males. What do you think about it?

7. Some people insist on giving advice even when it's not requested. Such an advice is generally not appreciated.

8. I am keeping the blue shirt I ordered from your catalog. This shirt fits fine. However, I am returning the sweater because this was much too small.

9. Did you hear her boast that she never has to study for her courses? The student misses the point of what an education means.

10. What do you think about the claim that teachers are more likely to give praise to female students? I disagree with the claim that teachers are more likely to give praise to female students.

Use Your English

ACTIVITY 1 listening

Listen to the two dialogues. Each dialogue illustrates a difference between male and female communication styles, according to Professor Deborah Tannen. After you have heard the dialogues, either discuss the following questions with a partner or write complete answers.

CD1 Tracks 7, 8

1. What communication differences do these dialogues illustrate?

2. Have you observed such differences in your own experience?

3. Can you think of exceptions to the generalizations that these dialogues illustrate?

ACTIVITY 2 writing/speaking/listening

In teams, make up lists of statements that include both amazing facts and "untruths." Good sources for hard-to-believe facts are reference books such as *The Guinness Book of World Records* or *Ripley's Believe It or Not* as well as almanacs. Mix in with the amazing facts some of your own statements that are **not** true. Each team should then read their list of statements to another group. The listeners must agree on which ones they believe and which they don't believe. Score a point for each correct judgment as to whether a statement is true or not.

Example: **Team A:** *The largest watermelon on record weighed 260 pounds.*
Team B: *We don't believe it.*
The statement is true. Team A gets the point.

ACTIVITY 3 speaking/writing

Write a paragraph comparing the language use of different groups based on a variable other than gender. For example, consider differences you are aware of based on age, social status, occupation, geographical location, or education. When you have finished, identify the reference forms you used.

ANSWER KEY

Exercise 13 1. The emotions (repetition is stylistically inappropriate)   2. this information   3. it is similar to Spanish (error: no referent for the second language in the two languages)   4. such an unkind man   5. these (such suggests other colors in the same class as blue and purple)   6. that 7. such advice   8. it (that one)   9. That student (or this student, depending on the discourse context)   10. this/this claim

Activity 1 Dialogue 1 shows the supposed difference between men and women in asking directions. (Women tend to readily ask for directions if lost; men often do not want to admit they need help and tend to ask only as a last resort. These, of course, are generalizations.)   Dialogue 2 illustrates the supposed difference between men and women regarding what they consider to be significant information to relate in conversation and the tendency for women to want to relate details about their experiences.

EXERCISE 13 [10 minutes]

In this exercise students identify and correct errors or inappropriate uses of reference forms in sentences.

1. As a class, read the directions and example. Could you replace *such* with *this advice?* Why or why not?

2. Tell students that some of the "errors" they will encounter in the sentences are not always, strictly speaking, ungrammatical, but rather are inappropriate because speakers and writers don't use them. Read the first item to give them another example. Point out that repeating the exact words (*the two emotions*) is not grammatically incorrect, but rather inappropriate in terms of usage: most native speakers would not repeat the phrase in the next sentence.

3. Have students work in pairs to complete the remainder of the exercise.

4. Ask volunteers to share their corrections—or their partner's corrections—with the class. See answers on LP page 130.

For more practice, use *Grammar Dimensions 4* Workbook page 53, Exercise 10.

EXPANSION [30 minutes]

Activity 5 (writing) on SB page 132 provides extra practice with *such* versus demonstrative determiners.

UNIT GOAL REVIEW [10 minutes]

Ask students to look at the goals on the opening page of the unit again. Refer to the pages of the unit where information on each goal can be found.

For a grammar quiz review of Units 4–6, refer students to pages 54–56 in the *Grammar Dimensions 4* Workbook.

 For assessment of Unit 6, use *Grammar Dimensions 4* ExamView®.

USE YOUR ENGLISH

The Use Your English activities at the end of the unit contain situations that should naturally elicit the structures covered in the unit. For a more complete discussion of how to use these activities, see To the Teacher, LP page xxvi.

ACTIVITY 1 listening [30 minutes]

You can use this activity after Exercise 3 on SB page 112. Students listen to two dialogues and then respond orally and/or in writing to questions.

CD1
Tracks 7
and 8

1. Tell students that they are going to listen to two dialogues about the difference between male and female communication styles.

2. Read the three questions with the class.

3. Have students listen to the audio once without taking notes.

4. Have them listen a second time, taking notes on their answers to the three questions.

5. Have students write their responses to the three questions.

6. Ask them to share their responses in small groups.

7. As a class, discuss students' reactions to the content of the dialogues.

ACTIVITY 2 writing/speaking/listening [45 minutes]

This activity might be used after Exercise 9 on SB page 124. In this activity students, working in teams, create lists of true and false "facts," and then read them to another team, which tries to identify which are true and which are false.

1. Have students work in teams of three or four for this exercise.

2. Read the directions and the example with the class.

3. Encourage students to use a variety of reference sources for their "facts," such as *The Guinness Book of World Records, Ripley's Believe It or Not,* almanacs, and the Internet.

4. Have each team compete against another in front of the class. Have one team read their entire list of facts, and the other team judge whether they are true or false. The listeners must agree on which ones they believe and which they don't believe.

5. Score a point for each correct judgment.

6. Then have the other team read their list of facts.

7. You might want to have a play off between winning teams.

ACTIVITY 3 speaking/writing [30 minutes]

Use this activity after Exercise 5 on SB page 115. Students write a paragraph comparing the language use of different groups based on a variable other than gender, and then identify the reference forms they used.

1. Brainstorm a list of factors that might influence styles of communication, such as age or education level, and write these on the board.

2. Have students work independently to choose one variable that might affect language use and write a paragraph about it.

3. Have students exchange papers with a partner and take turns identifying the reference forms they used.

4. Give students some time to discuss the content of their papers.

5. Ask volunteers to read their paragraphs aloud.

 **ACTIVITY 4** writing

Write a letter to either a business to complain about unsatisfactory merchandise or one of your political representatives (for example, a senator or the President) to voice your opinions about an issue that is important to you. Exchange letters with a classmate. The classmate should check your use of reference forms to see if they are appropriate and then write a response to your letter, playing the role of the company or person to whom you addressed it.

 **ACTIVITY 5** writing

Choose one of the sentences below to include in a paragraph. Then write the rest of the paragraph, creating a context appropriate for including the sentence. (The sentence could occur anywhere in the paragraph after the first sentence.)

Those subjects just aren't worth studying.
Those TV programs should be taken off the air.
Such advice should be helpful to anyone visiting _____. (Choose a city or country to fill in the blank.)
Such a person is to be avoided whenever possible.
Such bad luck shouldn't happen to anyone.

 **ACTIVITY 6** reading

As you do reading for other courses or for your own interests, write in a notebook examples of *such* reference forms that you find. Include the *such* phrase and the phrase(s) or sentence(s) to which each refers. Make a note of the context (for example, an explanation of a chemical process, a comment on people's behavior, a description of a product in an advertisement). At some point you may want to compare your findings with your classmates' to see the ways in which reference forms with *such* references are used in written texts.

 **ACTIVITY 7** research on the web

 Use the keywords "gender differences and food" and search for articles on comfort foods and gender differences in *InfoTrac® College Edition*. Poll your class or a group of 15–20 people about the comfort foods listed, asking them to agree or disagree with the choices on a 5-point scale (1 = strongly disagree, 5 = strongly agree). Give an oral or written report on your findings, using a variety of reference forms to link ideas.

 **ACTIVITY 8** reflection

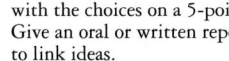 Review three textbooks and/or Web sites that you have found helpful for your learning. For each, write one or two sentences that describe in brief something about their usefulness. Use a demonstrative adjective and a classifier word. You could also use descriptive modifiers either before or after the classifier word. This kind of writing, called an annotation, is a common academic assignment. If time permits, compile the annotations written by class members and share them with the class in a handout or via e-mail attachment.

Examples:

Grammar Dimensions 4	This advanced-level grammar book helps students with many structures used in academic writing.
Randall's ESL Cyber Listening Lab	This Web site offers dialogues for listening practice at several levels of difficulty.

USE YOUR ENGLISH

ACTIVITY 4 writing
[45 minutes]

This activity is a good follow-up to Exercise 7 on SB page 119. Students write letters to businesses or a public representative expressing opinions. Partners review the letters and write responses to them.

1. Tell students that they are going to write a letter to either (a) a business to complain about unsatisfactory merchandise or (b) one of their political representatives to voice their opinions about an important issue.
2. Brainstorm a list of examples of each, and write these on the board.
3. Give students a set time within which to write their letters, such as 20 minutes.
4. Have them exchange letters with a partner, who should review it for the use of reference forms.
5. Have students write a response to their partner's letter, playing the role of the company or person to whom it was addressed.
6. Ask volunteers to read both letters to the class.

VARIATION

1. Ask students to write real complaint or appreciation letters or emails that they will send to a business or political representative.
2. Have students exchange their papers with a partner and edit them.
3. Give students time to revise their letters.
4. Have them actually send the letters or emails.
5. Ask students to report back to the class on any responses they receive.

ACTIVITY 5 writing
[30 minutes]

Use this activity after Exercise 13 on SB page 130.

1. Have students chose a sentence and then write a paragraph that includes it.
2. Have them exchange papers with a partner.
3. The partner should evaluate the paragraph in terms of whether the sentence makes sense in the context of that paragraph, or not.
4. Ask volunteers to share their partner's paragraphs with the class, and discuss.

ACTIVITY 6 reading
[30 minutes]

Assign this activity as homework after Exercise 10 on SB page 126. Students keep records of examples of *such* reference forms they encounter in their readings, and the contexts for these. This activity could represent an ongoing assignment during the course.

1. Tell students that you'd like them to keep a notebook in which they write down examples of *such* reference forms they find in their readings outside your class.
2. Tell them that they should write down the *such* phrase and the phrase(s) or sentence(s) to which each refers. They should also make a note of the context (for example, an explanation of a chemical process, a comment on people's behavior, a description of a product in an advertisement).
3. Periodically ask volunteers to share some of the entries in their notebooks with the class.

ACTIVITY 7 research on the web
[45 minutes]

 In this activity students research comfort foods and gender differences, create and conduct a survey, and report on the results using a variety of reference forms to link ideas. It is a good expansion activity after Exercise 4 on SB page 114.

1. This activity could be done in class if students have access to computers, using student passwords to *InfoTrac® College Edition*. Otherwise, assign it as homework.
2. Have students work in pairs, if possible.
3. Tell them to do a keyword search for *gender difference and food*, and to read several articles on the topic.
4. Have students create a survey in which they list five to ten comfort foods.
5. Have them use their survey to poll the class or a group of 15–20 people.
6. Ask them to analyze the results and give an oral or written report to the class using a variety of reference forms to link ideas.

ACTIVITY 8 reflection
[30 minutes]

 Activity 8 can be used after Exercise 8 on page 121 for extra practice with demonstrative determiners.

1. Tell students that they are going to practice a kind of writing called *annotation* that is very common in academic writing.
2. Ask students to choose three textbooks and/or Web sites that have helped them in their learning.
3. Have them write one or two sentences about each, describing their usefulness. In each sentence they should use a demonstrative adjective and a classifier word.
4. If time permits, compile the annotations written by students and share them with the class in a handout or via e-mail attachment.

RELATIVE CLAUSES MODIFYING SUBJECTS

UNIT GOALS

- **Use restrictive relative clauses to modify subjects**
- **Use restrictive relative clauses to make nouns more specific**
- **Know how to reduce restrictive relative clauses**

OPENING TASK

Trivia Challenge

■ **STEP 1**

The object of this game is to get the most answers right in a trivia game. Student A looks at page 135. Student B looks at page A-17.

■ **STEP 2**

To begin, Student A will create definitions or descriptions of a person or thing, offering three options. Student B will listen and repeat the definition, completing the sentence with the correct word or phrase. If correct, he or she will receive one point.

■ **STEP 3**

Student B will now create definitions or descriptions in the same way. The partner with the most points wins the game.

Example: a person
explores and studies caves
Options: (a) transducer,
*(b) spelunker, (c) coanchor

Student A creates a definition: *A person who explores and studies caves is called a (a) transducer, *(b) spelunker, or (c) coanchor*
(The correct answer is asterisked (*).)

Student B makes a guess: *A person who explores and studies caves is called a spelunker*.
Congratulations to Student B. He or she will be awarded one point for the correct answer.

Create a Definition or Description:

1. an animal
   It mates for life.
   (a) seahorse, (b) boa constrictor, *(c) Canada goose

2. a book
   Its original title was changed six times.
   (a) *War and Peace* by Leo Tolstoy, *(b) *The Great Gatsby* by F. Scott Fitzgerald, (c) *Pride and Prejudice* by Jane Austen

3. an inventor
   Teachers gave him poor report cards.
   *(a) Thomas Edison, (b) Alexander Graham Bell, (c) Robert Fulton

4. a person
   He or she fits the interior parts of pianos.
   (a) mucker, (b) hooker inspector, *(c) belly builder

Guess the Correct Answer:

5. (a) dragonfly, (b) flycatcher, (c) firefly

6. (a) cornball, (b) impostor, (c) daytripper

7. (a) amphora, (b) amulet, (c) aspartame

8. (a) bodice, (b) causerie, (c) bloomers

UNIT OVERVIEW

Unit 7 reviews the different types of relative clauses and then focuses on a less frequent type—relative clauses that modify subjects. Besides providing multiple opportunities for practice, this unit also reviews how to reduce relative clauses.

UNIT GOALS

Some instructors may want to review the goals listed on Student Book (SB) page 134 after completing the Opening Task so that students understand what they should know by the end of the unit. These goals can also be reviewed at the end of the unit when students are more familiar with the grammar terminology.

OPENING TASK [20 minutes]

The following task is a trivia game where clues in the form of definitions are given by one student of each pair and the opposite student guesses the response from the multiple choice answers on another page. Then students switch roles. Both students have the multiple choice answers in front of them. The example on page 134 demonstrates how to use relative clauses in the definition to be given and in the response; however, students are not required to use this structure if they are not yet familiar with it. This game will, however, reveal student ability to work with relative clauses. The object for the students is simply to find the correct answer to each question.

More generally, the problem-solving format is designed to show the teacher how well the students can produce the target structures implicitly and spontaneously when they are engaged in a communicative task. For a more complete discussion of the purpose of the Opening Task, see To the Teacher, Lesson Planner (LP) page xxii.

Setting Up the Task

■ STEP 1

1. Read the title of the task and make sure that students understand the word *trivia* and the nature of this game.

2. Discuss similar games students have played with others or seen on TV.

3. Ask all students to cover page 135 and look at the example on page 134 as you read through the steps. Tell Student A not to look at the next page (SB page 135) and Student B not to turn to the back of the textbook (SB page A-17) until you say so.

Conducting the Task

■ STEPS 2 AND 3

1. Model other definitions that have relative clauses modifying subjects. Write the following example on the board: a person; this person teaches at a college or university *A person who teaches adult students at a university is called (a) a student, (b) a professor, or (c) an assistant.*

2. Elicit *a professor* or longer response with relative clauses if students seem able. Don't press the point if students are unfamiliar with relative clause structures at this point. This is meant to be a fun trivia game.

3. Have students work in pairs to complete Steps 2 and 3. Remind students that each correct answer scores Student A or B a point for the correct response. Also, tell students that the answers with asterisks are the correct answers. Both Students A and B have the multiple choice answers from which to choose.

4. Circulate around the room, making sure that Student A is looking at SB page 135 and Student B is looking at SB page A-17. Explain vocabulary from the multiple choice answers as needed.

Closing the Task

1. Identify the winners from each pair.

2. Discuss as a class which items were the most challenging to create definitions for.

3. Check answers as a class. (Reminder: the answers with asterisks are the responses.)

4. Don't worry about the accuracy of relative clauses used at this point, though you may want to take notes of errors in meaning, form, or use in order to focus on those problems later.

GRAMMAR NOTE

Typical student errors (form)

- Omitting the relative pronoun in a relative clause:—e.g., * *The man lives next door is an engineer.* (See Focus 1.)

- Using a personal pronoun instead of a relative pronoun:—e.g., * *I like people they are friendly.* (See Focus 2.)

- Failing to move the adjective before the noun in the main clause when deleting the relative pronoun and *be* in a sentence:—e.g., * *An author very famous wrote this book.* (See Focus 3.)

Typical student errors (use)

- Using the wrong relative pronoun:—e.g., * *The man whom is talking is my brother.* (See Focus 1.)

- Omitting the relative pronoun that replaces the subject of the embedded clause:—e.g., * *The girl speaks Korean is my friend.* * *We know the girl speaks Korean.* (See Focus 3.)

Overview of Restrictive Relative Clauses

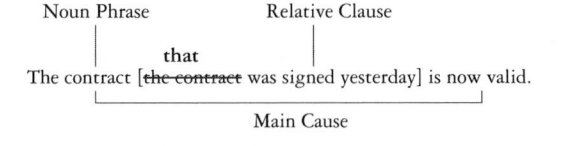

form   meaning

A restrictive relative clause modifies a noun phrase in a main clause. It is placed as close to the noun phrase as possible and is used to identify the noun. A relative pronoun (*that* in this sentence) is used to replace the noun being identified.

Noun Phrase   Relative Clause

that

The contract [~~the contract~~ was signed yesterday] is now valid.

Main Cause

There are four general types of restrictive relative clauses. They may modify main clause subjects or objects. Relative pronouns may be subjects or objects in their own clauses. Note the function of the labeled nouns in each clause:

Main clause: The contract is now valid ("contract" is the **subject**).

Relative clause: that was signed yesterday ("that" is the **object**)

TYPES OF RELATIVE CLAUSES	NOUN PHRASE IN MAIN CLAUSE	RELATIVE PRONOUN IN RELATIVE CLAUSE
S S (a) *The contract* **that was signed yesterday** is now valid.	Subject	Subject
S O (b) *The contract* **that he signed yesterday** is now valid.	Subject	Object
O S (c) I have not read *the contract* **that was signed** yesterday.	Object	Subject
O O (d) I have not read *the contract* **that he signed** yesterday.	Object	Object

This unit will focus on restrictive relative clauses that modify subjects in main clauses (like (a) and (b) on page 136). These clauses can have various relative pronouns, and the relative pronouns can fulfill various grammatical functions. *Whose* can function as a relative determiner. This unit will also deal with *whose* as a relative determiner.

EXAMPLES	SUBJECT BEING MODIFIED	RELATIVE DETERMINER	FUNCTION OF RELATIVE DETERMINER
(e) A person **who/that** sells houses is a realtor.	person	*who/that*	subject
(f) The secretary **whom/that** she hired is very experienced.		*whom/that*	direct object
(g) The employees **to whom** she denied a pay raise have gone on strike.		*whom*	indirect object
(h) The mansions **that/which** were sold last week were expensive.*	thing or animal	*that/which*	subject
(i) The computer **that/which** they purchased operated very efficiently.*		*that/which*	direct object
(j) The place **that/which** you spoke about is Denver.*		*that/which*	object of a preposition
(k) Clerks **whose** paychecks were withheld are in trouble.	person, thing, or animal	*whose*	possessive determiner
(l) The division **whose** sales have reached a million dollars will go to Hawaii.		*whose*	possessive determiner

* In many formal contexts, *that* is considered the only correct choice of relative determiner when a thing or animal is modified.

FOCUS 1 [20 minutes]

Focus 1 provides an overview of restrictive relative clauses that modify subjects in main clauses.

1. **Lead-in:** Write the two clauses, the main clause and the full embedded clause, of the example with the same subject on the board or an overhead projector —e.g., *The contract is now valid. The contract was signed yesterday*.

2. Demonstrate how the embedded clause is placed near a noun phrase in the main clause and how *that* substitutes for the repeated noun phrase (a).

3. Point out the different word order of relative pronouns, which function as objects in the relative clause—i.e., they do not follow the usual word order of statements (b) through (d).

4. Read with the class through all of the chart examples on page 137, carefully noting the use of *whose* in (k) and (l), which acts as a substitute for *his, her*, and *its* in the embedded clause.

5. Ask students to work in pairs to create two sentences without relative clauses for each of the twelve examples with relative clauses.

6. Have volunteer pairs come forward to write their two sentences for each example (a) through (l) on the board (or overhead projector).

7. Ask seated students to explain how to substitute relative determiners for the subjects and objects they are replacing. The volunteer pair should follow seated students' directions to change their sentences back to the original examples.

   Suggestion: Have students close their books while they are working to push them to recall how relative clauses are created.

8. Continue to work through all of the examples with different pairs of students coming forward.

LANGUAGE NOTE

How relative clauses are ordered and marked may be different in English than they are in other languages. In English, relative clauses follow the head noun. This is also true for some other languages, such as most European languages, Farsi, and Arabic. However, Japanese, Chinese, and Korean place the relative clause before the head noun, and native speakers of those languages may tend to reproduce this order in English. Also, English uses a relative pronoun, such as *who*, to mark a relative clause. Japanese, in contrast, uses particles in the relative clause itself. Native speakers of Japanese will need extra practice to master this distinction.

EXERCISE 1

STEP 1
Here is a picture of a rather complex invention created by the artist Rube Goldberg. What do you think this device is used for?

From Charles Keller, *The Best of Rube Goldberg*, 1979. RUBE GOLDBERG™ and © of Rube Goldberg Inc. Distributed by United Media.

STEP 2
Read the passage and underline all of the relative pronouns/determiners. Then, with your partner, identify and write down the function of the relative pronouns/determiners in each relative clause (subject, direct object, etc.). There may be more than one relative clause in a sentence. The first one has been done for you.

Example: Sentence (1) *that* —*subject function in relative clause*

(1) A kerosene lamp that is set near the window has a high flame that catches on to the curtain. (2) A fire officer whom a neighbor calls puts out the flame with a stream of water that the officer shoots from outside the window. (3) The water hits a short man who is seated below the window. (4) He thinks it is raining and reaches for an umbrella which is attached to a string above him. (5) The upward pull of the string on one side of a platform causes an iron ball that is resting on the other side of the platform to fall down. (6) The ball is attached to a second string that wraps around a pulley and connects to a hammer. (7) The downward pull of the ball on the second string causes a hammer to hit a plate of glass. (8) The crashing sound of the glass causes a baby pup that is in a cradle to wake up. (9) In order to soothe the pup, its mother rocks the cradle in which the pup was sleeping. (10) The cradle, to which a wooden hand is attached, is on a high shelf above a stool. (11) A man who is sitting on the stool below the shelf and whose back is positioned in front of the wooden hand smiles as the wooden hand moves up and down his back.

STEP 3
Without looking at the sample passage, summarize the process shown in the picture.

EXERCISE 2

For each of the phrases below, write two sentences describing a person who will do the following things. Use a *who* relative clause for one and a *whose* relative clause for another.

Example: will not get a job
A person who is not skilled will not get a job.
A person whose interview skills are poor will not get a job.

1. will not pass the course
2. will be a good leader
3. will make a lot of friends
4. can never take a vacation
5. is prepared to take a test
6. should not drive a car

---

meaning

FOCUS 2   Making Noun Phrases More Specific with Relative Clauses

LESS SPECIFIC	MORE SPECIFIC	EXPLANATION
(a) A man walked into the office.	(b) A man **who was wearing a pinstriped suit** walked into the office.	A relative clause makes the meaning of the noun it modifies more specific.
(c) The secretary can type 70 words per minute.	(d) The secretary **whom Dolores hired yesterday** can type 70 words per minute.	
(e) A computer is sitting on the desk.	(f) A computer **that has a high-speed Internet connection** is sitting on the desk.	

Exercise 1   Step 1: This device is used for or by someone with an itchy back.
Step 2: The underlined words are given above; their functions are as follows.   1. that is set (subject); that catches (subject)   2. whom a neighbor (object of verb); that the officer (object of verb)   3. who is seated (subject)   4. which is attached (subject)   5. that is resting (subject) 6. that wraps around (subject)   8. that is in a cradle (subject)   9. in which the pup (object of preposition)   10. to which a wooden hand (object of preposition)   11. who is sitting (subject); whose back is positioned (possessive adjective)

Exercise 2   Answers will vary. Possible answers are: 1. A person who does not study will not . . . /A person whose grades are poor will not . . .   2. A person who knows how to delegate will be . . . /A person whose public speaking skills are good will be . . .   3. A person who is kind and generous will make . . ./A person whose personality is extremely generous will make . . .   4. A person who works all of the time can never take . . . /A person whose bank account is empty can never take . . . 5. A person who does not delay studying is prepared . . . /A person whose study habits are good is prepared . . .   6. A person who does not have a license should not drive . . . /A person whose eyesight is poor should not drive. . .

EXERCISE 1 [20 minutes]

In this exercise students identify and write down the function of the relative pronouns/determiners in each relative clause in a paragraph.

STEP 1

1. Students will need time to study the picture. Read the description of it, and as a class discuss what is happening in the picture.

2. Tell students that each letter in the picture stands for a particular stage in a process. Guide them in identifying what is happening in each step. For example, say, *In step A, a lamp seems to be burning brightly. In step B, water is coming through the window. Why do you think that is happening? That's right, to put the flame out. Then what is happening in step C?*

STEP 2

1. Read the directions for Step 2 and the example as a class.

2. Have students work in pairs to complete Step 2.

3. Review the relative pronouns/determiners in each relative clause as a class. See answers on LP page 138.

STEP 3

1. Have students work with their partner to summarize the process shown in the picture.

2. Ask a group to read their summary to the class.

 For more practice, use *Grammar Dimensions 4* Workbook, page 57, Exercise 1.

EXPANSION 1 [30 minutes]

You may wish to use Activity 3 (speaking) on SB page 146 after Exercise 1. Students create a diagram similar to that in Exercise 1 for another device and explain how it works.

EXPANSION 2 [45 minutes/homework]

Activity 7 (research on the web) on SB page 147 is another good follow-up to Exercise 1. Students print out four articles on inventions from the Internet. They then identify and draw conclusions about the types of relative clauses in the articles.

EXERCISE 2 [15 minutes]

In this exercise students write two sentences, one with a *who* relative clause, and the other with a *whose* relative clause.

1. Read the directions and example as a class.

2. Have students work independently to write their sentences.

3. Have them exchange papers with a partner, review each other's sentences, and discuss them.

4. Ask volunteers to share their sentences with the class. See possible answers on LP page 138.

 For more practice, use *Grammar Dimensions 4* Workbook page 58, Exercise 2.

EXPANSION [30 minutes]

Use Activity 6 (writing/speaking) on SB page 147 after Exercise 2. In it, students play a trivia game similar to the one they played in the Opening Task, creating and making guesses about definitions.

FOCUS 2 [15 minutes]

1. **Lead-in:** Ask how students came to school today. Some might say *on foot*, but others will probably say *by bicycle, by car, by bus*, etc.

2. Ask them to imagine that they each have left something in their vehicle and they want a friend to retrieve it. Ask what they might have left. Some might say, *a scarf, a wallet, a book*, etc.

3. Now tell them that you need to know specifically what they left. Ask them to describe the item. Some may say, *The jacket is blue. Its collar is torn.* Prompt them to restate this in one sentence: *A blue jacket whose collar is torn was left on the bus.* Do a few more examples before reading sentences (a) through (f).

   Suggestion: Have students explain why there can be more than one verb tense in this example as well as in sentence (d).

4. Read the examples and explanation with the class. Ask volunteers to substitute the contents of each relative clause with other information that would make sense in the context of each sentence.

5. Encourage students to ask questions about anything they might not understand.

EXERCISE 3

Imagine that you are a new employee for a company. One of your co-workers has agreed to orient you to the new office. Ask a question about the objects in each of the pictures in the left column while covering up the right column. Have your partner distinguish these objects or persons, explaining what he or she knows by looking at the pictures in the right column.

Example:

New Employee:
Ask about what you see
(cover up the right column)

Experienced Employee:
Tell about what you know
(cover up the left column)

box/contains file folders

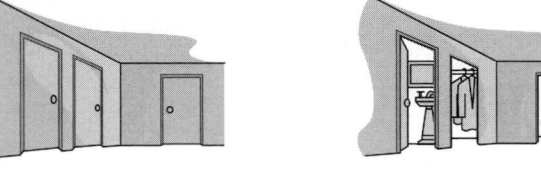

New Employee: *Which box contains the file folders?*
Experienced Employee: *The box that is sitting on the shelf.*

1. project/I should work on first

2. door/leads to the restroom

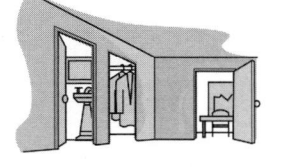

3. telephone number/belongs to the Moesler Corporation

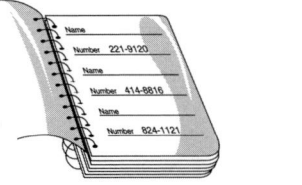

Now switch roles with your partner.

4. computer/has the Internet connection

5. light switch/illuminates the front of the conference room

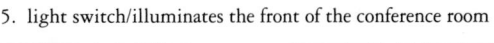

REAR   FRONT

6. book/our boss, Mr. Blake, wrote

ANSWER KEY

Exercise 3 1. New employee (A): Which projects should I work on first this morning? Experienced employee (B): The one that is face down on the desk and is labeled Housing Project.   2. New employee (A): Which door leads to the bathroom? Experienced employee (B): The first door that is on the left.   3. New employee (A): Which telephone number belongs to the Moesler Corporation? Experienced employee (B): The number that is second on the list.   4. New employee (B): Which computer has the Internet connection? Experienced employee (A): The one that is on the left.   5. New employee (B): Which light switch illuminates the front of the conference room? Experienced employee (A): The switch that is on the right.   6. New employee (B): Which is the book that our boss, Mr. Blake, wrote? Experienced employee (A): The book that is the second one from the left.

EXERCISE 3 [20 minutes]

In this information-gap exercise students take turns looking at different pictures of objects and asking and answering questions about them using relative clauses.

1. Read the directions and example as a class. Ask volunteers to think of other questions the new employee might ask, using relative clauses.

2. Have students work in pairs. Before they begin, make sure that Student A (New Employee) of the pair has covered the right side of items 1–3. Student A asks the questions and Student B (Experienced Employee) responds.

3. Have students do 1–3, and then switch roles (New vs. Experienced) for 4–6. Student B will now cover the right hand picture and ask the questions while Student B responds.

4. Ask pairs to perform their questions and answers with the class. Encourage others to share different questions and answers they came up with. See answers on LP page 140.

 For more practice, use *Grammar Dimensions 4* Workbook page 59, Exercises 3 and 4.

EXPANSION [30 minutes]

You may wish to use Activity 1 (listening) on SB page 145 after Exercise 3 for additional practice with relative clauses. Students listen to a lecture that explains important business terms. They take notes and then complete sentences using their notes.

FOCUS 3   Review of Reduced Relative Clauses

EXAMPLES	EXPLANATIONS
(a) The letter ~~that~~ he sent was never received.	We can delete relative pronouns if they function as objects in relative clauses. In examples (a) and (b), *that* and *whom* can be deleted.
(b) The accountant ~~whom~~ he corresponded with was well qualified.	
(c) NOT: The accountant with ~~whom~~ he corresponded was well qualified.	Relative pronouns cannot be deleted if they follow prepositions such as *with* or *to*.
(d) The conference room ~~that is~~ situated at the end of the hall is closed.	We can delete relative pronouns in relative clauses with auxiliary *be* in progressive or passive constructions. Both the relative pronoun and *be* are deleted.
(e) The water ~~that was~~ left in the pitcher evaporated.	
(f) The customer ~~who is~~ complaining to the manager is my aunt.	
(g) A child ~~who had been~~ playing on the equipment was asked to leave.	
(h) Chairs ~~that are~~ in the conference room cannot be moved.	We can delete relative pronouns in relative clauses with *be* + preposition phrases. Both the relative pronoun and *be* are deleted.
(i) A board member ~~who was~~ at the meeting decided to resign.	
(j) People ~~who have~~ credentials can be hired. with ^	In relative clauses with *have* or *have not* (= possession or lack of possession), we can delete the relative pronoun and paraphrase *have* or *have not* with *with* or *without*.
(k) The workers ~~who did not have~~ identification were asked to leave. without ^	

ANSWER KEY

Exercise 4 Answers will vary. Possible answers are: 1. . . . (that) the officer used to put out the fire hit a short man (who was) seated below the window.   2. . . . (that/which) the short man grabbed was attached to a string (that/ which was) attached to a wooden platform.   3. . . . that hit a plate of glass was connected to a pulley and a string.   4. . . . (that) the hammer broke made a crashing sound that woke up a baby pup.   5. The mother rocked the cradle in which her pup was sleeping./The mother rocked the cradle (that) her pup was sleeping in.   6. . . . (that/which was) attached to the cradle scratched the back of the man (who was) sitting on a stool.

EXERCISE 4

Look again at the stages of the drawing in Exercise 1 and analyze the operation of the backscratcher. Look particularly at how the objects listed below were affected during each stage in the process. Then, write a sentence containing a relative clause with an object relative pronoun. Put parentheses around the words that can be deleted.

Example: (Stage B) The curtain *(that) the flame touched caught on fire.*

1. (Stage C) The water _____
2. (Stage E) The umbrella _____
3. (Stage J) The hammer _____
4. (Stage K) The plate of glass _____
5. (Stage N) The cradle _____
6. (Stage O) The wooden hand _____

EXERCISE 5

Read the following sentences. Identify relative clauses that can be reduced. Mark your suggested revisions directly on the text. Then explain your revisions to your classmates.

Example: A person ~~who is~~ in a new job should act confidently.
I changed the sentence to "A person in a new job should act confidently" because the relative clause contains "be" + preposition.

1. The decision maker in an American business meeting is usually a person ~~who is~~ leaning toward the other members of the group and ~~who is~~ giving direct eye contact.

2. Body language ~~that is~~ composed of many gestures can communicate 80 percent of a message.

3. Anyone ~~who has been~~ working in the same position for a while will receive criticism at one time or another.

4. A person ~~who is~~ dressing for success in an American business setting should worry about the material, color, and style of his or her clothing.

5. Generally, a suit ~~that is~~ made of an expensive wool appears authoritative.

6. If you are someone ~~who is~~ feeling unsatisfied with your personality, do not be discouraged.

7. Anyone ~~who has~~ with ^ the determination to keep a mental picture of what he or she wants to be in mind can make his or her new image a positive reality.

Exercise 5 Answers will vary. Possible answers are: 1. I changed the sentence to "...a person leaning toward the other members of the group and giving direct eye contact" because we can delete the relative pronoun and *be* in a clause containing *be* in a progressive construction. 2. I changed the sentence to "Body language composed of many gestures can..." because we can delete the relative pronoun and *be* in a passive construction.   3. I changed the sentence to "Anyone working in the same position for a while will receive..." because we can delete the relative pronoun and *be* in a clause containing *be* in a progressive construction.   4. I changed the sentence to "A person dressing for success in an American business setting should worry..." because we can delete the relative pronoun and *be* in a clause containing *be* in a progressive construction.   5. I changed the sentence to "Generally, a suit made of expensive wool appears authoritative" because we can delete the relative pronoun and *be* in a clause containing *be* in a passive construction.   6. I changed the sentence to "If you are someone feeling unsatisfied with your personality, do not be discouraged" because we can delete the relative pronoun and *be* in a clause containing *be* in a progressive construction.   7. I changed the sentence to "Anyone with the determination to keep..." because we can delete the relative pronoun and paraphrase the word *has* in a relative clause with the word *with*.

FOCUS 3 [20 minutes]

1. **Lead-in:** Tell students that this focus chart is an excellent reference tool for them to use throughout the course.
2. Read the first group of examples (a–c). Ask volunteers to identify the relative pronouns that function as objects in the relative clauses.
3. Ask volunteers to create alternative examples.
4. Read the next two groups (d–i). Emphasize that both the relative pronoun and the auxiliary *be* must be deleted.
5. Read the next examples (j–k). Emphasize that the adjective is usually moved to *in front of* the noun in the main clause.
6. Read the remaining two examples, and ask volunteers to create alternative examples.

METHODOLOGY NOTE

Because this focus chart is fairly complex, it might be best to present it using an "uncover technique." Copy the chart onto an overhead transparency. Discuss the examples and explanations for one group of sentences in the grid (e.g., (a–c)) and then continue with the next group. If you do not have access to an overhead projector, have students cover and uncover the rows in their books with a piece of paper as you read them.

EXERCISE 4 [20 minutes]

Students refer to the picture of the invention in Exercise 1 and analyze it, creating sentences with a relative clause and an object relative pronoun.

1. Read the directions and example as a class.
2. Have students work independently to write their sentences.

3. Have them exchange papers with a partner, review each other's sentences, and discuss them.
4. Ask volunteers to share their sentences—or their partner's sentences—with the class. If other students came up with different analyses for each operation, encourage them to share these with the class. See possible answers on LP page 142.

EXPANSION [25 minutes]

Activity 5 (speaking/writing) on SB page 146 is a good follow-up to Exercise 4. In this activity students discuss and write definitions of business terms, using relative clauses in each definition.

EXERCISE 5 [20 minutes]

In this exercise students edit sentences by reducing the relative clauses in them.

1. Read the directions and example as a class. Point out how, in the first example, the adjective is moved to *before* the noun (*person*) in the main clause.
2. Have students work independently to edit the sentences.
3. Have them share and discuss their edits with a partner.
4. Review answers as a class. Encourage students to ask questions about anything they might not understand. See possible answers on LP page 142.

 For more practice, use *Grammar Dimensions 4* Workbook page 60, Exercise 5, and page 61, Exercise 6.

EXPANSION [45 minutes/homework]

Use Activity 4 (writing) on SB page 146 after Exercise 5. In this activity, students write a description of a complex outline, chart, or flow diagram using sentences with relative clauses. They then edit their work, reducing those relative clauses that can be reduced. The research for this task can be done as homework.

EXERCISE 6

Look at the pictures in Exercise 3 and write six sentences with reduced relative clauses that distinguish the objects. Share your sentences with your classmates.

Example: *The box sitting on the top shelf has file folders.*

EXERCISE 7

Below you will find information about four homes that celebrities sold for various reasons. Write sentences about this information using as many relative clauses modifying subjects as you can. Put parentheses around words that can be deleted.

Example: *The mansion (that) the oil tycoon sold for $2,000,000 has three fireplaces.*
The penthouse whose owner was a world-renowned physician sold for $4,000,000.

VILLA

Owner: country western singer

Reason for sale: divorce

Price: $3,000,000

Enter through walled gates and find sophisticated hacienda. 2-acre home with horse corral. 6 bedrooms/ 8 baths. Pool, tennis, jacuzzi, spa.

MANSION

Owner: oil tycoon

Reason for sale: bankruptcy

Price: $2,000,000

European chateau with hardwood floors, 50 miles from the coast. 4 bedrooms/4 bathrooms. 3 fireplaces. View of lake. Very private acre far from crowds.

PENTHOUSE

Owner: world-renowned physician

Reason for sale: death

Price: $4,000,000

Towering 20 stories above downtown. 3 bedrooms/4 bathrooms. Close to Music and Performing Arts Center. Modern design. 20 minutes from beach.

BEACHHOUSE

Owner: corporate executive

Reason for sale: job move

Price: $5,000,000

On the beach. 3 acres + private 120 ft. of beachfront. Bright and spacious. Pool room. 3 stories. State-of-the-art sound/ video system. 5 bedrooms/ 4 bathrooms. Greenhouse.

Use Your English

ACTIVITY 1 listening

■ **STEP 1** Listen to the audio of a lecture that explains various important business terms. On a separate piece of paper take notes about the terms introduced.

CD1 Track 9 ■ **STEP 2** Use your notes to fill in the blanks of the following quiz.

1. The process in which someone decides how their property will be distributed after their death is called _____.

2. A term which means to substitute an inoffensive term for an offensive one is a/an _____.

3. A person who has died is referred to as a/an _____.

4. A term which means to die leaving a will is _____.

5. The action which describes someone dying without a will is _____.

6. The land and property which someone owns is called _____.

7. _____ is called "personal property."

8. _____ is called "a gift."

ACTIVITY 2 writing

Write a letter of complaint to a store or company about a defective item that you bought recently. Try to include at least two sentences with relative clauses modifying main clause subjects.

Example: *Dear Sir:*

The toaster that I bought in your store last week is defective. The selector lever that determines how dark the toast will be is stuck.

ANSWER KEY

Exercise 6 Answers will vary. Possible answers are: 1. You should work on the project at the end of the stack. 2. The first door on the left leads to the restroom. 3. The second telephone number belongs to the Moesler Corporation. 4. The computer on the left has the Internet connection. 5. The light switch located on the right illuminates the front of the conference room. 6. Our boss, Mr. Blake, wrote the book second from the left on the shelf. **Exercise 7** Answers will vary. Possible answers are: 1. The house that/which has a $3,000,000 selling price is owned by a country western singer. 2. The physician whose accomplishments are world-renowned died last month. 3. The house (that) the oil tycoon is selling for $2,000,000 is on a very private acre of land. 4. The executive whose business has moved to another city must sell her beachfront house as soon as possible.

Activity 1 1. estate planning 2. euphemism 3. decedent 4. testate 5. intestate 6. realty property 7. Property such as stocks, cash, furniture, pets, jewelry, and clothing . . . 8. Property that you transfer freely

EXERCISE 6 [20 minutes]

In this exercise students look at the pictures in Exercise 3 and write sentences with reduced relative clauses.

1. Read the directions and example as a class.
2. Ask volunteers to create variations that describe something else about the box.
3. Have students write independently.
4. Have them exchange papers with a partner, review each other's sentences, and discuss them.
5. Ask volunteers to share their sentences—or their partner's sentences—with the class. See possible answers on LP page 144.

For more practice, use *Grammar Dimensions 4* Workbook page 62, Exercise 7.

EXPANSION [30 minutes]

Activity 8 (reflection) on SB page 147 is a good expansion activity to use after Exercise 6. In this activity students create a mnemonic device to remember the four ways that relative clauses may be reduced.

EXERCISE 7 [20 minutes]

Students write sentences about celebrity homes using relative clauses modifying subjects.

1. Read the directions and the first example.
2. Ask students to look in Focus 3 to find the explanation for why *that* could be deleted. (First explanation: *We can delete relative pronouns if they function as objects in relative clauses*.)
3. Read the second example. Ask students what function the relative clause serves in this sentence (Focus 2: *It makes the meaning of the noun it modifies more specific*).
4. Have students work in pairs to complete the exercise.

5. Ask volunteers to share their sentences—or their partner's sentences—with the class. See possible answers on LP page 144.
6. Encourage others to share different sentences they wrote.

EXPANSION [25 minutes]

Activity 2 (writing) on SB page 145 is a good follow-up to Exercise 7. In this activity students write a letter of complaint about a defective item they purchased using relative clauses that modify main clause subjects.

UNIT GOAL REVIEW [5 minutes]

Ask students to look at the goals on the opening page of the unit again. Refer to the pages of the unit where information on each goal can be found.

ExamView For assessment of Unit 7, Test Generator use *Grammar Dimensions 4 ExamView®*.

USE YOUR ENGLISH

The Use Your English activities at the end of the unit contain situations that should naturally elicit the structures covered in the unit. For a more complete discussion of how to use the Use Your English activities see To the Teacher, LP page xxvi.

ACTIVITY 1 listening [30 minutes]

CD1 Track 9

You may wish to use this activity after Exercise 3 on SB page 140–141. Students listen to a lecture that explains important business terms. They take notes and then complete sentences using their notes.

STEP 1

1. Inform students that they are going to listen to a lecture that explains various important business terms.
2. Tell them to take notes about the terms on a separate piece of paper.
3. Have students listen to the audio once, taking notes.
4. Have them listen a second time, completing and checking the notes they took.

STEP 2

1. Have students use their notes to complete the sentences.
2. Review answers as a class. See audio script on LP page S-4.

ACTIVITY 2 writing [25 minutes]

You may wish to use this activity after Exercise 7 on SB page 144. In this activity students write a letter of complaint about a defective item they purchased using relative clauses that modify main clause subjects.

1. Read the directions and example as a class.
2. Have students work in pairs to write a letter of complaint to a store or company about a defective item they bought recently.
3. Tell them to include at least two sentences with relative clauses modifying main clause subjects.
4. Ask volunteers to share their letters with the class. Ask the class to identify the sentences with relative clauses modifying main clause subjects.

Suggestion: If students have difficulty thinking of defective items, suggest one or more of the following problems:

a computer—the screen goes blank

a lamp—the switch doesn't turn the light on

a car—you hear a strange sound

a CD player—no sound comes out

 ACTIVITY **3** speaking

Exercise 1 described an unusual invention—a backscratcher. Working with a partner, try to draw a similar diagram for another device. Then describe the various features of the device, following the format of Exercise 1. Choose one of the following ideas or one of your own. Explain to the class how your invention works.

fly swatter   cheese cutter   door opener

window washer   pencil sharpener   adjustable chair

  ACTIVITY **4** writing

Find an outline, chart, or flow diagram that has various levels or interdependent steps in one of your textbooks or a magazine or newspaper. Describe the diagram using at least three sentences with relative clauses.

Example:

Unemployment

functional   cyclical   seasonal   structure

There are several types of unemployment. A person who is functionally unemployed has lost his or her job and is looking for another. A person who is a victim of a temporary downswing in the trade cycle is cyclically unemployed. A person who is seasonally unemployed means that he or she is not working during a particular season. . . .

After you have written your description, reduce all of the relative clauses that can be reduced according to the rules discussed in this unit.

  ACTIVITY **5** speaking/writing

Discuss the following business-related terms with a partner. Then write a definition for each term. Use a relative clause in each of your definitions. For example, term: per capita income; definition: *The average annual income that a particular population earns is called "per capita income."*

bankruptcy   gross national product   exchange rate
sales commission   prime rate   mortgage

 ACTIVITY **6** writing/speaking

Create your own "Trivia Challenge" game, like the one you played in the Opening Task on pages 134–135.

Example: an animal

It doesn't carry its young in a pouch.

*(a) seahorse, (b) kangaroo, *(c) ostrich*

■ **STEP 1**   Work with a partner. Think of five items and definitions/descriptions (you may use your dictionary for ideas).

■ **STEP 2**   Get together with another pair. See if they can guess the correct option. The team with the most correct guesses wins the game.

 ACTIVITY **7** research on the web

 With a partner, go to *InfoTrac® College Edition* and locate and print out four articles on *inventions*. Underline all examples of relative clauses. Then, place a check next to relative clauses in which the relative pronoun is a subject. What generalization can you make about the frequency of relative clauses in which the relative pronoun is a subject versus the frequency of relative clauses in which the relative pronoun is an object in formal written discourse?

ACTIVITY **8** reflection

Review Focus 3 and create a mnemonic device to remember the four ways that relative clauses may be reduced. A mnemonic device is a strategy for remembering a set or sequence of ideas using word or sound associations. For example, one way to remember the three branches of government in the United States is to remember the word "jel." The word "jel" sounds like "gel," as in gelatin, a substance that combines everything together. The Judicial, Executive, and Legislative branches help gel or "jel" the nation together. Note that these letters begin each of the key terms that you want to remember. Try to create a similar mnemonic strategy to remember ways that you can reduce relative clauses.

ACTIVITY 3 speaking [30 minutes]

You may wish to use this activity after Exercise 1 on SB page 138. Students create a diagram similar to that in Exercise 1 for another device and explain how it works.

1. Read the directions and ideas for devices as a class.

2. Review the diagram in Exercise 1 on SB page138. Point out how the letters in the diagram represent steps in the process.

3. Have students work in pairs or small groups. Ask them to choose one of the devices from the list or think up one of their own.

4. Ask them to draw a diagram for the device similar to the one shown in Exercise 1. Assure students that they need not be great artists to do this; stick figures and simple geometric shapes will be fine to illustrate their concept.

5. Have the pairs or small groups tell the class how their invention works, describing each step.

ACTIVITY 4 writing [45 minutes/homework]

You may wish to use Activity 4 after Exercise 5 on SB page 143. The research for this activity is a good homework assignment. Students write a description of a complex outline, chart, or flow diagram using sentences with relative clauses.

1. Write the categories from the chart on the board: *functional cyclical seasonal structure*

2. Ask students to read the example paragraph silently and underline the adverb form of these four terms. Remind students that the adverb form will end in –ly.

3. Read the example one sentence at a time. After reading each sentence, ask students to identify the relative clause in each sentence and what it modifies.

4. For homework, have students find an outline, chart, or flow diagram that has various levels

or interdependent steps in a textbook, a magazine, or an online site.

5. Have them write a description of the diagram using at least three sentences with relative clauses.

6. During the next class, have students share their writings with a partner.

7. Ask students to rewrite their writing, reducing all relative clauses.

ACTIVITY 5 speaking/writing [25 minutes]

You may wish to use this activity after Exercise 4 on SB page 143. In this activity students discuss and write definitions of business terms, using relative clauses in each definition.

1. Read the directions and example as a class. Ask students to identify the relative clause.

2. Have students work in pairs. Ask them to discuss the terms listed, and then write a definition for each of the terms. Each definition should contain a relative clause.

ACTIVITY 6 writing/speaking [30 minutes]

You may wish to use this activity after Exercise 2 on SB page 139. In it, students play a trivia game similar to the one they played in the Opening Task, creating and making guesses about definitions.

1. Read the directions and example as a class.

2. Have students work in pairs to think of and create definitions for five things. Tell them they can use a dictionary or encyclopedia for ideas

3. Have pairs get together with another pair. One pair should read all their definitions and the other pair should guess, and then switch roles.

4. The team with the greatest number of correct guesses wins the game.

ACTIVITY 7 research on the web [45 minutes]

 Activity 7 is a good follow-up to Exercise 1 on SB page 138. Using four articles printed from *InfoTrac® College Edition*, students identify and draw conclusions about the types of relative clauses in the articles.

1. Read the directions as a class.

2. Have students work in pairs. Tell them to locate four articles on *inventions* on *InfoTrac® College Edition*.

3. Ask them to print out the articles and underline all examples of relative clauses.

4. Tell them to then place a check next to relative clauses in which the relative pronoun is a subject. Encourage them to refer back to Focus 1 if they are uncertain about how to identify these.

5. Have students work together to analyze the four articles in terms of the frequency of relative clauses in which the relative pronoun is a subject versus the frequency of relative clauses in which the relative pronoun is an object.

ACTIVITY 8 reflection [30 minutes]

You may wish to use this activity after Exercise 6 on SB page 144. In this activity students create a mnemonic device to remember the four ways that relative clauses may be reduced.

1. Review Focus 3 with the class.

2. Tell students that they are going to create a mnemonic device to remember the four ways that relative clauses may be reduced.

3. Read the text of Activity 8, which describes and gives an example of a mnemonic device.

4. Ask volunteers to create mnemonic devices to remember other things.

5. Have students work in pairs to create their mnemonic devices.

6. Ask volunteers to share their creations with the class, and write these on the board.

UNIT 8

RELATIVE CLAUSES MODIFYING OBJECTS

UNIT GOALS

- **Use restrictive relative clauses to modify objects**
- **Use multiple restrictive relative clauses in a sentence**
- **Reduce relative clauses by deleting relative pronouns**
- **Choose appropriate relative clause forms for formal and informal communication**

OPENING TASK

Describing Inventions

Work on this task with a partner. Student A should look at the inventions and the invention dates on page 149, and Student B should look at the pictures and dates on page A-18. Take turns describing one of the inventions on your page without actually naming it. Your partner will guess what you have described.

Example: Student A: *I'm thinking of something that was invented in 1593 and that you use to measure the temperature.*
Student B: *Is it a thermometer?*
Student A: *Good guess!*

Thermometer 1593

Example: Student B: *I'm thinking of something that was invented about 1590 and that you can look through.*
Student A: *Is it glasses?*
Student B: *No, but it has a lens that you can look through to make small substances appear large.*
Student A: *Oh, it's a microscope.*
Student B: *That's right!*

Compound Microscope about 1590

Student A

Telescope 1608

Polaroid Land Camera 1947

Jet Engine Aircraft 1939

X-ray Machine 1895

Radio 1895

Zipper 1893

Skyscraper 1885

Air Conditioning 1902

Safety Razor 1901

UNIT OVERVIEW

Unit 8 continues the analysis of relative clauses begun in Unit 7. Whereas Unit 7 examined relative clauses modifying subjects; this unit looks at the form, meaning, and use of relative clauses modifying objects. This unit will be much easier for students if they have already completed Unit 7.

GRAMMAR NOTE

This unit covers several different types of relative clauses that modify objects. Some will be easier for students to understand and use than others. In general, those relative clauses that come at the end of sentences are more easily understood than clauses that are embedded in the midst of a sentence. So, for example, the sentence *My friend is the boy who speaks German* will be more comprehensible to most students than the sentence *The boy who speaks German is my friend.*

UNIT GOALS

Some instructors may want to review the goals listed on Student Book (SB) page 148 after completing the Opening Task so that students understand what they should know by the end of the unit. These goals can also be reviewed at the end of the unit when students are more familiar with the grammar terminology.

OPENING TASK [20 minutes]

The purpose of this activity is to create a context in which students will need to use relative clauses in an appropriate context. The problem-solving format is designed to show the teacher how well the students can produce relative clauses implicitly and spontaneously when they are engaged in a communicative task. For a more complete discussion of the purpose of the Opening Task, see To the Teacher, Lesson Planner (LP) page xxii.

Setting Up The Task

1. Have a brief class discussion about inventions. Students might discuss what they feel are the most important inventions in the last decade or recent years. Write the names of some inventions on the board, such as hybrid cars, cell phones with video, the Braille Glove.

2. Ask students to name other inventions within the past 50 years, then the past 100 years. Ask a volunteer to write these on the board.

3. Model and have students create sentences describing some of the inventions: *Hybrid cars are cars that use electric power as well as gasoline to run.*

Conducting the Task

1. Read the instructions as a class. Ask a pair of volunteers to read the first example, and ask students to identify the relative clause in the first sentence. What does it describe? (*something*)

2. Ask another pair of volunteers to read the second example, and have students again identify the relative clause and what it modifies.

3. Divide students into pairs.

4. Ask students to be careful not to glance at their partners' pages, where the answers are contained. Student A refers to SB page 149. Student B refers to SB page A-18.

5. You may want to walk around and listen in order to diagnose students' facility with relative clauses modifying objects. Is a student having problems with the form, meaning, and/or use of relative clauses?

6. Make sure the first student is using a phrase such as *I'm thinking of/imagining something/an object/a useful item that/which . . .* in order to produce the target structure—a relative clause modifying an object.

Closing the Task

1. Ask volunteers to share some of their answers with the class. Which inventions were the most challenging to describe? To guess?

2. If time permits, engage students in a discussion of the five most important inventions among the 20 listed on pages 148–149 and page A-18. How do we judge whether an invention is important, or not?

GRAMMAR NOTE

Typical student errors (form)

- Mixing up the word order of sentences with relative clauses modifying objects:—e.g., * *That he is working on the paper about global warming.* (See Focus 1.)

- Retaining *be* when deleting a relative pronoun followed by *be*:—e.g., * *They are going to a restaurant is in the center of town.* (See Focus 4.)

- Deleting relative pronouns that are the subject or a relative clause that uses a verb other than *be* or *have*:—e.g., * *I'd like to rent a car gets good mileage.* (See Focus 4.)

Typical student errors (use)

- Using *who* to refer to animals of things:—e.g., * *She threw a bone to the dog who was barking.* (See Focus 1.)

- Deleting relative pronouns that are needed for understanding:—e.g., * *She works with people are retired.* (See Focus 4.)

- Using a formal construction in informal speech:—e.g., * *He phoned the guy with whom he worked.* (See Focus 5.)

Types of Relative Clauses Modifying Objects

form

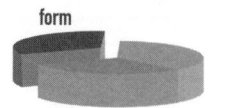

Relative clauses that modify objects can have various relative pronouns/determiners and different functions:

EXAMPLES	OBJECT BEING MODIFIED	RELATIVE PRONOUN	FUNCTION OF RELATIVE PRONOUN
(a) She knows a girl **who/that** can dance very well.	person	*who/that*	subject
(b) He looked for the banker **whom/that** he had met at the party.		*whom/that*	direct object
(c) He was angry at the person **whom/that** he had written a letter to.		*whom/that*	indirect object
(d) She talked to the students **whom/that** she was best acquainted with.		*whom/that*	object of a preposition
(e) OR She talked to the students with **whom** she was best acquainted.		*whom*	object of a preposition (directly following preposition)
(f) I have noticed the trash **that/which** is piled on the street.*	thing or animal	*that/which*	subject
(g) Did you see the apartment **that/which** he furnished himself?*		*that/which*	direct object
(h) He patted the dog **that/which** he had given a bone to.*		*that/which*	indirect object
(i) Toronto has a tall tower **that/which** you can get a great view from.*		*that/which*	object of a preposition
(j) Toronto has a tall tower from **which** you can get a great view.		*which*	object of a preposition (directly following preposition)

EXAMPLES	OBJECT BEING MODIFIED	RELATIVE PRONOUN	FUNCTION OF RELATIVE PRONOUN
(k) I need to find the man **whose** credit card has expired.	person	*whose*	possessive determiner
(l) I was impressed by the trees **whose** branches seemed to touch the sky.	thing or animal	*whose*	possessive determiner

* In many formal contexts, *that* is considered the only correct choice of relative determiner when a thing or animal is modified.

EXERCISE 1

Read the following story. Underline all relative clauses that modify objects. Circle the noun that is modified by each relative clause.

(1) When my mother and I came to the United States, I experienced a move from which I felt that I would never recover. (2) My mother and I never got along very well. (3) She was a glamorous fashion model, but I looked like a plain Jane who was clumsy and overweight.

(4) I was often left alone as my mother left for fancy parties at which she mingled with famous actors, artists, and musicians. (5) I desperately wanted to return to the country from which we had fled in Eastern Europe.

(6) My mother was fortunate when she first arrived, for she got her first job through friends of a fellow countryperson who had married an American millionaire. (7) These friends immediately introduced her to everyone that they knew. (8) However, most of these friends were childless, and I had no one with whom I could share my loneliness and misery.

(9) Not knowing where I could find happiness, I decided to begin copying the standards of style for which my mother was famous. (10) It had worked for her; perhaps it could work for me. (11) I followed numerous diets that would help me resemble a starved model. (12) Nothing delighted my mother more than the attempts that I made to become more like her. (13) I did not really believe in my new preoccupation with fashion. (14) It actually sent me into deep depressions which lasted weeks.

(15) As the years went by, I went away to a prestigious college which provided me with many opportunities to travel abroad and meet famous people. (16) I always seemed to be looking for something that I had not obtained in my youth. (17) Finally, I met someone who could liberate me from all of the fashion nonsense. (18) The love of my life turned out to be a scientist who liked to climb mountains and build things. (19) In fact, he built the first home that we lived in. (20) Believe it or not, this country cottage made possible the quiet life that I had always dreamed of as a teenager.

METHODOLOGY NOTE

You may want to review the different functions a relative pronoun (*who, whom, that, which, whose*) can have when modifying a subject before presenting Focus 1. It would also be helpful to review Focus 1 in Unit 7, on SB page 136, which gives an overview of restrictive relative clauses.

FOCUS 1 [20 minutes]

Focus 1 identifies the object being modified, the relative pronoun used, and the function of that relative pronoun in each example sentence.

1. **Lead-in:** Have students cover all but the first column of the chart on pages 150 and 151. Write a two-column chart on the board: *Object: person/thing/animal;* and *Relative Pronoun: who/whom/that/which/whose.*

2. Read the first example (a). Ask students to identify the object being modified: Is it a person, thing, or animal? Ask a volunteer to write the answer (*person*) in the chart on the board.

3. Ask students to say what relative pronoun is used in the example (*who/that*), and have the volunteer write this in the chart.

4. Finally, ask students to identify the function of the relative pronoun (*subject*).

5. Continue with this process for the remainder of the chart.

6. Ask volunteers to create other example sentences.

LANGUAGE NOTE

Point out that, in informal discourse, *that* is more commonly used than *which* or *who(m)*. In writing, however, *who(m)* is used for persons, and *that* and *which* are used for animals and things.

EXERCISE 1 [20 minutes]

In this exercise students practice identifying the relative clauses that modify objects in sentences and the noun that is modified in each case.

1. Read the directions and first example as a class. Could the relative clause be modifying *Mother and I*? Why or why not?

2. Have students work in pairs to complete the exercise.

3. Walk around the room to observe how well students seem to have understood the concepts in Focus 1.

4. Review the answers as a class. If students came up with other answers, ask them to explain them. See answers on LP page 150.

For more practice, use *Grammar Dimension 4* Workbook page 63, Exercise 1.

EXPANSION [45 minutes]

You may wish to use Activity 1 (listening/writing) on SB page 161 after Exercise 1 to give students more practice in listening to and writing descriptions that use a variety of relative clauses modifying objects. Students listen to a story about the intertwining lives of two people, Kimi Tamura and Fred Escobar, who were born on the same day in different cities in the United States and ended up living in the same building in Los Angeles.

EXERCISE 2

Take turns asking and answering questions about the story in Exercise 1. In each response, use a relative clause that modifies an object.

Examples: Student A: *What kind of move did the author experience?*

Student B: *She said that it was a move from which she would never recover.*

Student A: *What did the young girl look like?*

Student B: *She looked like "a plain Jane" who was clumsy and overweight.*

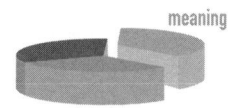

FOCUS 2	Using Relative Clauses to Modify Nouns

meaning

EXAMPLES	EXPLANATION
(a) The police caught a criminal who **had robbed three banks.** (b) He applied for work at companies **that his father recommended.**	A relative clause provides information that is necessary to identify or limit the noun it modifies. The clause specifies what type of thing(s) or person(s) is being described.

EXERCISE 3

STEP 1 A crime was committed at the Royal Restaurant. In pairs, take the roles of a criminal investigator and a witness. The investigator demands that the witness give certain information from the left column below. The witness provides a response with a relative clause modifying an object using events, people, conditions, etc. in the right column.

Example: Investigator: *Tell me the name of the man whom you saw at the Royal Restaurant.*

Witness: *I don't remember the name of the man that I saw.*

INVESTIGATOR INFORMATION REQUIRED	WITNESS EXPERIENCES/OBSERVATIONS
1. Name of the man the witness saw at the Royal Restaurant.	You don't remember the name.
2. Name of a woman the man was with.	Nobody told you the name, but you think the name is Jones or Johnson.
3. Type of car the witness saw parked near the Billings Bank.	You saw a blue compact car. It had a scratch on the right side.
4. Type of tip the suspect left at the last meal.	He left a large tip. You found it under the salt and pepper shakers.
5. Name of the company. Its truck was seen across the street from the Royal Restaurant.	You forgot the name of the company.
6. Type of sound the witness heard near the restaurant.	You heard a scream. The scream startled you.
7. Type of button the witness picked up at the scene of the crime.	You picked up a gold button. You think it fell from the robber's jacket.
8. Sequence of events following the robbery.	You saw the man run down the stairs to a car. Its license plate was XXX 123.
9. Type of dog in the car.	You saw a small, black dog. It had blue eyes.
10. Name of a relative close to the female suspect.	You know she had a son. His name was Biffo.

STEP 2 Using some of the information obtained at the interview, write one paragraph about the Royal Restaurant crime. Include at least five relative clauses in your narrative.

Exercise 2 Answers will vary.

Exercise 3 Step 1: 2. Tell me the name of the woman whom the man was with./I believe the name of the woman was Jones or Johnson.   3. Tell me the type of car that you saw parked near the Billings Bank./I saw a blue compact car that had a scratch on the right side.   4. Tell me about the tip that the suspect left at the last meal./He left a large tip which I found under the salt and pepper shakers. 5. Tell me the name of the company whose truck was seen across from the Royal Restaurant./I forgot the name of the company whose truck was seen there.   6. Tell me about the type of sound that you heard near the restaurant./I heard a scream which startled me.   7. Tell me about the type of button you picked up at the scene of the crime./I picked up a gold button that I think fell from the robber's jacket.   8. Tell me about the sequence of events that followed the murder./I saw a man who ran down the stairs to a car whose license plate was XXX 123.   9. Tell me about the type of dog that was in the car./I saw a small, black dog that had blue eyes.   10. Tell me the name of a relative who is close to the female suspect./I know that she had a son whose name was Biffo.

■ EXERCISE 2 [15 minutes]

Exercise 2 builds on the work students did in Exercise 1, asking students to describe the story in Exercise 1 using relative clauses that modify objects, much as they did in the Opening Task.

1. Read the directions as a class. Ask two volunteers to read the two example questions and answers. Ask students to identify the relative clause that modifies an object in the two responses. What is the noun that is modified in each?

2. Have students work in pairs. Tell them to take turns asking and answering questions about the sentences in Exercise 1. Remind them to use a relative clause that modifies an object in each response.

3. Ask volunteers to share their responses with the class. Write some of the responses on the board, and ask other students to identify the relative clause that modifies an object and the noun that is modified in each sentence.

For more practice, use *Grammar Dimensions 4* Workbook page 64, Exercise 2.

EXPANSION [30 minutes/homework]

Activity 2 (speaking/writing) on SB page 162 is a good follow-up to Exercise 2. Step 1 can be done in class and Step 2 assigned as homework. Students, in pairs, will describe a picture filled with detail, and then describe it in writing, using relative clauses modifying objects.

FOCUS 2 [10 minutes]

1. **Lead-in:** Before introducing the focus chart, describe a student: *I'm thinking of a student who is from (Brazil) and who is wearing (red shoes). Who am I thinking of?* Have the class guess the answer.

2. Ask several students to describe others using the same format, and have the class guess the answers.

3. Read the explanation in Focus 2. Emphasize that relative clauses are used to specify who or what is being described.

4. Ask a volunteer to read the two examples, and have the class say whether a person, thing, or animal is being described. How is the information in the relative clause essential?

5. Ask volunteers to supply other examples, write these on the board, and discuss them with students.

METHODOLOGY NOTE

Once students understand how to form relative clauses, they will need lots of practice to become proficient in using them correctly. Having students identify clauses with brackets and circling the nouns they modify helps them visualize how the sentences are constructed.

■ EXERCISE 3 [25 minutes/homework]

In this exercise students role-play an investigator interrogating a witness to a crime. Students must use relative clauses that modify nouns in their sentences. The information for this exercise continues on SB page 153.

STEP 1   It may be difficult for students to figure out how to do this exercise. To demonstrate the process, ask two students to come to the front of the room. Ask one student to play the role of witness and the other to act as the criminal investigator.

1. Do the example and the first two or three items to get the class started. The witness will need to be reminded to give a complete response that includes a relative clause. Be patient as students struggle to produce this difficult structure.

2. Have students work in pairs to do Step 1. Have them read through the investigator information and the witness observations before role-playing the interrogation.

3. Walk around the room to observe students' facility with generating relative clauses that modify nouns. See answers on LP page 152.

4. If time permits, ask students to switch roles and role-play the interrogation again.

STEP 2

1. Have students work independently to write a paragraph describing the crime. They should include a minimum of five relative clauses in their paragraphs. This might be completed as homework.

2. Ask several volunteers to share their paragraphs with the class. Did they include at least five relative clauses in their paragraphs?

For more practice, use *Grammar Dimensions 4* Workbook page 65, Exercise 3.

EXPANSION [60 minutes/homework]

1. For homework after Exercise 3, ask students to either make up a crime or find an account of a real crime—in a newspaper, on TV or the radio, or online. Have them write down as many details as possible about the crime. Suggest they use a 5-W chart (*who/what/where/when/why/how*) to take notes. Then, have them write five to ten statements that a witness to the crime could make, such as *I saw the two men who robbed the store walk in around 8 P.M. The one who had a gun . . .*

2. During the next class, have students work in pairs and exchange papers. They should then write a list of five to ten questions an investigator could ask, based on the witness information.

3. Have them take turns role-playing the interrogations.

FOCUS 3   Multiple Relative Clauses

use

EXAMPLES	EXPLANATIONS
(a) **Do you need a sleeping bag** which resists rain **and** which you can stuff into a pouch?	It is possible to use more than one relative clause in a sentence. These relative clauses may modify the same or different nouns.
(b) **She was wearing a hat** that my friend designed for a woman who had a funeral to attend.	
(c) AWKWARD: Marissa wrote a letter. The letter complained about cosmetics. She had ordered cosmetics last week.	Multiple relative clauses are used in formal writing to be specific and concise.
(d) BETTER: **Marissa wrote a letter** that complained about cosmetics that she had ordered last week.	With multiple relative clauses, we can communicate more information using fewer words and/or sentences.

EXERCISE 4

The following patented inventions were never sold on a wide-scale basis. Write sentences for each one, describing for whom the inventions were probably made. Use two relative clauses modifying objects in each sentence. Then, share your responses with a partner.

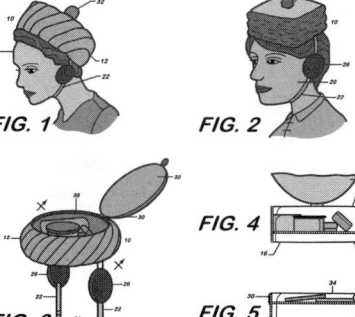
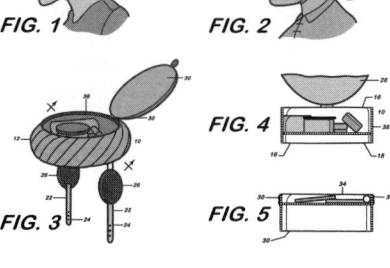

FIG. 1   FIG. 2

FIG. 3   FIG. 4   FIG. 5

Example: carry-all hat

The carry-all hat was probably invented for someone who does not want to carry a purse and who always needs her cosmetics nearby.

1. combination deer carcass sled and chaise lounge

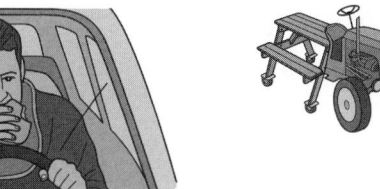

2. eyeglass frame with adjustable rearview mirrors

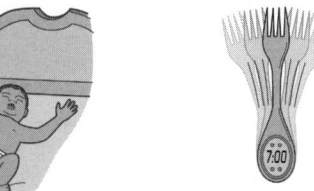

3. power-operated pool cue stick

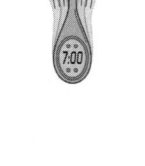

4. toilet-lid lock

5. baby-patting machine

6. alarm fork

7. car bib

8. motorized picnic table

ANSWER KEY

Exercise 4   Answers will vary. Possible answers are: 1. The combination deer carcass sled and chaise lounge was probably made for someone who likes to hunt and who wants to take a rest after the excitement of the day.   2. The eyeglass frame with adjustable rearview mirrors was probably made for someone who had poor eyesight and who was also a little paranoid.   3. The power-operated pool cue stick was probably invented for someone who liked to play pool and who also had a slow stroke.   4. The toilet lid lock was probably invented for people who had a child or who had a pet that they did not want to get into the toilet.   5. The baby-patting machine was probably made for someone who had a very fussy baby and who got tired of patting the baby all by him or herself.   6. The alarm clock fork was invented for someone who wants to know when to start eating or who wants to know when to stop eating.   7. The car bib was designed for drivers who want to protect clothing from food which falls while they are eating or from a drink that dribbles while drinking.   8. The motorized picnic table was invented for someone who likes to eat outside and who frequently likes to eat in different places.

FOCUS 3 [15 minutes]

Focus 3 explains the use of multiple relative clauses. This information will be particularly useful to students in their writing.

1. **Lead-in:** To illustrate how multiple relative clauses can be used in place of multiple individual sentences, write some sentences describing a student in class on the board: (*Angelica*) *has a backpack. The backpack contains her books. She uses the books for her English classes.*

2. Elicit how these sentences could be combined using relative clauses: *Angelica has a backpack that contains the books that she uses for her English classes.*

3. Read the explanations before you read the examples in this focus chart, and then ask students to analyze the examples in terms of the explanations. For example, read the first explanation, and then the first example. Write the example on the board. Ask, *How many relative clauses are there in this sentence?* (*two*). Ask a volunteer to draw brackets around the clauses. Ask, *What noun does each clause modify?* (*sleeping bag*). Ask the volunteer to circle the noun.

4. Read examples (c) and (d), and ask students to think of other ways of combining the sentences, such as *Marissa wrote a letter about cosmetics that she had ordered last week.* Do students find it easier to understand the series of single sentences, or the sentences with relative clauses? What words signal the relative clauses? (*that, which*).

METHODOLOGY NOTE

Point out to students that the use of multiple relative clauses in sentences occurs much more frequently in writing than in speech—though it does, of course, occur in speech as well. Encourage them to practice using multiple relative clauses when they write. Suggest that, when they are writing an outline or draft of their ideas for a paper, they first jot down all their thoughts, and then combine several into one sentence. They should then reread the sentence and see if they need to add or delete information.

EXERCISE 4 [15 minutes]

In this exercise students practice using multiple relative clauses in sentences describing a series of somewhat silly inventions.

1. Read the directions and first example as a class. Can students imagine themselves or anyone they know wearing such a hat?

2. To get students thinking, ask if they have ever invented something or known someone who has. You can mention that little inventions like the self-stick note have made their inventors rich.

3. Have students work in pairs. Have them take turns describing each invention using at least two relative clauses in each sentence.

4. Ask volunteers to share their sentences with the class. See possible answers on LP page 154.

EXPANSION [30 minutes]

As an expansion of the work with multiple relative clauses students began in Exercise 4, have them work in small groups to come up with their own silly inventions.

1. Have students work in small groups of three or four. Ask each student to think of at least three silly inventions. The inventions could save time, money, or effort.

2. Have each student write a description of each invention using multiple relative clauses.

3. Have each student take turns describing their inventions to their group. The others should draw a picture of the invention being described.

4. Ask students to share their best inventions with the class.

5. Ask each group to share the description that used the greatest number of relative clauses.

Combine the following groups of sentences into one sentence that contains two relative clauses modifying objects.

Example: Molly purchased a house. The house's former owner had made movies. The movies were box-office successes.

Molly purchased a house whose former owner had made movies which were box-office successes.

1. Students should be given scholarships. Scholarships cover all college expenses. College expenses include tuition and living expenses.

    _____

2. I am amazed at the invention. The man created the invention for some people. These people are disabled.

    _____

3. Most people did not buy chocolates. The youths were selling chocolates at a booth. The booth was located outside a supermarket.

    _____

4. Salespeople require an official contract. Clients have provided their signatures on the official contract. Their signatures are legible.

    _____

5. She admires one teacher. The teacher knew her subject area. The teacher was fair in grading.

    _____

6. A man was held hostage by thugs. Their main interest was obtaining money for drugs. The drugs could be sold for thousands of dollars on the black market.

    _____

7. The women applauded the policy. The company instituted the policy for pregnant employees. The pregnant employees needed a three-month leave after their children were born.

    _____

8. The woman tightly clasped a locket. Her son had given her the locket before he left for an assignment. The assignment was in Saudi Arabia.

    _____

---

form

FOCUS 4 Deleting Relative Pronouns

EXAMPLES	EXPLANATIONS
	You can delete relative pronouns with the following functions:
(a) I sent a letter ~~which~~ he never received.	• direct object
(b) The faculty admired the student ~~whom~~ they gave the award to.	• indirect object
(c) Tom saw the movie ~~which~~ Sahib talked about.	• object of preposition
(d) They hope to find an apartment ~~which is~~ in a quiet area of town.	You can also delete relative pronouns that serve as subjects when the subject is followed by the *be*-verb. When you delete the relative pronoun, the *be*-verb must be deleted as well. The resulting sentences can have:
(e) NOT: They hope to find an apartment is in a quiet area of town.	
(f) I met the athlete ~~who was~~ chosen as "Player of the Year."	• passive and progressive participles
(g) The child is delighted with the puppy ~~that is~~ licking her face.	
(h) The realtor sold the home ~~which is~~ located **on Elm Street**.	• prepositional phrases
(i) She doesn't know anyone ~~that is~~ **smart enough** to pass the test.	• adjective phrases
(j) I do not want to be around a person **who has** the flu.	When the subject is followed by *have (not)* to indicate possession, you can paraphrase with *with (without)* for the relative pronoun + *have (not)*.
(k) I do not want to be around a person **with** the flu.	
(l) Have you ever considered a job **that doesn't have** benefits?	
(m) Have you ever considered a job **without** benefits?	
(n) Could you recommend a book that appeals to all ages?	You cannot delete relative pronouns if they are subjects of a relative clause that uses a verb other than *be* or *have*.
(o) NOT: Could you recommend a book appeals to all ages?	

ANSWER KEY

Exercise 5 1. Students should be given scholarships that cover all college expenses which include tuition and living. 2. I am amazed at the invention that the man created for some people who are disabled. 3. Most people did not buy the chocolates which the youths were selling at a booth that was located outside a supermarket. 4. Salespeople require an official contract on which clients have provided signatures that are legible. 5. She admires one teacher who knew her subject area and who was fair in grading. 6. A man was held hostage by thugs whose main interest was obtaining drugs that could be sold for thousands of dollars on the black market. 7. The women applauded the policy that the company instituted for pregnant employees who needed a three-month leave after their children were born. 8. The woman tightly clasped a locket that her son had given her before he left for an assignment that was in Saudi Arabia.

EXERCISE 5 [15 minutes]

In this exercise students continue to practice combining several sentences into one using multiple relative clauses.

1. Read the directions and first example as a class.
2. Have students work independently to combine the sentences into one sentence with multiple relative clauses.
3. Have them exchange papers with a partner and place brackets around the relative clauses and circle the nouns that are modified by the clauses.
4. Ask volunteers to share their sentences with the class. See answers on LP page 156.

 For more practice, use *Grammar Dimensions 4* Workbook page 66, Exercise 4.

EXPANSION [30 minutes]

This expansion activity will give students additional practice in combining sentences using multiple relative clauses.

1. Have students work in small groups of three or four. Ask each group to agree on a topic that they will write sentences about.
2. Tell each student in each group to write at least three short sentences about the topic. These sentences should not contain any relative clauses.
3. Have students and then pass their paper with the written sentences to another member of their group. This other student should combine the new sentences into one sentence using multiple relative clauses. Every member of the group should have written sentences and combined someone else's sentences when this activity is completed.

4. Have the writers take turns reading their sentences aloud to their group. At this point students can help correct any errors they hear.
5. Ask volunteers from several groups to share some of the group's best sentences with the class.

FOCUS 4 [25 minutes]

This box is similar to Focus 3 in Unit 7, but in addition it describes how relative pronouns can be deleted when they function as objects.

1. **Lead-in:** Write example (a) on the board without the deletion. As in the example, draw a line through the relative pronoun *which,* and ask a volunteer to read the sentence. Repeat this process with the next two examples.
2. Read the explanation in the first row. Ask students to analyze the three examples on the board and say what function the deleted relative pronoun serves in each.
3. For the second row, read the explanation first, and then the examples (d–i). Ask students to identify the relative pronoun that is deleted in each and the *be*-verb. Ask them to say whether the sentences have passive or progressive participles, prepositional phrases, and/or adjective phrases.
4. For the third row, again read the explanation first, and then call on volunteers to read the examples (j–m). Ask students to point out the subjects and the verb *have* in each.
5. For the last row, read the examples (n) and (o) first, then the explanation. Ask volunteers to offer other examples with verbs other than *be* or *have*.

METHODOLOGY NOTE

The whole concept of deleting relative pronouns is a sophisticated one, even for advanced students. Many students will still tend to translate word-for-word in their heads, and omitting a word can cause confusion. Point out that it is much more common to delete relative pronouns in informal speech than in writing; students will always be correct if they retain the relative pronouns in their writing. Also point out that, in speech, nonhuman relative pronouns (those that refer to animals or things) tend to be deleted much more often than the relative pronouns that refer to persons.

With a partner, write descriptions of one or more sentences for the following pictures. Use at least one relative clause in each description. Then revise each description, deleting as many relative pronouns as possible. (Follow the rules in Focus 4.)

Exercise 6 Answers may vary and are listed below. Likely deletions are indicated in parentheses.

Example: A man brought flowers to a woman whom he admires.

Revision: *A man brought flowers to a woman he admires.*

1. A man (who is) wearing a hat is sitting on a boat (which is) in the middle of a lake.

3. A woman is giving a snack to a dog (that is) sitting in a field (that is) near some flowers.

2. A woman (who is) sitting on a stool is showing a girl (who is) wearing a striped shirt how to adjust a bicycle wheel.

4. A customer (who is) wearing an interesting necklace is taking a bag from a store clerk (who is) wearing a pink shirt.

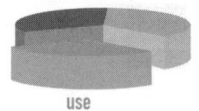
use

FOCUS 5 Relative Clauses in Formal and Informal Communication

EXAMPLES	EXPLANATIONS
Formal ↑ (a) I know the person **whom** he hired. (b) I know the person **who** he hired. (c) I know the person **that** he hired. (d) I know the person he hired. ↓ *Informal*	The use or omission of object relative pronouns may vary according to formality. *Whom* is used in formal writing but is often reduced to *who* or *that* in speaking. It can be omitted altogether in informal speech.
Formal ↑ (e) He met the person **to whom** she had written. (f) He met the person **whom** she had written **to**. (g) He met the person **who** she had written **to**. (h) He met the person she had written **to**. ↓ *Informal*	In formal written English, the preposition should always precede the object relative pronoun.

EXERCISE 7

Reread the story in Exercise 1. Mark word-order changes and cross out relative pronouns that will make the story less formal.

Example: When my mother and I came to the United States, I experienced a move ~~from which~~ I felt that I would never recover. ^from^ I was often left alone as my mother left for fancy parties ~~at~~ which she mingled with famous actors, artists, and musicians ^at^

ANSWER KEY

Exercise 7 Answers will vary and are listed below. Italicized and black words are used to denote word-order changes.

Paragraph 1 (1) When my mother and I came to the United States, I experienced a move ~~from which~~ I felt that I would never recover *from*. (2) My mother and I never got along very well. (3) She was a glamorous fashion model, but I looked like a "a plain Jane", ~~who was~~ clumsy and overweight.

Paragraph 2 (4) I was often left alone as my mother left for fancy parties ~~at which~~ *where* she mingled with famous actors, artists, and musicians. (5) I desperately wanted to return to the country ~~from which~~ we had fled *from* in Eastern Europe. **Paragraph 3** (6) My mother was fortunate when she first arrived, for she got her first job through friends of a fellow countryperson ~~who had~~

(Answers continued under SB page 158.)

---

married to an American millionaire. (7) These friends immediately introduced her to everyone ~~that~~ they knew. (8) However, most of these friends were childless, and I had no one ~~with whom~~ I could share my loneliness and misery *with*. **Paragraph 4** (9) Not knowing where I could find happiness, I decided to begin copying the standards of style ~~for which~~ my mother was famous *for*. (10) It had worked for her; perhaps it could work for me. (11) I followed numerous diets that would help me resemble a starved model. (12) Nothing delighted my mother more than the ~~attempts~~ that I made to become more like her. (13) I did not really believe in my new preoccupation with fashion. (14) It

actually sent me into a deep depression ~~which~~ *that* lasted weeks. **Paragraph 5** (15) As the years went by, I went away to a prestigious college ~~which~~ *that* provided me with many opportunities to travel abroad and meet famous people. (16) I always seemed to be looking for something that I had not obtained in my youth. (17) Finally, I met someone who could liberate me from all of the fashion nonsense. (18) The love of my life turned out to be a scientist who liked to climb mountains and build things. (19) In fact, he built the first home ~~that~~ we lived in. (20) Believe it or not, this country cottage made possible the quiet life ~~that~~ I had always dreamed of as a teenager.

EXERCISE 6 [20 minutes]

This exercise applies the principles enumerated in Focus 4. It asks students to write descriptions of pictures using relative clauses, and then edit their descriptions, deleting relative pronouns.

1. Read the directions and first example as a class. What relative pronoun was deleted? (*whom*) Is that pronoun a direct object, an indirect object, or an object of a preposition?
2. Have students work in pairs. Ask them to each compose a sentence or two about each picture.
3. Write numbers 1 through 4 across the board.
4. Ask one member of each pair to write one of the sentences on the board. Depending upon the size of your class, several sentences should be written under each number. See possible answers on LP page 158.

 For more practice, use *Grammar Dimensions 4* Workbook page 69, Exercise 5; page 70, Exercise 6.

EXPANSION [60 minutes/homework]

Activity 3 (research on the web) on SB page 163 makes an excellent homework assignment after Exercise 6. Students search the Internet for information on several topics related to inventions, and then answer questions using reduced relative clauses.

FOCUS 5 [20 minutes]

Focus 5 explores the differences in use of relative clause in formal and informal communication. These are important distinctions for students to be able to make as they become more proficient in English.

1. **Lead-in:** Ask volunteers to read the first four examples (a–d). Ask students if there is any difference in meaning between the four sentences.

(*No.*) Ask students to identify the differences between the four examples (*the use of a specific relative pronoun—or the deletion of one*).
2. Read the explanation. Ask students to say which of the examples are probably examples of informal speech, and which of formal writing.
3. Review examples (e–h) in the same manner. Which style are students more familiar with? Formal or informal?

VARIATION

1. Distribute sentence strips to four students with sentences (a–d) written on them. Write informal on the far left side and formal on the far right side of the board.
2. Ask the four students with strips to stand up and order themselves according to formality across the room. The students with sentences (a) and (b) should be on the left and the students with (c) and (d) should be on the right.
3. For the second row, read the explanation first, and then ask volunteers to read examples (e–h). Have students identify where the preposition is in each example. Which is an example of the most formal written English, and why?

EXERCISE 7 [20 minutes]

In Exercise 7 students return to the story in Exercise 1 and rewrite it, making it more informal by deleting relative pronouns and changing word order. It practices concepts presented in both Focus 4 and Focus 5.

1. Read the directions and first example as a class. Elicit that in the example the prepositions are moved to the end of the sentences. Refer students to the second explanation in Focus 5 to review how this reflects a less formal type of communication.
2. Have students work independently to edit the story in Exercise 1.
3. Have them share and discuss their edits with a partner.
4. Ask volunteers to share their sentences with the class. Ask them to identify the type of changes they made. See possible answers on LP page 158.

 For more practice, use *Grammar Dimensions 4* Workbook page 70, Exercise 7.

EXPANSION [30 minutes]

Use Activity 4 (reflection) on SB page 163 after Exercise 7 for additional practice with using reduced relative clauses in informal writing. In this activity, students think and write about effective study techniques.

In pairs, read the following dialogue aloud. Then, edit the dialogue to create a less formal style. The first line has been done for you as an example. (Be sure to focus on relative clauses modifying objects and contractions.) Finally, reread the dialogue aloud, including the revisions that you have made.

Luca: *Did you hear from the accountant ~~to whom~~ we talked* to *last month?*

Maya: No, I did not. Is he concerned about the bank account ~~which~~ we closed in January?

Luca: No, he is calling about personal taxes ~~that~~ you have not paid yet.

Maya: That makes another item ~~that~~ I do not need now—a reminder that I owe money.

Luca: I know what you mean. The accountant ~~with whom~~ I deal with is always asking me if I have any earnings ~~that~~ I neglected to mention.

Maya: Well, this year has been especially bad for me. I bought a car for one of my daughters who has very expensive tastes. I came up short at the end of the year, and I still owe taxes on the book royalties ~~that~~ I earned in April and the horse race ~~that~~ I won in September.

Luca: Sometimes I wish the United States collected a tax which is a strict percentage of a person's salary. A lot of other countries collect this type of "flat" tax.

Maya: Well, until that happens, I guess I will have to deal with the accountant after all. Let me know if he calls again.

Use Your English

ACTIVITY 1 listening/writing

STEP 1 Listen to the audio and take notes on descriptive information about the following items. You may want to listen a second time to check your notes.

CD1 Track 10

Example: *an apartment building* near downtown

1. braids —————————————
2. a joke —————————————
3. excuses —————————————
4. a ring —————————————
5. a model car —————————————
6. a writer —————————————
7. an engineer —————————————
8. colleges —————————————
9. a nurse —————————————
10. an artist —————————————
11. the hotel —————————————
12. a carnation —————————————
13. unattractive man —————————————
14. a phone booth —————————————

STEP 2 Now describe how each item fits into the story. Create sentences using relative clauses modifying objects.

Example: *Kimi and Fred lived in the same apartment building which was located near the downtown of Los Angeles.*

STEP 3 What do you think will happen next? Write a short paragraph that describes your thoughts. Use at least one relative clause modifying an object in your paragraph.

Activity 1 Step 1: Answers may vary. Possible answers are: 1. long, beautiful/ tied her braids in a knot to chair 2. teacher made Fred stay after school 3. Fred thought to knock on her door: newspaper? Paper to borrow? Walk to school? 4. gave Kimi a ring/ "My true love forever" 5. gave Fred a bright red model car/ on hood "My heart races for you" 6. Kimi wanted to write the Great American Novel 7. Fred wanted to design a famous bridge 8. on different coasts (CA and NY) 9. Fred married/ college classes 10. Kimi married/ church 11. met in lobby / high school prom 12. agreed to wear 13. smoked a cigar, scruffy beard, filthy clothes, gained weight 14. Kimi dialed the phone **Step 2:** Answers may vary. Possible answers are: 1. Kimi had long braids which Fred tied

3. Fred made excuses which would get Kimi to talk to him. 4. Fred gave a ring to Kimi which read "My true love forever." 5. Kimi gave Fred a model care on which was written "My heart races for you." 6. Kimi wanted to be the writer who wrote The Great American Novel. 7. Fred wanted to be an engineer who designed a famous bridge. 8. They went to colleges which were on different coasts. 9. Fred married a nurse whom he met in college classes. 10. Kimi married an artist that she met in church. 11. They agreed to meet in a hotel lobby which was where their prom was held. 12. They agreed to wear carnations which was how they would recognize each other. 13. Kimi saw an unattractive man who she thought was Fred. 14. Kimi went to a phone booth in which she made

EXERCISE 8 (OPTIONAL) [25 minutes]

In this final exercise students edit a dialogue to make it more informal, and then read it aloud.

1. Read the directions as a class. Ask a volunteer to read the two examples. What changed? How is the second sentence more informal than the first?

2. Have students work in pairs to edit the dialogue to make it more informal. Ask them to delete any object relative pronouns they think can be deleted and to use contractions whenever possible.

3. Have students role-play the dialogue.

4. Have a pair of volunteers act out the dialogue for the class in two ways: first, they should read the unedited lines of dialogue, then their edited version. Ask students to comment on the differences in tone. Is one style easier for them to understand than the other?

 For more practice, use *Grammar Dimensions 4* Workbook page 71, Exercise 8.

EXPANSION [25 minutes]

1. Ask students, in pairs, to look at picture 4 in Exercise 6 and write a dialogue between the two women. They should first write four or five lines of informal conversation for each woman.

2. Then, have them modify the dialogue so that it is more formal in style.

3. Ask two pairs of volunteers to act out their dialogues.

UNIT GOAL REVIEW [5 minutes]

Ask students to look at the goals on the opening page of the unit again. Refer to the pages of the unit where information on each goal can be found.

 For assessment of Unit 8, use *Grammar Dimensions 4 ExamView®*.

USE YOUR ENGLISH

The Use Your English activities at the end of the unit contain situations that should naturally elicit the structures covered in the unit. For a more complete discussion of how to use the Use Your English activities, see To the Teacher, LP page xxvi. While students are doing these activities in class, you can circulate and listen to see if they are using the structures accurately. Errors can be corrected after the activity has finished.

ACTIVITY 1 listening/writing [45 minutes]

CD1 Track 10

You may wish to use this activity after Exercise 1 on SB page 151. Students listen to a story about the intertwining lives of two people, Kimi Tamura and Fred Escobar, who were born on the same day in different cities in the United States and ended up living in the same building in Los Angeles. The audio contains numerous descriptions that use a variety of relative clauses modifying objects.

■ STEP 1

1. Tell students that they are going to listen to a story about the lives of two people who fell in love. Tell them that the story contains a number of descriptions that use a variety of relative clauses modifying objects.

2. Have students listen to the story and take notes on the listed items.

3. Then ask them to listen again to complete and check their notes, if they want to.

■ STEP 2

1. Read the directions and examples as a class. You may also want to do the first item together, making sure to include a relative clause modifying an object in your example.

2. Have students work in pairs to complete this step, in which they write sentences with relative clauses modifying objects. Encourage students to listen to the audio again if they cannot remember all the information.

3. Ask volunteers to share their answers with the class. Did any other students come up with different answers? Ask them to share theirs, as well.

■ STEP 3

1. Have students work independently to complete Step 3, in which they write a short paragraph about what they imagine will happen next in the story. Remind them to use relative clauses modifying an object where possible.

2. Ask volunteers to share their paragraphs with the class.

ACTIVITY 2 speaking/writing

■ **STEP 1**   In pairs, look at the following picture and describe what you see.

Eviction by Dierdre Luzwick

■ **STEP 2**   Write a paragraph using at least five relative clauses modifying objects.

Example: *This picture depicts the dangers of pollution on the environment. Animals are standing in line on a beach which is littered with boxes and cans . . .*

ACTIVITY 3 research on the web

 Using an Internet search engine such as Google® or Yahoo®, search for information on inventions, inventors, inventors' groups, or the Yankee Invention Exposition, then answer the questions below using reduced relative clauses.

Example: *Who do inventors look for at the Yankee Invention Exposition?*

 Inventors look for anyone ~~that has~~ the ability to inspect their widgets.

1. What inventions have a greater chance of being successful?

2. Why do inventors like to join clubs?

3. Who leads inventors' groups?

4. Where can inventors go to display or market their inventions?

ACTIVITY 4 reflection

Imagine that you are setting up the perfect study session. How do you normally organize your time? What kinds of materials, writing implements, locations do you prefer? Do you ever study with other students? What tasks or subjects do you study first? Write a short paragraph answering these questions about arranging and planning your time. Use at least five relative clauses that modify objects in your paragraph. When possible, try to reduce the relative clauses for greater conciseness.

Example: *I like to choose a desk (which is) near a well-lit window to begin my study session. I always use a pencil (~~that has~~) a brand-new eraser. . . .*

USE YOUR ENGLISH

ACTIVITY 2 speaking/writing
[30 minutes/homework]

You may wish to use this activity after Exercise 2 on SB page 152. Students, in pairs, describe a picture filled with detail, and then describe it in writing, using relative clauses modifying objects.

■ STEP 1

1. Read the directions. Have students work in pairs to do this step, in which they will take turns describing what they see in the picture. Remind them to use relative clauses that modify objects in their sentences, whenever possible.

2. Ask several pairs to share some of their descriptions with the class. Ask the class to identify the relative clauses and objects in the descriptions.

■ STEP 2

1. Ask for a volunteer to read the example. Ask students to identify the relative clauses in the sentence. What do they modify? (*objects*) Ask them to identify the objects that are modified. Are they people, animals, or things?

2. Have students work independently to write a paragraph describing the picture. Tell them to use at least five relative clauses modifying objects in their paragraphs.

3. Ask several volunteers to share their paragraphs with the class. Encourage others to share their most interesting observations with the class, as well.

METHODOLOGY NOTE

Lessons in fine art viewing and appreciation during language instruction allow students to engage in a perceptual experience with their peers while developing descriptive language ability. The development of this skill through art "encourage[s students] to value and respond to their own perceptions, observations, emotions, and intuition." Bring art postcards and books for your students to view and describe through presentations or in journals. Visit your program's art classrooms, or local galleries and museums with your class as time allows. Alongside the study of grammar, the study of art as part of the language learning experience encourages "self-expression and constitutes a powerful tool for self-discovery and development. It functions as a basic language and provides an essential bonding agent that connects and socializes us."

Source:
The University of Chicago, Laboratory Schools
http://www.ucls.uchicago.edu/academics/curriculum/
art.shtml (Accessed July 2007)

ACTIVITY 3 research on the web
[60 minutes/homework]

You may wish to use this activity, which makes an excellent homework assignment, after Exercise 6 on SB page 158. Students search the Internet for information on topics related to inventions, and then answer questions using reduced relative clauses.

1. Read the directions aloud to the class. Then write the example sentences on the board, but do not include the edits to the second sentence: *Who do inventors look for at the Yankee Invention Exposition? Anyone that has with the ability to inspect their widgets.*

2. Ask students what relative pronoun other than *that* could have been used in the second sentence. (*who*) Ask students to suggest ways to reduce the relative clause, and write responses on the board.

3. Have a volunteer write the edited sentence from the book on the board.

4. Ask volunteers to read the questions aloud.

5. Answer any questions students may have.

6. During the next class, ask students to share their written responses with the class.

ACTIVITY 4 reflection
[30 minutes]

In this activity, students think and write about effective study techniques using reduced relative clauses. You may wish to use Activity 4 after Exercise 7 on SB page 159 for practice with using reduced relative clauses in informal writing.

1. Ask a volunteer to read the introductory paragraph and the example.

2. Reread the paragraph, asking volunteers to give one or two answers to each question, and write responses on the board. Encourage them to use reduced relative clauses whenever possible.

3. Review the sentences on the board and discuss other ways to reduce the clauses.

4. Ask students to work independently to write a short paragraph answering the questions about arranging and planning their study time. Tell them to include at least five object-embedded relative clauses in their paragraphs.

5. Have volunteers read their paragraphs to the class. Ask others to identify the reduced clauses, and write these on the board.

UNIT GOALS

- **Distinguish restrictive from nonrestrictive relative clauses**
- **Use nonrestrictive relative clauses in definitions**
- **Use relative clauses to comment upon an entire idea**
- **Use nonrestrictive relative clauses with quantifying expressions**

OPENING TASK

The travel section of the newspaper is often filled with descriptive stories about interesting and exotic travel ideas. What kind of trip would you like to go on? What types of activities would you prefer? How could you persuade someone to take a similar tour?

■ STEP 1

With a classmate, select one of the following types of tours in which you would like to participate.

☐ Take a safari or other wildlife trek
☐ Go backpacking or hiking in the mountains
☐ Take a guided expedition
☐ Take a cross-country bike trip
☐ Take a cruise to one or more destinations
☐ Explore ancient ruins

☐ Take a wine-tasting tour
☐ Travel the route of a famous explorer
☐ Visit historic battlegrounds
☐ Tour one or more great castles
☐ Take a wellness vacation
☐ Visit one or more amusement parks
☐ Go camping
☐ Visit a ranch

■ STEP 2

With a partner, jot down notes to answer these questions about the tour you have selected.

- Where will you go? (*Go to a coast and swim with dolphins*) Where exactly is this located? (*Maui; one of the Hawaiian Islands in the U.S.A.*)

- What will you do? (*Swim with dolphins; intelligent mammals*) What equipment or skills are necessary for this activity? (*Snorkel; masks, snorkels, and fins*) What more can you say about this?

- In the evenings, what kind of cuisine will you eat? (*Luau*) What are the specific foods of this type of cuisine? (*roast pig, salmon, long rice, Haupia*)

■ STEP 3

Write a short paragraph for the travel section of the newspaper, convincing your reader to take this tour. Explain locations of special places and details about special equipment so that your reader will understand.

Example:

Anyone who is planning a trip should not forget the idea of going to Maui, which is the closest island to the big island of Hawaii in the Hawaiian Islands. Dolphins will be your morning swim companions. In the afternoon, you can rent masks, snorkels, and fins to snorkel around the beautiful coral reefs, which ring the island. In the evening, you can enjoy a traditional Hawaiian luau with roast pig, salmon, long rice, and Haupia, which is a traditional coconut pudding.

UNIT OVERVIEW

Unit 9 begins with a contrast between the form and meaning of nonrestrictive and restrictive relative clauses, and then explores three uses of nonrestrictive relative clauses: in definitions, to comment on an entire idea, and with quantifying expressions. This unit assumes that students have already studied restrictive relative clauses (see Units 7 and 8). It addresses the difficulties many students may have in distinguishing restrictive from nonrestrictive relative clauses and using nonrestrictive relative clauses appropriately in writing and speaking.

Due to the length of this unit, it has been divided into three lessons. Should a quicker review of the material be necessary, review each focus and the first exercise that follows it.

UNIT GOALS

Some instructors may want to review the goals listed on Student Book (SB) page 164 after completing the Opening Task so that students understand what they should know by the end of the unit. These goals can also be reviewed at the end of the unit when students are more familiar with the grammar terminology.

OPENING TASK [20 minutes]

The aim of this activity is to create a context in which students will need to review restrictive and use nonrestrictive relative clauses. The problem-solving format is designed to show the teacher how well the students can produce the target structures implicitly and spontaneously when they are engaged in a communicative task. For a more complete discussion of the purpose of the Opening Task, see To the Teacher, Lesson Planner (LP) page xxii.

Setting Up the Task

1. Discuss interesting and/or exotic trips students have taken or would like to take. Where did they go, and what did they see and do? Where did they stay, and what kinds of food did they eat?

2. Discuss different sources for tourism information: pamphlets, newspapers and magazines, TV shows, the Internet. If students wanted to take an exotic trip, what kinds of information would they look for, and where would they look for it?

Conducting the Task

1. Ask students to comment on the Hawaii travel ad. What does the ad seem to offer visitors to Hawaii?

2. Read the introductory paragraph as a class.

■ STEP 1

Ask a pair of volunteers to read Step 1 and the list of tours. Have students work in pairs to determine which ones are particularly attractive to them. Why did they choose those trips?

■ STEP 2

Have students work in pairs to answer the questions. You may want to walk around and listen in order to diagnose students' errors and to see if they are familiar with nonrestrictive relative clauses.

■ STEP 3

1. Read the directions and example as a class. What attractions and activities are mentioned in the example?

2. Were students surprised by anything they read in the paragraph?

3. Have students work independently to write a short paragraph for the travel section of the newspaper.

4. Have them work in small groups and take turns reading their paragraphs to the group.

Closing the Task

1. Ask several volunteers to share their paragraphs with the class.

2. Don't worry about accuracy at this point, though you may want to take notes of errors in meaning, form, or use in order to focus on those problems later.

GRAMMAR NOTE

Typical student errors (form)

- Using *that* rather than *which* to describe places or things in a nonrestrictive clause:—e.g., * *She handed me a sweater, that was made in Ireland, to keep me warm.* (See Focus 1.)

- In writing, setting off a restrictive clause with commas:—e.g., * *The player, who is the winner, receives the award.* (See Focus 1.)

- In writing, not setting off nonrestrictive clause with commas:—e.g., * *She's going to visit Sarah who is a good friend of hers.* (See Focus 1)

Typical student errors (use)

- When commenting on an entire idea, using a plural verb with *which*:—e.g., * *She discovered she did not have to take the tests, which are really good news.* (See Focus 3.)

- Using *which* rather than *whom* to refer to persons in quantifying expressions:—e.g., * *They asked five nurses, most of which worked during the day, to work all night last Saturday.* (See Focus 4.)

FOCUS 1 — Restrictive versus Nonrestrictive Relative Clauses

EXAMPLES	EXPLANATIONS
Meaning	A restrictive clause . . . A nonrestrictive clause . . .
(a) I tip tour guides who **provide good tours.**	• is necessary to identify the head noun it describes (not all tour guides, only the ones who give good tours).
(b) I tipped my tour guide, **who provided a splendid tour.**	• adds additional information; it does not help identify the tour guide in (b).
Form	
(c) I prefer to fly on airlines **that have direct routes to major cities.**	• is not set off by commas.
(d) When I return home to Chicago, I will telephone my mother, **who lives in Joliet.**	• is set off by one or more commas; it adds additional information to an already identified noun preceded by possessive adjective (*my mother*).
(e) Joliet, **which is a suburb of Chicago,** was a wonderful place to grow up.	• adds additional information to an already identified proper noun (*Joliet*).
(f) My mother will pick me up at O'Hare (**which is the international airport near Chicago**).	• is sometimes set off by parentheses.
(g) She usually meets me at the baggage claim, **which exits onto the street,** rather than at the gate inside the building.	• uses *which* (not *that*) to describe places or things; it adds additional information to a noun preceded by a definite article which is identifiable by inference (*the baggage claim (at the airport)*).
(h) NOT: She usually meets me at the baggage claim, that exits onto the street, rather than at the gate inside the building.	
(i) I always take the midnight flight, [*pause*] **which is never crowded.**	• is set off by a pause and a drop in intonation in speech.

EXERCISE 1

STEP 1   With a partner, underline the relative clauses in the following sentences and double underline the corresponding head nouns they refer to.

STEP 2   Determine if the clause carries essential information needed to identify the head noun or additional information by writing E (essential) or A (additional) next to each sentence.

STEP 3   Punctuate the relative clauses which carry additional information with commas.

STEP 4   Discuss why the information in the restrictive relative clause is essential and the information in the nonrestrictive relative clause with commas is additional and not necessary.

Example:

a. *The smog that covers Mexico City has become a serious health hazard.*

b. *Smog, which is a fog that has become polluted with smoke, is a pervasive problem in many large cities.*

a. *The smog that covers Mexico City has become a serious health hazard.*   E

The smog is specific smog in Mexico City that has become a serious health hazard. Therefore, the relative clause contains essential information and should not be separated from the head noun by commas.

b. *Smog, which is a fog that has become polluted with smoke, is a pervasive problem in many large cities.*   A

This nonrestrictive relative clause between commas adds additional information that is not essential to identifying which smog since the sentence is referring to all smog as a problem in many large cities.

E   1. a. The son who lives in New York will visit his mother in California.
A   b. Her only son who lives in New York will visit her in California.
E   2. a. The teacher who got married last year will not be returning this year.
A   b. Your English teacher who has a thorough knowledge of English grammar can help you with your grammar problems.
A   3. a. I studied at the University of Illinois which has a very good undergraduate program.
E   b. I studied at a university in Illinois which has a very good undergraduate program.
E   4. a. People who drink should not drive.
A   b. People who require water to survive may someday run out of pure water.

(Exercise 1 is continued on LP page 168.)

Exercise 1 Answers will vary. The following are suggested answers.   1. a. The son is a specific son who will visit his mother. The relative clause (RC) is restrictive as it contains essential information about one son (of many, we presume) and should not be separated from the head noun by commas. b. Her only son who lives in New York provides additional information about the one son and it isn't essential to identifying which son since the sentence is referring to only one son.   2. a. The teacher mentioned needs specific information to identify which teacher at a particular school or program. Therefore this information shouldn't be separated from the head noun. b. This information is not necessary to identify the teacher and is therefore separated with commas.   3. a. The University of Illinois is the specific university where the

speaker studied. All other information in the relative clause is additional and should be set off by commas. b. The clause is restrictive pointing out which university in Illinois the speaker is indicating. Therefore, the clause shouldn't be set off by commas.   4. a. People who drink are specific people who might but should not drive. The RC is restrictive as it contains essential information about what kind of people should receive the warning, and therefore people should not be separated from the head noun by commas. b. People, who require water to survive, provides additional information to the statement about the future of water availability. It isn't essential to identify which people since the sentence is referring to all people, not specific people. (The Exercise 1 answer key is continued on the following student book and lesson planner pages.)

FOCUS 1 [20 minutes]

Focus 1 first contrasts the difference in meaning between the two types of clauses, and then gives a detailed explanation of the differences in form between them.

1. **Lead-in:** Write the following two sentences on the board. *I admire teachers who are* _____. *I admire my English teacher,* _____. Ask students to comment on the two sentences: *What is similar? What is different?* If students don't explain, point out that the first sentence is speaking about teachers in general, but the second one is speaking about their particular English teacher.

2. Brainstorm on the board some characteristics of admirable teachers. Students may say: *well organized, fair, trustworthy, knowledgeable*, etc.

3. Brainstorm some characteristics of you, their teacher (or another teacher in the school). In this case, the qualities may be more specific: *red hair, knowledgeable about pronunciation, New Yorker*, etc.

4. Quickly review the explanations in Units 7 and 8 of how relative clauses are to combine several thoughts into one sentence. Write: *I admire teachers who are fair*. Ask students what this means. Clarify that they do not admire *all* teachers—they admire a certain type of teacher, *fair* teachers. Point out that this relative clause is used to clarify *which* kind of teachers are admired.

5. Write this sentence on the board: *I admire my English teacher, who is knowledgeable about pronunciation.* Ask students whether the information in the relative clause is needed for them to identify their English teacher. They should say *no* because they are all familiar with this talent of their teacher and this is extra or incidental information, stated almost as an afterthought. State that this is the purpose of a nonrestrictive relative clause: to add additional information that is not essential to defining the noun it modifies.

6. Write the terms *restrictive clause* and *nonrestrictive clause* on the board. Ask students to define *restrictive* (*something that limits*).

7. Read example (a) in the focus chart. Ask students to identify the relative clause (*who provide good tours*) and the noun that it modifies (*guides*). Ask if they need the information in the clause to identify the noun (*yes*).

8. Tell students that this type of relative clause is an example of a *restrictive clause*, and point to the term on the board. Explain that the clause *restricts*, or limits, the noun: in this sentence, the speaker is only referring to those *guides who provide good tours*. Ask a volunteer to read the explanation of a restrictive clause in the chart.

9. Read example (b), and elicit that the information in the *clause* is not needed to identify the noun. This is a *nonrestrictive clause.*

10. Have volunteers read the examples in the Explanations (Form) section of the focus chart.

11. Encourage students to ask questions about anything they do not understand.

LANGUAGE NOTE

Elicit that nonrestrictive clauses are often preceded by a pause and are spoken in a lower pitch than the rest of the sentence. Read examples from Focus 1, such as (b), (d), (e), (f), and (g), and ask students to raise their hands when they hear you pause and when they hear your pitch change.

EXERCISE 1 [25 minutes]

In this exercise students practice identifying and analyzing restrictive and nonrestrictive clauses, using the information they learned in Focus 1. Exercise 1 continues on SB page 168.

STEP 1

1. Read the directions, and write the first example on the board.

2. Ask a volunteer to underline the relative clause and double underline the corresponding head noun in the sentence. Have the students work in pairs to complete Step 1.

STEP 2

1. Ask, *Is the information in the clause needed to identify the head noun, or is it additional information?* Elicit that it is essential, and write an *E* beside the sentence on the board.

2. Repeat this process with the second example. Guide students in identifying that the information is additional. Have the pairs complete Step 2.

STEP 3 AND 4

1. Have students, in pairs, complete Steps 3 and 4.

2. Review answers with the class. Ask students to explain, in each case, why the information in each clause is essential or additional. Encourage them to refer back to Focus 1 as needed for their explanations. See answers on LP pages 166, 168, and 169.

For more practice, use *Grammar Dimensions 4* Workbook page 73, Exercise 1.

EXPANSION [30 minutes/homework]

Activity 1 (listening/writing) on SB page 176 is a good follow-up to Exercise 1, either as an in-class activity or as homework. Students listen to excerpts from tour guides of three different places, take notes, and then summarize the descriptions using nonrestrictive relative clauses.

E 5. a. When I get to New York, I'm going shopping at a store which I heard about from a friend.

A   b. When I get to New York, I'm going shopping at Saks Fifth Avenue which is located in downtown Manhattan.

E 6. a. We have spent a great deal of time refining a document which will be sent to the Grants and Contracts Office.

A   b. We have spent a great deal of time refining this document which will be sent on to the Grants and Contracts Office.

A 7. a. The world which is actually pear-shaped was once thought to be flat.

E   b. The world which we live in today is very different from the world a century ago.

A 8. a. He took an IQ test which refers to "intelligent-quotient" test before he moved to a different school.

E   b. He took an IQ test which measured verbal and math ability before he moved to a different school.

E 9. a. Have you heard about the Fulbright Scholars who receive scholarships to work and study in other countries?

A   b. Have you heard about the Fulbright Scholars who received scholarships to work and study in Hungary?

A 10. a. I would like to introduce the Professor Smith who chaired the task force report.

E   b. I would like to introduce Professor Smith who chaired the task force report.

A 11. a. We praise the university community which came forward and volunteered in a time of need.

E   b. We praise a university community which can come forward and volunteer in a time of need.

A 12. a. Internet addiction which has become more common today has many harmful effects.

E   b. Internet addiction which affects one's sense of self control is a harmful effect of computer use.

EXERCISE 2

Reread your notes from the Opening Task on pages 164–165. Write sentences from your notes with restrictive and nonrestrictive relative clauses. Write N next to the nonrestrictive relative clauses and R next to the restrictive relative clauses. Then, read your sentences aloud, inserting pauses with your nonrestrictive clauses.

Example: *Why not take an expedition to Macchu Picchu, which is the old capital of the Inca empire?* N

You can explore the ruins which the ancient Peruvians built on steep mountainsides. R

EXERCISE 3

For each numbered sentence, put brackets around the nonrestrictive relative clauses and circle the noun phrases they modify.

(1) The Specialty Travel Index, [which was founded in 1980 by C. Steen Hansen and Andy Alpine,] is an excellent source of information for travel agents as well as the average person interested in travel. (2) More than 400 tour operators advertise in this index, [which is available in paper and online versions (www.specialtytravel.com).] (3) The paper version, [which is published twice a year,] offers alphabetical listings of tour operators with accompanying websites, e-mails, addresses, and telephone numbers. (4) Entries are organized by subject matter and geographical emphasis and are cross-indexed for convenience. (5) In the online version, if travelers want to visit Aruba, [which is an island in the Caribbean,] they only need to search under "A" in the geographical location index. (6) If they would like a tour which specializes in "ranching," "river rafting," "rock climbing," or "romance," they only need to look under "R" in the "interest/activity" index. (7) "Cooking classes," "walrus-watching tours," "astrology tours," and "film festival tours" are some of the other special interest tours listed in the index.

(8) The Specialty Travel Index, [which is considered the "bible" of the special interest and adventure tour industry,] includes many interesting and experienced advertisers. (9) Expo Garden Tours, [which was established in 1988,] provides an opportunity for individual gardeners to explore some of the most beautiful gardens in the world. (10) Travelers can see tulip blooms in Holland, [which are most exquisite in the spring.] (11) Another "must-do" tour is the fourteen-day tour to gardens in Japan, [which features spectacular views of cherry blossoms and kurume azaleas as well as visits to cultural sites.] (12) Margaret Sanko and Heidi Beaumont, [who are co-founders of International Ventures, Ltd.,] specialize in trips to Eastern and Southern Africa. (13) They feature several types of safaris which would delight any traveler. (14) They have "highlight safaris," [which are for those who want to see the animals in premier game parks.] (15) They have "ventures," [which involve travel by road (often dusty and bumpy) with experienced guides from start to finish.] (16) They also have "wing safaris," [for travelers who would like to see the animals and landscape by air.] Finally, Jay and Annette Ciccarelli, a husband-wife team, sponsor culinary tours in Mallorca, [where they lead morning tours through food markets, wineries, cultural sites, and restaurants and spend the afternoons and evenings doing hands-on cooking workshops and serving travelers the creations which they have made.]

(17) Anyone planning a trip should not forget to consult The Specialty Travel Index, [which describes tours that fit any interest!]

5. a. The restrictive relative clause (RC) after a store identifies which store out of the many stores in New York: no commas necessary. b. A comma is necessary before the clause located after the name of a famous New York Store "Saks Fifth Avenue". The information that the store is located in downtown Manhattan is additional (commas needed) as the speaker is eagerly speaking about going to the store itself and the location is nonessential or additional.   6. a. Because the RC identifies a specific document and this information is essential, no commas are used to separate it from the

additional information is separated by a comma.   7. a. This clause adds additional information about the subject, and it is non-essential to the core meaning of the sentence. The RC is separated by commas. b. This sentence is talking about the modern world. To identify which world (and time period) the speaker means, we don't separate this head noun from the RC. It is a restrictive relative clause and essential to the meaning of the sentence (comparing today vs. a century ago).

(Exercise 1 answers are continued on LP page 169.)

EXERCISE 2 [20 minutes]

Exercise 2 builds on the work students did in the Opening Task. Students write sentences containing restrictive and nonrestrictive relative clauses using their notes from that task, and identify the different types of clauses.

1. Read the directions and two examples as a class. Ask volunteers to say how the clause in the first example is nonrestrictive, and in the second example is restrictive. What are the differences in punctuation between the two sentences?

2. Have students work independently to write their sentences, using their notes from the Opening Task. Remind them to include both restrictive and nonrestrictive relative clauses in their sentences.

3. Have students work in pairs to read and analyze their sentences. Remind them to pause before reading a nonrestrictive clause, and to lower their pitch.

4. Ask volunteers to read their partners' sentences to the class, and discuss these as a class.

EXPANSION [40 minutes]

Activity 2 (writing/speaking) on SB page 177 is a good follow-up to Exercise 2. Students, in groups of three, create and share sentences that describe celebrities using both restrictive and nonrestrictive relative clauses.

EXERCISE 3 [20 minutes]

In this exercise students continue their practice of the material from Focus 1, reading a passage from *The Specialty Travel Index* and identifying the nonrestrictive relative clauses and the noun phrases they modify.

1. Read the directions and the first sentence as a class. Ask students to locate commas in the sentence. Is the clause contained within the commas a restrictive or nonrestrictive relative clause?

2. Have students work in pairs to read all of the passage's sentences. Have them put brackets around the nonrestrictive relative clauses, and circle the noun phrases they modify.

3. Ask each pair to get together with another pair and compare and discuss answers.

4. Ask volunteers to read their answers to the class. Did they pause before each nonrestrictive clause, and lower their pitch when reading it? See answers on LP page 168.

EXPANSION [40 minutes]

Activity 4 (speaking/writing) on SB page 178 gives students the opportunity to interact and share information with their classmates about their home countries, orally and in writing, using a variety of nonrestrictive relative clauses. It is a good follow-up to the work students do in Exercise 3.

(Exercise 1 is continued from LP page 168.)

8. a. The RC should be separated by commas as the additional information adds little to the main intention of the main clause, only defining the main. b. No commas are used around the relative clause as it provides essential information about the subject for the sentence. Ability levels are important for schools to know. 9. a. This is non-restrictive relative clause and it needs commas because it adds additional information about the already identified Fulbright Scholars. b. This is a restrictive clause because it explains which particular group of Fulbright Scholars it is asking about. 10. a. By using the, it becomes clear that the introduction of the person is most important rather than the additional information presented about the professor. b. No commas are needed as we need to understand this essential information about this professor. 11. a. The praise is for a specific (the) university community therefore the remaining information is additional to whom the praise is for. Commas are used. b. The RC identifies which university community (of thousands) and is therefore essential information. 12. a. The RC adds non-essential, or additional, information. It is about when it occurs rather than what Internet addiction is. b. The information in the RC (the effect of the Internet on one's self-control) is essential information that describes the subject of the sentence.

Imagine you are a tourist visiting Vancouver, British Columbia, on your own. To entertain yourself, you took several tours of the city, which are listed below. Describe three tours you took in a letter to a friend. Use at least one nonrestrictive relative clause in each tour description.

Example:

Dear Owen,

I've really been enjoying myself in Vancouver. I've already spent a lot of money on tours, but it has been worth it. First, I took the City of Vancouver Tour, which was a five-hour tour of important sights around the city . . .

Regards,

Your Name

Name: City of Vancouver Tour
Price: $35.00
Description: five-hour bus tour of important points of interest: Stanley Park, Queen Elizabeth Park, Capilano Suspension Bridge

Name: Dinner Theatre Evening
Price: $70.00
Description: bus transportation, six-course dinner, tip, and ticket to theatre to see *A Streetcar Named Desire*

Name: Victoria City Tour
Price: $75.00
Description: 12-hour bus ride to the capital of British Columbia, ferry toll included, world famous Butchart Gardens

Name: Whistler Resort
Price: $100.00
Description: one day of skiing at world-class resort, lunch, ski rentals not included

Name: Fishing Trip
Price: $175.00
Description: half-day of fishing on Pacific Coast, private boat, guide, tackle, bait, license, lunch

---

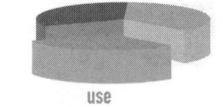

FOCUS 2	Nonrestrictive Relative Clauses in Definitions

use

EXAMPLES	EXPLANATION
(a) Gastroenteritis, **which is an inflammation of the stomach and the large intestines,** is on the rise because of passengers eating contaminated food or drinking tainted water on some cruise ships.	Nonrestrictive relative clauses are often used for defining terms in sentences.
(b) When a higher than normal number of passengers or crew become sick on a cruise, ships implement the "vessel sanitation program," **which requires additional cleaning procedures and restriction of sick passengers to their cabins.**	

EXERCISE 5

Review your answers to Exercise 3 and identify which nonrestrictive relative clauses are used for describing terms. Rewrite these sentences on a separate sheet of paper.

EXERCISE 6

Imagine you are a world traveler describing to an inexperienced traveler what you bring on a trip. Look at the list below, and add one more item of your own. Then, write sentences describing the items you always take with you and why. Use a nonrestrictive relative clause to define each item.

Example: laptop
I always bring a laptop, which is a portable computer, so that I can work on the plane and in my hotel room. OR
To assure that I can do my work while I am away, the first thing I pack is a laptop, which is a portable computer.

1. luggage cart
2. money belt
3. travel iron
4. adapter
5. travel calculator
6. Swiss army knife
7. book light
8. _____

Exercise 4   Answers will vary. The following is an example answer:

Dear _____,

I just got back from my trip to Vancouver. What a wonderful time I had! To orient myself, I took the City of Vancouver Tour, which was a five-hour bus ride to important points of interest. Then, that first evening, I paid $70 for the Dinner Theatre Evening, which consisted of a six-course dinner and the play *A Streetcar Named Desire*.

On the next full tour day, I took the Victoria City Tour, which was a 12-hour bus ride to the capital of British Columbia. I especially loved seeing the Butchart Gardens, which are world famous.

The next day I decided to go skiing at the Whistler Resort, but I did not realize how expensive it would be. I paid $100 for the ski tows and for my lunch, which was a gourmet feast.

On my last full day I took the Fishing Trip, which included lunch as well as fishing on the Pacific Coast and cost $175. Although the weather wasn't very good, I enjoyed the boat ride, which came with a private guide, tackle, bait, a license and lunch.

Well, I'll fill you in on more of the details when I return.

(Suggested answers to Exercise 5 and Exercise 6 are found on LP page 173.)

EXERCISE 4 (OPTIONAL) [25 minutes]

In this exercise students practice writing descriptions of travel tours using nonrestrictive relative clauses.

1. Read the directions and example as a class. Ask students to identify any nonrestrictive relative clauses they see in the example.
2. Have students work independently to write their descriptions of three tours. Remind them to use at least one nonrestrictive relative clause in each description.
3. If students are having difficulty using nonrestrictive relative clauses, remind them that proper nouns are considered "identifiable" and can be followed by nonrestrictive relative clauses, which require the comma.
4. Ask students to take turns reading their descriptions to a partner. Then, have them exchange papers and edit them for proper punctuation.
5. Ask volunteers to share their descriptions with the class. See sample answer on LP page 170.

EXPANSION [60 minutes/homework]

Activity 5 (research/speaking) on SB page 179 makes a good homework assignment after students study Focus 1 and complete Exercise 4. Students collect information about places they would like to visit and discuss them in small groups, using nonrestrictive relative clauses.

LESSON PLAN 2

FOCUS 2 [15 minutes]

Focus 2 explains the use of nonrestrictive relative clauses in definitions. This information will be particularly useful to students in their writing.

1. **Lead-in:** Write *gastroenteritis* on the board and ask several volunteers to define it in a sentence that uses a nonrestrictive relative clause. Write their definitions on the board.
2. Ask a volunteer to read the explanation in the focus chart, and then the first example. Is this definition of *gastroenteritis* similar to any of those on the board?
3. Ask another volunteer to read the second example. What term is defined by the nonrestrictive relative clause?
4. After reading the focus chart examples together, ask students to brainstorm computer-related terms, such as *floppy disk, DVD, hard drive, search engine*, etc., and write these on the board.
5. Ask students to create sentences in which they define these terms using nonrestrictive relative clauses. For example: *I copy all my files onto a DVD, which is a type of removable disc.*

EXERCISE 5 [15 minutes]

In this review exercise students revisit their answers to Exercise 3 and identify the nonrestrictive relative clauses that are used to define terms.

1. Ask students to look back at *The Specialty Travel Index* passage in Exercise 3, in which they have already put brackets around the nonrestrictive relative clauses and circles around the noun phrases the clauses modified.
2. Have students rewrite the sentences that contain the nonrestrictive relative clauses used in the passage to define terms on a separate piece of paper.
3. Ask students to underline the defining clause and double-underline the term that is defined in each case. See the answer key on LP page 173.

 For more practice, use *Grammar Dimensions 4* Workbook page 74, Exercise 2.

EXPANSION [60 minutes/homework]

Activity 6 (research on the web) on SB page 179 is an excellent homework assignment following Exercise 5. Students locate scientific articles on the Internet and analyze the use of nonrestrictive relative clauses in each.

EXERCISE 6 [20 minutes]

Students practice writing sentences with nonrestrictive relative clauses that are used to define terms, applying what they learned in Focus 2.

1. Read the directions as a class. Ask three different volunteers to read the two examples. Ask others to identify the nonrestrictive relative clause in each. Where in each sentence does the nonrestrictive relative clause occur?
2. Have students work independently to write sentences describing the list of travel items. Ask them to add one item of their own to the list, and describe it.
3. Have students, in pairs, take turns reading their definitions. Then, have them exchange papers and correct any punctuation mistakes. See possible answers on LP page 173.

For more practice, use *Grammar Dimensions 4* Workbook page 75, Exercise 3.

EXPANSION [30 minutes/homework]

Activity 7 (reflection) on SB page 179 will give students additional writing practice with nonrestrictive relative clauses used in definitions. It can be done in class or assigned as homework. In this activity students find and write definitions for five new terms they find in a textbook, using nonrestrictive relative clauses.

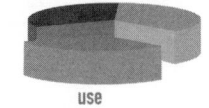

FOCUS 3 — Using a Relative Clause to Comment on an Entire Idea

use

EXAMPLES	EXPLANATION
(a) Last week I returned from a three-week cruise, **which was a relief.** (b) I had eaten too much food, **which was a big mistake.**	Some nonrestrictive relative clauses comment on a whole idea in the main clause. These are used most often in informal conversation and always begin with *which*.

EXERCISE 7

STEP 1 Below are excerpts from letters you have written to friends and family about your travel mishaps. How would you characterize these mishaps to your next-door neighbor in conversation? Use one of the following adjectives in your comments or one of your own:

disappointing	frightening	painful
exasperating	tiring	embarrassing
expensive	stressful	upsetting

Example: My brother and I were traveling in Mexico City. We got stuck in a horrible traffic jam in our taxi.

When my brother and I were traveling in Mexico City, we got stuck in a horrible traffic jam, which was very exasperating.

1. My friend and I wanted to save money in Venice. We walked from the train station all the way to our hotel.
2. I went hiking in the Sierra Nevada Mountains. I almost fell off a mountain trail.
3. I went on a bike tour of Canada. I fell down and broke my leg.
4. I left my traveler's checks in my hotel room. I did not have any way to pay my bill at an expensive Tokyo restaurant.
5. Last year I flew to Paris. I had to wait three extra hours to catch my return flight home.
6. I went on a ski trip and broke my wrist. I did not have health insurance so I had to pay for the X-ray myself.
7. I almost missed my flight to London. I had to run to the check-in counter with my suitcase and only had two minutes to spare.
8. I ate something in a restaurant that I had never tasted before. I got sick and could not sleep the entire night.

STEP 2 In groups of three, talk about a travel mishap similar to the ones in Step 1. Student A tells about a mishap. Student B comments on Student A's travel mishap. Student C summarizes the mishap and comments on it using a relative clause.

Example: **Student A:** *When I was in San Francisco, I took the wrong bus to Fisherman's Wharf.*

Student B: *That must have been frustrating.*

Student C: *When Kathy (Student A) was in San Francisco, she took the wrong bus to Fisherman's Wharf, which was really frustrating.*

ANSWER KEY

Exercise 7 Answers will vary. Possible answers are: 1. When my friend and I wanted to save money in Venice, we walked from the train station all the way to our hotel, which was tiring. 2. When I went hiking in the Sierra Nevada Mountains, I almost fell off a mountain trail, which was frightening. 3. When I went on a bike tour of Canada, I fell down and broke my leg, which was painful. 4. When I left my traveler's checks in my hotel room, I did not have any way to pay my bill at an expensive Tokyo restaurant, which was embarrassing. 5. Last year, when I flew to Paris, I had to wait three extra hours to catch my return flight home, which was exasperating. 6. When I went on a ski trip and broke my wrist, I did not have health insurance, so I had to pay for the X-ray myself, which was expensive. 7. When I almost missed my flight to London, I had to run to the check-in counter with my suitcase and only had two minutes to spare, which was stressful. 8. When I ate something in a restaurant that I had never tasted before, I got sick and could not sleep the entire night, which was upsetting.

FOCUS 3 [25 minutes]

1. **Lead-in:** Ask four volunteers to tell you something *scary, entertaining, painful,* or *humorous* that happened to them. Each volunteer should choose a different kind of story to relate.

2. Summarize what each student says in a sentence that comments on an entire idea using a nonrestrictive relative clause. For example: *Last year Yuko was almost attacked by a bear while she was camping, which was really scary.* Write your summary sentences on the board.

3. Read the contents of the focus chart.

4. Ask students to identify the nonrestrictive relative clause in each of the four sentences on the board, and ask them to say what they think the function of each clause is. They should mention that it is used to comment on an entire idea in the main clause. Point out to students that this structure is usually used in casual conversation.

EXERCISE 7 [25 minutes]

Exercise 7 asks students to apply what they have just learned in Focus 3 about using nonrestrictive relative clauses to comment on an entire idea.

STEP 1

1. Read the directions and the list of adjectives as a class.

2. Ask a volunteer to read the example. Elicit the changes between the two sentences: the first begins with *when,* and adds a nonrestrictive relative clause at the end of the second sentence. Elicit that that clause begins with *which.*

3. Have students work independently to combine each pair of sentences into one sentence that includes a nonrestrictive relative clause and one of the adjectives from the list or one of their own.

4. Review answers as a class. Encourage students who came up with different constructions to also share these. See possible answers on LP page 172.

STEP 2

1. Read the directions and example as a class.

2. Students work in groups of three to complete Step 2. If students don't have any travel mishaps, they can make one up or tell one that happened to a friend. They might even choose a story from Step 1 to expand on.

3. Ask several groups to act out their exchanges for the class. Does any group have a summary sentence that they are particularly proud of? Ask them to share it with the class.

 For more practice, use *Grammar Dimensions 4* Workbook page 77, Exercise 4.

EXPANSION [25 minutes]

Have students work in small groups to continue their work with commenting on a whole idea using nonrestrictive relative clauses.

1. Have students work in small groups of three or four. Ask them to choose a general topic to discuss, such as new federal legislation or energy consumption in the United States and abroad.

2. Model how to comment on an idea using nonrestrictive relative clauses—e.g., *Many Americans drive SUVs, which contributes to excessive gasoline consumption in this country.*

3. Ask several volunteers to make statements about the topic.

4. Have each student write two sentences about the topic their group has chosen. They should use nonrestrictive relative clauses to comment on an entire idea.

5. Ask them to share their sentences with the group, and discuss the topic.

6. Ask volunteers to summarize their group's discussion.

ANSWER KEY

Exercise 5 Answers are the sentences that contained nonrestrictive relative clauses that are defining terms.

(5) In the online version, if travelers want to visit Aruba, which is an island in the Caribbean, they only need to search under "A" in the geographical location index. (8) The Specialty Travel Index, which is considered the "bible" of the special interest and adventure tour industry, includes many interesting and experienced advertisers. (12) Margaret Sanko and Heidi Beaumont, who are co-founders of International Ventures, Ltd., specialize in trips to Eastern and Southern Africa. (14) They have "highlight safaris," which are for those who want to see the animals in premier game parks. (15) They have "ventures," which involve travel by road (often dusty and bumpy) with experienced guides from start to finish. (17) Anyone planning a trip should not forget to consult *The Specialty Travel Index*, which describes tours that fit any interest!

Exercise 6 Answers will vary. Possible answers are: 1. To save my back, I always use a luggage cart, which carries suitcases that weigh up to 300 pounds. 2. With thieves and pickpockets rampant around the world, I would never forget my money belt, which wraps around my waist under my shirt. 3. I always bring a travel iron, which is smaller and lighter than a regular iron, because I often need to touch up my shirts after they have been sitting in a suitcase for hours. 4. I would never forget my adapter, which allows me to plug in any electrical appliance in any electrical outlet around the world. 5. To orient myself to the value of currency in the country I am visiting, I always bring my travel calculator, which numerically converts my currency to the currency of the new country in a push of a button. 6. Because I never know where I will be, I always bring my Swiss army knife, which contains fifteen different tools for every occasion. 7. To save my eyesight, I always pack my book light, which takes three small batteries but provides a lot of light.

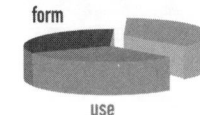

form

use

FOCUS 4

Using Nonrestrictive Relative Clauses to Quantify and Comment about Features

EXAMPLES	EXPLANATIONS
(a) There are many benefits to the new plan, **many of which** are not quantifiable.	Some nonrestrictive relative clauses comment on all of or some portion of a group of persons or things. To form this type of clause, combine a quantifier or number (such as *all of, the rest of, none of, many of, each of, two of, one-hundred of*) with a relative pronoun.
(b) I need three volunteers, **one of whom** must be strong.	
(c) Dr. Tom is the President of the Pharmaceutical League, **the title of which** is less important than the responsibility.	Other nonrestrictive relative clauses comment upon some features or aspects of persons, things, or ideas by combining a noun phrase (such as *purpose, title, design, sense, appearance, result, news*) with a relative pronoun *which*. Note that the relative pronoun is an object of a preposition in (c) and (d).
(d) **They could not agree on anything**, the result of which **was a divorce**.	

EXERCISE 8

A group of teachers are traveling to Vietnam this summer; however, because of different travel interests, they will be arriving and departing at different times from the same three cities: Ho Chi Minh City (HCMC), Hue, and Hanoi.

Study the following schedule with the dates and times (morning or afternoon) of arrival. Then, write a fax to a travel service in Vietnam that will arrange to pick up the teachers from the airport and deliver them to their hotels. The beginning of the letter appears on the next page.

NAME	CITY	ARRIVE	DEPART	CITY	ARRIVE	DEPART	CITY	ARRIVE	DEPART
Peterson	HCMC	6:15 AM	6:20 AM	Hue	6:20 AM	6:21 PM	Hanoi	6:21 PM	7:30 PM
McGill	HCMC	6:18 AM	6:20 AM	Hue	6:20 AM	6:27 AM	Hanoi	6:27 AM	7:30 PM
Orselli	HCMC	6:15 AM	6:20 AM	Hue	6:20 AM	6:27 AM	Hanoi	6:27 AM	7:30 AM
Hopf	HCMC	6:18 PM	6:22 AM	Hue	6:22 AM	6:27 AM	Hanoi	6:27 AM	7:30 AM
Nguyen	HCMC	6:18 PM	6:22 AM	Hue	6:22 AM	6:27 PM	Hanoi	6:27 PM	7:30 AM

Date: _____   Time: _____

To: Vietnam Travel Service   Phone: _____   Fax: _____

From: _____   Phone: _____   Fax: _____

Number of Pages: ___1___

Comments:

To Whom It May Concern:
A group of teachers will be coming to Vietnam for a visit. I would very much appreciate it if you could arrange airport transportation for the teachers, all of whom have slightly different schedules. Peterson and Orselli, both of whom will arrive at Ho Chi Minh City on June 15, must be picked up in the morning . . .

EXERCISE 9

Create sentences using nonrestrictive relative clauses containing the following nouns/clauses and noun phrases followed by *of-which* clauses.

Example: the city hall (the design of which)

Mapleton built a new city hall, the design of which was meant to inspire its citizens.

1. a mining accident (the news of which)
2. A man leaped out from behind the bushes (the appearance of which)
3. a civil war (an event of which)
4. They opened some new nursery schools (the result of which)
5. poverty (circumstances of which)
6. two papers (the purpose of which)
7. His children were all failures in the business world (an observation of which)
8. the robbery (the circumstances of which)

ANSWER KEY

Exercise 9 Answers will vary. Possible answers are: 1. Four men were killed in a mining accident, the news of which reached their families after 72 long hours. 2. A man leaped out from behind the bushes, the appearance of whom scared the girls. 3. Tensions resulted in a civil war, an event from which the nation would never recover. 4. They opened some new nursery schools, the result of which was improved childhood education. 5. After the floods, poverty, the circumstances of which had never been experienced by the people, gripped the entire region. 6. Two papers are required, the purpose of which is screening for graduate school. 7. His children all went into show business, an achievement of which the banker was not proud. 8. The robbery, the circumstances of which were a little unclear, took place at 3 p.m.

FOCUS 4 [20 minutes]

Focus 4 explains the use of nonrestrictive relative clauses to quantify and comment about all or a portion of a group of persons or things.

1. **Lead-in:** Write the quantifying expressions in the focus chart on the board: *all of, most of, none of, many of, each of, two of.*
2. Read the explanation and the first example. Which expression does it use? (*many of which*) What does the clause modify? (*many benefits*) How does it quantify the noun? (*It refers to* many of *the calls, not* all *of them.*)
3. Ask a volunteer to read the second example, and ask students to analyze this example, as well.
4. Tell students that this construction in examples (a–d) is much more common in writing than in speech although these constructions are certainly used in formal speech.

EXERCISE 8 [20 minutes]

In this exercise students write a fax using nonrestrictive relative clauses to quantify and comment about features of a travel itinerary, using the principles outlined in Focus 4.

1. Read the text, the schedule and the sample part of the fax as a class. Ask students to identify the nonrestrictive relative clauses in the sample sentences. What does each refer to?
2. Have students work in pairs to write a fax using the information in the table. Explain that they should fill in the information about date, time, etc., and then write sentences with nonrestrictive relative clauses to quantify and comment about features of the travel itineraries of each person in the Comments section.
3. Have each pair exchange faxes with another pair, and review and discuss them.
4. Ask several volunteers to read their faxes to the class.

 For more practice, use *Grammar Dimensions 4* Workbook page 78, Exercise 5.

EXPANSION [30 minutes/homework]

Activity 3 (writing) on SB page 177 can be assigned after Exercise 8, either as in-class work or homework. It could also be used as a diagnostic or a testing activity in which students demonstrate their ability to use nonrestrictive relative clauses. Encourage students to try to use all the different types of nonrestrictive relative clauses they studied in this unit.

EXERCISE 9 [20 minutes]

In this final exercise students continue practicing the principles they learned in Focus 4 of using nonrestrictive relative clauses to quantify and comment about features.

1. Read the directions and example as a class. Ask students to look back at Focus 4 and give the explanation for when to use this type of construction.
2. Remind students that this *of-which* type of construction is much more common in writing than in informal speech.
3. Have students work independently to write their sentences.
4. Have them exchange papers with a partner and review and discuss their choices.
5. Ask volunteers to share their sentences with the class. Encourage students who came up with different constructions to share these with the class, as well. See possible answers on LP page 174.

 For more practice, use *Grammar Dimensions 4* Workbook page 79, Exercise 6.

UNIT GOAL REVIEW [5 minutes]

Ask students to look at the goals on the opening page of the unit again. Refer to the pages of the unit where information on each goal can be found.

 For a grammar quiz review of Units 7–9, refer students to pages 80–82 in the *Grammar Dimensions 4* Workbook.

ExamView Test Generator For assessment of Unit 9, use *Grammar Dimensions 4* ExamView®.

Use Your English

ACTIVITY 1 listening/writing

CD1 Tracks 11, 12, 13

Listen to the audio, which gives excerpts from tour guides of three different places. Take notes about the famous sights. Afterwards, summarize the tour or portions of the tour using nonrestrictive relative clauses.

Sights	Characteristics
Example: Lafayette Park	one of the best-groomed parks in Washington, D.C.
The White House	construction began in 1792
Treasury Building	Andrew Jackson wanted to keep his eye on people handling cash

First, they saw Lafayette Park, which is one of the best-groomed parks in Washington, D.C. Then, they saw the White House, whose construction began in 1792. Finally, they saw the Treasury Building, which Andrew Jackson wanted to watch carefully because it housed the money.

ACTIVITY 2 writing/speaking

■ STEP 1

In groups of three, name two facts that are common knowledge about the following people. Then, create one or more sentences that contain relative clauses about these individuals.

John Lennon	Winston Churchill	Abraham Lincoln
Mother Teresa	Princess Diana	Joan of Arc
Fidel Castro	Mahatma Gandhi	

Example: *John Lennon (lead singer of the Beatles, born in Liverpool, England, was killed in New York) John Lennon, who was the lead singer of the Beatles, was born in Liverpool, England.*

■ STEP 2

Now think of another famous person you are familiar with. Present facts about this person to your classmates.

ACTIVITY 3 writing

You are preparing to be a tour guide of the city or your hometown or the city you are presently living in. Think of 5 sights that are in a two-mile radius and write the script you would use, incorporating as many details as possible about the sights, such as historical origin, age, and unique aspects.

Example: *At the beginning of the tour, we will start with the most important place in my town, which is the Plaza Leon. The Plaza Leon, which is more than one hundred years old, is the gathering place for young people on Friday and Saturday nights and for parents and children on Sunday afternoons. Four streets extend out from the Plaza, which have wide sidewalks and are tree-lined. Hernandez Street, which was named after the first mayor of the city, contains all of the food stores—bakeries, fish markets, vegetable stands, etc. Fernando Street, which the first mayor named after his only son, is where all of the professional offices are housed. Via del Mar Street, whose pavement is made of cobblestone, is the only street which still has its original surface. Finally, two universities, one of which is the most famous university in my home country, are located on Horatio Street, which is my favorite street of all.*

USE YOUR ENGLISH

The Use Your English activities at the end of the unit contain situations that should naturally elicit the structures covered in the unit. For a more complete discussion of how to use the Use Your English Activities, see To the Teacher, LP page xxvi. While students are doing these activities in class, you can circulate and listen to see if they are using the structures accurately. Errors can be corrected after the activity has finished.

ACTIVITY 1
listening/writing
[30 minutes]

CD1 Tracks 11,12,13

You may wish to use this activity after Exercise 1 on SB page 167. Students listen to excerpts from tour guides of three different places, take notes, and then summarize the descriptions using nonrestrictive relative clauses.

1. Tell students that they are going to listen to excerpts from tour guides of three different places.

2. Write these place names that students will hear on the board, so that they know how to spell them: *Number 1: Flagstaff House, Cotton Tree Drive, Victoria Peak Tram Terminus, Botanical and Zoological Gardens; Number 2: Monastery of San Lorenzo de El Escorial, parallelogram, slate columns, dome of the temple, cloister; Number 3: Getty Center, panoramic view*

3. Read the directions and example as a class. Ask students to identify the nonrestrictive clauses in the example. What does each modify?

4. Have students listen to the audio once without taking notes.

5. Ask students to listen again and take notes about the places that are described.

6. Encourage students to listen a third time to complete and check their notes, if they want to.

7. Ask students to summarize the tour, in its entirety or in parts, using nonrestrictive relative clauses.

8. Ask volunteers to share their answers with the class. Did any other students come up with different answers? Ask them to share theirs, as well.

ACTIVITY 2
writing/speaking
[40 minutes]

This activity is a good follow-up to Exercise 2 on SB page 168. Students, in groups of three, create and share sentences that describe celebrities using restrictive and nonrestrictive relative clauses.

■ STEP 1

1. Ask one volunteer to read the directions and the list of celebrities' names in Step 1, and ask another to read the example. Ask students to point out the relative clause. What does it modify? Is it restrictive, or nonrestrictive? Is the information it contains necessary to identify the noun it modifies?

2. Have students work in groups of three to complete Step 1. Encourage them to write more than one sentence about each celebrity.

3. Have students take turns reading their sentences to the group. Remind them to pause before a nonrestrictive relative clause and to lower their pitch when reading it.

VARIATION

Have students not name the person in their sentences, but rather refer to the person as "this man" or "this woman." Have the other members of the group guess who it is.

■ STEP 2

1. Have students work independently to write a description of another famous person not on the list, and share it with their group.

2. Ask volunteers from each group to share their group's best descriptions with the class.

ACTIVITY 3
writing
[30 minutes/homework]

Activity 3 can be assigned after Exercise 8 on SB page 174, either as in-class work or homework. It could also be used as a diagnostic or a testing activity in which students demonstrate their ability to use nonrestrictive relative clauses. Encourage students to try to use all the different types of nonrestrictive relative clauses they have studied. Encourage them to use quantifying expressions, and give overall comments when appropriate.

1. Read the directions aloud to the class. Then read the example slowly, line by line, and ask students to raise their hands when they hear a nonrestrictive relative clause. Reread the sentence, and have students say what kind of nonrestrictive relative clause it is and what the clause modifies.

2. Have students work independently to write a tour of a two-mile area of their hometown or city, describing at least five sights in detail. Ask them to use the different types of nonrestrictive relative clauses they studied in this unit.

3. Have students exchange papers with a partner and review them. You may want to ask students to identify each nonrestrictive relative clause, say what kind it is and what it modifies, as you did with the example.

4. Ask several volunteers to read their descriptions to the class. How many students were able to use all the types of nonrestrictive relative clauses covered in this unit?

ACTIVITY **4** speaking/writing

Interview several members of your class about various aspects of their native countries. Record that information below. Then, write several sentences on a separate sheet of paper, summarizing what you have learned using nonrestrictive relative clauses

Example: *María, who is from Mexico, likes mariachi music. She also likes horchata, which is a popular white milky drink.*

1. Name _____ Native Country _____

National Foods, Sports, Dances, etc. _____
_____
_____

2. Name _____ Native Country _____

National Foods, Sports, Dances, etc. _____
_____
_____

3. Name _____ Native Country _____

National Foods, Sports, Dances, etc. _____
_____
_____

4. Name _____ Native Country _____

National Foods, Sports, Dances, etc. _____
_____
_____

5. Name _____ Native Country _____

National Foods, Sports, Dances, etc. _____
_____
_____

 research/speaking

Visit a travel agency and bring in various travel brochures for places you would like to visit. In small groups, compare different destinations and places to stay.

Example: *I want to go to Hong Kong, which has many four-star hotels.*

ACTIVITY **6** research on the web

 With a partner, go to *InfoTrac® College Edition* and locate four scientific articles on any topic of your choice. Then, locate examples of nonrestrictive relative clauses in each one. Identify whether each nonrestrictive relative clause is used to provide a definition or to comment upon an entire idea or some portion of a group of persons, animals, or things.

 reflection

Select one of your textbooks which contains some subject matter which is new to you. Skim through the pages to identify at least five words you do not know. If the words are not described, try looking them up in a dictionary or by referring back to your textbook. Then, write five sentences describing these words. Be sure to use nonrestrictive relative clauses.

Example: *A debit card, which looks like a credit card, is used to obtain instant cash from an automatic teller.*

USE YOUR ENGLISH

ACTIVITY 4 speaking/writing [40 minutes]

This activity gives students the opportunity to interact and share information with their classmates about their home countries, orally and in writing, using a variety of nonrestrictive relative clauses. It is a good follow-up to the work students do in Exercise 3 on SB page 169.

1. Read the directions and example as a class. Ask students to identify the two nonrestrictive relative clauses in the example. What does each modify, and how?

2. Model how to interview classmates. Make a three-column chart on the board with the headings *Name/Native Country, National Foods, Sports, Dances,* etc. Ask a volunteer to interview another volunteer, and write the information on the board.

3. Have students reproduce the chart from the text on a separate piece of paper. Give them a time limit for interviewing their classmates, such as 15 minutes.

4. Give them another time limit, such as 10 minutes, for writing several sentences about the interviewees.

5. Ask several volunteers to read their sentences to the class. Discuss their use of nonrestrictive relative clauses.

VARIATION

Have volunteers read their description without naming the interviewees, and have the class guess who is being described.

ACTIVITY 5 research/speaking [60 minutes/homework]

Activity 5 makes a good homework assignment after students study Focus 1 and complete Exercise 4 on SB page 170. Students collect information about places they would like to visit and discuss them in small groups, using nonrestrictive relative clauses.

1. Read the directions and example as a class. Brainstorm a list of places in the world students would like to visit, and write these on the board.

2. Ask the class to call out any facts they know about each place, and write those on the board.

3. Have volunteers combine the facts into one- or two-sentence descriptions of each place, using nonrestrictive relative clauses.

4. Tell students that they can gather travel information by visiting a travel agency, researching information in the library, and/or on the Internet. Ask them to find information about places to stay, things to see and do, and places to eat.

5. Ask students to find information about at least two places they would like to visit.

6. During the next class, have students describe their locations in small groups of three or four.

7. Ask volunteers from each group to share several descriptions with the class. Who else would like to visit these places?

ACTIVITY 6 research on the web [60 minutes/homework]

In Activity 6 students locate scientific articles using InfoTrac and analyze the use of nonrestrictive relative clauses in each. This activity is an excellent homework assignment following Exercise 5 on SB page 171.

1. Ask a volunteer to read the directions.

2. If possible, have students work in pairs. They could also complete the activity on their own, and share their results with a partner.

3. Tell students to print out the four scientific articles they found on InfoTrac. Ask them to bracket all the nonrestrictive relative clauses and circle the nouns they modify.

4. Have them analyze each clause in terms of whether each nonrestrictive relative clause is used to provide a definition or to comment upon an entire idea or some portion of a group of persons, animals or things.

ACTIVITY 7 reflection [30 minutes]

In this activity, students find and write definitions for five new terms they find in one of their own textbooks. You may wish to use Activity 7 after Exercise 6 on SB page 171 for additional writing practice with nonrestrictive relative clauses used in definitions.

1. Read the directions and example as a class. Ask students to identify the nonrestrictive relative clause in the example. What does it modify? How does it modify *debit card*? (*by defining it*). What punctuation marks are used to set off the clause?

2. Have students work independently to choose a textbook that contains some subject matter that is new to them. They should identify at least five new words and write sentences defining them, using nonrestrictive relative clauses.

4. Tell students that they can look up the meanings of the new words in a dictionary or other reference source. Remind them that they need to create original definitions.

UNIT GOALS

- Know when relative adverbs can be used in place of relative pronouns

- Know the different patterns for using relative adverb clauses and use them correctly

- Know when to use the different patterns in speaking versus writing

OPENING TASK

What Do You Do to Stay Healthy?

As we all know, just as important as work are the activities that help us to maintain physical and mental health. Such activities could include working out in a health club, playing individual sports or team sports, dancing, gardening, playing chess, or meditation as just a few examples.

■ STEP 1

Pair up with a classmate. Take turns interviewing each other to find out two things that each of you do to promote your physical or mental health. For each activity, ask and respond to the following information.

1. the date or time period when you started this activity (for example, when you were a certain age or a certain number of months or years ago)
2. the main reasons why you engage in the activity (for example, to enjoy the out of doors, to get aerobic exercise)
3. the place or places where you do the activity
4. your favorite times for doing the activity (for example, a certain time of day or a certain day or days of the week)

■ STEP 2

Share some of the information that you have gathered about each other with your classmates.

UNIT OVERVIEW

This unit shows students how to use the relative adverbs *where, when, why,* and *how* in place of preposition + relative pronoun. It provides instruction and practice with a variety of relative adverb clause forms: those with head nouns + relative adverbs, those with relative adverbs only, and those with head nouns only. The unit ends with a focus on when to use the three patterns based on such variables as how specific the head noun's meaning is and how formal the communicative situation is.

GRAMMAR NOTE

The most difficult concept in this unit for most students will be Focus 3, relative adverbs without head nouns. Many students will need a lot of practice with this pattern, and will need to be reminded to delete the head noun when the adverb *how* is used in order to produce grammatically correct sentences.

UNIT GOALS

Some instructors may want to review the goals listed on Student Book (SB) page 180 after completing the Opening Task so that students understand what they should know by the end of the unit. These goals can also be reviewed at the end of the unit when students are more familiar with the grammar terminology.

OPENING TASK [20 minutes]

The purpose of the Opening Task is to create a context in which students will need to use a variety of relative adverb clauses. Students work in pairs to interview each other about what they do to stay healthy. The problem-solving format is designed to

show the teacher how well the students can produce the target structures implicitly and spontaneously when they are engaged in a communicative task. For a more complete discussion of the purpose of the Opening Task, see To the Teacher, Lesson Planner (LP) page xxii.

Setting Up the Task

1. Brainstorm a list of activities people engage in to stay healthy, and write these on the board— e.g., *work out, play sports, walk, take exercise classes,* etc.
2. Ask students how often they engage in these activities, and where they do them, and write responses on the board.

Conducting the Task

1. Read the introductory paragraph as a class.
2. Write a four-column chart on the board with these headings: *what/when/why/where.* Ask students to copy it in their notebooks.

■ STEP 1

Have students work in pairs to interview each other about activities they engage in to stay healthy. Ask them to fill out their charts with the information they gather in their interviews.

Closing the Task

■ STEP 2

Have students share their information with the class. Don't worry about accuracy at this point, though you may want to take notes of errors in meaning, form, or use in order to focus on those problems later.

GRAMMAR NOTE

Typical student errors (form)

- Not deleting the head noun in sentences with the relative adverb *how*:—e.g., * *That is the way how he writes.* (See Focus 3.)
- Incorrectly omitting relative adverbs:—e.g., * *This is the office I work.* (See Focus 4.)

Typical student errors (use)

- When replacing *in which* with *how,* failing to delete the preceding noun phrase:—e.g., * *We were amazed at the way how they ran the race.* (See Focus 1.)
- Using both *the way* and *how* in a sentence:—e.g., * *This is the way how they cook vegetables here.* (See Focus 2.)

Relative Adverbs versus Relative Pronouns

meaning

Relative adverbs *where, when, why,* and *how* can replace prepositions + the relative pronoun *which* when these prepositions refer to place, time, reason, or manner.

RELATIVE ADVERB	MEANING
where	place
when	time
why	reason
how	manner

RELATIVE ADVERB	REPLACES PREPOSITION + *WHICH*
(to which) (a) A spa is a place **where** you go either to exercise or relax.	*to* *at* $\Big\}$ *which* *from* *in*
(during which) (b) Summer is the time **when** many people take vacations.	*during* *at* $\Big\}$ *which* *in* *on*
(for which) (c) One reason **why** people join health clubs is to take a variety of group exercise classes.	*for which*
(the way in which) (d) I'd like to find out **how** the game of soccer originated.	*(the way) in which*
(e) I admire **how** you dance.	Note that when *how* replaces *in which* you must also delete the noun phrase *the way* before it.
(f) NOT: I admire the way how you dance.	

EXERCISE 1

Substitute relative adverbs for preposition + *which* whenever possible. Make necessary deletions. In one sentence you cannot replace *which* with a relative adverb; explain why.

Example: The beginning of a new year is a time ~~during which~~ *when* many Americans decide to make changes in their lifestyles.

1. On January 1, the day on which resolutions for the new year are often made, we hear people vowing to lose weight, quit smoking, or perhaps change the way in which they behave toward family or friends.

2. Those who want to shed pounds may go to weight loss centers; these are places which offer counseling and diet plans.

3. Others may join a health club at which they can lose weight by exercising.

4. Still others choose a less expensive way to lose weight: They just avoid situations in which they might snack or overeat.

5. People who want to quit smoking may contact organizations that can help them to analyze the times at which they have the greatest urge to smoke and to develop strategies to break the habit.

6. Those who decide to change their behavior toward others may also seek professional help, to find out the reasons for which they act in certain ways.

7. Most people are sincere about their promises on the day on which they are made; however, by February, many New Year's resolutions are just a memory!

JANUARY						
Sun.	Mon.	Tue.	Wed.	Thur.	Fri.	Sat.
			①1	2	3	4
5	6	7	8	9	10	11
12	13	14	15	16	17	18
19	20	21	22	23	24	25
26	27	28	29	30	31	

ANSWER KEY

Exercise 1 1. . . . day when resolutions; . . . perhaps change how they behave. . .   2. (cannot replace which here; not the object of the preposition)   3. . . . club where they   4. . . . situations where they (could use *when* here too, if situation is perceived as a time)   5. . . . times when they   6. . . . reasons why they   7. . . . time when they

FOCUS 1 [20 minutes]

This focus chart introduces the relative adverbs *where, when, why*, and *how* and explains their meanings in relation to the preposition + *which* clauses they may replace in sentences.

1. **Lead-in:** Write the relative adverbs in four columns on the board: *where/when/why/how.*

2. Read the opening paragraph and text of the box to the class. Ask a volunteer to read the first example and the list of prepositions + relative pronoun. Ask students if *where* refers to a place, time, reason, or manner. (*place*)

3. Write a few different place names on the board, such as *the beach* and *the mountains*, and have volunteers use them to create new examples using *where.*

4. Repeat this process for example (b). Write *winter* and *Thanksgiving* on the board for students to use in new sentences.

5. For example (c), write on the board: *A reason why people go to the beach is* _____ and ask students to complete it with an infinitive clause (e.g., *to cool off, to swim, to sail*, etc.).

6. To prompt additional examples of *how* clauses (such as those in d–f), write phrases with *I* + verb + *how* for students to expand—e.g., *I wonder how . . .; I am amazed at how . . .; I can't figure out how . . . .*

7. Emphasize that when *how* replaces *in which* students must also delete the noun phrase before *in which.*

METHODOLOGY NOTE

Review the meaning of the term *head noun*: a noun that is the head of the clause that comes after it. The clause modifies the noun.

EXERCISE 1 [20 minutes]

In this exercise students apply the information they just learned in Focus 1 by substituting relative adverbs for preposition + *which* in a series of sentences.

1. Read the directions and example. What does *when* refer to? A place, time, reason, or manner? (*A time*)

2. Have students work independently to substitute the relative adverbs for preposition + *which* in the sentences.

3. Caution students that in one sentence they will not be able to replace *which.*

4. Review answers with the class. Ask them why they were unable to replace *which* in one sentence. See answers on LP page 182.

 For more practice, use *Grammar Dimensions 4* Workbook page 83, Exercise 1 and page 84, Exercise 2.

EXPANSION [45 minutes]

Activity 1 (listening) on SB page 193 provides a very entertaining context in which students can practice replacing relative pronouns with relative adverbs. First they listen to 20 phrases that contain preposition + *which* clauses. They then form teams and compete to correctly identify each phrase using sentences with adverbial clauses.

FOCUS 2 — Pattern 1: Relative Adverb Clauses that Modify Nouns

form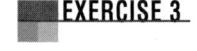

EXAMPLES

Head Noun	+	Relative Adverb	+	Clause
a place		where		you can relax
a time		when		I can call you
a reason		why		you should attend

Place

(a) A hardware store **where** we can get gardening tools is just around the corner.

Place

(b) Hilton Head, South Carolina, is an island **where** many people go to play golf.

Time

(c) I'll always remember the day **when** I ran in my first marathon.

Time

(d) We read about the period **when** the Olympics were first developed in Greece.

Definite Noun	Indefinite Noun
the day when	**a day** when
the reason why	**one reason** why
	some reasons why
the place where	**places** where

(e) The nutritionist explained to us
the way } to balance carbohydrates
how } and proteins in our meals.

(f) NOT: The nutritionist explained to us **the way how** to balance carbohydrates and proteins in our meals.

EXPLANATIONS

Relative adverb clauses often modify nouns. The modified noun is called a head noun because it is the head of the clause that follows.

The head noun is often a general word such as *place, time,* or *reason,* but it can also be a more specific word, especially for places and times.

The head noun can be definite (*the* + noun) or indefinite (*a, an, one, some,* or Ø modifier + noun). The head noun can also be singular or plural.

When you use *how,* you must delete the head noun. *How* adverb clauses have only two patterns: (1) *the way;* (2) *how.*

EXERCISE 2

Identify each of the head nouns in the Focus 1 chart on page 182. What other phrases could you substitute for these head nouns? Are your substitutions more general or more specific in meaning than the original ones?

Example: A spa is a place where . . .
Head noun: a place
Substitution: A spa is *a kind of health club* where . . .
(More specific than *place*)

EXERCISE 3

STEP 1   **Match each of the times in the first column with an event in the second column. Then make sentences using an appropriate head noun + a relative adverb.**

Example: 1897 the first Boston Marathon held
*1897 was **the year when** the first Boston Marathon was held.*

1. 1958	*d.*	a.	one of the earliest forms of soccer played in Japan
2. February 24	*e.*	b.	most health clubs are not very crowded
3. 5 A.M.	*b.*	c.	many people in the United States take skiing vacations
4. Mesozoic Era	*f.*	d.	Brazil won the World Cup in soccer for the first time
5. 1004 BCE	*a.*	e.	Mexicans celebrate Flag Day
6. December	*c.*	f.	dinosaurs roamed the earth

(Exercise 3 is continued on LP page 186.)

ANSWER KEY

Exercise 2   Answers will vary for the second part of each. Possible answers are:

(b) the time: summer is the season . . . (more specific)

(c) one reason: an explanation why . . . (more general)

(d) the way: the manner in which (synonym for way)

(e) the way: the manner in which (synonym for way)

Exercise 3   **Step 1:** Answers will vary. Possible answers are:

1. d; 1958 was the year when Brazil won the World Cup in soccer for the first time.

2. e; February 24 is the day when Mexicans celebrate Flag Day.

3. b; 5 A.M. is a time when most health clubs are not very crowded.

4. f; The Mesozoic Era is a time period when dinosaurs roamed the earth.

5. a; 1004 BCE was the year when one of the earliest forms of soccer was played in Japan.

6. c; December is a month when many people in the United States take skiing vacations.

FOCUS 2 [25 minutes]

Focus 2 explains the use of nonrestrictive relative clauses in definitions. This information will be particularly useful to students in their writing.

1. **Lead-in:** Remind students that the term *head noun* refers to the noun that is modified by a clause. Students will have encountered the concept of head nouns if they worked on subject-verb agreement in Unit 3.

2. Ask a volunteer to read the boxed text and the first explanation.

3. Write the first example on the board and read it aloud. Ask a volunteer to underline the head noun, circle the relative adverb, and place brackets around the clause. Ask students how they could rephrase this sentence using preposition + *which* (*A store is a place in which . . .*).

4. Repeat this process with examples (b–d).

5. For the second section of the focus chart, take a moment to review the concepts of definite and indefinite nouns.

6. Ask a volunteer to read examples (e–f), and then ask another to read the explanation.

7. Encourage students to ask questions about anything they do not understand.

EXERCISE 2 [15 minutes]

Exercise 2 asks students to identify the head nouns in Focus 1 and think of phrases they could use to replace the head noun in each instance.

1. Read the directions and example as a class. How is the substitution in the example more specific?

2. Have students work independently to complete the exercise. Ask them to write at least one alternative sentence for each example in Focus 1.

3. Have students share and discuss their sentences with a partner.

4. Ask volunteers to read their partners' sentences to the class, and discuss these as a class. See possible answers on LP page 184.

 work book For more practice, use *Grammar Dimensions 4* Workbook pages 85–87, Exercise 3.

EXPANSION [60 minutes/homework]

Activity 5 (writing) on SB page 195 makes a good homework assignment after students study Focus 1 and complete Exercise 2. Students create a booklet with information about their city for tourists and newcomers, using relative adverb clauses to modify nouns.

EXERCISE 3 (OPTIONAL) [25 minutes]

This exercise has four steps, ending on SB page 187, each dealing with a different relative adverb (*when, where, why, how*). Like many of the exercises in this book, this one is content-based, so that students can learn information about a variety of topics while working with the target grammatical structures.

1. For each step, read the directions and example as a class. Have students work independently to match the sentences, and then have them share their answers with a partner.

2. After students have completed Step 4, review answers to all four steps as a class. Encourage students to share different answers they may have come up with. See possible answers on LP pages 184 and 186.

EXPANSION [40 minutes/homework]

Activity 3 (writing/speaking) on SB page 194 is a good follow-up to Exercise 3. Students create lists of places and times/dates, modeled on the format of the sentences in Exercise 3, and then identify them, using relative adverb clauses that modify nouns. To save time in class, have students create their lists as homework.

STEP 2 Now match places with events. Again, make sentences using an adverb clause with an appropriate head noun. Try to use nouns other than *place* if possible.

Example: Shanghai, China Basketball star Yao Ming was born here.

*Shanghai, China is **the city where** basketball star Yao Ming was born.* (Note that *here* is deleted.)

1. Beijing *c.*	a. you can get a sandwich here
2. the kidneys *f.*	b. you can hike underground here
3. Uruguay *d.*	c. site for the 2008 Olympics
4. basement *e.*	d. the first World Cup soccer competition held here
5. deli *a.*	e. sports equipment often stored here
6. caves *b.*	f. the water in your body gets regulated here

STEP 3 Match the following reasons to the statements in the second column. Again, give a sentence for each match.

Example: reduce stress people try meditation because of this

Reducing stress is one reason why people try meditation.

1. improve heart health *e.*	a. some people look forward to the new year for this reason
2. fear of sharks *d.*	b. some people eat frozen yogurt instead of ice cream because of this
3. the chance to "turn over a new leaf" *a.*	c. many people love autumn hikes for this reason
4. lack of sleep *f.*	d. people sometimes avoid swimming in the ocean because of this
5. beautiful foliage *c.*	e. people take up jogging or bicycling for this purpose
6. low fat content *b.*	f. students sometimes don't perform well in class for this reason

STEP 4 Finally, match processes or methods in the first column to statements in the second. Make sentences for your matches using either the head noun *way* or the relative adverb *how*.

Example: Practicing swings you do this to improve your tennis game

*Practicing swings is **the way** you improve your tennis game.*

*Practicing swings is **how** you improve your tennis game.*

1. studying kinesiology *f.*	a. you do this to teach a dog to walk by your side
2. trimming dead flowers and fertilizing plants *c.*	b. you can do this to help prevent heart disease
3. conducting an opinion poll *e.*	c. you can promote new growth of flowers in your garden
4. repeating commands and giving rewards *a.*	d. the championship golfer Tiger Woods did this to improve his golf shots
5. eating healthy food and not smoking *b.*	e. people do this to survey the attitudes of large populations
6. reducing his head movements *d.*	f. someone does this to prepare for a career as a chiropractor

EXERCISE 4 Answers will vary. Possible answers are provided below.

Complete each of the blanks with appropriate words or phrases about yourself.

Example: <u>The shoreline</u> is a place where I <u>go to watch the birds</u>.

<u>Starting with my conclusion</u> is the way I <u>often begin to write a draft for a paper</u>.

1. <u>The year 1990</u> was the year when I <u>moved to the United States</u>
2. <u>Griffith Park</u> is the place where I <u>go to bicycle</u>
3. The reason why I don't like <u>the subway</u> is <u>that it is so noisy</u>
4. The way I get to school/work is <u>on the bus</u>
5. <u>Sunday</u> is a/the day when I <u>try to do something fun</u>
6. <u>To get money</u> is a reason why I <u>work</u>
7. A <u>place</u> where I <u>like to shop</u> is <u>the clothing outlet.</u>
8. <u>Studying at night</u> is how I <u>get my homework done</u>

Step 2 Answers will vary. Possible answers are: 1. c; Beijing is the site where the 2008 Olympics will be held. 2. f; The kidneys are organs where the water in your body gets regulated. 3. d; Uruguay is the city where the first World Cup soccer competition was held. 4. e; A basement is part of a home where sports equipment is often stored. 5. a; A deli is a store where you can get a sandwich. 6. b; Caves are a part of the earth where you can hike underground. **Step 3** Answers will vary. Possible answers are: 1. e; Improving heart health is one reason why people take up jogging or bicycling. 2. d; A fear of sharks is one reason why people sometimes avoid swimming in the ocean. 3. a; The chance to "turn over a new leaf" is one of the reasons why some people look forward to the

5. c; Beautiful foliage is one reason why many people love autumn hikes. 6. b; A low fat content is one reason why some people eat frozen yogurt instead of ice cream. **Step 4** Answers will vary. Possible answers are: 1. f; Studying kinesiology is how someone prepares for a career as a chiropractor. 2. c; Trimming dead flowers and fertilizing plants is how you can promote new growth of flowers in your garden. 3. e; Conducting an opinion poll is the way people can survey the attitudes of large populations. 4. a; Repeating commands and giving rewards is how you teach a dog to walk by your side. 5. b; Eating healthy food and not smoking is the way you can help prevent heart disease. 6. d; Reducing his head movements is how the championship golfer Tiger Woods

EXERCISE 4 (OPTIONAL) [15 minutes]

1. Ask a volunteer to read the directions and examples to the class.
2. Have students work independently to write their sentences.
3. Have students work in groups of three and take turns reading their sentences to each other.
4. Ask volunteers from each group to share sentences with the class. See possible answers on LP page 186.

EXPANSION 1 [20 minutes]

In this activity students should have fun completing the sentences from Exercise 4 as a pair.

1. Have students work in pairs.
2. Tell them to take turns filling in the blanks of the sentences in Exercise 4. To model, ask a volunteer to fill in the first blank in sentence #1 with a year—e.g., *2002*. Then, you fill in the second blank with something silly—e.g., *climbed Mount Everest twice*. Then switch roles: you say a year, and have the volunteer fill in the second blank.
3. Encourage students to be as outrageous as they like.
4. Have volunteers share their sentences with the class.

EXPANSION 2 [40 minutes/homework]

Activity 6 (research on the web) on SB page 195 is a good homework assignment following Exercise 4. In it, students research significant events that occurred during the year they were born and write about them using relative adverbs clauses.

FOCUS 3 — Pattern 2: Relative Adverbs without Head Nouns

form

EXAMPLES		EXPLANATIONS

Relative Adverb	+	Clause
where		he lives
when		the term starts
why		I called
how		she knows

(a) This is **where** we will meet tomorrow.

(b) That was **when** I decided to go to work.

(c) **Why** she left is a mystery.

(d) She explained **how** to change a tire.

A second pattern with relative adverbs has no head noun. As with Pattern 1, this pattern can express:

* place
* time
* reason
* manner

EXERCISE 5

Restate each of the sentences you made in Exercise 3 without the head nouns (except for the ones in Step 4 for which you used *how*).

Example: *1897 was **when** the first Boston Marathon was held.*

EXERCISE 6

Working with a partner or in a small group, decide whether each statement is true or false. If a statement is false, replace the phrase in italics with something that will make the statement true.

Example: *Spring is* when birds in the northern hemisphere begin their migration south.

Answer: *False. **Autumn** is when they migrate south.*

1. *New York* is where you can see the Lincoln Memorial.

2. *Late November* is when we celebrate the winter solstice.

3. *Religious persecution* is why many Europeans first settled in what became the United States of America.

4. *Majoring in mathematics* is how most undergraduate students prepare for a career in medicine.

5. *The 1970s* was the decade when Ronald Reagan was president.

6. *The drugstore* is where a bibliophile would go to add to her collection.

7. *Either July or August* is when a person born under the zodiac sign of Leo will celebrate his or her birthday.

8. *Using a meat barometer* is how you check to make sure meat is cooked well enough in the oven.

FOCUS 4 — Pattern 3: Head Nouns without Relative Adverbs

form

EXAMPLES		EXPLANATIONS

Head Noun	+	Clause
the place		we moved to
the time		I start school
the reason		they left
the way		you do this

(a) Sports Galore is **a store** I go to for exercise equipment.

(b) August 10th is **the day** Ecuadorians celebrate Independence Day.

(c) **The reason** spiders can spin perfect webs is that they have an innate ability to do so rather than having learned it.

(d) Public transportation is **the way** many city dwellers get to work.

A third pattern uses only the head noun and its modifying clause.

This pattern can also express:

* place
* time
* reason
* manner

(e) Dominic's is the restaurant I go **to** for pizza.

(f) NOT: Dominic's is the restaurant I go for pizza.

(g) Denver is the city I live **in**.

(h) NOT: Denver is the city I live.

(i) Dominic's is the place I $\left\{ \begin{array}{c} \text{go} \\ \text{go to} \end{array} \right\}$ for pizza.

With specific head nouns that express place, you must often include a preposition of direction or position.

The preposition is often optional in informal English when *place* is the head noun.

ANSWER KEY

Exercise 5   Step 1: 1. 1958 was when . . .   2. February 24 is when . . .   3. 5 a.m. is when . . .
4. The Mesozoic Era is when . . .   5. 1004 BCE was when . . .   6. December is when . . .
Step 2: 1. Beijing is where . . .   2. The kidneys are where . . .   3. Uruguay is where . . .
4. The basement is where . . .   4.   A deli is where . . .   5. Caves are where . . .
Step 3: 1. To improve heart health is why . . .   2. Fear of sharks is why . . .   3. The chance to "turn over a new leaf" is why . . .   4. Lack of sleep is why . . .   5. Beautiful foliage is why . . .   6. Low fat content is why . . .

Exercise 6   1. False. Washington, D.C. is where . . .   2. False. Late December is when . . .   3. True.
4. False. Majoring in biology is how . . .   5. False. The 1980s was the decade when . . .   6. False. The bookstore is where . . .   7. True.   8. False. Using a meat thermometer is how . . .

FOCUS 3 [25 minutes]

Focus 3 explains the second pattern in this unit for forming relative adverb clauses: no head noun + relative adverb + clause. Advanced students should be familiar with this pattern even though they may not be aware of it as a "formal" pattern.

1. **Lead-in:** Read the boxed text in the chart, and then the explanation. Ask two volunteers to read the four examples.
2. To relate this pattern to that shown in Focus 2, ask students to supply head nouns before the boldfaced relative adverbs so that they can see where there is a "Ø-head noun." Model one or two examples and ask for substitutions—e.g.: *This is the corner where we will meet tomorrow; That was the week when I decided to go to work.*
3. Have volunteers create other examples using each adverb.

EXERCISE 5 [25 minutes]

In Exercise 5 students apply what they have learned in Focus 3 by restating the sentences they created in Exercise 3, but this time without the head nouns.

1. Ask a volunteer to read the directions and example. What head noun does *when* replace in the example? (*1897*)
2. Have students work independently to rewrite their sentences from Steps 1–3 of Exercise 3 without head nouns. Tell them that they will not be able to do this with the sentences from Step 4.
3. Have students share and discuss their sentences with a partner.
4. Ask volunteers to share their sentences, and discuss these as a class. See answers on LP page 188.

For more practice, use *Grammar Dimensions 4* Workbook page 88, Exercises 4 and 5.

EXPANSION 1 [30 minutes]

This expansion activity could be done in class or assigned as homework. If done as homework, have students research and write their sentences at home, and complete the exercise in class.

1. Have students, in pairs, make up sentences modeled after the ones in Exercise 3. They should create at least three or four sentences for each step (1–3).
2. Suggest that students research information for their sentences on the Internet or in the library.
3. Have pairs exchange papers with another pair and rewrite the sentences without head nouns.
4. Have pairs take turns reading their sentences to each other.
5. Ask volunteers to share their most interesting sentences with the class.

EXPANSION 2 [30 minutes/homework]

In Activity 4 (speaking/writing) on SB page 194 students take turns discussing dates and places that have been significant to them in their lives using relative adverb clauses. Then share this information with the class. It is a good follow-up to the work students do in Exercise 5. It can be done in class, or assigned as homework, with students interviewing a friend or family member and reporting back to the class.

EXERCISE 6 [15 minutes]

Students replace head nouns in sentences with adverbial clauses, applying what they learned in Focus 2.

1. Read the directions and example as a class. Ask students what *spring* and *autumn* are (*head nouns*). Ask them to identify the relative adverb and clause.

2. Have students work independently to decide whether each sentence is true or false, and to correct the false statements.
3. Have students, in pairs, take turns reading their sentences.
4. Ask volunteers to share their answers with the class. Does everyone agree with those answers? See answers on LP page 188.

EXPANSION [40 minutes]

Activity 2 (writing/speaking) on SB page 193 is a good follow-up to Exercise 6. Students complete a list of statements with adverbial clauses using personal information, and then consult with classmates to find answers to their questions.

FOCUS 4 [20 minutes]

Focus 4 explains the third pattern in this unit for forming relative adverb clauses: head noun + no relative adverb + clause.

1. **Lead-in:** Read the boxed text, and then the explanation for the first group of examples in the focus chart. Ask students what adverbs refer to *place, time, reason,* and *way* (*where, when, why, how*).
2. Ask a volunteer to read the first example. Ask students to identify the head noun (*a store*). Ask another volunteer to restate the sentence using a relative adverb. (*Sports Galore is a store where I go to buy exercise equipment.*)
3. Explain that the relative adverb is understood. It does not have to be expressed.
4. Continue this process with examples (b–d).
5. Read the explanations in the second group of the focus chart. Then ask volunteers to read the examples.
6. Point out that the relative adverbs could *not* be inserted in (e) or (g) unless the prepositions *to* (in e) and *in* (in g) were deleted first.
7. Ask students to say where friends and relatives live using the sentence structure in example (g).

EXERCISE 7

Make sentences using Pattern 3 (head nouns without relative adverbs) to provide information about yourself.

Example: where you live

Winnipeg, Manitoba, Canada, is the city I live in.

1. where you were born

2. the date (month, day) when you were born

3. the way you make a certain food you like

4. the reason you are taking a specific course

5. a place you like to go to relax or have fun

6. a reason you like or dislike a course you are taking

7. the way people say "good luck" in your native language

FOCUS 5 | Contents for Relative Adverb Patterns

use

Here are some general guidelines for using the three patterns.

EXAMPLES	EXPLANATIONS
	Pattern 1: Head Noun + Relative Adverb + Clause We tend to use this pattern:
(a) Today is **a day when** all nations will want to join in prayers for peace in the world. (b) This is **the field where** we used to play softball every summer as kids.	• to focus on or emphasize the time, place, reason, or manner.
(c) I know **a nursery where** you can get beautiful orchids.	• when the meaning of the head noun is specific.

EXAMPLES	EXPLANATIONS
(d) Barton's is **a store where** one can find ski equipment discounted. (Less formal: Barton's is **where** you can get a fantastic deal!)	• when the context is more formal (such as written versus spoken English).
(e) **A place where** you can take dance lessons is at the corner of Hammond and Belknap. (f) The corner of Hammond and Belknap **Predicate** is **where** we usually meet.	• when the head noun is the subject of a sentence rather than the predicate. In example (e), **a place** helps to introduce new information.
	Pattern 2: Relative Adverb + Clause We often omit the head noun:
(g) I know **where** you can find tomato sauce in this market. (h) She told us **when** to show up. (i) Greece is **where** the Olympics started. (inferred: the country) (j) 1901 was **when** ping pong became a trademark name for table tennis. **Less formal**	• when the head noun has a general meaning (the time, the place) rather than a specific one. • when you can infer the head noun from the context or from general knowledge.
(k) **Why** she did that is a mystery to me!	• when the context of speech or writing is informal.
	Pattern 3: Head Noun + Clause This pattern tends to be used in contexts similar to ones for Pattern 1:
(l) Let us know **the day** you will arrive.	• when the head noun has a more specific meaning.
(m) Please state **the reason** you are seeking this position.	• when the context is more formal.

ANSWER KEY

Exercise 7 Answers will vary. Some sample answers are: 1. Bogotá, Colombia, is the city I was born in. 2. July 20 is the day I was born. 3. Sautéing with olive oil and onions is the way I like to cook zucchini. 4. To improve my speaking skills in public is the reason I am taking a speech course. 5. The beach is the place I go to relax. 6. The reason I like this course is the teacher and students. 7. The way people say "good luck" in my language is "Bonne chance."

EXERCISE 7 (OPTIONAL) [20 minutes]

In Exercise 7 students use this third pattern (head nouns without relative adverbs) to write about themselves and their lives.

1. Read the directions and example as a class. What relative adverb is omitted in the example? (*where*) Ask a volunteer to restate the example using the relative adverb.
2. Have students work independently to write their sentences.
3. Have them next work in small groups, exchange papers, and then read each other's sentences aloud.
4. Ask volunteers to share sentences with the class. See possible answers on LP page 190.

For more practice, use *Grammar Dimensions 4* Workbook page 89, Exercise 6.

EXPANSION [60 minutes]

This exercise can be done as a follow-up to Exercise 7. Students could do the whole exercise in class, or conduct their interviews outside of class and report back on the results.

1. As you did in Focus 1, write a four-column chart on the board with the headings: *where/when/why/how*. Ask students to copy the chart.
2. Tell students that they are going to interview others about their lives. Ask them to write a list of four to eight questions, using the relative adverbs on the board.
3. Brainstorm a list of questions students could ask, such as *Where were you born? Where were your parents born? When did you come to this country?* Ask a volunteer to write these on the board.

4. Have students interview at least four people, and note their responses in the chart.
5. Ask them to write a short paper summarizing the results. They should use head nouns without relative adverbs in their sentences.
6. Ask volunteers to share their results with the class.

FOCUS 5 (OPTIONAL) [25 minutes]

Focus 5 outlines the contexts in which the preceding three patterns of relative adverb clauses are used.

1. **Lead-in:** Read the first explanation, then the first two examples. Ask students to identify the head noun, relative adverb, and clause in the two examples. What is emphasized in each sentence—the time, place, reason, or manner?
2. Ask a volunteer to read the second explanation and example (c).
3. For example (d), ask students to say how the first sentence is more formal than the second.
4. Have a volunteer read the last explanation and examples (e) and (f).
5. Ask volunteers to create several other examples using *where* and *when*.
6. For the next two patterns, read (or have a volunteer read) the explanation, then the corresponding examples. Ask students to identify the patterns in each example.
7. Encourage students to ask questions about anything they do not understand.

METHODOLOGY NOTE

Explain to students that the guidelines in Focus 5 are not hard and fast rules, and that they can expect to hear and read exceptions to these rules. For example, although a context may be formal, if the head noun can be easily inferred, many people will omit it.

Decide whether the form given in (a) or (b) would be more typical or appropriate for each context. Use the guidelines given in Focus 5. Explain your choices.

1. **Ethel:** Max! What did you just turn off that light for?

   Max: Dear, if you'll wait just a minute, you'll find out . . .
   a. the reason why I did it.
   (b.) why I did it.

2. (a.) The day I got married
   b. When I got married
   . . . was one of the happiest days of my life.

3. (a.) A place where you can get a great cup of coffee
   b. Where you get a great cup of coffee
   . . . is right across the street.

4. Oh no! Can you believe it? I forgot . . .
   a. the place where I put my keys again.
   (b.) where I put my keys again.

5. (a.) One reason many people feel stress
   b. Why many people feel stress
   . . . is that they don't have enough spare time.

6. I would now like all of you in this audience to consider . . .
   (a.) the many times your families offered you emotional support.
   b. when your families offered you emotional support. It's hard to count them all, isn't it?

7. Let me show you . . .
   a. the way this MP3 player works.
   (b.) how this MP3 player works.

8. Ms. Cordero just told us . . .
   a. the time when we should turn in our papers.
   (b.) when we should turn in our papers.

9. Last year my family took a trip to see . . .
   (a.) the house where my great-grandfather grew up.
   b. where my great-grandfather grew up.

Exercise 8 Reasons for answers may vary. Possible answers are: 1. (b) informal, head noun is direct object, general 2. (a) head noun is subject 3. (a) head noun is subject 4. (b) informal, head noun is direct object, general 5. (a) head noun is specific (one reason), subject 6. (a) head noun is specific (the many times); emphasizes the head noun 7. (b) informal context, head noun is direct object, general 8. (b) head noun is general (can be assumed), direct object 9. (a) specific noun, makes clear the place is a house and not a city, area, neighborhood, etc.

Use Your English

ACTIVITY 1 listening

CD1 Track 14

Form groups of three or four and compete in teams. The audio you'll hear will consist of 20 phrases that need to be identified with a place, time, reason, or manner. The phrases will use preposition + *which* clauses. Your instructor will pause the audio after each phrase. Taking turns, each team needs to identify the phrase by using a sentence with a relative adverb clause. You may use any of the patterns discussed in this unit. If a team gives the wrong answer, the next team will have a chance to correct it. Award points for each correct answer.

Examples: Audio: The continent on which the country of Rwanda is located.

   Answer: *Africa is the continent where Rwanda is located.*

   Audio: The month in which we celebrate both Lincoln's and Washington's birthdays.

   Answer: *February is the month when we celebrate both birthdays.*

   Audio: The way in which you say "Thank you" in French.

   Answer: *"Merci" is how you say "Thank you."*

ACTIVITY 2 writing/speaking

How would you complete statements that begin as follows?

• I'd like to know the date (day, year, century, etc.) when . . .
• I'd like to find out the place (country, city, etc.) where . . .
• I wish I knew the reason(s) why . . .
• I am interested in finding out how . . .

   Write a list of statements using each of the relative adverbs above (with or without head nouns) to express things you'd like to know. Use the patterns given in the list above to begin your sentences. Share your statements with others in your class to see if anyone can provide the answers.

Activity 1 Answers may vary. Possible answers are: 1. Wyoming . . . where, 2. February 14 . . . when, 3. San Francisco . . . where, 4. December/January . . . when, 5. Remembering those who have died for the United States . . . why, 6. Washington . . . how, 7. To lift the car and help change a tire . . . why, 8. "Ill-ǝ-noy" . . . how, 9. A pharmacy . . . where, 10. Depression/physical abuse/Drug addiction/Advice . . . why, 11. The 19th century . . . when, 12. Australia . . . where, 13. Pennsylvania . . . where, 14. Heavy traffic or a law of no stopping . . . why, 15. Halloween . . . when, 16. Dial 0 or 411 . . . how, 17. Egypt . . . where, 18. May/June . . . when, 19. To find the area of a triangle . . . why, 20. N.O.W. . . . how,

EXERCISE 8 (OPTIONAL) [20 minutes]

In this final exercise students analyze a series of sentences and choose an answer based on the principles outlined in Focus 5.

1. Read the directions as a class. Have two volunteers read #1. Ask students what they think the answer should be, and write the whole clause on the board. Then, ask them to find the reason to support their answers in Focus 5, and write those reasons on the board.
2. Have students work in pairs to choose the correct form for each context.
3. Have each pair exchange papers with another pair, and review and discuss their choices.
4. Review answers as a class. See possible answers on LP page 192.

For more practice, use *Grammar Dimensions 4* Workbook page 90, Exercise 7 and page 91, Exercises 8 and 9.

EXPANSION [45 minutes/homework]

Assign Activity 7 (reflection) on SB page 195 as homework after Exercise 8 for additional writing practice with relative adverb clauses. In this activity, students reflect on their academic goals as well as the optimal conditions they might create for various kinds of learning.

UNIT GOAL REVIEW [10 minutes]

Ask students to look at the goals on the opening page of the unit again. Refer to the pages of the unit where information on each goal can be found.

 ExamView Test Generator
For assessment of Unit 10, use *Grammar Dimensions 4 ExamView®*.

USE YOUR ENGLISH

The Use Your English activities at the end of the unit contain situations that should naturally elicit the structures covered in the unit. For a more complete discussion of how to use the Use Your English Activities, see To the Teacher, LP page xxvi. While students are doing these activities in class, you can circulate and listen to see if they are using the structures accurately. Errors can be corrected after the activity has finished.

ACTIVITY 1 listening [45 minutes]

Activity 1 should be very enjoyable for students. First they listen to 20 phrases that contain preposition + *which* clauses. They then form teams and compete to correctly identify each phrase using sentences with adverbial clauses. This activity is a good sequel to Exercise 1 on SB page 183.

CD1 Track 14

1. Tell students that they are going to listen to 20 phrases that contain preposition + *which* clauses.
2. Write a four-column chart on the board with these headings, and ask students to copy it: *place/time/reason/manner*.
3. Have students listen to the audio once without taking notes.
4. Ask students to listen again and write each sentence in the appropriate column on their charts. Tell them to replay the audio as needed.
5. Encourage students to listen a third time to complete and check their notes, if they want to.
6. Divide the class into teams: either two teams, or smaller pairs of teams. Appoint one student to be the moderator for each pair of teams.
7. Have the moderator read each phrase from the audio. Teams should take turns identifying the phrase using a sentence with a relative adverb clause.

8. Tell students that they can use any of the three patterns they studied in this unit in their sentences.
9. If a team gives a wrong answer, the other team gets a chance to correct it.
10. Award points for each correct answer.
11. If you have more than two teams, you may want to have a play off.

ACTIVITY 2 writing/speaking [40 minutes]

This activity is a good follow-up to Exercise 6 on SB pages 188–189. Students complete a list of statements with adverbial clauses using personal information. Then consult with classmates to find answers to their questions.

1. Ask a volunteer to read the list of four questions. Ask other volunteers to complete the first sentence, *I'd like to know the date (day, year, century, etc.) when . . .* and write their responses on the board. Did they use a head noun, or not?
2. Have students work independently to complete the list of statements with information that expressed things they would like to know.
3. Have students work in groups of five or six. Have them take turns reading their statements. The other members of the group should supply them with the information they seek, if at all possible.
4. Ask each group to compare and contrast their questions: Did anyone ask for similar information?
5. Have a representative from each group summarize the similarities and differences for the class.

VARIATION

Have students work in pairs. Have them write their statements, and then exchange papers with their partners. The partners should research the answer to the questions in the library or on the Internet, and write an answer to each, using an adverbial clause.

 **ACTIVITY 3** writing/speaking

Make a new list of places and times/dates such as are shown in Exercise 3 on page 185, either individually or in teams. Then present the items on your list one by one to others who must define or identify the word or phrase in some way with a relative adverb clause. (If you prefer to do this as a competitive game, you could set time limits for responses and award points.) The following are a few examples of items and responses.

PLACE/DATE/TIME	POSSIBLE RESPONSE
February 14	*That's a day when people exchange valentines.*
Switzerland	*It's a country in Europe where skiers like to go because of the Alps.*
Trattoria	*It's a restaurant where you can get Italian food.*

 **ACTIVITY 4** speaking/writing

With a classmate, take turns telling each other about dates and places that have been important or memorable in your lives. These could be times and locations of milestone events such as birth and graduation, but they could also include a few humorous incidents or dates/places that may not seem so important now but were when you were younger.

Examples: *1990 was the year when I broke my leg playing Frisbee.*

I'll never forget a trip to Florida, the place where I first saw the ocean.

Take notes on your partner's events. Then report some of them orally to the class, using relative adverb clauses in some sentences. (In addition to *when* and *where*, you might also use the relative adverb *why* in giving reasons why a date or place was important.)

 **ACTIVITY 5** writing

Create a booklet providing information for tourists or new students about the city where you now live. The following are some ideas for possible categories; you may come up with additional ones.

- the places where you think visitors would most like to go
- the reasons why you think visitors would enjoy spending time in this city
- the places where it's fun to go shopping or to get the best food

You could divide the project so that individuals or small groups would each be responsible for a section or two of the guide.

 **ACTIVITY 6** research on the web

 What were some of the interesting and important events that happened during the year when you were born? Using the date of your birth as the topic of a search, find four or five things on the Internet that took place during that year. Write down your findings, using relative adverbs clauses.

Example: *October 17, 1989 was the day when a 7.1 magnitude earthquake struck San Francisco.*

 **ACTIVITY 7** reflection

In developing good academic study skills, it is helpful to reflect on your goals as well as the optimal conditions you might create for various kinds of learning, whether it's reading, writing, thinking, or a combination of different skills. Write responses to the following questions using relative adverb clauses.

1. Consider one of your courses or a major/program of study you are pursuing right now. What is one of the reasons why you are taking the course or program?
2. What are the times of the day when you can generally study the best? Why?
3. What are the times of the day when you are least able to study well? Why?
4. What are the places where it is easiest for you to study?
5. What are the places where it is difficult for you to get studying done?
6. What are the places where you can write most comfortably?

USE YOUR ENGLISH

ACTIVITY 3 writing/speaking
[40 minutes/homework]

Activity 3 can be assigned after Exercise 3 on SB paged 185–187. Students create lists of places and times/dates, modeled on the format of the sentences in Exercise 3, and then identify them, using relative adverb clauses that modify nouns. To save time in class, have students create their lists as homework.

1. Divide students into teams of three or four. Have each team create a list of places and times/dates following the format of Exercise 3, Steps 1 and 2. They could research information to use in the library or on the Internet. Ask them to write at least five times/dates and five place names.

2. Have teams compete with each other. They should take turns presenting the items on their lists one-by-one to the other team, who must then identify the word or phrase in some way using a relative adverb clause. For each correct answer, they get one point.

3. Set a competition time limit of 15 minutes.

ACTIVITY 4 speaking/writing
[30 minutes/homework]

In this activity students take turns discussing dates and places that have been significant to them in their lives using relative adverb clauses. It is a good follow-up to the work students do in Exercise 5 on SB page 188. It can be done in class, or assigned as homework, with students interviewing a friend or family member and reporting back to the class.

1. Have students work in pairs. Have them take turns telling each other about dates and places that have been significant to them in their lives.

2. Tell students to use relative adverb clauses with *when* and *where* in their sentences. Explain that

they may also want to use *why* when explaining why a date or place was important to them.

3. Write on the board: *1990 was the year when I broke my leg playing Frisbee.* Ask volunteers to relate something that occurred in a certain year, and write their sentences on the board.

4. Ask students to take notes and report on what their partners say using sentences with relative adverb clauses.

ACTIVITY 5 writing
[60 minutes/homework]

Activity 5 makes a good homework assignment after students study Focus 1 and complete Exercise 2 on SB page 185. Students create a booklet with information about their city for tourists and newcomers, using relative adverb clauses to modify nouns.

1. Read the directions and list of categories as a class. Brainstorm a list of other kinds of information that someone new to your city might like to know, and write these on the board.

2. Guide the class in dividing the categories into four groups, such as *restaurants, places to go, things to do,* and *where to shop.*

3. Have students work in groups of four. Assign each student one of the four main topics on the board.

4. Tell students that they are to research their topic and write one section of the tourism booklet. They should use relative adverb clauses modifying nouns in their sentences. Give an example: *The restaurant where you can get the best Chinese food is Chin Fun, on Main Street.*

5. During the next class, have students compile their four reports into one booklet.

ACTIVITY 6 research on the web
[40 minutes/homework]

 In Activity 6 students research significant events that occurred during the year they were born and write about them using relative adverb clauses. This activity is a good homework assignment following Exercise 4 on SB page 187.

1. Read the directions, and ask two volunteers to read the two examples. Ask students to identify the relative adverb clause in each sentence.

2. Ask students if they know any significant events that occurred during the year they were born. Write these on the board, and then ask students to create sentences about them using relative adverb clauses.

3. Have students search the Internet for four or five things that happened during the year they were born. Ask them to take notes and write sentences using relative adverb clauses.

ACTIVITY 7 reflection
[45 minutes/homework]

In this activity, students reflect on their academic goals as well as the optimal conditions they might create for various kinds of learning. You may wish to assign Activity 7 as homework after Exercise 8 on SB page 192 for additional writing practice with relative adverb clauses.

1. Read the directions and list of questions as a class. Ask several volunteers to respond to the first question using a relative adverb clause, and write their responses on the board. What does the clause modify?

2. Have students write answers to the questions as homework using relative adverb clauses.

CORRELATIVE CONJUNCTIONS

UNIT GOALS

UNIT GOALS

- Use correlative conjunctions for emphasis

- Join phrases and clauses with correlative conjunctions

- Write sentences with parallel correlative constructions

OPENING TASK

Planning a Course Schedule

Imagine that you would like to enter the New World Alternative College in order to earn an Associate's degree. The following list contains the classes that are offered and the number of courses and electives required in each category to obtain a degree.

NEW WORLD ALTERNATIVE COLLEGE
Course Offerings, Requirements, and Electives

English Composition
(1 course)
Expository Writing
Technical Writing
Humanities (2 courses)
Linguistics
Philosophy
Religious Studies
Social Sciences
(2 courses)
Anthropology
Communication Studies
Economics
Geography
Physical Sciences
(2 courses)
Geology
Astronomy
Physics
Mathematics (1 course)
General Mathematics
Computer Science

Life Sciences
(2 courses)
Psychology
Biology
Microbiology
**Environmental
Sciences (4 courses)**
The Greenhouse
Effect
Air Pollution
Garbage Disposal
Hazardous Waste
Acid Rain
Endangered Wildlife
History (1 elective)
U.S. History
World History
Foreign Language
(1 elective)
Chinese
French

STEP 1

In the following table, write in two courses from each category that you would be interested in taking. In some cases, there are only two courses to choose from. These are written in for you.

COURSES I WOULD LIKE TO TAKE	CHOICE 1	CHOICE 2
English Composition	Expository Writing	Technical Writing
Humanities		
Social Sciences		
Physical Sciences		
Mathematics	General Mathematics	Computer Science
Life Sciences		
Environmental Sciences		
History	U.S. History	World History
Foreign Language	Chinese or French	

STEP 2

Discuss your choices in groups of four. Are there any courses you would *not* like to take?

STEP 3

Summarize the results of your discussion.

Examples: *All of us must take either expository writing or technical writing.*

Maria is interested not only in Geology but also in Astronomy.

Neither Tom nor Gustaf would like to take Garbage Disposal.

UNIT OVERVIEW

Unit 11 assumes that students have already studied correlative conjunctions but may still be having some difficulty using them to join phrases and clauses appropriately, especially in writing.

GRAMMAR NOTE

Although the simple coordinating conjunctions rarely cause many problems for students, some can have difficulties with two-part correlative structures where one part of a sentence comes before the first conjunction and the other precedes the second conjunction.

UNIT GOALS

Some instructors may want to review the goals listed on Student Book (SB) page 196 after completing the Opening Task so that students understand what they should know by the end of the unit. These goals can also be reviewed at the end of the unit when students are more familiar with the grammar terminology.

OPENING TASK [20 minutes]

The aim of this activity is to give students the opportunity to use correlative conjunctions as they perform a task that many advanced level students will do at one time or another—plan a college schedule. The problem-solving format is designed to show the teacher how well the students can produce the target structure implicitly and spontaneously when they are engaged in a communicative task. For a more complete discussion of the purpose of the Opening Task, see To the Teacher, Lesson Planner (LP) page xxii.

Setting Up the Task

1. Discuss with the class the differences between Associate's and Bachelor's degrees and between required and elective courses.
2. Ask students to say what courses are required in their fields of study.
3. Discuss how the courses offered in an alternative college might differ from those offered in a regular college.

Conducting the Task

1. Read the introductory paragraph as a class.
2. Ask students to read through the list of courses and say which ones are different than those offered in their school. Are the required courses similar, or not?

■ STEP 1

Have students work independently to complete the chart with courses they would like to take.

■ STEP 2

Have students discuss their choices in groups of four. Instruct them to look back at page 196 to select courses they'd dislike taking. Encourage students to discuss specific reasons why they wouldn't like the courses they've chosen.

■ STEP 3

1. Read the directions for Step 3, and ask a volunteer to read the example.
2. Ask each group to write a summary of their discussion.

Closing the Task

1. Have a representative from each group share their results with the class.
2. Don't worry about accuracy at this point, though you may want to take notes of errors in meaning, form, or use in order to focus on those problems later.

GRAMMAR NOTE

Typical student errors (form)

- Using a plural verb in *either . . . or* constructions:—e.g., * *Either Mr. Soto or Mr. Davis are going to teach the class.* (See Focus 1.)
- Using *and* rather than *or* in making *either . . . or* statements:—e.g., * *Either it's going to rain and it's going to snow tonight.* (See Focus 1.)
- Using *neither* rather than *nor:*—e.g., * *They didn't want to go to the game, neither did I.* (See Focus 1.)
- Not inverting the first auxiliary verb in *not only . . . but also* constructions:—e.g., * *Not only they are buying a new house but they are also buying a new car.* (See Focus 2.)

Typical student errors (use)

- Using *both . . . and* to join two complete sentences:—e.g., * *Both Eliza likes to garden and she likes to read.* (See Focus 3.)
- Needlessly repeating information in a sentence with parallel structures:—e.g., * *Katie realized either that she should ask Tom or that she should ask George to drive her to school.* (See Focus 3.)

FOCUS 1 — Correlative Conjunctions for Emphasis

EXAMPLES		EXPLANATIONS
Coordinating Conjunctions	Correlative Conjunctions	Coordinating conjunctions and correlative conjunctions can be used to show different types of relationships:
and	*both . . . and* *not only . . . but also*	• additive
or	*either . . . or*	• alternative
nor	*neither . . . nor*	• negative
		In general, the correlative conjunctions are more emphatic.
(a) **A:** I hope Pablo **and** Karl come to the debate next Saturday. **B:** You're in luck! **Both** Karl **and** Pablo are coming.		**Additive Relationships** • less emphasis • more emphasis
(b) **C:** I hope Pablo is coming to the debate next Saturday. **D:** Guess what? **Not only** is Pablo coming, **but** Karl is **also**.		• even greater emphasis (*not only* usually comes before already known information, and *but* introduces new or surprising information)
(c) **A:** Can you come on Wednesday **or** Thursday? **B:** Yes, I can come on **either** Wednesday **or** Thursday		**Alternative Relationships** • less emphasis • more emphasis
(d) **A:** Milly doesn't want to take calculus or trigonometry, **nor** do I. **B:** You mean **neither** you **nor** Milly likes mathematics?		**Negative Additive Relationships** • less emphasis • more emphasis

EXERCISE 1

Answer the following questions with correlative conjunctions for emphasis. Write your answers in complete sentences.

Example: Spain doesn't border on Portugal or France, does it?
> *Yes, it borders on both Portugal and France.*

1. President's Day and Valentine's Day aren't in February, are they?
2. Cameroon and Algeria are in South America, aren't they?
3. Honey or sugar can be used to sweeten lemonade, can't it?
4. Whales and dolphins are members of the fish family, aren't they?
5. Niagara Falls is situated in Brazil and Uruguay, isn't it?
6. Martin Luther King Jr. and Jesse Jackson were prominent black lawyers, weren't they?
7. You can travel from California to Hawaii by boat or airplane, can't you?
8. Ho Chi Minh City and Saigon refer to different places in Vietnam, don't they?

EXERCISE 2

Using the information in parentheses, respond to the following statements with *not only . . . but also*.

Example: I heard that Samuel has to work on Saturdays. (Sundays)
> *Samuel has to work **not only** on Saturdays **but also** on Sundays.*

1. Shirley Temple could dance very well. (sing)
2. The language laboratory is great for improving pronunciation. (listening comprehension)
3. Nola should exercise twice a week. (go on a diet)
4. Becky has to take a test on Friday. (finish a project)
5. Thomas Jefferson was a great politician. (inventor)
6. The dictionary shows the pronunciation of a word. (part of speech)
7. The International Student Office will help you to locate an apartment. (get a part-time job)
8. It rained all day last Tuesday. (last Wednesday)

ANSWER KEY

Exercise 1 Answers will vary. Possible answers are: 1. Yes, both President's Day and Valentine's Day are . . . 2. No, neither Cameroon nor Algeria is . . . 3. Yes, either honey or sugar can be . . . 4. No, not only whales but also dolphins are mammals. 5. No, Niagara Falls is situated neither in Brazil nor in Uruguay. 6. No, both Martin Luther King Jr. and Jesse Jackson were prominent ministers. 7. Yes, you can travel from California to Hawaii by either boat or airplane. 8. No, both Ho Chi Minh City and Saigon refer to the same city in Vietnam.

Exercise 2 1. Shirley Temple could not only dance but also sing very well. 2. The language laboratory is great for improving not only pronunciation but also listening comprehension. 3. Nola should not only exercise twice a week but also go on a diet. 4. Becky has to not only take a test on Friday but also finish a project. 5. Thomas Jefferson was not only a great politician but also an inventor. 6. The dictionary shows not only the pronunciation of a word but also the part of speech. 7. The International Student Office will help you not only to locate an apartment but also get a part-time job. 8. It rained all day not only last Tuesday but also last Wednesday.

FOCUS 1 [20 minutes]

This focus compares and contrasts coordinating conjunctions and correlative conjunctions, and explains how correlative conjunctions are used for emphasis.

1. **Lead-in:** Read the first section of the chart with the class.

2. For the second section, read the explanation, then have a pair of volunteers read the lines of dialogue in the examples.

3. Ask students to create other example sentences using these conjunctions.

4. Repeat this process for the third and fourth sections of the chart.

5. Answer any questions students might have.

METHODOLOGY NOTE

Students should already be familiar with these coordinating conjunctions. Most will find it interesting to compare these with the pairs of correlative conjunctions.

EXERCISE 1 [15 minutes]

In this exercise students apply the information from Focus 1 by writing answers to a series of questions, using correlative conjunctions for emphasis.

1. Read the directions and example. What coordinating conjunction is used in the question? (*or*) What correlative conjunctions are used in the answer? (*both . . . and*) How does the use of the correlative conjunctions affect the meaning of the answer? (*They make the statement more emphatic.*)

2. Have students work independently to write their answers to the questions, using correlative conjunctions for emphasis.

3. Remind students to use all of the structures. They may be tempted to use *both . . . and* more than *not only . . . but*, and *either . . . or* more than *neither . . . nor*. Encourage them to practice alternate forms.

4. Have students compare their answers with a partner.

5. Ask volunteers to share their answers with the class. Did anyone come up with different constructions? See possible answers on LP page 198.

 For more practice, use *Grammar Dimensions 4* Workbook page 92, Exercise 1.

EXPANSION [30 minutes/homework]

In Activity 1 (listening) on SB page 206, students listen to a college advisor and a student discussing required and elective courses using correlative conjunctions. This activity is a good sequel to Exercise 1. It could be done in class or assigned as homework.

EXERCISE 2 [20 minutes]

Students continue their work with the material from Focus 1 in this exercise, responding to statements using *not only . . . but also*.

1. Read the directions and example as a class.

2. Write this alternative response on the board: *Samuel has to work on Saturdays and Sundays.* Ask students to compare this statement with the example in their books. Elicit that the correlative conjunctions indicate an additive relationship, and make the example statement more emphatic.

3. Have students work independently to write their responses to the statements using *not only . . . but also*.

4. Have students, in pairs, take turns reading and responding to the questions, using the answers they wrote.

5. Ask pairs of volunteers to read and respond to the questions in front of the class. See answers on LP page 198.

 For more practice, use *Grammar Dimensions 4* Workbook page 93, Exercise 2.

EXPANSION [30 minutes/homework]

Have students do Activity 2 (writing) on SB pages 206–207 after Exercise 2 either in class or as homework to give them additional practice with using correlative conjunctions for emphasis. In this activity they are asked to write a memo to a fictional boss using the information supplied and correlative conjunctions.

Joining Phrases and Clauses with Correlative Conjunctions

form

EXAMPLES	EXPLANATIONS
(a) **Neither** the pedestrian **nor** the bicyclist saw the car approaching. (b) Mary will **not only** complete her coursework **but also** write her Master's thesis by June. (c) Mrs. Thomas was **both** surprised **and** jubilant that her daughter was awarded a scholarship. (d) Mark usually eats **either** at home **or** on campus.	All four correlative conjunction pairs can join phrases.
(e) **Either** the teacher has to slow down the lecture pace **or** the students need to take notes faster. (f) **Not only** was Mr. Jones strict **but** he was **also** unfair.	Only two of the correlative conjunction pairs can join clauses.
(g) **Not only is she** taking physics **but** she is also taking biology. (h) NOT: Not only she is taking physics but she is also taking biology.	In combinations with *not only . . . but also*, the position of the subject following *not only* is inverted with the first auxiliary verb, *be,* or *do.*

EXERCISE 3

Underline the correlative conjunction pairs in the sentences and identify what type of structure is being conjoined: adjective phrase, adverb phrase, noun phrase, prepositional phrase, verb phrase, or clause.

1. The improvement of education has to do not only with content knowledge but also with higher-order thinking skills.

2. We think it is both appropriate and important to restate our position on the new performing arts center.

3. Not only is this an issue for students to discuss at school but also for their parents to discuss at home.

4. I appreciate both the progress that has been made and the planning that went into the business school.

5. Either they will use the laboratory equipment now or they will use it later.

6. We tried to calculate what it will take not only to attract new students into the engineering program but also to keep them there.

7. They can shop for supplies either by phone or on the web.

8. We commend you both in terms of how the advertising was done and in terms of how the ticket sales were made.

9. He is active in the club as not only the vice-president but also the activities chair.

10. We can use the achievement test as a measure of not only how well a student is doing but also how effective the new program is.

11. They can either demonstrate the problem experimentally or describe the problem conceptually.

12. Not only do I have to provide the question but I also have to provide the answer.

13. Both students and faculty have spoken out against the war.

14. They have been unsuccessful either because they do not try or because they do not care.

15. We need to approach the athletics problem both quickly and efficiently.

EXERCISE 4

Write a few of your own sentences using correlative conjunction pairs and the words provided.

1. urgent . . . important

2. silently . . . slowly

3. required courses . . . electives

4. in the cafeteria . . . at the snack bar

5. to construct . . . to remodel

6. they will succeed in their mission . . . they will die trying to achieve their dream

7. to suggest an alternative . . . to solve the problem

8. before the play begins . . . at the intermission

ANSWER KEY

Exercise 3   The correlative conjunctions are underlined above and on SB page 201. They are identified as: 1. prepositional phrase   2. adjective phrase   3. clause   4. noun phrase   5. clause   6. verb phrase   7. prepositional phrase   8. prepositional phrase   9. noun phrase   10. clause   11. adverb phrase   12. clause   13. noun phrase   14. clause   15. adverb phrase

Exercise 4   Answers will vary.

FOCUS 2 [20 minutes]

1. **Lead-in:** Read the first explanation, then tell students that correlative conjunctions can join different types of phrases. Ask a volunteer to read the first example, and ask students to identify the type of phrases it contains. (*noun phrases*)

2. Have volunteers read the next three examples (b–d), and ask students to identify the type of phrase used in each. (*verb phrases, adjectives, prepositional phrases*)

3. Read the second explanation, then ask volunteers to read the two examples (e–f).

4. Ask students to try substituting *either . . . or* in example (e) with *neither . . . nor* and *both . . . and*. Do they see how those correlative conjunctions sound wrong?

5. Read the last explanation, then ask volunteers to read the two examples (g–h). Ask students to identify the inversion of the subject and verb following *not only* (*is she*, rather than *she is*).

6. Provide two more examples of inversion using *do* and *have*: *Not only did he miss work on Wednesday but he also missed work on Monday and Tuesday. Not only has he ridden in a hot air balloon but he has also parachuted from an airplane.*

7. Encourage students to ask questions about anything they do not understand.

EXERCISE 3 [25 minutes]

In Exercise 3 students apply what they have just learned in Focus 2.

1. Read the first sentence as a class. What correlative conjunctions are used? (*not only . . . but also*) What kind of phrases do they join? (*prepositional phrases*)

2. Have students work independently to underline the correlative conjunction pairs in the sentences and to identify the type of structure they join.

3. Have students share and discuss their sentences with a partner. See answers on LP page 200.

EXPANSION [60 minutes/homework]

Activity 5 (research on the web) on SB page 209 makes a good homework assignment after students study Focus 2 and complete Exercise 3. Students research and make comparisons about course requirements at two different schools using correlative conjunctions.

LESSON PLAN 2

Review information covered in Focus 2 briefly.

EXERCISE 4 [20 minutes]

In Exercise 4 students continue to practice what they have learned in Focus 2. In this case they supply their own context to fit the words given.

1. Have students complete sentences on their own.

2. Ask students to share sentences with a partner.

3. Have pairs of students choose their most successful sentences to share with the class.

4. The class should listen carefully for proper placement of correlative conjunctions.

 For more practice, use *Grammar Dimensions 4* Workbook page 94, Exercise 3.

EXPANSION 1 [25 minutes]

To give students more practice in using correlative conjunctions to join phrases and clauses, ask them to write about courses they plan to take in the future.

1. Write this chart, which is similar to the one in the Opening Task, on the board and ask students to copy it:

Discipline	Course	Type
ESL	ESL 101	Required
	ESL 102	Required
	Conversation 303	Elective

2. Have students fill in or expand the chart with information about courses they are required to take for their fields of study, and elective courses.

3. Ask them to write 8–10 sentences describing the courses they plan to take, would like to take, and will not be taking, using the correlative conjunctions.

4. Have them read their sentences to a partner, and discuss their choices.

EXPANSION 2 [60 minutes/homework]

Assign the first part of Activity 4 (listening/writing/speaking) on page 208 as homework following Exercise 4. Students watch a TV program, note statements they hear that use correlative conjunctions, and then discuss how the conjunctions were used and which types were most frequently used.

Using the information you obtained in the Opening Task on pages 196–197, write sentences about your classmates' preferences.

Examples: *Natasha may take either U.S. History or World History.*

She wants to enroll in microbiology and either psychology or biology.

EXERCISE 6

Think of a couple you know who have lived together for a long time. Fill out the grid with information about the couple (putting each name at the top of a column). Then, with a partner, discuss the couple's appearance, preferences, habits, or other features of their lives together. Use as many correlative conjunctions as you can.

Examples: Appearance: *Both Chau and George have black hair.*

Preferences: *On weekends Chau and George like to go either out to eat or to the movies.*

Habits: *Chau and George neither smoke nor drink.*

	NAME 1:	NAME 2:
Appearance:		
Preferences:		
Habits:		

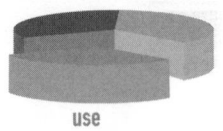

FOCUS 3	Correlative Conjunctions: Parallelism; Being Concise

use

NOT PARALLEL	PARALLEL	USES
clause/noun phrase (a) Not only was he an honors student but also a scholarship recipient.	**noun phrase/noun phrase** (b) He was not only an honors student but also a scholarship recipient.	In formal usage, the two phrases that correlative conjunctions join must have the same grammatical structures. If they do not, the sentence will not be parallel and should be rephrased.
gerund/infinitive (c) Both **gaining work experience** and **to earn academic credit** are important benefits of an internship.	**gerund/gerund** (d) Both **gaining work experience** and **earning academic credit** are important benefits of an internship.	

NOT CONCISE	CONCISE	USES
(e) She knew either **that she needed an A** or **that she needed a B** to pass the course. (g) Not only was **John** disqualified because of poor attendance but **Betty** was also disqualified for poor attendance.	(f) She knew that she needed **an A** or **a B** to pass the course. (h) Not only **John** but also **Betty** was disqualified because of poor attendance.	In addition, parallel structures should be concise, without unnecessary repetition.

ANSWER KEY

Exercise 5 Answers will vary.

Exercise 6 Answers will vary.

EXERCISE 5 [20 minutes]

In Exercise 5 students write about their classmates' preferences, using the information they gathered in the Opening Task (Steps 2 and 3) and applying what they have learned in Focus 2.

1. Read the directions and examples as a class. What correlative conjunctions are used? (*either . . .or*) What kind of phrases do they join? (*noun phrases*)

2. Have students look at the information they obtained about their classmates' preferences in the Opening Task and write sentences using the correlative conjunctions to join phrases and clauses.

3. Have students share and discuss their sentences with a partner.

4. Ask volunteers to read their partners' sentences to the class, and discuss these as a class.

5. If students disagree with the structure of a sentence, make sure they supply an alternative revised sentence.

EXPANSION [30 minutes]

Activity 3 (speaking) on SB page 208 can be assigned after Exercise 5 for extra practice with using correlative conjunctions to join phrases and clauses. Students role-play a working couple who are discussing how they each would like to divide the household chores.

EXERCISE 6 [20 minutes]

In Exercise 6 students discuss couples they know using correlative conjunctions.

1. Read the directions and examples as a class. Ask students to point out the correlative conjunctions used in the examples.

2. Brainstorm with the class what additional categories they could include, such as hobbies, family backgrounds, and organizational affiliations.

3. Have students work independently to fill out the grid with information about a couple who has lived together for a long time.

4. Have them work in pairs to discuss the couples. Tell them to use as many correlative conjunctions in their descriptions as they can.

5. Ask volunteers from several pairs to share their descriptions with the class. Ask another volunteer to write all the correlative conjunctions they use on the board.

EXPANSION [30 minutes]

Have students do this expansion work after Exercise 6 for more practice with joining phrases and clauses with correlative conjunctions. It is a variation of the task they perform in Activity 3 after Exercise 5, but with a humorous twist.

1. Discuss how difficult it can be to get *toddlers* to do anything you want them to do. Ask students to give examples of asking toddlers to do something and the responses they've been given.

2. Divide students into pairs. Ask them each to create a two-column chart: in the first column, they should list things they might ask a toddler to do, such as *Eat your dinner.*

3. Have students exchange papers, and fill in the second column with a second request, using a correlative conjunction. Model and elicit some examples: *Either you eat your dinner or you go to bed. / Not only do I want you to stop yelling, I want you to sit quietly for a moment.*

4. Tell students that they do not have to be realistic in what they write: their commands can be as outrageous as they like.

5. Have pairs of volunteers read their lists to the class, using lots of expression as if they are talking to a toddler.

FOCUS 3 [25 minutes]

Focus 3 explores parallelism and how it is used to achieve conciseness in expression.

1. **Lead-in:** Write the following three sentences on the board, with the correlatives written in one color and the other words in another color: *Kim was not only tired but he was also hungry. Neither the boys heard the shouts nor the girls from their tents. We will talk either at the coffee shop or chat in the bookstore.*

2. Ask students what they think is incorrect about the sentences. Elicit that the phrases or clauses following the correlatives are not of the same type.

3. Ask two volunteers to read the Not Parallel and Parallel columns in the focus chart. Read the Uses column to the class.

4. Ask students to identify the types of clauses used in both the Not Parallel and Parallel examples.

5. Follow the same procedure for the second section of the chart. Ask students to identify what words are deleted from the Not Concise examples to create the Concise examples.

6. Answer any questions students might have.

Read each sentence. Write OK next to sentences that are well-formed, parallel, and not repetitious. Rephrase the rest for concise, formal style. The first two have been done as examples.

1. I cannot stand to eat either liver or raw fish. OK

2. Not only is Maria tired but also sick. Maria is not only tired but also sick.

3. Not only *The New York Times* carried but also *The Los Angeles Times* carried the story of the train disaster in Algeria.

4. Juanita will both major in English and in sociology.

5. The Boston Red Sox either made the finals in the baseball competition or the Detroit Tigers did.

6. Suzuki neither found her watch nor her wallet where she had left them.

7. The Smith family loves both cats and dogs.

8. Mr. Humphrey thinks either that I should cancel or postpone the meeting with my advisor.

9. Not only am I going to the dentist but also the barber tomorrow.

10. Mary is going to either quit her job or is rearranging her work schedule to take astronomy.

11. I hope that the musicians are both well-rehearsed and that they are calm before the concert.

12. Todd neither saw or talked to his roommate, Bill.

13. Both bringing a bank card and cash is necessary for any trip.

14. Nor my two daughters nor my son wants to take an aisle seat on the airplane.

The following paragraphs have some nonparallel, inconcise structures with correlative conjunctions. Identify and rephrase them for formal usage.

(1) In the last 40 years, family life trends have changed dramatically in the United States. (2) In the past, it was expected that everyone would get married in their early twenties. (3) Now having to choose either between a family or a career, many are opting for the career and remaining single. (4) Others are postponing first marriages until their thirties or forties.

(5) If and when couples decide to marry, many are deciding to limit their family size. (6) Not only couples are having fewer children but they are also deciding to have no children at all. (7) On the other hand, some singles are either deciding to raise their own or adopt children by themselves. (8) In addition, many same-sex partners are not only choosing to form binding relationships but also to become parents.

(9) In the past, women worked either for personal satisfaction or to earn extra money for luxuries. (10) Today both husband and the wife must work in order to survive. (11) Because of this, husbands and wives do not always adhere to traditional sex roles. (12) Now either the husband might do the cooking and cleaning or the wife might do the cooking and cleaning.

(13) Both because of the greater stress of modern life and the greater freedom that each partner feels, divorce is becoming more and more common. (14) Neither the rich are immune nor the poor. (15) In some states, the divorce rate approaches fifty percent. (16) Marriage cannot be all bad, though. (17) Not only many people get divorced but these same people also get remarried one or more times throughout their lifetimes.

ANSWER KEY

Exercise 7 3. Not only *The New York Times* but also *The Los Angeles Times* carried . . . 4. . . . both in English and in sociology./ . . . major in both English and sociology. 5. Either the Boston Red Sox or the Detroit Tigers . . . 6. . . . neither her watch nor her wallet . . . 7. OK 8. . . . either cancel or postpone . . . 9. . . . not only to the dentist but also to . . . 10. . . . either quit her job or rearrange . . . 11. . . . both well-rehearsed and calm . . . 12. . . . neither saw nor talked . . . 13. Both a bank card and cash are . . . 14. Neither my two daughters nor my . . .

Exercise 8 (3) Now having to choose between either a family . . . (6) Not only are couples having fewer children, but they are also . . . (7) . . . are deciding to either raise their own or adopt . . . (8) . . . choosing not only to form binding relationships but also . . . (9) . . . either to achieve personal satisfaction or to . . . (10) Today both the husband and . . . (12) Now either the husband or the wife might do the cooking and cleaning. (13) Because of both the greater stress of modern life and the . . . (14) Neither the rich nor the . . . (17) Not only do many people get divorced these . . .

EXERCISE 7 [25 minutes]

In Exercise 7 students review a series of sentences and correct errors in form and parallel construction and delete unnecessary repetitions. It applies what they learned in Focus 3.

1. Read the directions and the first two sentences, which are examples, as a class. How else could students rephrase the second sentence?
2. Have students work independently to write OK next to the sentences that are well-formed, parallel, and concise. Ask them to rewrite the others.
3. Have students, in pairs, take turns reading their sentences. Which constructions are the most concise?
4. Ask volunteers to share their answers with the class. Does everyone agree with those answers? See answers on LP page 204.

 For more practice, use *Grammar Dimensions 4* Workbook page 96, Exercise 4.

EXPANSION [25 minutes]

This exercise will give students extra practice in identifying and correcting errors in parallelism in a résumé.

1. Talk about students' experiences with résumés: Have they ever written one? What information did they include? How did they structure the information?
2. Write the following portion of a résumé on the board, or write it in a word processing program, print it out, and hand it out to students.
3. Students could work independently or in pairs to correct the phrases.
4. Review answers as a class.

5. Ask students to write a similar description of a job they have had.
6. Have volunteers share their résumé entries with the class.

GOALS

A position as a senior computer programmer in a software development company. My degree, my work experience, and ability to develop business software programs qualify me for a job as a senior computer programmer.

Computer Programmer, ACME Business Systems

- Analyzed needs of business clients
- Software development and testing
- Implementation of software program on company computers
- Trained users in the software program
- Documentation writing

EXERCISE 8 (OPTIONAL) [25 minutes]

This exercise continues the practice students began in Exercise 7. This time, they review and correct sentences in a series of paragraphs, applying the principles outlined in Focus 3.

1. Read the directions as a class.
2. Ask volunteers to find a sentence that needs to be rewritten, and suggest an alternative construction. Write their responses on the board, and discuss the original and the rewritten sentence as a class.
3. Have students work independently to review the sentences in the paragraphs. Tell them to rewrite any that are not well formed. Tell them to double-check all parallel constructions, and rewrite any that are faulty. Remind them to delete any unnecessary repetitions.
4. Have students share their work with a partner.
5. Review students' rewrites as a class. Which rewritten sentences are the clearest and most concise?

 For more practice, use *Grammar Dimensions 4* Workbook page 97, Exercise 5.

EXPANSION 1 [30 minutes]

To give students additional practice with the form, meaning, and use of correlative conjunctions, have them do this expansion work, either in class or at home.

1. Ask students to choose at least three papers they have written in the past year. Ask them to review their writing and analyze it in terms of their use of correlative conjunctions. Have them refer to the three focus boxes in this unit to analyze their writing.
2. Ask students to rewrite 5–10 sentences from their papers using correlative conjunctions.
3. Have students share their work with a partner.
4. Ask volunteers to share their work with the class.

EXPANSION 2 [60 minutes/homework]

In Activity 6 (reflection) on SB page 209 students reflect and write a short composition about the strategies that are most beneficial to them in their language learning. This activity is a good final homework assignment.

UNIT GOAL REVIEW [5 minutes]

Ask students to look at the goals on the opening page of the unit again. Refer to the pages of the unit where information on each goal can be found. Review as needed.

 For assessment of Unit 11, use *Grammar Dimensions 4 ExamView®*.

Use Your English

ACTIVITY **1** listening

CD1 Track 15

Listen to the audio of a dialogue between a college advisor and a student. As you listen to the conversation, fill in the grid as the student responds to the advisor's questions.

NEW WORLD ALTERNATIVE COLLEGE STUDY PLAN		
	Fall	Spring
Year 1		
Year 2		

ACTIVITY **2** writing

Imagine that you are a supervisor for a company that allows fairly flexible hours for its part-time employees. Your boss recently called you to find out which day and time would be most convenient for each employee's evaluation conference. In order to help you in your decision, you asked the four workers you are supervising to indicate which hours they are available on the following blank schedule forms. An "A" indicates that a worker is available during a particular hour.

Conference Availability Charts

Pepita

	M	T	W	Th	F
9–10	A		A		A
10–11	A	A			
11–12		A	A	A	
12–1					
1–2		A	A		A

Tuan

	M	T	W	Th	F
9–10					
10–11					
11–12		A	A	A	
12–1	A	A	A	A	A
1–2			A		A

Tom

	M	T	W	Th	F
9–10					
10–11	A	A			
11–12			A		
12–1	A	A	A	A	A
1–2		A		A	

Laleh

	M	T	W	Th	F
9–10	A		A		A
10–11					
11–12			A		
12–1					
1–2		A		A	

Now write a memo to your boss, detailing who is and who is not available at various times for their evaluation conferences. Try to use the words *both, either,* or *neither* in your writing.

Example:

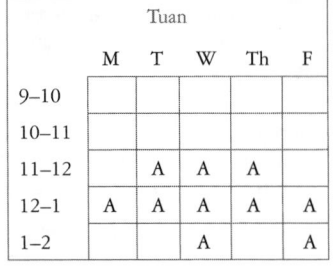

Memo

Dear Mr. Masters,
Both Pepita and Laleh are available from 9 to 10 on Monday, but neither Tuan nor Tom can come at that time . . .

ANSWER KEY

Activity 1 *Year 1:* **Fall:** Expository Writing, Psychology, Computer Science, French; **Spring:** World History, Anthropology, Communication Studies, Greenhouse Effect;
Year 2: **Fall:** Linguistics, Philosophy, Astronomy, Air Pollution; **Spring:** Biology, Geology, Acid Rain, Garbage Disposal

USE YOUR ENGLISH

The Use Your English activities at the end of the unit contain situations that should naturally elicit the structures covered in the unit. For a more complete discussion of how to use the Use Your English activities, see To the Teacher, LP page xxvi. While students are doing these activities in class, you can circulate and listen to see if they are using the structures accurately. Errors can be corrected after the activity has finished.

 **ACTIVITY 1** **listening**
[30 minutes/homework]

CD1
Track
15

In Activity 1 students listen to a college advisor and a student discussing required and elective courses using correlative conjunctions. This activity is a good sequel to Exercise 1 on SB page 199. It could be done in class or assigned as homework.

1. Tell students that they are going to listen to a discussion between a college advisor and a student about required and elective courses for the student. Explain that they will hear all the correlative conjunctions they studied in Focus 1.

2. Have students listen to the audio once without taking notes.

3. Ask students to listen again and fill in the grid as the student responds to the advisor's questions. Ask them to include the correlative conjunctions they hear used. Tell them to replay the audio as needed.

4. Encourage students to listen a final time to complete and check their notes, if they want to.

5. Have students compare notes with a partner.

6. Review answers as a class.

ACTIVITY 2 **writing**
[30 minutes/homework]

You may wish to have students do Activity 2 after Exercise 2 on SB page 199 either in class or as homework to give them additional practice with using correlative conjunctions for emphasis. In this activity they are asked to write a memo to a fictional boss using the information supplied and correlative conjunctions. The schedule forms and example memo are on SB page 207.

1. Read the directions with the class.

2. Have students look at the four charts.

3. Ask a volunteer to read the instructions for writing the memo, and ask another volunteer to read the example. What correlative conjunctions are used in the memo?
(*both . . . and; neither . . . nor*)

4. Have students write the memo to their "boss," indicating who is and who is not available for an evaluation conference at certain times. Remind them to use *both, either,* and *neither* in their memos.

5. Students could work independently or, if the activity is done in class, in pairs.

6. Ask volunteers to share their memos with the class. Encourage others to correct any errors in reporting availability that they might make.

 **ACTIVITY 3** speaking

Imagine that you have two children and both you and your spouse have to work outside the home, which leaves little time for running a household. In the chart below, choose which chores you would like to do and which chores you would like your spouse to do by marking an "X" under the appropriate column. If you feel that any of the tasks should be shared, write "B" (for both) under each column. Discuss your choice of respective duties with a classmate, using as many of the expressions you have learned in this unit as possible.

Example: *Both my spouse and I should share cooking meals because we both work.*

CHORES	MY CHORE	MY SPOUSE'S CHORE
cook meals	B	B
wash dishes		
vacuum floors and dust		
care for the yard		
shop for food		
shop for clothes		
pay bills		
clean toilets and fixtures		
do laundry		
take out garbage		
get the children dressed		
give the dog a bath		
take care of a child who is sick		

 **ACTIVITY 4** listening/writing/speaking

Listen carefully to a television program and jot down the statements you hear that contain *both/and, not only/but also, either/or,* or *neither/nor.* Share your notes and discuss which types of correlatives were used often and if they were used to show emphasis or not.

Example: *You can use either butter or margarine in the recipe. (cooking program)*
Not only did he strike out but he also got hit by a flying bat. (sports program)

 **ACTIVITY 5** research on the web

 Search the Web using a search engine such as Yahoo® or Google® to compare course offerings in the same major at one or more different universities, colleges, or vocational schools. You may compare your present school with another school or compare two entirely new schools to each other. Using correlative conjunctions, make several comparisons about course requirements.

Example: Dance Division at the Juilliard School and Dance/Theatre Department at California State University, Fullerton

Both Juilliard and CSU Fullerton require dance majors to take ballet and modern dance.
Neither Juilliard nor CSU Fullerton requires courses in piano.
Not only does Juilliard require courses in acting but it also requires courses in anatomy.

 **ACTIVITY 6** reflection

Some researchers feel that the following strategies contribute to more effective language learning:

- Arranging and planning your learning
- Evaluating your learning after a period of study
- Lowering your anxiety levels by eliminating stressful events in your environment
- Encouraging yourself
- Evaluating your emotional state after a period of study
- Asking questions of peers or others more knowledgeable about new material
- Creating mental images when learning sets of ideas or sequences of terms
- Reviewing what you have learned
- Analyzing and reasoning through new material
- Making intelligent guesses about new material

Write a short composition about which activities are most beneficial to you during your learning sessions. Use several examples with *either/or, neither/nor,* or *not only/but also* structures in your response to explain what you do, what you would like to do, and what you do not find beneficial during your study sessions.

Example: I have found my own set of learning strategies that work during my learning sessions. Although some people find studying with others useful, I neither study in groups nor ask questions of peers or others when learning new material. Instead, I . . .

ACTIVITY 3 speaking
[30 minutes]

Activity 3 can be assigned after Exercise 5 on SB page 202 for extra practice with using correlative conjunctions to join phrases and clauses. Students role-play a working couple who are discussing how they each would like to divide the household chores.

1. Discuss couples students know who have children and who both work. Who takes care of what chores in the house? Do they share the chores?
2. Ask a volunteer to read the directions. Do students think that most couples would be able to calmly and rationally discuss dividing household chores? How might different couples behave when discussing this topic?
3. Have students work in pairs. Have them each complete the chart and then role-play a discussion of chores, using the information in the charts.
4. Tell students to try to use as many of the expressions they have learned in this unit as possible in their discussion. Also, encourage them to overact a bit.
5. Ask several pairs to role-play the discussion.

ACTIVITY 4 listening/writing/speaking
[60 minutes/homework]

You may wish to assign Activity 4 as homework following Exercise 4 on page 201. Students watch a TV program, note statements they hear that use correlative conjunctions, and then discuss how the conjunctions and which types were frequently used.

1. Tell students that, for homework, you'd like them to watch a TV show and write down statements they hear that use correlative conjunctions.
2. Discuss what TV programs students like to watch. Which types of programs do they think might

contain a number of correlative conjunctions? (*Ones that compare and contrast things.*)
3. During the next class, have students work in small groups to share the statements they wrote down. What types of correlative conjunctions were used the most in each program? In all the programs members of the group watched? What were the conjunctions used for?
4. Ask a representative of each group to report the group's results to the class. Have a volunteer note their conclusions on the board. Tally the results for the class.

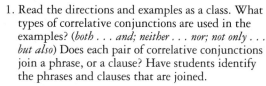

ACTIVITY 5 research on the web
[60 minutes/homework]

Activity 5 might make a good homework assignment after students study Focus 2 and complete Exercise 3 on SB pages 200–201. Students research and make comparisons about course requirements.

1. Read the directions and examples as a class. What types of correlative conjunctions are used in the examples? (*both . . . and; neither . . . nor; not only . . . but also*) Does each pair of correlative conjunctions join a phrase, or a clause? Have students identify the phrases and clauses that are joined.
2. Tell students that you would like them to research at least two different universities, colleges, or vocational schools on the Internet. They should take notes on the course offered, and on which courses are required, and which are elective. They may want to use a chart like the one in the Opening Task to organize their notes.
3. Explain to students that they can compare their current school with another school or compare two entirely new schools to each other.
4. Ask students to make at least four comparisons about course requirements at the two schools using sentences with correlative conjunctions.

5. During the next class, have students read and discuss their comparisons with a partner. What correlative conjunctions did they use?

ACTIVITY 6 reflection
[60 minutes/homework]

This activity is a good homework assignment following Exercise 8 on SB page 205.

1. Brainstorm a list of strategies students use to help them in their language learning, and write these on the board.
2. Ask a volunteer to read the directions and list of strategies to the class. Which strategies do most of the students use? Are there any very unusual strategies that others might consider using?
3. Write one or two of the strategies on the board. Ask students to comment on how they employ them, and write responses on the board in the form of notes—e.g., for *Arranging and planning learning,* you might write: *estimate time for each assignment/do hardest assignments first.*
4. Guide students in creating sentences using the information on the board and correlative conjunctions—e.g., *Not only do I estimate the time it will take me to do each assignment, but I also do the hardest assignment first.*
5. Ask students to create their own lists of strategies they use, and make notes about how they use them. Have them write a short composition about those strategies that are most beneficial to them in their language learning. Encourage them to use as many of the expressions and constructions they have learned in this unit as possible.
6. During the next class, have students exchange papers with a partner and discuss their strategies.

SENTENCE CONNECTORS

- **Understand the differences between conjunctions and sentence connectors**

- **Use appropriate sentence connectors to express various logical meanings**

- **Choose appropriate sentence connectors for formal and informal contexts**

- **Use correct punctuation for sentence connectors in writing**

OPENING TASK

How Things Came to Be

Cultures all over the world have creation myths, which explain how life on earth came to be.

▪ STEP 1

Read the two creation myths from Finland and Polynesia that are summarized on the next page. They describe how the earth, the sky, and the first people on earth came to exist.

▪ STEP 2

Write a paragraph describing the similarities and differences between the two creation myths. In comparing the stories, consider the following questions:

1. What existed at the beginning of creation?
2. In what order were things created?
3. How were the earth and sky created?
4. Who was responsible for creating the first people and how were they created?

From Finland:

In the beginning there was only Water, Air, and Air's daughter, Ilamatar. Ilamatar spent her time wandering around the world. One day Ilamatar sank down to rest upon the ocean's face as she was very tired. When she lay down, the seas rolled over her, the waves tossed her, and the wind blew over her. For seven hundred years, Ilamatar swam and floated in the sea. Then one day while she lay floating with one knee up out of the water, a beautiful duck swooped down and landed on her knee. There it laid seven eggs. As the days went by, the eggs grew hotter and hotter until Ilamatar could no longer endure the heat and pulled her knee into the water. Because of this, the eggs rolled into the ocean and sank to its bottom. Eventually, one of the eggs cracked. From the lower half of its shell, the earth was formed. From the egg's upper shell, the sky formed over the land and sea. From the yolk of the egg, the sun rose into the sky. From the white of the egg, the moon and stars were created and took their place in the heavens. Later, Ilamatar gave birth to the sea's child, whom she called Vainamoinen. For seven years Vainamoinen swam the seas. Then he went ashore and became the first person on earth.

From Polynesia:

In the beginning there was Darkness and the Sea. While soaring over the Sea, Old Spider discovered a large clam shell and climbed inside it. It was very dark inside the clam shell, and Old Spider was feeling cramped. Then she found a snail inside and asked the snail to open the shell a little. After the snail opened the shell, the Old Spider took the snail, put it in the West and made it into the Moon. Old Spider, however, felt the space was still too tight and wanted to raise the shell higher. It turned out there was another snail around to help the Old Spider raise it. In this way, the sky, called Rangi, was created. After the sky had been created, Old Spider pushed down hard on the lower part of the shell, and it became the earth, called Papa. Together Rangi, God of the Sky, and Papa, Goddess of the Earth, created all of the plants and animals. Finally they produced the first people. Everyone lived together in the clam shell. Because of the crowded conditions, the many children begged Kane, the god of the forests, to separate Rangi and Papa to create more space. Kane obliged; as a result, Rangi and Papa were no longer together.

UNIT OVERVIEW

Knowledge and appropriate use of logical connectors are important features of grammatical competence for advanced level students. This unit starts with a review of connector types and then focuses on sentence adverbs, or sentence connectors. We have called them **sentence connectors** so that students will be more aware of how they differ from the subordinating conjunctions that join clauses within a sentence.

Please note that because this unit is unusually long, it has been divided into five separate lessons. To review this unit more quickly, read each focus chart with students and complete one exercise with a second exercise, expansion, or activity assigned as homework for each chart.

GRAMMAR NOTE

The sentence connectors in this unit are presented in **semantic sets**—i.e., they are grouped according to the types of logical meanings they represent. Within these sets, distinctions are made between the various connector words and phrases in terms of their meaning and use. The unit contains eight very detailed focus boxes. Tell students that these can be used as reference tools throughout the course.

UNIT GOALS

Some instructors may want to review the goals listed on Student Book (SB) page 210 after completing the Opening Task so that students understand what they should know by the end of the unit. These goals can also be reviewed at the end of the unit when students are more familiar with the grammar terminology.

OPENING TASK [20 minutes]

The purpose of this task is to create a compelling context in which students can exhibit their command of various reference forms. Here, students read and then write a comparison of two creation myths, one from Finland and one from Polynesia, that contain several types of sentence connectors. The problem-solving format is designed to show the teacher how well the students can produce the target structures implicitly and spontaneously when they are engaged in a communicative task. For a more complete discussion of the purpose of the Opening Task, see To the Teacher, Lesson Planner (LP) page xxii.

Setting Up the Task

Ask students to share what they know about different creation myths. What myths do they know from other cultures? How does each myth explain the creation of the earth and of people? Are there any similarities between the myths?

Conducting the Task

■ STEP 1

1. Read the directions for the first step as a class.
2. Divide students into groups of four. Have them take turns reading the two creation myths aloud, each student reading several sentences.
3. Ask students to take turns summarizing the two myths.

■ STEP 2

Ask students to each write a paragraph describing the similarities and differences between the myths. The paragraph writing task is designed to elicit comparison and contrast connectors, but students may also use other types of connectors in summarizing various parts of the two stories. Remind them to respond to the four questions in Step 2 as they write.

Closing the Task

1. Ask students to take turns reading their paragraphs to their groups.

2. Ask volunteers to read their paragraphs to the class, and discuss these.
3. Don't worry about accuracy at this point, though you may want to take notes of errors in meaning, form, or use in order to focus on those problems later.

VARIATION

You might want to collect students' papers and use sentences from them for later work on sentence connector types, such as adding connectors to sentence pairs or changing sentences with subordinating conjunctions to two sentences joined by a connector (or to two main clauses joined by a semicolon and connector). You may also be able to use some sentences for error analysis and correction.

GRAMMAR NOTE

Typical student errors (form)

- Using a comma rather than a semicolon in sentences in which a connector begins an independent clause after another independent clause in the same sentence:—e.g., * *We were careful to keep the temperature at 68 degrees in the house all winter, as a result, none of our plants died.* (See Focus 8.)
- Adding unnecessary commas to sentences with connectors:—e.g., * *I read the book she gave me, although, I would not recommend it to my friends.* (See Focus 8.)

Typical student errors (use)

- Repeating previously stated information word for word when using a similarity connector: —e.g., * *John and I often go to the movies on Saturdays. Similarly, Alex and Maria often go to the movies on Saturdays.* (See Focus 5.)
- Using different constructions to contrast two ideas:—e.g., * *We see lots of commercials on the network TV channels; in contrast, I know there are very few on the public broadcasting stations.* (See Focus 6.)

FOCUS 1   Connectors

Connector Relationships

Many types of meaning relationships can exist within one sentence or from one sentence to another. Words or phrases that express these relationships are called **connectors**. The chart below shows some of these relationships.

EXAMPLES	TYPES OF RELATIONSHIPS	EXAMPLES WITH CONNECTORS
(a) Old Spider climbed inside the clam shell. She discovered a snail there.	time sequence	**After** Old Spider climbed inside the clam shell, she found a snail there.
(b) Old Spider lived in a clam shell. Two snails lived there.	added idea	Old Spider lived in a clam shell. Two snails lived there **as well.**
(c) In the Finnish myth, the heavens were created from an egg. The sun was formed from the yolk of the egg.	example	In the Finnish myth, the heavens were created from an egg. The sun, **for example,** was formed from the yolk of the egg.
(d) In the Finnish myth, the earth did not exist in the beginning. In the Polynesian myth, at first there was only darkness and the sea.	similarity	In the Finnish myth, the earth did not exist in the beginning. **Similarly,** in the Polynesian myth, at first there was only darkness and the sea.
(e) In the Polynesian myth, the moon was a snail. In the Finnish myth, the moon came from an egg white.	contrast	In the Polynesian myth, the moon was a snail, **whereas** in the Finnish myth the moon came from an egg white.
(f) Ilamatar was very tired. She lay down on the ocean's face.	result	Ilamatar was very tired, **so** she lay down on the ocean's face.
(g) Creation myths are universal. They are found throughout the world.	clarification	Creation myths are universal. **That is,** they are found throughout the world.

Note: Refer to Appendix 3, page A-6, for a complete chart of sentence connectors.

Types of Connectors

There are three main types of connectors: coordinating conjunctions, subordinating conjunctions, and sentence connectors.

EXAMPLES	EXPLANATIONS
Independent Clause (h) Ilamatar kept the eggs on her knee, **Independent Clause** **but** eventually they got too hot.	• **Coordinating conjunctions** connect the ideas in two independent clauses. The coordinating conjunctions are *and, but, for, or, nor, so,* and *yet*. In written English, we usually write these clauses as one sentence, separated by a comma.
Dependent Clause (i) **After** Old Spider made the sky, **Independent Clause** she created the earth. **Independent Clause** (j) Old Spider made the sky **Dependent Clause** **before** she created the earth.	• **Subordinating conjunctions** connect ideas within sentences. They show the relationship between an idea in a dependent clause and an idea in an independent clause. Common subordinating conjunctions include: Time *after, before, once, since, until, when, whenever, while* Reason *as, because, since* Result *in order that, so that, that* Contrast *although, even though, though, whereas* Condition *if, even if, provided that, unless* Location *where, wherever*
Independent Clause (k) Rangi and Papa created the plants and animals. **Independent Clause** **In addition,** they produced the first people. **Independent Clause** (l) Ilamatar could not endure the heat from the eggs; **consequently,** **Independent Clause** she put her knee back into the water.	• **Sentence connectors** usually express relationships between two or more independent clauses. The independent clauses may be separate sentences, as in (k). They may also be in the same sentence, separated by a semicolon, as in (l). The remainder of this unit is concerned with the third type of logical connector, sentence connectors.

Note: Refer to Appendix 3, page A-6, for a complete chart of sentence connectors.

METHODOLOGY NOTE

If your students didn't do the Opening Task, they should at least read the two creation myth stories before studying this focus chart. Otherwise, the example sentences, many of which refer to the stories, may be harder to understand.

FOCUS 1 [25 minutes]

This focus gives an overview of logical connectors and summarizes the three types of structures that signal logical relationships between ideas: coordinating conjunctions, subordinating conjunctions, and sentence connectors. Sentence connectors, the focus of this unit, are also called "sentence adverbs."

1. **Lead-in:** Begin with a focus on meanings (relationships between ideas) rather than on the three grammatical categories of connectors. Make sure students understand that the connector examples in the third column are rewrites of the examples in the first column.

2. Write the categories of relationships listed in column 2 on the board. Ask students for other connector words or phrases of each type. At this point, don't be concerned with the grammatical categories of their responses (i.e., whether it is a coordinating conjunction, subordinating conjunction, etc.).

3. Review the three types of connectors in the second part of this focus chart (coordinating conjunctions, subordinating conjunctions, and sentence connectors). Check off the words and phrases you listed on the board as you progress through the chart. Students will probably be most familiar with the first two types, though many may not know all of them, and they may not have learned or remember their grammatical labels. Remind students that subordinating conjunctions are sometimes called *subordinators*.

4. Let students know that sentence connectors are generally the most formal of the connectors. Tell students that these occur most frequently in academic writing and formal speech.

5. For an example, say these sentences and ask students to tell you what sounds odd about them: *I was really hungry this morning after my first class. Thus, I got a snack at the cafeteria.* Most students will know that *thus* sounds too formal in this context. Ask them to rephrase the thoughts in a less formal manner. Responses could include joining the ideas by *so* or using a reason subordinator like *because* with the first clause.

For each of the sentence pairs below, state what the relationship of the second sentence is to the first: *time sequence, added idea, example, similarity, contrast, result,* or *clarification.*

Example: Ilamatar's child swam the seas for seven years. He went ashore.
Relationship: *time sequence*

1. The myths of many cultures include a god of thunder. The Mayan god of thunder was Chac. _____*example*_____

2. In Greek mythology, Ares, the god of war, was often violent and belligerent. The goddess Athena was a peacemaker. _____*contrast*_____

3. Myths help us to understand human behavior. They also entertain us.
_____*added idea*_____

4. Ancient civilizations did not know the scientific explanations for natural phenomena such as storms. They made up stories to explain these events. _____*result*_____

5. In North American Indian cultures, cosmogony is a major theme in myths. These myths explain how the universe was created. _____*clarification*_____

6. In a Chinese creation myth, a man named Pan Gu lived in an egg for eighteen thousand years. He woke up and chopped the egg in two with an ax. _____*time sequence*_____

7. The village represents a place of order in African folktales. The bush, or jungle, represents a place of mystery and destructive forces. _____*contrast*_____

8. Jason, the leader of the Argonauts in Greek mythology, went on a long sea voyage to get the Golden Fleece. The Greek hero Odysseus embarked on a long voyage. _____*similarity*_____

9. In an Indonesian myth, the first woman in the world caused a great flood that washed away her garden. She was punished with a malformed child who had only one eye, one arm, and one leg. _____*result*_____

10. A common animal in many myths and folktales is the trickster. In Asia, the trickster is often a rabbit or a monkey. _____*example*_____

FOCUS 2   Addition Connectors

meaning

use

Simple Addition

CONNECTORS	EXAMPLES	MEANINGS
also	(a) Myths often tell stories about how things originated. They **also** attempt to explain why things occur in nature.	These connectors express simple addition. They have the meaning of *too* or *and*.
in addition	(b) In oral traditions, cultures passed myths down to later generations. **In addition,** many cultures told historical stories, known as legends.	
furthermore	(c) Many creation myths begin with a formless universe, or chaos. **Furthermore,** they often explain how the earth and sky are formed by separating the matter of the universe.	
moreover	(d) In many creation myths, the world is first covered by a great sea. **Moreover,** the sea is often the origin of the first animals.	

Emphatic Addition

CONNECTORS	EXAMPLES	MEANINGS
what is more (informal: *what's more*)	(e) Some African myths emphasize the need for individuals to help the community. **What is more,** even the animals are expected to help out.	Emphatic connectors signal an idea that stresses some aspect of what has been previously stated. Their meaning is similar to "Not only *that* (what I just said), but also *this* (what I am saying now)."
as well	(f) The Polynesian sea-god Tangaroa sometimes appeared as a huge fish. He could take on the form of a green lizard **as well.**	
*besides (this)**	(g) Myths may represent cultural values. **Besides this,** they can reflect fears about forces beyond control.	

* In this example and others in the unit, the word ***this*** refers to the idea that has been previously mentioned. The word THIS will often be a demonstrative pronoun (*this, that, these,* or *those*) or a demonstrative determiner + noun phrase (for example: as well as *this fact*).

Note: Refer to Appendix 3, page A-6, for a complete chart of sentence connectors.

■ EXERCISE 1 [20 minutes]

This exercise requires analysis of the underlying logical relationships between sentences. This is an important academic skill for students to develop for reading as well as writing. Obviously, they need to understand these relationships in order to choose appropriate connectors.

1. Read the directions and example as a class. Ask students to identify what type of relationship exists between the two sentences (*time sequence*).

2. Have students work in pairs, taking turns reading the sentences and identifying the relationship between each pair of sentences.

3. Many students will have the most difficulty with 5, a clarification relationship. The second sentence in 5 paraphrases the statement *cosmogony is a major theme in myths* and could be related to the first sentence by *in other words* if a connector were added.

4. Another difficult sentence is 7, which shows contrast. If your students don't grasp this relationship, ask them to identify or draw boxes around the contrasting terms: *village/order; bush (jungle)/mystery* and *destructive forces*.

5. Review answers as a class. See answers on LP page 214.

work book | For more practice, use *Grammar Dimensions 4* Workbook page 98, Exercise 1 and page 99, Exercise 2.

FOCUS 2 [30 minutes]

Focus 2 continues on SB page 216. The first three sections of Focus 2 explain the difference between the meanings and uses of simple addition and emphatic addition connectors. The fourth section on page 216 explains and exemplifies intensifying connectors, and the final section on this page distinguishes these intensifying connectors from emphatic ones.

1. **Lead-in:** Write on the board: *This summer, I have a lot of plans for how to spend my time. One of them is to do a lot of traveling. Besides that, (leave space for several sentences). In fact . . . (leave space for a sentence).*

2. Ask students what other things they might like to do during the summer besides travel. Have a volunteer write responses in full sentences after *besides that*. Ask these same students to give specific examples of the other things they might like to do. Model an example: *Besides that, I'd like to learn how to scuba dive. In fact, I plan to enroll in a scuba diving class in June.* Have a volunteer write responses on the board after *In fact . . .*

3. Ask students to explain in their own words the difference between the two additions. (*besides that* adds information, with emphasis; *in fact* shows support for the preceding statement)

4. Have a group of three volunteers read the focus chart, each reading one column at a time.

5. Ask students to glance through the focus chart and note the various placements of connectors within sentences: initially, medially and, in the case of as well, finally. Tell students that although they may have used many of the connectors, they may tend to always put them at the beginning of a sentence. Encourage them to consider placing connectors in other places in a sentence to focus more sharply on a logical connection. For example, in (a) placement of *also* focuses on *tell(ing) stories about how things originated as well as attempt(ing) to explain why things occur in nature.*

6. Note that in spoken and informal written English, *what is more* is often expressed with a contraction: *what's more.*

7. Answer any questions students may have.

METHODOLOGY NOTE

Advanced students should be familiar with the simple addition connectors. They may be less familiar with those expressing emphatic or intensifying addition. Most of the vocabulary should be familiar to them, but they may not have learned these connectors as a semantic set.

Some students may tend to use only one connector (e.g., *also*) as a simplification strategy and may need to be encouraged to expand their repertoire. (This will be true for many of the focus charts in this unit.) Encourage them to use forms they haven't used before, or have used infrequently, and to focus on making those forms part of their active vocabulary.

Simple Addition versus Emphatic Addition

EXAMPLES	MEANINGS
(h) Urban legends, a kind of contemporary folktale, have been written about in a number of recent books. **Simple Addition** (i) They are **also** the topics of a recent television series and a horror film. **Emphatic Addition** (j) A number of Web sites dedicated to discussing urban legends have been developed **as well.**	We often use simple addition and emphatic addition in the same contexts. The emphatic connector simply stresses the added information more than the simple connector does.

Intensifying Addition

CONNECTORS	EXAMPLES	MEANINGS
in fact	(k) Some myths tell stories of terrible destruction. **In fact,** in many stories the entire world is destroyed.	Intensifying connectors show that an idea will strongly support another one.
as a matter of fact	(l) Urban legends are often communicated in writing rather than orally. **As a matter of fact,** e-mail has become the source of many urban legends.	
actually	(m) In one well-known urban legend, a woman with an elaborate hairdo was killed by spiders nesting in it. **Actually,** this never happened.	

Intensifying Addition versus Emphatic Addition

EXAMPLES	EXPLANATIONS
(n) Urban legends, despite the name, do not always take place in an urban setting.	(Introductory sentence)
Emphatic Addition (o) **Besides that,** urban legends are not historical tales as were the ancient legends such as "King Arthur" or "Saint George and the Dragon."	We use emphatic connectors when we add a related idea. (o) adds another fact that makes the term "urban legend" rather inaccurate.
Intensifying Addition (p) **In fact,** many urban legends are more like a folktale or a joke with a dark theme.	We use intensifying connectors to elaborate an idea. (p) supports the idea of urban legends not being historical tales as many ancient legends were.

Note: Refer to Appendix 3, page A-6, for a complete chart of sentence connectors.

Use an appropriate sentence connector from the list below to show the kind of addition relationship expressed in the last sentence of each pair or group of sentences. More than one connector could be appropriate for most contexts. Try to use each connector in the list once.

also	moreover	besides
in addition	what is more	in fact
furthermore	as well	as a matter of fact
		actually

Example: The study of folklore includes legends. It includes proverbs.
> The study of folklore includes legends and proverbs as well.

1. In ancient myths, the possession of fire is a common theme. It is often a source of conflict between gods and humans.

   _____

2. The Greek hero Prometheus stole fire from the king of gods, Zeus, and was seriously punished. He was chained to a rock.

   _____

3. Our teacher asked us if we had ever read the myth of Prometheus. I hadn't. I had never even heard of it. (Connect ideas in the second and third sentences.)

   _____

4. The Aztec deity Quetzalcoatl was the god of the sun and the air. He was the god of wisdom and a teacher of the arts of peace.

   _____

5. The primordial sea is present in many creation myths. It is one of the most common elements in these stories.

   _____

6. Many of the gods in ancient myths acted very much like the humans they created. They fall in love with each other and fight with each other. They make mistakes and regret their actions. (Connect ideas in the second and third sentences.)

   _____

7. I read about some of the most well-known urban legends on a Web site. I can't believe that people think some of those stories are true. I can't believe that they would tell them to others.

   _____

8. Humankind has always tried to explain questions about the origins of the universe. We are still trying to answer some of these questions today.

   _____

ANSWER KEY

Exercise 2   Answers will vary. Possible answers are: 1. As a matter of fact, it is often a source . . . 2. In fact, he was chained . . .   3. I hadn't. Moreover, I had never even heard . . .   4. In addition, he was the god of wisdom . . .   5. Actually, it is one of the most common elements . . .   6. What is more, they make mistakes . . .   7. . . . on a Web site, and I can't believe . . . Furthermore, I can't believe . . .   8. . . . some of these questions today as well.

In this exercise students apply what they have just learned in Focus 2. They link sentences using connectors from a list to express specific addition relationships.

1. As a class, read the directions and example. What other connectors could be used in the example? How would they affect the meaning?
2. Have students work in pairs to complete the exercise.
3. Remind students that *also* is the most general of the connectors and can fit many contexts, but some of the other connectors offer more precise meanings for particular contexts. Encourage students to use connectors that are less familiar to them wherever possible and to try putting the connectors in positions other than the beginning of the sentence. (*As well*, of course, has to be placed at the end of the sentence.)
4. Ask volunteers to share their answers with the class. See possible answers on LP page 216.

 For more practice, use *Grammar Dimensions 4* Workbook page 99, Exercise 3.

EXPANSION [45 minutes]

Activity 2 (writing) on SB page 236 can be assigned after Exercise 2. In this activity students, working in groups, create lists of facts and opinions, exchange them with another group, and add facts to each statement, using addition connectors.

Make up two sentences for each of the following instructions. Use an addition connector to link ideas between sentences. An example has been given for the first one.

1. Give two reasons why you enjoy something you often do in your spare time.

Example: *I enjoy volunteer work with children at the hospital because I like children. Besides that, it gives me work experience for my future career in medicine.*

2. Give two reasons why you like one movie or television show you've seen more than another.

_____

_____

3. State two advantages of flying over driving when a person goes on a long trip.

_____

_____

4. State two uses for computers.

_____

_____

5. Give two reasons why people tell stories about themselves.

_____

_____

6. Give two reasons why you would want to improve your English grammar skills.

_____

_____

7. State two differences between English and your native language.

_____

_____

8. Give two reasons why someone should visit a particular city or country.

_____

_____

9. Give two reasons why someone should get to know you.

_____

_____

10. State two things that you are very good at doing.

_____

_____

FOCUS 3   Alternative Connectors

meaning

use

CONNECTORS	EXAMPLES	MEANINGS
on the other hand *alternatively*	(a) We can read myths simply as stories. **On the other hand,** we can see them as reflections of cultural values and ideas. (b) You could take the history course you eventually need this semester. **Alternatively,** you could complete your schedule with a science course.	These connectors indicate a possibility in addition to the one just mentioned. *On the other hand* and *alternatively* have similar meanings. *Alternatively* is a more formal connector. It is used mainly in written English.
	(c) Washington, D.C. might be fun to visit this summer.	The "other possibility" could be various parts of a previously mentioned idea. (d) through (f) are some alternative statements that might follow example (c).

	Other possibility	Part changed in (c)
	(d) **On the other hand,** it might be too crowded.	fun
	(e) **On the other hand,** Minneapolis might be a better city to visit in the summer.	Washington, D.C.
	(f) **On the other hand,** it might be better to go there in the fall.	this summer

Note: Refer to Appendix 3, page A-6 for a complete chart of sentence connectors.

ANSWER KEY

Exercise 3   Answers will vary.

Briefly review information covered in Focus 2. Have students provide you with examples of, words of intensifying addition.

EXERCISE 3 [20 minutes]

In this exercise students respond to instructions by creating sentences whose ideas are linked with addition connectors.

1. Read the directions and example as a class. What other connectors could be used in the example? How would they affect the meaning?
2. Have students work in pairs. Tell them to take turns making up two sentences for each set of instructions.
3. Students should discuss each sentence with their partner, including what other connectors could be used and how each would change the sentence's meaning, before going on to the next.
4. Ask volunteers to share some examples with the class. Ask the class to raise their hands if they came up with a similar response to each instruction.

EXPANSION [30 minutes]

Have students do this expansion work for more practice with addition connectors. They do the first part as homework, and complete the activity in class.

1. For homework, ask students to make up five instructions modeled after the ones in Exercise 3.
2. During the next class, ask students to work in pairs and take turns giving and responding to instructions. Monitor the pair work production.

VARIATION

This activity could also be done as a whole-class activity, with individual students calling on others

in the class to respond—e.g., *Katya, state two courses that you like and explain why*. (Note: As with any activity in which you are not able to "screen" students' requests in advance, give students the option to "pass" if they are asked something personal to which they don't want to respond.)

LESSON PLAN 2

FOCUS 3 [20 minutes]

Focus 3 explores the meanings and uses of alternative connectors, which are used after stating one possibility to indicate another.

1. **Lead-in:** Write the two connectors—*on the other hand* and *alternatively*—on the board. Ask one volunteer to read the first two examples, and another to read the meanings.
2. To help students understand the second part of this chart, write this example on the board: *I could buy a cake for dessert tonight. On the other hand . . .*
3. Draw a box around *I*. Ask students to substitute a name for *I*. Write a new sentence after *on the other hand*, using a shortened form rather than repeating the entire original sentence (e.g., *On the other hand, Kevin could buy one*.). Model saying the sentence, and elicit that the name is stressed. Have students practice saying the sentence.
4. Repeat this procedure with other parts of the sentence, boxing *make*, then *cake*, then *tonight* and writing each new sentence with the substitutions under the previous one. For each, vary some of the words and phrasing of the original (e.g., *On the other hand, I might wait to get one until tomorrow*.) to avoid making your additions sound unnatural.
5. If time permits, and if students easily grasped the concept of different possibilities, ask them to tell you another place in the sentence where they could position *on the other hand* instead of at the

beginning of the sentence. (The most natural place would be after *could*.)

METHODOLOGY NOTE

The first part of this chart gives students two common alternative connectors. *On the other hand* will probably be the most familiar one. Remind students that the preposition for this connector is *on* and never *in,* and that the article *the* cannot be omitted in this construction.

EXERCISE 4

Add a statement after each sentence below and on the next page that would express another possibility. Use *on the other hand* or *alternatively* to signal the connection.

Example: I could get a job this summer.
On the other hand, I could take a few courses in summer school.

1. I could stay home this weekend.
<u>On the other hand, I could go to a movie.</u>
2. The theory of the Big Bang, explaining the origins of the universe, could be correct.
<u>On the other hand, perhaps there really was an Almighty Creator.</u>
3. If you're looking for a used car to buy, you could check the classified ads in the newspaper.
<u>Alternatively, you could visit a car dealer.</u>
4. Legalizing heroin in the United States could help decrease crime.
<u>On the other hand, it could increase the number of drug users in the country.</u>
5. Parents who are upset with the violence that their children see every day on television could write letters to the television stations.
<u>Alternatively, they could limit the kinds of television shows they allow their children to watch.</u>

EXERCISE 5

Form small groups. Read each of the statements below. Then take turns forming alternative statements for each one. Each person must focus on a different part of the statement. Use *on the other hand* or *alternatively*.

Example: It could be fun to get a job making pizzas this summer.
On the other hand, it could get boring after awhile.
(focus: fun)
It might be more interesting to get work at a television studio.
(focus: a job making pizzas)
It would probably be more fun to eat the pizzas!
(focus: making)

1. Chile might be a good place to go for our winter vacation.
2. Advanced Composition could be a good course for me to take next quarter.
3. It might be fun to go to the art museum on Saturday.
4. You could call your family this weekend.

FOCUS 4   Exemplifying, Identifying, and Clarifying Connectors

EXEMPLIFYING CONNECTORS	EXAMPLES	MEANINGS
for example	(a) The struggle between gods and their offspring is a frequent theme in ancient myths. The Greek god Zeus, **for example,** fought with the Titans.	These connectors introduce examples of what has been mentioned.
e.g.	(b) Mythic stories about floods are told in many cultures (e.g., Scandinavian, Celtic and Turkish mythology all have such stories).	The abbreviation *e.g.* (from Latin *exempli gratia*) is sometimes used as an abbreviation for *for example*. In professional writing, the sentence beginning with *e.g.* is put in parentheses, Note that a comma follows *e.g.*
for instance	(c) Some urban legends involve food contamination. Take, **for instance,** the story about the mouse in the fried chicken.	*For example* and *for instance* introduce a typical member of a group or a typical instance.
especially	(d) Violence in movies seems to be increasing. Action films **especially** are getting more violent.	*Especially* and *in particular* introduce an important member of a group or an important instance.
in particular	(e) Learning the rules for article usage in English is a challenge. **In particular,** the use of articles with generic nouns may be confusing.	
to illustrate	(f) The steps for saving your computer files are quite simple. **To illustrate,** we will save the file you have just created.	*To illustrate* and *as an example* often introduce a lengthy example such as a process or narrative.
as an example	(g) Many great composers have had their share of misery. **As an example,** consider the life of Mozart.	

IDENTIFYING CONNECTORS	EXAMPLES	MEANINGS
namely	(h) Many fairy tales have common features; **namely,** they often involve magical events and royalty, such as kings or princesses.	These connectors identify something either previously mentioned or implied. They introduce a more specific or detailed elaboration.
specifically	(i) I have a question about connectors. **Specifically,** when do you use *in fact*?	

ANSWER KEY

Exercise 4   Answers will vary. Possible answers are shown above.
Exercise 5   Answers will vary. Possible answers are: 1. On the other hand, it might be too crowded then./ . . . Hawaii would be a lot cheaper./ . . . it might be better to go there during Easter break. 2. Alternatively, my schedule might be too busy./ . . . Intermediate Composition would be more appropriate./ . . . fall quarter might be a lighter quarter to take it.   3. On the other hand, usually the museum is very crowded on Saturdays./ . . . I might prefer to go swimming./ . . . maybe I should

wait until next Tuesday.   4. On the other hand, you could visit them./ . . . you could call your best friend./ . . . you could call them on Thursday.

EXERCISE 4 [15 minutes]

In this exercise students practice using the alternative connectors they studied in Focus 3.

1. Read the directions and example as a class. Could *alternatively* be used in the example, as well? (*yes*)

2. Have students work independently to add a statement to each of the sentences using *on the other hand* or *alternatively*.

3. Have students work in pairs and take turns reading the statements they wrote.

4. Ask volunteers to share some examples with the class. Which connector did students use the most, *on the other hand* or *alternatively?* See possible answers on LP page 220.

EXERCISE 5 [15 minutes]

This exercise gives students oral practice in using alternative connectors.

1. As a class, read the directions and example.

2. Have students work in small groups of three or four. Tell them to take turns creating alternative statements to each of the sentences using *on the other hand* or *alternatively.* Each student should focus on a different part of the original statement.

3. You might want to walk around the class and check that students are all responding to different portions of the statements.

4. Ask different groups to share responses with the class.

work book For more practice, use Grammar Dimensions 4 Workbook page 100, Exercise 4.

LESSON PLAN 3

FOCUS 4 [20 minutes]

This focus is continued on SB page 222.

1. **Lead-in:** Have students read this focus for homework. Ask them to note which connectors are ones they have used and which are new for them.

2. Note that most of the connectors in this chart are used in formal contexts with the exception of *I mean.*

3. Assign Exercise 6 along with the reading of Focus 4. This will give students a chance to select appropriate connectors for specific contexts and provide motivation for reviewing the explanations in this focus chart.

CLARIFYING CONNECTORS	EXAMPLES	MEANINGS
that is	(j) Some fairy tales are morality tales in disguise; **that is,** they were created to teach a lesson about how people should or should not behave.	These connectors signal that something will be rephrased or clarified.
i.e.	(k) Fairy tales are part of an oral tradition (**i.e.,** the stories were first told orally rather than being written down).	In written English, we sometimes use *i.e.* (from Latin *id est*) as an abbreviation for *that is*. In professional writing, the sentence beginning with *i.e.,* is put in parentheses. Note that a comma follows the abbreviation.
in other words	(l) Fairy tales are not usually historical. **In other words,** they are not set in a particular time or place.	We use *that is* and *in other words* in both spoken and written English.
I mean	(m) I don't quite understand the difference between legends and epics. **I mean,** they seem very similar to me.	*I mean* is less formal; we generally do not use it in formal academic English to clarify a statement.

Note: Refer to Appendix 3, page A-6, for a complete chart of sentence connectors.

■EXERCISE 6

Use an exemplifying, identifying, or clarifying connector from the list below that would be appropriate for each blank. The first has been done as an example.

for example	especially	to illustrate	that is
for instance	in particular	as an example	in other words

1. Many words in English have origins in Greek myths. *Chaos*, <u>for example</u>, is a word the Greeks used to describe the unordered matter that existed before creation.

2. Some natural objects have English names that derive from Roman words for mythological characters. Planets, <u>in particular</u>, have been given such names. <u>To illustrate</u>, here are a few of them. Jupiter is named after the god of the sky. Neptune, in Roman mythology, was the god of springs and rivers. And Saturn was one of the gods of agriculture.

3. Some English names for metals also derive from myths. The metal uranium, <u>for instance</u>, comes from the Latin *Uranus* (the god of the sky). The metal tellurium comes from the Latin *Tellus* (the goddess of the earth).

4. Sometimes we may refer to an idea as *chimerical*; <u>in other words</u>, it is unrealistic or fanciful. This word comes from the name for a Greek monster, the Chimeaera, which had a lion's head, a goat's body, and a dragon's tail.

5. Some English names for bodies of water also derive from Greek words. This is true <u>especially</u> in the case of oceans. The name for the Arctic Ocean, <u>as an example</u>, comes from the Greek word for *bear: arkto*. The name for the Atlantic Ocean derives from *Atlantides*, who were sea nymphs. And the word ocean itself comes from *Oceanus*, the oldest member of the mythological race, the Titans.

6. Some governments are known as *plutocracies*; <u>that is</u>, they are governments run by the wealthy. The word *plutocracy* comes from *Plutus*, the god of wealth.

■EXERCISE 7

For each sentence below, fill in the correct abbreviation, *e.g.* or *i.e.* Then explain your choice.

Example: There are many kinds of fruit trees that grow in our state (e.g., there are orange, pear, and peach trees).
The second sentence gives examples of fruit trees, so e.g. is the correct connector.

1. The caterpillar underwent a metamorphosis (<u>i.e.</u>, it became a butterfly).

2. Cows are herbivores (<u>i.e.</u>, they do not eat meat).

3. American folktales often use exaggeration for humor (<u>e.g.</u>, in the tale of the giant lumberjack Paul Bunyan, his pancake griddle was so big that to grease it, men had to skate across it with bacon on their skates).

4. Many fairy tales have a heroine who is treated very badly (<u>e.g.</u>, in the story of Cinderella, her stepmother and stepsisters are very unkind to her).

5. *Young* and *old* are antonyms (<u>i.e.</u>, they are opposite in meaning).

6. Some words in English can be spelled several ways (<u>e.g.</u>, *theater* can also be spelled *theatre*).

7. Ancient stories were sometimes recited as epic poems (<u>i.e.</u>, long poems about a heroic mythological person or group of persons).

8. Some of the epic poems were sung (<u>e.g.</u>, in Ukraine during the sixteenth and seventeenth centuries, epic poems called *dumy* were performed by traveling musicians).

ANSWER KEY

Exercise 6   Answers will vary. Possible answers are shown above and on SB page 223.

Exercise 7   The text in parentheses . . .   1. . . . clarifies what the caterpillar becomes during metamorphosis.   2. . . . clarifies what an herbivore is.   3. . . . gives an example of an American folktale that uses exaggeration for humor.   4. . . . gives an example of a fairy tale where the heroine is treated badly.   5. . . . clarifies the meaning of an antonym.   6. . . . gives an example of a word that can be spelled in a different way.   7. . . . clarifies what an epic poem is.   8. . . . gives an example of an epic poem that was sung.

EXERCISE 6 [20 minutes/homework]

This exercise can be assigned with reading Focus 4 for a good homework assignment. Working on their own outside of class will give students time to think about the underlying relationships of the sentences in this exercise.

1. As a class, read the directions and example.
2. Some students will need more time than others to understand some of the less familiar relationships expressed by connectors such as *in particular, especially, that is,* and *in other words*. Remind them that some statements define or explain words or phrases in a previous statement. This constitutes a clarification (*that is, in other words*) relationship. Thus, they may need dictionaries to check words they don't know (e.g., *plutocracy* in #6).
3. Have students work independently (preferably outside of class) to complete the exercise.
4. Have them exchange papers with a partner, review each other's answers, and discuss them.
5. Review answers as a class. See possible answers on LP page 222.

work book For more practice, use *Grammar Dimensions 4* Workbook page 101, Exercise 5.

EXPANSION [30 minutes/homework]

Activity 7 (reflection) on SB page 239 will give students additional practice in thinking about and articulating the underlying relationships between thoughts in sentences. In this activity, students reflect on and write about specific things they could do to improve their language proficiency within the next few months.

EXERCISE 7 [20 minutes]

In this exercise students practice using and explaining the use of *i.e.* and *e.g.*, in a series of sentences.

1. Ask students what *i.e.* and *e.g.* stand for (*that is* and *for example*). As a class, read the directions and example.
2. Have students work independently to complete the exercise.
3. Have them compare answers with a partner, explaining their reasons for each choice.
4. Review answers as a class. See answers on LP page 222.

Add an identification statement after each of the following sentences to further specify information conveyed. Use *namely* or *specifically* to indicate its relationship to the sentence before it.

Example: There is one thing I really like about you.
<u>Namely, you never blame other people when something is your fault.</u>

1. I'd like to know a few things about you.

   _____

2. I have one bad habit I wish I could break.

   _____

3. There are several things you might do to improve your financial situation.

   _____

4. There are two movies I'd like to see.

   _____

5. There are a few things about my future I often wonder about.

   _____

6. There is one thing I would like to have accomplished by this time next year.

   _____

EXERCISE 9

Following is a list of words along with their definitions. Make up one sentence using each word. Then for each, add an independent clause that explains the word. Use *in other words, that is,* or *I mean* to signal the relationship between the clauses. Use a semicolon to punctuate them.

Example: intractable, difficult to manage or get to behave
Our new Labrador puppy is intractable; in other words, it is hard to make him behave.

1. digress   (verb)   to stray from the main topic in speech or writing
2. equivocate   (verb)   to avoid making a direct statement about something
3. incessant   (adj.)   continuing without interruption
4. polychromatic (adj.)   having many colors
5. xenophobic   (adj.)   having a fear or dislike of strangers or foreigners

---

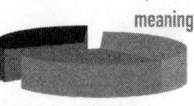

FOCUS 5   Similarity Connectors

CONNECTORS	EXAMPLES	MEANING
similarly	(a) Mythological stories were often handed down orally from generation to generation. **Similarly,** folk tales were part of the oral traditions of many cultures throughout the world.	These connectors signal that two or more ideas or situations are alike.
likewise	(b) If you practice speaking a second language everyday, you will most likely improve your fluency. **Likewise,** if you write in a journal every day, you will probably become a better writer.	
in the same way	(c) Learning to play a musical instrument well requires practice. **In the same way,** developing athletic abilities cannot be accomplished without practice.	

Using Similarity Connectors

EXAMPLES	EXPLANATIONS
(d) Blake likes to read folk tales. **Likewise,** this has been one of Karen's favorite leisure reading activities. (e) NOT: Blake likes to read folk tales. **Likewise,** Karen likes to read folk tales.	Paraphrase the information after the connector. Don't just repeat the previous information word for word.
(f) Football players try to carry a football across their goal line. **Similarly,** soccer players try to kick a soccer ball into a goal.	The comparison can involve differences in several terms: FOOTBALL SOCCER *players* ⟷ *players* *carry* ⟷ *kick* *football* ⟷ *soccer ball*
(g) Patrice bought some new clothes when we went shopping. **Likewise,** Mara purchased a few new outfits. (h) The spots on leopards help to camouflage them in the jungle. **Similarly,** colorations on deer help to hide them in the woods.	*Likewise* and *in the same way* often suggest greater similarity, or sameness, than *similarly* does.
(i) Dogs may get disturbed during an electrical storm. Cats may react **in the same way.** (j) A man in the audience started to heckle the speaker. Others behaved **similarly.**	You can use similarity connectors at the end of sentences when you are expressing the point of similarity in a verb phrase.

Note: Refer to Appendix 3, page A-6, for a complete chart of sentence connectors.

ANSWER KEY

Exercise 8 Answers will vary. Possible answers are: 1. Namely, I'd like to know what your hobbies are and what you're studying in school.   2. Specifically, I wish I could stop chewing my fingernails. 3. Specifically, you could get a roommate to save on rent, eat out less, and begin saving 5 percent of your income each month in case of emergency.   4. Namely, I'd like to see *Shakespeare in Love* and *The Sixth Sense*.   5. Specifically, I wonder if I'll ever get married and if I'll have children.   6. Namely, I'd like to have finished my mathematics requirements.

Exercise 9 Answers will vary. Possible answers are: 1. It seems as if I have digressed. That is, I have strayed from the topic.   2. Have you noticed how Danielle always equivocates? That is, she never answers a question directly.   3. I find her lectures incessant; in other words she speaks continuously without interruption.   4. My new bag is polychromatic. I mean, it is very colorful. 5. Cultures that have been isolated from other people by geography or language sometimes tend to be xenophobic. That is, they fear strangers or foreigners.

EXERCISE 8 [15 minutes]

In this exercise students add statements to the sentences using *namely* or *specifically* to give additional information. Unlike some of the other sentence connectors in this unit, *namely* and *specifically* are ones many students will not be very familiar with and may not have used productively.

1. As a class, read the directions and example. Could *specifically* be used here, as well? (*yes*)
2. Have students work in pairs and take turns adding a sentence beginning with *namely* or *specifically* to give an example or a more specific and detailed elaboration of each statement.
3. Ask volunteers to share their answers with the class. Did anyone else come up with a similar statement? Ask students who created very different statements to share them with the class, as well. See possible answers on LP page 224.

EXERCISE 9 [15 minutes]

Students continue applying what they have learned in Focus 4 by creating definitions for a list of words and adding independent clauses using *in other words, that is,* or *I mean*.

1. As a class, read the directions and example. Could *that is,* or *I mean,* be used instead of *in other words?* (*yes*)
2. Have students work independently to write their sentences.
3. Have them share answers with a partner.
4. Review answers as a class. See possible answers on LP page 224.

EXPANSION 1 [15 minutes]

This expansion work continues the practice begun in Exercise 9 with *in other words, that is,* and *I mean*.

1. Divide students into small groups. Give groups strips of paper with five or six words and definitions, with the word on one strip and the definition on another.
2. Ask students to match the words to their definitions and create sentences modeled after the example in Exercise 9.
3. Ask volunteers from various groups to share their sentences with the class.

VARIATION

1. Ask each group to create the word and definition strips, using their dictionaries to find words.
2. Have them exchange strips with another group, and then match and create sentences.

EXPANSION 2 [30 minutes]

Activity 3 (writing/research) on SB page 237 is also a good follow-up to Exercise 9. Students make and exchange a list of five new words, look them up, and then write sentence pairs defining and using each word in context, using clarification connectors.

LESSON PLAN 4

FOCUS 5 [15 minutes]

Focus 5 concentrates on the meaning and use of similarity connectors, used to indicate that two or more ideas or situation are alike.

1. **Lead-in:** Write a 3-column chart on the board with these headings: *Connector/First Sentence/Second Sentence.* In the first column, write the three similarity connectors: *similarly, likewise, in the same way.* Elicit that they all are used to indicate that two or more ideas or situations are alike.

2. Read the first example, and ask students to point out what is similar in both sentences, and write their responses on the board in the second and third columns. (*Mythological stories → folk tales* and *handed down orally from generation to generation → were part of the oral traditions of many cultures throughout the world.*)

3. Ask a volunteer to read the next two examples, have students identify the similar elements in each, and add this information to the chart on the board.

4. Follow this procedure for the remainder of the chart. Emphasize that the element in the first sentence is rephrased—not repeated—in the second sentence. For example, in (g), *some new clothes* becomes *a few new outfits;* in (h), the idea of *camouflage* is referred to in the second sentence with *hide.*

5. Point out that rephrasing can include the connector. For example, in (i), *get disturbed during an electrical storm* is paraphrased as *react in the same way.*

METHODOLOGY NOTE

The number of connectors used to express similarity is limited in English. Your students will probably be familiar with *similarly* and *likewise. In the same way* is perhaps less common. Although advanced learners may have seen these connectors as part of a list during previous grammar study, they may be uncertain about how to use them in communicative situations.

The second half of the focus chart should be particularly helpful to students. Many students who repeat previously stated information are unaware that this is a very awkward construction in English. This section gives them useful tools for paraphrasing information.

The second section also explains the nature of comparisons made using these connectors, the shades of difference in meaning among the connectors, and the various positions in a sentence where connectors can be placed, other than just at the beginning of the sentence.

The chart below gives information about myth and folklore spirits in Western Europe. Imagine that you are a folklorist, and that you have been asked to write a summary of the ways in which these spirits are similar. As preparation for your summary, use the information in the chart to make at least five pairs of sentences expressing similarity. Use a similarity connector with the second sentence of each pair.

Example: *Pixies enjoy playing tricks on humans; elves, **likewise**, enjoy fooling people.*

Name of Spirit	fairy	pixie	brownie	elf
Where found	Ireland, England, Scotland	England	Scotland	Scandinavian countries
Typical residence	forests, underground	forests, under a rock	humans' houses, farms	forests
Appearance	fair, attractive, varied size	handsome, small	brown or tawny, small, wrinkled faces	varied: some fair and some dark
Visibility to humans	usually invisible; visible by use of a magic ointment	usually invisible	usually invisible	usually invisible; visible at midnight within their dancing circle
Clothing color	green, brown, yellow favorite: green	always green	brown	varied
Favorite pastime(s)	dancing at night	dancing at night; playing tricks on humans	playing tricks on humans	dancing at night; playing tricks on humans
Rulers	fairy king and queen	pixie king	none	elf-king

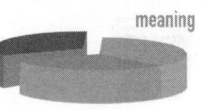
meaning

use

FOCUS 6 **Contrast and Concession Connectors**

CONTRAST CONNECTORS	EXAMPLES	MEANINGS
however	(a) In some creation myths, the sun exists before people do. In others, **however,** people create the sun.	These connectors show that two ideas contrast.
in contrast	(b) The characters in legends may be based on people who actually lived. **In contrast,** the characters in fables, often animals, are fictional.	
on the other hand	(c) The proposed new hotel complex will benefit our city. **On the other hand,** it will create serious problems with increased traffic.	
though	(d) This lake is not very good for fishing. It's great for swimming and water skiing, **though.**	
in fact	(e) Early civilizations thought *the earth was the center of the universe.* **In fact,** *the earth revolves around the sun.*	These connectors signal that the following statement is contrary to something previously stated. The contrary parts are shown in italics.
however	(f) Some people think that *whales are fish.* **However,** *these animals are actually mammals.*	

ANSWER KEY

Exercise 10 Answers will vary. Some possible answers are:
- Fairies live in Ireland, England, or Scotland. However, pixies live in England only.
- All fairies are fair. On the other hand, some elves are fair and some are dark.
- Fairies, pixies, and elves have rulers, but brownies have no formal rulers.
- Fairies, pixies, brownies, and elves are usually invisible. However, fairies can be made visible by use of a magic ointment and elves are visible at midnight within their dancing circle.
- Elves live outside. On the other hand, brownies live in houses and farms.

EXERCISE 10 [25 minutes]

Exercise 10 gives students a very enjoyable way to practice using the similarity connectors they studied in Focus 5. This exercise could be done individually, in pairs, or in small groups. You could also conduct the exercise orally with the class as a whole, writing responses on the board.

1. Discuss what students know about the nature spirits of myths and folklore, such as fairies and elves. What do they look like? Where do they live? How do they act?

2. Ask a volunteer to read the directions and example. Is the information from the first sentence repeated in the second sentence, or paraphrased? (*paraphrased*)

3. Divide students into groups of three or four. Ask one student to be the note taker. Have students take turns creating sentences using the information in the chart and similarity connectors.

4. Remind students that similarity connectors can be placed in different positions in a sentence—they do not always need to come at the beginning of a sentence.

5. Ask the note taker from each group to report several sentences the group created. See possible answers on LP page 226.

For more practice, use *Grammar Dimensions 4* Workbook page 102, Exercise 6 and page 103, Exercise 7.

FOCUS 6 [20 minutes]

Focus 6 provides detailed information about the meanings and uses of contrast and concession connectors. This chart should be a useful reference tool for students. Note that the focus chart continues on SB page 228.

1. **Lead-in:** Have students read through the column of connectors and identify any they are not familiar with or any they are not sure how to use.

2. Read the examples and explanations with the class. In each, ask students to identify where the connector is in the sentence.

3. To help students understand the difference between contrastive and concessive relationships, write examples (f) and (g) on the board. Underline the elements in each pair of sentences that are being compared and label them (A) and (B).

4. Ask students to identify what is true and not true according to these statements. Example (f) can be described this way: *Some people think (A); however, (A) is not true. (B) tells what is true.*

5. Example (g) does not offer two contrary statements. In this instance, the connector indicates doubt or reservation on the part of the speaker. It offers additional information that also needs to be considered.

6. Have volunteers create other examples using contrast and concession connectors.

7. Answer any questions students may have.

LANGUAGE NOTE

Although most advanced students should be familiar with the majority of these connectors, they may only use several of them in actual communication. Encourage them to experiment with using all the connectors in the chart when creating sentences.

CONCESSION CONNECTORS	EXAMPLES	MEANINGS
even so	(g) The heroes in myths often had superhuman powers such as great strength. **Even so,** they also had weaknesses that could lead to their downfall.	These connectors signal a reservation about something. The first statement is true, but the second statement is also true or needs to be considered.
however	(h) Both parables and allegories are stories that have moral lessons; parables, **however,** are much briefer and usually convey a single principle or moral.	
nevertheless	(i) Native Americans have often had difficulty preserving their traditions in modern society. **Nevertheless,** they have been able to pass down old stories about their culture to the new generations.	The second statement may also express surprising or unexpected information.
nonetheless	(j) I know mountain climbing can be dangerous. I'd like to try it **nonetheless.**	
despite (this)	(k) Chifumi has to get up at 5 A.M. to get to school on time. **Despite this,** she has never missed a class.	
in spite of (this)	(l) The day was cold and rainy. **In spite of the inclement weather,** we decided to take a hike.	
on the other hand	(m) Learning a new language can be frustrating sometimes. **On the other hand,** it can be a lot of fun.	

Note: Refer to Appendix 3, page A-6, for a complete chart of sentence connectors.

EXERCISE 11

Use the information in the chart from Exercise 10 to make up five sentence pairs expressing differences between the various European folklore spirits.

Example: *The favorite pastime of fairies is dancing at night. Brownies, in contrast, enjoy playing tricks.*

EXERCISE 12

The chart below gives information about people who have made remarkable achievements in the face of adversity. Use the information to make up sentence pairs linked by a concession connector.

Example: *Helen Keller was deaf and blind. In spite of these difficulties, she became an eloquent communicator.*

Person	Difficulty	Achievement
Helen Keller	was deaf and blind	became an eloquent communicator
Martin Luther King, Jr.	encountered racial prejudice	preached nonviolence toward adversaries
Beethoven	became deaf	continued to write symphonies
Charles Dickens	grew up in poverty	became a famous novelist
Stephen Hawking	is confined to a wheelchair by Lou Gehrig's disease	became an internationally acclaimed physicist
Jim Abbott	had only one hand	played professional baseball as a pitcher

ANSWER KEY

Exercise 11   Answers will vary.

Exercise 12   Answers may vary. Possible answers are: • Despite the fact that Helen Keller was deaf and blind, she was able to become an eloquent communicator.   • Martin Luther King Jr., encountered much racial prejudice. Nonetheless, he preached nonviolence toward adversaries.   • Beethoven became deaf; even so, he continued to write symphonies.   • Charles Dickens grew up in poverty. Nevertheless, he became a famous novelist.   • In spite of being confined to a wheelchair by Lou Gehrig's disease, Stephen Hawking has become an internationally acclaimed physicist.   • Jim Abbott had only one hand. Even so, he played professional baseball as a pitcher.

■ EXERCISE 11 [20 minutes]

In Exercise 11 students use the information about folklore spirits from Exercise 10 to create sentences using the contrast connectors from Focus 6.

1. As a class, read the directions and example. What kind of connector is used in the example? (*a contrast connector*)

2. Have students work in pairs. Ask them to create at least five sentence pairs that express the differences between the folklore spirits in the chart in Exercise 10.

3. Ask volunteers to share sentences with the class. Ask the class to say where in the sentence each connector is located.

 For more practice, use *Grammar Dimensions 4* Workbook page 105, Exercise 8 and 9.

EXPANSION [30 minutes]

Use Activity 1 (listening/writing) on SB page 236 after Exercise 11. Students listen to two versions of the Greek myth of Echo and Narcissus, take notes, and then compare the two versions using contrast and similarity connectors.

■ EXERCISE 12 [15 minutes]

Students practice using the concession connectors in this exercise, creating sentence pairs about famous people.

1. As a class, read the directions and example. What kind of connector is used in the example? (*a concession connector*) Ask students to identify the elements that are compared in the two sentences. Does the second sentence refute the information in the first one?

2. This would be a good time to review two connectors students often confuse: *despite (THIS)* and *in spite of (THIS)*. Remind them that *despite* is never followed by the preposition *of*.

2. Have students work independently to write sentence pairs using the information about the famous people in the chart.

3. Have them take turns sharing their sentences with a partner.

4. Ask volunteers to share sentences with the class. See possible answers on LP page 228.

EXPANSION [30 minutes]

Activity 5 (speaking/listening/writing) on SB page 238 makes a good sequel to Focus 6 and Exercise 12. In this activity students interview each other and write about their similarities and differences, using similarity and contrast connectors.

As you have seen in this unit, some sentence connectors may signal more than one meaning relationship. These include *on the other hand* (alternative, contrast, concession), *in fact* (intensifying addition, contrast), and *however* (contrast, concession). Review these connector meanings in Focus 2, Focus 3, and Focus 6. Then write down which relationship each signals in the sentences below. You may also want to refer to Appendix 3 on page A-6.

Example: You could drive to Denver if you have time. <u>On the other hand</u>, you could consider flying there.

Relationship: *alternative*

1. The mechanic told me the fuel pump in my car needed to be replaced. In fact, the fuel pump was fine.
   Relationship: <u>contrast</u>

2. Your research paper on Hindu epic poems is very good. It could use some more variety in vocabulary, however.
   Relationship: <u>concession</u>

3. I might take biology next quarter. On the other hand, I may take geology if it fits my schedule better.
   Relationship: <u>alternative</u>

4. In the distance, the next city looked fairly close. However, as it turned out, it wasn't very close at all.
   Relationship: <u>contrast</u>

5. That plasma television set is expensive. In fact, it costs triple what my old one cost.
   Relationship: <u>intensifying addition</u>

6. The weather forecast predicted heavy rain all weekend. On Saturday, however, there was not a cloud to be seen anywhere.
   Relationship: <u>contrast</u>

7. This soup has a really good flavor. On the other hand, it could use a little salt.
   Relationship: <u>concession</u>

8. Nylon is a very light material. It is, however, very strong.
   Relationship: <u>concession</u>

9. I'm having a hard time following these cell phone directions for creating an address book. In fact, it seems impossible to figure them out.
   Relationship: <u>intensifying addition</u>

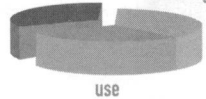
meaning

use

FOCUS 7   Connectors Expressing Effects/Results and Purposes

EFFECT/RESULT CONNECTORS	EXAMPLES	MEANINGS
accordingly	(a) Rain is an important theme in many African religions. **Accordingly,** their rituals often focus on rain-making and rain-stopping.	These connectors signal that a statement is an effect or result of something. They differ mainly in their degrees of formality. We use *as a result (of), because of,* and *due to* in both spoken and written English. We use *therefore, consequently, thus,* and *hence* more in written English. *Thus* and *hence* are the most formal connectors.
as a result	(b) English spelling rules can be confusing. **As a result,** some have proposed simplified spelling.	
as a result of (this)	(c) Some people suffer from acrophobia. **As a result of this phobia,** they avoid heights.	
because of (this)	(d) Rainbows look like bridges in the sky. **Because of this image,** in many cultures rainbows were thought to be gateways to the heavens.	To express cause-effect or reason-result relationships in conversation, speakers tend to use subordinating conjunctions like *because* and *since* as in (j), more than sentence connectors.
due to (this)	(e) A megaphone is a hollow cone. **Due to its shape,** it can amplify sound.	
consequently	(f) Some of the older fairy tales were thought to have too much violence for children. **Consequently,** later versions of these stories removed the violence.	
therefore	(g) The plot of this book is not very original. The ending, **therefore,** is easy to predict.	
thus	(h) In myths, fire was considered the property of the gods. **Thus,** anyone caught stealing it was usually punished severely.	
hence	(i) With the invention of print, long stories could be published in books; **hence,** epic poems are no longer recited orally.	
because	(j) The ending of this book is very easy to predict **because** the plot isn't very original.	

EXERCISE 13 [25 minutes/homework]

This is another exercise that might be best done as a written homework assignment to give individuals time to think about the relationships expressed in the sentence pairs. Reviewing students' papers will also give you the opportunity to assess their grasp of the differences in meaning and use of the various connectors they have studied in Focus 2, 3, and 6.

1. As a class, read the directions and example. Ask students to complete the exercise as homework.

2. Ask students to read through the examples, and answer any questions they might have.

3. During the next class, review answers as a class and collect student papers to judge overall class comprehension. See answers on LP page 230.

EXPANSION [30 minutes/homework]

Activity 4 (writing) on SB page 237 is a good homework assignment following Exercise 13. Students write an essay about three turning points in their lives, using reason-result connectors.

LESSON PLAN 5

FOCUS 7 [15 minutes]

Many of the connectors used in Focus 7 are found only in more formal contexts, and so may be less familiar to many students. This chart continues on SB page 232.

1. **Lead-in:** Ask students to read through the first column, which lists the different connectors, and write down any that are not familiar to them.

2. Read the first paragraph of explanation in the third column, and then ask volunteers to read examples (a–g). Guide students in identifying the results in each sentence pair.

3. Read examples (h) and (i) with the class. Write this similar example on the board: *The television show I was watching last night was really boring. _____ I turned it off.* Write *Hence* in the blank.

4. Ask a volunteer to read the sentence aloud, and ask students how they think it sounds (they should think it sounds strange or funny). Ask them what connector would sound more natural (*therefore* could be used, but, in conversational English, the coordinating conjunction *so* would be more common.)

5. Read the examples and explanations of the purpose connectors. Tell students that these are usually used only in formal contexts. Explain that, in conversation, English speakers tend to use coordinating conjunctions to express purpose rather than use the purpose connectors. (*In rewriting fairy tales for children, authors wanted to make the stories more pleasant,* so *they sometimes changed unhappy endings.*)

PURPOSE CONNECTORS	EXAMPLES	MEANINGS
in order to (do this)	(k) You should check your computer for possible viruses. **In order to check it,** you'll need to close all programs.	Purpose connectors also express causal relationships.
with this in mind	(l) In rewriting fairy tales for children, authors wanted to make the stories more pleasant. **With this in mind,** they sometimes changed unhappy endings to happy ones.	
for this purpose	(m) Throughout human history, people have wanted to convey moral lessons in a way that would interest their audiences. **For this purpose,** they created fables, parables, and other kinds of moralistic stories.	Of the connectors shown here, *for this purpose* is the most formal.

Note: Refer to Appendix 3, page A-6, for a complete chart of sentence connectors.

EXERCISE 14

The two charts on the next page give information about various characters from myths and legends. Use the information from Chart A to make sentence pairs expressing reason-result relationships. Use Chart B to make sentence pairs expressing purpose relationships. For all sentence pairs, use an appropriate sentence connector.

Examples: *The Norse gods believed nothing could harm Balder, the sun god. Consequently, they thought it fun to hurl weapons at him.*

Robin Hood wanted to help the poor. For this purpose, he robbed the rich.

Chart A

Character(s)	Event/Situation	Result
1. Norse gods	believed nothing could harm Balder, the sun god	thought it fun to hurl weapons at him
2. Con, relative of Pachacamac, Incan god of fertility	was defeated in battle by Pachacamac	left Peru and took the rain with him
3. Gonggong, Chinese god of the waters	had his army destroyed by Zhurong, god of fire	fled in disgrace to the west and smashed into a mountain pillar holding up the sky
4. Paris, Trojan hero	wanted the beautiful Helen of Troy for his wife	gave the goddess Aphrodite a golden apple to win her favor

Chart B

Character(s)	Action/Event	Purpose
1. Robin Hood	robbed the rich	help the poor
2. Haokah, Sioux god of thunder	used the wind as a drumstick	create thunder
3. The Pied Piper of Hamlin	played his musical pipe so the rats would follow him out of town	rid Hamlin Town of rats
4. Momotaro	left his Japanese village and made the dangerous journey to Oni Island	conquer the horrible Oni ogres and bring back the priceless treasures they had stolen

ANSWER KEY

Exercise 14 Answers will vary. Possible answers are:
Chart A 2. Con was defeated in battle by Pachacamac, the Incan god of fertility. Consequently, he left Peru and took the rain with him. 3. Gonggong, the Chinese god of the waters, had his army destroyed by Zhurong, god of fire. As a result, he fled in disgrace . . . 4. Paris, a Trojan hero, wanted the beautiful Helen of Troy for his wife. Because of this, he gave the goddess Aphrodite a golden apple to win her favor.

Chart B 2. In order to create thunder, Haokah, the god of thunder, used the wind as a drumstick. 3. Hamlin was swarming with rats. With this in mind, the Pied Piper of Hamlin played his pipe so the rats would follow him out of town. 4. In order to bring back the priceless treasures stolen by the Oni ogres, Momotaro left his village and made the dangerous journey to Oni Island.

EXERCISE 14 [20 minutes]

To practice using effect/result and purpose connectors, students create sentences about characters from myths and legends, using the information in the two charts.

1. Ask students to read through the list of characters from myths and legends in Charts A and B. What do they know about any of them? Do they remember any stories about any of them?

2. Read the directions, and then ask a volunteer to read the first row of Chart A on SB page 233. Then, read the first example, which uses the information in the first row of Chart A.

3. Ask students to suggest other connectors they might use in the example to express a result, such as *accordingly* or *therefore*.

4. Ask a volunteer to read the first row of Chart B on SB page 233. Then, read the second example, and ask students to suggest other connectors they might use to indicate purpose, such as *in order to do this* or *with this in mind.*

5. Have students work in pairs. One student should create sentences using the information in Chart A, and the other in Chart B. Then, have them switch charts and create new sentences.

6. As with other exercises in this unit, encourage students to use connectors that are less familiar to them and to vary their choices.

7. Ask volunteer pairs to share their sentences with the class. See possible answers on LP page 232.

For more practice, use *Grammar Dimensions 4* Workbook page 106, Exercise 10 and page 107, Exercise 11.

FOCUS 8 Punctuation of Sentence Connectors

form

Many sentence connectors can be used at the beginning, the middle, or the end of a sentence or independent clause. The punctuation surrounding a sentence connector depends on where it appears in a sentence.

EXAMPLES	EXPLANATIONS
(a) Apollo is the god of the sun in Greek mythology. **Similarly,** Balder is the sun god in Norse myths.	If the connector begins a sentence, use a period before it (ending the previous sentence) and a comma after it.
(b) Balder was much loved by the other gods; **however,** he was accidentally killed with a mistletoe dart by one of them.	If the connector begins an independent clause after another independent clause in the same sentence, use a semicolon before it and a comma after it.
(c) Many mythological characters have more than one name. Some, **in fact,** have several name variations.	If the connector is in the middle of a sentence or an independent clause, we usually separate it from the rest of the clause with commas.
(d) Aphrodite is the Greek goddess of love. She is **also** the goddess of beauty.	We do not usually use commas with *also* when it is in the middle of a sentence.
(e) Balder died from his dart wound. His wife Nanna died **as well,** having suffered a broken heart.	We do not use commas before *as well* when it follows a verb.
(f) The gods were grief-stricken when Balder died. The mortals reacted **in the same way.**	If the connector comes at the end of the sentence, punctuation is usually not necessary except for two connectors: *however* and *though.*
(g) Tu, known in Polynesian myths as the angry god, was quite belligerent. He could sometimes be very kind, **however.**	

Add, delete, or change punctuation in the following sentences to make them correct.

1. The rainbow plays a role in the myths and religious stories of cultures throughout the world.;in fact, most cultures hold symbolic beliefs about what rainbows consist of and what they represent.

2. In some Native American myths, the rainbow is thought to be a bridge or ladder to other worlds;likewise,in Norse myths the rainbow Asbru is a bridge connecting heaven and earth.

3. The rainbow has also been perceived as an object similar to manmade ones.;for example,in a German creation myth,it is a bowl holding the paint God used to color the birds.

4. The Mojave Tribe of Arizona sees the rainbow as a manmade object also unlike the German myth;however,they believe it is a toy used by the creator to stop rain storms.

5. Some Native Americans say that the rainbow was created from the souls of wildflowers that once lived in the forest. They believe that lilies from the prairies were used to complete it, as well.

6. In Islam,four colors of the rainbow are thought to correspond to the four elements.,; some Buddhists,on the other hand,believe there are seven colors of the rainbow which relate to the seven planets and the seven regions of the earth.

7. In some cultures,the rainbow represents reconciliation between God and humanity; e.g. in Mayan mythology,the rainbow stands as a promise that God will not destroy the world again after devastating rains, ~~similarly,~~in the Old Testament of the Bible, a rainbow appears to Noah after the great flood.
. Similarly

EXERCISE 16

As a review of the connectors in this unit, go back to Exercise 1 on page 214. Rewrite the second sentence in each numbered pair, adding an appropriate sentence connector and punctuation where needed.

ANSWER KEY

Exercise 15   Answers may vary. Possible answers noted above.

Exercise 16   Answers will vary. Possible answers are: 1. For example, the Mayan god . . .   2. In contrast, the goddess Athena . . .   3. In addition, they help us . . .   4. As a result, they made up . . . 5. That is, they explain . . .   6. Then he woke up . . .   7. On the other hand, the bush . . .   8. Similarly, the Greek hero . . .   9. Consequently, she was . . .   10. For instance, in Asia . . .

FOCUS 8 [15 minutes]

Students have now seen multiple examples of using sentence connectors in different places in a sentence. This focus explains the rules for punctuating sentences with connectors.

1. **Lead-in:** Read the first example and explanation with the class. This is the construction that most students will be most familiar with.

2. Read the second example and explanation. This is the trickiest of all the examples in this chart. Point out a common error to students—that of putting a comma between two main clauses joined by a sentence connector. Explain that this is called either a *comma splice* or a *run-on sentence*. Explain that the semicolon indicates a sharper division between the parts of a sentence than does a comma.

Suggestion: Review the sentence connectors students will tend to use most frequently in their writing—e.g., *also, furthermore, for example, however, on the other hand, therefore, consequently, nevertheless.* Write these on the board and ask students which ones they tend to use a lot. Suggest that they pay special attention when editing their writing to sentences that have these words.

EXERCISE 15 [15 minutes]

In Exercise 15 students edit a series of sentences, applying the principles of punctuation outlined in Focus 8.

1. Read the directions to the class. You may want to do #1 as an example.

2. Have students work independently to edit the punctuation of the sentences.

3. Have them compare answers with a partner.

4. Review answers as a class. See answers on LP page 234.

EXPANSION [30 minutes]

Assign Activity 6 (research on the web) on SB page 238 as homework after Exercise 15. Students research two creation myths from different cultures on the Web and write about them, using similarity and contrast connectors. Remind them to review their writing for proper punctuation.

EXERCISE 16 [20 minutes]

In this final exercise students rewrite the sentences in Exercise 1, adding connectors and the proper punctuation. This exercise could be done in class or assigned as homework.

1. Read the directions to the class. You may want to do the first pair of sentences in Exercise 1 on SB page 214 as an example.

2. Have students work independently to add connectors and punctuation to the sentence pairs in Exercise 1.

3. Have them compare answers with a partner.

4. Review answers as a class. See possible answers on LP page 234.

 For more practice, use *Grammar Dimensions 4* Workbook page 108, Exercise 12.

EXPANSION [20 minutes]

1. To give students extra practice in using connectors and properly punctuating sentences, ask them to review and revise a paper they have written recently, adding connectors and the proper punctuation.

2. Have them exchange papers with a partner and review them, or ask them to hand in the papers. Do they think their writing improved with the use of connectors? Are the relationships between ideas now clearer?

UNIT GOAL REVIEW [5 minutes]

Ask students to look at the goals on the opening page of the unit again. Refer to the pages of the unit where information on each goal can be found.

 For a grammar quiz review of Units 10–12, refer students to pages 110–112 in the *Grammar Dimensions 4* Workbook.

 For assessment of Unit 12, use *Grammar Dimensions 4 ExamView®.*

ACTIVITY 1 listening/writing

CD1 Tracks
16, 17

There are a number of Greek myths that explain how certain flowers came to be. Like many myths, different versions exist of these stories; they usually have common elements but vary in some details of the story. Listen to the audio for two versions of the Greek myth of Echo and Narcissus, which tell how the Narcissus flower came to be. Listen once to both versions to get a general idea of how they are similar and how they differ. Listen a second time and take notes on each version. When you have finished, briefly collaborate with two or three classmates to fill in any details you might have missed. From your notes, write a description of the similarities and differences of the two versions. Use a variety of contrast and similarity sentence connectors.

ACTIVITY 2 writing

In groups, create a list of ten facts or opinions on different topics. Below each fact, leave several spaces. Then pass the list to another group. The members of that group have to add another fact to each statement, using an addition sentence connector to signal the relationship. When they are finished, they should pass the list to another group who will do the same thing until several groups have added sentences to each list.

Examples: Group 1: ***Tomatoes*** *are very good for you.*

            Group 2: *In fact, they are a good source of vitamins.*

            Group 3: *In addition, they taste good.*

            Group 4: *Furthermore, you can use them in a lot of different ways, such as in making sauces or salads.*

            Group 1: ***San Francisco*** *is a beautiful city.*

            Group 2: *It also has great restaurants.*

            Group 3: *It's a book lover's city as well.*

            Group 4: *What's more, you can go sailing in the bay.*

ACTIVITY 3 writing/research

■ **STEP 1**   Make a list of five words that you think others in the class might not be very familiar with. Use a dictionary if necessary. Try to find words that could be useful additions to someone's vocabulary.

■ **STEP 2**   Exchange lists with one of your classmates. Each of you should look up the words you have been given in the dictionary to see its range of meanings. Then write one sentence using the word in a context and add a statement defining the word, using one of the clarification sentence connectors (*that is* or *in other words*) as was done in Exercise 9. If you wish, you can connect the sentences with a semicolon to show their close relationship.

Example: *Some folktales are moralistic; in other words, these stories instruct people on how to behave.*

■ **STEP 3**   Give your sentences to your partner; check each other's sentences for correctness.

ACTIVITY 4 writing

"Turning point" is a term we sometimes use to describe an event that has changed or influenced someone in an important way. Consider three turning points in your life. Write an essay in which you explain how each turning point has changed your life. Use reason-result sentence connectors in your explanations.

Example: *One of the major turning points in my life was when my family left Bosnia for the United States. Because of this, we had to start a new life and adjust to an entirely different culture. . . .*

USE YOUR ENGLISH

The Use Your English activities at the end of the unit contain situations that should naturally elicit the structures covered in the unit. For a more complete discussion of how to use the Use Your English activities, see To the Teacher, LP page xxvi.

ACTIVITY 1 listening [30 minutes]

CD1 Tracks 16,17

You may wish to use this activity after Exercise 11 on SB page 228. Students listen to two versions of the Greek myth of Echo and Narcissus, take notes, and then compare the two versions using contrast and similarity connectors.

1. Before having students listen to the stories, bring in a picture of Echo and Narcissus from a mythology book. This myth is included in most collections of Greek myths. The children's section of a library is a good source for mythology books with attractive pictures. You could also bring in a picture of a Narcissus flower.
2. Tell students that they are going to listen to two versions of the Greek myth of Echo and Narcissus, which tells a story about how the Narcissus flower came to be. Tell them that the two stories are somewhat different.
3. Have students first simply listen to the audio once.
4. Have them listen a second time, taking notes on the two stories.
5. Have students work in pairs or groups of three. Ask them to compare notes and to fill in their notes with any details they may have missed.
6. Ask them to work independently to write a description of the similarities and differences between the two stories. Tell them to refer to Focus 5 and 6 for lists of similarity and contrast connectors to use.

ACTIVITY 2 writing [45 minutes]

Use this activity after Exercise 2 on SB page 217. Students work in groups to create lists of facts and opinions, and then pass them to other groups, who add facts to each statement, using addition connectors.

1. Have students work in groups of three or four for this exercise.
2. Read the directions, and ask two volunteers to read the two examples. What addition sentence connectors are used?
3. Have each group create a list of ten facts or opinions on different topics, leaving space beneath each one for other groups to add to them. If students have Internet access, they could use the Internet to gather information for their lists.
4. Have the groups pass their lists to another group. The second group should then add a fact to each sentence, using an addition connector. Tell students to refer back to Focus 2 for a list of addition connectors they might use.
5. Then, ask the groups to pass the papers on to another group. Continue this process until at least three groups have added their sentences to the originals.

ACTIVITY 3 writing/research [30 minutes]

Activity 3 is a good follow-up to Exercise 9 on SB page 224. Students make and exchange a list of five new words, look them up, and then write sentence pairs defining and using each word in context, using clarification connectors.

■ STEP 1 Read the directions for Step 1 with the class, and have students create a list of five words they think others will not know. They can use a

dictionary to find words—but they should be words that other people might actually find useful to know and use.

■ STEP 2 Read the directions and example for Step 2 with the class. Have students exchange lists with a partner, look up the meanings of the words in a dictionary, and write one sentence using each word in context followed by a statement that defines the word. Tell them to look back at Exercise 9 for examples of such sentences.

■ STEP 3 Have students exchange papers with their partner and correct them, as needed. Ask volunteers to share sentences with the class.

ACTIVITY 4 writing [30 minutes/homework]

This activity is a good homework assignment following Exercise 13 on SB page 230. Students write an essay about three turning points in their lives, using reason-result connectors.

1. Write *turning point* on the board and elicit a definition. Discuss some turning points in your and students' lives.
2. Read the directions and examples with the class. What connector is used in the example? Could others be used, as well? What does the connector express about the relationship between the ideas in the two sentences?
3. Have students work independently to write an essay about three turning points in their lives, using reason-result connectors.
4. During the next class, have students exchange papers with a partner and discuss them.
5. Ask for a few volunteers to read their essays to the rest of the class.

■ **STEP 1**   Pair up with another classmate. Your task is to find out six things that you have in common and six things that are different about you. The similarities and differences should not be things that are apparent (for example, do not use similarities or differences in physical appearance or the similarity of both being in the same class). Consider topics such as goals, hobbies, travels, language learning, families, and various likes and dislikes (foods, sports, courses, books, movies, etc.).

■ **STEP 2**   As you discover the similarities and differences, make a list of them. Then, each of you should write six sentence pairs expressing your discoveries, using similarity and contrast connectors. Divide the task equally so that each of you states three similarities and three differences. Share some of your findings with your classmates.

Examples: *Sven started learning English when he was 12.* **Similarly,** *I first started taking English courses when I was 13.*

Wenxia loves to read science fiction. **In contrast,** *I read mostly nonfiction books.*

I love math. Tina, **on the other hand,** *hopes she never has to take another math course in her life.*

 ACTIVITY **6** research on the web

 Creation myths from around the world often have similarities; for example, in many myths, the earth and sky are formed by dividing an egg. Using Internet search engines such as Google® or Yahoo®, find two more creation myths from different cultures. Prepare a report in which you summarize each myth and describe similarities and differences between the two myths.

 ACTIVITY **7** reflection

To make progress in your language learning at advanced levels, it is sometimes useful to focus on a few areas at a time in which you would especially like to improve.

■ **STEP 1**   Identify one area of language proficiency that you would especially like to improve (e.g., academic writing, reading, listening comprehension, vocabulary, pronunciation, oral presentation skills) in English or another language.

■ **STEP 2**   Think of three specific things you could do within the next few months to develop this area, and write a sentence for each.

■ **STEP 3**   Finally, state what you hope will be the result of your efforts.

Example:

Language area: *Improve oral skills for seminar presentations*

Specific activities: *To improve my oral presentation skills, I will pay close attention to the talks that will be given for the next six weeks in my engineering seminar class, and I will make notes on both the positive and negative features. Besides that, I plan to watch a videotape at the skills center that shows how to use transitional expressions for introducing and changing topics. I'll also prepare a short talk using a slideshow program on my laptop and ask a few friends in my department to be my audience and give me feedback. As a result of these activities, I expect to learn more about what makes a good research presentation in my field. In addition, I hope to make the ideas in my presentation easier for the audience to follow. Finally, I'd like to become more aware of what I most need to work on.*

USE YOUR ENGLISH

ACTIVITY 5 — speaking/listening/writing [30 minutes]

In this activity students interview each other and write about their similarities and differences, using similarity and contrast connectors. It makes a good sequel to Focus 6 and Exercise 12 on SB page 229.

▪ STEP 1

1. Tell students that they are going to pair up and interview each other to find out about their similarities and differences. After reading the Step 1 directions as a class, ask students to say what comes to mind first when they think about comparing themselves with their classmates (Remind students that these comparisons should not be to physical appearance).

2. Have students work in pairs to discover six things they have in common and six things that are different. Emphasize that these should not be qualities that are immediately apparent, such as appearances. Have them take notes as they interview each other.

▪ STEP 2

1. Ask a volunteer to read the directions for Step 2.

2. Read the example. What other contrast connectors might they use in these examples?

3. Have students organize the notes they took into a list of similarities and differences.

4. Have students write six sentence pairs about what they have discovered about each other using similarity and contrast connectors. Tell them to look back at Focus 5 for a list of similarity connectors and at Focus 6 for a list of contrast connectors.

5. Have each pair of students work with another pair and take turns talking about what they have found, using the sentences they have written.

6. Ask volunteers to share some of their findings with the class, and discuss.

ACTIVITY 6 — research on the web [30 minutes/homework]

You may wish to assign this activity as homework after Exercise 15 on SB page 235. Students research two creation myths from different cultures on the Web and write about them, using similarity and contrast connectors.

1. Read the directions with the class, and assign this activity as homework.

2. Remind students about how they compared and contrasted myths and folklore in Exercise 15.

4. Ask them to research myths on the Internet, chose two, and write an essay comparing and contrasting them.

5. During the next class, ask volunteers to read their essays to the class.

ACTIVITY 7 — reflection [30 minutes/homework]

In this activity students reflect on and write about specific things they could do to improve their language proficiency within the next few months. It is a good expansion activity after Exercise 6 on SB page 222.

1. This activity could be done in class or assigned as homework.

2. Read the directions and example for Steps 1–3 with the class.

3. Ask volunteers to mention specific actions they might take within the next few months to improve some aspect of their language proficiency, and write responses on the board.

4. Encourage students to refer to the focus charts in this unit, as needed, for ideas about which connectors to use in their writing.

5. During the next class, ask volunteers to share their writing with the class.

MODAL PERFECT VERBS

- Use the correct forms of modal perfect verbs

- Choose correct modals to express judgments, obligations, and expectations

- Choose correct modals to make deductions and guesses

- Choose correct modals to express results of past conditions and to make predictions

OPENING TASK

Mr. Retrospect's Hindsight and Sage Advice

Mr. Retrospect is an advice columnist who specializes in telling people what they should have done—after the fact.

■ STEP 1

Read the following letter sent to Mr. Retrospect and his reply.

Dear Mr. Retrospect:

Like many people my age, I joined a social Web site to make new friends. After corresponding on this site for several weeks with a young woman in my area—I'll call her Annie—I arranged to contact her by telephone. We had a very nice conversation during which we found out that we both love out-of-doors activities. Annie then asked me if I liked to shop. That seemed like a rather abrupt topic change, but I said "Oh, sure," thinking that going shopping together might be a good way to get to know more about her. We made plans to meet the next weekend. When I arrived at her house, Annie came to the door with a big smile and, then after chatting just a few minutes, ushered me out into her backyard . . . to chop wood for her fireplace! I suddenly realized what she had asked me on the phone had nothing to do with shopping! I didn't know what to say, so I grabbed the axe and went to work, but I felt I had been taken advantage of. What do you think I should have done?

Henry

Dear Henry:

Sorry, but from what you have written, it's clear that you misheard Annie's question, so you can hardly fault her. I don't think you could have done anything much differently at the time, but perhaps you should have just laughed at yourself for the amusing misunderstanding and made the most of the outdoor activity. Besides, it must have been great exercise for your biceps! You might have thought of some way that she could have returned the favor—maybe chopping vegetables for a dinner at your place. Better luck next time!

Mr. Retrospect

■ STEP 2

Write responses to the following letters.

Dear Mr. Retrospect:

On a recent trip, I visited a relative I don't know very well, one of my great-aunts. She lives in a remote rural area; the nearest large city is three hundred miles away. I'm her only nephew, so she was really looking forward to my visit. Everything was fine until we sat down to eat. When I asked her what was in the stew she had just served, she announced, "Possum and squirrel, dear." I was so shocked that I refused to eat anything and had to leave the table. I'm afraid that I hurt my great-aunt's feelings even though later I said I was sorry. Now I am wondering what I could have said to be more polite.

Wild animal lover (well, squirrels anyway)

Dear Mr. Retrospect:

My hairdresser recently talked me into a new hairstyle that makes me look like a porcupine! I hated it! Unfortunately, he thought it was the perfect style for me. After he finished styling my hair he proclaimed "Oh Sally, it's *so you!*" I was speechless. How do you think I should have responded?

Sally

■ STEP 3

In small groups, share the responses you wrote.

UNIT OVERVIEW

This unit begins with a review of the forms of modal perfect verbs, and then explores their various meanings and uses in a variety of circumstances, concluding with a focus that summarizes the forms, meanings, and uses of all of them.

Please note that due to its length, this unit has been divided into four lesson plans. To review this unit more quickly, review focus charts and complete the first exercise to observe students' grasp of the grammar topics.

GRAMMAR NOTE

Modal verbs present challenges to almost every student of English. Very few other languages employ modal auxiliaries to the extent that English does, and as a distinct class of verbs with distinct syntactic properties. A thorough treatment of the modal perfect verbs is, therefore, an important part of an advanced grammar course.

UNIT GOALS

Some instructors may want to review the goals listed on Student Book (SB) page 240 after completing the Opening Task so that students understand what they should know by the end of the unit. These goals can also be reviewed at the end of the unit when students are more familiar with the grammar terminology.

OPENING TASK [20 minutes]

The aim of the Opening Task is to create a context in which students will need to use modal perfect verbs as they respond in writing to a request for advice about a past situation. The problem-solving format is designed to show the teacher how well the students can produce the target structures implicitly

and spontaneously when they are engaged in a communicative task. For a more complete discussion of the purpose of the Opening Task, see To the Teacher, Lesson Planner (LP) page xxii.

Setting Up the Task

1. To help students appreciate the humor in this task, before they start Step 1, ask if they are familiar with the word *retrospect* and the idiom *in retrospect*. You could elicit a definition by asking if they know the prefix *retro-* (back) and the root *spect* (look), both of which are parts of many other English words. Give them a few contextual examples of the idiom *in retrospect* using modal perfect verbs, such as: *Last year, I spent all of my savings to buy a new car. In retrospect, I should have bought a used car; I should have kept some of my savings for emergencies.*

Conducting the Task

■ STEP 1

1. Have students work with a partner to do Step 1, with one student reading the letter aloud and the other reading the response.
2. Have students discuss with their partner if they would have given different advice to Henry.

■ STEP 2

Have students read the letters, and then write responses to them. You can have them work with a partner or individually.

■ STEP 3

Have them work in small groups, in which they share their responses to the letters. Circulate and listen in to note if students are easily employing modal perfect verbs. Do not correct any errors in the conversations at this point.

Closing the Task

1. As a class, discuss the different kinds of suggestions students came up with. Was one of the situations more challenging to respond to than the others? Why?
2. Don't worry about accuracy at this point, though you may want to take notes of errors in meaning, form, or use in order to focus on those problems later.

GRAMMAR NOTE

Typical student errors (form)

- In negative forms of perfect modal verbs, placing *not* after *have*:—e.g., * *They might have not seen the movie.* (See Focus 1.)
- Omitting *will* when predicting the completion of a future event:—e.g., * *In another year they have moved to Florida.* (See Focus 8.)

Typical student errors (use)

- Using *should have* rather than *must have* to express an inference that something almost certainly happened:—e.g., * *If the cookies are gone, the kids should have eaten them.* (See Focus 4.)
- Using *might have* in *if* clauses to express the results of unreal situations:—e.g., * *If we might have bought that lottery ticket, we would have won a million dollars.* (See Focus 6.)

FOCUS 1 — Review of Modal Perfect Verbs

Although modal perfect verbs have a number of meanings, the forms are fairly simple.

EXAMPLES	EXPLANATIONS
(a) Henry **should have listened** more carefully to Annie. (b) They **must have come** from miles away.	**Active voice:** modal + *have* + past participle
(c) That concerto **should have been played** slowly. (d) Her house **must have been built** during the last century.	**Passive voice:** modal + *have* + *been* + past participle
(e) I **must have been dreaming**! (f) They **could have been waiting** for us somewhere else.	**Progressive:** modal + *have* + *been* + present (*-ing*) participle
(g) The game **might not have ended** yet. (h) You **may not have read** the instructions correctly.	**Negative:** In negative forms, *not* comes after the modal.
(i) That **must've** (/must əv/) been Ted on the phone. (j) NOT: That **must of** been Ted. (k) You **should've** (šud ə/) told me sooner! (l) Oh, I **could've** (/kud ə/) done that.	**Pronunciation in Contractions and Fast Speech** Speakers often contract *have* when using perfect modals in informal speech, pronouncing *have* as /əv/. This often leads writers to use *of* instead of *have* in modal perfect verbs, but this is not correct for written English. In fast speech, /əv/ may be further reduced to /ə/ as shown in (k) and (l).

Summary of Modal Perfect Forms

		SUBJECT + MODAL (NOT) + HAVE BEEN		PAST PARTICIPLE	PRESENT PARTICIPLE	
ACTIVE	He	could (not)	have —	eaten	—	all that food.
PROGRESSIVE	He	could (not)	have been	—	eating	all day.
PASSIVE	It	could (not)	have been	eaten	—	so quickly.

Note: There is also a passive progressive form for perfect modals: modal + *have* + *been* + *being* + past participle: *The food* **could have been being eaten** *during the week that we were gone.* This verb form, however, is not very common in either spoken or written English.

EXERCISE 1

Complete each blank with a modal perfect verb, using the cues in parentheses. The first one has been done as an example.

My friends and I discussed the letters Mr. Retrospect received and the responses we would make to them. Andrew thought that Henry (should/listen) (1) <u>should have listened OR should have been listening</u> more carefully during the phone conversation. Celeste added that Henry's new friend Annie (must/think) (2) <u>must have thought</u> he was a pretty nice guy to be so willing to chop wood. Takiko agreed with Mr. Retrospect that Henry (might/ask) (3) <u>might have asked</u> Annie to help him with something later if he felt taken advantage of. For a response to his letter, we (would/inform) (4) <u>would have informed</u> Henry that in the future, he should repeat what he thinks he heard if something sounds a little strange in the context. As for the Wild Animal Lover's dining experience, we all agreed that we (not/could/eat) (5) <u>couldn't have eaten</u> that dinner either, but we (not/would/want) (6) <u>wouldn't have wanted</u> to hurt the great-aunt's feelings. I suggested that he (might/say) (7) <u>might have said</u> he was allergic to squirrel or possum. That excuse (not/would/stray) (8) <u>wouldn't have strayed</u> too far from the truth since he probably (would/get) (9) <u>would have gotten</u> sick from eating it. Finally, concerning the last letter, we disagreed about how Sally (should/respond) (10) <u>should have responded</u> to her hairdresser. Rosa thought Sally (could/ask) (11) <u>could have asked</u> the hairdresser to restyle her hair. Marty said she (might/suggest) (12) <u>might have suggested</u> to him that her spiked hair could hurt someone. We all concurred that Sally (should/find out) (13) <u>should have found out</u> what her hairdresser planned to do before he styled her hair. We also agreed that the hairdresser (must/think) (14) <u>must have been thinking</u> only of his own preferences at the time and that Sally should look for a new stylist.

FOCUS 1 [20 minutes]

Of the eight focus boxes in this unit, this is the only one that focuses solely on perfect modal forms.

1. **Lead-in:** To practice active, passive, and progressive forms of modal perfects, write a 3-column chart on the board with these headings: *Active (modal + have + past participle)/Passive (modal + have been + past participle)/Progressive (modal + have been + present (-ing))*.

2. Divide the class into teams of four or five students.

3. Give each team a chance to give examples of the three types of verbs, and write these on the board. If they cannot, then they forfeit their turn.

4. Continue until each team has had at least two chances to respond.

5. Ask two volunteers to read the chart, one reading the examples, and the other the explanations. You could then read the summary.

6. Answer any questions students may have.

EXERCISE 1 [15 minutes]

In this exercise students apply the information they just learned in Focus 1 by completing sentences with modal perfect verbs.

1. Read the directions and example. What modal form is used in the example? (*the active voice*)

2. Have students work independently to complete the sentences with modal perfect verbs, using the cues in parentheses.

3. Review answers with the class. See answers on LP page 242.

For more practice, use *Grammar Dimensions 4* Workbook page 113, Exercise 1.

Expressing Judgments about Past Situations: *Should Have, Could Have, Would Have, Might Have*

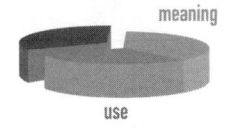

meaning

use

EXAMPLES	EXPLANATIONS
(a) You **should have gone** to bed earlier. (But you didn't.)	The modal forms *should have* (and negative *should not have*), *could have*, and *might have* express judgments about something that did not happen.
(b) They **shouldn't have spent** so much money. (But they did.)	
(c) The teacher **could have warned** us that we would have to know all the math formulas for the test. (But she didn't.)	
(d) Robert **might have written** us that he was coming. (But he didn't.)	
	These modals can express a variety of attitudes:
(e) You **shouldn't have taken** the day off from work. It created a burden for everyone else.	• *Should have* and *should not have* with second- or third-person subjects often imply criticism.
(f) Carmelita **should have treated** her sister better.	
(g) I **shouldn't have taken** the day off from work. Now I'm even more behind.	• With *I* or *we* as the subject, *should have* and *should not have* may express regret.
(h) We **should have treated** our sister better. Now she won't even talk to us, and it's all our fault.	
(i) If I had known years ago what I know now, I **would have made** much better use of my time in school.	• *Would have* may also express regret when used in the result clause of a conditional sentence.
(j) You $\left.\begin{array}{l}\text{could}\\ \text{might}\end{array}\right\}$ **have called** us when you were in town. We didn't even know you were here.	• *Should have, could have,* and *might have* can all express irritation, anger, or reproach. In certain contexts, they may express the speaker's judgment that someone has shown a lack of thoughtfulness or courtesy.
(k) You **might have asked** me if I wanted some dessert before you told the waiter to bring the bill.	
(l) Ian **could have offered** to contribute to the cab fare. He certainly had the money to do so.	• *Could have* also expresses capability more directly than *should have* and *might have* do.

EXERCISE 2

English speakers sometimes use the expression *coulda woulda shoulda** informally to refer to past opportunities that went unfulfilled: things they could have done or should have done, for example, but didn't do.

STEP 1   In the following passage, the writer discusses some regrets about college years. Underline each modal perfect verb. Which sentence explicitly states the *if*-clause that is implied for the modal perfect verbs with *would have*?

Coulda, Woulda, Shoulda!

(1) At some point in life, most people wish they had done something they instead passed up. (2) There are very few times in my life that I would go back and redo. (3) But I do have several regrets when I look back at my time at college. (4) What would I have done differently? (5) What are my coulda, woulda, shouldas?

(6) Well, I would have looked more carefully into the courses I selected, especially those in my majors, art and history. (7) I also should have picked up my education courses. (8) Even though I wasn't interested in teaching at that time, trying to pick up those courses later is a struggle. (9) I could have picked up my teaching credentials or another backup plan while I was already in school.

(10) Take advantage of all the opportunities available to you in college. (11) I should have gone to more plays, attended more sports events, gone to more concerts and art exhibits, and joined more groups. (12) After college, those opportunities are never as available as when you are right there on campus. (13) I would have done more if I knew what I know now.

(14) I would have gotten to know more people, different kinds of people. (15) I would have gone up to more people to say hello. (16) I would have asked more questions. (17) I wouldn't have waited for others to notice me first. (18) I would have taken the initiative to meet new friends and acquaintances.

From John Naisbitt and Patricia Aburdene. Megatrends 2000. Copyright © 1990 by Megatrends LTD.

STEP 2   Next write down three things that you could have, should have or, given what you now know, would have done during this past year. Share your responses with classmates.

ANSWER KEY

Exercise 2   Step 1: The implied *if*-condition is expressed in sentence #13. The modal perfect verbs are underlined above.   **Step 2:** Answers will vary.

FOCUS 2 [15 minutes]

1. **Lead-in:** Ask students questions that elicit modal perfect answers. *Lisa, what should you have done this past week that you didn't do? What could I have explained better in class this week? Bernard, what might you have done to prepare for your classes better?*

2. Ask students to describe a past situation in which someone behaved inappropriately (inconsiderately, rudely, etc.). The situation could be from real life or fiction; it could be from their personal lives or from a movie. Then ask questions as needed to prompt use of modal perfects expressing judgments (e.g., *Well, what do you think he might have done instead?*).

3. Read the first explanation. Emphasize that these modal perfect verbs are used to express things that did not really happen, but that the speaker wishes had, in fact, happened.

4. Ask volunteers to read the first four examples.

5. For the second portion of the chart, read each explanation first, and then the examples that illustrate it.

6. Encourage students to ask questions about anything they do not understand.

EXERCISE 2 [25 minutes]

In Exercise 2 students read a passage in which the author expresses certain regrets about college years. They practice first identifying and then using modal perfect verbs.

STEP 1

1. Read the introductory paragraph and directions for the first step. You may want to do the first sentence as an example with the class.

2. Have students work independently to underline the modal perfect verbs in the passage. See answers on LP page 244.

3. Ask them to work with a partner and take turns stating which sentence explicitly states the *if*-clause that is implied for the modal perfect verbs with *would have*.

STEP 2

1. Have students work independently to write three things that they could have, should have, or would have done during this past year.

2. Ask volunteers to share their lists with the class, and discuss these.

EXPANSION [30 minutes/homework]

Activity 5 (reflection) on SB page 259 makes a good homework or in-class assignment after students study Focus 2 and complete Exercise 2. They reflect on how they should have, could have, or would have better used the opportunities they have had to learn another language.

EXERCISE 3

Make a statement expressing a judgment about each of the following situations. Use *should have*, *could have*, or *might have* + verb in your response.

Example: A friend failed a test yesterday.
> She **could have spent** more time studying.
> She **might have asked** her teacher for help before the test.

1. One of your classmates returned a paperback book to you with the cover torn. When you gave it to him, the book was new.

2. Someone you know said she found a pair of sunglasses lying on the ground near a classroom building on her school campus and kept them since she didn't know who they belonged to.

3. You were stopped by the police while driving your car. Your license plates had expired.

4. A neighbor locked herself out of her apartment and didn't know what to do. So she just sat down on the front steps and waited for someone to notice her.

5. A friend wanted to get a pet but her roommates didn't like cats or dogs. So she moved out of the house she shared with them.

EXERCISE 4

The following story describes the unfortunate experiences of the Park family—Seung, Eun Joo, and their daughter Sophie—at a hotel where they recently spent a vacation. For each situation, state what you think the hotel staff or the Parks should have, could have, or might have done.

Examples: When the Parks arrived at the hotel, the front desk clerk was talking on the phone to her boyfriend and ignored them.
> *The clerk could have at least acknowledged their presence.*
> *The Parks should have looked for another hotel!*

1. When the clerk got off the phone, she told the Parks that their rooms had been given to someone else. However, other rooms would be available in four hours.

2. The Parks decided to have lunch in the hotel restaurant. Their waiter, who had a bad cold, kept coughing on their table as he took their orders.

3. When the food arrived, Eun Joo's soup was so salty she could feel her blood pressure rising by the second. Seung's pork chop was about as edible as a leather glove. Sophie's spaghetti looked like last week's leftovers and it tasted worse.

4. When the Parks were finally able to check into their rooms, the bellman forgot one of their bags in the lobby. Instead of getting it, he rushed off, explaining that he had to catch a train. Mr. Park ended up bringing the bag up by himself, which made him quite angry.

5. When Sophie tried to take a shower, she discovered there was no hot water.

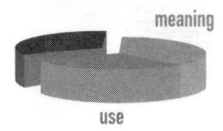

meaning

use

FOCUS 3 Expressing Obligations and Expectations: *Be Supposed to Have, Be to Have*

Be supposed to have and *be to have* are perfect forms of phrasal modal verbs. Their meanings depend somewhat on the tense of the *be* verb.

EXAMPLES	EXPLANATIONS
(a) We **were supposed to have taken** our exam on Friday, but our teacher was sick.	We use the past tense of *be supposed to have* + past participle to refer to something that was planned or intended but that did not happen.
(b) We **are supposed to have made up** the exam by next week.	We use a present tense form of *be supposed to have* when we expect something to be completed in the future.
(c) I **was to have graduated** in June, but I need to take two more courses for my degree.	*Be to have* expresses similar meanings as *be supposed to have*. *Be to have* is more common in formal English. Like *be supposed to have*, *be to have* refers to a past event that did not occur when *be* is past tense. It refers to a future expectation when *be* is present tense.
(d) Governor Carroll **is to have submitted** his resignation by next Friday.	

EXERCISE 5

Complete the sentences below to express obligations or expectations. The first has been done as an example.

Example: I was supposed to have <u>transferred to another college</u> this year, but <u>I needed more financial aid than I was offered.</u>

1. I was supposed to have <u>studied in Paris</u> this year, but <u>my French wasn't good</u> enough

2. In my <u>communication</u> class, I was supposed to have <u>handed in an essay</u> by (put in a day or date here) <u>Monday</u>, but <u>I didn't finish it on time</u>

3. I was to have <u>finished my paper</u> last (insert time phrase: weekend/month, etc.) <u>weekend</u>, but <u>I forgot</u>.

4. My family was <u>supposed to have taken a cruise to Alaska, but we had to postpone the trip until next summer.</u>

EXERCISE 6

Interview a classmate to find out three things that she or he was supposed to have done during the last few months but didn't do. Report at least one of them to the class.

Example: *Fan was supposed to have gone to the mountains last weekend, but her car broke down before she even got out of town.*

Exercise 3 Answers will vary. Possible answers are: 1. He should have replaced it./He could have offered to pay for it. 2. She could have brought them to the campus lost and found./She could have put a free ad in the campus newspaper. 3. I should have renewed the plates./I shouldn't have been driving. 4. She could have called a locksmith./She might have checked to see if a window was open. 5. She might have considered getting fish or a hamster instead.
Exercise 4 Answers will vary. Possible answers are: 1. The clerk should have offered something, such as a free meal, while they were waiting./The Parks could have demanded to see the manager. 2. The waiter should have stayed home if he was sick./The Parks should have left the restaurant.

3. The Parks should have refused to eat their food./They might have asked for the maître d'.
4. The bellhop should have gone back to get their bag./The Parks, after all this bad service, should have asked the hotel to reduce their bill. 5. She should have called the front desk and complained.
Exercise 5 Answers will vary. Possible answers are above.
Exercise 6 Answers will vary. Sample answers: Rudy was supposed to have bought his new motorcycle last week, but he didn't have enough money./Amy was supposed to have visited her cousins, but they had to go back to Tokyo for a month.

EXERCISE 3 (OPTIONAL) [15 minutes]

1. Read the directions and example as a class. How are the two sample judgments different? Does one imply that the friend was more capable of passing the test than the other? How are the two sample judgments different? Does one imply that the friend was more capable of passing the test than the other? (*Yes*—could have spent *implies more capability.*) Does either response indicate a stronger opinion?

2. Have students work in pairs to discuss and then make a judgment about each situation using *should have, could have,* or *might have* + verb.

3. Ask volunteers to share their judgments with the class. Encourage those with different judgments to share those, as well. See possible answers on LP page 246.

 For more practice, use *Grammar Dimensions 4* Workbook page 114, Exercise 2.

EXPANSION [30 minutes/homework]

Activity 2 (writing) on SB page 258 is a good follow-up to Exercise 3.

EXERCISE 4 (OPTIONAL) [20 minutes]

1. Read the directions, and then ask a volunteer to read the examples to the class. Ask students to suggest other things the Parks or the desk clerk *should/could/might have* done, and write these on the board.

2. Have students work in pairs to discuss each situation and to write their sentences.

3. Ask volunteer pairs to read their sentences to the class. Encourage them to read with a lot of expression. See possible answers on LP page 246.

EXPANSION [30 minutes]

Activity 1 (listening/speaking) on SB page 258 is a good follow-up to Exercise 4.

Suggestion: Have student pairs perform their conversations. The class could vote for the pair with the most helpful advice. Discuss the levels of politeness of tone and language encountered in the responses.

LESSON PLAN 2

FOCUS 3 [10 minutes]

1. **Lead-in:** Read the examples and explanations in the first section, and then ask volunteers to supply additional examples. Write these on the board.

2. Ask two volunteers to read the examples and explanation in the second row. Have students heard or read these constructions before?

3. Answer any questions students may have.

LANGUAGE NOTE

Native speakers of English often use nonperfective infinitive forms in informal English (e.g., a speaker might say *We were supposed to have taken our exam on Friday . . .*) Native speakers may also contract these phrasal modals in informal spoken English—e.g., "*We were **supposedt've** bought our tickets yesterday.*" However, it would be incorrect for students to write a sentence in this manner.

EXERCISE 5 [10 minutes]

1. Ask a volunteer to read the directions and example. What perfect form of a phrasal modal verb is used in the example? (*supposed to have*)

2. Have students work independently to complete the sentences with information about themselves.

3. Have students share and discuss their sentences with a partner.

4. Ask volunteers to share their sentences, and discuss these as a class. See possible answers on LP page 246.

 For more practice, use *Grammar Dimensions 4* Workbook page 115, Exercise 3.

EXERCISE 6 [20 minutes]

1. Read the directions and example as a class. Ask volunteers to describe something they were supposed to have done in the past few months, but didn't do.

2. Have students work in pairs and take turns interviewing each other to find out three things they were supposed to have done in the past few months, but didn't do. Ask them to write these down—but to not write down either their name or the name of their partner.

3. Collect the papers, shuffle them, and hand them out to students.

4. Have students read the papers, and ask the rest of the class to guess whose life is being described in each. See sample answers on LP page 246.

EXPANSION [30 minutes/homework]

1. For homework, have students interview two or three people about the same subject (three things they were supposed to have done in the past few months, but didn't do).

2. Ask them to write down the responses and to note any similarities or differences between them. Then ask volunteers to share their findings with the class.

FOCUS 4

Inferring/Making Deductions from Past Evidence: *Must (Not) Have, Can't Have, Should (Not) Have, Would (Not) Have*

meaning

use

Modal perfect verbs can express two kinds of past inference: We may infer that something (1) almost certainly did or did not happen or (2) probably did or did not happen.

EXAMPLES	EXPLANATIONS
	Inferring Near Certainty
(a) **Myla:** Our chemistry experiment failed. We **must have followed** the procedures incorrectly. (We **must not have done** it the right way.)	We use *must have* when we infer that something almost certainly happened.
(b) **Alberto:** We **can't have done** them incorrectly! I read every step carefully before the experiment and checked each one afterwards, too.	*Can't have* is the opposite of *must have*. We use it to express a belief that something is almost impossible or unbelievable.
(c) If the test tubes aren't here, Brian **must have taken** them.	These examples express strong inferences, not facts. Since both (a) and (b) refer to the same event, one of them must be wrong. Unlike *must have*, *should have* does not express an inference that something almost certainly happened.
(d) **NOT:** If the test tubes aren't here, Brian **should have taken** them.	
	Inferring Probability
(e) Let's check on our second experiment. The powder **should have dissolved** by now.	We use *should have* to express an expectation about a past event. We may infer that something happened, but we don't know for sure.
(f) We **should have gotten** a chemical reaction when we heated the solution, but nothing happened. I wonder what went wrong.	Sometimes we use *should have* to express an expectation about a past event that we know did not occur.
(g) If our observations are correct, the burglary **would have occurred** shortly after midnight.	*Would have* may also express an inference that something probably happened. We use it to speculate about what happened if we accept a certain theory or if we assume certain conditions. Sometimes the condition is stated in an *if*-clause as in (g).
(h) About one hundred seconds after the big bang, the temperatures **would have fallen** to one thousand million degrees.	The condition may be implied rather than directly stated. In (h), the implied condition is: if we accept the big bang theory as a model of how the universe began. The writer uses *would have fallen* instead of *fell* because the big bang theory is hypothetical.

EXERCISE 7

According to one model of how the universe began, between ten and twenty thousand million years ago the density of the universe and the curvature of space-time became infinite; this point in space-time was termed the "big bang." The following passage describes what some physicists believe probably happened after the big bang. Underline or write down the modal perfect verbs that express probability. Why does the author use these forms instead of simple past tense?

> (1) Within only a few hours of the big bang, the production of helium and other elements <u>would have stopped.</u> (2) And after that, for the next million years or so, the universe <u>would have</u> just <u>continued</u> expanding, without anything much happening. (3) Eventually, once the temperature had dropped to a few thousand degrees, and electrons and nuclei no longer had enough energy to overcome the electromagnetic attraction between them, they <u>would have started</u> combining to form atoms. (4) The universe as a whole <u>would have continued</u> expanding and cooling, but in regions that were slightly denser than average, the expansion <u>would have been slowed down</u> by the extra gravitational attraction. (5) This would eventually stop expansion in some regions and cause them to start to recollapse.

EXERCISE 8

The following sentences express some hypothetical statements about how native languages are learned. Fill in the blanks, using *must have, can't have,* or *should have* and the correct form of the verb in parentheses.

Example: *Researchers believe children <u>can't have</u> learned their first languages just by memorizing words.*

1. The number of possible sentences in any language is infinite. For this reason, we (learn) _____ our native languages by simply storing all the sentences we heard in a "mental dictionary." That would be impossible!

2. Children (develop) _____ their ability to speak their native languages by learning rules from adults because adults are not conscious of all grammar, pronunciation, and meaning rules either.

3. A child (acquire) _____ his or her native language by the age of 5; if not, we suspect that something is physically or psychologically wrong.

4. When a native English-speaking child says words like *ringed* and *doed*, this shows that he or she (apply) _____ a familiar rule for the past tense.

5. Similarly, if a child says words like *tooths* and *childs,* we speculate that he or she (overgeneralize) _____ the rule for regular plurals.

ANSWER KEY

Exercise 7 The modal perfect verbs are underlined above. Would have is used here to express inferred probability that the big bang theory is accepted although hypothetical.

Exercise 8 1. can't have learned 2. can't have developed 3. should have acquired 4. must have applied 5. must have overgeneralized

FOCUS 4 [20 minutes/homework]

Focus 4 describes how modal perfect verbs are used to express two kinds of inferences about the past. You may want to assign this focus as homework, so that students have a chance to study it and formulate questions. Then, go over the focus chart as a class, addressing any questions students might have.

1. **Lead-in:** Before class begins, hide something from the classroom that is usually there (e.g., an eraser, chalk, a calendar).
2. When students come in, ask them if they notice anything missing from the room. Give clues as needed.
3. When they have identified the missing item(s), ask, *What must have happened to (the eraser)?*
4. Elicit statements of probability. Note the time, and ask students to say what must have happened by now. Model an example: *Let's see, it's three o'clock; that means the mail carrier should have delivered my mail by now, and my daughter should have finished her last class.*
5. Ask different volunteers to read the examples and explanations in the focus chart.
6. Encourage students to ask questions about anything they do not fully understand.

LANGUAGE NOTE

Some students may tend to use *should have* rather than *might have* to express an inference that something almost certainly happened: Make sure they understand the difference between these two verbs.

EXERCISE 7 [20 minutes]

In Exercise 7 students read about what some physicists think may have happened after the "big bang." They identify the modal perfect verbs that express probability, implementing what they learned in Focus 4.

1. Introduce this exercise by asking if anyone knows of Stephen Hawking. Hawking is a famous physicist and the subject of a documentary film. He has made remarkable achievements despite having a severe disability.
2. Read the directions as a class. You may want to do the first sentence with the class as an example.
3. Have students work independently. Ask them to either underline or to write down the modal perfect verbs in the passage that express probability.
4. Have them compare answers with a partner.
5. Ask volunteers to read their answers to the class. See answers on LP page 248.
6. Discuss the final sentence of the passage: that matter in the universe is recollapsing. What could this mean for life on earth?

EXPANSION [30 minutes]

1. For further practice using modal perfect verbs to express probability, bring in copies of another excerpt by another scientist on the origin of another planet, such as Mars or Venus. Alternatively, you could ask students to find information on the Internet.
2. Ask students to underline all the modal perfect verbs used in the passage.
3. Have them read the article or passage to a partner. Then, ask them to exchange papers and check each other's work.
4. Ask volunteers to share the most interesting facts they learned with the class.

EXERCISE 8 [15 minutes/homework]

Students complete sentences about language acquisition in children using the modal perfect verbs *must have, can't have,* and *should have* that they studied in Focus 4.

1. Ask students for their ideas on how children acquire languages. Do they learn them word-by-word? Do they learn grammar by being taught rules?
2. Ask a volunteer to read the directions and example. Why would *must have* and *should have* not be good choices?
3. Have students work independently to complete the sentences.
4. Have them work in small groups to compare answers. Then, ask them to come up with one additional sentence about language acquisition that uses one of the modal perfect verbs.
5. Ask representatives of groups to share their new sentences with the class.

Suggestion: This would also make an excellent homework assignment, giving students more time to consider the concepts.

 For more practice, use *Grammar Dimensions 4* Workbook page 116, Exercise 4.

FOCUS 5 — Expressing Guesses About Past Situations: *May Have, Might Have, Could Have, Can Have*

We use certain modal perfects to make statements about the past when the speaker is not sure what happened.

EXAMPLES	EXPLANATIONS
(a) The movie **may have** already **started**. There are only a few people in the lobby. (b) I **might have gotten** an A on the test. I think I knew most of the answers.	*May have* and *might have* indicate that the speaker doesn't know if an event has occurred but has reason to believe that it has.
(c) I **may have met** him a long time ago. Both his name and face are very familiar. (d) I **might have met** him a long time ago, but I doubt it. He doesn't look at all familiar.	From the speaker's viewpoint, *might have* sometimes expresses less possibility of a past event having occurred than *may have* does.
(e) I don't think insects killed our strawberry plants. We **could have used** the wrong kind of soil. Or maybe we didn't fertilize them enough.	*Could have* often expresses one possible explanation among others. The speaker may imply that other explanations are possible.
(f) **Might** Carol **have been** the one who told you that? (g) **Could** too much water **have killed** the plants? (h) **Can** that **have been** Tomás on the phone? I didn't expect him to call back so soon.	*Might have, could have, can have* (but not *may have*) are also used in questions. *Might have* and *could have* in questions express guesses about a past event. We use *can have* only in questions. Usually a form of *be* is the main verb. The first sentence of (h) can be paraphrased: *Is it possible that Tomás was on the phone?*

EXERCISE 9

Each numbered group of statements below expresses certainty about the cause of a situation. For each, give an alternate explanation, using a perfective modal that expresses possibility. Can you think of any others?

Example: Look! The trunk of my car is open! Someone must have broken into it!
Alternate explanation: *You may have forgotten to shut it hard and it just popped open.*

1. Rebecca made a lot of mistakes on her economics assignment. She must not have studied the material very carefully.
   Alternate explanations: _____

2. Our English teacher didn't give us back our homework today. He must have been watching TV last night instead of reading it.
   Alternate explanations: _____

3. We invited Nora and Jack to our party but they didn't come. They must have found something better to do.
   Alternate explanations: _____

4. There was so much food left over from the party. Our guests must not have liked what we served.
   Alternate explanations: _____

5. Carlos usually gets off of work at five and is home by six. It's now eight and he's still not home. He can't have left work at five.
   Alternate explanations: _____

6. The crowd was laughing at the politician's speech last night. They must have thought she was really funny.
   Alternate explanations: _____

EXERCISE 10

To review the uses of perfect modals so far, return to the letters at the beginning of this chapter. Which of the letters in the Opening Task on pages 240 and 241 has a modal expressing advisability? Which has an inference modal? Which one includes a modal expressing possibility? Identify the perfective modals the letter writers used. Did you use these same modals in your answers? If you did, share some of your answers with the class. If not, give a one-sentence answer to each, now using these modals in perfective forms.

Exercise 9 Answers will vary. Possible answers are: 1. She could have misunderstood what she studied./She might not have been concentrating on her work. 2. He could have been grading homework for another class./He may not have been feeling well. 3. They could have gone out of town./They might have had a previous invitation. 4. Some guests might have eaten before they came to the party./We could have prepared too much food for the number of people who came. 5. He might have had an accident./He may have stopped to visit someone. 6. They could have thought what she was saying was ridiculous./They may have disagreed with her.

Exercise 10 Note: Advisability modals are those in Focus 2 that express judgments about past situations. *Modals expressing advisability:* should have done (Henry); should have just laughed at yourself; might have thought; could have taken (Mr. Retrospect); should have responded (Sally) *Inference modal:* must have been great exercise (Mr. Retrospect) *Modal expressing possibility:* could have done; could have returned (Mr. Retrospect); could have said (Wild animal lover)

FOCUS 5 [20 minutes]

Focus 5 explores how certain modal perfects are used to express uncertainty about past events.

1. **Lead-in:** Describe one or two well-known "unsolved mysteries," such as the "Bermuda or Devil's Triangle," an area off the southeastern Atlantic coast of the United States, which has had a number of unexplained losses of ships, small boats, and aircraft. Say, *People wonder: If a ship disappears in the Bermuda Triangle, could it have been due to strange magnetic forces there?*

2. Ask students to describe other such mysteries, and express what *may/might/could have* happened.

3. Have volunteers read the examples and explanations. Ask volunteers to give other examples for (c) and (d), so that students understand the difference in probability between *may have* and *might have*.

4. Encourage students to ask questions about anything they do not understand.

EXERCISE 9 [20 minutes]

In Exercise 9 students practice the material from Focus 5, using modal perfects to express a lack of certainty about past events.

1. Read the directions and example as a class. Ask volunteers to suggest two other alternate explanations, and write these on the board.

2. Have students work in pairs to give at least one alternate explanation for the cause of each past event, using a perfective modal.

3. Have pairs get together with another pair and take turns reading their sentences.

4. Ask volunteers to share their best explanations with the class. See possible answers on LP page 250.

 For more practice, use *Grammar Dimensions 4* Workbook page 116, Exercise 5.

EXERCISE 10 [20 minutes]

In Exercise 10 students reread the letters to and from Mr. Retrospect during the Opening Task and analyze the types and uses of modals.

1. Read the directions with the class. Draw a 4-column chart on the board. Label the first column *Expressing Judgments.* Ask students to look back at previous focus charts and dictate the headings for the next three columns (*Expressing Obligations and Expectations/Inferring/Making Deductions/Expressing Guesses*).

2. As a class, go back and reread the first letter to Mr. Retrospect on SB page 240. Ask students to find the first instance of a modal verb, and write the phrase on the board (*What do you think I should have done?*). What does that modal express? (*a judgment*)

3. Have students work independently to review the material from the Opening Task, including what they wrote.

4. Ask them to share their conclusions with a partner.

5. Review the letters to and from Mr. Retrospect as a class, and ask volunteers to share their analyses of their own work with the class. See answers on LP page 250.

 For more practice, use *Grammar Dimensions 4* Workbook page 118, Exercise 6.

EXPANSION [25 minutes/homework]

1. For homework, ask students to read an advice column—in a newspaper, a magazine, or online—and write a response to one of the letters, using modal perfect verbs.

2. During the next class, have students share the original letters and their responses in small groups.

FOCUS 6

Expressing Results of Unreal Conditions: *Would Have, Could Have, Might Have*

meaning

EXAMPLES		EXPLANATIONS
Unreal Condition	**Hypothetical Result**	*Would have, could have,* and *might have* express hypothetical results of conditions that did not happen (unreal conditions).
(a) If Bruno had arrived before noon,	he would have seen us.	
Actual Condition	**Actual Result**	
(b) Bruno arrived after noon,	so he missed seeing us.	
		The following modals express different degrees of probability of the results:
(c) If I had been at that intersection ten minutes earlier, **I would have seen** the accident.		• high probability
(d) If the car had stopped for the light, the accident **could have been avoided.**		• capable of happening
(e) If Grace had been wearing her seat belt, she **might have escaped** injury.		• a chance of happening

We also use these modals in statements that only **imply** the condition rather than state it directly. These statements may express a missed opportunity or a rejection of one option for another.

EXAMPLES	IMPLIED UNREAL CONDITION	IMPLIED FACT
(f) Tim **would have been** a great father.	if he had been a father	He was not a father.
(g) I **could have gone** to medical school.	if I had wanted to go to medical school	I did not go to medical school.
(h) Fiona **might have made** the debate team.	if she had tried out for the debate team	She did not try out for the debate team.

EXERCISE 11

Modal perfect verbs in the sentences that follow express unreal conditions. Identify each modal perfect verb. Then decide whether each of these modal perfects is the result of a stated condition or the result of an implied condition. If the condition is implied, state what you think a possible condition might be.

Example: I could have driven you to your doctor's appointment. *Implied condition*
Possible condition: *If I had known you needed a ride, . . .*

1. Seth would have turned in your assignment for you yesterday if you had let him know you wouldn't be able to attend class.
2. I'm sorry you got stuck in traffic. You could have gotten off the freeway and taken street routes to get here.
3. If I had known the grammar class would be offered in the spring, I might have waited to take it then.
4. I could have told you that the swimming pool was closed today.
5. If that lecture had gone on any longer, I might have fallen asleep.
6. We could have gone out of town for our vacation, but we decided to stay home and remodel the kitchen instead.
7. I think my sister would have been a good math teacher.
8. That car accident might have been worse than it was.

EXERCISE 12

For each sentence, give two result modals (*would have, could have,* or *might have*) that would be appropriate, using the verb in parentheses as the main verb. For each, explain the difference in meaning and/or use between the two modals you choose.

Examples: If the weather had been nicer, they (stay) _____ longer at the beach.
(1) *would have stayed*
(*They definitely wouldn't have left so early; they had intended to be there longer.*)
(2) *could have stayed*
(*It would have been possible to stay longer; this form might be used if cold or rainy weather forced them to leave.*)

1. If Sam had been prepared for the interview, he (get) _____ the job.
2. If you had let me know you needed transportation, I (drive) _____ you to your appointment.
3. If we had been more careful about our environment, we (prevent) _____ damage to the ozone layer.
4. The chairperson (call off) _____ the meeting if she had known so many committee members would not be here today.

ANSWER KEY

Exercise 11 Note: Answers for implied conditions will vary. 1. would have turned in; Stated condition: If you had let him know . . . 2. could have gotten off; Not an unreal condition but a judgment of past event; Implied condition: (if you had known the traffic was going to be so bad) 3. I might have waited; Stated condition: If I had known the grammar class . . . 4. could have told you; Implied condition: (if you had asked me) 5. might have fallen; Stated condition: If that lecture had gone on . . . 6. could have gone; Implied condition: (if we had wanted to) 7. would have been; Implied condition: (if she had decided to be a math teacher) 8. might have been worse; Implied condition: (if the car had been moving faster)

Exercise 12 Answers will vary. Possible answers are: 1. might have/would have got(ten) 2. could have/would have driven 3. could have/might have prevented 4. would have/might have called off

FOCUS 6 [15 minutes]

Focus 6 illustrates how the modal perfect verbs *would/could/might have* are used to express the results of hypothetical conditions and events.

1. **Lead-in:** Write *would have, could have,* and *might have* on the board. Then, give an example such as: *If I had bought stock in Microsoft twenty years ago, I would have been rich today.* Ask students whether your statement refers to something that actually happened, or not (*no*). Ask a volunteer to give another example using *would have.*

2. Repeat, using *could have* and *might have*: *If I had left the soup cooking on the stove for ten hours, I could have burned down the house. If we had gone to the gym, we might have felt better.* Ask volunteers to supply other examples.

3. Read the first section of the chart as a class.

4. For the second section, read the explanation first. Then have volunteers read the examples. Discuss the degrees of probability expressed in each example.

5. Examples (f–h) may be more difficult for some students to understand, since the meanings are implied, rather than directly stated. To help students understand implied conditions, give them statements about yourself similar to (f–h) and ask them to tell you the implied conditions and implied facts. Examples: *I could have been a concert pianist. I would have made a terrific rocket scientist.*

6. Encourage students to ask questions about anything they do not understand.

EXERCISE 11 [20 minutes]

In Exercise 11 students apply what they have just reviewed in Focus 6, analyzing whether the modal perfects refer to a stated or implied condition.

1. Read the directions and example as a class. Ask volunteers to suggest two other possible conditions, and write these on the board.

2. Have students work in pairs. They should discuss and decide whether each condition is stated or implied and, if implied, what that condition might be.

3. Have pairs get together with another pair and discuss their conclusions.

4. Ask volunteers to share their analyses with the class. See possible answers on LP page 252.

EXERCISE 12 (OPTIONAL) [15 minutes]

Students complete sentences with result modals, and then explain the differences in meaning and/or use between the two modals they chose.

1. Read the directions and examples as a class. Review the explanation of degrees of probability in the second section of Focus 6.

2. Ask a volunteer to create another example using *might have*, and write this on the board.

3. Have students work independently to complete the sentences.

4. Have them share their sentences in small groups, explaining the differences in meaning and/or use between the two modals they chose for each.

5. Ask volunteers to share sample answers with the class, and discuss. See possible answers on LP page 252.

work book For more practice, use *Grammar Dimensions 4* Workbook page 118, Exercise 7.

EXPANSION [30 minutes/homework]

Activity 3 (writing) on page 259 is a good sequel to Focus 6 and Exercise 12. Students think of how things in their pasts might have been different, list five of these, and then write one or two paragraphs about one of them using perfect modal verbs to express the results of unreal conditions. This would also make a good homework assignment.

■ EXERCISE 13

Choose three of the five conditions below. Make up three hypothetical results to follow each condition. Use *would have*, *could have*, and *might have*. Explain your choices of modal based on the degree of probability of each result.

Example: If I had lived in the nineteenth century, *I would have owned a horse instead of a car. I could have learned how to make ice cream instead of buying it from the supermarket. I might have wanted to be a farmer instead of going into business.*

Explanation: *It is quite likely that I would have owned a horse rather than a car. It is somewhat probable that I would have learned to make ice cream. It's possible, but not very likely, that I would have wanted to be a farmer.*

1. If I could have picked any city to grow up in,

2. If I had been the leader of my country during the last decade,

3. If I could have been present at one historical event before I was born,

4. If I had been born in another country,

5. If I had been able to solve one world problem of this past century,

■ EXERCISE 14

What might be an implied condition for each of the following hypothetical statements? Write down a few of your answers for each sentence. Share your responses with your classmates.

Example: I could have won the race.
Possible implied conditions:
If I had just run a little faster at the beginning, I could have won the race.
I could have won the race if I had trained harder.

1. This could have been a much better year for me.

2. My parents might have been even more proud of me than they are.

3. My financial situation would have been improved.

4. I could have been a more fluent speaker of (*state a language here*).

5. I might have considered being a (*state a career or profession here*).

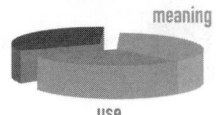

meaning

use

| FOCUS 7 | Predicting the Completion of a Future Event: *Will Have, Shall Have* |

Will have and *shall have* are future perfect modal forms. They express the completion of a future event before another future time.

EXAMPLES	EXPLANATIONS
(a) By the time you get this postcard, **I will have left** Portugal.	Possible meaning: You will get this postcard in a week or so. I'm leaving Portugal tomorrow.
(b) At the end of this week, **I'll have been** in Athens for four months.	In spoken English, *will* is often contracted.
(c) By this date next year, we **shall have reduced** our air pollution by 30 percent.	*Shall have* has the same meaning as *will have*. American English speakers rarely use this form in everyday English. Some types of formal English, such as speeches or legal documents, use *shall have*.

■ EXERCISE 15

The following predictions have been posted to the Long Bets Foundation Web site, which provides a forum for bets, debates, and discussions about the future. Rewrite the information in the chart below as predictions with future perfect modal verbs. You can use the verb in parentheses to create your sentence or some other verb. Make other sentence structure changes as needed. If time permits, discuss which predictions, if any, you think will come true. An example has been provided for the first one.

Example: *By 2020, technology will have been developed that allows people to "fax" (teleport) objects such as books, clothing, and jewelry.*

Event or condition:	Predicted to happen by:
1. technology allows people to "fax," or teleport, objects such as books, clothing, and jewelry (develop)	2020
2. technology for tracking and identification is inside the bodies of at least 50 percent of U.S. citizens (embed)	2025
3. computers instead of surgeons administer and monitor all surgical anesthesia (replace)	2030
4. intelligent signals from outside our solar system (received)	2050
5. governments of the world legally permit global mobility: people may live anywhere on earth if they obey local laws (legalize)	2103
6. mandatory classes in defending against robot attacks in over 50 percent of schools in the USA or Europe (require)	2150

Exercise 13 Answers will vary. Possible answers are: 1. I might have chosen Madrid/my hometown.   2. I would have worked for racial equality/raised taxes.   3. I would have participated in the French Revolution/witnessed the first Olympics.   4. I might not have had as many opportunities as I do now/might have spoken another language as my native language.   5. I would have put an end to world hunger/would have found a cure for AIDS.

Exercise 14 Answers will vary. Possible answers are: 1. if I had gotten more of my required classes out of the way.   2. if I had made the Dean's List this semester.   3. If I had been able to work more hours at my job.   4. . . . Spanish, if I had participated in a language program in Mexico

---

5. . . . professional musician if I had been a more talented violinist.

Exercise 15 Clause order and phrasing of responses may vary. Note that in some cases, an effort has been made to keep subjects from being too long, as in #6.   2. By 2025, technology for tracking and identification will have been embedded . . .   3. By 2030, computers will have replace surgeons in administering and monitoring all surgical anesthesia.   4. By 2050, we will have received intelligent signals from outside our solar system.   5. By 2103, governments of the world will have legalized global mobility.   6. By 2150, mandatory classes in defending against robot attacks will have been required in over 50%.

EXERCISE 13 [15 minutes]

Students create hypothetical results to conditions, expressing the degrees of probability outlined in Focus 6.

1. Read the directions, and ask two volunteers to read the two parts of the example to the class. Are there other possible explanations?
2. Have students work independently to write three hypothetical results to each condition.
3. Have them share their sentences in small groups, explaining their choices of modal based on the degree of probability of each result. Encourage them to refer back to Focus 6, as needed.
4. Ask volunteers to share their sentences with the class, and discuss. See possible answers on LP page 254.

EXERCISE 14 [15 minutes]

In Exercise 14 students write what might be implied conditions for a series of hypothetical statements.

1. Read the directions and example as a class. Ask volunteers to suggest other implied conditions, and write these on the board.
2. Have students work independently to write at least one implied condition for each statement.
3. Have them share their work with a partner.
4. Ask volunteers to share their answers with the class, and discuss. See possible answers on LP page 254.

EXPANSION [20 minutes]

For additional practice with using modals to express the results of unreal conditions, have students do this expansion activity.

1. Divide students into small groups.
2. Have each group write at least three hypothetical statements similar to those in Exercise 14.
3. Have groups exchange papers, and write what might be an implied condition for each statement.
4. Have the groups take turns reading what they have written.
5. Ask volunteers to share a few statements and implied conditions with the class.

LESSON PLAN 4

FOCUS 7 [25 minutes]

Focus 7 is a short and direct explanation of the meaning and use of future modal perfect forms to predict the completion of a future event.

1. **Lead-in:** Draw a time line on the board with two or three future dates (weeks, months, or years from now, depending on what you want to describe):
   now   December   July   October
2. Under the time line, write the beginnings of sentences for your timeline: *By December, I will have . . .*
3. Give an example of a completion for your first sentence (e.g., *I will have bought a new computer*). Ask volunteers to tell you what they will have done/seen/written/bought/tried, etc., by that date.
4. Ask two volunteers to read the explanations and examples in the chart.
5. Emphasize that *shall have* is not common in American English, particularly in speech.

LANGUAGE NOTE

Although native English speakers do use *will have* in future perfect modal forms in speech and informal writing, they often use simple future forms instead. This may require changing the lexical verb. For example, (a) could be restated as: *By the time you get this postcard, I won't be in Portugal any longer* (or *I'll be back home*). Consequently, some students may not have heard these forms much in spoken English and may think they sound "strange." They may also have heard contracted forms and not have been aware that *'ll* represents *will*.

EXERCISE 15 [20 minutes]

Students rewrite the information as predictions with future perfect modal verbs, applying the principles they learned in Focus 7.

1. Read the directions and example as a class. Ask volunteers what else might be developed by 2020.
2. Ask students to work in pairs to make predictions with future perfect modal verbs.
3. Ask several volunteers to share their predictions to each statement with the class, and discuss the implications of these predictions. See possible answers on LP page 254.

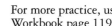 For more practice, use *Grammar Dimensions 4* Workbook page 119, Exercise 8.

EXPANSION [40 minutes/homework]

Activity 4 (research on the web) on SB page 259 is a good sequel to Focus 7 and Exercise 15. It could be assigned as homework. Students research global warming on the Internet, find five predictions, and write them down using perfect modal verbs.

FOCUS 8 — Summary of Modal Perfect Verbs

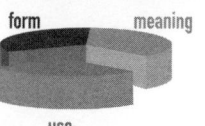

form meaning
use

EXAMPLES	MODAL PERFECT VERBS	IMPLIED FACT	MEANING/USE
(a) You **should have told** me.	*should have could have might have*	You didn't tell me.	Judgment of past situation
(b) We **were supposed to have left** before Thursday.	*be supposed to have be to have*	We didn't leave.	Expectation, obligation
(c) Our professor **must have cancelled** class today.	*must have can't have*	—	Inferring near certainty about past situations
(d) The film I dropped off **should have been developed** yesterday.	*should have would have*	—	Inferring probability about past situations
(e) She **may have missed** the bus. I don't see her anywhere.	*may have might have could have can have*	—	Expressing guesses about past situations
(f) He **would have written** if he had known you wanted him to.	*would have could have might have*	He didn't write.	Result of stated unreal condition
(g) You **could have stayed** with us.	*would have could have might have*	You didn't stay with us.	Result of implied real condition
(h) By next month, they **will have finished** the first stage of the project.	*will have shall have*	—	Predicting completion of a future event.

EXERCISE 16

Edit the following sentences to correct any errors in modal perfect verb form or use.

Example: I think I might met you at Diane's party last month.
　　　　　Correction: *I think I might have met you . . .*

1. In my presentation to the class on learning strategies, I should have ~~emphasize~~ *emphasized* more the need to try out different strategies and then to evaluate them.

2. I am glad that my grandmother was able to get out of New Orleans before the hurricanes. That might ~~of~~ *have been* been a very frightening experience for her.

3. Our advisor ~~would have being~~ *might have been* very proud of us if he had known we won the award for the best poster at the engineering poster session, but he was away for a conference.

4. That movie was interesting, but it was so long! I think it could *have* been edited to make it about a half hour shorter.

5. We were ~~suppose~~ *supposed* to have turned in our projects at the beginning of class last Friday.

6. If the prize for the Biology Department raffle had been something I really wanted, I would ~~buy~~ *have bought* a ticket.

7. You lost your sweater? Well, let's go back to our English classroom to see if you might've ~~leave~~ *left* it there.

8. My brother and my sister-in-law got married in 2005. So if they stay married, by 2055, they will ~~be~~ *have been* married 50 years!

FOCUS 8 [15 minutes/homework]

Focus 8 gives a summary of all the modal perfect verbs presented in this unit.

1. **Lead-in:** You may want to assign this chart as homework, and then discuss it in the next class.
2. Ask volunteers to give another example for each statement.
3. Encourage students to ask questions about anything they do not understand.

METHODOLOGY NOTE

Remind students that this summary can serve as a good reference for their future work and study. They may want to keep a separate notebook of *Grammar Dimensions* focus charts that provide summary information. Remind them that the charts in the appendix are also excellent reference tools.

EXERCISE 16 (OPTIONAL) [15 minutes]

As a final exercise, students read sentences and correct any errors in modal perfect verb forms or use.

1. Read the directions and example as a class. What is wrong with the example sentence?
2. Have students work independently to correct the sentences.
3. Have them share their work with a partner.
4. Ask volunteers to share their answers with the class, and discuss. See answers on LP page 256.

For more practice, use *Grammar Dimensions 4* Workbook page 120, Exercise 9.

UNIT GOAL REVIEW [10 minutes]

Ask students to look at the goals on the opening page of the unit again. Refer to the pages of the unit where information on each goal can be found.

ExamView Test Generator For assessment of Unit 13, use *Grammar Dimensions 4 ExamView®*.

Use Your English

 **ACTIVITY 1** listening/speaking

 Listen to the audio. You will hear two telephone conversations. The first is between friends; the second is a business conversation. Each conversation elicits some type of advice or judgment from one of the speakers.

CD2 Tracks
1, 2

■ **STEP 1** Listen to the two conversations once to get the meaning.

■ **STEP 2** Listen to each conversation a second time. At the end of each one, take the role of the person who offers advice or makes a judgment. Provide an appropriate response to the person asking for your advice or opinion. Use a perfect modal verb. Write down your responses; then compare them with those of some of your classmates.

ACTIVITY 2 writing

Write three brief scenarios that describe thoughtless, rude, or somehow inappropriate behavior. Exchange scenarios with a classmate and write at least one judgment about each of the situations your classmate has written, using *could have, might have,* or *should have.* Use a variety of modals in responding. Afterwards, if time permits, share a few of your situations and responses with the class.

Example: *You were riding a subway train to school. You were standing up because it was very crowded, and suddenly the train stopped. A woman next to you spilled her diet soda all over your new jacket.*

Judgments:
She shouldn't have been drinking a soda on the train.
She could at least have offered to pay for dry cleaning the jacket.

 **ACTIVITY 3** writing

Write five sentences stating situations that would (could, might) have happened in the past if circumstances had been different. Choose one of your sentences to explain in more detail. Write a paragraph based on the sentence you selected.

Example: *If my family had not moved to the United States, I might not have learned English . . .*

 **ACTIVITY 4** research on the web

 In Unit 14, Exercise 7, page 270, some of the current effects of global warming are described. Read the descriptions in that exercise. Then, using a search engine such as Google® or Yahoo®, research the topic of global warming on the Internet to find some specific claims about changes that will have occurred by a particular time period. Write down four or five of the predictions you find using perfect modal verbs, citing the source for your information.

Example: *According to the National Resources Defense Council, scientists project that if the current rates of ice cap melting continue, by 2100, the sea level will have risen by 3 feet.*

 **ACTIVITY 5** reflection

In trying to develop proficiency in a language other than our native language, almost all of us have had some second thoughts—or "coulda, shoulda, woulda's," as the expression goes—about what we might have done differently. In many cases, our second thoughts involve ideas about what we could have or should have done both inside and outside the classroom. Reflect on your experiences learning English or another language. Write down at least three things you think you could have, should have, or, given your feelings now, would have done to make the most of opportunities for language learning. One example is given here:

In revising my last paper, I could have paid more attention to the vocabulary suggestions that my teacher made.

The Use Your English activities at the end of the unit contain situations that should naturally elicit the structures covered in the unit. For a more complete discussion of how to use the Use Your English activities, see To the Teacher, LP page xxvi.

ACTIVITY 1 listening/speaking
[30 minutes]

This activity is a good sequel to Exercise 4 on SB page 246. Tell students that they are going to listen to two phone conversations.

CD2
Tracks 1,2

Note: Please disregard student book track numbers 18 and 19.

■ **STEP 1** Have students listen to the audio once without taking notes.

■ **STEP 2**

1. Ask students to listen again and make notes about what the people are asking.
2. Ask students to write responses or advice to the people on the audio. Tell them to replay the audio as needed.
3. Have students work in small groups and share their responses with the group. Ask them to note similarities and differences in their responses.
4. Ask representatives of each group to read several responses to the class, and discuss.

ACTIVITY 2 writing
[30 minutes/homework]

This activity is a good follow-up to Exercise 3 on SB page 246. It could be completed in class or assigned as homework, with students exchanging papers during the next class.

1. Ask several students to describe examples of rude or thoughtless behavior they have seen. Then ask

others to comment on these: What should people have done? What could they have done? What might they have done?

2. Read the directions and examples as a class. Ask a volunteer to create another sentence using *might have* to add to the example.
3. Ask students to write three brief scenarios about instances of bad behavior. Tell them they can describe real situations or ones they make up.
4. Have them exchange papers with a partner, and write a judgment about each situation using *could/might/should have*. Encourage them to use all three modals.
5. Have pairs get together with another pair, and exchange papers. Ask them to take turns reading the situations and the judgments. Then, ask them to discuss these: Do they have other ideas about how people *could/might/should have* behaved?
6. Ask several volunteers to share their best situations and judgments with the class.

ACTIVITY 3 writing
[30 minutes]

You may wish to assign Activity 3 after Focus 6 and Exercise 12 on SB page 253.

1. Ask volunteers to think of something they might have done differently in their pasts had circumstances been different. Model an example, such as: *If I had learned to swim when I was young, I might not be so afraid of the water now.*
2. Read the directions and examples as a class.
3. Ask students to list five things that might or could have been different in their pasts. Then chose one of these to focus on while writing a paragraph about it. Tell them to use *could/couldn't have* and *might have/might not have* in their writings.
4. Ask volunteers to read their writings to the class, and discuss.

ACTIVITY 4 research on the web
[40 minutes]

This activity is a good sequel to Focus 7 and Exercise 15 on SB page 255.

1. Discuss what students know and think about global warming. Do they think global warming is having any effect on our environment now? Are they worried about the effects it might have in the future?
2. Read the directions and examples as a class.
3. Have students use an Internet search engine such as Google® or Yahoo!® to find information about global warming. Have them write down five specific predictions about future effects of global warming using future perfect modal forms. Ask them to look for predictions that include dates, as in the example.
4. Ask volunteers to share their findings with the class, and discuss these.

ACTIVITY 5 reflection
[30 minutes/homework]

Activity 5 makes a good homework or in-class assignment after students study Focus 2 and complete Exercise 2 on SB page 245.

1. Read the directions and examples as a class.
2. Have students work independently to list at least three things they would change about how they acted in the past.
3. Have them share these insights with a partner. How might things have been different if they had acted differently?
4. Ask volunteers to share some insights with the class, and discuss.

- Know how discourse organizers help listeners and readers understand information

- Use appropriate connectors to introduce, organize, and summarize topics

- Use *there* + *be* appropriately to introduce topics

- Use rhetorical questions to introduce and change topics and to focus on main points

OPENING TASK

Analyzing Issues

What global, national, or local issues interest you most?

STEP 1

With a partner, choose one of the following topics. Each of you will be writing a paragraph about some aspect of the topic.

- pollution
- the homeless
- illiteracy
- global warming
- an important health issue (e.g., smoking, obesity)
- censorship on the Internet

- immigration policies
- a social or political problem in the area where you live
- something that needs to be changed at your school or campus (course requirements, needed facilities, methods of teaching, etc.)

STEP 2

With your partner, explore the topic by writing four or five questions about it. Here is an example for the topic of overpopulation:

1. Is overpopulation becoming a more serious problem?
2. How should the problem of overpopulation be dealt with in developing countries?
3. Does anyone have the right to tell others how many children they should have?
4. What are the religious, cultural, and individual factors we need to consider in addressing the population problem?
5. Can we ever solve the problem of overpopulation?

STEP 3

Each of you should select one of the questions you wrote in Step 2 to answer in one paragraph. Save the questions and the paragraphs you wrote for exercises later in this unit.

UNIT OVERVIEW

This unit covers structures in English that serve to introduce, connect, and focus topics in discourse. These organizers are especially important in academic and business writing and in formal speaking contexts.

Please note that due to its length, this unit has been divided into three lesson plans. To review this unit more quickly, review focus charts and complete the first exercise to observe students' grasp of the grammar topics.

GRAMMAR NOTE

It is important to emphasize the functions of these discourse organizers. Most students will appreciate their usefulness in organizing spoken and written material. The most challenging material is presented in Focus 5 and 6: rhetorical questions. Some students will automatically assume that any question is meant to be answered. After reviewing the multiple examples and explanations in the focus charts, the function of rhetorical questions should become much clearer to them.

UNIT GOALS

Some instructors may want to review the goals listed on Student Book (SB) page 260 after completing the Opening Task so that students understand what they should know by the end of the unit. These goals can also be reviewed at the end of the unit when students are more familiar with the grammar terminology.

OPENING TASK [20 minutes]

The purpose of the Opening Task is to create a context in which students will need to use discourse organizers to brainstorm ideas about a topic and then write a paragraph about it. The problem-solving format is designed to show the teacher how well the students can produce the target structures implicitly and spontaneously when they are engaged in a communicative task. For a more complete discussion of the purpose of the Opening Task, see To the Teacher, Lesson Planner (LP) page xxii.

Setting Up the Task

Have students brainstorm issues at the global, national, and local levels. They can brainstorm individually, on paper, and then share their ideas, or they can brainstorm as a class, with you writing on the board. Emphasize that "issues" tend to be topics about which people can agree or disagree.

Conducting the Task

■ STEP 1

1. Read the directions and list of topics as a class. If the topics listed here do not appeal to you or your students, modify or expand them to fit your context and interests. You could use topics from the previous brainstorming activity.

2. Have students work with a partner and choose a topic to write about.

■ STEP 2

Have them write four or five questions about the topic. Give them a 10-minute time limit for this step.

■ STEP 3

Have students work independently to choose one of the questions they wrote in Step 2 and write a one-paragraph answer to it. Set a time limit for their writing, such as 15 minutes.

Note: Given that they are only writing a paragraph, students cannot be expected to produce the full range of discourse organizers in this unit. They will review the products of this task and add organizers, where appropriate, in later exercises.

Closing the Task

1. As a class, discuss some of the topics and ideas students wrote about. Which problems are the most difficult to solve? What were some of the most interesting solutions?

2. Tell students to hold on to their papers—they will use them again later in the unit.

3. Don't worry about accuracy at this point, though you may want to take notes of errors in meaning, form, or use in order to focus on those problems later.

GRAMMAR NOTE

Typical student errors (form)

- Using *firstly* as a sequence connector, rather than *first*:—e.g., * *Firstly, mix the flour and butter together.* (See Focus 1.)

- Using the wrong form of *to be* in *there + be* constructions:—e.g., * *There is three kinds of cheeses to choose from.* (See Focus 3.)

Typical student errors (use)

- Mixing tenses when asking rhetorical questions:—e.g., * *They really want to stay here, didn't they? Open the door, won't you?* (See Focus 5.)

- Responding to rhetorical questions with a *yes/no* answer: —e.g., *Who wants to work 70 hours a week?* * *No.* (See Focus 6.)

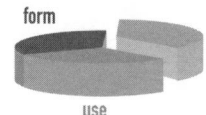
form

use

FOCUS 1 — Overview of Discourse Organizers

This unit presents structures that speakers and writers use to signal or emphasize the organization of discourse. These structures help the listener or reader follow the discourse, focus on main points, and understand how parts are related. The following are uses of the discourse organizers covered in this unit.

EXAMPLES	EXPLANATIONS
(a) **First,** we need to examine the root causes of crime in our city, such as lack of education. (b) **After that,** the existing laws and programs should be evaluated. (c) **Finally,** we need to determine who will pay for new programs.	**Form:** sequential connectors **Use:** to show the sequence of topics or main point
(d) **There are** many reasons why crime is increasing in our cities.	**Form:** *there + be,* **Use:** to introduce topics
(e) **Is crime really increasing as much as everyone thinks it is?** The answer to this question may surprise you.	**Form:** rhetorical questions **Use:** to introduce topics
(f) So far, we have considered the positive side of general education requirements. **Next,** let's look at some of their drawbacks.	**Forms:** sequential connectors, rhetorical questions **Use:** to signal topic shifts
(g) Lack of education may be one cause of crime. **But what about parental responsibilities in cases of juvenile crime?**	
(h) **To summarize,** the statistics just presented indicate that air quality has been steadily improving during the last decade.	**Form:** summary connectors **Use:** to introduce or make a summary of what has been or will be discussed
(i) This paper examines the contributions of recent immigrants to the state economy. **Overall,** my research will show that immigrants have played a significant role in economic development.	
(j) **Should we be paying more tuition when we cannot even get the courses we need to graduate on time?**	**Form:** rhetorical questions **Use:** to emphasize key points, especially in argumentative discourse

EXERCISE 1

Match each of the sentences containing discourse organizers in the first column with topics in the second column. Then identify the form of discourse organizer in each and its apparent use. More than one use might be possible. The first has been done as an example.

Example: 1. i. (kinship systems); Form: *there + be*; Use: *to introduce a topic*

_i_ 1.	There are two types of family relatives I will discuss today: those involving blood relations and those resulting from marriage.	a. How the universe was created and evolved
_f_ 2.	What does your clothing reveal about your identity?	b. Basics of the Internet
_e_ 3.	To summarize, I have described several types of behavior that are typically regarded as masculine.	c. Violence on television
_h_ 4.	So far I have discussed the benefits of regular exercise. But what about people who become obsessed with workouts and spend half their lives at the sports club?	d. Parking problems on campus e. Gender roles
_g_ 5.	Lastly, I will talk about adrenaline, which is produced by the adrenal gland and raises blood pressure in stress situations.	f. How people express themselves through their style of dress
_j_ 6.	Is there any reason why women and minorities should earn less than white males in comparable jobs?	g. Major hormones in the human body
_b_ 7.	To start with, we will describe one of the most widely used services, known as e-mail. After that, we will discuss news bulletin boards.	h. Starting a physical fitness program
_c_ 8.	Thirdly, let's consider programs that feature real-life police on patrols dealing with violent criminals.	i. Kinship systems in anthropology j. Job equality
_a_ 9.	There are two main types of theories that can categorize most of modern cosmology: evolutionary theories and continuous creation theories.	
_d_ 10.	In summary, my presentation today will provide several compelling reasons why our campus needs more space for cars.	

ANSWER KEY

Exercise 1 The correct matches are shown above. The form and use are as follows: 2. rhetorical question; to introduce a topic 3. summary connector; to introduce a summary of what has been discussed 4. rhetorical question; to signal topic shift 5. sequential connector; to show sequence of topics 6. rhetorical question; to emphasize a key point 7. sequential connectors; to show sequence of topics 8. sequential connectors; to introduce a topic 9. there + be; to introduce a topic 10. summary connector; to introduce a summary of what will be discussed

FOCUS 1 [15 minutes/homework]

This focus box gives an overview of the forms and uses of the various discourse organizers that are covered in this unit.

1. **Lead-in:** Read the introductory paragraph and the first three examples (a), (b), and (c) in the chart. Point out another sequential organizer—*next*—in example (f). Ask a volunteer to read the explanation. Elicit other sequential organizers students may know, such as *then*.

2. Write *rhetorical question* on the board and elicit what it means (*a question that is not meant to be answered, but rather is posed to introduce a topic*).

3. Ask a volunteer to read examples (d) and (e), and ask another student to read the explanations.

4. Ask students to identify the rhetorical question. Is the speaker expecting the listener to respond to this question? (*no, it introduces the topic*)

5. Read the fourth explanation, and have volunteers read the two examples (f) and (g). Ask students to identify the two topics mentioned in each example.

6. Read the remaining examples (h), (i), and (j), as well as the explanations with the class.

7. Answer any questions students may have.

Suggestion: Have students read through the examples and explanations for homework. Then assign Exercise 1 as a review and have students name the kinds of organizers that are explained in Focus 1.

METHODOLOGY NOTE

This focus chart introduces all of the many organizers covered in this unit. The chart is organized according to how each organizer is used to organize discourse. Most of the forms will be familiar to advanced learners; however, they will probably need practice using all of them in communicative contexts. For example, they may be familiar with all of the sequential connectors, but may not know which ones are appropriate for chronological connections and which are appropriate for logical connections. This distinction will be made in Focus 2.

EXERCISE 1 [20 minutes/homework]

In this exercise students match sentences with topics, and then identify the form and use of the discourse organizer used in each. This exercise could be done in class, or assigned as homework.

1. Read the directions, first sentence, and the answer (given in the example). Where in the sentence does *there + be* occur? (*the beginning*) Ask students to look at Focus 1 and find the explanation for its use (in the second section).

2. Have students work in pairs to match the sentences containing discourse organizers with the topics in the second column. Tell students to use Focus 1 as a reference to identify the types of discourse organizers.

3. Ask pairs to compare answers with another pair.

4. Review answers as a class. See answers on LP page 262.

 For more practice, use *Grammar Dimensions 4* Workbook page 122, Exercise 1.

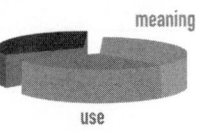

FOCUS 2 Sequential Connectors:
Chronological and Logical

EXAMPLES	EXPLANATIONS
	Sequential connectors may be chronological, logical, or both.
(a) **At first,** the lake seemed very cold. **Later,** after we had been swimming for a while, it seemed warmer.	Chronological connectors signal the sequence of events in time, such as the events of a story or the steps of a procedure.
(b) I have several items of business to share with you at this meeting. **First,** I will report on our latest expenditures. **Then,** I will present a proposal for our next ad campaign. **Lastly,** I will tell you about holiday party plans.	Logical connectors organize the sequence of events in a text, such as the parts of a speech or an essay. They are especially common in formal spoken English contexts, such as presentations and academic lectures.

Chronological

EXAMPLES		CONNECTORS	USES
(c) **At first,** Frederick didn't like his new neighbor.		*at first*	beginning continuation
(d) Eva was running slowly in the race at first. **Eventually** she pulled ahead, though.		*eventually*	
(e) Our first destination was Seoul, Korea. **Subsequently** we went to Bangkok, Thailand.		*subsequently*	
(f) **At last** they reached Vancouver, where they planned to spend the night.		*at last*	conclusion
(g) **In the end,** both our hero and his adversary die.		*in the end*	

Chronological or Logical

CHRONOLOGICAL	LOGICAL	CONNECTORS	USES
(h) **First,** turn on the ignition.	(i) **First,** let's consider the main issues.	*first*	beginning
(j) **First of all,** check the gas level.	(k) **First of all,** I will discuss the arguments against building the new subdivision.	*first of all*	
(l) **To start with,** open a new file and save it.	(m) **To start with,** the developers have not done an environmental impact study.	*to start with*	beginning
(n) **To begin with,** Matt went to Costa Rica.	(o) **To begin with,** let's look at the effects of air pollution in the valley.	*to begin with*	
(p) **Next,** he flew to Venezuela.	(q) **Next,** I will explain my opponent's stand on this issue.	*next*	continuation
(r) **Then,** he traveled to Brazil.	(s) **Then,** I will summarize the main points of the debate.	*then*	
(t) **After that,** he visited a friend in Argentina.	(u) **After that,** I will evaluate the various arguments.	*after that*	
(v) **Finally,** he spent a few weeks in Chile.	(w) **Finally,** I will present the implications of my position.	*finally*	conclusion
(x) **Lastly,** check the oil level.	(y) **Lastly,** new jobs are needed.	*lastly*	

FOCUS 2 [15 minutes/homework]

Focus 2 offers an extensive explanation of the meanings and uses of chronological and logical sequential connectors. Since it is so detailed, you may want to assign it as homework and quickly review it during the next class. Tell students that they can use this chart as a reference tool. The Focus 2 charts begin on SB page 264 and conclude on page 266.

1. **Lead-in:** Explain the distinction between chronological and logical connectors by pointing out a few examples in the focus chart or providing a few of your own. Note that *chronological* can include narratives and procedures.

2. Give students an overview of how the chart is organized: chronological connectors are listed in the second chart, followed by connectors that could be used for both types of sequence, and concluding in the third chart on page 266 with examples of specifically logical connectors.

3. Ask students to skim the chart and check any boldfaced connectors that are unfamiliar to them.

4. Use the chart to explain those connectors which are new to students.

5. Tell students to use the chart for reference and review as they work through the practices in Exercises 2, 3, and 4.

LANGUAGE NOTE

As mentioned earlier, students sometimes confuse logical and chronological sequence connectors. For example, they may use *at first*, a chronological connectors, to introduce the first point of an argument in an essay.

EXAMPLES		CONNECTORS	USES
(z)	**The first type of pollution** I'd like to discuss is that caused by automobiles.	*the first* + noun	beginning
(aa)	**One cause of prejudice** is ignorance.	*one* + noun	
(bb)	**In the first place,** we need to get more legislation to help the disabled.	*in the first place*	
(cc)	**Secondly,** we also have a problem with noise pollution.	*secondly*	continuation
(dd)	**The second point** concerns the issue of whether . . .	*the/a second*	
(ee)	**A second question we might ask** is who should take responsibility for the homeless?	*(third, fourth, etc.)* + noun	
(ff)	**In the second place,** we need to change our attitudes.	*in the second place*	
(gg)	**The last reason** is one I am sure everyone is aware of.	*the last* + noun	conclusion
(hh)	**A final question** might be how we will fund our project.	*a final* + noun	
(ii)	**To conclude,** pollution is obviously getting worse in our city.	*to conclude*	
(jj)	**In conclusion,** parents must take a more active role in schools.	*in conclusion*	

Make up a sentence with a beginning sequential connector that could follow each of the sentences below. Try to use a variety of connectors.

Example: *My family is very special.* **In the first place,** *my father and mother have worked very hard to provide all of us an education.*

1. My family is very special.

2. Making a plane reservation on the World Wide Web is easy.

3. I appreciate many of the things my friends do for me.

4. Smoking can cause a lot of health problems.

5. We need to start taking major steps to save our planet.

6. When I started learning English, I encountered many difficulties.

7. A person who has really had an influence on my life is (*put person's name here*).

For five of the sentences below, list ideas that could follow, using beginning, continuation, and concluding sequential connectors in your list. Try to use a variety of connectors.

Example: I can think of several things I don't have that I'd like to have. *To start with, I'd like to have a really good camera. Next, I wouldn't mind having a new car. Lastly, I'd love to have my own house.*

1. There are several things I'd like to do on my next vacation.

2. Our school could use a few improvements.

3. I have a few gripes about _____. (*You pick the topic.*)

4. I think I have made progress in several respects during the past few years.

5. My home (apartment/room) is a comfortable place for several reasons.

6. Several world problems seem especially critical to me right now.

7. I have several goals for my future.

Exchange the paragraph you wrote for the Opening Task with either your partner for that task or another classmate. Did your classmate use any sequential connectors in the paragraph? If so, which ones? If not, would any of the connectors in the Focus 2 charts on pages 264–266 be appropriate to organize ideas in the paragraph? Discuss your analysis with your classmate.

Exercise 2 Answers will vary. Possible answers are: 1. In the first place, my father and mother have worked very hard to provide all of us an education. 2. The first thing you need to do is decide whether to book with an airline company or an online travel agent. 3. One thing I appreciate is their helping me out with transportation. 4. One problem is that it can lead to heart disease. 5. One thing we need to do is stop the destruction of the ozone layer. 6. To begin with, the word order of sentences in English is different from that of my native language. 7. . . . my aunt. First of all, she was the one who encouraged me to go to college.

Exercise 3 Answers will vary.

Exercise 4 Answers will vary.

Focus 2 is continued from LP page 264.

EXERCISE 2 [10 minutes]

In Exercise 2 students use the sequential connectors they just studied in Focus 2 to create sentences.

1. Read the directions and example as a class. What other sequential connectors might students use to begin the second sentence? Have them look back at Focus 2 for ideas. (*first of all, to start with*)
2. Have students work independently to complete the exercise. Encourage them to refer to Focus 2 and try to use a variety of connectors.
3. Have students share and discuss their sentences with a partner.
4. Ask volunteers to read their partners' sentences to the class, and discuss these as a class. See possible answers on LP page 266.

 For more practice, use *Grammar Dimensions 4* Workbook page 123, Exercise 2.

EXPANSION [25 minutes/homework]

As a homework assignment following Exercise 2, have students choose one of the statements in Exercise 2 and write a paragraph on that topic. Encourage them to refer to Focus 2 and try to use a variety of connectors.

EXERCISE 3 (OPTIONAL) [25 minutes]

Students create lists of ideas, using sequential connectors.

1. Read the directions and example as a class. Are the connectors chronological or logical, or both?
2. Have students work independently to list ideas that could follow five of the sentences. Tell them

to use a variety of beginning, continuation, and concluding sequential connectors in their lists. Encourage them to refer to Focus 2 for ideas.

3. Have students share and discuss their sentences with a partner.
4. Ask volunteers to read their sentences to the class, and discuss these as a class.

 For more practice, use *Grammar Dimensions 4* Workbook page 123, Exercise 3 and page 124, Exercise 4.

EXPANSION [20 minutes/homework]

As a homework assignment following Exercise 3, have students use one of the sentences and list of ideas they created in Exercise 3 and write a paragraph on that topic. Encourage them to elaborate on each of the sentences in their list with an additional sentence that describes, gives reasons, or in some other way explains each sentence. Tell them to refer to Focus 2 and try to use a variety of connectors.

EXERCISE 4 (OPTIONAL) [20 minutes]

In this exercise students analyze the paragraphs they wrote for the Opening Task in terms of the use of sequential connectors.

1. Have students work in pairs and exchange the paragraphs they wrote for the Opening Task.
2. Ask them to analyze each other's papers, identifying which sequential connectors were used. Ask them to make notes on which connectors might be added to the papers to improve their organization.
3. Ask students to discuss their analyses with each other.
4. Ask volunteers to share their analyses with the class.

EXPANSION 1 [20 minutes]

Activity 2 (reading/writing) on SB page 278 is an enjoyable follow-up to Exercise 4. Students rewrite a recipe for apple pie in the proper sequence using sequential connectors.

EXPANSION 2 [25 minutes/homework]

1. For homework, ask students to take a recipe and scramble the steps, as they were scrambled in the apple pie recipe in Activity 2.
2. During the next class, have them exchange recipes with a partner and rewrite the recipe in order, using sequential connectors.
3. Have pairs read their scrambled and rewritten recipes to the class.

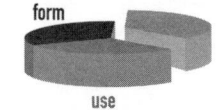
form

use

FOCUS 3	*There + Be* as a Topic Introducer

There + be often introduces a topic that the speaker or writer has classified into different parts.

EXAMPLES	EXPLANATIONS
(a) **There are** three ways to get to the freeway from campus. (b) **There were** four principal causes for the recession. (c) **There could be** several explanations for this child's behavior.	The *be* verb can be any tense and can follow a modal verb such as *can, could,* or *may.*
(d) There are { three, a few, several, many, a number of } { aspects, causes, effects, factors, methods, principles, reasons, rules, stages, steps, strengths, theories, ways } to consider.	Noun phrases that come after the *be* verb often include a number or a quantifier (for example, *four, several*) and an abstract general noun (for example, *aspects, reasons*).
(e) There are **three kinds of** rhetorical questions. (f) There are **several types of** students.	Classifying phrases such as *kinds of* or *types of* often follow *there + be.*
(g) There are many driving rules to keep in mind when you get behind the wheel. **The first** rule of the road is to be courteous to other drivers. (h) There are five stages in this process. **In the first stage,** water is drawn through a tube.	You may use sequential connectors, as shown in Focus 2, to organize topics that follow an introduction with *there + be.*

Beginning	Continuing	Ending
first	*second, third, etc.*	*last*
first of all	*secondly*	*finally*
to start with	*next*	*lastly*
the first + noun	*the second, the third, etc.* + noun	*the last* + noun
one	*a second, a third, etc.*	*the last*
one + noun	*a second* + noun, etc.	*a final* + noun
in the first place	*in the second place*	*finally*

The sequential connectors in this chart are most often used for subtopics after *there + be* introducers.

Guides to writing often caution writers against overusing *there + be.* This is good advice to avoid wordiness; keep in mind that this is not the only way to introduce a topic.

Fill in the blanks with appropriate words or phrases from the chart on page 268. Use different forms of connectors for each passage. Add commas where needed.

Example: ___There are___ two ___kinds___ of twins. ___The first___ is called identical. ___The second___ is called fraternal.

1. (a) ___There are___ three (b) ___types/kinds___ of extrasensory perception, or ESP, that I will be discussing in today's lecture. (c) ___To begin,___ I will talk about telepathy, perhaps the best known and most researched area. (d) ___Then,___ I will explain telekinesis, which concerns the ability to move a distant object through will power alone. (e) ___Last,___ I will describe the phenomenon of precognition, which involves knowing ahead of time about an event.

2. If you have pollen allergies, (a) ___there are___ a number of (b) ___things___ that you might try to avoid pollen. (c) ___First of all,___ stay in an air-conditioned room. (d) ___Secondly,___ when you drive, keep your windows up and your air-conditioning on. (e) ___Next,___ shower as soon as you go inside after being exposed to a lot of pollen. (f) ___Finally,___ get an air-filter system in your home. (g) ___Then,___ if you live in the United States, move to Europe! That continent does not have the ragweed pollen that plagues people in the United States.

3. (a) ___There are___ three main (b) ___steps___ in the process of making rayon, a fabric produced from soft woods and other vegetable materials. (c) ___To start with,___ the material is pulped. (d) ___Next,___ it is treated with caustic soda, nitric acid, and other substances until it turns into a liquid. (e) ___Last,___ it is forced through tiny holes in metal, forming liquid filaments which solidify into threads.

4. (a) ___There are many types___ of pasta, with a great variety of shapes. (b) ___One___ is macaroni, which is a curved tube. (c) ___A second___ is fettuccine, which looks like a thin ribbon. Capelletti is (d) ___another___; it is shaped like a hat. (e) ___A fourth type___ is ravioli; it is square-shaped or round-shaped and stuffed with cheese or meat. (f) ___A fifth type___ is rotelle, which has a corkscrew shape. And these are only a few of them!

ANSWER KEY

Exercise 5   Answers will vary. Possible answers are listed above.

FOCUS 3 [25 minutes]

Focus 3 explores how *there + be* is used to introduce topics. It includes information about how sequential connectors follow introductions with *there + be*, as well.

1. **Lead-in:** Read the explanation and examples in the first section. What modal verb is used in example (c)? (*could*)

2. Remind students that subject-verb agreement is needed between *be* and the noun phrase that follows the verb. Note that all the examples here requiring subject-verb agreement have plural forms of *be,* except for the example where *be* is used with the modal *could.*

3. For the next two examples, (e) and (f), ask volunteers to read the sentences. Elicit a definition of *rhetorical question*, which students first encountered in Focus 1 and review the explanation.

4. Read the last section, with examples (g) and (h). Call attention to the sequential connectors in the box. Note that the inset box offers parallel forms of sequential connectors as illustrated in columns. Although some are interchangeable (e.g., *first, secondly*), others are not, so students need to be careful with their choices. Remind them that *firstly* is not used as a sequential connector when citing multiple steps or ideas.

5. Ask students to think of step-by-step processes, such as how to cook or make something. Ask a volunteer to describe the process, using *there + be + sequential connectors.*

LANGUAGE NOTE

This chart includes a list of quantifiers and abstract nouns following *there are* in (d), which should provide useful vocabulary to students in formal writing and speech contexts.

EXERCISE 5 [20 minutes]

Students use *there + be* to introduce topics and different connectors to complete sentences. It applies what they just learned in Focus 3.

1. Ask a volunteer to read the directions and example. What kind of sequential connectors are used? (*beginning* and *continuing*)

2. Have students work independently to complete the sentences. Encourage them to use a variety of connectors, referring to Focus 3.

3. Have students exchange papers with a partner and review each other's work.

4. Ask volunteers to share their answers. Encourage others with different answers to share their choices, as well. See possible answers on LP page 268.

For more practice, use *Grammar Dimensions 4* Workbook page 125, Exercise 5.

Write a sentence with *there* + *be* to introduce a classification for each topic below. Then write at least two or three sentences that could develop the topic.

Example: Topic: Three grammar points

There are three grammar points to study this week. One is relative clauses. A second is correlative conjunctions. The last is generic articles.

1. Types of books you like the best
2. Things that you think make a good movie or TV program
3. Topics that you are covering in a particular class for a specific amount of time (a week, a quarter, a semester)
4. Steps for performing a procedure that you know how to do (replacing a printer cartridge, solving a math problem, studying for an exam, parallel parking)
5. Professions or careers that would be good for someone who likes people
6. A topic of your choice

EXERCISE 7

The paragraph below has too many uses of *there* + *be* verb. Rewrite the paragraph, eliminating some of these forms to improve the information flow of the paragraph.

There is increasing evidence that our oceans have been warming up because of human activity. There are a number of serious ecological problems that have already resulted from an increase in ocean temperatures. For example, in Alaska's Bering Sea, there is a decrease in the population of some coldwater fish. In addition, the sea ice that polar bears live on near Hudson's Bay has been melting earlier, which has decreased their hunting season on the ice. There have also been negative effects on the ecology of the tropics. For instance, there were many coral reefs severely damaged by El Niño conditions in the late 1990s. Scientists believe that the upper regions of oceans are becoming more acidic from all of the CO_2 humans have put into the atmosphere, much of which ends up in the oceans. There are many organisms, including corals, that have difficulty growing shells with this increased acidity. Scientists worry that there will only be an increase in these disruptive effects of global warming on our planet's ecology.

EXERCISE 8

Look again at the paragraph you wrote for the Opening Task on page 261. Did you use a *there* + *be* introductory phrase? If so, read your sentence to the class. If not, make up a sentence that might be used to develop one of your questions, using *there* + *be* as an introducer.

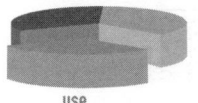

FOCUS 4 Summary Connectors

use

Summary connectors also help to organize discourse. Some of these connectors signal that the ideas expressed summarize what has been said before.

EXAMPLES	CONNECTORS	USE
(a) **In summary,** drug abuse is a major problem today.	*in summary*	general summary
(b) **To summarize,** we should all exercise our right to vote.	*to summarize*	
(c) **As has been previously stated,** many people did not consider AIDS a serious problem at first.	*as (has been) previously stated/ mentioned*	review of main idea

Some summary connectors can be used either for introductions—summarizing what is to be presented—or for conclusions, summarizing what has already been stated.

LINK TO FOLLOWING DISCOURSE (INTRODUCTION)	LINK TO PRECEDING DISCOURSE (CONCLUSION)	CONNECTORS	USE
(d) I have been asked to report on our recent experiments. **All in all,** they have been very successful.	(e) From the presentation I have just given, I hope you will agree that, **all in all,** our experiments have been successful.	*all in all*	summary of points
(f) **Overall,** the quality of television appears to be declining. For example, the news is becoming more and more like entertainment.	(g) From the evidence I have presented in this essay, it appears, **overall,** the quality of television is declining.	*overall*	
(h) **Briefly,** the arguments for gun control can be summed up so far in the following way.	(i) **Briefly,** so far I have discussed three of the arguments for gun control.	*briefly*	condensation of points
(j) **In short,** the arguments against euthanasia, which I will discuss next, are mostly religious ones.	(k) **In short,** as I have shown, the arguments against euthanasia are mostly religious ones.	*in short*	

Exercise 6 Answers will vary.

Exercise 7 Answers will vary. Students should revise at least two or three sentences with *there are*. A sample revised paragraph shows revisions in the underlined sentences: There is increasing evidence that our oceans have been warming up because of human activity. <u>A number of serious ecological problems have already resulted from an increase in ocean temperatures.</u> For example, in Alaska's Bering Sea, <u>the population of some coldwater fish has decreased.</u> In addition, the sea ice that polar bears live on near Hudson's Bay has been melting earlier, which has decreased their hunting season on the ice. There have also been negative effects on the ecology of the tropics. For instance, there were many coral reefs severely damaged by El Niño conditions in the late 1990s. Scientists believe that the upper regions of oceans are becoming more acidic from all of the CO_2 humans have put into the atmosphere, much of which ends up in the oceans. <u>Many organisms, including corals, have difficulty growing shells with this increased acidity. Scientists worry that the disruptive effects of global warming on our planet's ecology will only increase.</u>

Exercise 8 Answers will vary.

EXERCISE 6 [25 minutes]

Students write sentences that introduce a given topic and that could develop it, using *there + be* and sequential connectors.

1. Read the directions and example as a class. Ask students what kinds of sequential connectors are used in the example. (*beginning, continuing, ending*).
2. Have students work in pairs to introduce each topic with a *there + be* sentence and to write two or three sentences that could develop each topic.
3. Have each pair get together with another pair and take turns reading their sentences.
4. Ask representatives of pairs to share their sentences with the class.

EXPANSION [20 minutes/homework]

For homework, ask students to choose one of the topics listed in Exercise 6 and write a paragraph about it, using *there + be* to introduce the topic, and developing the topic with sentences in which they use sequential connectors.

EXERCISE 7 [20 minutes]

Exercise 7 addresses a common flaw in writing: overuse of *there + be*. Students rewrite a paragraph, eliminating unnecessary uses of these forms.

1. Read the directions as a class.
2. Ask students to underline all instances of *there + be* in the paragraph. How many do they find?
3. Have them work independently to rewrite the paragraph, eliminating some of these forms to improve the information flow of the paragraph.

4. Before reviewing answers, ask students to count and report how many instances of *there + be* they eliminated, and write the number of eliminations (e.g., 1–7) on the board.
5. Review answers as a class. Encourage discussion of why some students chose to eliminate instances of *there + be,* and others did not. See a sample revised paragraph on LP page 270.

EXERCISE 8 (OPTIONAL) [20 minutes]

Exercise 8 has students return, once again, to the paragraph they wrote for the Opening Task. This time, they analyze it in terms of whether or not they used *there + be* as an introductory phrase, applying the principles they learned in Focus 3.

1. Ask students to look back on the paragraph they wrote for the Opening Task. Did they use a *there + be* introductory phrase?
2. Ask those students who did to read their sentence to the class.
3. Ask others to write a sentence with *there + be* to introduce an idea.
4. Ask various volunteers to share their sentences with the class.

EXPANSION [20 minutes/homework]

Activity 3 (writing) on SB page 279 can be coordinated with the work students do in Exercise 8 or Exercise 9. The essay can be assigned as homework although it's important that students are instructed how to organize and outline a persuasive essay. Students write an essay based on an opinion on one of the issues mentioned in the Opening Task (or on another issue). Students should be encouraged to use discourse organizers effectively, but not with a heavy hand.

LESSON PLAN 3

FOCUS 4 [20 minutes]

Focus 4 divides the various summary connectors by use: as a general summary, to review a main idea, to summarize all points, and to give a synopsis of all points.

1. **Lead-in:** Read the introductory text for the two sections of the chart. Then, ask students to look at the boldfaced terms and state whether connectors are (1) unfamiliar, (2) part of passive vocabulary (discourse connectors) they have encountered but haven't used, or (3) part of their active vocabulary (connectors they use in their own writing or speech). *All in all* and *In short* are expressions that students may have heard but may not have ever used.
2. Read the first section of the chart. Tell students that these summary connectors alert the listener or reader to the fact that a summary is coming.
3. Ask two volunteers to read the second section. You may want to tell students that another phrase people use in speech for *in short* is *to make a long story short*.
4. Answer any questions students may have.

METHODOLOGY NOTE

Most of your students will probably be familiar with the most common summary connectors (*in summary, to summarize*). However, the second part of this chart, which shows connectors that link to both following and preceding discourse, may be new information to many.

Choose three of the sentences or brief passages below. Write a summary statement for each. Use the summary connector indicated in parentheses. In small groups, compare the summary statements you wrote with those of your classmates.

Example: My paper will discuss the problem of overpopulation. (briefly)
Summary statement: *Briefly, overpopulation is a serious threat to the survival of all life on earth.*

1. Today, I'd like to talk about something I know every one of you is concerned about. (briefly)

2. By hooking a computer into a national electronic system, you can communicate and get information in a number of ways. For example, you can send and receive messages from others who have subscribed to the system or get the weather report for the day. You can take courses or play computer games. You can make travel reservations or look up information in an encyclopedia. (all in all)

3. Without iron, the body wouldn't have hemoglobin, which is an essential protein. Hemoglobin, found in red blood cells, carries oxygen to the rest of the body. A deficiency of iron can cause headaches and fatigue. (in short)

4. Good friendships do not develop easily; they require effort. You need to make time for your friends. You should be prepared to work out problems as they arise, since things will not always go smoothly. You shouldn't expect perfection from your friends. (in summary)

5. So far I have discussed several of the causes and effects of divorce. (as has been previously mentioned)

6. There are several things to keep in mind if you want to train a dog to obey you. First, you need a lot of patience. Secondly, you should not punish your dog for misbehaving but rather correct the inappropriate behavior. You should never hit a dog unless it is threatening to bite someone. Finally, remember to praise your dog for behaving properly. (all in all)

7. Fellow classmates: We have finally reached this proud moment, when we will receive our diplomas as testimony of our many achievements. In my speech to you this afternoon, I would like to stress what I believe is one of the most important purposes of education. (briefly)

8. In many American cities, it's difficult to get much real news from the local television news programs. For example, the local news on a typical hot summer day might feature interviews with people who are complaining about the weather and perhaps take a look at this season's swimwear fashions. You may find out how much money a blockbuster movie made at the box office over the weekend. Another "news" segment might tell you about some new product that you can buy. (overall)

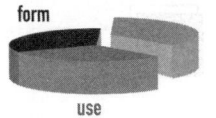

form

use

| **FOCUS 5** | Rhetorical Questions to Introduce and Shift Topics |

Rhetorical questions, unlike other questions, are not used to ask for information. In discourse, rhetorical questions are used to introduce topics and to shift from one topic to a new one.

EXAMPLES	EXPLANATIONS
(a) How does nitrogen circulate? (b) What are the most common causes of fatigue? (c) Is aggression a part of human nature? (d) Can Congress save the budget?	The form of a rhetorical question may be either a *Wh*-question (*who, what, when, where, why*) or a *yes/no* question.
(e) "What Is a University?" by John Henry Newman (f) "Are Women Human?" by Dorothy Sayers (g) "Were Dinosaurs Dumb?" by Stephen Jay Gould	Titles of books, articles, and speeches also use rhetorical questions to introduce topics.
(h) Remember the great health care debate?*	Rhetorical questions may introduce background information about a topic.
(i) So far, we have looked at some of the causes of teenage gangs. But what are the effects on the communities in which they live?	We also use rhetorical questions to signal a shift from one subtopic to another.

* Note that this question leaves off the first two words, "*Do you,*" of the full question form for an informal, conversational tone.

■ **EXERCISE 10**

The excerpts below use rhetorical questions to introduce topics. For each, predict what the topic is about.

1. What do we know about the universe, and how do we know it? Where did the universe come from, and where is it going? Did the universe have a beginning, and if so, what happened before then? What is the nature of time? Will it ever come to an end?

2. Have you ever heard the sound a duck makes as it dies a slow and painful death? In other words, have you ever heard a sixth grader with no musical experience try to play the oboe?

3. Do you believe that the more you diet, the harder it is to lose weight because your body adapts and turns down your rate of burning calories—your metabolism?

Exercise 9 Answers will vary. Possible answers are: 1. Briefly, the following is an issue every one of you is concerned about. 2. All in all, there are numerous benefits in connecting to one of these systems. 3. In short, we can't do without iron. 4. In summary, the result of patience and hard work is a good and lasting friendship. 5. As has been previously mentioned, there are several key causes and significant effects of divorce. 6. All in all, positive reinforcement and patience are the best ways to get your dog to behave properly. 7. Briefly, these diplomas reflect our educational achievements and our readiness to achieve further in the future. 8. Overall, local news shows seem more about vacation planning than about the serious issues and stories that affect us all.

Exercise 10 Answers may vary. Sources and actual topics are below. 1. A book explaining what we know to date about the universe and how this knowledge has developed. (Source: *A Brief History of Time: From the Big Bang to Black Holes*, by Stephen Hawking, Bantam Books, 1988, p. 1) 2. An essay describing the writer's experiences learning a new musical instrument. (Source: "Quacking UP: My Trials and Tribulations with the Oboes," Halyey Whilte, Kaplan/*Newsweek* "My Turn" Competition, 2004) 3. A nutrition article presenting research evidence that this popular belief about dieting is not true. (Source: "A False Belief in a Diet Slowdown," by Jean Carper, *Los Angeles Times*, March 29, 1990, p. 34)

EXERCISE 9 [20 minutes]

In Exercise 9 students use the summary connectors they just studied in Focus 4 to summarize brief passages.

1. Read the directions and example as a class. Ask volunteers to suggest two other summary statements beginning with *briefly*.
2. Have students work independently to choose three passages and write summary statements for each, using the summary connectors in parentheses.
3. Have students work in small groups and take turns reading and comparing their summaries. What kind of summary connectors did they use?
4. Ask representatives of groups to share their sentences with the class. See possible answers on LP page 272.

 For more practice, use *Grammar Dimensions 4* Workbook page 126, Exercise 6.

EXPANSION [45 minutes/homework]

Activity 4 (research on the web) on SB page 279 is a good follow-up to the work students do in Exercise 9. It can be done in class if students have Internet access in class, or assigned as homework. Students research ecotourism articles on the Internet and write a summary of one, using a variety of discourse organizers.

FOCUS 5 [15 minutes]

Focus 5 is the first of two charts (Focus 6 is the second) that explain the forms and uses of rhetorical questions in organizing texts. This one explores how rhetorical questions are used to introduce topics and to shift between topics.

1. **Lead-in:** Elicit the meaning of *rhetorical question*, which students defined in Focus 1.
2. Discuss the reasons why writers and speakers might use rhetorical questions to introduce or to shift topics. Write two titles on the board: *The Most Common Cause of Fatigue is a Lack of Oxygen* and *Does a Lack of Oxygen Cause Fatigue?*
3. Ask students which title captures their interest the most.
4. With a volunteer, read the explanation and examples in each section of the chart. Where have students heard or read similar rhetorical questions? Ask volunteers to suggest similar examples after each section, and write these on the board.

LANGUAGE NOTE

Writers and speakers use rhetorical questions to engage their readers and listeners—i.e., to make them active participants in the reading or listening activity. They also show the writer's/speaker's awareness of an audience since the rhetorical questions suggest a dialogue between writer/reader or speaker/listener.

EXERCISE 10 [10 minutes]

In this exercise, students read excerpts that begin with rhetorical questions and predict what content each might be introducing.

1. Read the directions as a class.
2. Have students work independently to write a prediction of what the rest of each passage might be about.
3. Have students share their predictions with a partner. Did they come to similar or different conclusions?
4. Ask volunteers to share their predictions with the class. See possible answers on LP page 272.

 For more practice, use *Grammar Dimensions 4* Workbook page 127, Exercise 7.

FOCUS 6 Rhetorical Questions to Focus on Main Points

use

Another kind of rhetorical question focuses the listener/reader on the main points of a topic and emphasizes the speaker/writer's viewpoint. It is sometimes called a "leading question."

EXAMPLES	SPEAKER/WRITER VIEWPOINT	EXPLANATIONS
(a) Haven't we had enough wars?	We have.	Leading rhetorical questions seek agreement from the listener or reader. They imply a *yes* answer. In other words, from the writer's or speaker's viewpoint, a negative answer is not possible.
(b) Don't divorced fathers as well as mothers have rights?	They do.	
(c) Isn't English hard enough to learn without all those different article usage rules?	It is.	
(d) We've had enough wars, haven't we?	We have.	Leading questions have the same meaning as negative tag* questions that seek agreement (falling tone in spoken English).
(e) What kind of solution is that to the rising cost of medical care?	It is a bad solution.	Another type of rhetorical question that focuses on main points implies a response in the negative. In other words, the speaker/writer will not take *yes* for an answer. Note that examples (e), (f), and (g) are all *wh*-questions.
(f) How much longer can we ignore the signs of global warming?	We can't ignore them any longer.	
(g) Who was more committed to nonviolence than Gandhi?	No one was more committed.	

*Note: A **tag question** is a short question that is added at the end of a statement seeking either agreement or confirmation. (e.g., *That's not right, is it? That's right, isn't it?*) When the speaker seeks agreement, he or she ends the sentence with falling intonation.

EXERCISE 11

Write a leading rhetorical question to express each of the following opinions. More than one form is possible, and some ideas need to be rephrased, not just transformed into a question. State the positive implication of each in parentheses.

Example: We've gone far enough in the space race.
Possible questions and implications:

Isn't it time to stop the space race? (It is.)
Haven't we gone far enough in the space race? (We have.)
Shouldn't we consider stopping the space race? (We should.)

1. Our senior citizens deserve more respect.

_____

2. We need to start thinking more globally.

_____

3. Our school already has too many required courses.

_____

4. Women deserve the same job opportunities as men.

_____

5. All people should have a place to live.

_____

6. (Your choice: Write your own rhetorical question about a topic.)

_____

ANSWER KEY

Exercise 11   Answers will vary. Possible questions and responses are: 1. Do our senior citizens deserve more respect? (They do.)   2. Is it time for Americans to think more globally? (It is.)   3. Does our school already have too many required courses? (It does.)   4. Don't women deserve the same job opportunities as men? (They do.)   5. Shouldn't everyone have a place to live? (They {Everyone} should.)   6. Answers will vary.

FOCUS 6 [25 minutes]

Focus 6 looks at another type of rhetorical question, the "leading question." These questions urge listeners or readers to agree with the speaker or writer about a topic.

1. **Lead-in:** Read the two explanations in the first section, and then the first example. Ask students what response the speaker is expecting: That we *have* had enough of wars, or *have not*. Then read the second column.

2. Ask volunteers to read the other three examples in the first section. Encourage them to be expressive.

3. Repeat this process with the second section. What kinds of tones of voice would a speaker use for examples (e–g)? (*an angry or insistent tone of voice*)

4. Discuss how students react to these types of questions. Do they find them engaging, persuasive, or intrusive?

5. Ask volunteers to create other examples.

Suggestion: Bring in some editorials or opinion essays that use a number of rhetorical questions so that students can see the questions in context. Ask them to identify the questions and what response the writer expects the reader to give to each.

CULTURE NOTE

The rhetorical questions explained here are those used to emphasize rather than introduce points. Students from some cultures may find these types of questions a bit offensive, since they assume or demand a certain response. In turn, native speakers may be surprised when students do not respond to leading questions as they anticipate. Emphasize how finding cultural "middle-ground" or point of agreement is often an important part of American conversational style.

EXERCISE 11 (OPTIONAL) [15 minutes]

Students focus on writing leading rhetorical questions that invite a positive response, using the skills outlined in Focus 6.

1. Read the directions and examples as a class.

2. Have students work in pairs to write at least two leading rhetorical questions for each opinion. (At least one question per student in each pair.) Remind them to ask questions that invite a positive response.

3. Ask volunteers to share their questions with the class. Encourage them to be expressive as they read the questions.

4. Encourage others who came up with different questions to share those, as well.

 For more practice, use *Grammar Dimensions 4* Workbook page 128, Exercise 8.

EXPANSION [60 minutes/homework]

In Activity 5 (reflection) on SB page 279 students listen to a lecture—either from one of their classes, or online—and note the discourse organizers used. This activity is a good homework assignment after Exercise 11.

EXERCISE 12

State the writer's viewpoint for the rhetorical questions in each of the following excerpts. Then state what you think is the thesis (the main point) of each text. Discuss which of the questions you find most effective in making their points.

Example: How many Americans can afford an $80,000 Mercedes-Benz?
Should auto safety be reserved only for the wealthy?

Writer's viewpoint: Not many Americans can afford a Mercedes and auto safety should not be reserved for only the wealthy. Thesis: Auto safety devices should be put on all cars, not just expensive cars.

1. Fair-minded people have to be against bigotry. How, then, can fair-minded people ignore, condone, or promote discrimination against divorced fathers—100 percent of whom are men—and make believe it isn't discrimination?

2. I am, I hope, a reasonably intelligent and sensitive man who tries to think clearly about what he does. And what I do is hunt, and sometimes kill. . . . Does the power that orchestrates the universe give a deer more importance than a fly quivering in a strip of sticky tape?

3. One of the more popular comic book characters is Wolverine, a psychopath with retractable metal claws embedded in his hands and a set of killer instincts that makes him a threat to friend and foe alike. This is a proper role model for children?

4. I will not lie: sometimes I doubt why I stay in orchestra. I question my devotion each time I get politely yelled at by my orchestra teacher. I especially regret my choice on those days when I seem to create my own horrifying pitch. Wouldn't my GPA, the school, and the world be better off without my violin screeching? Wouldn't my parents get a better night's sleep? Wouldn't I?

5. My hands are restless. They drum on the top of the desk. It seems my hands have something to say. If my hands could talk, you'd have trouble getting them to stop. They would apologize to my grandma, because what kind of Chinese hands can't figure out how to use chopsticks?!

EXERCISE 13

The following excerpts from an essay by Isaac Asimov use six rhetorical questions to develop an argument about the need for population control. Identify the rhetorical questions. Then discuss how the author uses them to develop his ideas. What is the overall effect of the questions? Discuss which ones you think are most effective in emphasizing key points and introducing subtopics.

Let's Suppose . . .

1 Suppose the whole world became industrialized
2 and that industry and science worked very
3 carefully and very well. How many people could
4 such a world support? Different limits have been
5 suggested, but the highest figure I have seen is
6 twenty billion. How long will it take before the
7 world contains so many people?
8   For the sake of argument, and to keep things
9 simple, let's suppose the demographic growth rate
10 will stay as it is, at two percent per annum. . . .
11 At the present growth rate our planet will contain
12 all the people that an industrialized world may
13 be able to support by about 2060 A.D. . . .
14   Suppose we decide to hope for the best. Let us suppose that a change *will* take
15 place in the next seventy years and that there will be a new age in which population
16 can continue rising to a far higher level than we think it can now. . . . Let's suppose
17 that this sort of thing can just keep on going forever.
18   Is there any way of setting a limit past which nothing can raise the human
19 population no matter how many changes take place?
20   Suppose we try to invent a real limit; something so huge that no one can imagine
21 a population rising past it. Suppose we imagine that there are so many men and
22 women and children in the world, that altogether they weigh as much as the whole
23 planet does. Surely you can't expect there can be more people than that.
24   Let us suppose that the average human being weighs sixty kilograms. If that's the
25 case then 100,000,000,000,000,000,000 people would weigh as much as the whole
26 Earth does. That number of people is 30,000,000,000,000 times as many people as
27 there are living now.
28   . . . Let us suppose that the population growth-rate stays at 2.0 percent so that the
29 number of people in the world continues to double every thirty-five years. How long,
30 then, will it take for the world's population to weigh as much as the entire planet?
31   The answer is—not quite 1600 years. This means that by 3550 A.D., the human
32 population would weigh as much as the entire Earth. Nor is 1600 years a long time.
33 It is considerably less time than has passed since the days of Julius Caesar.
34   Do you suppose that perhaps in the course of the next 1600 years, it will be
35 possible to colonize the moon and Mars, and the other planets of the solar system?
36 Do you think that we might get many millions of people into the other world in the
37 next 1600 years and thus lower the population of the Earth itself?
38   Even if that were possible, it wouldn't give us much time. If the growth-rate
39 stays at 2.0 percent, then in a little over 2200 years—say by 4220 A.D.—the human
40 population would weigh as much as the entire Solar system, including the Sun.

ANSWER KEY

Exercise 12   1. Fair-minded people cannot ignore, condone, or promote discrimination against divorced fathers. Nor can they make believe it isn't discrimination.   2. The power that orchestrates the universe does not accord a deer more importance than a fly quivering in a strip of sticky tape. 3. The comic book character Wolverine is not a proper role model for children.   4. My GPA, the school, and the world would be better off without my violin screeching.   5. No kind of Chinese hands would be ignorant of how to use chopsticks.

Exercise 13   The rhetorical questions are underlined in the passage above.
Discussion: In this excerpt, Asimov uses all of these questions to introduce the topics that follow by providing answers to the questions. These questions help to organize Asimov's hypothetical situation and to involve the reader in wondering about the answers to the questions. (If X happened, what would Y be like? What could we do about X?) They also anticipate possible reader responses as in the last paragraph.

EXERCISE 12 (OPTIONAL) [20 minutes]

In Exercise 12 students read a variety of passages and analyze the use and effectiveness of the rhetorical questions used in each.

1. Read the directions and example as a class. Do students agree with the conclusions about the writer's viewpoint and thesis? Ask a volunteer to state these two points differently.

2. Explain a few words students may not know, such as *bigotry* (prejudice) and *condone* (approve of).

3. Have students work in pairs to state the writer's viewpoint and thesis for each passage.

4. Have each pair get together with another pair and compare answers. Then, ask them to discuss which rhetorical questions they found most effective.

5. Ask a representative of each group to report which questions the group thought were most effective, and discuss these as a class. See answers on LP page 276.

For more practice, use *Grammar Dimensions 4* Workbook page 129, Exercise 9.

EXERCISE 13 (OPTIONAL) [25 minutes]

Students read part of an essay by Isaac Asimov on population control and analyze his use of rhetorical questions.

1. Find out if any of your students are familiar with the work of Isaac Asimov. What have they read by him? How would they describe his work?

2. Read the directions as a class.

3. If time permits, call on students to read paragraphs aloud. After each paragraph, ask other students to identify the rhetorical questions and analyze what functions they serve to develop the essay.

4. Poll the class: Which rhetorical questions are most effective in this essay? Why?

Note: Some students may challenge the logic of Asimov's argument.

EXPANSION [30 minutes]

In Activity 1 (listening/writing/speaking) on page 278 students listen to a psychology lecture and note the variety of discourse organizers used and the ideas they introduce. Since the organizers include many of the types studied in this unit, this activity is a good follow-up to Exercise 13.

UNIT GOAL REVIEW [10 minutes]

Ask students to look at the goals on the opening page of the unit again. Refer to the pages of the unit where information on each goal can be found.

 For assessment of Unit 14, use *Grammar Dimensions ExamView®*.

Use Your English

 **ACTIVITY 1** listening/writing/speaking

CD2 Track 3

You may at times have wished you had a photographic memory—that is, one that remembers everything it receives as input—especially when you need to study for an exam. However, not being able to forget anything can be detrimental, as case histories in abnormal psychology have shown. Listen to the audio. You will hear a brief psychology lecture on the benefits of forgetting. Listen for the discourse organizers (sequential connectors, *there + be*, summary connectors, rhetorical questions) that the speaker uses as cues to introduce topics and focus on the main points. Take notes on the main ideas of the lecture on a separate sheet of paper. Then, listen to the audio one more time and write down the discourse organizers the speaker used to organize the lecture. Compare your notes and the list of discourse organizers with several classmates.

ACTIVITY 2 reading/writing

Are you familiar with the saying "It's as American as baseball, motherhood, and apple pie"? The apple pie reference probably means eating it rather than making it, but here's a chance to test your knowledge of American cooking. The recipe below explains how to make an apple pie. The directions, however, are not in the proper sequence. In small groups or with a partner, rewrite the steps of the recipe. Add sequential connectors to some of the sentences to help organize the text.

APPLE PIE
- Stir the mixed ingredients with the apples until the apples are well coated.
- Dot the top of the pie with 1/2 tablespoon of butter before putting on the top crust.
- Line a 9-inch pie pan with a pie crust; put aside while you prepare the apple filling.
- Cover the pie with a top crust and bake it in a 450-degree oven for 30 minutes.
- Peel, core, and cut 5 to 6 cups of apples into very thin pieces.
- Place the coated apples in layers in the pie shell.
- When the pie comes out of the oven, sprinkle 1 cup of grated cheese on top and put it under a broiler to melt the cheese.
- Combine and sift over the apple slices 1/2 cup of brown sugar, 1/8 teaspoon of salt, 1 tablespoon of cornstarch, and 1/4 teaspoon of cinnamon.

 **ACTIVITY 3** writing

Choose one of the topics from the Opening Task on page 261 or another issue that interests you. Write a persuasive essay in which you express an opinion on the topic. Try to convince your readers of the validity of your viewpoint. Use appropriate discourse organizers in developing your essay.

 **ACTIVITY 4** research on the web

A recent trend in international travel has been greater attention on the part of tourists to ethical issues such as respecting and enhancing the environment and promoting the welfare of the people who live in the places visited. These trends are known by such names as ecotourism and geotourism.

Find an article about the topic of ecotourism or geotourism on *InfoTrac® College Edition*. Write a summary of the article, using a variety of discourse organizers.

Example: *To start with, the author describes different kinds of "ethical tourism" and gives examples of questions tourists may ask about places they plan to visit.*

 **ACTIVITY 5** reflection

One of the ways to improve your comprehension of academic lectures is to pay attention to the kinds of discourse organizers that speakers use to introduce topics and to change topics. Speakers use these organizers to signal or "signpost" the structure of a lecture. Often professors will also give a preview of the lecture to students beforehand, such as handing out an outline of topics to be covered in the next lecture. Listen carefully to a lecture for one of your classes or download one of the many lectures available from Web sites, and note the kinds of discourse organizers that are used. Write them down and report on your findings to your class.

ANSWER KEY

Activity 1 Results of notetaking will vary.   Discourse organizers used: Who has not wished for a photographic memory? All in all; at first; later; finally; first of all; secondly; a third problem; in short

Activity 2 Order of directions: 1. Line 9-inch pan . . . ;   2. Peel, core, and cut . . . ;   3. Combine and sift . . . ;   4. Stir mixed ingredients . . . ;   5. Place coated apples . . . ;   6. Dot top of the pie . . . ; 7. Cover the pie . . . ;   8. When the pie comes out of the oven . . .

Possible sequential connectors: (1) To start with, (2) Second, (3) Third, (4) Then, (5) Next, (6) After that, (7) (Ø) Not all sentences require a sequential connector), (8) Finally

The Use Your English activities at the end of the unit contain situations that should naturally elicit the structures covered in the unit. For a more complete discussion of how to use the Use Your English activities, see To the Teacher, LP page xxvi.

ACTIVITY 1 listening/writing/speaking
[30 minutes]

CD2
Track 3

This activity is a good follow-up to Exercise 13 on SB pages 276–277. Please disregard the former CD track number (20) listed in the student book.

1. Ask students if any of them have problems remembering things. Then, ask them to imagine what it would be like if they always remembered everything, including very painful experiences.

2. Tell students that they are going to listen to a short psychology lecture on the benefits of forgetting. They will listen for the discourse organizers used and the ideas they introduce. They may hear any of the discourse organizers they have studied in this unit, including sequential connectors, *there + be*, summary connectors, and rhetorical questions.

3. Have students listen to the audio once without taking notes. Then have them listen again and write each discourse organizer they hear.

4. Ask them to listen a third time and write down what topics and main points each discourse organizer introduces or summarizes. Tell them to replay the audio as needed.

5. Have students work in small groups and compare their lists.

6. Ask volunteers to share their lists with the class, and discuss. See answers on LP page 278.

ACTIVITY 2 reading/writing
[20 minutes]

This activity is a good follow-up to Exercise 4 on SB page 267.

1. Discuss recipes with students: Who uses them? What kinds of recipes do they like best—simple ones, ones with pictures, ones that number every step? Ask if anyone has made an apple pie from a recipe.

2. Have students work in pairs or small groups to rewrite the steps of the apple pie recipe in order. Tell them to use sequential connectors as needed to organize the material.

3. Ask volunteers to read their recipes. What sequential connectors did they use? Did anyone come up with a different order? See answers on LP page 278.

ACTIVITY 3 writing
[20 minutes/homework]

Activity 3 can be assigned after Exercise 8 on SB page 270 or after Exercise 9 on SB page 272.

1. Have students chose a topic of interest to them—one from the Opening Task, or another—and write an essay in which they persuade the reader to agree with their viewpoint. Emphasize the importance of organizing their arguments.

2. Remind students to use the various discourse organizers they have learned in this unit to introduce and sequence topics.

3. Have students exchange papers and discuss them, suggesting places where discourse organizers could be used or removed to improve the flow of the text.

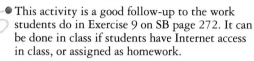

ACTIVITY 4 research on the web
[45 minutes/homework]

This activity is a good follow-up to the work students do in Exercise 9 on SB page 272. It can be done in class if students have Internet access in class, or assigned as homework.

1. Write *ecotourism* and *geotourism* on the board and ask students to define the terms. Discuss what they know about these forms of tourism. Has anyone ever been on an ecotour? Which countries offer a lot of ecotours?

2. Read the directions and example as a class. What organizer is used? (*to start with*)

3. Have students search *InfoTrac*® for articles on ecotourism/geotourism. Ask them to write a summary of one of the articles, using a variety of discourse organizers. Encourage them to refer back to the focus charts in this unit for ideas on organizers they might use.

4. Have volunteers read their summaries to the class, and discuss.

ACTIVITY 5 reflection
[60 minutes/homework]

This activity is a good homework assignment after Exercise 11 on SB page 275.

1. Ask student to think of lectures they have heard in their classes. What discourse organizers have speakers used to introduce topics? To sequence points? To summarize? Write responses on the board.

2. Ask students to listen to a lecture—either from one of their classes, or online—and note the discourse organizers used. Ask them to list all the organizers they hear and, as they are able, to note the purpose of each.

3. During the next class, have students describe the lectures to a partner and share the organizers they recorded, and their purposes. Were certain organizers used in both lectures?

CONDITIONALS
If, Only If, Unless, Even Though, Even If

- Know the different kinds of conditional sentences in English

- Use *if, only if, unless, not unless,* and *if not* correctly to express conditions

- Know the difference between *even though* and *even if* and use them correctly

- Use conditional forms to give advice

OPENING TASK

When They Were Young

"When I was growing up, we went out to eat only if it was a special occasion."

"When I was a child, our parents wouldn't let us stay up late even if we begged them!"

"When I was your age, we couldn't leave the dinner table unless we asked permission."

Do these comments sound familiar? Part of the process of growing up is listening to your parents, grandparents, or other older relatives or adults tell you how things were different "back then" or "when we were your age."

■ STEP 1

In many societies, life in the past was more difficult than it is now, and children had less freedom than they do today. Consider what your older relatives (parents, aunts and uncles, grandparents, etc.) have told you about the way life was for them when they were younger. List some of the rules, restrictions, and hardships they have described.

■ STEP 2

In small groups, discuss and write down some of the things your older relatives *could not do* or *had to do* as a result of family customs, cultural rules, or simply the lifestyle of past generations.

Examples: *Lucy's mother couldn't drive a car even after she got her license unless one of her parents went with her.*

Antonio's great-aunt could go out on dates only if one of her older brothers went along.

To help out his family, Hyung's grandfather started working full-time when he was 16 even though he had wanted to finish high school.

■ STEP 3

Report some of your group's most interesting descriptions to the rest of the class.

UNIT OVERVIEW

This unit covers conditional sentences with a variety of structures. It examines the uses of *only if, unless, even though,* and *even if* clauses in factual, future (predictive), and subjunctive sentences.

Please note that due to its length, this unit has been divided into four lesson plans. To review this unit more quickly, review focus charts and have students complete the first exercise after each chart to observe students' grasp of the grammar topics.

GRAMMAR NOTE

Conditional sentences are one of the most difficult aspects of English grammar for many students. The semantics of the wide variety of conditional clauses can be very hard to grasp. Students will need a good command of the English tense system, of modals, and of negation in order to master conditional sentences in English. These have been covered in previous units, so your students should now be well prepared to take on the material in this unit.

UNIT GOALS

Some instructors may want to review the goals listed on Student Book (SB) page 280 after completing the Opening Task so that students understand what they should know by the end of the unit. These goals can also be reviewed at the end of the unit when students are more familiar with the grammar terminology.

OPENING TASK [20 minutes]

The purpose of the Opening Task is to create a context in which students will need to use conditionals as they discuss the rules, regulations, and hardships experienced by older family members when those members were young. The problem-solving format is designed to show the teacher how well the students can produce the target structures

implicitly and spontaneously when they are engaged in a communicative task. For a more complete discussion of the purpose of the Opening Task, see To the Teacher, Lesson Planner (LP) page xxii.

Setting Up the Task

To engage students in the topic, tell them a story you heard growing up about the restrictions or hardships of your own older relatives. Use some examples of this unit's conditional structures in your story.

Conducting the Task

■ STEP 1

Read the directions as a class. Brainstorm a list of rules, regulations, and hardships that students have heard their older relatives talk about, and write these on the board.

■ STEP 2

1. Read the directions for Step 2 as a class. Ask three volunteers to read the three examples.
2. Have students work in small groups and write a list of things that rules, restrictions, and hardships prevented their older relatives from doing.

Closing the Task

■ STEP 3

1. Ask representatives from several groups to share their lists with the class, and discuss.
2. Ask some questions about the groups' lists using conditional forms: *So, Pietro, you say that your grandfather had to work seven days a week. Did he have to work even if there was a special holiday?*
3. Don't worry about accuracy at this point, though you may want to take notes of errors in meaning, form, or use in order to focus on those problems later.

GRAMMAR NOTE

Typical student errors (form)

- Mixing tenses in conditional sentences: —e.g., *If I were an American, I were speaking better English. If she had bought the paper, she read the story.* (See Focus 1.)
- Using *only if* when the main clause is negative: —e.g., *Only if you lend me the book, I won't buy it.* (See Focus 2.)
- Not inverting the subject and verb in the main clause when using *only if* or *not unless* at the beginning of a sentence: —e.g., *Only if you visit Costa Rica in December, you could see the turtles on the beach.* (See Focus 3.)

Typical student errors (use)

- Using *unless* rather than *if . . . not* to express a statement that is contrary to fact: —e.g., *The boys would not feel so tired unless they had slept better last night.* (See Focus 4.)
- Using *only if* rather than *if* in sentences giving advice: —e.g., *Be sure to eat three meals a day only if you want to be healthy.* (See Focus 6.)

FOCUS 1 — Review of Conditional Sentences with *If*

form   meaning

EXAMPLES	EXPLANATIONS
General Truth (a) If you **are** 65 or older, you **qualify** for senior citizen discounts.	**Factual Conditionals** One common type of factual conditional describes general truths. This type of conditional is often used in the sciences to describe physical laws.
Habitual Present (b) If my great-grandmother **comes** over, we usually **go** to the park. **Habitual Past** (c) When my mother was young, if relatives **visited** on Sunday, they **stayed** all day. **Inference: Explicit** (d) If that **was** grandmother on the phone, she **must have missed** the train. **Inference: Implicit** (e) If that **is** grandmother on the phone, she **is** still in Connecticut.	Another common type of factual conditional refers to habitual events. The event may be present or past. A third type of factual conditional infers something. The inference may be explicit or implicit. In explicit inference, the main-clause verb includes the modal *must* or *should*.
(f) If my great-grandmother **comes** tomorrow, we **may go** to a restaurant.	**Future Conditionals** These conditionals describe future events.
Present Hypothetical (g) If we **lived** closer to our grandparents, we **would see** them more often. (We don't live close to our grandparents; we don't see them as often as we would like to.) (h) If my great-grandmother **were** alive today, she **might** not **approve** of the tattoos that many young people have. **Past Hypothetical** (i) If my great-aunt **had been born** about 50 years later, she **might have been** a doctor instead of a nurse.	**Hypothetical Conditionals** The present hypothetical conditional describes conditions that are untrue or hypothetical. Past hypothetical conditionals describe conditions and results that were unreal or untrue in the past.

Summary of Verb Tenses Used with Conditional Sentences

TYPE OF CONDITIONAL	IF-CLAUSE	MAIN CLAUSE
Factual: general truth Factual: habitual	simple present simple present simple past	simple present simple present simple past
Factual: inferential	simple present simple past *will* / *be going to* } + base verb	various tenses
Future	simple present	*will* *could* *may* *might* *be going to* } + base verb
Hypothetical: Present	simple past or subjunctive *were*	*would* *could* *might* } + base verb
Hypothetical: Past	past perfect (*had* + past participle)	*would have* *could have* *might have* } + past participle

EXERCISE 1

To review verb tenses for conditional tenses, complete each of the blanks by writing the appropriate form of the verb in parentheses. The first has been done as an example.

1. If my aunts and uncles (go) _____*go*_____ out for dinner, they always (eat) _____*eat*_____ at the same Italian restaurant.

2. My mother has two older sisters. She told me that she was glad that she was the youngest child because if she (be) _____*had been*_____ the oldest, her parents (expect) *would have expected* her to do much of the housework.

3. If my brother (come) _____*comes*_____ for a visit from Ecuador next summer, he (bring) _____*will bring*_____ his entire family, including two dogs and a parrot.

4. I (telephone) _____*might telephone*_____ my family this weekend if I (stay) _____*stay*_____ on campus.

(Continued on next page)

FOCUS 1 [20 minutes/homework]

This focus gives an overview of the forms and uses of the various discourse organizers that are covered in this unit.

1. **Lead-in:** To review the various conditional tenses, ask students questions that elicit the various forms: If you miss the registration deadline for classes, what happens? Midori, if you have free time on the weekends, what do you usually do? When you were younger, how did your parents usually act if they didn't want you to do something or go somewhere with your friends? Write responses on the board, label the types (e.g., general truth, etc.) and note the corresponding examples in the focus chart.

2. Ask a series of volunteers to read the examples and explanations.

3. The second part of the chart is a good reference tool for students to use as they continue through the course.

4. Answer any questions students may have.

Suggestion: As homework, have students review the three types of conditionals (and their subclassifications) listed on the first page of this chart. When reviewing the assignment in the next class, focus on examples (a–i).

METHODOLOGY NOTE

The focus chart provides an overview of conditional forms. The four exercises that follow help students review their previous study of conditional tenses before focusing on the special forms in this unit.

EXERCISE 1 [20 minutes/homework]

Exercise 1 asks students to complete sentences using conditional tenses, practicing the material reviewed in Focus 1. It is continued on SB page 284. This exercise could be done in class, or assigned as homework.

1. Read the directions and example (the first sentence) as a class. What kinds of factual conditionals are these? (*habitual events*)

2. Have students work independently to complete the sentences by writing the correct form of the verbs in parentheses in the blanks.

3. Review answers as a class. See answers on LP pages 282 and 284.

 For more practice, use *Grammar Dimensions 4* Workbook page 130, Exercise 1.

5. My parents said that if they (have) _____had_____ the time, they (like) _____would like_____ to organize a big family reunion, but for the time being they are just too busy with their jobs.

6. If the man in this photo (be) _____is_____ my great-grandfather, that (must, be) _____must be_____ my great-aunt next to him.

7. If family members (disagree) _____disagree_____ about values, they (should, remember) _____should remember_____ that it is natural for different generations to think differently.

8. Gretchen (spend) _____will spend_____ the whole year with her grandfather in Berlin if she (finish) _____can finish_____ her senior project before June.

9. Could you see who's at the door? If that (be) _____is_____ my sister, she (have) _____will have_____ the charcoal for the barbecue.

10. We're not going on vacation until next month. If we (go) _____went_____ now, we (miss) _____would miss_____ seeing my cousins, who are touring the east coast this summer.

EXERCISE 2

With a partner, take turns asking and answering the following questions about the school or schools you have attended. Answer each question with a complete conditional statement. If necessary, think of a particular class in a school you attended.

Examples: What happened if a student got into a fight at your school?

Possible answers:
In my elementary school, if a student got into a fight, the principal called up the parents.
If a student got into a fight in my high school, he or she was suspended for a few days.

What happened in one of your classes in elementary, middle, or high school if:

1. a student walked in 20 minutes late to class?
2. a student didn't turn in the homework assignment?
3. a student cheated on an exam?
4. a student constantly interrupted the teacher?
5. a student broke a classroom rule such as not to chew gum, not to forget textbooks, etc.?

EXERCISE 3

Complete each of the following past conditional statements. First complete the conditional statement with any other information you want to add; then express a hypothetical past result.

Examples: If my elementary school had . . .

If my elementary school had offered English classes, I would have learned English more easily.

If my elementary school had been less strict, I would have enjoyed it more.

1. If I had had a chance to . . .
2. If my parents (or mother or father) had lived . . .
3. If my grandparents had been able . . .
4. If my family had been . . .
5. If my English teacher had given . . .

EXERCISE 4

Add a condition to each of these past hypothetical statements.

Example: I would have studied more

If I had known I was going to get a C in my biology course last quarter, I would have studied more.

1. I would have worked harder
2. I would have been happier
3. the last year in school would have been easier for me
4. my parents would have been upset with me
5. my life would have been less complicated

Exercise 2   Answers may vary. Sample answers are: 1. In my high school, if . . ., the student would have been marked absent for the whole period.   2. In my English class, if . . ., the student would have received a zero.   3. If . . ., the student would have been sent to the principal's office.   4. If . . ., the student might be suspended from class.   5. If . . ., the student might be asked to stay after school.
Exercise 3   Answers will vary. Possible answers are: 1. . . . take guitar lessons, I could have been in a band.   2. . . . during 1800s they might not have come to the United States.   3. . . . to move here, they would probably have done so.   4. . . . less adventurous, we might not have moved so much. 5. . . . us less homework, I would have been able to go dancing last night.
Exercise 4   Answers may vary. Possible answers are: 1. . . . on my essay if I had known some of my classmates would be reading it.   2. . . . if I could have gone back to Athens for the summer. 3. . . . if I hadn't had to take so many courses each quarter.   4. . . . if I had dropped out of school. 5. . . . if my parents hadn't gotten sick last fall.

EXERCISE 2 [10 minutes]

In Exercise 2 students ask and answer questions using a complete conditional statement in their answers. Have students think of specific schools they attended as children.

1. Read the directions, example questions, and sample answers as a class. Have students look back at Focus 1 about the habitual past for another example.
2. Have students work independently to complete the exercise. Encourage them to refer to the Focus 1 Summary of Verb Tenses to recall which verb tenses to use.
3. Have students share and discuss their sentences with a partner.
4. Ask volunteers to read their partners' sentences to the class, and discuss these as a class. See possible answers on LP page 284.
5. Make a chart comparing responses to the five questions. Have students comment on whether schools are similar or very different? Which schools are better? Which schools are more formal and which are informal? Encourage discussion.

EXPANSION [15 minutes]

Choose one or two of the topics from the list and conduct a brief class discussion in which you encourage students to use conditional forms. Ask questions related to the topic, such as: *If a student in high school was caught smoking, what happened?*

EXERCISE 3 [15 minutes]

In Exercise 3 students complete past conditional statements with information they add, and then they express a hypothetical past result.

1. Read the directions and examples as a class. Ask students to suggest other alternatives. Then,

ask them to find the explanation for this form and meaning in Focus 1; see example (i).
2. Have students work independently to complete the exercise.
3. Have students share and discuss their sentences with a partner.
4. Ask volunteers to read their partners' sentences to the class, and discuss these as a class. See possible answers on LP page 284.

EXPANSION [15 minutes]

1. Have each student write down the beginning of a sentence using a conditional *if* phrase and pass it to the person to his or her right.
2. Have students complete the sentences. Remind them not to write anything that might embarrass another student.
3. Ask volunteers to share their sentences with the class.

EXERCISE 4 [15 minutes]

Students use past hypothetical statements to construct new sentences using conditionals.

1. Read the directions. Ask a volunteer to read the example. Ask students to suggest other alternatives using conditionals.
2. Have students work in pairs to create new sentences.
3. Have pairs share their sentences with another pair.
4. Ask volunteers to share their sentences with the class, and discuss these as a class. See possible answers on LP page 284.

EXPANSION [60 minutes/homework]

In Activity 6 (research on the web) on SB page 299 students use the Internet to research the lives and hardships of people in the United States or Canada during a period in the past. Then they write a report using conditional sentences. This activity is a good homework assignment after Exercise 4.

FOCUS 2 — Exclusive Conditions: *Only If* and *Unless*

We use both *only if* and *unless* to express the only condition under which an event will or should take place.

EXAMPLES	EXPLANATIONS
Main Clause: Affirmative (a) As a girl, my grandmother went shopping **Condition** **only if** she had finished her assigned chores.*	Use *only if* when the main clause is affirmative. It means "only on the condition that."
Main Clause: Negative (b) As a girl, my grandmother didn't go **Condition** shopping **unless** she had finished her assigned chores.	Use *unless* when the main clause is negative. It means "except on the condition that."
Main Clause: Affirmative (c) As a girl, my grandmother visited cousins **Condition** on Saturday **unless** her mother needed her to help at home.	You can also use *unless* when the main clause is affirmative. The implication, however, is negative. In (c), the implication is that Grandmother didn't visit cousins on Saturday if her mother needed her.
(d) Nowadays, my grandmother would spend the day shopping **only if** she **were** bored.	For hypothetical present, use the subjunctive form *were* in formal written English, just as with other hypothetical conditionals.

*In spoken English, native speakers often separate *only if,* placing *only* before the main verb and *if* after it: As a girl, my grandmother *only* went shopping *if* she had finished her chores; she would *only* spend the day shopping now *if* she were bored.

Decide whether *if, only if,* or *unless* should be used in each blank. The first one has been done for you.

In the Old Days . . .

As each generation matures, it tends to judge the younger generations as somehow not quite measuring up to those of the past: the new generation may be regarded as a bit lazier, less disciplined, or less imaginative. My family was no exception.

"Drive to school!" my father would exclaim to my siblings and me. "Why, when we were your age, we walked everywhere (1) _____unless_____ there was a severe snowstorm. And if we couldn't walk, we went by car (2) _____only if_____ the buses weren't running." The meal options were generally fewer for my parents' generation also: (3) "_____if_____ we didn't like what was served for dinner," my mother would remind us, "we had to eat it anyway." According to my parents, entertainment was more active before television watching became the main leisure activity, and obligations were more strictly enforced. As children, they usually played games outside (4) _____unless_____ the weather was terrible. And outdoor play was allowed (5) _____only if_____ all homework had been completed. When my mother was in high school, her parents wouldn't let her go out on dates (6) _____unless_____ her school grades were acceptable, and then (7) _____only if_____ her mother and father had a chance to meet the potential date.

Perhaps people shouldn't talk about the past (8) _____unless_____ they promise not to gripe about how easy the younger generation has it today!

FOCUS 2 [20 minutes]

Focus 2 takes a look at the use of *only if* and *unless* to express an exclusive condition governing an event.

1. **Lead-in:** Write *only if* and *unless* on the board. Read the first explanation, and then the first example. Is the main clause affirmative or negative? *(affirmative)*

2. Read the footnote in the chart about spoken English.

3. Read the second explanation, and then the second example. Is the main clause affirmative or negative? *(negative)* What makes it negative? *(the words didn't go)*.

4. Ask students to imagine that they are the parents of a teenaged boy who wants to go out with his friends on Saturday. They, as the parents, want him to get some chores done first. Model two examples of what they might say, one with *only if* and another with *unless*: *You can go out with your friends only if you clean your room first. You can't go out unless you've cleaned your room.* Ask a volunteer to write students' sentences on the board.

5. The third example, (c), will be difficult for many students to understand. Model rephrasing some of the sentences on the board in the third person, such as: *Our son stayed home on Saturdays unless he had cleaned his room.*

6. Read the fourth explanation and example.

7. Encourage students to ask questions about anything they do not understand.

METHODOLOGY NOTE

Many students find the logical concepts underlying these conditionals confusing. Give them ample practice converting *only if* to *unless* statements and vice versa so that they understand the reverse relationship between these two subordinating conjunctions. (This is the focus of Exercise 6 also.)

EXERCISE 5 [15 minutes]

Students apply what they have just learned in Focus 2, completing sentences with *if, only if,* or *unless.*

1. Ask a volunteer to read the directions and example. Is the main clause in the example affirmative or negative? *(affirmative)* Is the implication affirmative, or negative? *(negative)*. Ask students to locate the explanation for this meaning of *unless* in Focus 2 (example and explanation (c)).

2. Have students work in pairs to complete the sentences.

3. Have pairs get together with other pairs and review their answers.

4. Review answers as a class. See answers on LP page 286.

Suggestion: This exercise provides a good diagnostic of students' understanding of the differences between *if, only if* and *unless.* You may want to ask students to hand in their papers so that you can assess their understanding at this point.

EXPANSION [30 minutes/homework]

Activity 3 (writing/speaking) on SB page 298 can be assigned after Exercise 5 as homework or as an in-class activity. In this activity students consider conditions that they think are very unlikely in their lives.

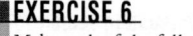

EXERCISE 6

Make each of the following a negative condition by using *unless* instead of *only if* and making other changes as necessary.

Example: When I was your age, we went to the movies only if it was a holiday.
*When I was your age, we **didn't go** to the movies **unless** it was a holiday.*

1. Back in the old days, we only locked our houses if we were going on a vacation.

   Back in the old days, we left our house unlocked unless we were going on a vacation.

2. We could have ice cream for dessert only if it was a special occasion.

   We couldn't have ice cream for dessert unless it was a special occasion.

3. We could only go out after dinner if we had cleaned up the kitchen.

   We couldn't go out after dinner unless we had cleaned up the kitchen.

4. In high school, we were permitted to stay overnight at our friends' houses only if all the parents had met each other.

   In high school we weren't permitted to stay overnight at our friends' houses unless the parents had met each other.

5. We were allowed to go to house parties only if they were chaperoned by adults.

   We weren't allowed to go to house parties unless they were chaperoned by adults.

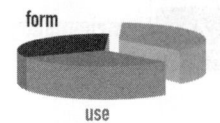

form

use

FOCUS 3 Fronted* *Only If* and *Not Unless* Clauses

EXAMPLES	EXPLANATIONS

(a) **Only if** our parents approved
  Verb Subject Verb
  could   we   go out on a date.
	You can use *only if* or *not unless* at the beginning of a sentence to emphasize a condition. Invert the subject and the first verb in the main clause.

(b) **Not unless** a party was chaperoned
  Verb Subject Verb
  did my parents allow me to attend.
	The first verb may be an auxiliary (*be, have, do*), a modal verb (*will, could, may*, etc.), or main verb *be*.

(c) **Unless** he finishes his chemistry project,
  Subject Verb
  he   is not going on the weekend trip.
	Do not invert the subject and first verb when you begin a sentence with *unless*. Separate the condition from the main clause with a comma.

* *Fronting* refers to putting words or structures that typically occur in other positions in sentences at the beginning of a sentence. Structures are often fronted for emphasis.

EXERCISE 7

Add an *only if* or *not unless* conditional clause to the beginning of each of the following statements to emphasize a condition. Make other changes as needed.

Example: It's fun to do calculus problems.
Only if you love mathematics is it fun to do calculus problems.

1. Learning the conditional forms in English is easy.
2. Going bungee jumping is fun.
3. Spiders make great pets.
4. I'll help you with your English homework.
5. I will get up at 4 A.M. tomorrow.
6. I'll quit (name a "bad habit" you have).

288 | UNIT 15

CONDITIONALS *If, Only If, Unless, Even Though, Even If* | 289

ANSWER KEY

Exercise 7 Answers will vary.

EXERCISE 6 [15 minutes]

In Exercise 6 students work with *unless* and negative main clauses, as explained in Focus 2.

1. Read the directions. Make sure students understand that, in spoken English, speakers often put *only* before the main verb and *if* at the end of the verb phrase, rather than saying the two words (*only if*) together. Refer to the footnote in Focus 2 for examples.

2. Read the first sentence of the example. Ask students to identify the main clause and say whether it is affirmative or negative (*affirmative*).

3. Read the second sentence in the example and ask the same questions. Elicit that the main clause is now negative.

4. Have students work independently to rewrite the sentences, making the main clause negative.

5. Have students exchange papers with a partner and review each other's work.

6. Ask volunteers to share their answers with the class. See answers on LP page 288.

 For more practice, use *Grammar Dimensions 4* Workbook page 131, Exercise 2.

EXPANSION [40 minutes/homework]

Activity 2 (writing/speaking) on SB page 297 is a good follow-up to Exercise 6. The first part could be given as homework, with students discussing their writings in groups during the next class. In this activity students create a list of rules they had to follow when they were younger. Then they compare and contrast these in groups.

FOCUS 3 [10 minutes]

Focus 3 shows the special emphatic forms of fronted *only if* and *not unless* clauses, which require subject-verb inversion.

1. **Lead-in:** Write the noninverted forms of examples (a) and (b) on the board (or elicit forms from the class) so students can see how the parts of the sentence change when we use fronted emphatic forms. These are the noninverted forms: (a) *We could go out on a date only if our parents approved.* (b) *My parents did not allow me to attend a party unless it was chaperoned.* Note how the negative moves to the main clause in (b) in the noninverted form.
   Note: Fronted forms for focus and emphasis are the topic of Unit 24.

2. Remind students that subject-verb agreement is needed between *be* and the noun phrase that follows the verb.

3. Read the explanation and examples as a class. Ask students to identify the inversion of subject and verb in the main clause in the first example.

4. Ask volunteers to give several other examples, and write these on the board.

5. Answer any questions students may have.

EXERCISE 7 [20 minutes]

Exercise 7, in which students add an *only if* or *not unless* clause to the sentences, is a creative task with potential for humor.

1. Read the directions as a class. Ask a volunteer to read the example. Ask students to create another example using *not unless*, and write this on the board.

2. Have students work in small groups to write their new sentences.

3. Ask a representative from various groups to share their best sentences with the class.

 For more practice, use *Grammar Dimensions 4* Workbook page 132, Exercises 3 and 4.

FOCUS 4 | *If . . . Not* versus *Unless*

EXAMPLES	EXPLANATIONS
Future Main Clause (a) Juana will take the computer science course . . . **Future Conditional Clause** . . . if it does not conflict with her work schedule. . . . unless it conflicts with her work schedule. **Future Main Clause** (b) She won't take a writing course . . . **Future Conditional Clause** . . . **if** it does **not** satisfy a requirement. . . . **unless** it satisfies a requirement.	**Future or Hypothetical Conditions** In statements that express future or hypothetical events, subordinators *if . . . not* and *unless* have roughly the same meaning. They describe the negative conditions under which something will or may happen.
Main Clause: Contrary to Fact (c) Violeta couldn't have passed her Latin exam . . . **Condition: Contrary to Fact** . . . if she hadn't had a tutor. **Main Clause** (d) Violeta couldn't have passed her Latin exam . . . **Condition** . . . **unless** she'd had a tutor.	**Past Conditions** In statements that express past conditions, use *if . . . not* to express a condition that is contrary to fact when the main clause is also contrary to fact. The meaning of (c) is that Violeta **did** pass the exam and she **did** have a tutor. Two meanings are possible when we use *unless* to state the condition. In (d) the most probable meaning is the same as example (c): Violeta **did** have a tutor; she **did** pass the exam. However, another possible meaning is that Violeta **did not** pass the exam and that only tutoring might have kept her from failing.
(e) Wen wouldn't have so much homework **if** he were **not** taking calculus. (f) **NOT:** Wen wouldn't have so much homework **unless** he were taking calculus. (g) Thanks for helping me get my new job. **If it weren't for** you, I would still be working at that horrible place. (h) **If it hadn't been for** the encouragement of her English-speaking friends, Pham wouldn't be so fluent in English. (i) **NOT: Unless** it were for you . . . (j) **NOT: Unless** it had been for the encouragement of her English-speaking friends . . .	**Present: Contrary to Fact Main Clause** To express a statement that is contrary to present fact, use *if . . . not* to state the condition. In (e), Wen is taking calculus, so he **does** have a lot of homework. We do not use *unless* for this meaning. We also use the expressions *if it weren't for* + noun and *if it hadn't been for* + noun to express conditions with main clauses that are contrary to present fact. In (g), the speaker is not working at the horrible place; in (h), Pham is fluent in English. The conditions have made these present facts possible. We do not use *unless* as shown in (i) and (j) when the main clause expresses a present result.

EXERCISE 8

For each situation below, choose the best paraphrase among the statements that follow.

1. Esther has made tentative plans to go to Greece for a vacation next summer. The only thing that might prevent her from doing so is if her mother needs to go away on business. In that case Esther would need to stay home to take care of her brother.
   a. Esther will go to Greece next summer if her mother takes a business trip.
   b. Unless her mother stays home, Esther will go to Greece next summer.
   c. Esther will go to Greece next summer unless her mother has to take a business trip.

2. The pioneers who settled the frontiers of North America confronted many dangers traveling to their new homelands, including fierce animals, terrible storms, and rivers they had to cross. Without great courage, they probably would have turned back.
   a. The pioneers would probably have turned back if they had not possessed great courage.
   b. The pioneers could not have reached their new homelands if they had possessed great courage.
   c. The pioneers could not have possessed great courage unless they had reached their new homelands.

3. My family went to my grandmother's house for dinner last night. We all ate so much pasta that no one could eat dessert. The only way we could have had room for dessert would have been to wait for three hours, but since we had tickets for a concert that evening, we had to leave shortly after we finished the main course.
   a. We couldn't have eaten dessert if we had not waited for 3 hours after our meal.
   b. We couldn't have eaten dessert unless we had waited for 3 hours after our meal.
   c. We could have eaten dessert unless we had waited for 3 hours after our meal.

4. David is on the college tennis team and has won all of his matches so far this year. He credits his high school coach for his success and says he wouldn't have even made the team without the excellent training his coach provided.
   a. David says he wouldn't be on the tennis team unless it had been for his coach's training.
   b. David says if it weren't for his coach's training, he wouldn't be on the tennis team.
   c. David says if it had been for his coach's training, he wouldn't be on the tennis team.

EXERCISE 9

Complete the following sentences with statements about yourself.

Example: If it hadn't been for my parents, *I might not have gone to college.*

1. If it hadn't been for my parents,
2. If it weren't for my friends,
3. If it weren't for (name)'s good advice,
4. If it hadn't been for my knowledge of (subject),

ANSWER KEY

Exercise 9 Answers will vary. Possible answers are: 1. . . . I would have considered a different career. 2. . . . I might not have tried out for the soccer team. 3. . . . I might not have decided to further my education. 4. . . . computer programming, I wouldn't have been offered that job I got.

FOCUS 4 [25 minutes]

Focus 4 explores the differences in meaning between various uses of *if . . . not* and *unless.*

1. **Lead-in:** Ask students to read the first section silently.
2. Write a work schedule for Juana (e.g., *Mon.–Thurs., 10–2*) on the board. List a time for the computer science course that doesn't conflict (e.g., *Tues., Thurs., 3–4*). Discuss example (a) with reference to the schedule.
3. Then say that the computer science class time has changed. Write a new time for the class that conflicts with Juana's work schedule. Ask if Juana will take a computer science course, based on this information.
4. Go over (b), which should be easier for students to process after discussing (a).
5. Read the explanations and examples in the second section of the chart. To supplement the examples of past conditions, give (1) an example about yourself that expresses something you wouldn't have been able to do without a lot of help, and (2) an example that involves students' lives (e.g., *The basketball team couldn't have won the game if Natasha hadn't scored so many points*).
6. Remind students that the condition in both examples (c) and (d) is probably contrary to fact. Present the meanings detailed in the third section in two steps: (1) the points represented by (e) and (f); (2) the expressions exemplified in (g) and (h), followed by the note about *unless* as shown in (i) and (j).
7. Answer any questions students might have.

METHODOLOGY NOTE

Since these grammatical concepts can be quite difficult for students—and since there is such an abundance of material in this focus chart—you may want to assign this as homework and then go over the contents during the next class.

EXERCISE 8 [10 minutes]

Exercise 8 has students choose the best paraphrase for sentences, applying the principles they learned in Focus 4.

1. Read the direction as a class.
2. Have students work independently to choose the sentence that best paraphrases the original statement.
3. Have students compare their answers with a partner.
4. Ask various volunteers to share their choices with the class. See answers on LP page 290.

EXPANSION [40 minutes/homework]

In Activity 5 (writing) on SB page 299 students imagine that they can make all the rules for their school or city. This activity is a good homework assignment after Exercise 8.

EXERCISE 9 [15 minutes]

In Exercise 9 students complete *if* sentences with information about themselves, practicing what they learned in Focus 4.

1. Read the directions and example as a class. Ask volunteers to suggest two other statements to complete the example.
2. Have students work independently to complete the statements with information about themselves.
3. Have students work in small groups and take turns reading their statements.
4. Ask representatives of groups to share their sentences with the class, and discuss. See possible answers on LP page 290.

 For more practice, use *Grammar Dimensions 4* Workbook page 133, Exercise 5.

EXPANSION [20 minutes/homework]

For homework, have students make up their own *if* statement to complete and develop the topic in a paragraph.

meaning

FOCUS 5 | *Even Though* and *Even If*

Both *even though* and *even if* emphasize conditions. However, their meanings are different.

EXAMPLES	EXPLANATIONS
(a) My uncle walked to work **even though Actual Condition** his job was five miles away. (His job was five miles away; nevertheless, he walked to work.)	*Even though* is an emphatic form of *although*. It means "despite the fact that." The condition after *even though* expresses a reality.
(b) My uncle will walk to work **even if Real or Not Real Condition** it is raining. (He walks when it rains as well as when it doesn't rain.)	*Even if* is an emphatic form of *if*. It means "whether or not." The condition after *even if* may or may not be a reality.
(c) My uncle {walks / used to walk} to work **even if it** {rains. / was raining.}	*Even if* can mean "even when" with habitual present conditions and past tense conditions. We can paraphrase (c): He walks to work even when it rains; he used to walk to work when it was raining.
(d) **Even if** I have to stay up all night, I will finish this paper. (e) NOT: **Even** I have to stay up all night, I'll finish this paper. (f) **Even though** it was late, we stayed up to find out who had won the election. (g) NOT: **Even** it was late, we stayed up to find out who had won the election.	**Even versus *Even If* and *Even Though*** *Even* cannot be used as a substitute for *even though* or *even if*. *Even* is not a subordinator. In your writing, you should check any uses of *even* to make sure that you don't mean *even if* or *even though*.

EXERCISE 10

Choose the correct form, *even though* or *even if*, for each blank.

Example: The children bought their mother a special gift last Mother's Day ___even though___ they didn't have much money.

1. Fran's mother was never without a car. However, she would often walk three miles to the market ___even though___ she could have driven if she had wanted to.

2. ___Even though___ Duane's grandfather had a daytime job, he also worked every evening for many years.

3. Our family had a rule for dinner: We had to eat at least a few bites of each kind of food. ___Even if___ the food was something we had tried before and didn't like, we still had to eat a mouthful.

4. Last Christmas Eve, ___even though___ the temperature dropped to below zero, my father insisted we take our traditional stroll through the neighborhood singing Christmas carols.

5. We'd love for you to spend the holidays with us. It would be wonderful if you could stay at least a week. But ___even if___ it's only for a day or so, we hope you'll plan to come.

EXERCISE 11

Choose five of the following quotations and write a brief explanation or paraphrase of what you think each means.

Example: Even if you do learn to speak correct English, whom are you going to speak it to? (Clarence Darrow)

Explanation: *Darrow jokingly implies that many people do not speak "correct English," which he seems to equate with formal English. He uses the word whom, which people rarely use in conversational English.*

1. A house is no home unless it contains food and fire for the mind as well as the body. (Margaret Fuller)

2. Make a decision, even if it's wrong. (Jarvis Klem)

3. We rarely think people have good sense unless they agree with us. (François de la Rochefoucald)

4. A loud voice cannot compete with a clear voice, even if it's a whisper. (Barry Neil Kaufman)

5. It is impossible to enjoy idling unless there is plenty of work to do. (Jerome K. Jerome)

6. The trouble with the rat race is that even if you win, you're still a rat. (Lily Tomlin)

7. Don't make use of another's mouth unless it has been lent to you. (Belgian proverb)

8. Even if you're on the right track, you'll get run over if you just sit there. (Will Rogers)

ANSWER KEY

Exercise 11 Answers will vary. Possible answers are: 1. One's home and family should provide intellectual as well as physical nourishment. 2. You need to take a stand sometimes and not worry about always making the right decision. 3. We tend to admire people who think the way we do about things. 4. Clarity is more powerful than volume in expressing ideas. 5. Doing nothing is enjoyable only when we are avoiding work! 6. You may be successful in a competitive society, but the end result may not be what you really enjoy. 7. When you are repeating what others have said, make sure it's okay with them (or give them credit for what they have said). 8. You may be headed in the right direction, but you need to move to get to your destination!

FOCUS 5 [20 minutes]

Focus 5 explores the differences in meaning between *even though* and *even if*. This is a source of a number of common errors.

1. **Lead-in:** To help students understand the meaning of *even though*, write *even though* on the board and, beneath it, one or two of your accomplishments that were difficult for some reason (e.g., *I learned how to ski*). Ask volunteers to state some difficult things they have accomplished, and write their responses on the board.

2. Next to your response, write a condition that made your accomplishment difficult (e.g., *I am not very coordinated*). Model a statement: *I learned how to ski, even though I am not very coordinated.*

3. Then ask the former volunteers to follow this pattern and make a statement about what they accomplished, using an *even though* clause. Write their sentences on the board.

4. To clarify the meaning of *even if*, tell students that you are determined to do something in the future, even if it may be difficult or unpleasant (e.g., *My house is really a mess. I am determined to clean my entire house from top to bottom this weekend*.) Have students suggest conditions that might prevent you from cleaning your house, such as, *Will you clean your house even if friends drop by.* If possible, respond to each question in the affirmative (with tongue in cheek if students try to ask questions that they think will make you lose your determination!): *Yes, I'll clean my house even if my friends drop over; Oh yes, I'll probably stay home and clean my house even if someone offers me free tickets to the Miami Dolphins game on Saturday afternoon.*

5. Ask different volunteers to read the examples and explanations in the chart.

6. Emphasize the very common error in example (g). Ask volunteers to suggest other example sentences using *even though*.

EXERCISE 10 [15 minutes]

Students practice what they have just learned in Focus 5, completing sentences with *even though* or *even if*.

1. Read the directions and example as a class. Why wouldn't *even if* be appropriate here? (because *even though* means *despite the fact that* here)

2. Have students work independently to complete the sentences.

3. Have students review their answers with a partner.

4. Ask volunteers to share their answers with the class. See answers on LP page 292.

For more practice, use *Grammar Dimensions 4* Workbook page 134, Exercise 6.

EXERCISE 11 [15 minutes]

In Exercise 11, students choose five quotations and paraphrase or write an explanation of them.

1. Ask a volunteer to read the directions and example. Ask another volunteer to read the explanation of the example.

2. Ask students to suggest other possible explanations of the example, and discuss these.

3. Have students work in pairs to explain or paraphrase the five quotations.

4. Review explanations as a class. Encourage all those with different explanations to share these with the class, as well. See possible sample answers on LP page 292.

5. Discuss what makes one explanation better than another by writing the various explanations and paraphrases on the board. Work on one sentence at a time.

EXPANSION [30 minutes/homework]

In Activity 7 (reflection) on SB page 299 students reflect on and write about what they have accomplished to date in their learning, and what they will try to accomplish in the future despite obstacles, using *even though* and *even if* clauses. This activity is a good homework assignment after Exercise 11.

use

EXAMPLES	EXPLANATIONS
(a) Don't make reservations at the Four Seasons restaurant **unless** you're prepared to spend a lot of money. (b) Take a foreign language course **only if** you're willing to do homework faithfully every day. (c) You should pay your taxes on time **even if** you have to borrow the money. (d) Be sure to take a trip to the waterfall **even though** it's a long drive on a dirt road. It's well worth the trouble!	We often use connectors such as *unless, only if, even if,* and *even though* in statements that offer advice to specify conditions under which the advice holds.
(e) Don't go to see the movie *Last Alien in Orlando* **unless** you need a nap. (Implication: The movie is really boring!) (f) Take English 4 **only if** you have nothing to do on the weekends. (Implication: The class is difficult; you'll have a lot of homework.)	We sometimes use humorous conditions with advice statements to make a point indirectly. The advice in (e) and (f) has an ironic tone; the conditions are not meant to be taken literally.

EXERCISE 12

Make advice statements by combining information in the Condition and Advice columns on the next page. First match each condition with an appropriate piece of advice. Then make a full statement, using an appropriate conjunction: *if, only if, unless, even if, even though*. Make any changes necessary. The Conditions statements can either begin or end your sentences.

Examples: Condition   Advice

you have plenty of water   take a hike in Death Valley

Unless you have plenty of water, don't take a hike in Death Valley.

Take a hike in Death Valley only if you have plenty of water.

Condition	Advice
1. you don't have a wetsuit to keep you warm	a. order the Jamaican spice chicken
2. you are taking a vacation in South Carolina	b. take a riverboat cruise on the Mississippi River
3. you don't mind huge crowds	c. try walking to the top of the cathedral in Seville, Spain
4. you love spicy food	d. visit the Grand Canyon in July
5. you are flying across time zones	e. treat yourself to a good meal in Paris
6. you like slow-moving leisurely travel	f. don't go swimming off the Oregon coast in winter
7. you don't mind climbing a lot of stairs	g. be sure to visit one of the old southern plantations
8. your budget is limited	h. be sure to set your watch accordingly if you have to change planes during travel

ANSWER KEY

Exercise 12 Advice statements will vary. Possible answers are: 1. f. Unless you have a wetsuit . . . 2. g. If you are taking a vacation . . . 3. d. Visit the Grand Canyon in July only if you . . . OR: Don't visit . . . unless . . . 4. a. If you love . . ., OR: Order the Jamaican jerk chicken only if . . . 5. h. If you are flying across time zones . . . 6. b. If you like . . . OR: Only if you like . . . 7. c. Unless you don't mind climbing . . . don't try walking to the top . . . 8. e. Even if . . . treat yourself . . . OR: Unless your

FOCUS 6 [25 minutes]

Focus 6 offers one common context of usage–advice–for the structures covered in this unit.

1. **Lead-in:** Read the explanation in the first section, and then the first example. Ask students to identify the condition in the sentence (*you must be prepared to spend a lot of money*), and the advice.
2. Repeat this procedure with the next three examples (b–d).
3. Read examples (e) and (f). Ask students to suggest other implications.
4. Read the explanation in the second section.
5. Encourage students to ask questions about anything they might not understand.

METHODOLOGY NOTE

Ask students to what extent ironic language such as that in (e) and (f) exists in their native languages, and whether these examples seem humorous to them. Discuss the importance of understanding humor in different cultures in order to develop communicative competence. (Advanced students often comment that the most difficult part of comprehending classroom discourse is understanding their classmates' and teachers' jokes!)

EXERCISE 12 [20 minutes]

In Exercise 12 put the information in Focus 6 into practice by matching conditions with advice and then crafting statements of advice. The columns and accompanying photos of the Northwest coast of the United States, the Grand Canyon, and a traditional plantation mansion in the South appear on SB page 295.

1. Read the directions and example as a class. Ask students to suggest other statements of advice using this information.
2. Have students work in pairs to match the conditions to the advice and create statements of advice.
3. Have pairs get together with another pair and share their sentences.
4. Ask a representative of each group to share their sentences with the class. See possible answers on LP page 294.

For more practice, use *Grammar Dimensions 4* Workbook page 135, Exercise 7.

EXPANSION [45 minutes/ homework]

Activity 4 (writing) on SB page 298 is a good group activity and homework assignment for students who have completed Focus 6 and Exercise 12. Students are asked to create guides (possibly online) for their peers about issues of concern to all such as safety, fashion, and travel.

EXERCISE 13

Working with a partner, make up sentences that offer advice for at least five of the following situations using an *only if* or a *not unless* clause.

Example: What to do or not to do in the city where you live

Don't plan to go out for dinner at a restaurant in my hometown unless you can get there before 10 P.M.

1. How not to get lost at a particular place (your campus, a shopping mall, a city)
2. What to wear or what not to wear for a night on the town where you live
3. How to be culturally appropriate on a trip to a particular country
4. A place someone shouldn't shop at because of high prices or poor quality
5. A course or subject not to take at your school
6. A movie someone should not waste time to see
7. A book someone should not bother to read

EXERCISE 14

The paragraph below has five errors involving the conditionals focused on in this unit. Identify and correct them.

How to Evaluate Health News

(1) These days we are constantly hearing and reading about biomedical studies concerned with factors that affect our health. (2) Even these studies often present results as general "facts," the conclusions are not always true. (3) Only if multiple studies have been done it is wise to generalize results to a larger population. (4) Furthermore, you shouldn't be too quick to believe a study unless the number of subjects involved isn't large, because generalizations cannot be made from a small sample size. (5) Even the sample size is big enough, the results may not be statistically significant. (6) In other words, a statistical difference between two factors may be important only the difference could not happen by chance.

Use Your English

ACTIVITY 1 listening

CD2
Tracks 4, 5

Listen to the audio. You will hear two brief passages providing advice about health and safety issues. After each one you will hear three statements. Only one is a correct paraphrase of an idea in the passage. Circle the letter of the correct paraphrase below. Compare your answers with those of your classmates.

1. (a) b c   2. a b (c)

ACTIVITY 2 writing/speaking

Consider some of the family or school rules that you, your siblings, and your friends had to follow when you were younger. Create a list of rules that could be expressed with *if, unless,* or *only if* conditions. Use the categories below for ideas. In small groups, compare your lists. If possible, form groups that include different cultural backgrounds and discuss some of the cultural similarities and differences revealed by your lists.

- Mealtime etiquette
- Eating snacks
- Watching television or playing computer games
- Having friends over or staying at friends' houses
- Dating
- Going out with friends at night
- Making long distance phone calls
- Classroom rules
- School cafeteria rules

Examples: *In my elementary school in Taiwan, we were allowed to speak in class only if we raised our hand and the teacher gave us permission.*

When I was in high school, I couldn't have any of my friends over to visit unless one of my parents was home.

ANSWER KEY

Exercise 13   Answers will vary. Possible answers are: 1. Don't attempt to get around the University of Michigan campus unless you have a map.   2. If you are a male, don't go to the Palace Restaurant unless you are wearing a jacket and tie.   3. In country X, tip the waitstaff only if the service has been exceptional.   4. Shop at Mimi's Boutique only if you don't mind spending over $100 for a blouse.   5. You should take Introduction to Computers only if you have had no experience with a computer.   6. Don't bother to see *Dumber Than Ever* unless you like really stupid jokes.   7. Don't read that politician's new autobiography unless you enjoy fiction.

Exercise 14   2. Even though these studies   3. have been done is it wise   4. involved is large   5. Even if   6. important only if

EXERCISE 13 [20 minutes]

Students offer advice for a variety of situations, applying what they have learned from Focus 6.

1. Read the directions and example as a class. Ask students to suggest other advice for the city or town in which they live, and write these on the board.
2. Have students work in small groups and choose at least five of the situations and write advice for each.
3. Ask representatives of groups to share their advice with the class, and discuss. Is this good advice? See possible answers on LP page 296.

 For more practice, use *Grammar Dimensions 4* Workbook page 136, Exercise 8.

EXPANSION [30 minutes]

1. Ask students to chose one of the topics from Exercise 13 and write a short essay about it.
2. Have students work in small groups and take turns reading their essays aloud, and discussing the topics.
3. Have several volunteers read their essays to the class, and discuss.

EXERCISE 14 [15 minutes]

In Exercise 14 students read a paragraph and identify five errors involving conditionals. These are very common errors that many students make.

1. Read the directions as a class.
2. Have students work in pairs to identify and correct the errors in the passage.
3. Review answers as a class, and discuss.

 For a review of Focuses 1–6, use *Grammar Dimensions 4* Workbook page 137, Exercise 9.

EXPANSION [30 minutes/homework]

Activity 1 (listening) on SB page 297 is a good follow-up to Exercise 14, either for in-class work or as homework. Students listen to two passages that give advice about health and safety issues and choose the correct paraphrase of this advice.

UNIT GOAL REVIEW [10 minutes]

Ask students to look at the goals on the opening page of the unit again. Refer to the pages of the unit where information on each goal can be found.

 For a grammar quiz review of Units 13–15, refer students to pages 138–140 in the *Grammar Dimensions 4* Workbook.

 **ExamView** Test Generator   For assessment of Unit 15, use *Grammar Dimensions 4 ExamView®*.

USE YOUR ENGLISH

The Use Your English activities at the end of the unit contain situations that should naturally elicit the structures covered in the unit. For a more complete discussion of how to use the Use Your English activities, see To the Teacher, LP page xxvi. While students are doing these activities in class, you can circulate and listen to see if they are using the structures accurately. Errors can be corrected after the activity has finished.

 ACTIVITY 1 listening [30 minutes]

In Activity 1 students listen to two passages that give advice about health and safety issues. They are asked to choose the correct paraphrase of advice details. This activity is a good follow-up to

CD2 Tracks 4,5

Exercise 12 on SB pages 294–295, as it is related to health. Note that the former CD track numbers (21, 22) are incorrectly listed in the student book.

1. Tell students that they are going to listen to two passages. After each passage, they will hear three statements summarizing each passage. Only one will be correct for each passage.
2. a) Before playing Passage 1, discuss any problems students—or people they know—have had with insomnia, or not being able to go to sleep.

   b) Before playing Passage 2, discuss what students do to prevent sports injuries, such as warming up and stretching.
3. Work on only one passage at a time. Have students listen to the audio once.
4. Ask students to listen again and circle the letter of the correct paraphrase.
5. Ask them to listen a third time and check their answers.
6. Have students work in pairs to compare their answers.
7. Ask volunteers to share their answers with the class, and discuss.

ACTIVITY 2 writing/speaking [40 minutes]

In this activity students create a list of rules they had to follow when they were younger. Then they compare and contrast these in groups. This activity is a good follow-up to Exercise 6 on SB page 288.

1. Discuss what rules student were taught about mealtime etiquette when they were young. Guide them in making statements about these using *if, only if,* and *unless* as they are used in the examples.
2. Have students work in small groups to create lists of rules they (or people they know) had to follow as a child, using *if, unless,* or *only if*.
3. Ask groups to get together with another group and exchange and discuss their lists.
4. Ask representatives from each group to share two of their lists with the class. Encourage others to respond with their lists, and discuss.

 **ACTIVITY 3** writing/speaking

Most of us have some strong opinions or beliefs about things that we would never do or that we would be very unlikely to do. For example, a person might believe that she would never accept a job that she hated or would never live in a very cold climate.

■ **STEP 1** Make a list of five things that you believe you would be very unlikely to do. For each item on your list, imagine a circumstance under which you might change your mind or be forced to behave differently, and write it down as a possible exception. Use either *unless* or *only if*.

Example: *I wouldn't live in a very large city.*

Exception: *I would do it only if I could be chauffeured wherever I wanted to go.*

■ **STEP 2** Compare your responses with those of your classmates.

 **ACTIVITY 4** writing

Here's a chance to share your knowledge. Either individually or as a collaborative project with some of your classmates, create a brief guide for one of the following topics. Your guide could be intended as a Web page for the Internet or a poster.

• A guide that informs students which courses at your school to avoid or which to take only under certain conditions
• Advice about what to do or not to do in your hometown or country
• A travel guide to some place you've been to that you like
• A guide for what to wear and how to behave at a formal occasion such as a wedding
• A guide for women on understanding men
• A guide for men on understanding women
• A guide of your choice

For as many items as possible, use condition statements with *only if, unless, even if,* or *even though.* Your conditions could be humorous or serious.

 **ACTIVITY 5** writing

Imagine that you could be in charge of your school or city for a year. You could make any rules or laws you wish, and everyone would have to obey them. Make a list of the regulations you would enforce, using conditional statements where they might be needed.

 **ACTIVITY 6** research on the web

 Use an Internet search engine such as Google® or Yahoo® or other Web source to learn more about the way people in the United States or Canada lived during some period in the past. Try to find out some of the hardships they endured and the ways in which their lives differed from our lives today. Enter keywords such as a decade (e.g., 1830's), the country's name and your area of interest (e.g., lifestyle). Write a brief report on your findings, using conditional sentences to express some of the information you found.

Example: *Even though the pioneers were afraid of thieves coming into their houses, they had no way to lock their houses when everyone was away. They could only latch the door from within.*

ACTIVITY 7 reflection

Accomplishing the goals we set for ourselves usually involves some sacrifice. No pain, no gain, as the saying goes! Think of three things that you have accomplished in your learning even though these were not easy for you, and another three things that you will try to accomplish even if you need to make sacrifices to do so. Write a sentence for each, using *even though* and *even if* conditions to express what you have done or will do to achieve your goals.

Examples: *Even though I don't like studying grammar, I memorized most of the irregular verb forms in English. I will try to read one book every month even if I have to give up some of my TV watching time.*

ACTIVITY 3 — writing/speaking
[30 minutes/homework]

Activity 3 can be assigned after Exercise 5 on SB page 287 as homework or as an in-class activity.

1. Ask students to describe things that they would never do. Model: *I would never eat insects.*
2. Ask them to think of, and describe, conditions that might make them do these things. Model: *I would never eat insects, unless I had nothing else to eat.*

■ STEP 1

1. Ask a volunteer to read the directions for Step 1.
2. Ask another volunteer to read the example. Ask students to suggest other exceptions.
3. Have students work independently to create lists of five things they would never do. Then, ask them to imagine what circumstances might make them do those things and write these down, using *unless* or *even if*.

■ STEP 2

1. Have pairs get together with other pairs and share their sentences.
2. Ask representatives of several groups to share their best sentences with the class, and discuss.

ACTIVITY 4 — writing
[45 minutes]

This activity a good follow-up to the work students do in Exercise 12 on SB page 294.

1. Write *Our Town (or City)* on the board. Ask students to say what are good activities and activities that are not recommended to do in the town or city where your class is held. Write responses on the board.

2. Ask several students to offer advice about what to do in your town, using conditionals.
3. Read the directions as a class.
4. Have students work in small groups of three or four to create a guide to one or more of the topics listed. Tell students that their recommendations may be placed on the Internet.
5. Ask students to use conditional statements with *only if, unless, even if,* or *even though* in their recommendations.
6. Have groups exchange their recommendations with another group, and discuss.
7. Have volunteers read their summaries to the class, and discuss.

Suggestion: Some students might also want to contribute their own artwork (drawings, cartoons, photographs) for the guides. Emphasize to students that they should not reproduce text or art from the Internet that they don't have written permission for.

ACTIVITY 5 — writing
[40 minutes/homework]

This activity is a good homework assignment after Exercise 8 on SB page 291.

1. Ask students to imagine that, for a year, each of them is the leader of their school. What rules would they make? What rules would they change?
2. Have students work in small groups to create statements about what rules and regulations they would create if they were in charge of their school and of their city.
3. Ask representatives of groups to share their lists with the class. Discuss whether these are good rules, or not.

ACTIVITY 6 — research on the web
[60 minutes/homework]

 This activity is a good homework assignment after Exercise 4 on SB page 285.

1. Discuss what students know about the hardships people faced in previous generations. Ask them to comment about what their parents went through, and their grandparents.
2. Read the directions as a class.
3. Have students use the Internet to research how people lived and the challenges they faced during a specific period in the past. Ask them to compare how their lives differed from the lives we lead today.
4. Ask them to write a brief report on their findings, using conditional sentences to express some of the information they found.
5. Have students share their writings with a partner.

ACTIVITY 7 — reflection
[30 minutes/homework]

This activity is a good homework assignment after Exercise 11 on SB page 293.

1. Discuss what students have accomplished in terms of learning English, even though they have faced certain obstacles.
2. Read the directions, and have volunteers read the examples.
3. Ask students to write about three things that they have accomplished in their learning even though these were difficult, and three things that they will try to accomplish even if they need to make sacrifices to do so.
4. Have students share their sentences with a partner.
5. Ask volunteers to share their sentences with the class, and discuss these.

REDUCING ADVERBIAL CLAUSES

- Know how to reduce adverbial clauses of time and cause

- Position and punctuate reduced adverbial clauses

- Reduce adverbial clauses with emotive verbs

- Avoid dangling participles in writing

OPENING TASK

The Lone Traveler

On one of your hiking trips to Mills Landing, you found an old diary with a few notes scrawled in it. Apparently, a lone traveler had kept a record of his travels about one hundred years ago.

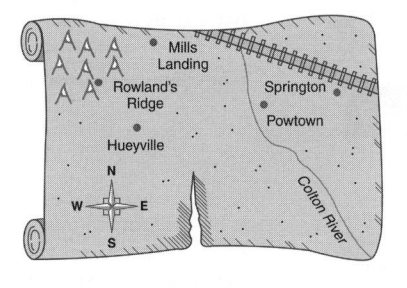

Jan. 30: Discouraged by poor crops. No cash. Left Springton by wagon in search of work.

Feb 4: Today searched for job in Powtown. No luck. All jobs require skills I don't have.

March 15: Crossed the Colton River but raft turned over. Lost everything except diary and watch. Walked to Hueyville.

March 18: No work in Hueyville. Met kind woman there. Told me about vacant house abandoned by miners near Rowland's Ridge.

March 21: Sold my watch for supplies. Hiked to Rowland's Ridge. Found shack and moved in.

March 27: Days and days of rainy weather. Decided to fix up place. Borrowed tools to fix roof, walls, and floors.

March 29: Hammering floorboards. Saw red bag. Opened it. Eureka! A bag full of money. I am rich.

April 8: Guilty conscience. Worry about possible owner. Hiked to Mills Landing and asked Sheriff what to do. Says the money is mine because money left long ago. No one will ever claim.

■ **STEP 1**

Using the map, trace the traveler's steps with a partner.

■ **STEP 2**

With your partner, write a brief article for the local newspaper about the lone traveler's story. Describe the traveler's route and what occurred along the way.

Example:

100-Year-Old Diary of Traveler Found

Yesterday a diary was found that tells the story of a former resident of the area. Apparently, one hundred years ago, a lone traveler, discouraged by poor crops and having no cash, had left Springton in order to find work. Searching for a job in Powtown, the traveler . . .

UNIT OVERVIEW

This unit looks at the form and meaning of a variety of adverbial clauses and examines ways of reducing them. It includes a focus chart on a common error in writing for native and nonnative speakers alike: dangling participles. Please note that due to its length, this unit has been divided into three lesson plans. To review this unit more quickly, review focus charts and have students complete the first exercise after each chart to observe students' grasp of the grammar topics.

GRAMMAR NOTE

Unit 16 assumes that students have a good understanding of complex sentence structures in which subordinate clauses of time and cause are joined to main clauses. Building on this foundation, the focus charts provide instruction on how to reduce and punctuate these clauses as well as how to avoid dangling participles, a recurring problem for developing writers.

UNIT GOALS

Some instructors may want to review the goals listed on Student Book (SB) page 300 after completing the Opening Task so that students understand what they should know by the end of the unit. These goals can also be reviewed at the end of the unit when students are more familiar with the grammar terminology.

OPENING TASK [30 minutes]

The purpose of the Opening Task is to create a context in which students will need to use adverbial phrases as they report the route of a traveler presumably living somewhere in North America in the 1800s; examples of the conditionals *only if* and *unless* are presented in the opening quoted statements. The problem-solving format is designed to show the teacher how well the students can produce the target structures implicitly and spontaneously when they are engaged in a communicative task. For a more complete discussion of the purpose of the Opening Task, see To the Teacher, Lesson Planner (LP) page xxii.

Setting Up the Task

Prior to class, wrap up several coins in a square of red cloth or felt and tie a string around it. Tell students they will be reading a story in which a red bag plays a part. To increase interest, ask them to guess the answers to the following questions: (1) *What is in the bag?* (2) *Who owned it?*, and (3) *Why is it important?* Then ask students to open their books and read the diary.

Conducting the Task

■ STEP 1

1. Read the directions for Step 1 as a class.
2. Ask students to work in pairs and trace the traveler's route using lines and arrows. (The route should be as follows: *Springton→ Powtown→ Hueyville→ Rowland's Ridge→ Mills Landing.*)

■ STEP 2

Have students work with the same partner. Ask them to write a short newspaper article about the traveler. They may copy the first few sentences of the example. Remind them to include as much detail as they can, or create a totally new story of their own. Prompt reduced clauses by telling students that they may want to begin one or more of their sentences using the following verbs: *crossing, selling, hiking, terrified, disheartened,* or *worried*.

Closing the Task

1. Have pairs of students exchange articles, read them, and comment on them.
2. Ask a few volunteers to read their stories to the class.
3. Don't worry about accuracy at this point, though you may want to take notes of errors in meaning, form, or use in order to focus on those problems later.

GRAMMAR NOTE

Typical student errors (form)

- In writing, omitting commas before or after a reduced adverb clause: —e.g.,* *The president having given his speech left the room.* (See Focus 3.)
- In writing, using dangling participles: —e.g., * *After barking for two hours, the dog's owner finally returned home.* (See Focus 5.)

Typical student errors (use)

- Reducing adverb clauses that have a different subject than the main clause: —e.g.,* *Following the recipe carefully, my cake was a great success.* (See Focus 1.)
- Using the *-ing* participle when the focus of the sentences is on the person experiencing the emotion: —e.g.,* *Annoying by the long lines in the store, she walked out.* (See Focus 4.)

FOCUS 1 — Reducing Adverbial Clauses of Time

We can reduce adverbial clauses of time that contain the words *before, after, while, when,* and *since.* To do this, the subject of the main clause and the adverbial clause must be the same. These reduced clauses are called participle phrases and use verb + *-ing.*

FULL ADVERBIAL CLAUSE	REDUCED ADVERBIAL CLAUSE*	TIME MEANING
(a) **While we are hiking/were hiking/hiked,** we admire/admired the scenery around us. *are/were* V + *-ing* ⟶	(b) **(While) hiking,** we admire/admired the scenery around us. V + *-ing*	A time happening at the same time as the time expressed in the main clause.
(c) **Since he has/had been living in Paris,** he has/had learned to speak French quite well. *has/had been* V + *-ing* ⟶	(d) **(Since) living in Paris,** he has/had learned to speak French quite well. V + *-ing*	A time occurring before and up to the point of the time expressed in the main clause.
(e) **After we have/had hiked around the canyon,** we are/were exhausted. *have/had* V + *-ed* ⟶	(f) **(After) having hiked around the canyon,** we are/were exhausted. *having* + V + *-ed*	A time occurring before the time expressed in the main clause.
(g) **While they are/were being searched,** they feel/felt nervous. *are/were* + *being* + V + *-ed* ⟶	(h) **(While) being searched,** they feel/felt nervous. *being* + V + *-ed*	A time occurring at the same time or immediately after the time expressed in the main clause.
(i) **When Sam gets tired,** we will leave.	(j) **NOT:** Getting tired, we will leave.	The subject of the main clause and the subject of the adverbial clause are not the same. The adverbial clause cannot be reduced.

*For some of these reduced adverbial clauses, you can either keep or leave out the adverbial (in parentheses), as in (b), (d), (f), and (h) above.

EXERCISE 1

Complete the following sentences about the out-of-doors. Give advice, using *should* or *shouldn't.*

Example: After getting lost in the woods, <u>you should look for familiar landmarks such as hills or trees</u>.

1. While walking along a narrow ridge, <u>you should stay close to the ridge wall</u>
2. When hiking in an area with poisonous snakes, <u>you should always look where you are going</u>
3. After having fallen into icy water, <u>you should change into dry clothes as quickly as possible</u>
4. Before entering a meadow filled with deer, <u>you should be still and take a photo</u>
5. When washing dishes in the wilderness, <u>you shouldn't use detergent that will pollute</u>
6. Before lighting a fire in the woods, <u>you should make sure you are not under a tree with dry limbs or leaves</u>.
7. Before being attacked by mosquitoes, <u>you should put on insect repellent</u>
8. After having spotted a bear, <u>you shouldn't make a noise</u>

EXERCISE 2

Read the following story. Reduce the full adverbial clauses of time where possible. The first one has been done for you.

            graduating
   (1) Since ~~he graduated~~ from high school, Juan has been working and studying very hard. (2) While he attends classes at a community college, he works part-time at a bank. (3) After he graduates from the community college, he would like to attend a four-year university in order to become an architect. (4) Some day Juan would like to get married and have a family. (5) However, before he gets married, he is planning to take a trip to Europe. (6) When he is traveling through Europe, he hopes to see the great architecture of France, Spain, and Italy. (7) After he returns, he will begin looking more seriously for a partner.

EXERCISE 3

Reflect on your last month of activities and write at least five sentences containing reduced adverbial clauses of time like those shown in in the chart on page 302.

Example: *After having taken my biology exam, I had to study for my history exam.*

ANSWER KEY

Exercise 1   Answers will vary. Possible answers are shown above.
Exercise 2   (2) While attending classes   (3) After graduating from   (5) Before getting married,
(6) When traveling through Europe   (7) After returning
Exercise 3   Answers will vary.

FOCUS 1 [20 minutes]

This focus chart describes how to reduce adverbial clauses of time.

1. **Lead-in:** Read the first section as a class. To emphasize that reduced adverb clauses are derived from full clauses and that they have the same subject as a main clause, write sentence (a) on the board, using one color for all words except *we*, which you should write in a different color. Underline the identical subjects. State that the subject of both must be the same in order to consider reducing the clause to the phrase (*While*) *hiking*.
2. Ask individuals to take turns reading examples (c–h), noting the time expressed in each.
3. Write example (i) on the board and ask students to identify the two separate subjects (*Sam* and *we*) in the sentence. Ask if it is possible to reduce the first clause. Students should acknowledge that it is <u>not</u> possible, since the subjects (*Sam* and *we*) are not the same.

METHODOLOGY NOTE

The great challenge with reduced adverbial clauses is to learn how to recognize the subject in both the main clause and the adverb clause, particularly when that subject is implied. This first focus concentrates on examples in which the subjects are explicit, setting the students up for success in their later work in this unit, when they will be required to work with implied subjects.

EXERCISE 1 [20 minutes/homework]

Exercise 1 asks students to complete sentences with adverbial clauses of time, practicing the principle of keeping the subject the same, as described in Focus 1. This exercise could be done in class, or assigned as homework.

---

1. Read the directions and example as a class. What is the subject of the adverbial clause? (*you*, implied)
2. Have students work independently to complete the sentences with advice for each situation. Tell students to be aware of time frames as they create their responses.
3. Review answers as a class. See possible answers on LP page 302.

For more practice, use *Grammar Dimensions 4* Workbook page 142, Exercise 2.

EXERCISE 2 [15 minutes]

In Exercise 2 students reduce adverbial clauses of time in a story. This exercise is good practice in how to make writing more concise.

1. Read the directions and example as a class. What is the time expressed in the adverbial clause? (*a time occurring before and up to the point of time expressed in the main clause*)
2. Have students work independently to complete the exercise. Remind them to search for subordinate clauses that contain the same subject as the main clause in order to identify a place to make a reduction. Encourage them to refer to Focus 1 for ideas.
3. Have students share and discuss their sentences with a partner.
4. Ask volunteers to read their partners' sentences to the class, and discuss these as a class. See answers on LP page 302.

For more practice, use *Grammar Dimensions 4* Workbook page 141, Exercise 1.

EXPANSION [30 minutes]

Activity 2 (writing) on SB page 311 is a good follow-up to Exercise 2. In this activity students write directions about how to make or do something, using reduced adverbial clauses.

EXERCISE 3 [15 minutes]

In Exercise 3 students write about their own lives using reduced adverb clauses of time.

1. Read the directions and examples as a class. Ask students to offer other examples from their lives.
2. Have students work independently to complete the exercise.
3. Have students share and discuss their sentences with a partner.
4. Ask volunteers to read their partners' sentences to the class, and discuss these as a class.

EXPANSION [60 minutes/homework]

You may wish to assign Activity 4 (research on the web) on SB page 312 after students complete Exercise 3 as homework. In this activity students research the California Gold Rush on the Internet, and then write a short fictional story about the life of a miner.

FOCUS 2

Reducing Adverbial Clauses That Show Cause

form   meaning

We can also reduce adverbial clauses containing *because, since,* and *as* to *-ing* phrases. Again, the subject in the main clause must be the same as the subject in the adverbial clause.

FULL ADVERBIAL CLAUSE	REDUCED ADVERBIAL CLAUSE*	CAUSAL MEANING
(a) **Because we take/took/are taking/were taking the bus,** we save/saved a lot of money.	(b) **Taking the bus,** we save/saved a lot of money.	The participle phrase contains the cause or reason. The main clause contains the result. The participle phrase can refer to present and past time as was shown in Focus 1.
(c) **Since I have/had been rehearsing every day,** I am/was ready to perform.	(d) **Rehearsing every day,** I am/was ready to perform.	
(e) **As I have/had never gone skiing,** I want/wanted to take lessons.	(f) **Never having gone skiing,** I want/wanted to take lessons.	In the reduced form, a negative word like *never* or *not* can precede the auxiliary verb. This means that the action did not occur.
(g) **Because he is/was not being watched by the police,** he is/was free to move.	(h) **Not being watched by the police,** he is/was free to move.	

*These reduced clauses do not include the adverbial. That is, it is not possible to say "Because taking the bus, we saved a lot of money."

EXERCISE 4

Tony and Maria have had several mishaps on their camping trip. Suggest a cause for each mishap by adding a reduced adverbial clause to each sentence below. Compare your completed sentences with a partner.

Example: They got lost on their hike.
Not having brought a map, they got lost on their hike.

1. Tony was bitten by mosquitoes.
2. They were very thirsty.
3. They were very hungry.

4. Maria jumped in fright.
5. Maria was shivering.
6. Tony developed a blister.

EXERCISE 5

Imagine that you have received a letter from a friend who is having a difficult time adjusting to life at a university in the United States. She is making excuses for several of her actions. Write a piece of advice for each problem, using a reduced causal adverbial clause.

Example: Because I arrived at my first class late, I waited outside the room and missed the entire lecture.
Having arrived to the class late, you should have quietly entered the room and sat down.

1. Because I have no computer, I do not type my papers.
2. Because I watched a lot of TV, I couldn't concentrate on my homework.
3. As I have not understood my instructor, I have stopped going to class.
4. Because I do not know anyone, I sit alone in my room for hours.
5. Since I hate the food on campus, I go out for dinner every night and now I'm almost broke.
6. As I am embarrassed by my accent, I do not speak to many people.
7. As I am very shy, I do not ask questions about my assignments in class.
8. As I got a D on my last test, I am planning to drop my class.
9. Because I made expensive long distance calls to my family every other night, I ran up a huge phone bill.
10. Since I did not have enough time to write my research paper, I copied most of the information from an encyclopedia.
11. Because I was put on academic probation, I have felt very depressed.
12. Since I do not speak English very well, I speak my native language with friends from my native country.

Exercise 4 Answers may vary. Possible answers are: 1. Not having remembered the insect repellent . . .
2. Having forgotten their water bottle . . . 3. Not having eaten all day . . . 4. Seeing a wolf . . .
5. Not having put on her down parka . . . 6. Having walked too long in boots that were too small . . .
Exercise 5 Answers may vary. Possible answers are: 1. Not having a computer, you should go to the school computer lab. 2. Watching too much TV, you should have had more self-control and turned it off so that you could concentrate on your homework. 3. Not having understood your professor, you should ask for clarification during the lecture or visit him or her during office hours. 4. Not knowing anyone, you should make a greater effort to get involved in clubs or extracurricular activities. 5. Hating the food

6. Being embarrassed by your accent, you should take a pronunciation class. 7. Being very shy, you should ask about your assignments during your professor's office hours. 8. Having gotten a "D" on your last test, you should get a tutor or study harder to do better on the next test. 9. Having made too many long distance calls to your family, you should think about e-mailing or faxing messages instead.
10. Not having had enough time for your research paper, you should not have plagiarized, no matter how short on time you were OR you should have asked for an extension on the due date. 11. Having been put on academic probation, you should meet with your advisor. 12. Not speaking English very well, you should try to practice English with some new English-speaking friends.

FOCUS 2 [15 minutes]

Focus 2 takes a look at how to reduce adverb clauses that contain *because, since,* and *as,* converting them to participle phrases with *-ing.*

1. **Lead-in:** Draw two columns on the board and label them *Cause* and *Effect.* Under *Cause* write the following examples: *standing on your head, pinching your nose, not tying your shoes,* etc.

2. Ask students to think of the possible effects of each activity. You should begin each sentence and allow individuals to finish it. For example: *Standing on your head, . . . might make your face turn blue. Pinching your nose, . . . might cause you to stop breathing. Not tying your shoes, . . . might make you trip on your laces.*

3. Ask students to silently read examples (a–h). After they have finished reading, highlight the fact that the participle phrase can refer to different time frames and can also be made negative by adding the words *not* and *never.*

4. Encourage students to ask questions about anything they do not understand.

Note: All students will benefit from extensive practice in reducing adverb clauses that begin sentences, such as is offered here.

EXERCISE 4 [15 minutes]

In Exercise 4 students apply the principles of Focus 2, adding reduced adverb clauses to sentences.

1. Read the directions. Ask a volunteer to read the example. Ask students to suggest other causes, using a reduced adverb clause.

2. Have students work in pairs to create new sentences.

3. Have pairs share their sentences with another pair.

4. Ask volunteers to share their sentences with the class. See possible answers on LP page 304.

 For more practice, use *Grammar Dimensions 4* Workbook page 143, Exercise 4.

EXPANSION [25 minutes]

This expansion activity will give students more practice in generating reduced adverb clauses.

1. Have students work in pairs. Ask them to think of a situation such as the one in Exercise 4, in which two people were on a camping trip.

2. Have them write 4–6 sentences describing mishaps that occurred.

3. Have them exchange papers with another pair. Ask the pairs to add reduced adverbial clauses suggesting the cause of each unfortunate event.

4. Have the pairs take turns reading their sentences to the other pair.

5. Ask representatives to share their best two sentences with the class.

EXERCISE 5 [25 minutes]

Students respond to a series of stated problems with advice, using reduced adverb clauses.

1. Ask a volunteer to read the directions and example. Ask another volunteer to give an example that uses *never* or *not.*

2. Have students work independently to write their lines of advice to each situation.

3. Have students take turns sharing their advice in small groups. See possible answers on LP page 304.

VARIATION

Ask one student to read the problem and the other student to give him or her oral advice about how to solve it using reduced adverb clauses. Then, ask students to do the exercise in writing for homework.

 For more practice, use *Grammar Dimensions 4* Workbook page 142, Exercise 3.

EXPANSION [60 minutes/homework]

Activity 3 (listening/speaking) on SB page 312 is a good homework assignment following Exercise 5. In this activity students listen to their choice of an audio book, identify one or two descriptive passages, and write down the examples of reduced adverbial clauses they hear.

FOCUS 3 — Position and Punctuation of Reduced Adverbial Clauses

EXAMPLES	EXPLANATIONS
(a) **Hiking alone in the mountains,** Diane always carries water and a compass.	Reduced adverbial clauses (participle phrases) may appear at the beginning, middle, or end of a sentence.
(b) The doe, **having been frightened by the noise,** disappeared from the clearing.	
(c) The trackers waded across the river, **holding tightly to the reins of their horses.**	
(d) The trackers waded across the river **while holding tightly to the reins of their horses.**	Commas are needed in all positions, except the sentence-final position with the adverbial included, as in (d).

EXERCISE 6

Insert commas where needed in the following story.

(1) Tiffany was a very lucky girl. (2) Being born into a very wealthy family she always got everything she wanted. (3) She was given a pony before celebrating her eighth birthday. (4) After turning 10 she had a tutor to teach her anything she wanted to learn. (5) Enjoying sports she learned how to sail, ski, and scuba dive. (6) Turning 12 her interests changed to travel. (7) Enjoying traveling she decided to have her sixteenth birthday on a ship. (8) For a whole weekend, she and her friends were eating, playing games, and dancing while cruising to Mexico.

(9) Tiffany's luck began to change, however, on her eighteenth birthday. (10) Her parents promised her a shiny red sports car, but they told her that she would have to pay for the registration and the insurance herself. (11) She paid for the first installment of her insurance, but not having a well-paying job she avoided paying for the second installment of the insurance and drove her car anyway. (12) One night, speeding along a winding road she saw another car coming towards her. (13) She beeped loudly, but the car did not move over. (14) She swerved her car to the right barely missing the other car as it drove by. (15) Her car hit a tree, but she was not hurt. (16) Arriving on the scene a police officer asked to see her driver's license and her up-to-date insurance identification. (17) Lucky Tiffany's luck ran out when she told him that her insurance had expired. (18) Unfortunately, her license was revoked and she had to pay for the damages to the car out of her own pocket not having adhered to her parents' agreement.

EXERCISE 7

Match the following main clauses and participle phrases. Try placing the participle phrases in different positions, using commas as necessary.

Example: *Returning to Europe, Christopher Columbus brought cocoa beans from the new world.* (7-f)
Christopher Columbus, returning to Europe, brought cocoa beans from the new world. (7-f)

Participle Phrases

1. Having healed numerous individuals from malaria   (h)
2. Conquering American tropical lands   (g)
3. Sold either as fresh fruit or made into juice   (d)
4. Upsetting the natural order of climate and ecology   (a)
5. Prompting explorers to leave on long voyages   (e)
6. Grown almost year-round   (b)
7. Returning to Europe   (f)
8. Extracting the sweet juice from the sugarcane   (c)
9. Dried   (i)

Main Clauses

a. agriculture and industry have ruined tropical lands.
b. bananas are available in every season.
c. the natives sucked on the tender green shoots.
d. pineapple has been an important cash crop.
e. pepper was a prized commodity in the Middle Ages.
f. Christopher Columbus brought cocoa beans from the new world.
g. the Spaniards were introduced to cocoa and chocolate.
h. quinine is a very useful medicinal plant.
i. cinnamon rolls up into small sandy-brown cigarette shapes.

ANSWER KEY

Exercise 7   The structure of final sentences may vary. The matches are: 1. h   2. g   3. d   4. a   5. e   6. b   7. f   8. c   9. i

FOCUS 3 [10 minutes]

Focus 3 gives the rules governing punctuation and placement of reduced adverb clauses in writing.

1. **Lead-in:** Read the first explanation, and ask volunteers to read the first three examples. Ask students to identify the position of each adverb clause in each example. (*beginning, middle, end*)

2. Read the second explanation and example (d) as a class. Ask students if you were to delete the word *while* from example (d), would they need to add a comma? (*yes*)

3. Answer any questions students may have.

EXERCISE 6 [15 minutes]

In Exercise 6 students add commas to a story, applying the principles stated in Focus 3.

1. Have students work independently to add commas as needed to the story.

2. Have students exchange papers with a partner and review each other's work.

3. Ask volunteers to share their answers with the class. See answers on LP page 306.

 For more practice, use *Grammar Dimensions 4* Workbook page 144, Exercise 5 and Exercise 6.

EXPANSION [30 minutes]

This activity will give students additional practice in punctuating text with reduced adverb clauses.

1. Have students work in pairs. Ask each pair to find one paragraph from a book that contains reduced adverb clauses. Have them copy the paragraph—but tell them to omit all punctuation.

2. Have them exchange papers with another pair and have the pairs punctuate the paragraph. Then exchange papers again. Students should review and correct the papers.

EXERCISE 7 [20 minutes]

Students create sentences by matching main clauses and participle phrases.

1. Read the directions and example as a class. Could the participle phrase be placed anywhere else in the sentence?

2. Have students work in pairs to write their sentences.

3. Have pairs share their sentences with another pair.

4. Ask a representative from various groups to share their best sentences with the class. See the matches on LP page 306.

 For more practice, use *Grammar Dimensions 4* Workbook page 145, Exercise 7.

EXPANSION [60 minutes/homework]

In Activity 5 (reflection) on SB pages 312 and 313, students edit an essay they have written in the past, reducing adverb clauses and paying attention to punctuation. This activity is a very effective homework or in-class assignment after Exercise 7.

FOCUS 4 Reduced Adverbial Clauses with Emotive Verbs

meaning

EXAMPLES	EXPLANATIONS
Emotive Verbs: *amuse* *confuse* *frustrate* *please* *annoy* *embarrass* *interest* *puzzle* *bewilder* *excite* *intrigue* *shock* *bore* *frighten* *irritate* *surprise* *captivate*	Reduced adverbial clauses often contain emotive verbs (verbs that express feelings or emotions).
(a) **Amused** by the movie, Tony laughed out loud. (b) **Frightened** (by the noise), Donna left to investigate.	If we use the *-ed* participle, the focus is on the person experiencing the emotion.
(c) The clown stood on his head, **amusing** the spectators. (d) Two students whispered in the back of the room, **annoying** the teacher.	If we use the *-ing* participle, the focus is on the person or thing causing the emotion.

EXERCISE 8

Circle the correct option.

Example: Nick jumped, _____ by the lighting.
  (a.) frightened   b. frightening

1. The hikers, _____, gazed at the lovely waterfall.
   (a.) surprised and bewildered   b. surprising and bewildering

2. _____ by mosquitoes, Miko could not sleep.
   (a.) Bothered   b. Bothering

3. The movie, while _____ and sensational, was inappropriate for children.
   a. intrigued   (b.) intriguing

4. _____ that the bears had invaded the camp, the family left.
   (a.) Irritated   b. Irritating

5. _____ by the lecture, many students fell asleep.
   (a.) Bored   b. Boring

6. _____ in Indian artifacts, Martin collected arrowheads.
   (a.) Interested   b. Interesting

7. They walked on their hands, _____ all of the bystanders.
   a. shocked   (b.) shocking

8. The play, while _____ and funny, did not keep us awake.
   a. amused   (b.) amusing

FOCUS 5 Avoiding Dangling Participles

meaning

Writers often use reduced adverbial clauses in their sentences. If the subject in the reduced clause is different from the subject in the main clause, the reduced clause is called a "dangling participle" and may result in a miscommunication. To avoid this error, writers need to make sure that the performer of the action in the main clause is the same as the performer of the action in the reduced clause. To correct this error, the subject of the main clause should be changed to match the subject in the reduced clause. Or the reduced clause should be expanded to a full adverbial clause.

DANGLING PARTICIPLES	MEANING AS WORDED
(a) The path was more visible **carrying a flashlight.**	Miscommunication: The path was carrying a flashlight. Reworded: Carrying a flashlight, I could see the path more visibly. OR The path was more visible when I was carrying a flashlight.
(b) **Using binoculars,** the pond was clearly defined.	Miscommunication: The pond was using binoculars. Reworded: Using binoculars, I could see the pond clearly defined. OR While I was using binoculars, the pond was clearly defined.
(c) **Enclosed in a waterproof can,** the hikers kept the matches safe.	Miscommunication: The hikers were enclosed in a waterproof can. Reworded: Enclosed in a waterproof can, the matches were kept safe by the hikers. OR Because the matches were enclosed in a waterproof can, the hikers kept the matches safe.
(d) **After carefully reading it over,** the diary should be revised for gaps and inconsistencies.	Miscommunication: The diary is reading itself over. Reworded: After you carefully read it over, the diary should be revised for gaps and inconsistencies. OR After carefully reading it over, you should revise the diary for gaps and inconsistencies. OR After carefully reading it over, revise the diary for gaps and inconsistencies.
(e) **When keeping a diary,** dates and places should be carefully recorded.	Miscommunication: Dates and places are keeping the diary. Reworded: When you are keeping a diary, dates and places should be carefully recorded. OR When keeping a diary, people should carefully record dates and places. OR When keeping a diary, it is important to carefully record dates and places.**

Note: Because the subject of the reduced adverbial clause is the same as the imperative "you" in the main clause, the reduced clause is not a dangling participle.
**When the adverbial clause contains a nonreferential "it," which is assumed to be the same subject as the generic people who keep diaries, the rule for the same subject in both clauses is relaxed.

FOCUS 4 [10 minutes]

Focus 4 examines reduced adverb clauses that contain emotive verbs.

1. **Lead-in:** Read the first explanation, and ask volunteers to read the emotive verbs.

2. Brainstorm a list of other emotive verbs, and write these on the board.

3. Read the second explanation, and ask a volunteer to read the first example. Ask whether *the movie* or *Tony* is amused. Ask other students to repeat the sentence, substituting one of the other emotive verbs for *amused*. Read the second example, and repeat.

4. Repeat this procedure with the third section of the chart.

5. Answer any questions students might have.

EXERCISE 8 [10 minutes]

Exercise 8 has students choose either an *-ed* or an *-ing* participle to complete sentences, using what they have just learned in Focus 4.

1. Have students work independently to complete the sentences.

2. Have students compare their answers with a partner.

3. Ask various volunteers to share their choices with the class. See answers on LP page 308.

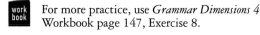

For more practice, use *Grammar Dimensions 4* Workbook page 147, Exercise 8.

FOCUS 5 [20 minutes]

Focus 5 addresses a prime source of errors for native and nonnative speakers: dangling participles.

1. **Lead-in:** Tell students a story about something that recently happened to you or someone else. For example, tell them that, while you were driving on a freeway Friday night, one of your tires suddenly went flat.

2. Write a sentence with a dangling participle summarizing your experience: *While driving on the highway, one of my tires suddenly went flat.*

3. Tell students you need to edit this sentence because it doesn't accurately express your meaning. Ask them who was driving. When they say it was you, ask them to identify where the subject, *I*, is in the sentence. (*It doesn't exist.*) Then ask them to identify the subject of the sentence (*one of my tires*). Erase the entire clause after the adverb clause and write *I*. Then ask students to complete the sentence to express what happened.

4. Read the summary of the focus chart.

5. For each section of the chart, ask students to identify the subject of the sentence. Elicit what the subject should be, and then read the revised sentence. Answer any questions students might have.

LANGUAGE NOTE

Dangling participles are a common error in writing even for native English speakers. Once students understand why dangling participles are ungrammatical structures in standard written English, they usually enjoy the unintended humor often created by such structures. For example, in the Focus 5 sentences we have paths carrying flashlights, ponds using binoculars, and hikers enclosed in waterproof cans! Tell students that the identification and/or correction of dangling participles is often part of advanced-level standardized English examinations.

EXERCISE 9

While hiking in the woods in some parts of the world, a person may encounter a skunk and be unexpectedly sprayed. The following sentences relate to Jane's experience with this, but some of them contain dangling participles. Identify which sentences are incorrect, explain why they are humorous as they are presently stated, and reword the main clause to make each sentence correct.

Example: Hiking in the woods, a skunk crossed Jane's path. *This sentence is humorous because it suggests that the skunk, not Jane, was hiking in the woods. The appropriate form would be "While Jane was hiking in the woods, a skunk crossed her path."*

1. Having been sprayed by a skunk, she screamed loudly.
2. Frightened and humiliated, we walked Jane back to the campground.
3. Having returned to the campground, we looked for some catsup.
4. Applying a thick coat of catsup all over her body, the skunk smell was neutralized.
5. Soaking her clothing for 30 minutes in vinegar and water, the smell diminished.
6. Having been victimized by a skunk, we were informed by Jane that she will think twice about hiking in the woods again.
7. It is wise to bring catsup and vinegar when camping in skunk country.

EXERCISE 10

Rewrite these sentences to correct the participle errors. There may be several ways to correct a sentence.

Example: After having been bitten by mosquitoes, the ointment felt soothing to her skin.
After having been bitten by mosquitoes, she rubbed a soothing ointment onto her skin.

1. James pet the dog, while barking.
2. While having a bath, water leaked over the sides of the tub.
3. The hurricane terrified people, being driven from their homes.
4. When amused by their children's naughty pranks, a straight face is always a good solution for parents.
5. Slithering along the path, I spied a snake.
6. Nearly suffocated by the heat, the room was packed with people.
7. The canned fruits and jams helped the family survive, having prepared for the winter.
8. Sobbing and wailing, the search party was able to locate many survivors.
9. Sitting on the beach, the waves seemed huge to Martin.
10. After carefully reading it over, the diary should be revised for gaps and inconsistencies.

Use Your English

ACTIVITY 1 listening/writing

CD2 Track 6

STEP 1 Relax, close your eyes, and listen attentively to the audio for five descriptions. Each one is unfinished. Use your imagination to create a mental image that completes each piece. Listen to each description a second time. Stop the audio after each one. What do you see? Write your ideas in complete sentences. Try to use as many participle phrases as you can.

Example: *Looking ahead, I see high jagged peaks. Each one is covered with snow. Dotting the landscape below, hundreds of lakes are nestled among groves of trees.*

STEP 2 Now listen again and write down any *-ed* or *-ing* participle phrases that you hear.

Example: *The propeller turning and the engine roaring, the plane is ready for takeoff. Ascending higher and higher, you see nothing but white fog in every direction.*

ACTIVITY 2 writing

We often use reduced adverbial clauses to give directions for carrying out some procedure. Consider something you know how to do very well that requires several motions (for example, making beef jerky, changing a tire, operating a video camera). Then, write the directions to do this activity, using at least two reduced adverbial clauses.

Example: *Before making beef jerky, purchase three pounds of lean beef. Cut strips of the beef about one-half-inch thick. Then, hang these strips on a wood framework about four to six feet off the ground. After building a smoke fire, allow the meat to dry in the sun and wind.*

Exercise 9 *Sentences 1, 3, and 7 are correct. For the incorrect sentences, here are some possible corrections: 2. Frightened and humiliated, Jane walked back to the camp with us. Because Jane was frightened and humiliated, we walked her back to the camp. 4. Applying a thick coat of catsup all over her body, Jane was able to neutralize the skunk smell. Because Jane applied a thick coat of catsup all over her body, the skunk smell was neutralized. 5. Soaking her clothing for 30 minutes in vinegar and water, Jane diminished the smell. Because Jane soaked her clothing for 30 minutes in vinegar and water, the smell diminished. 6. Having been victimized by a skunk, Jane informed us that she will think twice about hiking through the woods again. After Jane/she*

had been victimized by a skunk, we were informed by her/Jane that she will think twice about hiking in the woods again.
Exercise 10 *Answers may vary. Possible answers are continued on LP page 312.*
1. James pet the dog while the dog was barking. While barking, the dog was petted by James.
2. While Mary was having a bath, the water leaked over the sides of the tub. While having a bath, I allowed the water to leak over the sides of the tub. 3. Being driven from their homes, people were terrified by the hurricane. The hurricane terrified people as they were being driven from their homes.

EXERCISE 9 [10 minutes]

1. Read the directions and example as a class. What is the subject of the example? (*skunk*) What should the subject be? (*Jane*)
2. Have students work independently to rewrite the sentences, correcting the dangling participle phrases.
3. Have students review their answers with a partner.
4. Ask volunteers to share their answers with the class. See possible answers on LP page 310.

 For more practice, use *Grammar Dimensions 4* Workbook page 148, Exercise 9.

EXPANSION [10 minutes]

For more practice in changing dangling participle clauses to subordinate adverb clauses, have students, in pairs, take turns restating the sentences using *after*. Use the first sentences as an example: *After Jane was sprayed by a skunk . . .*

EXERCISE 10 [20 minutes]

1. Read the directions and example as a class. Ask students to identify the subject of the example and what the subject should be.
2. Ask volunteers to suggest other ways of rephrasing the example.
3. Have students work in pairs to rewrite the sentences.
4. Have pairs get together with other pairs and share their answers.
5. Ask volunteers to share their answers with the class. Encourage students to share other ways of rephrasing the sentences. See possible answers on LP pages 310 and 312.

EXPANSION [45 minutes]

Activity 1 (listening/writing) on SB page 311 is a good follow-up to Exercise 10, Students listen to five descriptions of situations, and then write descriptions of what comes to their "mind's eye" using participle phrases. Students then listen for and write down the *-ed* and *-ing* participles they hear in the descriptions.

UNIT GOAL REVIEW [10 minutes]

Ask students to look at the goals on the opening page of the unit again. Refer to the pages of the unit where information on each goal can be found.

 For assessment of Unit 16, use *Grammar Dimensions ExamView®*.

USE YOUR ENGLISH

The Use Your English activities at the end of the unit contain situations that should naturally elicit the structures covered in the unit. For a more complete discussion of how to use the Use Your English activities, see To the Teacher, page xxvi.

ACTIVITY 1 listening/writing [45 minutes]

 CD2 Track 6

This activity is a good follow-up to Exercise 10 on SB page 310. Note that the former CD track number (23) is incorrectly listed in the student book.

Discuss students' experiences with listening to very vivid descriptions of situations, such as a description of a beautiful place or of a terrifying situation. Do they get very vivid mental pictures when they hear such descriptions? Ask several students to describe

something vivid they have heard, and say what images it evoked for them.

STEP 1

1. Read the directions and example as a class.
2. Have students listen to the audio once.
3. Ask students to listen again, stop the audio after each description, and write sentences about what images they see, using as many participle phrases as they can.

STEP 2

1. Read the directions and example as a class. Ask students to listen to the audio a third time and write down any *-ed* or *-ing* phrases they hear.
2. Have students work in pairs to share their written descriptions and their lists of participles.
3. Ask volunteers to share their work with the class.

ACTIVITY 2 writing [30 minutes]

This activity is a good follow-up to Exercise 2 on SB page 303.

1. Ask a volunteer who likes to cook to tell you how to make something simple, such as pasta. Ask anther volunteer to write these directions on the board.
2. Work with the class to add as many reduced adverb clauses to this description as possible.
3. Read the directions for Activity 2, and ask a volunteer to read the example.
4. Have students work independently to write directions about how to make or do something, using reduced adverb clauses.
5. Have students work in pairs to share their directions.
6. Ask several volunteers to read their directions to the class.

ACTIVITY 3 listening/speaking

Check out a book recorded on audiotape or CD novel (for example, Charles Dickens's *A Tale of Two Cities*, Mark Twain's *Huckleberry Finn*, Willa Cather's *O, Pioneers!*) from your local library or video store. Listen to the audio and identify one or two descriptive passages. Within these passages, listen for examples of reduced adverbial clauses. Share these examples with your classmates.

ACTIVITY 4 research on the web

Go to the Internet and use an Internet search engine such as Google® or Yahoo® to research the topic "California Gold Rush." Read and take notes on several articles to familiarize yourself with when it happened, who was involved, what challenges were encountered, what successes were achieved, etc. Then, write a short fictional piece about a miner's life during that time.

Example: *Living near the town of Coloma, California, Peter Jacobson, one of the many California gold miners at the time of the Gold Rush experienced many hardships . . .*

ACTIVITY 5 reflection

Review an essay that you wrote previously. Analyze it sentence by sentence and reduce adverbial clauses appropriately. See the example on page 313.

Examples:

> Many people have been moving to Southern California from colder regions of the United States. <u>When people have been living in Southern California for a while</u>, they assume new habits and lifestyles. It does not take long for them to begin wearing shorts and sandals. <u>While they were living in Minnesota or New York</u>, they got used to winters where they bundled up from head to toe. <u>Since they arrived to the west coast</u>, they wear shorts and sandals all year round. In the past, they often watched Hollywood movies on TV in their living room. Now, <u>because they are living near the entertainment industry</u>, they can drive to see movie premieres or even live filming of TV dramas.

■ **STEP 1** Underline time or causal adverbial clauses.

Examples:

TIME:
<u>When people have been living in southern California for a while</u>, they assume new habits and lifestyles.
<u>Living in southern California for a while</u>, they assume new habits and lifestyles.

CAUSAL:
Now, <u>because they are living near the entertainment industry</u>, they can drive to see movie premiers or even live filming of TV dramas.
Now, <u>living near the entertainment industry</u>, they can drive to see movie premiers or even live filming of TV dramas.

■ **STEP 2** Label each type of clause and determine whether or not one or more clauses can be reduced or reordered. Revise the sentences for greater conciseness and clarity.

■ **STEP 3** Submit your revised paper to your instructor for feedback.

Exercise 10 Possible answers (continued):
4. When amused by their children's naughty pranks, parents should keep a straight face. When parents are amused by their children's naughty pranks, a straight face is always a good solution.
5. Slithering along the path, a snake was spied by me. While a snake was slithering along the path, I spied it.   6. Nearly suffocated by the heat, the people were packed in the room. Because the room was packed with people, they nearly suffocated in the heat.   7. Having prepared for the winter, the family was able to survive on their canned fruits and jams. The canned fruits and jams, having been prepared in the summer, helped the family survive in the winter.   8. Sobbing and wailing, many survivors were located by the search party. Because the survivors were sobbing and wailing, the search party was able to locate many of them.   9. Sitting on the beach, Martin perceived the waves as huge. Because Martin was sitting on the beach, the waves seemed huge to him.
10. After carefully reading over the diary, it is important to revise it for gaps and inconsistencies. After carefully reading over the diary, the author should revise it for gaps and inconsistencies.   After it is read over, it should be revised for gaps and inconsistencies.

ACTIVITY 3 — listening/speaking
[60 minutes/homework]

Activity 3 is a good homework assignment following Exercise 5 on SB page 305. In this activity students listen to their choice of an audiobook or book-on-tape, identify one or two descriptive passages, and write down the examples of reduced adverbial clauses they hear.

1. Read the directions as a class.
2. If time allows, read a descriptive passage from a book of fiction and ask students to write down any reduced adverb clause they hear. Compare notes as a class.
3. Have students, for homework, go to the library and check out an audiobook and listen to at least one chapter of it. Ask them to choose one or two descriptive passages, and write down the examples of reduced adverbial clauses they hear.
4. During the next class, have several volunteers share their lists with the class.

ACTIVITY 4 — research on the web
[60 minutes]

In this activity students research the California Gold Rush on the Internet, and then write a short fictional story about the life of a miner. It is a good follow-up to the work students do in Exercise 3 on SB page 303.

1. Discuss what students know about the California Gold Rush. Talk about any books or movies they have seen that portray the lives of gold miners during that time.
2. Read the directions as a class.

3. Have students research the California Gold Rush on the Internet and download several articles on when it happened, who was involved, what challenges were encountered, what successes were achieved, etc.
4. Ask students to write a short fictional description of a miner's life during that time. Encourage them to use as many adverb clauses of time as they can.
5. During the next class, have students exchange papers with a partner, and read and comment on them.
6. Ask several volunteers to read their writings to the class, and discuss.

ACTIVITY 5 — reflection
[60 minutes/homework]

In Activity 5 students edit an essay they have written in the past, reducing adverb clauses and paying attention to punctuation. This activity is a very effective homework or in-class assignment after Exercise 7 on SB page 307.

Make sure students have a formerly written essay or provide one for them before you begin this task. With the class, read the directions and sample of an essay on SB pages 312–313.

■ STEP 1

1. Read the examples of adverbial clauses and the sampled reductions. Ask students to suggest other phrasings. Ask students whether each underlined clause is an adverbial clause of *time* or *cause*.
2. Have students underline adverbial clauses in an essay of their own.

■ STEP 2
Have students work independently to reduce or reorder the clauses in their essays, reducing adverb clauses and paying attention to punctuation. Tell them to follow the same procedure they followed in the example with their own essays: determine what kind of adverb clause each underlined clause is, and then rephrase them.

■ STEP 3

1. Ask several volunteers to share their work with the class, and discuss.
2. Collect papers from students and give them feedback on their rewrites.

PREPOSITION CLUSTERS

- Use verbs with the correct preposition clusters
- Use adjectives with the correct preposition clusters
- Use common multiword preposition clusters
- Use preposition clusters to introduce a topic or identify a source

OPENING TASK

■ STEP 1

Look at the following pictures and captions describing immigrants and refugees from around the world.

Guatemalans fleeing to Mexico during civil war

Turks displaced to Europe after earthquake

■ STEP 2

Now think about one group of refugees or immigrants that has recently settled in your native country or in a country you are familiar with. Think about the circumstances surrounding the group's departure from their homeland and present living conditions in the new country. Jot down notes about these circumstances in the chart below.

Immigrant or Refugee Group _____	
1. Why they departed from their country	
2. What they hope for in their new country	
3. What group (if any) they are at odds with in the new country	
4. What aspects of life they are unaccustomed to in the new country	
5. Who they associate with in the new country	
6. What geographical areas they are attracted to in the new country	
7. How their contributions result in a richer cultural heritage for the new country	

■ STEP 3

Discuss the results of your brainstorming with your classmates.

UNIT OVERVIEW

This unit looks at preposition clauses: verb + specific preposition clusters, adjective + preposition clusters, and preposition clusters used to introduce a topic or identify a source. Please note that due to its length, this unit has been divided into three lesson plans. To review this unit more quickly, review focus charts and have students complete the first exercise after each chart to observe students' grasp of the grammar topics.

GRAMMAR NOTE

Prepositions can be one of the most difficult language structures to master in English. Unit 17 assumes that students have already learned how to locate objects in space (e.g., *The pencil is on the desk*) and have learned various peculiarities of prepositions (viz., that they are deleted in sentences such as *She went home*). The focus of this unit, instead, is on the co-occurrence of prepositions with verbs, adjectives, and nouns in speech and writing.

UNIT GOALS

Some instructors may want to review the goals listed on Student Book (SB) page 314 after completing the Opening Task so that students understand what they should know by the end of the unit. These goals can also be reviewed at the end of the unit when students are more familiar with the grammar terminology.

OPENING TASK [20 minutes]

The purpose of the Opening Task is to create a context in which students will need to use preposition clusters to make observations and draw conclusions about groups of people who move from one country to another. The problem-solving format is designed to show the teacher how well the students can produce the target structures implicitly and spontaneously

when they are engaged in a communicative task. For a more complete discussion of the purpose of the Opening Task, see To the Teacher, Lesson Planner (LP) page xxii.

Setting Up the Task

■ STEP 1

Ask students to look at and describe the photos. What country might these people be from? What is happening in the photos? Listen to the way students use prepositions as they share their knowledge of immigration in small groups.

Conducting the Task

Bring in additional photos from magazines or books. Encourage students to tell their classmates what they know about these different groups.

■ STEP 2

1. Read the directions for Step 2.
2. Have students work independently to write notes about the circumstances under which groups of refugees or immigrants left their countries, and what their present living conditions are like in their current country.

■ STEP 3

Ask students to work in small groups to discuss what they have written.

Closing the Task

Ask volunteers to share the results of their group with the class. Don't worry about accuracy at this point, though you may want to take notes of errors in meaning, form, or use in order to focus on those problems later. Take note of the way students use prepositions as they share their knowledge of immigration issues.

CULTURE NOTE

Be aware that this topic may be sensitive for certain students, especially those who are from war-torn areas or from regions of profound poverty. Also be aware that certain stereotypes may be stated, which you and other students may not agree with. Use this discussion as an opportunity for greater communication and understanding among students as you and the class discuss reasons for emigration and immigration.

GRAMMAR NOTE

Typical student errors (form)

- Using the wrong preposition in adjective + preposition clusters: —e.g.,* *We're unfamiliar about that topic.* (See Focus 5.)
- Using the wrong preposition in multiword preposition clusters: —e.g.,* *The Democrats were in favor for the health care plan.* (See Focus 6.)

Typical student errors (use)

- Using the wrong preposition in verb + preposition clusters: —e.g.,* *She did not want to deal to the screaming child.* (See Focus 1.)
- Omitting the preposition in verb + preposition clusters: —e.g.,* *You can rely me.* (See Focus 1.)
- Omitting *for* in verb + *for* clusters: —e.g., * *I was hoping better weather today.* (See Focus 4.)

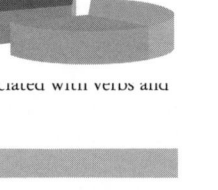
form

FOCUS 1 | Verb + Preposition Clusters

Preposition clusters are prepositions that follow and are closely associated with verbs and adjectives or prepositions that appear in common phrases.

EXAMPLES	EXPLANATION
(a) Refugees **differ from** immigrants in that they have not left their homelands by choice.	These verb + preposition clusters must be followed by noun phrases (a) or gerunds (b).
(b) Refugees usually **plan on** returning to their homeland as soon as the hostilities are over.	(Gerunds will be covered more fully in Unit 18.)

Other examples of verb + preposition clusters are:

consist of	count on
hope for	deal with

EXERCISE 1

There are four verb + preposition clusters in the chart prompts in the Opening Task. Can you identify them? Now, use your notes from the chart and write four sentences about the immigrant or refugee group you described, using verb and preposition clusters.

Example: *The Vietnamese departed from Vietnam in order to find better economic and political conditions.*

EXERCISE 2

The following incomplete sentences contain verb + preposition clusters. Complete them in two ways, with a noun phrase and with a gerund.

Example: The new parents marveled at
- the beauty of their child. (noun phrase)
- seeing their son for the first time. (gerund)

1. A healthy diet consists of
   - a carefully monitored diet
   - eating lots of fruits and vegetables

2. The plan called for
   - billions of dollars in funds
   - entering the country from the north

3. Does anyone object to
   - a drink on the way home ?
   - leaving the party early ?

4. Ever since I was a child, I have counted on
   - your love and support
   - becoming a doctor

5. As it is very late, you can dispense with
   - the introduction
   - unloading the cargo

6. After the accident, Jaime withdrew from
   - his friends
   - playing sports

7. Will the president succeed in
   - the fight against drugs ?
   - winning the election ?

8. The protesters were demonstrating against
   - the war
   - opening the new nuclear plant

9. Why can't she distinguish between
   - the two girls ?
   - helping and smothering her friends ?

10. I don't agree with the politician who believes in
    - the amendment
    - banning citizens' possession of weapons

ANSWER KEY

Exercise 1 The verb + preposition clusters are: (1) *depart from* (2) *hope for* (3) *be at odds with* (4) *be unaccustomed to* (5) *associate with* (6) *be attracted to* (7) *result in* Sentences will vary. Possible answers are: (1) They *departed from* their country because of an ongoing civil war. (2) They *hoped for* an opportunity to live freely. (3) Their political beliefs *are at odds with* the current government. (4) They *are unaccustomed to* speaking about the government in public. (5) They *associate* mostly *with* themselves.

(6) They *are attracted to* the opportunities in that country. (7) Their refined aesthetic sense has *resulted in* many contributions to the arts.

Exercise 2 Answers will vary. Possible answers are shown above.

FOCUS 1 [10 minutes]

Focus 1 describes how verb + preposition clusters must be followed by noun phrases and gerunds.

1. **Lead-in:** Ask student pairs to brainstorm any verbs that they know that must be followed by a preposition. Students might mention verbs in the focus chart as well as some of their own.
2. Call on one student from each pair to provide examples.
3. Ask volunteers to read the focus chart.

METHODOLOGY NOTE

Note that some of the verbs by themselves are **transitive** (e.g., *plan, count*) and others are **intransitive** (e.g., *differ, consist*). Review this concept with students.

EXERCISE 1 [10 minutes]

Exercise 1 asks students to identify the verb + preposition clusters in the Opening Task chart, and then write sentences about the group they described in that task, using verb + preposition clusters.

1. Read the directions and example as a class. What is the verb + preposition cluster?
2. Have students work independently to write sentences about the group they described in that task, using verb + preposition clusters.
3. Review answers as a class. See possible answers on LP page 316.

 For more practice, use *Grammar Dimension 4* Workbook page 150, Exercise 1.

EXPANSION [60 minutes/homework]

In Activity 3 (listening/writing) on SB page 329 students watch an animal nature show and jot down examples of preposition clusters they hear. This activity makes a good homework assignment following Exercise 1.

EXERCISE 2 [15 minutes]

In Exercise 2 students complete sentences in two ways, with a noun phrase and a gerund, applying what they have learned in Focus 1.

1. Read the directions and example as a class. Ask students to suggest other noun phrases and gerunds to complete the example, and write these on the board.
2. Have students work independently to complete the exercise. Remind them to complete the sentences in two ways.
3. Have students share and discuss their sentences with a partner.
4. Ask volunteers to read their partners' sentences to the class, and discuss these as a class. See possible answers on LP page 316.

 For more practice, use *Grammar Dimension 4* Workbook page 151, Exercise 2.

FOCUS 2 Verb + *With* Clusters

EXAMPLES

(a) The laborers **consulted with** their union.

(b) They decided not to **cooperate with** management.

EXPLANATION

Verb + *with* clusters show association between or among people.

Other examples of verb + *with* **clusters are:**

associate with	join with	unite with
deal with	side with	

EXERCISE 3

Ask and answer *should* questions with a partner. Use the subject in the first column and then make sentences with the verb + preposition clusters and the objects in the second and third columns

Example: Q: Should homeowners deal with realtors to sell their homes?

A: No, they shouldn't deal with realtors; they should try to sell the houses themselves.

Subject	Verb + Preposition	Object
1. homeowners	associate with	their children
2. criminals	cooperate with	students
3. the rich	consult with	ophthalmologists
4. parents	deal with	the police
5. patients	join with	realtors
6. young people	side with	gangs
7. teachers	unite with	the poor

FOCUS 3 Verb + *From* Clusters

EXAMPLES

(a) The garage was **detached from** the house.

(b) Rice pudding **differs from** bread pudding.

EXPLANATION

Verb + *from* clusters imply separation.

Other examples of verb + *from* **clusters are:**

abstain		emerge		prevent		retire	
desist	from	escape	from	prohibit	from	separate	from
deviate		flee		recede		shrink	
dissent		migrate		recoil		withdraw	

EXERCISE 4

Fill in one of the verbs + *from*, using the examples above, in each blank below. You may need to change the verb form in some examples.

1. Certain groups follow restrictive dietary laws. For example, Orthodox Jews (a) __abstain from__ pork and shellfish. Sometimes these and other groups who (b) __deviate from__ the status quo or (c) __differ from__ the norm are considered strange by outsiders but extremely religious by those from within the same community.

2. Refugees come to a foreign country to live for many different reasons. They want to (a) __escape from__ persecution, war, disaster, or epidemics. Certain Southeast Asians have (b) __emerged from__ tragic conditions in their native lands but have become successful in their new homes around the world.

3. Some newcomers to a country go through culture shock. This phenomenon makes some people (a) __shrink from__ social relationships. Because of depression, they also sometimes (b) __recoil from__ responsibilities. They may even (c) __withdraw from__ psychological help because they are not used to dealing with doctors for psychological problems.

4. Mr. Johnson is getting older. His hair (a) __is receding from__ his forehead. Next year he plans to (b) __retire from__ his job.

ANSWER KEY

Exercise 3   Answers will vary. Possible answers are: 2. Should criminals cooperate with the police to reduce their jail terms?   3. Shouldn't the rich unite with the poor in the fight against AIDS? 4. Should parents side with their children under all circumstances?   5. Should patients consult with ophthalmologists about their eyes?   6. Should young people join with gangs who are breaking rules of law and order?   7. Should teachers associate with students outside of class?

Exercise 4   Answers will vary. Possible answers are listed above.

FOCUS 2 [10 minutes]

1. **Lead-in:** Read the explanation; then ask two volunteers to read the two example sentences.

2. Ask another volunteer to read the other examples shown in the vocabulary box.

3. Ask students to give other example sentences using these examples, and write these on the board.

4. Encourage students to ask questions about anything they do not understand.

EXERCISE 3 [15 minutes]

In Exercise 3 students apply what they have just learned in Focus 2 by asking and responding to *should* questions.

1. Read the directions and examples as a class. Ask students to offer other possible responses to the example question.

2. Have students work in pairs, taking turns asking and answering the questions.

3. Have pairs share and discuss their sentences with another pair.

4. Ask representative of groups to share their questions and answers with the class. See possible answers on LP page 318.

 For more practice, use *Grammar Dimension 4* Workbook page 152, Exercise 3.

EXPANSION [15 minutes]

For additional practice with verb + *with* clusters, ask students to create seven new sentences using the seven verb + preposition clusters from Exercise 3.

FOCUS 3 [10 minutes]

1. **Lead-in:** Ask one student to read examples (a) and (b) and the explanation for the class.

2. Ask students to give synonyms for the phrases in the vocabulary box—e.g., *abstain from* = refrain from, *desist from* = discontinue, *detach from* = separate from, *deviate from* = diverge from.

3. As with Focus 2, you could give (or elicit) additional examples related to your class or to an academic context: *The student's ideas **differed from** the teacher's.*

4. Encourage students to ask questions about anything they do not understand.

EXERCISE 4 [15 minutes]

In Exercise 4 students complete sentences using one of the verbs + *from* from Focus 3.

1. Have students work independently to complete the sentences using one of the verbs + *from* from Focus 3. Encourage them to use past, present, and infinitive verb forms to fill in the blanks.

2. Have students share their sentences with a partner.

3. Ask volunteers to share their sentences with the class. See possible answers on LP page 318.

 For more practice, use *Grammar Dimension 4* Workbook page 152, Exercise 4.

FOCUS 4 — Verb + *For* Clusters

meaning

EXAMPLES	EXPLANATION
(a) I **long for** a cigarette every morning. (b) I **pray for** the strength to stop smoking.	Several verb + *for* clusters relate to desire or need.

Other examples of verb + *for* clusters are:

ask for	thirst for	hope for	yearn for	wish for

EXERCISE 5

Use several of the verb + preposition clusters above to describe desires for yourself or someone you love.

Example: I hope for better health for my whole family.

EXERCISE 6

Select one or two of the groups of preposition clusters below. Create one to two short paragraphs for each group of verb + preposition clusters and then share the results with your class.

Example: rebel at, shudder at, jeer at

The people held up their fists and **jeered at** *the tanks as they moved into the city. They had been* **rebelling at** *following the central government for the past 25 years. They* **shuddered at** *the thought of military rule in their own quiet neighborhoods.*

1. talk of, think of, disapprove of
2. listen to, object to, reply to
3. plan on, embark on, live on
4. believe in, persist in, result in
5. look at, laugh at, point at

EXERCISE 7

Study the chart on the next page about immigration movements to the United States. Use different verbs + *for* to describe why the different groups came to the United States.

Example: Cubans *The Cubans longed for freedom in a non-Communist country.*

1. Irish
2. Germans
3. Norwegians
4. Poles
5. Jews
6. Austrians
7. Italians
8. Mexicans
9. Haitians
10. Vietnamese

What other immigrant groups are coming to the United States today? Why?

MAJOR IMMIGRATION MOVEMENTS TO THE UNITED STATES

Group	When	Number	Why
Irish	1840s and 1850s	About 1½ million	Famine resulting from potato crop failure
Germans	1840s to 1880s	About 4 million	Severe economic depression and unemployment; political unrest, and failure of liberal revolutionary movement
Danes, Norwegians, Swedes	1870s to 1900s	About 1½ million	Poverty; shortage of farmland
Poles	1880s to 1920s	About 1 million	Poverty; political repression; cholera epidemics
Jews from Eastern Europe	1880s to 1920s	About 2½ million	Religious persecution
Austrians, Czechs, Hungarians, Slovaks	1880s to 1920s	About 4 million	Poverty; overpopulation
Italians	1880s to 1920s	About 4½ million	Poverty; overpopulation
Mexicans	1910 to 1920s 1950s to present	About 700,000 About 2 million	Mexican Revolution of 1920; low wages and unemployment Poverty; unemployment
Cubans	1960s to present	About 700,000	Communist takeover in 1959
Dominicans, Haitians, Jamaicans	1970s and 1990s	About 900,000	Poverty; unemployment
Vietnamese	1970s and 1990s	About 500,000	Vietnam War 1957 to 1975; Communist takeover
Iranians	1980s to 2000s	About 200,000	Political unrest; religious persecution
Chinese	1990s to 2000s	About 600,000	Poverty; Communist takeover of Hong Kong

Adapted from U.S. Immigration and Naturalization Service and Bureau of U.S. Citizenship and Immigration Service sources.

Exercise 5 Answers will vary.

Exercise 6 Answers will vary. Possible answers are: 1. The group talked of forming a committee to help the homeless. They thought of several projects they could pursue. Most disapproved of distributing "free handouts." 2. She listened to all of the arguments against the new shopping mall. She objected to many of them. That is why she decided to reply to the most offensive ones with a series of letters to the mayor. 3. We are planning on a South Seas trip, which we will embark on in the middle of February. We will live on our boat for the next few months, only getting off at major ports. 4. I believe in equal rights for women. I will persist in supporting the Equal Rights Amendment until it is passed. This will hopefully result in better living and working conditions for future generations of women. 5. We looked at the funny antics of the clown. My daughter laughed at his big, red nose. My son pointed at his very large black shoes.

Exercise 7 Answers will vary. Possible answers are: 1. The Irish longed for a land where they could raise good crops. 2. The Germans wished for better economic times. 3. The Norwegians yearned for good farmland. 4. The Poles thirsted for a place with no political repression. 5. The Jews prayed for a place where they would have religious freedom. 6. The Austrians hoped for a less populated land. 7. The Italians prayed for an escape from poverty. 8. The Mexicans longed for a peaceful existence. 9. The Haitians thirsted for employment opportunities. 10. The Vietnamese hoped for an escape from the war.

FOCUS 4 [10 minutes]

Focus 4 examines the meaning of verb + *for* preposition clusters.

1. **Lead-in:** Point out that in each of these examples, *for* could be replaced by the expressions *to get* or *to have*. For example, *I yearn to have a cigarette every morning. I wish to get a new job.* As with Focuses 2 and 3, you could provide additional examples related to your class or to an academic context: *After two hours, the students long for a break.*
2. Answer any questions students might have.

EXERCISE 5 [15 minutes]

Students use verb + preposition clusters to describe their desires for themselves and their loved ones.

1. Read the directions and example as a class.
2. Ask students to work independently to write their sentences.
3. Have students share their sentences with a partner.
4. Ask volunteers to share their sentences with the class, and discuss them.

EXERCISE 6 [20 minutes]

One of the best ways to teach preposition clusters is by grouping together verbs that take the same preposition. This exercise contains several common verb + preposition combinations.

1. Read the directions and example as a class.
2. Ask students if they can determine the general meanings of *at, of, to, on,* and *in* in each item group. They should induce meanings such as: *of + concerning, to + towards, on + entering on, in + within some type of limits, at + toward or in the direction of.*

3. Ask students to work independently to write their paragraphs.
4. Have students share their paragraphs with a partner.
5. Ask volunteers to share their paragraphs with the class, and discuss these. See possible answers on LP page 320.

METHODOLOGY NOTE

When grading compositions, be selective in your grading by ignoring all grammar errors except the targeted grammar point (in Exercise 6, the preposition clusters). In this way, students will know that they should focus on mastering this specific structure at this time. Too many various grammar-focused corrections are often overwhelming and discouraging for students trying to communicate their ideas on topics important to them (such as immigration).

 For more practice, use *Grammar Dimension 4* Workbook page 154, Exercise 5.

EXPANSION [30 minutes/homework]

In Activity 2 (writing) on SB page 328 students respond to the inscription at the base of the Statue of Liberty by writing a short composition in which they use at least five preposition clusters. This activity is a good follow-up to Exercise 6, either as homework or as a class activity.

EXERCISE 7 (OPTIONAL) [30 minutes]

In Exercise 7 students describe the reasons why different groups immigrated to the United States, applying the principles stated in Focus 4.

1. Read the directions and example as a class.
2. Have students work in pairs, taking turns making sentences using the information in the chart.
3. Ask the class to brainstorm other groups that are immigrating to the United States today. Write these names on the board—e.g., Russians, Tibetans, Kosovics, etc.
4. Collaboratively write a paragraph about what these groups *yearn for, pray for, ask for, thirst for, hope for, wish for,* or *long for* in leaving their native countries. See possible answers on LP page 320.

FOCUS 5 — Adjective + Preposition Clusters

EXAMPLES	EXPLANATION
(a) The house stands **adjacent to** the river.	Adjective + preposition clusters
(b) The town is **dependent on** fishing.	
(c) We **are burdened with** high taxes.	*Be* + adjective (*-ed*) + preposition clusters
(d) Miwa **is accustomed to** eating three meals a day.	

Other examples of adjective + preposition clusters are:

free / immune / safe } from	eager / homesick / sorry } for	compatible / unfamiliar / content } with
expert / good / swift } at	proficient / rich / successful } in	careless / happy / enthusiastic } about
ignorant / afraid / proud } of		

EXERCISE 8

Create your own questions for the following answers, using two different adjective + preposition phrases from the chart above.

Examples: A healthy mathematician   *Who is **free from** disease and **good at** math?*

A sloppy executive   *Who is **careless about** his appearance and **successful in** his job?*

1. A calm athlete

   Who is free from stress and expert at sports?

2. A claustrophobic politician

   Who is afraid of closed spaces and is also successful in politics?

3. An anxious addict

   Who is concerned about too many things and addicted to drugs?

4. A clean mechanic

   Who is free from dirt and expert at fixing cars?

5. A weary worrier

   Who is tired of work and concerned about everything?

6. A joyful seamstress

   Who is happy about life and good at sewing?

7. A repentant runner

   Who is sorry for what she did wrong and swift at running?

8. (Your suggestion)
   (Answers will vary.)

EXERCISE 9

Discuss what the following organizations are *interested in, concerned about, accustomed to, committed to, dedicated to*, and/or *preoccupied with*. Also, come up with another organization to discuss.

Example: The World Bank

   The World Bank is interested in aiding the world's poor.

1. Greenpeace
2. European Community
3. The Peace Corps
4. The United Nations
5. The Red Cross
6. The Red Crescent
7. UNICEF
8. The Fulbright Program
9. Amnesty International
10. (Your suggestion)

ANSWER KEY

Exercise 8   Answers will vary. Possible answers are listed above.

Exercise 9   Answers will vary. Possible answers are: 1. Greenpeace is interested in saving the environment.   2. The European Community is dedicated to regulating the finances of the European nations.   3. The Peace Corps is committed to helping underdeveloped nations.   4. The United Nations is concerned about world peace.   5. The Red Cross is accustomed to providing medical help during times of war, natural disaster, or famine.   6. The Red Crescent is committed to giving medical help to people in the Muslim world.   7. UNICEF is dedicated to curing children's diseases. 8. The Fulbright Program is preoccupied with giving opportunities to scholars to share their knowledge in other parts of the world.   9. Amnesty International is dedicated to exposing and stopping inhumane activities throughout the world.   10. (Answers will vary.)

FOCUS 5 [20 minutes]

Focus 5 explains adjective + preposition clusters. It includes a long list of these clusters, which can serve as a good reference tool for students.

1. **Lead-in:** Write the following statements on the board:
   (a) *I am homesick for my birthplace.*
   (b) *I am confident in my research skills.*
   (c) *I am close to my parents.*
   (d) *I am interested in reading fiction.*
   (e) *I am satisfied with my English ability.*

2. Then, write a 4-column chart on the board:

Statement	Usually	Sometimes	Rarely
a			
b			
c			
d			
e			

1. Conduct a short survey with the class. Read the statements and ask students to raise their hands to indicate the answers *usually, sometimes,* or *rarely.* Tally the results in the chart you drew on the board by adding slash marks to represent the opinions.

2. Ask volunteers to summarize the results: *Our class is usually homesick for our birthplaces, Our class is only sometimes confident in our research skills,* etc.

3. Ask students to look at the five sentences and notice what follows the verb. They should note that there are two types of adjectives—common ones like *close* and others derived from participles like *interested.*

4. Ask volunteers to read examples (a–d) aloud.

5. Ask the class to read the list of other examples, in the box, silently.

EXERCISE 8 [20 minutes]

In Exercise 8 students engage in an activity where they create questions for answers they are given, using two different adjective + preposition phrases from Focus 5.

1. Read the directions as a class. Ask two volunteers to read the two examples. Ask students to identify the adjective and the preposition in each.

2. Have students work in pairs. Each person should write a list of questions for the answers given, and then take turns asking and answering them.

3. Ask volunteer pairs to share their questions with the class. See possible answers on LP page 322.

 For more practice, use *Grammar Dimension 4* Workbook page 154, Exercise 6.

EXERCISE 9 (OPTIONAL) [25 minutes]

In Exercise 9 students discuss various international organizations, using adjective + preposition clusters explained in Focus 5.

1. Read the directions and example as a class. Ask volunteers to suggest other sentences about the World Bank, such as *The World Bank is dedicated to helping poor people around the world.*

2. If students are unfamiliar with these organizations, give them a few hints. Write, in random order, the following nouns and phrases on the board and ask students to match the noun with the appropriate organization and create a sentence describing the organization's main purpose: *stopping inhumane activities, curing sick children, working for world peace, regulating finances, protecting the environment, providing medical help, helping underdeveloped nations, funding opportunities for scholars.* (Example: environment + Greenpeace, *Greenpeace is interested in saving the environment.*)

3. Have students work in small groups, taking turns creating sentences using adjective + preposition clusters.

4. Ask representatives of groups to share two of their best sentences and one of their suggestions. Discuss these with the class. See possible answers on LP page 322.

 For more practice, use *Grammar Dimension 4* Workbook page 155, Exercise 7.

EXPANSION [20 minutes]

For more practice with adjective + preposition clusters:

1. Have students work in small groups.

2. Write these additional adjective + preposition combinations on the board: *capable of, certain of, different from, famous for, faithful to, fond of, guilty of, jealous of, popular with, ready for, superior to,* and *useful to.*

3. Ask groups to create five or six more statements about well-known people using the clusters on the board.

4. Ask representatives of groups to share two of their best sentences with the class, and discuss.

FOCUS 6 | Multiword Preposition Clusters

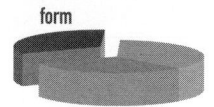

form

Some preposition clusters consist of three or more words.

EXAMPLES	EXPLANATIONS
(a) Some refugee groups are **at odds with** immigrants from other countries.	Multiword preposition clusters follow this pattern: *preposition + (article) noun + preposition*.
(b) **In case of** an emergency, please call campus security.	Many clusters use *in* or *on* as the first preposition and *of* as the second preposition.

Common multiword clusters:

in + noun + *of*	*on* + noun + *of*	*in* + *the* + noun + *of*	*on* + *the* + noun + *of*
in case of	on account of	in the course of	on the advice of
in charge of	on behalf of	in the event of	on the basis of
in place of	on top of	in the habit of	on the part of
in lieu of	on grounds of	in the name of	on the strength of
in favor of		in the process of	on the face of

Less regular combinations:

by means of	in return for	at odds with	with the exception of
with respect to	in addition to	for the sake of	

EXERCISE 10

Write *in (the)* or *on (the)* in the following blanks; the first one has been done for you.

Example: _On the_ basis of the evidence, the defendant was acquitted.

1. _____In_____ case of an emergency, duck under your desks and cover your heads.

2. _____On_____ account of his great skill, he completed the task with ease.

3. _____On the_____ advice of my physician, I must take these pills and get plenty of rest.

4. I have decided to buy the warehouse _____on the_____ strength of expert opinion.

5. _____In the_____ event of an earthquake, do not panic.

6. She wants a divorce _____on_____ grounds of mental cruelty.

7. He will pay the bail _____in_____ lieu of staying in jail.

8. She is _____in the_____ habit of joking when she should be serious.

9. _____On_____ behalf of the committee, I would like to thank you for all of your work.

10. _____In the_____ course of the evening, everyone laughed and had a good time.

EXERCISE 11

Working with a partner, fill in the following blanks with the expressions below. Compare your answers with those of your classmates.

in the habit of	with reference to	for the sake of
as a consequence of	with the purpose of	in lieu of
for lack of	with an eye to	for fear of
on account of	in addition to	

Example: _With reference to_ your question, many Afghans are living in Pakistan and Iran.

1. The United States is _____ turning back many Mexicans from its southern border.

2. Bulgarians of Turkish descent are emigrating from Bulgaria _____ reuniting with their families in Turkey.

3. European Jews and North American Jews have inhabited Israel _____ recreating a Jewish homeland.

4. _____ economic incentives, many British have been lured to move to New Zealand.

5. Indonesians live in tents and makeshift huts _____ funds to rebuild their homes after the tsunami.

6. Salvadoreans do not want to return to El Salvador from the United States _____ encountering dangerous gangs and sexual discrimination.

7. After 1975 many Cambodians escaped into Thailand _____ humane treatment.

8. _____ Moroccans and Tunisians, Senegalese have immigrated to Italy to find work.

9. _____ starvation, Nigerians, Ugandans, Sudanese, and Chadian have fled to other African countries.

10. _____ staying in Romania, many Romanians of Hungarian descent are moving to Hungary.

ANSWER KEY

Exercise 11 Answers may vary. Possible answers are: 1. in the habit of 2. with the purpose of/with an eye to 3. for the sake of/with the purpose of/with an eye to 4. On account of/As a consequence of 5. for lack of 6. for the sake of/with an eye to 7. for lack of 8. In addition to 9. On account of/As a consequence of 10. In lieu of

FOCUS 6 [15 minutes]

Focus 6 examines preposition clusters that contain three or more words.

1. **Lead-in:** Dictate the following sentences to your students:
   (a) *In case of emergency, leave the building through the rear exit.*
   (b) *On behalf of John, we want to thank you for being here.*
   (c) *In the event of an earthquake, do not use the elevator.*
   (d) *On the advice of Dr. Smith, you should take your pills.*
2. Ask students to underline the multiword preposition clusters in each sentence.
3. Ask them to describe how they are similar and different.
4. Ask them to read the columns in the box silently for more examples.
5. Answer any questions students might have.

EXERCISE 10 [20 minutes]

Students continue correcting participle errors in Exercise 10.

1. Read the directions and example as a class. Ask students to identify the multiword preposition cluster in the example.
2. Have students work in pairs to complete the sentences with the correct preposition cluster.
3. Have students work in pairs to rewrite the sentences.
4. Have student pairs circle the completed cluster in each sentence and together write a new sentence using that cluster.

5. Students should take turns reading new sentences to the class. The class should make suggestions if the use of the cluster could be improved.

For more practice, use *Grammar Dimension 4* Workbook page 156, Exercise 8.

EXPANSION [30 minutes]

In Activity 1 (listening/writing) on SB page 328 students hear about the administration of President John F. Kennedy, and then answer questions using preposition clusters. This activity is a good follow-up to Exercise 10.

EXERCISE 11 (OPTIONAL) [20 minutes]

Students complete sentences using multiword preposition clusters they encountered in Focus 6.

1. Read the directions and example as a class. Could any other cluster from the list be used in the example, rather than *with reference to?* (*no*)
2. Ask students to work independently to write their sentences.
3. Have students share their sentences with a partner.
4. Ask volunteers to share their sentences with the class, and discuss these. See possible answers on LP page 324.

For more practice, use *Grammar Dimension 4* Workbook page 156, Exercise 9.

EXPANSION [20 minutes]

For additional practice:

1. Have students work independently to create at least five original sentences using the expressions in the box in Focus 6.
2. Have them exchange papers with a partner.
3. Randomly ask one member of a pair to read one sentence to the rest of the class.

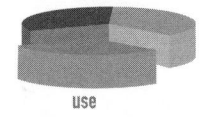

FOCUS 7 | Preposition Clusters: Introducing a Topic/Identifying a Source

use

EXAMPLES	EXPLANATIONS
(a) **Pertaining/Relating to** immigrant quotas, the United States has tightened its restrictions in recent years. (b) **Speaking about/of** persecution, certain immigrant groups have endured more than others. (c) **With respect/reference to** culture shock, most immigrant groups experience it in one form or another.	Some preposition clusters can introduce a topic.
(d) **Based on/upon** immigration statistics, more men than women emigrate from their native countries. (e) **According to** Professor Herbert, many immigrants decide to return to their native countries after a few years.	Other preposition clusters can identify a source.

EXERCISE 12

Complete the following sentences.

Example: Based on the weather report, _hurricane conditions will prevail for this week_ .

1. According to scientists, _the ozone layer is quickly depleting_ .
2. With respect to our solar system, _we are discovering new planet-like objects beyond Pluto_
3. With reference to recent political events, _something needs to be done about settling racial tensions_
4. Speaking about discrimination, _laws should be passed to protect the civil rights of all citizens_
5. Relating to my last conversation with my family, _I have decided to spend the summer in Paris_
6. Based upon my own observations, _he will never make a good baseball player_
7. According to the dictionary, _the word advisor has two spellings: a-d-v-i-s-o-r and a-d-v-i-s-e-r_
8. Pertaining to the death penalty, _I don't believe it is ever justified_ .
9. With respect to the students in this class, _we are all very good at taking tests_ .
10. Speaking of good movies, _did you see the new Spanish film yet?_ .

EXERCISE 13

Supply the appropriate prepositions for the blanks in the following passage.

People have migrated (1) _from_ one country to another throughout time. The first humans emerged (2) _from_ Africa and spread throughout the globe. A momentous movement of "barbarians" (consisting (3) _of_ such groups as the Huns, Goths, Visigoths, and Vandals) departed (4) _from_ Central Asia and were successful (5) _at_ toppling the Roman Empire. The Islamic Moors crossed over (6) _to_ Arabia into Europe, Central Asia, and the Balkans. The Vikings migrated (7) _from_ Norway and Sweden into Russia.

Recent migrations include a large number of Europeans and Africans moving (8) _to_ North and South America, Indians moving (9) _to_ all parts of the former British Empire, Chinese settling (10) _in_ Southeast Asia, and Mexicans crossing (11) _over_ to the United States.

Why do people migrate (12) _from_ one region (13) _to_ another? They may flee (14) _from_ serious environmental conditions like earthquakes and floods or dangerous political situations like wars and rebellions. They may be in search (15) _of_ better economic conditions. Or on the advice (16) _of_ family or friends, they decide that a new location will be better for raising a family or for retirement.

According (17) _to_ experts, several barriers limit migration. People may be ignorant (18) _of_ what exists in other places. They may be accustomed (19) _to_ their own homes and find it too difficult to leave. They may be unfamiliar (20) _with_ foreign immigration policies. In addition (21) _to_ these factors, there are other personal characteristics which limit migration, including age, gender, and education. For example, a well-educated young male differs (22) _from_ a poor uneducated female in his ability and willingness to move (23) _from_ one country to another.

ANSWER KEY

Exercise 12 Answers will vary. Possible answers are listed above.

FOCUS 7 [25 minutes]

Focus 7 explains the uses of preposition clusters that introduce a topic or identify a source.

1. **Lead-in:** Explain to students that the preposition cluster *speaking about/of* is often used to introduce a topic.
2. Explain that you will play a simple game with them in which you will talk about a particular topic and you will have them interrupt you using one of the expressions from Focus 7, followed by a question. For example, you will say: *The weather has been very hot today.* And a student will reply: *Speaking of/about the weather, hasn't this been a hot autumn in general?*
3. Practice with a few more examples:
   (a) *I plan to assign a lot of homework tonight.*
   (b) *I very much enjoy going to the movies.*
   (c) *I hope that there won't be much traffic on the way home tonight.*
   (d) *I need to buy some new clothes.*
4. Ask students to read the focus chart and identify other preposition clusters that are used to introduce a topic or to identify a source.
5. Give students a little oral practice in identifying a source by having them report one piece of advice that their mother or father gave to them in the past. For example: *According to my mother, it is not advisable to swim after eating a big meal.* Answer any questions students might have.

EXERCISE 12 [20 minutes]

Students first practice the principles of Focus 7 in a controlled exercise, completing sentences that begin with preposition clusters.

1. Read the directions and example as a class. Ask students to suggest several other possible endings to the example sentence.
2. Have students work independently to complete the sentences.
3. Have them exchange papers with a partner, and review and discuss each other's work.
4. Ask different volunteers to share their answers with the class. See possible answers on LP page 326.

EXPANSION 1 [homework]

For homework, ask students to look for paragraphs in the newspaper (either a current newspaper, one in the library, or one online) that illustrate the various preposition clusters described in this chapter. Ask them to share their results with the class.

EXPANSION 2 [30 minutes/homework]

In Activity 5 (reflection) on SB page 329 students discuss groups of words that derive from similar roots. This activity is a good final activity for the unit, assigned whether as homework or for in-class work after Exercise 12.

EXERCISE 13 (OPTIONAL) [15 minutes]

In Exercise 13 students supply missing prepositions in a passage about migration.

1. Read the directions and example (the first sentence) as a class. Are other prepositions possible here? (*no*)
2. Have students work independently to complete the sentences.
3. Have them exchange papers with a partner, and review and discuss each other's work.
4. Ask volunteers to share their answers with the class. See answers on LP page 326.

 For more practice, use *Grammar Dimension 4 Workbook* page 157, Exercise 10.

EXPANSION [60 minutes/homework]

Activity 4 (research on the web) on SB page 329 has students research definitions of terms that describe the movements of people within a culture and between nations. It is a good follow-up to the work students do in Exercise 13. The activity involves both in-class work and homework.

UNIT GOAL REVIEW [5 minutes]

Ask students to look at the goals on the opening page of the unit again. Refer to the pages of the unit where information on each goal can be found.

 For assessment of Unit 17, use *Grammar Dimensions 4 ExamView®*.

Use Your English

ACTIVITY 1 listening/writing

Listen to the audio and take notes about the administration of President John F. Kennedy, one of the most famous U.S. presidents of the twentieth century. After listening to the audio, answer the following questions, using preposition clusters in each response.

CD2 Track 7

Example: What is one positive cause that JFK contributed to?
He contributed to the establishment of the Peace Corps.

1. What was Kennedy's administration known for?
2. How did he unite with Americans of all colors and religions?
3. What were the elderly happy about?
4. Speaking about school segregation, what did Kennedy do?
5. Who cooperated with local technicians to build roads in Tanganyika, Africa?
6. Who did the United States join with to form the Organization for Economic Cooperation and Development?
7. What were the Latin Americans enthusiastic about in 1962?
8. Why did the United States and Russia consult with each other?

ACTIVITY 2 writing

> Give me your tired, your poor
> Your huddled masses yearning to breathe free,
> The wretched refuse of your teeming shore.
> Send them, the homeless, tempest-tossed to me,
> I lift my lamp beside the golden door!

Do you believe it is possible for countries such as the United States to have an open-door policy? How has the open-door immigration policy of the United States changed over the last few decades? Do you agree or disagree with the changes? Write a short composition on this topic, incorporating at least five preposition clusters you have learned in this unit.

ACTIVITY 3 listening/writing

Watch 15 minutes of a nature TV show or video that describes the life cycles, migration patterns, communication habits, etc. of an animal (for example, polar bear, bumblebee, salmon, jackrabbit, Canada goose). Jot down examples of preposition clusters that you hear.

Example: *Canada geese depart from their homes in the north and fly south for the winter.*

ACTIVITY 4 research on the web

The following terms relate to intercultural contact or movement from, to, or within a country. Find definitions of the following terms on the Internet, using a search engine. Give definitions of these terms while citing your specific sources, using the expression *according to,* for example, "*According to the Internet, a refugee is any uprooted person who has a well-founded fear of persecution for reasons of race, religion, nationality, membership in a particular social group, or political opinion."*

1. refugee
2. emigrant
3. guest worker
4. brain drain
5. multiculturalism
6. political correctness
7. melting pot
8. xenophobia

ACTIVITY 5 reflection

Knowing vocabulary means knowing how different words collocate or group together. With a partner, consider words you encounter in your academic texts and brainstorm:

a. What words depend on this word as a root?

Example: migrate   *migration, migratory, immigration, immigrant*

b. What other words are associated with or co-occur with this word?

Example: migrate   *migrate to, migrate away from*

c. What words are similar to and/or different from this word? Does the word have a synonym or antonym?

Example: migrate   *similar: immigrate, move   different: remain stationary*

USE YOUR ENGLISH

The Use Your English activities at the end of the unit contain situations that should naturally elicit the structures covered in the unit. For a more complete discussion of how to use the Use Your English activities, see To the Teacher, LP page xxvi.

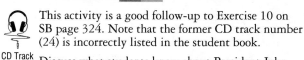

ACTIVITY 1 listening/writing
[30 minutes]

This activity is a good follow-up to Exercise 10 on SB page 324. Note that the former CD track number (24) is incorrectly listed in the student book.

CD Track 7

Discuss what students know about President John F. Kennedy. What did he accomplish during his presidency? How did his administration change the lives of people in the U.S. and abroad?

1. Read the directions and example as a class.
2. Have students listen to the audio once.
3. Ask students to listen again and answer the questions, stopping the audio as needed to write their answers.
4. Ask students to listen to the audio a third time to complete and check their answers.
5. Have students work in small groups to share their answers and then share answers with the class.

VARIATION

Ask students to write a short paragraph about John F. Kennedy's administration based on the audio. Ask them to include at least 3 preposition clusters in their paragraph.

ACTIVITY 2 writing
[30 minutes/homework]

In this activity students respond to questions about U.S. immigration policy and to a portion of the poem ("The New Colossus" by Emma Lazarus) which is inscribed on a plaque inside the base of the Statue of Liberty. This activity is a good follow-up to Exercise 6 on SB page 320, either as homework or as a class activity.

1. Discuss what students know about the Statue of Liberty, and who has visited it. Talk about what it has represented to people. Ask if anyone knows the inscription at its base.
2. Ask a volunteer to read the inscription. Ask another volunteer to read the text that follows.
3. Ask students to work independently to write a short composition in which they address these questions, using at least five preposition clusters.
4. Have students work in small groups, exchange their papers, and discuss them.
5. Ask several volunteers to read their compositions to the class.

ACTIVITY 3 listening/writing
[60 minutes/homework]

This activity makes a good homework assignment following Exercise 1 on SB page 316.

1. Read the directions and example as a class. Ask students to identify the preposition clusters in the example.
2. Have students watch an animal nature show and note the preposition clusters they hear for homework.
3. Have students share their findings in small groups.
4. Ask representatives of groups to share several findings with the class.

ACTIVITY 4 research on the web
[60 minutes/homework]

This is a good follow-up to the work students do in Exercise 13 on SB page 327. The activity involves both in-class work and homework.

1. Divide the class into five or six groups and ask them to find definitions of the eight on the Internet for homework.
   Suggestion: Each group could be assigned a different source—e.g., Internet, dictionary, encyclopedia, classmates, textbooks on immigration, the teacher (you may need to make yourself available during an office hour for this), or their family members.
2. After completing their research, students should form groups and report the information they obtained from different sources according to the sample in the student book.

ACTIVITY 5 reflection
[30 minutes/homework]

This activity is a good final activity for the unit, and can be assigned as homework or for in-class work after Exercise 12 on page 326.

1. Read the directions and examples as a class.
2. Have students work in pairs to identify a word's roots, what words it is associated with, and words that are similar or different.
3. Ask the pairs to share their conclusions with another pair and then with the class.

GERUNDS AND INFINITIVES

UNIT GOALS

- Identify the functions of gerunds and infinitives in a sentence
- Use a variety of gerund and infinitive structures correctly
- Distinguish gerunds from infinitives
- Use *for* with infinitives and *'s* with gerunds
- Use gerunds as objects of prepositions and phrasal verbs

OPENING TASK

Skills and Qualifications

You and a partner have been asked to consider the strengths and weaknesses of the following ten applicants described on the next page for "Altacreat," an artistic community in the northwestern United States designed to provide artistic space for ten artists in residence for periods of up to three months. Specially designed studios inspire "cutting-edge" artistic creations and common eating, and conversation spaces provide contexts for global intellectual exchange after the day's work is done.

Altacreat has individual apartments and studios for each artist, all room and board paid for by scholarships, a library, a computer center, and communications facilities for all artists, the capability to receive international newspapers, mail, and television broadcasts, 24-hour computer access, and interactions with the public through on-site visits by local schools and businesses.

■ STEP 1

In pairs, jot down ideas about why you think each person in the chart that follows might like to be a candidate. Think about why he or she would want to be part of the center and what positive skills or characteristics he or she could bring. The first one has been done as an example.

CANDIDATE	RATIONALE
Composer: Female, wife of architect, Korean, 25 years old Specialization: classical piano	Playing the piano could entertain and inspire the other artists to design better creations. She might also want to co-design with her husband (if he is also selected) modern piano studios for home and commercial use.
Architect: Male, husband of piano composer, Japanese, 35 years old Specialization: modern styles mixed with very traditional	
Novelist: Female, Hungarian, 40 years old, married, expects to have a baby in one month Specialization: novels about gypsies in Europe	
Opera Singer: Female, Russian, 32 years old, single Specialization: dramatic, passionate roles in Italian operas	
Screenplay Writer: Female, wife of filmmaker, 39 years old, American (U.S.) Specialization: detective mysteries	
Filmmaker: Male, husband of screenplay writer, 60 years old, Mexican Specialization: love stories	
Poet: Male, 28 years old, Vietnamese, widowed Specialization: effects of technology on everyday life	
Landscape Architect: Female, 23 years old, Brazilian, single Specialization: sunken gardens	
Artist: Female, 36 years old, Turkish, married Specialization: geometric mosaics	
Digital Artist: Female, 28 years old, Chinese, single Specialization: collecting photos from Webcams and arranging them in displays	

■ STEP 2

Share the results of your brainstorming with your classmates.

UNIT OVERVIEW

Unit 18 provides an overview of gerunds and infinitives in their perfective, progressive, and passive forms. It also contrasts the two types of structures and provides numerous exercises to help students select and use the appropriate verb form.

Please note that due to its length, this unit has been divided into three lesson plans. To review this unit more quickly, review focus charts and have students complete the first exercise after each chart to observe students' grasp of the grammar topics.

GRAMMAR NOTE

Students of English are often confused by the numerous complementation options for English verbs. Many common errors occur when students pair the wrong complement with the wrong main verb. Often, they will have learned the form and meaning for one verb + complement construction, and substitute other verbs: *The teacher told us to read this chapter.* * *The teacher demanded us to read this chapter.* This unit systematically explains two structures that often confuse students: gerunds and infinitives. Perfective infinitives are introduced in this unit, and fully explored in Unit 19.

UNIT GOALS

Some instructors may want to review the goals listed on Student Book (SB) page 330 after completing the Opening Task so that students understand what they should know by the end of the unit. These goals can also be reviewed at the end of the unit when students are more familiar with the grammar terminology.

OPENING TASK [25 minutes]

The purpose of the Opening Task is to create a context in which students will need to use gerunds and infinitives to evaluate candidates for an artist-in-residence community in the northwestern United States. The problem-solving format is designed to show the teacher how well the students can produce the target structures implicitly and spontaneously when they are engaged in a communicative task. For a more complete discussion of the purpose of the Opening Task, see To the Teacher, Lesson Planner (LP) page xxii.

Setting Up the Task

Discuss artist-in-residence programs students are familiar with, in the United States and other countries.

Conducting the Task

■ STEP 1

1. Have students work in pairs to read about the artist-in-residence program, Altacreat.
2. Ask the pairs to evaluate the list of applicants and write down their ideas about why they think each person might like to attend Altacreat, and what positive skills or characteristics he or she could bring.

Closing the Task

■ STEP 2

Ask volunteer pairs to share their ideas with the class, and discuss. Don't worry about accuracy at this point, though you may want to take notes of errors in meaning, form, or use in order to focus on those problems later.

GRAMMAR NOTE

Typical student errors (form)

- Using the *-ing* form of *be* rather than the infinitive after *want, need, appear, promise, hope*: —e.g.,* *They hope being arriving at the airport around 9.* (See Focus 4.)

- Not using infinitive complements with explicit subjects after verbs such as *advise, invite,* and *warn*: —e.g.,* *He warned to avoid that road.* (See Focus 4.)

- Omitting *for* before the stated subject of an infinitive: —e.g.,* *Her desire was them go to a good school.* (See Focus 5.)

Typical student errors (use)

- Omitting *to* in infinitive constructions: —e.g., * *The owner of the company was forced pay taxes.* (See Focus 1.)

- Using gerunds rather than infinitives in sentences, and vice versa: —e.g.,* *She stopped to talk when he walked in the room.* * *I liked to watch the sun set yesterday.* (See Focus 3.)

- Omitting *for* in verb + *for* clusters: —e.g., * *I was hoping better weather today.* (See Focus 4.)

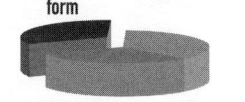

form

FOCUS 1 — Overview of Gerunds and Infinitives

EXAMPLES	EXPLANATIONS
	Infinitives (*to* + verb) or gerunds (verb + *-ing*) can have various functions in a sentence:
(a) **Speaking English** is fun. (b) **To compose a sonata** would take months. (c) It would take months **to compose a sonata**.	**Subject:** Gerunds and infinitives can function as subjects. However, it is more common for infinitives that are subjects to move to the end of the sentence with *it* as the new subject.
(d) His dream was **to direct the ultimate Mexican love story.** (e) Her hobby is **weaving baskets.**	**Subject Complement:** A subject complement follows *be* and refers back to the subject of the sentence.
(f) I don't understand the need **to take a ten-minute break.** (g) The instruction **to wear safety goggles** has saved many people's eyes.	**Noun Complement:** Noun complements explain the nouns that they refer to. The infinitive can be a complement to certain abstract nouns (for example, *advice, decision, desire, fact, opportunity, order, plan, possibility, proposal, request, refusal, requirement, suggestion, way, wish*). (See Unit 21, Focus 1, for a more extensive list of abstract nouns.)
(h) I am sorry **to inform you of the delay.** (i) They were pleased **to meet you.**	**Adjective Complement:** Certain adjectives can be followed by infinitives. These include: *afraid · disappointed · pleased* *amazed · eager · proud* *anxious · eligible · ready* *apt · (un)fit · reluctant* *ashamed · fortunate · sad* *bound · glad · shocked* *careful · happy · sorry* *certain · hesitant · sure* *content · liable · surprised* *delighted · likely · upset* *determined*
(j) Paco hopes **to see the play.** (k) Carol remembered **mailing the package.**	**Direct Object:** A direct object follows a verb. Depending upon the verb and accompanying meaning, the object may be an infinitive or a gerund.
(l) **By studying hard,** you can enter a good school. (m) Thank you **for helping me.** (n) **NOT:** He lost the deal because of wait too long.	**Object of Preposition:** Gerunds, not infinitives, are objects of prepositions.

EXERCISE 1

Read the following text and underline all gerunds and infinitives. Then identify the function of each one (subject, subject complement, noun complement, adjective complement, direct object, or object of preposition).

(1) Alan Loy McGinnis in his book *Bringing Out the Best in People* (Augsburg Publishing House, Minneapolis, 1985) describes 12 important principles or rules for <u>helping</u> people <u>to perform</u> to the best of their ability. (2) The first rule is <u>to expect</u> the best from the people you lead. (3) A true leader needs <u>to drop</u> the role of "watch-dog" and <u>to display</u> a positive attitude toward everyone who works under him or her. (4) The second principle is <u>to make</u> a thorough study of the other person's needs. (5) <u>Walking</u> a mile in another person's shoes will allow a leader <u>to truly understand</u> someone he or she is working with. (6) The third rule is <u>to establish</u> high standards of excellence. (7) Many people have never learned the pleasure of <u>setting</u> high standards and <u>living</u> up to them. (8) The fourth rule is <u>to create</u> an environment where failure is not fatal. (9) People who expect <u>to succeed</u> all of the time often cannot rise from a failure. (10) An effective motivator needs <u>to know</u> how to help people deal with their failure.

(11) "<u>Climbing</u> on other people's bandwagons" is the fifth principle that McGinnis suggests. (12) A good leader needs <u>to identify</u> the beliefs and causes of the people that he or she works with. (13) By <u>using</u> these good ideas, he or she can encourage them <u>to pursue</u> as many of these goals as possible. (14) <u>Employing</u> models <u>to encourage</u> success is the sixth rule. (15) Everyone loves <u>hearing</u> about true success stories of others <u>to build</u> confidence and motivation. <u>Recognizing</u> and <u>applauding</u> achievement is the seventh rule. (16) A good leader tries <u>to look</u> for strengths in people and catch them "<u>doing</u> something right" so that he or she can compliment them.

(17) The eighth rule is <u>to employ</u> a mixture of positive and negative reinforcement. (18) <u>Using</u> praise is only one of many methods used <u>to motivate.</u> (19) Sometimes a person does his or her best because he or she is afraid <u>to be punished.</u> (20) The ninth and tenth rules relate to <u>appealing</u> sparingly to the competitive urge and <u>placing</u> a premium on collaboration. (21) Some competition is good; however, the decision <u>to work</u> with other people creates good morale and allows the job <u>to be completed</u> more efficiently.

(22) The eleventh principle is <u>to learn</u> how to deal with troublemakers in a group. (23) A leader who does not learn how <u>to handle</u> a problematic person will never learn how <u>to stay</u> in difficult situations and solve them. (24) Finally, the twelfth rule is <u>to find</u> ways to keep the motivation of the leader, himself or herself, high. (25) <u>Renewing</u> oneself through sports, <u>reading</u>, <u>going</u> to a restful spot, etc. are all necessary for the good leader <u>to become energized</u> and <u>to</u> successfully <u>perform</u> the other eleven principles.

Which functions of gerunds and infinitives are most common in this selection? Is the "*to*-verb" structure always a complement? What other meaning can it have? (Hint: Review sentences 15 and 18.)

ANSWER KEY

Exercise 1 *The gerunds and infinitives are underlined above. The functions are:* (1) subj.; obj. of prep.; noun comp.; (2) subj. comp.; (3) object, object; (4) subj. comp.; (5) subject, object; (6) subj. comp.; (7) obj. of prep., obj. of prep.; (8) subj. comp.; (9) object; (10) object; (11) subject; (12) object; (13) obj. of prep., object; (14) subj.; noun comp.; (15) object, noun comp., subject, subject; (16) object, object; (17) subj. comp.; (18) subject, obj of prep.; (19) adj. comp.; (20) obj. of prep., obj. of prep.; (21) noun comp.; object; (22) subj. comp.; (23) object, object; (24) subj. comp.; (25) subject, subject, subject, adj. comp., adj. comp.

FOCUS 1 [25 minutes]

Focus 1 gives students an overview of the various forms of gerunds and infinitives and their functions in sentences.

1. **Lead-in:** Explain that English has several *clause-within-a-clause* constructions. Relative clauses are one type that students may be familiar with. Write this example on the board: *A lawyer who passes the bar exam may practice in this state.* Ask one student to put brackets around the embedded clause.

2. Explain that they may also be familiar with full clausal *that*-complements with tensed verbs. Write these examples on the board: *They hope that she is better. They said that she speaks French.*

3. Ask one student to come to the board and bracket the embedded clauses (*that she is better; that she speaks French*).

4. Add that students will also encounter subjunctive complements. Write the following example on the board: *The woman insisted that we be ready by 5:00 a.m.* Ask students to identify the embedded clause. (If they notice the *be*-verb, explain that this will be discussed in more detail in Unit 22.) Once identified, bracket the embedded clause (*that we be ready*) on the board.

5. State that the gerunds and infinitives represented in the focus chart are actually "tenseless" clauses in which the subject is understood to be the same subject as the one in the "tensed" clause, as in (j), where the person seeing the play is Paco. Write: *Paco hopes {Paco sees the play}* on the board. Also explain that the subject may be easily inferred from the context, as in (a). Write this sentence on the board: *{For someone} to compose a sonata would take months.*

6. Ask various individuals to read the examples and explanations for the different functions of gerunds and infinitives while the rest of the class listens.

METHODOLOGY NOTE

Although students at this level will generally have had experience with gerunds and infinitives as direct objects, most will need to expand their knowledge of the other functions.

EXERCISE 1 [20 minutes]

In Exercise 1 students identify gerunds and infinitives and their functions in a reading passage, applying what they have just learned in Focus 1.

1. Read the directions as a class. Ask a volunteer to identify the gerunds and the infinitive in the first sentence. (*bringing out, helping people, to perform*)

2. Have students work in pairs to underline the gerunds and infinitives in the passage

3. Have pairs get together with another pair. Have students take turns identifying the function of each gerund or infinitive. Encourage them to refer to Focus 1, as needed.

4. Review answers as a class. See answers on LP page 332.

 For more practice, use *Grammar Dimensions 4* Workbook page 158, Exercise 1.

FOCUS 2 — Infinitives and Gerunds in Perfective, Progressive, and Passive

EXAMPLES	EXPLANATIONS
(a) Eva's plan has always been **to return** to her homeland.	simple infinitive (*to* + verb)
(b) She hoped **to have earned** an Olympic gold medal by the time she was 20.	perfective infinitive (*to* + *have* + past participle)
(c) Their goal is **to be working** by March.	progressive infinitive (*to* + *be* + present participle)
(d) We wanted **to have been swimming** by now.	perfective progressive infinitive (*to* + *have* + *been* + present participle)
(e) The suggestion **to be seen** by a surgeon was never followed.	passive infinitive (*to* + *be* + past participle)
(f) They were happy **to have been chosen** for the award.	perfective passive infinitive (*to* + *have* + *been* + past participle)
(g) Part of the problem **is not knowing** enough.	simple gerund (verb + *-ing*)
(h) She was excited about **having watched** the race from start to finish.	perfective gerund (*having* + past participle)
(i) **Being appointed** to the board of directors is a great responsibility.	passive gerund (*being* + past participle)
(j) **Having been selected** for the experiment gave her career a boost.	perfective passive gerund (*having been* + past participle)

EXERCISE 2

With a partner, discuss the following topics using infinitives and gerunds. Use the appropriate simple, perfective, progressive, or passive form and give reasons for your response for each item.

Example: a movie you enjoyed seeing
I enjoyed seeing "Star Wars I" because I like science fiction.

1. a holiday food you like to eat
2. a present you would like to be surprised with
3. a sport you enjoy playing
4. a place you are excited about having seen
5. another name you would like to have been named
6. a job you would like to be doing right now
7. a famous person in history you would like to have met
8. a topic you would like to have been studying by now
9. a story you liked being told as a child
10. a feeling you had after having been recognized for something

EXERCISE 3

A woman received a $1000 prize for winning a short-story writing contest. Her acceptance speech appears below. Fill in the appropriate gerund or infinitive. In some cases, more than one answer may be correct.

It is a great honor (award) _to be awarded_ this generous prize tonight. (1) _To be presented_ (present) an award for something that I enjoy doing anyway thrills me. (2) _Saying/To say_ (say) that I am indebted to my parents would be an understatement. (3) _To have/Having/To have had_ (have) parents who were trained as teachers gave me an important start. From the time I was very young, (4) _studying_ (study) four hours every day after school was required. It was a frequent sight (5) _to see_ (see) my siblings discussing main points and rehearsing the answers to problems. (6) _Being scolded/To have been scolded_ (scold) by our parents for not paying enough attention to our work would have been the greatest shame.

Besides doing my homework for school, (7) _reading_ (read) fiction and nonfiction books took up much of my leisure time. (8) _Having read_ (read) so many types of books by the time I got to college proved to be a marvelous advantage. (9) _Having seen_ (see) so many good written models allowed me to creatively and effortlessly produce my own work for my university English classes.

Today, it requires more discipline for me (10) _to be_ (be) a good writer. (11) _Being married_ (marry) with three children leaves less time to write. It requires initiative (12) _to arise/arising_ (arise) every day at 5:00 A.M. to write. (13) _Writing_ (write) in this manner is the only way that I have been able to produce several short stories and a few poems. (14) _Not having received_ (not receive) very good marks on my essay pieces in college, I have left essay writing to some other writer! Well, I can see that my time is up. It has been an honor (15) _to be selected/being selected_ (select) as the winner of this contest and I thank my parents, family, and all of you for your recognition today.

ANSWER KEY

Exercise 2 Answers will vary.

Exercise 3 Answers will vary. Possible answers are listed above.

FOCUS 2 [20 minutes]

1. **Lead-in:** Copy the examples and explanations onto two different-colored pieces of paper, with examples on one color, and explanations on the other. Pass out the 20 strips to either individuals or pairs, depending upon your class size.

2. Ask students to walk around the class and try to match the examples with the explanations. Once all students have found their matches, ask them to write the sentence strips on the board in a chart such as that on SB page 334 or on an overhead projector. The resulting chart should resemble Focus 2. It's fine if it doesn't follow the exact order.

3. Ask two volunteers to take turns reading the examples and explanations aloud.

4. Encourage students to ask questions about anything they do not understand.

METHODOLOGY NOTE

Most students will probably be familiar with the different verb tenses (if they have completed Units 1 and 2). This focus chart will allow them to see how tense is incorporated with gerund and infinitive forms.

EXERCISE 2 [20 minutes]

In Exercise 2 students discuss topics of interest, applying the various forms of gerunds and infinitives they have just studied in Focus 2.

1. Read the directions and example as a class. Ask students to identify the form of the gerund in the example. (*a simple gerund*)

2. Have students work in pairs to discuss the topics. Ask them to use as many of the forms from Focus 2 as possible in their talks.

3. Ask volunteers to share their answers and report on their partners' answers.

 work book For more practice, use *Grammar Dimensions 4* Workbook page 159, Exercise 2.

EXPANSION [20 minutes/homework]

For further practice, ask students to write one original sentence for each of the forms in Focus 2, either in class or for homework. Give an example for the first form, the simple infinitive: *To become a doctor has always been Maria's plan.*

EXERCISE 3 (OPTIONAL) [20 minutes]

In Exercise 3 students continue working with various forms of gerunds and infinitives, completing sentences in an acceptance speech.

1. Read the directions and example as a class. Ask students to identify the form of the infinitive in the example. (*perfective infinitive*)

2. Have students work independently to complete the sentences with the correct gerund or infinitive.

3. Ask students to compare their answers with a partner.

4. To check answers, ask three different students to read the three different paragraphs aloud, using the answers they wrote. See possible answers on LP page 334.

5. Discuss any incorrect answers.

EXPANSION [30 minutes]

Activity 1 (listening) on SB page 349 is a good follow-up to Exercise 3. In this activity students listen to a story about a famous unsolved mystery, and then complete sentences using infinitives or gerunds.

EXERCISE 4

Fill in the following blanks with appropriate infinitives. More than one answer may be possible.

Example: The requirement <u>to wear</u> a spacesuit is an essential rule for the astronaut to follow.

1. Few people have made the decision _____<u>to become</u>_____ an astronaut.

2. The proposal _____<u>to replace</u>_____ expendable rockets with rockets that could return to Earth saved a great deal of money for the taxpayer.

3. The space program strictly heeded the advice _____<u>to isolate</u>_____ the astronauts for 18 days after their flight to the Moon in order to assure their good health.

4. The suggestion _____<u>to create</u>_____ a "moon base" would allow much useful scientific research.

5. A precaution _____<u>to take</u>_____ after every spaceflight includes isolating lunar samples until the scientific team is satisfied that no risk of contamination remains.

6. The decision _____<u>to do</u>_____ space-walks occurred in 1964 with Project Mercury.

7. The first words _____<u>to be stated</u>_____ by Neil Armstrong as he stepped on to the surface of the moon were "That's one small step for a man; a giant leap for mankind."

8. The next challenge _____<u>to be pursued</u>_____ is a mission to Mars.

EXERCISE 5

With a partner, take turns asking and answering the following questions. Use an adjective complement in each of your responses.

Example: What are you bound to do after you finish your schooling?
I am bound to get a job as a computer technician.

1. What type of food are you hesitant to eat?

2. What are you apt to do in the next few weeks?

3. Which clubs here or in your native country are you eligible to join?

4. What sport are you reluctant to try?

5. What movie are you likely to see in the next few weeks?

6. Which country would you be delighted to visit?

7. Which student in your class is most liable to be successful?

8. What are you sure to do after your class today?

9. Which friend are you most happy to know?

10. What movie star or musical star would you be ready to meet?

meaning

FOCUS 3 Gerunds versus Infinitives

Certain types of verbs (verbs of emotion, verbs of completion/incompletion, and verbs of remembering) can be affected by the choice of infinitive or gerund.

EXAMPLES	EXPLANATIONS
(a) **To eat** too much sugar is not healthy. (b) **Eating** too much sugar is not healthy.	Infinitive and gerunds as objects and subjects sometimes have equivalent meanings.
(c) **ACTUAL:** For the time being, **I prefer being** a housewife. (d) **POTENTIAL:** When my children are grown, I would **prefer** *to get* a job outside the home. (e) **ACTUAL: Playing** golf every day is boring. (f) **POTENTIAL: To play** golf every day would be my idea of a happy retirement.	In other cases, we choose an infinitive or gerund by the meaning of an action. We often use gerunds to describe an actual, vivid, or fulfilled action. We often use infinitives to describe potential, hypothetical, or future events.

(Continued on next page)

ANSWER KEY

Exercise 4 Answers will vary. Possible answers are listed above.

Exercise 5 Answers will vary. Possible answers are: 1. I am hesitant to eat raw oysters.   2. I am apt to take a test.   3. I am eligible to join the golf club and the speech club.   4. I am reluctant to try windsurfing.   5. I am likely to see Rob Roy.   6. I would be delighted to visit Turkey   7. Tom is most liable to be successful.   8. I am sure to stop by the post office.   9. I am most happy to know

EXERCISE 4 (OPTIONAL) [15 minutes]

In Exercise 4 students focus only on using infinitives.

1. Read the directions and example as a class. Ask students to identify the form of the infinitive in the example. (*simple infinitive*)
2. Have students work independently to complete the sentences with the correct infinitive. Remind them that there may be more than one correct answer to some sentences.
3. Ask volunteers to share their sentences with the class. See possible answers on LP page 336.

EXERCISE 5 (OPTIONAL) [20 minutes]

Exercise 5 reviews adjective complements, explained in Focus 1.

1. Read the directions and example as a class. Ask students to look back at Focus 1 and find the list of adjectives that can be followed by infinitives. Is *bound* in this list? (*yes*)
2. Ask students to work in pairs and take turns asking the questions and answering them using adjective complements.
3. Ask volunteers to share their responses with the class, and discuss these. See possible answers on LP page 336.

LESSON PLAN 2

FOCUS 3 [30 minutes]

Focus 3 explains how certain verbs are affected by the choice of an infinitive or a gerund. This is an excellent reference tool for students. The Focus 3 charts are continued on SB page 338.

1. **Lead-in:** Write the following pairs of sentences on the board:
   A. *I forgot to call Ana yesterday.*
   B. *(A few minutes ago) I forgot calling Ana yesterday.*
2. Draw a time line that shows the different times of forgetting and discuss the differences in meaning.
3. Explain that, in case A, you forgot that you needed to call Ana and you didn't call her at all.
4. Explain how, in case B, you did call Ana, but you forgot (a few minutes ago) the fact that you had called her.
5. Emphasize that this is a dramatic example of the difference in meaning that the choice of gerund or infinitive can make. The verb *remember* can also have a distinct meaning when followed by the gerund versus the infinitive.

GRAMMAR NOTE

Other types of *emotion* and *completion/incompletion* verbs (refer to Appendix 4B List A on SB page A-8 and List C on SB page A-9) may also take a gerund or an infinitive depending upon whether one is referring to an actual or potential event.

1. Ask students to tell you whether the infinitive or the gerund form of the verb *study* would be most suitable in the following blanks:
   I will begin _____ my homework after school gets out today.
   I will begin _____ right now.
2. Ask them to identify which sentence suggests something that has not yet happened and which one suggests an event that is ongoing. (They should supply *to study* in the first blank and *studying* in the second.)
3. Ask students to silently read the rest of the focus chart, or assign it as homework.

Verbs of Emotion

ACTUAL EVENT	POTENTIAL EVENT
(g) Did you **like** *dancing* that night? You seemed to be having a good time.	(h) Do you **like** *to dance*? I know a good nightclub.
(i) Tim **hates** *quarreling* with his wife over every little thing.	(j) Tim **hates** *to quarrel* with his wife. It would be the last thing he would want to do.
(k) **I preferred** *studying* astronomy over physics.	(l) **I prefer** *to study* physics next year.

Verbs of Completion/Incompletion

ACTUAL EVENT	POTENTIAL EVENT
(m) I **started** *doing* my homework. Question #1 is especially hard.	(n) Did you **start** *to do* your homework?
(o) Did you **continue** *watching* the program yesterday after I left?	(p) Will you **continue** *to watch* the program after I leave?
(q) He **began** *speaking* with a hoarse voice that no one could understand.	(r) He **began** *to speak*, but was interrupted by the lawyer.
(s) She **stopped** *listening* whenever she was bored.	(t) She **stopped** *to listen* to the bird that was singing. (Note: *to* means "in order to.")
(u) They **finished** *reading* the book.	(v) I will **finish** *reading* this book before I go shopping. (Note: *Finish* always requires a gerund.)
	(w) **NOT:** I will finish to read the book.

Verbs of Remembering

EXAMPLES	TIME SEQUENCE	EXPLANATION
(x) Tom **remembered** *closing* the door.	First: Tom closed the door. Then: Tom remembered that he did so.	Besides the real event and potential event meanings, *remember, forget,* and *regret* signal different time sequence meanings when we use a gerund or an infinitive.
(y) Tom **remembered** *to close* the door.	First: Tom remembered that he needed to close the door. Then: Tom closed the door.	

In the Opening Task on pages 330 and 331, you and your classmates considered the candidates for Altcreat. At the last minute, the media released new information about the candidates based on several confidential interviews. Read and select the correct verb in each of the quotes that follow. In some cases, both verbs may be correct. Explain why one verb or both verbs are correct.

Example: **Composer:** I would like (to go/going) only if my husband could go.
   (***To go** is preferred because the situation is hypothetical.*)

1. **Composer:** (To work/working) at Altacreat without my husband would be dreadful.
2. **Poet:** I love (to smoke/smoking). As a matter of fact, I smoke three packs of cigarettes a day.
3. **Artist:** (To paint/painting) in silence is impossible. I cannot get anything done unless two or three people are talking around me.
4. **Novelist:** I mean (to stay/staying) at Altacreat only until my baby is born.
5. **Landscape Architect:** I hated (to work/working) in cold weather when I went to school in Wisconsin. That's why I transferred to another university where the climate was warmer.
6. **Architect:** (To pass/passing) the Architectural Boards Exam this fall is my intention. Unfortunately, I have already failed it twice.
7. **Opera Singer:** I would not like (to fly/flying) to Altacreat in the United States because I have acrophobia.
8. **Digital Artist:** I regret (to inform/informing) the committee in my application that I was a digital artist because I actually have limited knowledge of computers.
9. **Filmmaker:** I will continue (to benefit/benefiting) from this experience even after I return to Mexico.
10. **Screenplay Writer:** Did I remember (to tell/telling) you that funding for future Altacreat projects will be one of my major publicity campaigns once my three-month project is finished?

ANSWER KEY

Exercise 6   The correct verbs are circled above. The reasons for choice are: 1. represents a future thought or emphasizes real action   2. is a habitual real action   3. represents a future thought or emphasizes real action   4. represents a future action   5. real, past action   6. refers to a future action   7. refers to a future action   8. refers to someone getting information right now   9. refers to a future action   10. question implies that this is not a completed action

EXERCISE 6 [25 minutes]

In this exercise students read new information about the applicants to Altacreat, the artist-in-residence community from the Opening Task. Students choose the correct verb to complete sentences about the applicants, and then explain their choices.

1. Read the directions and example as a class.
2. Have students work in pairs to complete the sentences.
3. Have pairs get together with another pair. Have students take turns sharing what verb they chose and saying why. Encourage them to refer to Focus 3, as needed.
4. Review answers as a class. See answers on LP page 338.

work book For more practice, use *Grammar Dimensions 4* Workbook page 160, Exercise 3.

EXPANSION [30 minutes/homework]

This activity gives students additional practice with gerunds and infinitives. It makes a good homework assignment.

1. Ask students to think of three other potential applicants to Altacreat. Have them write a short description of each applicant.
2. Ask them to write two or three sentences giving information about each applicant, following the models in Exercise 6.
3. Ask students to exchange papers with a partner and discuss them.

FOCUS 4 — Gerunds and Infinitives as Direct Objects

form

EXAMPLES	EXPLANATIONS
	Another way to predict the form of a direct object complement (either gerund or infinitive) is by the choice of verb in the base sentence.
(a) Scientists **appear** to be getting close to an explanation. (b) **NOT:** Scientists appear being getting close to an explanation.	• An infinitive must follow *want, need, hope, promise,* and *appear* (and other verbs in List A on page A-8). Notice here that many of these verbs (although not all) signal potential events, a meaning of infinitives discussed in Focus 3.
(c) Juan **hates** (for) **Grace** to worry.	• Some verbs from List A (*desire, hate, like, love,* and *prefer*) may optionally include *for* with the infinitive complement when the infinitive has an explicit subject.
(d) Einstein **convinced other scientists** to reject Newtonian physics. (e) **NOT:** Einstein convinced to reject Newtonian physics. (f) **NOT:** Einstein convinced other scientists rejecting Newtonian physics.	• *Advise, convince, invite,* and *warn* (and other verbs in List B on page A-9) are followed by infinitive complements with explicit subjects.
(g) Einstein **risked** introducing a new theory to the world. (h) **NOT:** Einstein risked to introduce a new theory to the world.	• *Appreciate, enjoy, postpone, risk,* and *quit* (and other verbs in List C on pages A-9 and A-10) take only gerunds. Notice that many of these verbs (although not all) signal actual events, a meaning of gerunds discussed in Focus 3.

EXERCISE 7

Read the following text. Underline all direct object infinitives, and circle all direct object gerunds. (Not every sentence may have one.)

Then, make a list of the verb + infinitive or gerund combinations that you find.

Example: Verb + Infinitive   Verb + Gerund
          learn   *to speak*   *prefer*   *saying*

Einstein's Early Education

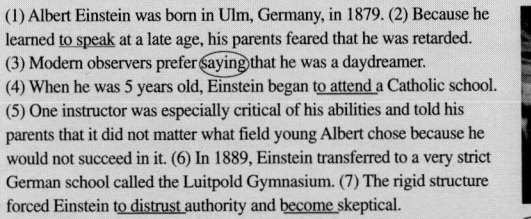

(1) Albert Einstein was born in Ulm, Germany, in 1879. (2) Because he learned to speak at a late age, his parents feared that he was retarded. (3) Modern observers prefer saying that he was a daydreamer. (4) When he was 5 years old, Einstein began to attend a Catholic school. (5) One instructor was especially critical of his abilities and told his parents that it did not matter what field young Albert chose because he would not succeed in it. (6) In 1889, Einstein transferred to a very strict German school called the Luitpold Gymnasium. (7) The rigid structure forced Einstein to distrust authority and become skeptical.

(8) At age 12, Einstein picked up a mathematics textbook and began teaching himself geometry. (9) By 1894, Einstein's father's business had failed to prosper, and the family moved to Italy. (10) Einstein, however, remained behind and began feeling lonely and unhappy. (11) Consequently, he paid less attention to his studies and was finally asked by one of the teachers to leave. (12) He joined his family in Italy but was not able to matriculate at a university because he did not have a diploma. (13) When he heard that a diploma was not necessary to enter at the Swiss Polytechnique Institute in Zurich, he decided to apply.

(14) Einstein traveled to Switzerland but did not pass the entrance examination. (15) He was not prepared well enough in biology and languages, so he enrolled in the Gymnasium at Aarau to prepare himself in his weaker subjects. (16) Albert enjoyed studying in Aarau more than at the Luitpold Gymnasium because the teachers wanted to teach students how to think. (17) He took the exam again and was finally permitted to matriculate into a four-year program. (18) Einstein did not excel during these years at the Institute. (19) In fact, he rarely attended the lectures. (20) He read his books at home and borrowed his classmates' notes to pass tests.

(21) When Einstein graduated in 1900, he failed to obtain a position at the Institute. (22) His professors did not intend to reward Einstein's lackadaisical attitude toward classes with a position. (23) Because he did not get an academic appointment, he worked at the Swiss Patent Office. (24) He worked there for several years until he was offered an appointment as Associate Professor of Physics at the University of Zurich. (25) It was there that Einstein's revolutionary theories of space-time began to take hold and threatened to destroy the reputations of other colleagues who had built their careers on Newton's ideas of a clockwork universe.

What meaning does the "*to*-verb" structure have in sentences 15 and 20?

ANSWER KEY

Exercise 7   The direct objects infinitives are underlined, the direct object gerunds circled above.
Note: The to-verb in (15) and (20) means "in order to."
2. to speak   3. saying   7. to distrust / (to)become   8. teaching   10. feeling   11. to leave
12. to matriculate   13. to enter / to apply   15. to prepare   16. studying   17. to matriculate
21. to obtain   22. to reward   25. to take hold / to destroy

FOCUS 4 [20 minutes]

Focus 4 explores how gerunds and infinitives are used as direct objects in sentences, and how this influences their forms.

1. **Lead-in:** Write the following three patterns on the board:

   Subject + _____ *to* + sit.

   Subject + _____ object + *to* + sit.

   Subject + _____ + sitting.

2. Ask students to create sentences based on each pattern. They might supply verbs such as *desire, choose,* or *manage* in the first blank; verbs such as *tell, allow,* or *help* in the second blank; and verbs such as *avoid, admit,* and *stop* in the third blank.

3. Ask students to turn to Appendix 4B on pages A-8 through A-10 and look at the different types of verbs comprising Lists A through C. Encourage them to associate the groups of verbs with their general meanings—e.g., emotion, mental activity, communication, causation, etc. Note that certain verbs in List A can optionally include *for*—e.g., *I expect (for) him to come early. They will desire (for) us to bring gifts. The man would love (for) them to help.*

4. Ask pairs of volunteers to read aloud each group of examples and explanations, and discuss these as a class.

■ EXERCISE 7 [15 minutes]

In Exercise 7 students first identify and then list the direct object infinitives and direct object gerunds in a reading about Albert Einstein.

1. Read the directions as a class. Ask a volunteer to read the first three sentences of the reading. Then read the example, which lists the verbs, the infinitive, and the gerund in the second and third sentences of the reading.

2. Have students work independently to underline the direct object infinitives and circle the direct object gerunds.

3. Have them work in pairs to create their lists, following the example.

4. Ask different students to read each paragraph, and ask volunteers to identify the direct object gerunds and infinitives. See answers on LP page 340.

work book

For more practice, use *Grammar Dimensions 4* Workbook page 161, Exercise 4 and page 162, Exercises 5 and 6.

EXPANSION [20 minutes/homework]

For further practice with direct object gerunds and infinitives, this activity can be completed in class or assigned as homework.

1. After doing Exercise 7, ask students to close their books and try to reconstruct Einstein's life history. Ask them to write a short paragraph summarizing his childhood, his youth, and his adulthood, using infinitives and gerunds as direct objects.

2. Ask them to use Appendix 4B on SB pages A-8 through A-10 to check their use of infinitives and gerunds.

3. Have volunteers from different pairs read their summaries to the class.

EXERCISE 8

Complete the following sentences based on the passage in Exercise 7. Use an infinitive or gerund. The first one has been done for you.

Example: As a baby, Einstein appeared _to be_ retarded.

1. As a young child, he failed ___to impress___ his teachers.
2. At age twelve, Einstein decided ___to teach___ himself geometry.
3. Einstein neglected ___to do___ his homework.
4. When Einstein's family left for Italy, he quit ___studying___.
5. Because of this, one teacher advised him ___to leave___ school.
6. Without his family, he couldn't help ___feeling___ lonely.
7. He didn't mind ___joining___ his family in Italy.
8. Unfortunately, he couldn't begin ___to study___ at a university without a diploma.
9. He tried ___to enter___ the Swiss Polytechnique but could not pass the entrance exam.
10. He regretted ___failing___ the entrance exam the first time.
11. Professors at the Polytechnique declined ___to give___ Einstein a position because of his lackadaisical academic performance.
12. As a clerk at the Swiss Patent Office, he continued ___thinking___ about physics.
13. The University of Zurich invited Einstein ___to become___ a faculty member.
14. Many professors couldn't help ___admiring___ Einstein's unusual ideas.
15. Soon he began ___to question___ well-established professors with his revolutionary theories.

EXERCISE 9

Look back at the notes you made for the Opening Task on page 331 and additional information you learned in Exercise 6. Assume that only five of the applicants can be chosen for the three-month project at Altacreat.

STEP 1 In pairs, rank order the applicants from 1 (= most desirable) to 10 (= least desirable). Consider what might be the appropriate mix of males and females, whether married couples or singles are preferable, what skills and abilities are most essential for global exchange, what compatibility factors should be considered, etc.

STEP 2 As a class, come to a consensus about which five applicants would be most desirable.

STEP 3 After this discussion, answer the following questions.

1. Who has the class chosen to be the top five finalists?
2. Was there any candidate that you personally regretted eliminating?
3. Did any of your classmates persuade you to select someone that you had not originally selected?

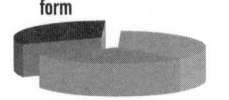
form

FOCUS 5	*For* with Infinitives and *'s* with Gerunds

EXAMPLES	EXPLANATIONS
(a) **(For people)** to see is a wonderful gift. (b) **(Your)** neglecting your teeth will cause an earlier return to your dentist.	The subject of an infinitive or a gerund is often not stated but can be implied from context. It will either have a general reference or a specific one that can be determined from other references in the sentence or paragraph.
(c) **For a Russian** to be the first man in space was commendable. (d) Her desire was **for them** to take a trip around the world.	When an infinitive functions as a subject or a subject complement, any stated subject of the infinitive should be preceded by *for*. If a pronoun follows *for*, it must be in object form.
(e) They hoped **for her** to be able to attend the concert. (f) I expected **(for)** him to be there when I finished. (g) We advised **the couple** to postpone their marriage.	When the infinitive functions as a direct object, its stated subject should take object form if it is a pronoun and may or may not be preceded by *for*. Three options are possible depending on the verb. (See Focus 4.)
(h) **Their denying the allegation** was understandable. (i) I didn't like **the dog's barking** all night.	When the subject of a gerund is stated, it takes the possessive form.

ANSWER KEY

Exercise 8   Answers will vary. Possible answers are listed above.

Exercise 9   Answers will vary.

EXERCISE 8 [20 minutes]

In Exercise 8 students complete sentences based on the reading about Einstein in Exercise 7, using infinitives and gerunds.

1. Read the directions as a class. Ask a volunteer to read the examples. Find the explanation in Focus 4 for choosing an infinitive. (the first explanation)
2. Have students work independently to complete the sentences.
3. Have them work in pairs to share and compare their answers.
4. Review answers with the class. See possible answers on LP page 342.

For more practice, use *Grammar Dimensions 4* Workbook page 163, Exercise 7; page 164, Exercise 8; and page 166, Exercise 9.

EXPANSION [60 minutes/homework]

Activity 3 (research on the web) on SB page 350 makes a good homework assignment following Exercise 8. In this activity students use the Internet to research and then to write about one of their favorite artists, musicians, architects, or writers using at least two gerund complements and four infinitive complements.

EXERCISE 9 (OPTIONAL) [30 minutes]

In Exercise 9 students refer to the notes they made in the Opening Task and the additional information they learned about the applicants in Exercise 6, and then work on choosing the top five applicants to Altacreat. Read the opening directions as a class.

STEP 1
Have students work in pairs to review and rank the applicants according to a variety of different criteria.

STEP 2
Have the class work together to choose the five best applicants.

STEP 3

1. Read the questions in Step 3 as a class. Elicit that, to answer the questions, students will use verbs from Lists A (e.g., *choose*), B (e.g., *persuade*), and C (e.g., *regret*) from Appendix 4B on SB pages A-8 through A-10.
2. Have students work in small groups and discuss their answers to the questions.
3. Ask representatives of different groups to report on their group's discussion.

LESSON PLAN 3

FOCUS 5 [15 minutes]

Focus 5 explains how infinitives are used with *for* and how, when the subject of a gerund is stated, it takes the possessive (*'s*) form.

1. **Lead-in:** Write on the board the following examples:

    We hoped [they would come to the graduation]. ⇒
    *We hoped for **them** to come to the graduation.*

    John postponed [his son will travel to Hawaii]. ⇒
    John postponed his son's traveling to Hawaii.

2. Emphasize that when a subject of an infinitive or gerund is stated, it is necessary to change the subject of the embedded clause to either an object pronoun or the possessive form, respectively.
3. Inform students that a less formal variant of the possessive gerund complement substitutes a noun phrase or object pronoun in place of the possessive form. Thus, in conversation, many native speakers will say: *John postponed his*

son traveling to Hawaii. OR *John postponed him traveling to Hawaii.*

4. Ask one volunteer to read the examples, and another to read the explanations in the chart.
5. Answer any questions students might have.

Read the descriptions of problem situations. Following each description is a statement about the problem. Fill in the blank with *for + noun/pronoun* or a possessive construction to complete each sentence.

Example: Sue went to a party. Ralph did not speak to her all evening. Sue disliked
Ralph's ignoring her at the party.

1. Burt did not get enough sleep last night. He ended up yelling at Mrs. Gonzalez, his boss. _____His_____ yelling at his boss was a big mistake.

2. Mrs. Sutherland warned students to do their own work during the test. Sue got caught cheating. _____For Sue_____ to get caught cheating was shameful.

3. Tony did not watch where he was going and ran into the rear end of the car in front of him. The driver of the car resented _____Tony's_____ hitting her car.

4. Nina always goes to bed at 9:00 P.M. Her friend, Nathan, forgot and called her house at 11:00 P.M. Nina was very angry. Nina expected _____(for) Nathan_____ to call at an earlier hour the next time.

5. Bill's grandmother mailed him a birthday package, which arrived a week before his birthday. Bill couldn't wait and opened the package early. Bill's mother was upset about _____his_____ opening the present before his birthday.

6. Ursula left the house when it was still dark. When she got to school, she noticed that she was wearing one black shoe and one brown shoe. _____For Ursula_____ to leave the house without checking her shoes was very silly.

7. Mrs. Lu has several children who make a lot of noise everywhere they go. All of her neighbors are very upset. _____For Mrs. Lu_____ to let her children run wild angers the neighbors.

8. Michelle has asked Than to go to the movies several times. Than always tells her that he can't because he has to watch a TV show, do his homework, call his mother, etc. Michelle is tired of _____Than's_____ making excuses.

Read the following sentences. Write *C* beside correct sentences and *I* beside the incorrect sentences and make all necessary corrections. Be sure to refer to Focuses 3, 4, and 5 to review the rules.

Example: _I_ He agrees speak at the convention.

1. __C__ I expected him to see me from the balcony, but he didn't.
2. __I__ They intended ~~interviewing~~ the ambassador the last week in November. *(to interview)*
3. __I__ I regretted ~~to tell~~ her that she had not been sent an invitation to the party. *(telling)*
4. __I__ Patty has chosen ~~attending~~ the University of Michigan in the fall. *(to attend)*
5. __C__ Have you forgotten to fasten your seat belt again?
6. __I__ ~~Terry~~ getting married surprises me. *(Terry's)*
7. __I__ Would you please stop ~~to talk~~? I cannot hear the presenter. *(talking)*
8. __I__ Did he suggest ~~us go~~ to a Japanese restaurant? *(our going)*
9. __C__ She can't stand to do her homework with the radio turned on.
10. __I__ Mr. and Mrs. Hunter forced their daughter's ~~joining~~ the social club against her will. *(to join)*
11. __I__ For ~~they~~ to be traveling in Sweden is a great pleasure. *(them)*
12. __I__ Please remember ~~working~~ harder. *(to work)*
13. __C__ Mary tends to exaggerate when she tells a story.
14. __I__ I don't mind Tai ~~to arrive~~ a little late to the meeting. *(arriving)*
15. __I__ Would you care ~~have~~ a drink before we eat dinner? *(to)*
16. __I__ John avoided ~~go~~ to the dentist for three years. *(going)*
17. __I__ They can't afford ~~taking~~ a trip to the Caribbean this year. *(to take)*
18. __I__ ~~She~~ coming late to the appointment was a disappointment. *(Her)*
19. __I__ Some schools decide ~~participating~~ every year. *(to participate)*
20. __C__ They ceased to comply with the rules.
21. __I__ Has he not offered ~~resign~~? *(to)*
22. __I__ ~~There~~ complaining about discrimination is understandable. *(Their)*
23. __I__ ~~You~~ starting a fight will have a negative end. *(Your)*
24. __I__ My hope is for my children ~~earn~~ a good living. *(to)*
25. __I__ I disliked ~~Tom~~ repetitive questions all through the meeting. *(Tom's)*

ANSWER KEY

Exercise 10 Answers will vary. Possible answers are listed above.

Exercise 11 The corrections needed may vary. Possible answers are listed above.

EXERCISE 10 [20 minutes]

Students complete sentences using *for* + noun/pronoun or a possessive construction, applying the principles they just learned in Focus 5.

1. Read the directions and example as a class. Ask students to identify the construction (*possessive construction*) and why that is appropriate (*the subject of the gerund*, Ralph, *is stated*).
2. Have students work in pairs. Ask them to take turns reading the sentences aloud, and then take turns choosing an answer to each
3. Review and discuss answers as a class. See possible answers on LP page 344.

For more practice, use *Grammar Dimensions 4* Workbook page 166, Exercise 10.

EXERCISE 11 [25 minutes]

Exercise 11 asks students to identify and correct errors in sentences, applying the principles of Focuses 3–5.

1. Read the directions and example as a class. What is wrong in the example? (*the infinitive* to *was omitted*)

Suggestion: At this point it might be helpful to ask volunteers to read and review the rules governing each choice from Focuses 3–5.

2. Ask students to work independently to identify and correct errors in the sentences.
3. Have students share and compare answers with a partner.
4. Review answers as a class. If the suggestion was followed, have students articulate which rule was followed to make the correction.

EXPANSION [40 minutes]

In Activity 4 (reflection) on SB pages 350–351 students evaluate a list of learning strategies and indicate which ones they like and dislike. They then discuss their evaluations with a partner and discuss ways to improve their learning strategies.

FOCUS 6 — Gerunds as Objects of Prepositions and Phrasal Verbs

form

EXAMPLES	EXPLANATIONS
(a) The Altacreat's selection committee could not **agree to** the poet's **being** on the list of finalists. (b) The members **argued about keeping** the novelist and the opera singer as well.	Gerunds generally follow verbs + prepositions, such as *agree to, look at, worry about,* etc.
(c) The teacher **asked for the committee to make** a decision within 20 minutes. (d) She **hoped for them to make** their announcement by 4:00.	An exception to this is when the preposition is *for* with such prepositional verbs as *ask for, ache for, care for, hope for, long for,* etc. In this case, use an infinitive with a "subject."
(e) The artists will be able to **depend on eating** gourmet meals at regular times. (f) They can **cut down on** disturbing distractions. (g) They will not **look forward to** returning to their routine lives after they leave Altacreat.	Phrasal verbs and phrasal verbs followed by prepositions (*put up with, cut down on, stand up for,* etc.) always take the gerund (not the infinitive) form. Note that the first *to* is not an infinitive marker in (g) but is a part of the phrasal verb + preposition *look forward to.*
(h) The artists are **accustomed to creating** things on their own. (i) They are **suspicious of relying** on others' intuitions.	We also use gerunds following adjective + preposition combinations such as *content with, surprised at, annoyed by.*

EXERCISE 12

Since the beginning of time, human beings have tried to understand who they were and where they came from through religious beliefs, theories, and rituals. Write general statements about these ideas, using the prompts below. Include a gerund or infinitive in each response.

Example: people believe in   (human beings evolved from apes)
Some people believe in human beings' having evolved from apes.

1. religions   insist on   (God has created living things)
Some religions insist on God's having created living things.

2. cultures   call for   (people have dietary restrictions)
Some cultures call for people to have dietary restrictions.

3. cultures   think about   (their ancestors are pleased or displeased with them)
Some cultures think about their ancestors' being pleased or displeased with them.

4. people   hope for   (relatives are reunited in an afterlife)
Some people hope for relatives to be reunited in an afterlife.

5. members   wait for   (God returns to the chosen people)
Some members wait for God to return to the chosen people.

6. believers   complain about   (other people don't believe)
Some believers complain about other people's not believing.

7. religions   argue about   (priests have proper authority)
Some religions argue about priests having proper authority.

8. members   agree to   (their children are baptized)
Some members agree to their children being baptized.

EXERCISE 13

Read the following notes about important figures in scientific history. Write sentences about each person, using one of the following expressions: *celebrated for, famous for, good at, proficient in, renowned for, skillful in,* or *successful in.*

Examples: Aristotle, Greek philosopher, laws of motion
Aristotle was a Greek philosopher who was famous for developing theories about motion.

1. Ptolemy, Egyptian philosopher and astronomer, made charts and tables from an observatory near Alexandria, Egypt

2. Descartes, French philosopher, developed a theory of knowledge by doubting, believed intuition was the key to understanding

3. Copernicus, Polish astronomer, concluded that the sun was at the center of the universe

4. Kepler, German astronomer and mathematician, realized that planets travel in ellipses rather than circles

5. Galileo, Italian astronomer and physicist, improved the telescope; wrote *The Starry Messenger*, which refuted the prevailing theory of an earth-centered universe

6. Newton, English mathematician, determined general laws of motion and the laws of gravity

7. Einstein, German physicist, published the Special Theory of Relativity and the General Theory of Relativity, introduced the concepts of gravitational fields and curved space

ANSWER KEY

Exercise 13 Answers will vary. Possible answers are: 1. Ptolemy was an Egyptian philosopher and astronomer who was successful in making charts . . .   2. Descartes was a French philosopher who is renowned for developing a theory . . .   3. Copernicus was a Polish astronomer who was famous for concluding that the sun . . .   4. Kepler was a German astronomer and mathematician who was celebrated for realizing . . .   5. Galileo was an Italian astronomer and physicist who was skillful in improving the telescope . . .   6. Newton was an English mathematician who was famous for determining the general laws . . .   7. Einstein was a German physicist who was proficient in developing new concepts such as gravitational fields and curved space . . .

FOCUS 6 [15 minutes]

1. **Lead-in:** Before reading the focus chart, ask students to read the boldfaced type in the examples and identify the prepositions used. Ask a volunteer to write these on the board.

2. Read the first section, and ask one volunteer to create an original sentence using *agree to*, and ask another to create a sentence using *argue about*.

3. Read the second section. This is a source of errors for many students. Ask several volunteers to create other sentences using *ask for, hope for, care for*.

4. Have two other volunteers read the next two sections.

5. Answer any questions students might have.

METHODOLOGY NOTE

The rules in this focus are fairly straightforward. Students need to remember that a gerund (not an infinitive) is an object of a preposition or a phrasal verb, except when the preposition is *for* (e.g., *She asked for Tom to go with her.* NOT: * *She asked for Tom going with her*).

EXERCISE 12 [25 minutes]

Students write sentences about general beliefs using gerunds and/or infinitives.

1. Read the directions and example as a class.

2. Have students work in pairs, using the prompts supplied and a gerund or infinitive in each response.

3. Remind students to pay attention to the preposition. If the preposition is *for*, students need to use the infinitive form; otherwise, they will use the gerund form.

4. Have pairs share their sentences with another pair, and discuss them.

5. Ask volunteers to share sentences with the class, and discuss. See answers on LP page 346.

 For more practice, use *Grammar Dimensions 4* Workbook page 167, Exercise 11 and page 168, Exercise 12.

EXPANSION [30 minutes/homework]

In Activity 2 (writing) on SB page 349 students write about an alien from another planet using gerund complements. This activity is a good follow-up to Exercise 12, either as homework or as a class activity.

EXERCISE 13 (OPTIONAL) [20 minutes]

In Exercise 13 students write sentences with the information provided, using gerunds as the objects of prepositions or phrasal verbs.

1. Read the directions and example as a class.

2. Have students work independently to complete the sentences.

3. Have them exchange papers with a partner, and review and discuss each other's work.

4. Ask volunteers to share their answers with the class. See possible answers on LP page 346.

 For more practice, use *Grammar Dimensions 4* Workbook page 169, Exercise 13.

EXPANSION [20 minutes/homework]

This activity can be assigned for in-class work or as homework for extra practice with gerunds as the objects of prepositions and phrasal verbs.

1. Have students work in pairs.

2. Ask them to write seven more sentences about famous or infamous people they are familiar with using the adjective + preposition combinations provided in Exercise 13. Give an example: *Adolph Hitler was renowned for the atrocities he committed in Europe.*

3. Have pairs share their sentences with another pair.

Fill in the following blanks with a gerund or infinitive.

After taking off on the last Mercury mission, Gordon Cooper settled in for a good night's sleep halfway through his journey. Compared with most of the duties of spaceflight, it seemed (1) _____to be_____ (be) an easy enough undertaking. But Cooper ended up (2) _____having to wedge_____ (have to wedge) his hands beneath his safety harness to keep his arms from (3) _____floating around_____ (float around) and (4) _____striking_____ (strike) switches on the instrument panel.

Since Cooper's flight, (5) _____sleeping_____ (sleep) in space has become a routine matter—maybe too routine. When carrying out an especially boring or tiring task, some astronauts have nodded off—only they didn't really nod: they simply closed their eyes and stopped (6) _____moving_____ (move). There are none of the waking mechanisms that we would expect (7) _____to have_____ (have) on earth—one's head (8) _____falling_____ (fall) to one side or a pencil (9) _____dropping_____ (drop) to the floor.

Space crews have also found that they don't need handholds and ladders to get around; they quickly learn (10) _____to push off_____ (push off) with one hand and float directly to their destinations. (11) _____To eat_____ (eat), use a computer, or do some other stationary task, astronauts now slip their stockinged feet into loops or wedges attached to the floor. Similarly, a single Velcro head strap suffices (12) _____to keep_____ (keep) sleeping astronauts from (13) _____drifting out_____ (drift out) toward the ventilation ducts.

A favorite recreation in space is (14) _____playing/to play_____ (play) with one's food. Instead of carrying food all the way to their mouths with a utensil, some experienced astronauts like (15) _____to catapult_____ (catapult) food from spoons. Although (16) _____drinking_____ (drink) coffee seems like the most natural thing on Earth, in space it won't work. If you tried (17) _____to tip_____ (tip) the cup back to take a drink, the weightless coffee would not roll out. One astronaut offers the following advisory: "Don't let your curiosity tempt you into (18) _____exploring_____ (explore) a larger clump of liquid than you're prepared (19) _____to drink/drinking_____ (drink) later." If you don't start (20) _____to drink/drinking_____ (drink) your blob with a straw, it eventually attaches itself to the nearest wall or window.

Although spaceflight has its irritations, these are necessary if astronauts are to soar. The whole idea of airborne testing is to make (21) _____living_____ (live) and (22) _____working_____ (work) in weightlessness easy and unremarkable for ordinary folk.

Adapted from: D. Stewart, "The Floating World at Zero G," *Air and Space* (August/September 1991): 38.

Use Your English

CD2 Track 8

ACTIVITY 1 listening

Listen to the audio, a story about a famous unsolved mystery. Use information from the audio to complete each sentence below. Use a phrase containing an infinitive or a gerund based on what you have heard.

Example: *Cullen was not good at* ___conversing___.

1. _____ describes Priscilla's fashion tastes.
2. Cullen finished _____.
3. _____ was one indication of Cullen's violence.
4. Priscilla and Cullen decided _____.
5. Priscilla allowed various characters _____.
6. Cullen probably resented Priscilla's _____.
7. Beverly Bass and her friend "Bubba" Gavel tried _____.
8. Soon after the crime, the police succeeded in _____.
9. _____ was "Racehorse" Haynes's best talent.
10. "Racehorse" Haynes convinced the jury _____.
11. The prosecutors failed _____.
12. The jurors admitted _____.

ACTIVITY 2 writing

You are a news reporter called to interview a visitor from another planet. Although this creature looks very much like a human being and speaks English, you find that she has some very different characteristics. Describe what you learned from the alien as a result of your interviews. You might include some information about what the alien is accustomed to, annoyed at, capable of, concerned about, desirous of, incapable of, interested in, suited for, susceptible to, sympathetic toward, and weary of. Use at least five gerund complements in your report.

Example: *The alien has a very unusual diet. She is used to eating tree bark and grass.*

ANSWER KEY

Activity 1 Answers will vary. Possible answers are: 1. Dressing racily 2. living conservatively 3. Breaking Priscilla's collarbone 4. to separate 5. to come into her home. 6. receiving support payments and attorney's fees 7. coming to Priscilla's aid 8. charging Cullen with murder 9. To discredit witnesses 10. to doubt Priscilla 11. to convince the jury Cullen was guilty beyond a reasonable doubt 12. not believing Cullen was innocent

EXERCISE 14 (OPTIONAL) [20 minutes]

In Exercise 14 students complete sentences in a reading about spaceflight, using gerunds and infinitives. This exercise makes a good homework assignment.

1. Read the directions and example (the second sentence) as a class. Could a gerund be used here? (*no*)
2. Have students work independently to complete the sentences.
3. Have them exchange papers with a partner, and review and discuss each other's work.
4. Review answers as a class. See answers on LP page 348.

EXPANSION [20 minutes]

As a review, ask students to refer back to Focus 1 and identify the function of each of the verb forms— e.g., subject, subject complement, noun complement, adjective complement, direct object, or object of preposition. For example, #1 functions as a direct object. #2 functions as an object of preposition.

UNIT GOAL REVIEW [10 minutes]

Ask students to look at the goals on the opening page of the unit again. Refer to the pages of the unit where information on each goal can be found.

For a grammar quiz review of Units 16–18, refer students to pages 171–173 in the *Grammar Dimensions 4* Workbook.

 For assessment of Unit 18, use *Grammar Dimensions 4 ExamView®*.

USE YOUR ENGLISH

The Use Your English activities at the end of the unit contain situations that should naturally elicit the structures covered in the unit. For a more complete discussion of how to use the Use Your English activities, see To the Teacher, LP page xxvi. While students are doing these activities in class, you can circulate and listen to see if they are using the structures accurately. Errors can be corrected after the activity has finished.

ACTIVITY 1   listening [30 minutes]

In Activity 1 students listen to a story about a famous unsolved mystery, and then complete sentences using infinitives or gerunds. This activity is a good follow-up to Exercise 3 on SB page 335. Note that the former CD track number (25) is incorrectly listed in the student book.

CD 2
Track 8

1. Discuss famous cases of unhappy marriages and murders, such as the O. J. Simpson trial and Scott Peterson. Tell students that, in the United States, a jury can only convict someone of murder when there is no "reasonable doubt" about his or her innocence. If they have any doubts at all, they cannot declare the person guilty.
2. Read the directions and example as a class.
3. Have students listen to the audio once.
4. Ask students to listen again and complete the sentences, stopping the audio as needed to write their answers.
5. Ask students to listen to the audio a third time to complete and check their answers.
6. Have students work in small groups to share their answers.
7. Ask volunteers to share their answers with the class. Discuss whether students think Cullen committed the murder, or not.

VARIATION

If students are familiar with the O. J. Simpson trial, which took place in Los Angeles and was broadcast throughout the world, ask them to create a paragraph comparing the two famous cases. Encourage them to use at least five infinitive and/or gerund structures in their paragraphs and to underline these forms wherever they are used.

ACTIVITY 2   writing [30 minutes/homework]

In this activity students write about an alien from another planet using gerund complements. This activity is a good follow-up to Exercise 12 on SB page 346, either as homework or as a class activity.

1. Discuss stories and movies about aliens visiting Earth from another planet. Ask students to describe the aliens.
2. Read the directions and example as a class.
3. List the verbs from the directions on the board and have students copy them:

accustomed to	*incapable of*
annoyed at	*interested in*
capable of	*suited for*
concerned about	*susceptible to*
desirous of	*sympathetic toward*
	weary of

4. Ask students to work independently to write a report summarizing the interviews with the alien. Tell them to use at least five gerund complements in their reports, using the verbs on the board.
5. Have students work in pairs, exchange their papers, and discuss them.
6. Ask several volunteers to read their reports to the class.

ACTIVITY 3 research on the web

Go to the Internet to read facts about the life of one of your favorite artists, musicians, architects, or writers, using a search engine such as Google® or Yahoo®, or another source you may know. Write a short composition in which you use at least two gerund complements and four infinitive complements in your writing.

Example: Leonardo Da Vinci

Leonardo Da Vinci was a famous painter, sculptor, architect, and musician who began displaying his artistic abilities early in life. In Florence, he loved to associate with gifted artists such as Botticeli . . .

ACTIVITY 4 reflection

Review the following learning strategies and indicate with a check (✓) the ones you enjoy doing, don't mind doing, can't stand doing, or simply forget to do. Share your chart with a partner, and discuss ways that you might improve your learning strategies.

	ENJOY DOING	DON'T MIND DOING	CAN'T STAND DOING	FORGET TO DO
Preview main ideas by skimming reading material before actually reading it.				
Check the accuracy of your oral production while you are speaking.				
Judge how well you have done a learning activity after you have completed it.				

	ENJOY DOING	DON'T MIND DOING	CAN'T STAND DOING	FORGET TO DO
Use reference materials such as dictionaries and encyclopedias to assist with learning.				
Write down key words and concepts during a listening or reading activity.				
Make a mental or written summary of information gained through listening or reading.				
Play back in your mind the sound of a word, phrase, or fact in order to assist comprehension.				
Use information in a reading text to guess meanings of new items, predict outcomes, or complete missing parts.				
Elicit from a teacher or peer additional explanations or examples.				
Work together with others to solve a problem.				
Reduce anxiety by using mental techniques to reduce stress.				

ACTIVITY 3 research on the web
[30 minutes/homework]

In this activity students use the Internet to research and write about one of their favorite artists, musicians, architects, or writers, using at least two gerund complements and four infinitive complements. This activity makes a good homework assignment following Exercise 8 on SB page 342.

1. Read the directions as a class. Ask a volunteer to read the example aloud.
2. Have students research one of their favorite musicians, architects, or writers on the Internet and write about him or her using at least two gerund complements and four infinitive complements.
3. Have students share their writings in small groups.
4. Ask a few volunteers to read their writings to the class, and discuss.

ACTIVITY 4 reflection
[40 minutes]

In this activity students evaluate a list of learning strategies and indicate which ones they like and dislike. They then discuss their evaluations with a partner and discuss ways to improve their learning strategies. It is a good activity for students after Exercise 11 on SB page 345.

1. Read the directions as a class. Ask a volunteer to read the headings of the columns aloud. Ask students to read through the list of learning strategies silently.
2. Have students work in pairs. Have them each check the appropriate column—enjoy doing, don't mind doing, can't stand doing, or simply forget to do. Then, have them share their responses and discuss ways to improve their learning strategies.
3. Ask students to share their best learning strategies with the class, and discuss.

PERFECTIVE INFINITIVES

UNIT GOALS

- Use the correct forms of perfective infinitives

- Use perfective infinitives to express ideas and opinions about past events

- Use perfective infinitives to express emotions and attitudes

- Use perfective infinitives to express obligations, intentions, and future plans

- Use perfective infinitives with *enough* and *too*

OPENING TASK

Time Travel to the Past

Have you ever wished you could go back in time and meet famous people from past eras, see things that no longer exist in the world, or participate in exciting historical events?

Confucius

Queen Cleopatra

Mount Fuji

■ **STEP 1**

Which of the following statements reflect things you'd like to have seen, heard, or done? Which sound less appealing to you? Rank the statements from 1 through 8, with 1 representing your first preference and 8, your last.

- observe dinosaurs when they roamed the earth _____
- speak with Confucius, the great Chinese philosopher _____
- live in an ancient Mayan city _____
- take a cruise on the Nile River in Queen Cleopatra's barge _____
- see the Japanese volcano Mount Fuji when it erupted in 1707 _____
- listen to Beethoven play his Fifth Symphony for the first time in Vienna in 1808 _____
- accompany Orville Wright on the first airplane flight in 1903 _____
- attend a performance by the famous twentieth-century American blues singer, Billie Holiday _____

■ **STEP 2**

Compare your ratings with those of a few of your classmates. Briefly explain the reasons for your top one or two choices.

Example: *I would like to have attended a performance by Billie Holiday because I've heard some of her songs, and I saw a movie about her life.*

■ **STEP 3**

Write two more statements expressing things that you would like to have seen, heard, or done.

UNIT OVERVIEW

Unit 19 reviews forms of perfective infinitives, explains their meanings, and presents some of the typical communicative contexts in which they are used.

Please note that due to its length, this unit has been divided into five lesson plans. To review this unit more quickly, review focus charts and have students complete the first exercise after each chart to observe students' grasp of the grammar topics.

GRAMMAR NOTE

The largest obstacle most students need to overcome when mastering perfective infinitives is that of understanding when events occur in relationship to other events in a sentence. This unit explains these relationships in time in detail, and gives students multiple opportunities to develop their understanding of and ability with these structures.

UNIT GOALS

Some instructors may want to review the goals listed on Student Book (SB) page 352 after completing the Opening Task so that students understand what they should know by the end of the unit. These goals can also be reviewed at the end of the unit when students are more familiar with the grammar terminology.

OPENING TASK [25 minutes]

The purpose of the Opening Task is to create a context in which student will need to use perfective infinitives as they read a series of statements about witnessing or participating in historical events and rank their appeal in terms of whether they would like to have seen, heard about, or in some way been involved in the event. The problem-solving format is designed to show the teacher how well the students can produce the target structures implicitly

and spontaneously when they are engaged in a communicative task. For a more complete discussion of the purpose of the Opening Task, see To the Teacher, Lesson Planner (LP) page xxii.

Setting Up the Task

1. Read the opening questions and ask students to answer the question about time travel while considering the art and photos on page 352.
2. Ask students to read through the bulleted fragments on page 353 and identify unfamiliar historical figures or vocabulary.
3. If time permits, ask students to share their knowledge about the events, places, or people.

Conducting the Task

■ STEP 1

Ask students to consider and rank the statements individually.

■ STEP 2

1. Have students work in small groups to complete Step 2, in which they compare and discuss their ratings and give reasons for their top choices.
2. Listen as students discuss their rankings to get a sense of their familiarity with perfective infinitives. Student may omit the *would* before *like*. Do not correct at this point.

■ STEP 3

Have students work independently to write at least two statements expressing things that they would like to have seen, heard, or done.

Closing the Task

1. Ask students to return to their small groups and take turns sharing the sentences they have written

2. Ask various volunteers to share their sentences with the class.
3. Don't worry about accuracy at this point, though you may want to take notes of errors in meaning, form, or use in order to focus on those problems later.

EXPANSION [10 minutes]

For further assessment, follow up the task with additional questions, prompting responses with lexical verbs. For example: *What would you like to have done if you lived in the nineteenth century?* (Make certain that students are aware that the nineteenth century indicates the 1800's.)

GRAMMAR NOTE

Typical student errors (form)

- Using the gerund rather than the past participle in perfective infinitive structures:—e.g., * *I'd like to be seeing the results of that test.* (See Focus 1.)
- Using the past participle rather than the gerund in progressive forms of perfective infinitive structures:—e.g., * *The boys have been watched the game on TV.* (See Focus 3.)

Typical student errors (use)

- Using the past progressive rather than the past perfect with perfective infinitives:—e.g., * *She prefers not to be having an early morning class.* (See Focus 5.)
- Using the present progressive rather than the past perfect when expressing uncertainty about past events:—e.g., * *Someone seems to be eating all the ice cream last night.* (See Focus 7.)

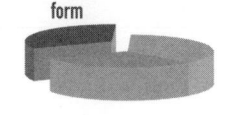

FOCUS 1 — Review of Perfective Infinitive Structures

Perfective infinitives (*to* + *have* + past participle) express events that are past in relation to a present, past, or future moment of focus.

EXAMPLES	EXPLANATIONS
Perfective Infinitive	**Forming the Perfective Infinitive**
(a) I'd like **to have been** at the first Olympic games in Greece.	Perfective infinitives have the form *to* + *have* + past participle (*-ed* or irregular verb form).
(b) Many people claim **to have seen** UFOs.	
(c) I expect **to have finished** my term paper by tomorrow night.	
	Types of Perfective Infinitive Clauses
	Like other infinitives, perfective infinitives occur in a number of clause types in sentences:
(d) **To have won** the Boston Marathon was a dream come true for her.	• subject
(e) It is helpful **to have reviewed** the chapter assignment before you attend the class lecture.	• postponed subject after introductory *it*
(f) I would love **to have seen** my friend's face when he opened his gift from all of us.	• object
(g) The question **to have been** debated at last week's meeting was whether our school needed a new swimming pool, but the meeting got postponed.	• adjective
(h) Research writing is a good course **to have taken**.	
(i) My sister was too young **to have known** she shouldn't have picked the flowers in the park.	• degree complement
(j) Those pants were big enough **to have fit** a giant!	

■ EXERCISE 1

In the following passage, Ted Turner, a well-known American businessman, talks with interviewer Studs Terkel about some of the things he would like to have done. Underline the perfective infinitives he uses. The first one has been done as an example.

(1) I would like <u>to have lived</u> a whole bunch of lives. (2) I would like <u>to have gone</u> to West Point or Annapolis and had a military career, I would like <u>to have been</u> a fireman, I would like <u>to have been</u> a state trooper, I would like <u>to have been</u> an explorer, I would like <u>to have been</u> a concert pianist, an Ernest Hemingway, an F. Scott Fitzgerald, a movie star, a big league ballplayer, Joe Namath. (3) I like it all.

(4) I would like <u>to have been</u> a fighter pilot, a mountain climber, go to the Olympics and run the marathon, a general on a white horse. (5) A sea captain, back in the days of sailing ships, sailed with Horatio Nelson. (6) I would like <u>to have gone</u> with Captain Cook to find the Spice Islands, with Columbus, with Sir Francis Drake. (7) I would like <u>to have been</u> a pilot, a privateer, a knight in shining armor, gone on the Crusades. (8) Wouldn't you? (9) I'd like <u>to have gone</u> looking for Dr. Livingston, right? (10) In the heart of darkest Africa. (11) I would like <u>to have discovered</u> the headwaters of the Nile and the Amazon River.

■ EXERCISE 2

Write three statements about things you would like to have done, using perfective infinitive clauses. Exchange the three statements you wrote with another classmate. Report one or more of your classmate's statements to the rest of the class or a small group, using a *that*-clause with a modal perfect verb.

Example: Statement: *I would like to have discovered the North Pole.*
Paraphrase: *Olivia wishes that she could have discovered the North Pole.*

Note that in the paraphrase, *could* is used as the modal with *wish* as the main clause verb.

■ EXERCISE 3

Complete the blanks with perfective infinitives. Use the verb in parentheses.

Example: She was happy (break) <u>to have broken</u> the record for the one-hundred-meter dash.

1. (a) The elderly gentleman next door considers himself (be) _____ quite a romantic fellow in his younger days. (b) He claims (write) _____ passionate love letters to more than a dozen women. (c) Not all of his letters got the responses he had hoped for, but in his opinion, as the saying goes, it was better (love) _____ and lost than never (love) _____ at all.

2. **David:** (a) It was really nice of Hector (give) _____ us his car for our trip to the Grand Canyon. We had a great time.
   Alana: (b) Oh, he was happy (be able to) _____ help you out. (c) I'd really like (go) _____ with you on your trip, but my cousins were visiting that weekend.

3. (a) Jeanne is too smart (believe) _____ the story Russ told her the other day. (b) His story was outlandish enough (convince) _____ her that it was far from the truth.

4. (a) Dear Fran: Accepting that job offer was a wise decision for you (make) _____. (b) We're glad (have) _____ you as our office mate for the past three years. (c) Good luck! With your talent, we expect you (receive) _____ a big promotion before long.

ANSWER KEY

Exercise 2   Answers will vary.
Exercise 3   1. to have been; to have written; to have loved; to have loved   2. to have given; to have been able to; to have gone   3. to have believed; to have convinced   4. to have made; to have had; to have received

FOCUS 1 [20 minutes]

Focus 1 shows the formation of perfective infinitives and where they can occur in a sentence.

1. **Lead-in:** Read the explanations, and have various volunteers read the examples.
2. To help students understand the syntactic roles of perfective infinitives, have them highlight or bracket the perfective infinitive clauses in the examples in their entirety (e.g., *to have been at the first Olympic games in Greece*).
3. Write each sentence on the board and ask students to come up and circle the perfective infinitive section.
4. Ask students seated to ask how this perfective infinitive functions: as a *subject, postponed subject after it, object, adjective,* or *degree complement*.

EXERCISE 1 [10 minutes]

In Exercise 1 students identify the perfective infinitives in a reading passage by Ted Turner, applying what they have just learned in Focus 1.

1. Ask students if they know of Ted Turner, who, among other things, started the CNN Broadcasting station, has owned a major league baseball team (the Atlanta Braves) and was married to the actor Jane Fonda.
2. Read the directions as a class. Ask a volunteer to read the first sentence. Ask students to say what kind of clause *to have lived* is. (object)
3. Have students work independently to underline the perfective infinitives in the passage.
4. Have them work in pairs to compare answers.
5. Review answers as a class. See answers on LP page 354.

 For more practice, use *Grammar Dimensions 4* Workbook page 174, Exercise 1.

EXERCISE 2 [20 minutes]

In Exercise 2 students write and talk about things they would have liked to have done, using perfective infinitive clauses.

1. Read the directions and example as a class.
2. Have students work independently to write their three statements.
3. Have them work in small groups to share their sentences.
4. Ask several volunteers to share their sentences, and ask others to identify the perfective infinitive clauses they used in them.

 For more practice, use *Grammar Dimensions 4* Workbook page 175, Exercise 2.

EXPANSION [25 minutes]

For additional practice—either in class or at home—have students choose one of their statements from Exercise 2 and write a paragraph about the topic, using the statement as the topic sentence for the paragraph. Ask them to support their statements with details and examples.

EXERCISE 3 [20 minutes]

In Exercise 3 students complete sentences with perfective infinitives, continuing their practice of the forms explored in Focus 1.

1. Read the directions and example as a class.
2. Have students work independently to complete the sentences with the correct perfective infinitive.
3. Ask students to compare their answers with a partner.

4. To check answers, ask four different students to read the four different passages aloud, using the answers they wrote.
5. Discuss any incorrect answers. See answers on LP page 354.

EXPANSION [30 minutes]

Activity 1 (listening/writing/speaking) on SB page 370 is a good follow-up to these first three exercises. In it students listen to a series of messages that have been left on their answering machines while they were away on (a fictional) vacation. They leave messages in response, using perfective infinitive forms.

FOCUS 2 — Expressing Past Events

EXAMPLES	EXPLANATIONS
	Past in Relation to the Present
(a) Jamie is happy **to have finished** her report last night so she can go to the soccer game with us today.	Perfective infinitives signal an event or condition in the past. The event or condition may continue to the present.
(b) Ben considers Phillipe **to have been** his best friend ever since they started college three years ago. (Ben still considers him to be his best friend.)	
	Past in Relation to the Past
(c) Dr. Yamada wanted **to have completed** her research before last August. However, her funds for the project ran out.	The event expressed by the infinitive clause may be unfulfilled.
(d) The driver claimed **to have stopped** for the traffic light before the accident occurred.	With verbs that express beliefs or attitudes, such as *claim* or *consider*, the event in the infinitive clause may or may not have actually happened.
	Past in Relation to the Future
(e) Winona expects **to have made** all of her plane reservations by next week.	The event expressed by the infinitive clause may be a future event that takes place before another time in the future.
(f) Winona expects **to make** all of her plane reservations by next week.	We also commonly use infinitives that are not perfective (*to* + verb) to carry the same meaning for future events.
Perfective: Past	**Past Tense vs. Present Tense Main Clauses**
(g) It **was** nice of you **to have done** that.	When the main clause is past tense, speakers often use nonperfective infinitives to express the same meanings as perfective ones.
Nonperfective: Past	
(h) It **was** nice of you **to do** that.	When the main clause is present tense, use:
Perfective: Past	
(i) It **is** nice of you **to have done** that. (You did something in the past.)	
Nonperfective: Present, Future	
(j) It **is** nice of you **to do** that. (You are doing something right now or will do something in the future.)	

Infinitive	*To Express*
perfective	past meaning
nonperfective	present or future meaning

EXERCISE 4

Complete each blank with a perfective infinitive, using the verb in parentheses. Then state which type of meaning each one expresses: past relative to the present, to the past, or to the future.

Example: I would like (accompany) <u>to have accompanied</u> the Castenada family on their travels across the country.

1. The Castenada family has been traveling in the United States all summer and has only two weeks left of their trip; by the end of August, the family plans (tour) <u>to have toured</u> most of the East Coast. (future)

2. The Castenadas intended (visit) <u>to have visited</u> all of their West Coast relatives before the end of June, but they couldn't because of car trouble. (past)

3. Eight-year-old Ruby Castenada says that she would like (spend) <u>to have spent</u> the entire summer at Disneyland. (present)

4. So far, Mr. and Mrs. Castenada consider the highlight of their vacation (be) <u>to have been</u> their camping trip in Michigan. (present)

5. At the beginning of the trip, Javier, their teenage son, was upset (leave) <u>to have left</u> all his friends for the whole summer. (past)

6. However, now Javier admits that he would like (see) <u>to have seen</u> even more of the country and hopes to travel again soon. (present)

7. The Castenadas' goal is (visit) <u>to have visited</u> all of the continental United States before Javier goes away to college. (future)

EXERCISE 5

Restate the infinitives in the following quotations as perfective infinitives. If you had to choose one of them for a maxim to live by, which one would you select? Can you think of any other sayings that use perfective infinitives?

Example: To win one's joy through struggle is better than to yield to melancholy.
(Andre Gide, French author)
To have won one's joy through struggle is better than *to have yielded* to melancholy.

1. What a lovely surprise to finally discover how unlonely being alone can be. (Ellen Burstyn, American actress)

2. To endure what is unendurable is true endurance. (Japanese proverb)

3. I would prefer even to fail with honor than to win by cheating. (Sophocles, Greek dramatist)

4. To teach is to learn twice over. (Joseph Joubert, *Pensées*)

5. It is better to be happy for a moment and burned up with beauty than to live a long time and be bored all the while. (Don Marquis, "the lesson of the moth," *Archy and Mehitabel*)

6. Youth is the time to study wisdom; old age is the time to practice it. (Rousseau, *Reveries of a Solitary Walker*)

ANSWER KEY

Exercise 5 1. to have discovered 2. To have endured what is unendurable 3. to have failed with honor rather than than to have won by cheating. 4. To have taught is to have learned twice over. 5. to have been happy . . . than to have lived and to have been bored. 6. to have studied wisdom . . . to have practiced it.

FOCUS 2 [25 minutes]

Focus 2 explores how perfective infinitives are used to express past events, and how they can reflect on the moment of focus.

1. **Lead-in:** Read the explanation in the first section, and ask two volunteers to read the two examples aloud.

2. Draw time lines on the board to illustrate when events occurred in relation to later or earlier ones:

report finished	can go to soccer game
(a) x	x
last night	today
started college	has been best friend
(b) ——— x ——— x ———	
3 years ago	(now/still)

3. Ask students to say when each event occurred. (*last night, today*)

4. Read the explanation in the second section, and ask two volunteers to read the two examples aloud.

5. Note that with (c) and (d), it is the main verbs that make the event either unfulfilled (c) or doubtful (d). To emphasize this point, substitute *is glad* for *wanted* in (c). This would make the event fulfilled (and of course then would not make sense with the sentence that follows).

6. Read the explanation in the third section, and ask two volunteers to read the two examples aloud.

7. The explanations and examples in the last section may be confusing at first to students because the sentences are so similar, with only the verb tenses and perfective infinitive forms changing. Explain that native speakers tend to use the forms for (g) and (h) for the same contexts: somebody did something in the past; it was a nice thing.

8. Point out that the comment clauses in (i) and (j) refer to different times: to a past event for (i) and to a present or future event for (j).

9. To further exemplify this last distinction, put a list of past and present events on the board and elicit comments: *My friend sent me some flowers. (It is nice of her to have done that.) The teachers will hold a farewell party for students tomorrow night. (It is nice of them to do that.)*

10. Encourage students to ask questions about anything they do not understand.

EXERCISE 4 [15 minutes]

In Exercise 4 students complete sentences using perfective infinitives, and then identify the meaning of each use.

1. Read the directions and example as a class. Ask students to refer to Focus 2 and identify the meaning of the perfective infinitive in the example.

2. Have students work independently to complete the sentences with the correct perfective infinitive.

3. Ask students to compare their answers with a partner. Have them take turns stating the type of meaning each expresses in relationship to the past, present, or future.

4. Ask volunteers to share their answers and state the meaning of each with the class. See answers on LP page 356.

work book For more practice, use *Grammar Dimensions 4* Workbook page 175, Exercise 3.

EXPANSION [30 minutes/homework]

Activity 5 (reflection) on SB page 371 makes a good homework assignment following Exercise 4. In this activity students reflect on their academic achievements and write about what they would like to have achieved by next year.

EXERCISE 5 [15 minutes]

In Exercise 5 students restate maxims using perfective infinitives, applying what they learned in Focus 2.

1. Read the directions and example as a class.

2. Ask students to work in pairs to rewrite the maxims using perfective infinitives.

3. Have each pair get together with another pair and take turns sharing their sentences.

4. Ask various volunteers to share a sentence with the class, and discuss these. See answers on LP page 356.

work book For more practice, use *Grammar Dimensions 4* Workbook page 176, Exercise 4.

EXPANSION [30 minutes/homework]

1. For homework, ask students to find five other quotations and rewrite them, using perfective infinitives. Suggest they consult a book of quotations from the library or, if possible, an Internet source.

2. Note that not all quotations with infinitives can be rewritten with perfective infinitives, but this fact could lead to further discussion of the meanings of perfective infinitives.

FOCUS 3 — Progressive and Passive Forms of Perfective Infinitives

EXAMPLES	EXPLANATIONS
	Progressive Form
(a) I'd like **to have been watching** when Bart received his award for bravery.	*to + have + been + verb + -ing*
(b) Mr. Ford believed the police **to have been guarding** his store when the robbery occurred.	
	Passive Form
(c) Bart would like me **to have been sent** a ticket to the ceremony.	*to + have + been + past participle*
(d) Mr. Ford believed his wife **to have been given** false information by the police.	

EXERCISE 6

Rewrite each of the following clauses as a perfective infinitive clause. The clauses begin with *that*, *Ø-that* (*that* has been deleted), or *when*. Make any word changes that are necessary.

Examples: *Ø-that* clause: Josef wishes he could have discovered the Cape of Good Hope with Bartolomeu Dias in 1488.

infinitive clause: *Josef would like to have discovered the Cape of Good Hope with Bartolomeu Dias in 1488.*

that-clause: Veronica believes that she was shortchanged.

infinitive clause: *Veronica believes herself to have been shortchanged.*

1. Our English teacher expects that we will finish our oral reports on our favorite celebrities by the end of next week.

2. Josh would prefer that he be the last one to present, but unfortunately for him, he is scheduled to be first.

3. Isela believes she was greatly misinformed by one of her interview subjects.

4. We wish we could have heard more about Shaun's talk with Beyonce. (Change *wish* to *would like.*)

5. Jocelyn hoped she would be given a chance to interview her favorite author, but the interview didn't work out.

6. Gerard claims that he was sent an autograph from a "major motion picture star," whose identity he is keeping a secret.

7. Sandra reported that Angelina Jolie, her favorite actress, had been sitting in front of her at a Carnegie Hall concert.

8. Ty thinks that he has gotten the most interesting interview with a celebrity. (Use *consider* for the main verb.)

9. Berta wishes that she had been eating dinner at the Hollywood restaurant last Friday night because someone told her that her favorite basketball player was there.

10. I will be relieved when I have presented my report since getting up in front of others makes me anxious.

FOCUS 4 — Negative Forms of Perfective Infinitives

EXAMPLES	EXPLANATIONS
	Formal English
(a) The three nations were wise **not to have signed** the agreement until they could discuss it further.	In formal written English, put negative forms (*not, never,* etc.) before the infinitive verbs.
(b) **Not to have been contacted** for a job interview was a big disappointment for Daniel.	
(c) Senator Bolan appears **never to have voted** in favor of extra funding for child care.	A paraphrase of (c) would be the following: *It appears that Senator Bolan has never voted in favor of extra funding for child care.* Note that in example (c), the person's name replaces the subject *it* when the perfective infinitive follows *appears*.
	Informal English
(d) **To have not been invited** to the party made her really upset.	In less formal English, speakers sometimes put negative forms after *have.*
(e) I seem **to have not brought** the book I meant to give you today.	
(f) That woman claims **to have never seen** the money that turned up in her purse.	

FOCUS 3 [20 minutes]

1. **Lead-in:** Read the explanations, and ask two volunteers to read the examples aloud.

2. To review the progressive and passive forms, write *Progressive* on the board. Beneath it, write several "dehydrated" phrases with the base forms of two verbs—i.e., *I'd like/swim.* Have students, using the focus chart, say the progressive infinitive forms. Write these on the board—i.e., *I'd like to have been swimming.*

3. Show students how to expand a few of the phrases: *I'd like to have been swimming last weekend instead of working in the chemistry lab.*

4. Repeat this procedure for passive forms. Write the label *Passive* on the board with "dehydrated" phrases beneath it for students to transform. For example: *I'd like/tell: I'd like to have been told the truth.*

5. Include some irregular verbs, such as *keep, leave, build, hear, make, meet, sleep, speak, win.* *Hope* could be used as a main verb instead of *like* for some of the phrases. Consult the list of common irregular verbs in Appendix 8, SB p. A-15 for other verbs.

EXERCISE 6 [20 minutes/homework]

In this exercise students rewrite clauses as perfective infinitive clauses, applying the principles of Focus 3. This exercise makes a good homework assignment.

1. Read the directions and first example as a class. Ask a volunteer to add *that* to the example sentence: *Josef wished that . . .*

2. Read the second example as a class. Ask a volunteer to rephrase the example sentence, omitting *that*: *Veronica believes she was . . .*

3. Have students work in pairs to rewrite the sentences.

4. Have pairs get together with another pair. Have students take turns sharing the sentences they wrote.

5. Review answers as a class. See answers on LP page 358.

VARIATION

Ask students to write out and turn in this assignment to assess their use of these forms in a controlled context. If assigned for homework, do the first one in class together to ensure that students understand the examples.

For more practice, use *Grammar Dimensions 4* Workbook page 177, Exercise 5.

LESSON PLAN 3

FOCUS 4 [15 minutes]

Focus 4 shows the placement of negative forms with perfective infinitives in both formal and informal English.

1. **Lead-in:** Write this sentence on the board and read it aloud: *Not to have traveled when she was younger saddened Joanna.*

2. Ask students whether this construction seems formal or informal. (*formal*) Ask how someone might express this thought when talking. (*To have not traveled when she was younger saddened Joanna.*) Elicit that, in more formal contexts, the negative *not* comes before the infinitive verb, and in less formal contexts, such as speech, it usually comes after *have.*

3. Ask three volunteers to read the first three examples. Read the explanation.

4. Ask volunteers to create other examples, and write these on the board.

5. Repeat this process with the second section of the chart.

6. Answer any questions students might have.

LANGUAGE NOTE

Remind students that, in informal English, speakers also use the nonperfective forms in some of the contexts shown here (e.g., *The three nations were wise not to sign the agreement . . .*). In other contexts, such as (e), it would be incorrect to use the nonperfective form—e.g., a speaker wouldn't say * *I seem to not bring the book,* but might avoid using a perfective infinitive by saying: *I think I forgot the book I meant to give you.*

The point here is not to encourage students to avoid complex structures but to help them understand (1) where these structures have meanings similar to others they have heard or seen, and (2) how the structures can be used to achieve more precise meaning, especially in formal contexts.

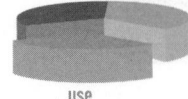

EXERCISE 7

In the following summary of a murder case, French Detective Henri Armand investigates the activities of a suspect, Dr. Moreau. Rewrite the underlined part of each of the following sentences so that it contains a negative perfective infinitive clause. Use the pattern for formal written English.

Example: It seemed that Dr. Moreau had not told the truth.
Dr. Moreau seemed <u>not to have told</u> the truth.

1. Contrary to what Dr. Moreau claimed, <u>it appeared he had not been out of town the last weekend in April.</u>

   he appeared not to have been out of town the last weekend in April.

2. It was quite strange, Detective Armand thought, <u>that Dr. Moreau had not told his housekeeper he would be away the weekend the murder occurred.</u> (Replace *that* with *for*.)

   for Dr. Moreau not to have told his housekeeper he would be away the weekend the murder occurred.

3. Furthermore, the doctor did not seem to remember much about the inn he claimed <u>he had stayed in</u> that weekend. How very odd!

   to have stayed in that weekend.

4. Also, the doctor claimed <u>that he had not known the victim, Horace Bix;</u> yet Bix's name was found in Dr. Moreau's appointment book.

   never to have known the victim, Horace Bix.

5. All in all, Detective Armand believed <u>that Dr. Moreau had not given the police truthful answers to most of their questions.</u>

   Dr. Moreau not to have given the police truthful answers to most of their questions.

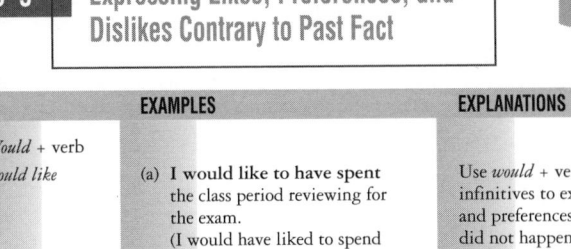

FOCUS 5	Expressing Likes, Preferences, and Dislikes Contrary to Past Fact

use

	EXAMPLES	EXPLANATIONS
Would + verb *would like*	(a) **I would like to have spent** the class period reviewing for the exam. (I would have liked to spend the class period reviewing for the exam.)	Use *would* + verbs with perfective infinitives to express likes, dislikes, and preferences about things that did not happen.
would love	(b) My parents **would love to have joined** us for dinner. (My parents would have loved to join us for dinner.)	Alternative forms of these sentences are given in parentheses. The alternative form has a perfective main clause verb and a nonperfective infinitive.
would prefer	(c) **I would prefer not to have had** an early morning class. (I would have preferred not to have an early morning class.)	
would hate	(d) **Wouldn't you hate to have been** in that crowded room? (Wouldn't you have hated to be in that crowded room?)	
	(e) **We would have liked to have spent** the class period reviewing for the exam. (incorrect) (f) **We would like to have spent** the class period reviewing for the exam. (correct)	Native English speakers sometimes use perfective forms for both clauses in speech. Although this pattern would sound fine to many native English speakers, it is not considered standard for written English.

EXERCISE 8

Choose any five of the following topics. For each topic, write a statement expressing a past wish. With a classmate, explain the reasons for one or two of your statements.

Example: An experience while traveling
I would prefer to have flown from England to France instead of going by boat across the channel.
Reason: *The sea was very rough that day and I got seasick.*

1. The way you spent your last vacation
2. Your participation in a sports event
3. A course you had to take
4. A paper you had to write
5. A meal you had recently
6. An experience you had at a party
7. (A topic of your choice)

ANSWER KEY

Exercise 8 Answers will vary. Possible answers are: 1. I would like to have spent last summer in Portugal. 2. I would like to have played soccer in high school. 3. I would prefer to have had more emphasis on poetry in my literature class. 4. I would like to have researched my topic more. 5. I would like to have tried the spicy mussels at the Thai restaurant we went to. 6. I would like to have danced a little more at the party last weekend.

EXERCISE 7 [15 minutes]

In Exercise 7 students practice rewriting sentences using the formal pattern of use for negative perfective infinitive clauses.

1. Read the directions as a class. Ask a volunteer to read the example. How is this construction "formal"? (*Not* precedes the infinitive verb.)
2. Have students work independently to rewrite the sentences.
3. Have them work in pairs, exchange papers, and review each other's work.
4. Ask different students to share their sentences with the class, and discuss. See answers on LP page 360.

For more practice, use *Grammar Dimensions 4* Workbook page 178, Exercise 6.

EXPANSION [60 minutes/homework]

Activity 2 (research/speaking/writing) on SB page 370 is a good follow-up to Exercise 7, either as homework or as a class activity. In this activity students survey people about regrets they have and share their findings with their classmates.

FOCUS 5 [15 minutes]

This focus and the three that follow it explain and illustrate communicative contexts in which perfective infinitives are used. Encourage students to learn and practice the structures with the commonly occurring *would* + verb phrases.

1. **Lead-in:** Ask students questions eliciting perfective infinitive forms: Serina, what would you have preferred to do instead of coming to class this morning? Yoshi, how would you like to have spent last weekend if you could have gone anywhere in the world?

2. If students give responses without perfective infinitives, assist them by writing their responses on the board and prompting the infinitive forms—e.g., *I wish I could have gone scuba diving* → *I'd like to have gone scuba diving.*

3. Read the explanations in the focus chart, and ask two volunteers to take turns reading the examples.

EXERCISE 8 [20 minutes]

In Exercise 8 students use cues to create sentences expressing likes, dislikes, and preferences about past events that did not end up happening.

1. Read the directions and example as a class.
2. Have students work independently to write the sentences using *would (like/love/hate/prefer)* + a perfective infinitive.
3. Have them work in pairs to share and compare their answers.
4. Review answers with the class. See possible answers on LP page 360.

For more practice, use *Grammar Dimensions 4* Workbook page 178, Exercise 7.

EXPANSION [20 minutes]

To practice asking questions using *would (like/love/hate/prefer)* + a perfective infinitive:

1. Have students work in pairs. Ask them to take turns phrasing the sentences they wrote in Exercise 8 as questions. Model, using the example in Exercise 8: *Would you like to have been asked to present your report first?* The other student should respond with the sentence he/she wrote: *Yes, I would like . . .*
2. Ask several pairs to share a question-and-answer with the class.

EXERCISE 9

Use the cues below to make sentences expressing a past wish that did not materialize or an unpleasant event that was avoided. Use the standard English pattern of *would like, would love, would prefer, would not like, would hate* followed by a perfective infinitive. Make any changes that are necessary, including any needed verb tense changes.

Example: be asked to present my report first
I would like to have been asked to present my report first.

1. take all of my final exams on one day instead of on several days
2. forget the answers to the vocabulary test questions
3. go to the movies instead of just staying home Saturday night
4. be the only one in our math class without the assignment done
5. be given true-false questions for the entire test rather than essay questions
6. study geology instead of biochemistry last semester
7. walk into the English classroom and find out the teacher was absent

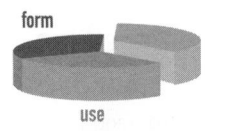

form

use

FOCUS 6	Expressing Other Emotions and Attitudes with Perfective Infinitives

EXAMPLES	EXPLANATIONS
(a) I **am sorry** to have missed your graduation party.	• *be* + adjective
(b) They **were shocked** to have been treated so rudely by the waiter.	
(c) It **was really generous of you** to have lent us your bicycles.	• *it + be* + adjective (+ *of* + noun)
(d) **It is annoying** to have been waiting so long to buy a ticket.	
(e) **It is such a pleasure** to have met you after reading many of your books.	• *it + be* + noun phrase
(f) **It was a miracle** to have found the contact lens in the swimming pool.	
(g) **It was fortunate for us** to have discovered the mistake so quickly.	• (*it + be* + adjective) *for* + noun/objective pronoun
(h) **For them** to have had three plane delays in one day was very unlucky.	
(i) It **must** be exciting to have lived in so many countries!	You may also use modal verbs before *be* with many of the expressions.
(j) It **would** be disappointing to have missed the parade. I'm glad we made it on time!	

EXERCISE 10

Choose five of the numbered items below. Make sentences with perfective infinitive clauses, using the cues. Use a variety of structures and add descriptive words or phrases to expand the cues into sentences. *Note:* For some phrases, either personal or impersonal, *it* could be the subject for a sentence, but some phrases allow only one choice.

Examples: Be foolish . . . think
John must be foolish to have thought that no one would notice he had taken the dangerous chemicals from the lab.
It was foolish of us to have thought no one would notice we were missing from class.

1. Be happy . . . find out
2. Be surprising . . . hear
3. Be unwise . . . build
4. Be kind . . . donate
5. Be so annoying . . . get
6. Be really thrilling . . . find out
7. Be a tragedy . . . lose
8. Be sad . . . learn

EXERCISE 11

Use an expression from Exercise 10, or a similar one, to make up a brief response for each of the situations below. Use a perfective infinitive in your response.

Example: You have recently spent three days at the beach house of your parents' friends while they were not there. You are writing them a thank-you note.
It was very generous of you to have let me stay in your beach house during my trip to the coast. I really appreciate your kindness. Thank you!

1. You have just remembered that today is the birthday of one of your friends who lives in another city, and you forgot to send her a birthday card. You buy a card and want to write a note to tell her you're sorry.
2. A friend helped you move to an apartment. You want to send him a thank-you note.
3. You are having a conversation at a party with someone you have just met. She has been telling you about her trip to see the Summer Olympics.
4. You recently went shopping. When you tried to purchase something, the salesman kept you waiting for several minutes while he chatted with a friend on the phone. You are writing a letter of complaint to the manager of the store.
5. You are writing a letter to a friend. You want to tell her how fortunate you were recently. You just heard that you were awarded two scholarships to attend school next year.
6. You call up the mother of a friend to thank her for having given a going-away party for you before you move to another city.
7. A friend did not show up for a class three sessions in a row. This strikes you as strange because he has never missed a class before. Another friend asks you if you know where he has been, but you don't.
8. A friend just wrote you an e-mail telling you that she enrolled a few weeks ago in a Web design class. You think she made a smart decision and want to let her know.

ANSWER KEY

Exercise 9 Answers may vary. Possible answers are: 1. I would like to have taken . . . 2. I would hate to have forgotten . . . 3. I would prefer to have gone . . . 4. I would not like to have been . . . 5. I would like to have been given . . . 6. I would prefer to have studied . . . 7. I would like to have walked . . . found out . . .

Exercise 10 Answers will vary.

Exercise 11 Answers will vary. Possible answers are: 1. I'm really sorry to have missed your birthday. 2. It was so nice of you to have helped me move. 3. Oh, I'd love to have seen some of the events live, especially the track and field events. 4. I was truly surprised to have received such poor service in your store. 5. I was fortunate to have been awarded two scholarships for next year. 6. It was very kind of you to have thrown me a party. 7. No, I have no idea. It's really unusual for Minhhuy to have missed so many classes. 8. I'm happy to hear you have enrolled in Web Design 204 and I think you have made a smart decision.

EXERCISE 9 [30 minutes]

In Exercise 9 students write sentences expressing a past wish using *would (like/love/hate/prefer)* + a perfective infinitive, and then explain them.

1. Read the directions as a class. Ask a volunteer to read the example. Ask another volunteer to give another reason why one would say the example, and write this on the board.
2. Have students work independently to write seven sentences expressing a past wish using *would (like/love/hate/prefer)* + a perfective infinitive.
3. Have students work in small groups to explain their reasons for one or two of their statements.
4. Ask random students to share a sentence and their reasons. See possible answers on LP page 362.

EXPANSION [30 minutes/homework]

For homework, ask students to choose two topics from Exercise 9 and write two short descriptions of their past wishes.

LESSON PLAN 4

FOCUS 6 [15 minutes]

1. **Lead-in:** Read the first two examples and explanation as a class. Write *be + adjective* on the board and the phrase from the first example underneath it: *I am sorry.* Ask students to supply other examples, and write these on the board.
2. Repeat this procedure with the remaining four explanations and the accompanying examples.
3. Encourage students to use the examples as models to create one more example for each explanation. Answer any questions students might have.

LANGUAGE NOTE

Tell students that while speakers do use other nonperfective as well as perfective forms in some of these contexts, the perfective forms express meaning more precisely. In other cases, nonperfective infinitives indicate a future event. Explain (or elicit an explanation) of the difference in meaning between *I am sorry to have missed your party* and *I am sorry to miss your party.*

Point out that *it was generous of you* and similar phrases are useful for expressing appreciation and gratitude in formal contexts such as thank-you notes or letters (e.g., *It was generous/kind/nice/thoughtful of you to do X*). Similarly, *It was a pleasure to have . . .* could be used in follow-up letters after job or college admissions interviews, etc.

EXERCISE 10 [20 minutes]

Students expand cues into sentences with perfective infinitive clauses, applying the principles they just learned in Focus 6.

1. Read the directions as a class. Ask two volunteers to read the two examples. Ask another volunteer to use the cues to create a sentence using a modal verb before *be*. (e.g., *It would be foolish to have thought we could go for two days without food.*)
2. Have students work independently to write sentences with perfective infinitive clauses. Encourage them to use a variety of structures and add descriptive words or phrases to their sentences.
3. Have them work in small groups and take turns reading the sentences they wrote.
4. Ask representatives of several groups to share their best sentences with the class, and discuss.

 For more practice, use *Grammar Dimensions 4* Workbook page 179, Exercise 8.

EXERCISE 11 [20 minutes]

Exercise 11 asks students to respond to situations using expressions from Exercise 10 and perfective infinitives.

1. Read the directions and example as a class. Ask volunteers to suggest two other sentences expressing gratitude.
2. Ask students to work independently to write a response to each situation.
3. Have students share and compare answers with a partner.
4. Ask random students to share their response to each situation. See possible answers on LP page 362.

EXPANSION [45 minutes/homework]

Activity 4 (research on the web) on SB page 371 is a good homework assignment following the work students do in Exercise 11. Students use *InfoTrac® College Edition* to research and write about the life of a famous composer using perfective infinitives to express emotion.

Expressing Uncertainty About Past Events

use

EXAMPLES	EXPLANATIONS
(a) **I seem to have forgotten** my homework assignment. Oh wait, here it is in my notebook!	After the verbs *seem* and *appear*, perfective infinitives express uncertainty about past events based on present evidence.
(b) This assignment **appears to have been written** rather hastily.	Sometimes the "uncertainty" is actually a way to avoid directly accusing or criticizing someone.
(c) Hmmm . . . someone **seems to have eaten** all the ice cream. I wonder who did that!	Note on informal English: When speakers use perfective infinitive in fast speech, *to have* tends to sound like "*to-uv.*"
(d) An increase in the medication **seems to have lowered** the patient's blood pressure.	*Appear* and *seem* followed by perfective infinitives are often used as "hedges" in formal speech and writing, such as medical reports, news reports, and academic writing,
(e) The election results **appear to have been influenced** by voters' opposition to the war.	both to express uncertainty and to avoid direct criticism.
(f) There **appears to have been** a storm during the time we were gone.	When *there* is the grammatical subject of *seem* or *appear* + perfective infinitive, the logical subject follows the verb if it is active.
(g) There **appear to have been** some conclusions **made** without evidence to support them.	If the verb is passive, as in (g), the logical subject comes between the auxiliaries and the main verb. In (g), the logical subject is *conclusions*.

Match each of the questions in the Questions column with a response from the Responses column to make conversational exchanges. With a partner, compare your answers and then read the exchanges out loud with appropriate expression.

Questions	Responses
1. Gee, it's already 8 o'clock. I guess I'd better get up! Have you looked to see what the weather is like this morning?	a. Uh-huh, it seems to have gone sour. You should ask the waiter to get you another glass.
2. Hmm . . . you know, that t-shirt looks kind of tight on you. Are you sure it's a medium? Maybe you should check with the sales clerk.	b. Well, there appears to have been a robbery there last night, so it's not going to open until the police have investigated.
3. Does this milk taste a little funny to you?	c. Yeah, I did just a few minutes ago. It appears to have stopped raining, at least for the time being,
4. Wow! I can't believe we've been sitting in this traffic for half an hour. What do you think is going on?	d. Oh, she seems to have found out we were awarded that big project for next month. So I guess she thinks we deserve it!
5. Hey, I just heard that the boss said we could all leave the office at noon today. What brought that on?	e. You're right. It seems to have been mismarked. I think it's actually a small.
6. How come the video store is closed? Shouldn't it have opened an hour ago?	f. I'm not sure, but from what I can see, there appears to have been some sort of accident up ahead.

ANSWER KEY

Exercise 12 1. c   2. e   3. a   4. f   5. d   6. b

FOCUS 7 [15 minutes]

Focus 7 looks at how *seem/appear* + perfective infinitives are used to express uncertainty about past events.

1. **Lead-in:** Review the past participles of some common irregular verbs. Write the infinitive of several verbs on the board, such as *forget, write, eat.* Elicit the past participles, and write these on the board.

2. Ask students to suggest other irregular verbs, and add these to the list on the board.

3. Since *seem* is the most common verb used with perfective infinitives to express uncertainty about the past, give students infinitive verb prompts and help them create sentences. Examples: *lose→ I seem to have lost my glasses. break→ I seem to have broken the chain on my bicycle. leave out → I seem to have left out a verb in this sentence.*

4. Ask two volunteers to read the first two explanations and examples.

5. Read the third section, and give several additional examples, speaking quickly and making *to have* sound like *to-uv*: *Huh . . . they seem to have sold out of ice cream! Well . . . the kids seem to have forgotten to do their chores.*

6. Read the remainder of the chart as a class.

7. Answer any questions students might have.

EXERCISE 12 [20 minutes]

In Exercise 12 students work in pairs, matching questions with responses to make conversational exchanges, and then practice the conversations.

1. Read the directions as a class.

2. Have students work in pairs to match the questions with the responses

3. Have them practice the conversations, speaking with expression.

4. Ask various volunteer pairs to practice each conversation in front of the class, using the answers they chose.

5. Discuss any different choices other students made. See answers on LP page 364.

EXERCISE 13

Rewrite each of the following statements with hedges, using an appropriate form of *appear* or *seem* followed by a perfective infinitive. (In some cases, either present or past tense of *appear* or *seem* may be used.)

Example: In this study, several of the formulas were miscalculated.
Rewrite: *In this study, several of the formulas appear to have been miscalculated.*

1. The train accident involved the conductor's error in judging the amount of time needed to clear the railroad tracks.

2. During the riots last night, bystanders stole goods from a number of stores on State Street.

3. Dr. Rushmore misdiagnosed the patient and treated him with an inappropriate medication.

4. The patient contracted malaria several weeks ago but ignored the symptoms.

5. The vases recently found by the archeologists were made during the 4th century BC.

6. Dogs evolved from wolves, differing only 1% in their mitochondrial DNA.

7. The migration of ancient animals thousands of miles from their original homes resulted from factors related to continental drift.

8. What caused the suspension bridge to collapse after the earthquake? According to preliminary investigations, it was not constructed according to engineering codes.

EXERCISE 14

Make up a sentence with *appear* or *seem* followed by a perfective infinitive for each of the following situations.

1. You go for a job interview. The interviewer asks to see your application form. You realize you must have left it at home. Respond to the question.

2. You are a teacher. One of your students looks as if she is on the verge of falling asleep. Make a comment to her.

3. As you are getting ready to leave the classroom, you discover that you no longer have your notebook, which was with you when you entered the room. Make a comment to your classmates as they are walking out.

4. You have just stopped reading a novel that is one of the worst ones you have ever read. Make a comment to a friend about the author of the book.

5. When your teacher starts going over a homework assignment, you realize that you did the wrong one. The teacher calls on you for an answer. Give an appropriate response.

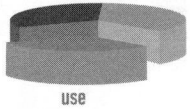

FOCUS 8	Expressing Obligations, Intentions, and Future Plans

use

EXAMPLES	EXPLANATIONS
(a) You **needed to have submitted** a petition by last Friday to drop your composition course. (b) You **will need to have completed** one more English course by the end of this year in order to graduate.	After *need to*, perfective infinitives can express past obligations not fulfilled or future obligations depending on the tense of the main verb. Note that a time *by-phrase* is often used.
(c) You **will want to have started** applying for jobs in early spring.	*Will want to* + perfective infinitive can also express future obligation.
(d) The engineers **were supposed to have checked** all the controls before the shuttle was launched. (e) Caroline **was to have spent** the entire summer sculpting, but she ended up working at a bank for a month.	Perfective infinitives may follow phrasal modals *be supposed to, be to*. With past forms of the main verbs, they express past obligations or plans that were or might not have been fulfilled.
(f) Do you **plan to have written** your report before Sunday? (g) The weatherman **expects** the rains **to have ended** by next weekend.	With verbs such as *plan, intend, hope,* and *expect*, perfective infinitives express a future time before another future time.

EXERCISE 15

Complete the following sentences with information about yourself; use a perfective infinitive clause in each.

Example: By tomorrow, I intend <u>to have bought my sister a birthday present</u>.

1. By next week, I plan _____.

2. I intend _____ within the next five years.

3. I was supposed _____ but I didn't because

_____.

4. By the end of the year, I will need _____.

5. I expect _____ before _____.

6. By _____ I hope _____.

Exercise 13   Answers may vary. (Note that *appears* is sometimes a more appropriate choice, though, than *seems*.) Possible answers are: 1. The train accident seems to have involved the conductor's error . . .   2. During the riots last night, bystanders appear to have stolen goods from a number of stores on State Street. (OR: A number of stores on State Street appear to have been broken into by bystanders)   3. Dr. Rushmore seems to have misdiagnosed . . .   4. The patient appeared to have contracted malaria . . .   5. The vases recently found by the archeologists appeared to have been made . . .   6. Dogs appeared to have been evolved . . .   7. The migration of ancient animals thousands of miles from their original homes seems to have resulted from . . .

Exercise 14   Answers will vary. Possible answers are: 1. I seem to have forgotten my application.   2. You appear not to have gotten enough sleep last night.   3. I seem to have lost my notebook.   4. The author appeared to have forgotten how to write by the end of that book.   5. I'm sorry. I seem to have done the wrong assignment.

Exercise 15   Answers will vary. Possible answers are: 1. to have finished that novel   2. to have completed my degree   3. to have become a senior this year . . . I was three credits short   4. to have finished my math requirements   5. to have gotten married . . . the end of the decade   6. next year . . . to have visited my grandparents in Indonesia

EXERCISE 13 (OPTIONAL) [20 minutes]

In Exercise 13 students apply what they have just learned about hedges in Focus 7, rewriting statements using an appropriate form of *appear* or *seem* followed by a perfective infinitive.

1. Read the directions and example as a class. Do students think the hedge in the example is used to express uncertainty or to avoid direct criticism? (*To avoid criticism. The speaker is certain that the formulas are incorrect, so there is no uncertainty.*)
2. Have students work independently to rewrite the sentences using hedges.
3. Have them share their sentences in small groups, and discuss.
4. Ask volunteers to share their answers with the class. See possible answers on LP page 366.

EXERCISE 14 (OPTIONAL) [25 minutes]

In Exercise 14 students write responses to a series of situations using *seem/appear* + perfective infinitive.

1. Read the directions as a class.
2. Have students work independently to write sentences. Encourage them to write more than one response to each situation using *seem/appear* + perfective infinitive.
3. Have them share their sentences in small groups. Ask them to explain the use of each response—to express uncertainty, to avoid criticism, or both.
4. Have one student from each group share two sentences the group created with the class and state the use of each. See possible answers on LP page 366.

 For more practice, use *Grammar Dimensions 4* Workbook page 180, Exercise 9.

EXPANSION [20 minutes/homework]

For further practice using hedges:

1. For homework, have students write a description of one or two situations in which someone would be likely to use a hedge. Collect students' papers during the next class.
2. Select two or three papers to read each class period during the next three classes, eliciting responses from response mode as a mini-review of this teaching point. You could vary how students respond (e.g., one day have students write down their responses, and then during the next class have them discuss the situation and their response to it with the person next to them, etc.).

LESSON PLAN 5

FOCUS 8 [15 minutes]

1. **Lead-in:** Write *need to + perfective infinitive* on the board. Ask two volunteers to read the first two examples.
2. Ask students to identify when each obligation in the two examples occurred: in the past, or the future. (*past, future*)
3. Read the first explanation.
4. Write *want to + perfective infinitive* on the board. Ask another volunteer to read example (c). Ask students to say when the obligation occurs (*in the future*), and then read the second explanation.
5. Follow this procedure for the next two explanations and their examples, writing *supposed to, be to,* and *plan/intend/hope/expect + perfective infinitive* on the board.
6. Answer any questions students might have.

EXERCISE 15 [20 minutes]

In Exercise 15 students complete sentences using perfective infinitives and their own personal information, practicing the uses they just studied in Focus 8.

1. Read the directions and example as a class. Ask several students to provide other examples, using information about their lives, and write these on the board.
2. Have students work independently to complete the sentences.
3. Have them exchange papers with a partner, and review and discuss them.
4. Ask random students to share a sentence with the class. See possible answers on LP page 366.

 For more practice, use *Grammar Dimensions 4* Workbook page 181, Exercise 10.

EXPANSION 1 [20 minutes]

For additional practice with the various uses of perfective infinitives to express obligations, intentions, and future plans:

1. Have students work in pairs. Ask them to take turns interviewing each other, creating questions out of the statements in Exercise 15, and taking notes on their partner's responses.
2. Have several students report on their partner's responses, using indirect speech: *By next week, Ari plans to have . . . .; Helen said she was supposed to have . . .*

EXPANSION 2 [30 minutes/homework]

Activity 3 (writing/speaking) on SB page 371 is a good homework assignment following Focus 8 and Exercise 15. In this activity students write about a topic of their choice using *will need* or *will want* + perfective infinitives.

FOCUS 9 — Perfective Infinitives with *Enough* and *Too*

use

EXAMPLES	EXPLANATIONS
adjective + *enough*	***Enough***
(a) The earthquake was **powerful enough** to have destroyed a whole city. (The earthquake could have destroyed a whole city.)	Following *enough*, perfective infinitives often express an event that could have happened but did not necessarily happen. In other words, they express past possibilities.
***enough* + noun**	
(b) I got **enough homework** on Friday to have kept me busy for a week. (The homework could have kept me busy for a week.)	
***too* + adjective**	***Too***
(c) We were **too tired** to have gone anywhere last night. (We didn't go anywhere last night because we were too tired.)	Following *too*, perfective infinitives may express events that did not occur. The main clause gives a reason.
***too* + *many/much* + noun**	
(d) She has **too much intelligence** to have done so poorly on the exam. (She did poorly, but I am surprised because she is so intelligent.)	The perfective infinitive after *too* may also express the speaker's disbelief that something did not occur.

EXERCISE 16

Use the phrases below to create sentences about past possibilities using perfective infinitives.

Example: poison . . . strong enough
The poison that the child accidentally swallowed was strong enough to have killed her, but fortunately she recovered completely.

1. music at the concert . . . loud enough

2. they made enough money . . .

3. fireworks . . . bright enough

4. wind . . . strong enough

5. the weather in (your hometown) . . . hot/cold enough

EXERCISE 17

The following sentences express disbelief about an event or explain why something didn't happen. Combine the ideas in each pair of sentences into one sentence, using a perfective infinitive clause. (*Hint:* Start with the sentence that has a *too* + adjective phrase, changing pronoun subjects if needed.)

Example: Rachel couldn't have done well in the marathon last fall. She had sustained too many minor injuries.

Combined: *Rachel had sustained too many minor injuries to have done well in the marathon last fall.*

1. My brother couldn't have cheated on a test. He is too honest.

2. You couldn't have stopped taking piano lessons! You have too much talent.

3. Stan couldn't have bought that wild tie himself. He is too conservative.

4. Charmaine didn't stay at that low-level job. She has too much ambition.

5. They couldn't have taken on any more debts. They have too many already.

ANSWER KEY

Exercise 16 Answers will vary. Possible answers are: 1. The music at the concert was loud enough to have broken the sound barrier. 2. They made enough money to have bought a new car years ago. 3. The fireworks were bright enough to have been seen for miles. 4. The wind was strong enough to have toppled several trees. 5. The weather in Houston was hot enough to keep us inside for days at a time.

Exercise 17 1. My brother is too honest to have cheated on a test. 2. You have too much talent to have stopped taking piano lessons! 3. Stan is too conservative to have bought that wild tie himself. 4. Charmaine has too much ambition to have stayed at that low-level job. 5. They have too many debts to have taken on any more.

FOCUS 9 [15 minutes]

Focus 9 looks at how perfective infinitives are used to express past possibilities or a speaker's disbelief that something did not occur in the past.

1. **Lead-in:** Ask two volunteers to read the first two examples, and ask another to read the explanation.

2. Write other sentences on the board with *could +* perfective verb and ask students to transform these into sentences with perfective infinitives, such as: *The food we had for dinner last night could have fed twenty people!* → *We had enough food for dinner last night to have fed twenty people!*

3. Ask two volunteers to read the next two examples, and ask another to read the explanations.

4. Write sentences similar to the ones in parentheses under (c) and (d). Example: *We didn't go swimming in the lake because it was too cold, so we took a boat ride instead.* → *The lake was too cold to have gone swimming in, so . . .*

5. Answer any questions students might have.

EXERCISE 16 [20 minutes]

In Exercise 16 students create sentences that express past possibilities using perfective infinitives, practicing the uses they just studied in Focus 9.

1. Read the directions, and have a volunteer read the example. Ask students to say when this possibility occurred. (*in the past*) Ask students to give two other examples of past possibilities using *poison* and *strong enough.*

2. Have students work in pairs to write sentences about past possibilities using the phrases provided.

3. Have each pair get together with another pair and take turns sharing their sentences

4. Ask various representatives of these small groups to share two of their group's best sentences with the class. See possible answers on LP page 368.

 For more practice, use *Grammar Dimensions 4* Workbook page 182, Exercise 11.

EXERCISE 17 [15 minutes]

Exercise 17 has students create sentences that combine two uses of perfective infinitives explored in Focus 9: expressing disbelief about an event and explaining why something didn't happen.

1. Read the directions as a class. Ask a volunteer to read the example aloud. Ask students to say what the example expresses: disbelief about an event or why something didn't happen. (*why*)

2. Have students work in pairs and take turns creating a single sentence that combines the ideas in each pair of sentences into one sentence, using a perfective infinitive clause.

3. Call on random students to share their sentences with the class. See answers on LP page 368.

 For more practice, use *Grammar Dimensions 4* Workbook page 182, Exercise 12.

UNIT GOAL REVIEW [10 minutes]

Ask students to look at the goals on the opening page of the unit again. Refer to the pages of the unit where information on each goal can be found.

 For assessment of Unit 19, use *Grammar Dimensions ExamView®*.

Use Your English

CD2 Tracks 9–12

Imagine that you have just returned from a two-week vacation. The dates of your vacation were July 14 through the 28th. Listen to the audio. You will hear four messages that have been left on your telephone answering machine.

■ **STEP 1** Take notes as you listen to each message.

■ **STEP 2** Use your notes to create responses that you could leave on the answering machines of the people who called. Use at least one perfective infinitive form in each response.

■ **STEP 3** Share your favorite responses with a small group of classmates.

ACTIVITY  **research/speaking/writing**

Interview five people about regrets—either their greatest regrets or most recent ones. Then write the results of your interviews using statements with perfective infinitives. Share the results with your classmates. Here are some examples of paraphrases:

Examples: Jack's regret: that he quit his job
Paraphrase: *Jack is sorry to have quit his job.*

Risa's regret: that she didn't go to Vienna for her vacation
Paraphrase: *Risa is sorry not to have gone to Vienna for her vacation.*

Blanca's regret: that she never learned Spanish from her mother
Paraphrase: *Blanca is sorry never to have learned Spanish from her mother.*

ACTIVITY  **writing/speaking**

■ **STEP 1** Consider a procedure from your major field of study or one of the following topics for which you can list a number of things that need to have been done in preparation. Possible topics: studying abroad, studying for a particular kind of exam (e.g., math, English), going out on a date, getting married, going fishing, playing a team sport.

■ **STEP 2** Create a list of 4–5 items using *will need* or *will want* + perfective infinitives. A few examples are given below.

Example: Taking a trip abroad
The travelers will need to have gotten a passport.
They will want to have checked to see if they need immunizations.

■ **STEP 3** When you have finished, share your information in small groups and answer any questions your classmates may have about your list.

ACTIVITY **4** **research on the web**

 Using *InfoTrac® College Edition* or other Web-based resources, research the life of a famous composer such as Beethoven, Mozart, Tchaikovsky, or Gershwin. With your classmates, take turns reporting on some of the information you learned, using perfective infinitives to express your emotional reaction toward it.

Examples: *I was surprised to have found out that Beethoven was mathematically illiterate.*
I was sad to have read how lonely Beethoven was.

ACTIVITY **5** **reflection**

Consider what you would like to have accomplished this year in English studies or any of your academic subjects. Make a list of at least five things you expect or hope to have achieved by next year at this time.

Example: *I hope to have improved my ability to use verb tenses correctly in writing essays.*

The Use Your English activities at the end of the unit contain situations that should naturally elicit the structures covered in the unit. For a more complete discussion of how to use the Use Your English activities, see To the Teacher, LP page xxvi.

ACTIVITY 1 listening/writing/speaking
[30 minutes]

CD2 Tracks 9–12

This activity is a good follow-up to Exercise 3 on SB page 355. Note that the former CD track numbers (26–29) are incorrectly listed in the student book.

1. Discuss how students get voice messages: Do they have an answering machine? Do they have voicemail?
2. Discuss messages they leave for others: What information do they always include? Do they leave short messages, or longer ones?

■ STEP 1

1. Read the directions as a class.
2. Have students listen to the audio once.
3. Ask students to listen again and take notes on the messages, stopping the audio as needed to write.

■ STEP 2 Have students work independently to write responses to the messages. Ask them to use at least one perfective infinitive form in each response.

■ STEP 3

1. Have students work in small groups to share their favorite responses.
2. Ask several volunteers to share their favorite responses with the class.

ACTIVITY 2 research/speaking/writing
[60 minutes/homework]

This activity is a good follow-up to Exercise 7 on SB page 360, either as homework or as a class activity.

1. Read the directions as a class. Ask three volunteers to read the three examples.
2. Ask students to share some regrets they have, or that people they know have.
3. Ask students to interview five people about their regrets, and then summarize their findings in writing, using perfective infinitives. If students will be interviewing people outside class, you might give them an opening line to use, such as: *I'm doing a class research project about the kinds of things that people regret. For example, some people regret not doing certain things, or some regret things they've done. Could you tell me one or two things that you have regrets about?*
4. Have students work in small groups to share their findings and discuss them.
5. Ask several volunteers to share their findings with the class.

ACTIVITY 3 writing/speaking
[30 minutes/homework]

This activity is a good follow-up for students after Exercise 15 on SB page 367.

■ STEP 1 Read the directions as a class.

■ STEP 2 Have students choose or think of a topic and write a list of 4–5 things that need to have been done in preparation using *will need* or *will want* + perfective infinitives.

■ STEP 3

1. Have students work in small groups and share their lists. Encourage group members to ask questions.
2. Ask several volunteers to share their lists with the class, and discuss.

ACTIVITY 4 research on the web
[45 minutes/homework]

This activity is a good follow-up to the work students do in Exercise 11 on SB page 363.

1. Read the directions as a class. Ask two volunteers to read the two examples.
2. Ask students to identify the focus that explains the use of perfective infinitives to express emotion. (Focus 6)
3. Have students research the life of a famous composer online. Ask them to write a description and to include expressions of emotions they have about the composer's life.
4. Ask different volunteers to read their descriptions to the class, and discuss.

ACTIVITY 5 reflection
[30 minutes/homework]

This activity makes a good homework assignment following Exercise 4 on SB page 357.

1. Read the directions as a class. Ask a volunteer to read the examples aloud.
2. Ask students to reflect on what they have achieved so far in their studies—either in English, and/or other studies. Ask them to write a list of at least five things they hope to have achieved by this time next year.
3. Have students share their lists in small groups.
4. Ask a few volunteers to read their lists to the class, and discuss.

ADJECTIVE COMPLEMENTS IN SUBJECT AND PREDICATE POSITION

UNIT GOALS

- Use three types of adjective complement structures

- Use adjective complements in subject and predicate position

- Choose among infinitives, gerunds, and *that*-clauses

- Order *that*-clauses and infinitives to introduce new information or to refer to known information in discourse

OPENING TASK

Human Beings' Relationship to Animals

■ STEP 1

Some things that further human progress, comfort, or enjoyment may have negative effects on animals. As you look over the following list, think about the positive and negative associations each term has.

■ STEP 2

Discuss five of the terms with a partner and jot down your ideas in the chart below.

TERM	POSITIVE	NEGATIVE
1. animal research	provides a way to test the safety of drugs and cosmetics	animals dissected, injected, and killed in experiments
2. fur coat		
3. zoo		
4. oil tanker		
5. veal		
6. ivory		
7. pesticide		
8. campground		
9. bullfight		
10. hunting		
11. highway construction		

■ STEP 3

After your discussion, write down statements about several of the terms, including both positive and negative associations. Here are some sample statements about the first term, *animal research*:

It is unethical for researchers to use animals like gorillas and chimpanzees in medical studies. That this research tests the safety of drugs and cosmetics is undeniable. But researchers' blindly generalizing the findings from these experiments to human beings does not make sense. In addition, injecting and killing these animals during experiments is inhumane.

UNIT OVERVIEW

Unit 20 introduces and expands students' knowledge of three adjective complement structures: *that*-clauses, infinitives, and gerunds. This unit focuses on the distinct differences in meaning and word order of these three types of adjective complements.

Please note that due to its length, this unit has been divided into three lesson plans. To review this unit more quickly, review focus charts and have students complete the first exercise after each chart to observe students' grasp of the grammar topics.

GRAMMAR NOTE

One of the challenges many students face in mastering the forms and uses of adjective complements is learning how to **extrapose**, or to move a clause generated in subject position to the end of a sentence. A failure to extrapose often results in awkward constructions that may even cause errors in interpretation. This unit addresses this common problem with its explanation of principles and ample opportunities to put these into practice.

UNIT GOALS

Some instructors may want to review the goals listed on Student Book (SB) page 372 after completing the Opening Task so that students understand what they should know by the end of the unit. These goals can also be reviewed at the end of the unit when students are more familiar with the grammar terminology.

OPENING TASK [30 minutes]

The purpose of the Opening Task is to create a context in which students will need to use adjective complements as they consider human beings' relationship with animals in a variety of contexts. The problem-solving format is designed to show the teacher how well the students can produce the target structures implicitly and spontaneously when they are engaged in a communicative task. For a more complete discussion of the purpose of the Opening Task, see To the Teacher, Lesson Planner (LP) page xxii.

Setting Up the Task

1. Bring in photos of some of the items in the grid on SB page 373, such as a picture of an animal research lab.
2. Bring in realia, such as a bottle of shampoo displaying a disclaimer that animals have not been used in testing the product. Use the realia and/or photos to spark a brief, general discussion about how humans use animals.

Conducting the Task

■ STEP 1

1. Read the directions as a class.
2. Ask students to think about the positive and negative aspects of animal research. Some students may know that animals have played a role in doctors' finding treatments for polio, cancer, diabetes, etc. They may also know that many animals have been killed as a result of these experiments.

■ STEP 2

1. Read the directions for Step 2.
2. Have students work in pairs. Ask them to read through the terms in the chart and discuss and then write down their ideas about at least five of them.

■ STEP 3

After their discussion, students should work individually to write several statements about their own positive and negative reactions to one or more specific terms above.

Closing the Task

1. Have students gather in small groups to share and discuss what they've written regarding their thoughts about the terms in the chart.
2. Ask representatives of several groups to report on what their group thought about several of the terms.
3. Don't worry about accuracy at this point, though you may want to take notes of errors in meaning, form, or use in order to focus on those problems later.

GRAMMAR NOTE

Typical student errors (form)

- In sentences in which the main subject and the complement subject are alike, not deleting the *for* phrase in infinitive adjective complements: —e.g., * *The boys are excited for themselves to win the game.* (See Focus 1.)
- Omitting *that* in *that* + clause constructions: —e.g.,* *The ozone is being depleted is very alarming.* (See Focus 1.)

Typical student errors (use)

- Using gerunds with *it* constructions:—e.g., * *It is depressing animals facing extinction.* (See Focus 2.)
- Omitting *it* + linking verb at the beginning of a sentence with an adjective complement in predicate position:—e.g., * *Interesting that black bears do not usually harm people.* (See Focus 2.)
- Omitting the complementizer *that*:—e.g.,* *She lost her keys is unfortunate.* (See Focus 3.)

FOCUS 1 — Overview of Adjective Complements

EXAMPLES	EXPLANATIONS
adjective complement + *be* + adjective (a) **Killing these animals** is inhumane.	Adjective complements can appear in subject position in front of linking verbs (such as *appear, be, become, look, remain, seem*) followed by adjectives.
(b) **That the blue whale is becoming extinct** seems sad. (c) **For campers to pollute streams** is irresponsible. (d) **Bulls' being killed** in bullfights appears brutal.	Adjective complements are of three types: • *that*-clause (consisting of *that* + clause) • infinitive (consisting of *for* + noun phrase + *to* + base verb) • gerund (consisting of *'s* + verb + *-ing*)
(e) The captain appears ready **for the media to interview** him about the shipping accident. (f) The senator is eager **for investigators to determine** the cause of the oil spill.	The adjectives that precede adjective complements and follow animate subjects generally show positive expectation (e.g., *ready, anxious, happy, eager, glad,* etc.).
(g) The senator is eager to win the next election. (h) **NOT:** The senator is eager for himself to win the next election.	If the main subject and the complement subject are alike, we delete the *for* phrase.

EXERCISE 1

Read the following text. Underline examples of adjective complements.

> Recently, the topic of animal research has become quite controversial. Animal rights activists believe that animal experimentation for medical purposes is not necessary because sophisticated computer modeling can accomplish the same result. Researchers disagree and claim that animal research should precede human research when serious health risks are involved. That 90% or more of the genes linked to diseases are the same in animals and humans is a convincing reminder that animal experimentation with rats, mice, pigs, and monkeys can successfully lead to medical advances and cures. That animals in research should be carefully guarded against disease and suffering is obvious. However, researchers' discontinuing the use of animals in experiments which could lead to cures for cancer and AIDS would be very unfortunate.

> In the past few years, animal rights activists from organizations like ALF (Animal Liberation Front) have targeted research labs across the United States. Last year, protesters broke into a university lab to release hundreds of research animals. They destroyed computers containing research data and painted slogans on the walls such as "Mice Have Feelings Too" and "Free the Animals." Others sent hate mail and made threats to families of university researchers. That individuals feel strongly about a cause is commendable. For them to trespass, destroy property, and harass researchers' family members is not. Animal rights activists have now become one of the top U.S. domestic terrorism threats. Several universities have been forced to investigate the backgrounds of their graduate student researchers, change keys to electronic security cards, and set up cameras to record who is entering or leaving the research facilities. It is unfortunate that this level of security has become necessary. It is tragic that many medical advances will be thwarted or slowed because of the activities of a few overzealous individuals.

EXERCISE 2

In the following short texts about animals and their unusual habits, complete the adjective complements with *that*-clauses, *for/to* infinitives, or gerunds.

Example: Elizabeth Mann Borghese, who was the daughter of the writer Thomas Mann, taught her dog to take dictation on a special typewriter. Her dog's <u>taking dictation</u> is hard to believe.

1. Once a woman was thrown off a yacht and three dolphins rescued her and led her to a marker in the sea. Another time, several fishermen were lost in a dense fog, and four dolphins nudged their boat to safety. Dolphins' _____ is well-documented.

2. Mrs. Betsy Marcus's dog Benjy was known to sing "Raindrops Keep Fallin' on My Head." For a dog _____ is incredible.

3. At one time, passenger pigeons were very numerous. Now there are none because of massive hunting and the destruction of their natural forest home. That hunters _____ is sad.

4. Jaco, an African gray parrot, could speak German. When his master left the house alone, he said, "God be with you." When his master left with other people, he said, "God be with you all." Jaco's _____ is fascinating.

5. The dwarf lemur and the mountain pygmy possum were considered extinct. However, in recent years, these animals have reappeared. For seemingly extinct animals _____ is inspiring.

6. Washoe, a female chimpanzee, was taught sign language. She was able to make up words like *drink-fruit* for watermelon and *water-bird* for swan. That Washoe _____ is intriguing.

ANSWER KEY

Exercise 2 Answers will vary. Possible answers are: 1. helping humans 2. to sing 3. kill these animals 4. speaking to singular and plural groups differently 5. to reappear 6. could communicate with sign language

FOCUS 1 [15 minutes]

Focus 1 introduces students to the different types of adjective complements and where they may appear in sentences.

1. **Lead-in:** Read the explanations and examples in the first two sections. Ask students to identify the position of the adjective complements in the four examples. (*in the subject position*)
2. Ask one volunteer to read the next two examples, and another to read the explanation. Ask two volunteers to create two more examples.
3. Read the last explanation and examples.
4. Answer any questions students might have.

EXERCISE 1 [20 minutes]

In Exercise 1 students read a selection about animal rights activists and underline the adjective complements, applying what they have just learned in Focus 1.

1. Discuss what students know and think about animal activists.
2. Read the directions as a class.
3. Have students work in pairs and take turns reading each sentence aloud and identifying the adjective complements.
4. Have pairs compare answers with another pair.
5. Review answers as a class. See answers on LP page 374.

EXPANSION [60 minutes/homework]

Activity 2 (research/writing) on SB page 381 is a good follow-up to Exercise 1, either as homework or as a class activity. In this activity students research animals facing extinction and write about their reactions to the fate of one of these using adjective complements.

EXERCISE 2 [20 minutes]

In Exercise 2 students complete sentences about animals and their unusual habits using one of the three types of adjective complements they studied in Focus 1.

1. Read the directions as a class. Ask a volunteer to read the example. Ask students to identify the type of adjective complement in the example, referring to Focus 1. (*gerund*)
2. Have students work independently to complete the sentences.
3. Have them compare answers with a partner.
4. Ask volunteers to share their answers with the class. See possible answers on LP page 374.

 For more practice, use *Grammar Dimensions 4* Workbook page 184, Exercise 1.

EXPANSION [60 minutes/homework]

For homework, assign Activity 6 (research on the web) on SB page 383. In this activity students search the Internet for information on how animals have been used in research and then give an oral report in which they express their opinions about using animals to further medical progress, using adjective complements.

■ EXERCISE 3

STEP 1 Imagine that you are an animal. What would make you happy if you were one of the following pets? Write your answers in first person and use one of the adjectives: *anxious, eager, glad, happy,* or *ready.*

Example: cat   *I would be **eager** for my owner to feed me a tuna casserole.*
*I would be **happy** to lie around in the sun.*

1. horse   3. dog   5. goldfish
2. parrot   4. mouse   6. snake

STEP 2 Write 3 more sentences like Step 1 and have the class guess which additional animals might express these thoughts.

FOCUS 2	Adjective Complements in Subject and Predicate Position

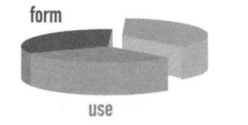
form
use

EXAMPLES	EXPLANATIONS
(a) I am sorry to say that certain businesses that sell sculptured ivory objects have hired poachers to kill elephants for their tusks. Known Information **For poachers to take the tusks from live elephants** is alarming. Known Information **That they sell them** is abominable. Known Information Worst of all, **elephants' becoming an endangered species because of this** is criminal.	In subject position, adjective complements usually contain a known idea, either previously mentioned or assumed through context.
***It* + linking verb + adjective + adjective complement** (b) It is interesting **that medical researchers have made important medical discoveries through animal research.** They need to continue this work. (c) It is necessary **for protesters to call for a moratorium on animal testing.** Animals have rights too!	When *that*-clauses and infinitives contain new information, they will more commonly appear in predicate position preceded by *It* + linking verb + adjective.
(d) **NOT:** It is abominable poachers' killing elephants.	Gerunds do not normally occur with *it* constructions.

■ EXERCISE 4

Fill in the blanks with a variety of appropriate linking verbs and adjectives from the following lists. More than one answer may be correct.

Linking Verbs	Adjectives		
appear	*apparent*	*improper*	*obvious*
be	*bad*	*inappropriate*	*odd*
become	*compulsory*	*irrational*	*sad*
look	*depressing*	*irritating*	*surprising*
remain	*disappointing*	*likely*	*true*
seem	*impossible*	*necessary*	*unfortunate*

Example: From all of the evidence, it ___was obvious___ that the defendant was guilty.

1. Crime is rampant in many parts of the world. That teenagers commit many of these crimes _____.
2. It _____ for children to attend elementary and secondary school in the United States.
3. It was a long, hard winter. Felicia's being shut inside every day _____.
4. It _____ that the president will be reelected if the economy continues to recover.
5. The young man stayed out until 3:00 A.M. For him not to listen to his parents _____.
6. All of the other men had been rehired by the company. John's still being unemployed _____.
7. It _____ for two wrongs to make a right.
8. Everyone knew that President Rabin had been shot. That he had been shot by one of his own people _____.
9. The fashion designer's clothes this season are very extreme. For vinyl to be mixed with fur _____.
10. I have stopped going to the theater on Saturday afternoons. Children's whispering and throwing popcorn in the air _____.

ANSWER KEY

Exercise 3   Answers will vary. Possible answers are: 1. I would be happy to gallop around freely. 2. I would be eager to practice new words.   3. I would be ready to take walks with my master.   4. I would be happy to eat food scraps on the floor.   5. I would be anxious to have the lights on so that everyone could look at me in my fish tank.   6. I would be happy to slither around on the ground.

Exercise 4   1. seems depressing   2. is compulsory   3. was depressing   4. 's likely   5. was inappropriate   6. seemed surprising   7. remains impossible   8. seemed sad   9. looks odd 10. has become irritating

EXERCISE 3 [20 minutes/homework]

In Exercise 3 each student takes on the role of six different animals and projects what it would be like for that animal to have specific emotions, using structures like those in the examples and in the overview of adjective complements in Focus 1.

STEP 1

1. Read the directions as a class. Ask a volunteer to read the two example sentences aloud.
2. Have students work individually to complete the sentences.
3. Ask students to work in pairs, reading sentences out of order so their partner can guess which animal they are describing. See possible answers on LP page 376.

STEP 2

1. Have students read directions and complete Step 2 (for homework if possible). They should write sentences about animals that aren't yet mentioned in this exercise, but remember not to mention the actual animal.
2. Organize students to work in small groups and make the review of their new animal sentences into a competition where other students try to guess the animal.
3. Discuss any incorrect sentences or answers.

 For more practice, use *Grammar Dimensions 4* Workbook page 185, Exercise 2.

LESSON PLAN 2

FOCUS 2 [15 minutes]

Focus 2 explores the forms and uses of adjective complements in subject and predicate position, highlighting how their function determines their location in a sentence.

1. **Lead-in:** Ask a volunteer to read the explanations, and read the examples aloud to the class.
2. Ask volunteers to create other examples of each form and use, and write these on the board.
3. Answer any questions students may have.

LANGUAGE NOTE

Focus 2 summarizes how English speakers manage information in discourse. If a person writes or talks to someone, they normally will refer to what they think their audience understands or refer to what their interlocutor has said before presenting something new that they want to say. This is why we sometimes put an adjective complement in subject position. However, if English speakers are beginning a new topic, they will often reserve the piece of information for the predicate position in the sentence. The reason for this is that the information will be more memorable for the audience listening to or reading it.

EXERCISE 4 [20 minutes]

In Exercise 4 students complete sentences with linking verbs and adjectives from a list, following the principles explored in Focus 2.

1. Read the directions as a class. Ask two volunteers to read the words in the box. Read the example aloud.
2. Have students work in pairs to complete the sentences with their choice of words in the box.

3. Ask students to work in small groups to compare their answers.
4. Ask volunteers to share an answer for each sentence. See answers on LP page 376.
5. Discuss any incorrect answers.

 For more practice, use *Grammar Dimensions 4* Workbook page 185, Exercise 3.

EXPANSION 1 [15 minutes]

To reinforce the idea that when the complement structure is in the predicate, it introduces a new idea that begs further comment, ask students to do this expansion activity:

1. Ask students to add a follow-up sentence to the first sentence that begins with *it*. (#2) Write an example on the board: *From all of the evidence, it was obvious that the defendant was guilty. No one ever really doubted it.*
2. Ask students if they have other ideas for a follow-up sentence. Write these on the board as well.
3. Repeat this process for sentences #3, 4, and 7 from Exercise 4. Encourage students to give several different follow up sentences for each.

EXPANSION 2 [45 minutes]

Activity 7 (reflection) on SB page 383 could be assigned following Exercise 4. In this activity students discuss their opinions about various study habits, using adjective complements in subject or predicate position.

EXERCISE 5

What do you think about the following activities or ideas? Use adjective complements in your answer.

Examples: (you) saving a little money every month
It's wise (for me) to save because I might need some extra money some day.
OR *My saving money has become essential to my future.*

1. (you) studying English grammar   My studying English grammar is improving my writing.
2. (you) slipping in a puddle of water in front of your friends   It is embarrassing to slip in a puddle in front of my friends.
3. (your friend) copying someone else's paper
   My friend's copying someone else's paper is dishonest.
4. (your relative) riding a motorcycle without a helmet   It's unwise for your relative to ride a motorcycle without a helmet.
5. (a single person) joining an online dating service   It isn't too dangerous for a single person to join an online dating service.
6. (a poor person) winning the lottery   For a poor person to win the lottery is very fortunate.
7. (cities) banning smoking in all public places   It is proper for a city to ban smoking in all public places.
8. (teachers) creating schools for profit rather than teaching in public schools   Teachers' creating schools for profit rather than service seems selfish.
9. (elderly people) skydiving (= jumping from a plane with a parachute on)   It's surprising for elderly people to skydive.
10. (the government) making alcohol illegal
    For the government to make alcohol illegal is controversial.

EXERCISE 6

Comment on the following facts found in the *Book of Lists 2* using a *that*-clause in subject position.

Example: Tigers do not usually hunt humans unless they are old or injured. However, a tigress, the Champawat man-eater, killed 438 people in the Himalayas in Nepal between 1903 and 1911.
That so many people were killed in Nepal by a tiger is tragic.

1. Black bears do not usually hurt humans unless they are hungry. When the Alaskan blueberry crop was poor in 1963, black bears attacked at least four people, one of whom they killed, because no other food was available.

2. In the central provinces of India, leopards have been known to enter huts and kill humans. One famous leopard, the Panawar man-eater, is reputed to have killed four hundred people.

3. On March 25, 1941, the British ship *Britannia* sank in the Atlantic Ocean. While the 12 survivors sat in a lifeboat, a giant squid reached its arm around the body of one of them and pulled him into the ocean.

4. In South America, people have reported losing fingers, toes, or pieces of flesh while bathing in piranha-infested waters.

5. In 1916, four people were killed as they were swimming along a 60-mile stretch of the New Jersey coast. The attacker was a great white shark.

EXERCISE 7

Consider your responses during the Opening Task on page 373 and what you know about environmental issues to create dialogues with facts about animals, using a *that*-clause and the adjective provided.

Example: shocking   Q: What's so shocking?
A: **It's shocking** that the oil from the grounded oil tanker killed thousands of innocent animals.

1. irresponsible   4. important
2. encouraging   5. outrageous
3. sad   6. fortunate

meaning

FOCUS 3	Infinitives, Gerund, and *That*-Clauses

EXAMPLES	EXPLANATIONS
(a) Many zoos have instituted stricter laws regarding the care of their animals. **That zoos protect their animals is important.** (b) **Zoos' protecting their animals** is important.	Infinitive, gerund, and *that*-clauses have different meanings. *That*-clauses and gerunds refer to actual or fulfilled events. In (a) and (b), the adjective complements refer to the fact that zoos actually do already protect their animals.
(c) Many zoos have reported higher numbers of animals dying in captivity. **For zoos to protect their animals is important.**	Infinitives refer to future ideas or potential events. In (c), zoos potentially can protect their animals (but they don't necessarily do so).

ANSWER KEY

Exercise 6   Answers will vary. Possible answers are: 1. That black bears were starving in 1963 was unfortunate.   2. That one leopard killed so many people is terrible.   3. That one person was drowned by a squid after surviving a ship sinking is ironic.   4. That people can lose a finger, toe, or piece of flesh while bathing is devastating.   5. That people were killed while swimming recreationally is tragic.

Exercise 7   Answers will vary. Possible answers are: 1. It is irresponsible that highways have destroyed natural animal habitats.   2. It is encouraging that zoos have begun treating their animals more humanely.   3. It is sad that calves are killed to provide veal for diners.   4. It is important that more politicians become aware of the illegal ivory trade.   5. It is outrageous that bulls are killed for sport.   6. It is fortunate that more people are becoming courteous campers.

EXERCISE 5 [20 minutes]

In Exercise 5 students express their opinions about a variety of topics using adjective complements.

1. Read the directions and examples as a class. Elicit another example using the complement in a predicate position: *For me to save money is . . .*
2. Have students work in groups of four. One pair should do the first five sentences, and the other should do the last five. Ask them to write at least two variations for each sentence.
3. Have the pairs take turns reading their sentences to each other.
4. Ask each pair to then write one additional sentence using an adjective complement in a way that has not been done by the other pair.
5. Have them read their sentences to each other.
6. Ask volunteers to share their two best sentences with the class. See possible answers on LP page 378.

EXPANSION [30 minutes]

Activity 1 (listening) on SB page 381 is a good follow-up to Exercise 5. Students listen to a series of messages and conversations in which adjective complements are used in subject and predicate positions and choose the most appropriate response.

EXERCISE 6 [15 minutes]

In Exercise 6 students comment on a series of facts using a *that*-clause in subject position.

1. Ask students if they have ever heard of animals harming humans in their native countries. Ask them to share these stories with the class.
2. Read the directions and example as a class. Ask a volunteer to give another example that begins with *That tigers . . .*

3. Ask students to work in pairs to comment on each set of facts using a *that*-clause in subject position.
4. Have pairs get together with another pair and take turns sharing their sentences.
5. Ask various volunteers to share a sentence with the class, and discuss these. See possible answers on LP page 378.

 For more practice, use *Grammar Dimensions 4* Workbook page 186, Exercise 4 and page 187, Exercise 5.

EXPANSION [30 minutes/homework]

Activity 3 (reading/speaking) on SB page 382 is a good homework assignment following Focus 2 and the work students do in Exercise 6. In this activity students use certain adjectives to comment on a current social problem that they feel strongly about.

EXERCISE 7 [25 minutes]

In Exercise 7 students return to the responses they made during the Opening Task, and use these to create short dialogues.

1. Read the directions and example as a class.
2. Ask students to work in pairs to write short dialogues about animals, using the responses they gave in the Opening Task and a *that*-clause and the adjective provided.
3. Have pairs get together with another pair and take turns sharing their sentences.
4. Ask various volunteers to report on how their group responded to a topic. See possible answers on LP page 378.

EXPANSION [40 minutes/homework]

Activity 4 (writing) on SB page 382 can be done in class or assigned as homework after Exercise 7. Students write a fictional letter of complaint to a company about a figure they bought that was made from illegally obtained ivory using adjective complements.

LESSON PLAN 3

FOCUS 3 [20 minutes]

1. **Lead-in:** Ask students to name a few activities that they do in your class on a regular basis. Write these on the board (e.g., *workbook exercises, speaking exercises, warm-up activities, composition assignments*, etc.).
2. Ask students to give you an adjective that describes how it feels to do each of these activities (e.g., *helpful, fun, useful, hard*, etc.), and write these on the board beside the names of the activities.
3. Give students a sample sentence combining these adjectives with an adjective complement. For example, *That we did workbook exercises every night was helpful. Our doing speaking exercises is fun.*
4. Ask students whether or not this structure indicates that the activity took place, is taking place now, or has not yet taken place.
5. Contrast this with another example: *For us to eat ice cream in every class would be unwise.* Ask students whether or not this action has taken place. Point to the *for/to* infinitive and explain that this relates to future or potential events.
6. Ask different volunteers to read the examples and explanations for (a), (b), and (c) aloud.

EXERCISE 8

Circle the best option and explain your decision.

Example: 1. (a) It is heartening that the Beauty Cosmetics Company of London has refused to test its products on animals since its establishment.
b. It would be heartening for the Beauty Cosmetics Company of London to refuse to test its products on animals.

*(The Beauty Cosmetics Company has actually refused already, so answer **a** with the **that**-clause is correct.)*

1. (a) It is shocking that commercial whalers have almost exterminated the blue whale.
b. It would be shocking for commercial whalers to almost exterminate the blue whale.

2. (a) It is sad that dolphins catch diseases from humans at dolphin recreational swim centers.
b. It would be sad for dolphins to catch diseases from humans at dolphin recreational swim centers.

3. a. After an oil spill, it will be important that animals are rescued.
(b) After an oil spill, it will be important for animals to be rescued.

4. (a) Companies' cutting down the Amazonian rain forests will lead to ecological disaster.
b. For companies to cut down the Amazonian rain forests would lead to ecological disaster.

5. (a) For healthcare workers to stop the AIDS crisis in Africa would be inspiring.
b. That healthcare workers' stopped the AIDS crisis in Africa is inspiring.

EXERCISE 9

What would be out of the ordinary for the following types of people to do or to have done? Comment on their activities using the following *-ly* adverb + adjective clusters: *wholly unexpected, particularly odd, really surprising, extremely unusual, virtually impossible, incredibly strange, terribly funny.*

Example: Inuits   *Inuits' living in grass huts would be incredibly strange.*

1. dictators
2. busybodies
3. bus drivers
4. procrastinators
5. professional athletes
6. English teachers
7. Hollywood stars
8. your mother
9. your friend's father
10. our class

Use Your English

ACTIVITY 1 listening

🎧 CD2 Tracks 13–17

Listen to the audio and circle the appropriate comment that would follow from what you have heard. Here is an example of the type of exchange you might hear.

Example: Tonya: Did you hear the good news?
Francisco: No, what?
Tonya: Rosa's parents just bought her a car for her birthday.
(a) That Rosa got a new car for her birthday is amazing.
b. For Rosa to get a new car will be amazing.

1. (a) It's annoying that such a smart aleck like Tom should have such luck!
b. For Harvard to give such an expensive scholarship is annoying.

2. a. It is essential for human beings to revere animals for their intelligence and strength.
(b) It is true that many human beings have killed animals in order to obtain food and clothing.

3. a. That citizens care so much about the needy in Los Angeles is encouraging.
(b) Citizens' neglecting the needy in Los Angeles will lead to serious consequences.

4. a. Scientists working in the Gobi Desert is extraordinary.
(b) That we now know something about dinosaur parental care is astonishing.

5. (a) It's great that she got a new computer.
b. It's great for her to get a new computer.

ACTIVITY 2 research/writing

Research several animals that are in danger of becoming extinct. Find out how they are dying or being killed. Then, write a short paragraph, giving your feelings and opinions about **one** of these animals. Several suggestions are given below.

California condor	spotted owl	blue whale
Arabian oryx	orangutan of Borneo	giant Panda

ANSWER KEY

Exercise 8 Letters of the correct sentences are circled above. The reasons are: 1. This is a true fact that whalers have almost exterminated the blue whale.   2. It is true that dolphins catch diseases from humans at these centers.   3. Focus is on a future event with After an oil spill.   4. This is a fact: companies are cutting down the Amazonian rain forests, but to do so in the future would be inspiring.   5. The AIDS crisis has not yet been stopped, but to do so in the future would be inspiring.

Exercise 9 Answers will vary. Possible answers are: 1. Dictators' allowing people to vote would be extremely unusual.   2. Busybodies' minding their own business would be terribly funny.

3. Bus drivers' allowing people to smoke on the bus would be wholly unexpected.   4. Procrastinators' doing things on time would be particularly odd.   5. Professional athletes' being humble would be really surprising.   6. English teachers' overlooking grammar errors is virtually impossible.   7. Hollywood stars' living in poor neighborhoods would be extremely unusual.   8. Your mother's not teaching you good manners would have been particularly odd.   9. Your friend's father remarrying would be virtually impossible.   10. Our class's being dismissed early would be wholly unexpected.

EXERCISE 8 [15 minutes]

In Exercise 8 students choose the sentence that makes the best use of an adjective complement.

1. Read the directions as a class. Ask a volunteer to read the example. Ask students what time is referred to here: past, present, or future? (*past*)
2. Have students work independently to circle their choices for each pair of sentences.
3. Have them work in pairs, exchange papers, and review each other's work.
4. Ask different students to share their sentences with the class, and discuss. See answers on LP page 380.

 For more practice, use *Grammar Dimensions 4* Workbook page 189, Exercise 7.

EXERCISE 9 [25 minutes]

In this final and entertaining exercise students create sentences expressing what would be strange for a number of different people to do or have done, using specific *-ly* adverb + adjective clusters.

1. Read the directions as a class. Ask a volunteer to read the example. Encourage two other students to create two other sentences.
2. Have students work independently to write at least one sentence for each person or group of people. Tell them not to write their names on their papers.
3. Collect all the papers, and then divide students into small groups. Pass out a paper to each student.
4. Have them take turns reading the sentences on their papers aloud to the group.
5. Ask different students to share their best sentences with the class.

 For more practice, use *Grammar Dimensions 4* Workbook page 188, Exercise 6.

EXPANSION 1 [25 minutes/homework]

For further practice, assign this activity as homework.

1. Have students write a list of 5–8 other groups of people.
2. Have them exchange papers with another student.
3. For homework, ask students to write two sentences about each group expressing what would be strange for them to do, using the *-ly* adverb + adjective clusters from Exercise 9.
4. During the next class, have students work in pairs, exchange papers, and read and comment on them.

EXPANSION 2 [40 minutes]

In Activity 5 (writing) on SB page 382 students write a short opinion paragraph in which students express their thoughts on the truth veracity of the statements in the Fox paragraph. They are encouraged to use 3 or more adjective complements. This is a good activity for students after Exercise 9, implementing what they've learned from the whole unit.

UNIT GOAL REVIEW [10 minutes]

Ask students to look at the goals on the opening page of the unit again. Refer to the pages of the unit where information on each goal can be found.

 For assessment of Unit 20, use *Grammar Dimensions 4 ExamView®*.

USE YOUR ENGLISH

The Use Your English activities at the end of the unit contain situations that should naturally elicit the structures covered in the unit. For a more complete discussion of how to use the Use Your English activities, see To the Teacher, LP page xxvi.

ACTIVITY 1 listening [30 minutes]

CD2 Tracks 13–17

This activity is a good follow-up to Exercise 5 on SB page 378. Note that the former CD track numbers (30–34) are incorrectly listed in the student book.

1. Read the directions and example as a class.
2. Have students listen to the audio once.
3. Ask students to listen again and circle the appropriate comment that would follow from what they have heard.
4. Have students work in pairs to compare their responses.
5. Ask volunteers to share their answers with the class. See answers on LP page 380.

ACTIVITY 2 research/writing [60 minutes/homework]

This activity is a good follow-up to Exercise 1 on SB pages 374–375, either as homework or as a class activity.

1. Read the directions and the list of animals as a class.
2. Ask students to research at least three of the animals listed.
3. Ask them to write a paragraph in which they express their feelings and opinions about one of the animals.
4. Have students work in pairs and exchange papers and discuss their writings.
5. Ask several volunteers to share their writings with the class, and discuss.

 **ACTIVITY 3** reading/speaking

Comment upon a current problem in your community, your country, or the world. Indicate how certain or impossible a solution will be in the near future using one of the following adjectives: *certain, likely, probable, possible, unlikely,* or *impossible.*

Example: *For the past few years the European Union has discussed a common constitution. It now appears likely that the majority will ratify the constitution in the near future.*

 **ACTIVITY 4** writing

Rosary beads, piano keys, and dice are all made of ivory, sometimes illegally obtained. Hunters cut the tusks from elephants with chainsaws and then sell the tusks to businesspeople who smuggle them out of the country. Often political officials collaborate in the crime by issuing false import permits.

Imagine that you have bought an ivory figure for $1000 and later learned that the ivory had been illegally obtained. Write a letter of complaint to the company from which you bought the figure. Use statements such as, "I have just learned that the figure I bought from you was made of illegally obtained ivory. Your selling me such an item is outrageous."

 **ACTIVITY 5** writing

Michael W. Fox, in his book *Inhuman Society: The American Way of Exploiting Animals*, has expressed his opinion on modern zoos in the following way:

Today's zoos and wildlife safari parks are radically different from the early iron and concrete zoos. It takes money to run a modern zoo, and zoo directors realize that they must compete with a wide variety of leisure-time activities. Concession stands, miniature railroads, and other carnival amusements, as well as dubious circuslike shows with performing chimps or big cats, lure many visitors to some of our large zoos and wildlife parks. What tricks and obedience the animals display are more a reflection of the power of human control than of the animals' natural behavior. Performing apes, elephants, bears, big cats, dolphins, and "killer" whales especially draw the crowds. Man's mastery over the powerful beast and willful control over its wild instincts is a parody of the repression and sublimation of human nature and personal freedom.

Individually, write a short paragraph explaining whether or not you agree with Fox. What statements are true? What are questionable? (Use at least three adjective complements in your writing.)

 **ACTIVITY 6** research on the web

 Using an Internet search engine such as Yahoo® or Google®, or another Web site or source you may know of, search the Internet to find out how animals have been used in research of one of the following diseases: polio, diphtheria, mumps, hepatitis, diabetes, arthritis, high blood pressure, AIDS, or cancer. As a result of your research, express your opinions in a short oral report on the use of animals in furthering medical progress. Do you feel that it is important or unnecessary?

Example: *It is important for researchers to use animals in their research . . .*

 **ACTIVITY 7** reflection

Students have to develop good study habits in order to get assignments finished and to pass their exams. With a classmate, discuss your opinions about the following activities. Give the reason why these are or are not suitable study options. In your discussion, use several adjective complements in subject or predicate position.

Example: Cramming for tests
Students' cramming for tests is not consistent with the type of regular, frequent study needed to learn a subject.
It's not good to cram for tests because it is difficult to retain material after the test is over.

1. Going to bed at 2:00 A.M. on weeknights
2. Designating particular times each day to devote to your studies
3. Staying out late every Saturday night
4. Surveying materials before you read them
5. Looking up every unknown word in a dictionary
6. Rehearsing learned material with a friend
7. Asking questions of your teacher if you do not understand something
8. Going to a movie instead of going to class
9. Getting involved in many extracurricular activities
10. Studying at a cafeteria

USE YOUR ENGLISH

ACTIVITY 3 reading/speaking
[30 minutes]

In this activity students use certain adjectives to comment on a current social problem that they feel strongly about. This activity makes a good assignment following Exercise 6 on SB page 378.

1. Read the directions as a class. Ask a volunteer to read the example aloud.
2. Have students work independently to write a short description of their feelings about a social problem, using the adjectives listed.
3. Have students share their writings in small groups.
4. Ask a few volunteers to read their writings to the class, and discuss.

ACTIVITY 4 writing
[40 minutes]

In this activity students write a fictional letter of complaint to a company about a figure they bought that was made from illegally obtained ivory using adjective complements. It is a good activity for students after Exercise 7 on SB page 379.

1. Write the following words on the board: *beads, pistol grips, dice.*
2. Ask students to brainstorm in pairs what these words have in common. They should determine that all these objects are made of ivory.
3. Ask one student to read the first paragraph.
4. Ask students to work in pairs to write the letter of complaint.
5. Ask one member of each pair to read the letter of complaint aloud to the class.

ACTIVITY 5 writing
[30 minutes/homework]

In this activity students discuss and write about a passage on modern zoos using adjective complements. It is a good follow-up to the work students do in Exercise 9 on SB page 380.

1. Read the directions as a class. Ask students to read the paragraph silently.
2. Have students work independently to write a paragraph (for homework) expressing their views on the passage. Tell them to include at least three adjective complements in their paragraph.
3. Ask different volunteers to read their paragraphs aloud, and encourage debate after all have had a chance to read.

ACTIVITY 6 research on the web
[60 minutes/homework]

In this activity students are asked to find information on the Internet about how animals have been used in research and then give an oral report in which they express their opinions about using animals to further medical progress, using adjective complements. It is a good homework assignment following the work students do in Exercise 2 on SB page 375.

1. Read the directions and example as a class.
2. Have students research the topic and write a short report.
3. During the next class, have students work in small groups and take turns presenting their reports to the group.
4. Ask several volunteers to share their reports with the class, and discuss.

ACTIVITY 7 reflection
[45 minutes]

In this activity students discuss their opinions about various study habits, using adjective complements in subject or predicate position. This activity could be assigned after Exercise 4 on SB page 377.

1. Read the directions as a class. Ask a volunteer to read the example.
2. Divide the class into two groups, A and B. Ask Group A to write about what they think of the first five study habits, and ask Group B to write about the last five habits.
3. Have students form groups of four: two students from Group A, and two from Group B.
4. Have them take turns sharing what they wrote with the group.
5. Ask various volunteers to report on similarities and differences in opinions in their groups, and discuss.

NOUN COMPLEMENTS
TAKING *THAT* CLAUSES

UNIT GOALS

- Use noun complements to explain abstract nouns

- Distinguish *that*-clause noun complements from restrictive relative clauses

- Use *that*-clause noun complements in subject position to signal known or implied information

- Use *the fact + that* noun complements appropriately

- Appropriately use *that*-clause noun complements after transitive adjectives and phrasal verbs

OPENING TASK

Explaining Natural Phenomena

How good are you at explaining natural phenomena? Would you be able to explain why the North American and South American eastern coastlines and the Eurasian and African western coastlines appear to be mirror images of each other? One account for this phenomenon is the theory that all of these continents once formed a single continent and subsequently moved apart.

■ STEP 1

Discuss at least five of the following questions with your classmates. Try to write down the facts that could explain these intriguing natural events.

1. What explains the observation that in some parts of the world leaves change color and fall from the trees each year?
2. What explains the observation that shooting stars speed across the sky?
3. What explains the fact that there are oases in desert environments?
4. What accounts for the fact that some rainbows are partial and some are full?
5. What could illustrate the idea that physical activity is difficult at high altitudes?
6. What could illustrate the law that heat flows from a warm place to a cooler place?
7. What fact could explain the reason for the sun and moon to appear larger near the horizon?
8. What fact could account for the reason for a person's reflection appearing upside down in a spoon?

■ STEP 2

Now add a few questions of your own concerning other intriguing natural events that you are curious about. Once you have written your questions, see if your classmates know the facts that explain them.

UNIT OVERVIEW

Unit 21 provides an overview of noun complements, distinguishes the *that*-clause from a restrictive relative clause, and introduces the function of the *that*-clause noun complement in discourse.

Please note that due to its length, this unit has been divided into three lesson plans. To review this unit more quickly, review focus charts and have students complete the first exercise after each chart to observe students' grasp of the grammar topics.

GRAMMAR NOTE

Unit 21 contains information about noun complements that can be quite challenging for advanced students, even though they may have had exposure to complement structures at earlier levels (e.g., *The fact that John was late bothered me*).

UNIT GOALS

Some instructors may want to review the goals listed on Student Book (SB) page 384 after completing the Opening Task so that students understand what they should know by the end of the unit. These goals can also be reviewed at the end of the unit when students are more familiar with the grammar terminology.

OPENING TASK [30 minutes]

The purpose of the Opening Task is to create a context in which students will need to use noun complements as students work to explain eight types of natural phenomena. The problem-solving format is designed to show the teacher how well the students can produce the target structures implicitly and spontaneously when they are engaged in a communicative task. For a more complete discussion of the purpose of the Opening Task, see To the Teacher, Lesson Planner (LP) page xxii.

Setting Up the Task

1. Read the introductory paragraph as a class. Ask students to look at the map and say whether the outlines of the coastlines look as though they could fit together to form one land mass.

2. Discuss any theories students may have heard or read about that suggest that the continents were once one large land mass.

Conducting the Task

■ STEP 1

1. Read the directions as a class.

2. Have students work in small groups. Assign half the groups questions 1–4, and the other half 5–8.

3. Encourage students to guess the explanations even if they do not understand exactly why these phenomena occur. If students do not use noun complements when discussing the questions, you may want to request that they use the following words in their explanations: *observation, fact, idea*, or *law*. Possible answers appear in the Exercise 3 answer key. These could be compared against students' explanations.

■ STEP 2

1. Read the directions as a class. Encourage the small groups to think of other intriguing natural events that other groups in the class might find difficult to explain. Have each group share one more natural event and have the other groups guess the explanation by writing down their responses on an overhead transparency or on the board.

2. Compare the explanations and give a prize to the group that comes the closest to the real explanation.

Closing the Task

1. Discuss which natural events the class is still unsure about, which theories seem the most plausible, and where the students might go to obtain the information. You could also encourage creative possibilities (or myth-making) to account for some of the unknown phenomena.

2. Don't worry about accuracy at this point, though you may want to take notes of errors in meaning, form, or use in order to focus on those problems later.

GRAMMAR NOTE

Typical student errors (form)

- Using a *for-to* infinitive rather than a *that*-clause after some abstract nouns such as *answer, suggestion, idea, news, thesis*, etc: —e.g., * *The suggestion for kids to go to school earlier was rejected by the board.* (See Focus 1.)

- Using a *that*-clause rather than a *for-to* infinitive after some abstract nouns such as *advice, requirement, proposal*, etc:—e.g., * *They ignored the requirement that people to drive slowly around the school.* (See Focus 1.)

- Omitting *the fact* (*idea/news*, etc.) before a *that*-clause noun complement:—e.g., * *He could not face up to that his girlfriend had left him.* (See Focus 5.)

Typical student errors (use)

- Omitting *the fact that* phrase in object position after certain verbs such as *accept, conceal, discuss, overlook*, etc:—e.g., * *The murderer concealed he knew the victim.* (See Focus 4 for other verbs.)

- Overusing *that*-clauses in object position with *the fact*, particularly in writing:—e.g., * *The lawyer said that the fact that his client held a good job and the fact that he coached the boys' softball team indicated the fact that he was an upstanding citizen.* (See Focus 4.)

FOCUS 1 — Overview of Noun Complements

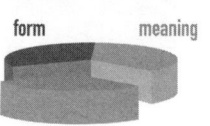

form   meaning

Noun complements explain or provide the complete content of certain nouns.

EXAMPLES	EXPLANATIONS
(a) The theory **that water expands when it is frozen** is testable. (b) The requirement **for workers to wear safety glasses** is important.	Noun complements are of two types: *that* clauses and infinitives. • The *that* clause is a way of explaining the noun. • The *for-to* infinitive also explains the noun. • Both types of complements follow abstract nouns. Many abstract nouns have verb counterparts (*requirement/require, advice/advise, reminder/remind*, etc.).
Abstract Nouns (+ *That* Clause): *answer news reply* *appeal notion request* *axiom possibility statement* *fact proposal suggestion* *hypothesis reason theory* *idea reminder thesis*	With the abstract nouns listed here, we use a *that* clause to form noun complements.
Abstract Nouns (+ Infinitives): *advice permission request* *appeal plan requirement* *command preparation suggestion* *instruction proposal tendency* *motivation recommendation* *order reminder*	Another group of abstract nouns takes infinitives.

EXAMPLES	EXPLANATIONS
(c) Most people understand the recommendation **that citizens should pay higher taxes.** (d) Most people understand the recommendation **for citizens to pay higher taxes.**	Some nouns, such as *request, recommendation,* and *suggestion* may take either a *that* clause or an infinitive as a complement.
(e) The fact **that the parties were able to meet** indicates the commitment of everyone to cooperate. (f) Does he understand the need **for leaders to establish some guidelines?**	Noun complements may appear with nouns either in subject or object position.

EXERCISE 1

Underline each noun complement. Circle the abstract noun that precedes it.

Example: Early scientists believed (the notion) that matter could be divided into four basic elements: earth, water, air, and fire.

1. (The tendency) for liquids to turn into gases is well known.

2. Moisture in the air provides (the catalyst) for industrial fumes to react and form acid rain.

3. Galileo proposed (the hypothesis) that all falling bodies drop at the same constant speed.

4. (The possibility) for scientists to intercept messages from space is increased by using radio telescopes.

5. (The idea) that songbirds may hear their own songs while they sleep is confirmed by a University of Chicago study.

6. (The fact) that overhead cables sag on a hot day proves that solids expand when heated.

FOCUS 1 [15 minutes]

Focus 1 introduces students to the form and meaning of the two types of noun complements: *that*-clauses and infinitives.

1. **Lead-in:** Ask students to work in pairs and take turns reading examples and explanations.

2. To help reinforce the abstract nouns, ask them to interact using a short 3-line dialogue:

   Student A: *I heard the request.* (fill in one of the words from the list)

   Student B: *What request?* (repeating the word that Student A has said)

   Student A: *The request that we turn off the lights before leaving the room/to turn off the lights before leaving the room* (fill in a *that* + clause or an infinitive)

3. Answer any questions students might have.

METHODOLOGY NOTE

Point out that this focus, and Focus 5, are both excellent reference tools for students to use.

EXERCISE 1 [15 minutes]

In Exercise 1 students identify the noun complements and the abstract noun that precedes each, applying what they have just learned in Focus 1.

1. Read the directions as a class.

2. Divide the class into pairs and ask one student to read three items aloud while the other underlines and circles the appropriate words. Then they switch roles.

3. Have each pair compare answers with another pair.

4. Review answers as a class. See answers on LP page 386.

For more practice, use *Grammar Dimensions 4* Workbook page 190, Exercise 1.

EXERCISE 2

Summarize the information from the text by completing the statements that follow.

> ### SOLAR RAYS AND OUR SKIN
>
> The increase of hydrofluorocarbons in the atmosphere is dangerously depleting the earth's ozone layer. The effect of this is that people are having greater exposure to ultraviolet light rays. Can these solar rays increase the chances of skin cancer? Yes, in fact, they increase the cases of malignant melanoma—the deadliest type.
>
>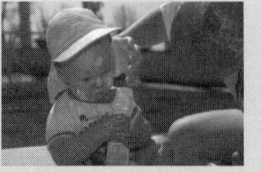
>
> According to The American Cancer Society, hundreds of thousands of new cases of skin cancer will be diagnosed in the United States each year. About 5 percent of these will be malignant melanoma. To prevent more cases, many doctors say that people should stay out of the sun altogether. This is especially true for redheads and blondes with freckled skin who have less natural protection against the sun's rays. At the very least, a person should cover up and wear a sunscreen with a high sun-protection factor (15, 25, or 30) during the periods of the day when ultraviolet rays are strongest.
>
> A good example of an anti-skin-cancer campaign comes from Australia. Life-guards in the state of Victoria wear T-shirts with the slogan "SLIP! SLOP! SLAP!"—which means slip on a shirt, slop on some sunscreen, and slap on a hat. Although these hints may not please all sunbathers on beaches around the world, they might very well save their lives.

Example: The news that <u>hydrofluorocarbons are depleting the ozone layer</u> is alarming.

1. The fact that _____ indicates why there has been an increase in cases of malignant melanoma.

2. The fact that _____ explains why blondes and redheads burn easily.

3. The fact that _____ is evidence that ultraviolet rays can cause skin cancer.

4. The doctors' recommendation for _____ is not very popular.

5. The amusing reminder for _____ has changed the sunbathing habits of people in Australia.

EXERCISE 3

Reread the questions in the Opening Task on page 385, Step 1, and answer at least five of them, using a *that* clause in subject position.

Example: What explains the observation that "shooting stars" speed across the sky?

The observation that "shooting stars" speed across the sky can be explained by meteorites' burning up as they hit the earth's atmosphere.

FOCUS 2 · *That* Clause Noun Complements versus Restrictive Relative Clauses

EXAMPLES	EXPLANATIONS
(a) The story that she opened a restaurant is untrue. (b) The requirement that criminals serve 85 percent of their time is strictly reinforced.	A *that* clause noun complement defines an idea. In (a), *opened a restaurant* is "the story." The sentence still makes sense even if *the story* is deleted. In this sentence, *which* cannot replace *that*. Likewise in (b), the main idea of the sentence is kept even if *the requirement* is omitted.
(c) The story that/which she told was untrue. (d) The requirement that/which most annoys criminals in prison is the "lights out" curfew.	A restrictive relative clause limits an idea. *The story* in (c) relates to a particular story, the one that she told. The sentence will not make sense if *the story* is deleted. In this sentence, *which* can replace *that*. The same is true in (d), where the sentence will not make sense if *the requirement* is deleted.

EXERCISE 4

Which sentence in each of the following pairs contains a noun complement? Circle your choice.

Example: (a.) The idea that they didn't question the witnesses was shocking.
       b. The idea that he had was exciting.

1. (a.) Many people dispute the fact that human beings evolved from apes.
   b. Many people accept the fact that he just mentioned.

2. a. The suggestion that she included in the letter will never be followed.
   (b.) The suggestion that a person should warm up before jogging is important.

3. (a.) The reply that she did not need help came as a surprise.
   b. The reply that contained important information was received too late.

4. (a.) I believe the theory that opposites attract.
   b. I believe the theory that my uncle proposed.

5. a. The students will select the answer that they think is correct.
   (b.) The students will select the answer that one oxygen and two hydrogen molecules constitute water.

6. a. They discussed the possibility that there may be additional concerns.
   (b.) They discussed the possibility that was predicted earlier.

7. (a.) I understand the statement that was made by the Turkish ambassador.
   b. I understand the statement that "two wrongs don't make a right."

Exercise 2 1. people are having greater exposure to ultraviolet rays   2. fair-headed people have less natural protection against the sun's rays   3. thousands of people have malignant melanoma 4. people to stay out of the sun altogether   5. people to slip on a shirt, slop on some sunscreen, and slap on a hat

Exercise 3 1. Leaf pigments (which assist some plants during photosynthesis) becoming visible when the leaf dies in the fall explains the observation that the leaves of some trees change color and fall to the ground during cold weather.   2. Bits of interplanetary matter (meteorites) entering the earth's atmosphere and burning up explains the observation that stars shoot across the sky.

are oases.   4. Rainfall not filling the air over a large enough area accounts for the fact that there is only a partial rainbow.   5. Troubled breathing during mild exercise in the mountains illustrates the idea that activity is difficult at high altitudes.   6. An ice cube melting in a glass of water illustrates the law that heat flows from a warm place to a cooler place.   7. The sun and the moon appearing larger than normal is explained by the fact that the eye evaluates the size of the sun and the moon against the size of objects on the earth near the horizon—e.g., trees, hills, buildings, etc. 8. A person's reflection appearing upside down is explained by the fact that the concave parts of a spoon act as a lens. If the spoon were flat, it would reflect like a mirror.

EXERCISE 2 [20 minutes]

In Exercise 2 students summarize information about the harmful effects of radiation, using the two types of noun complements they just studied in Focus 1. This exercise is quite challenging, since students must understand and summarize some complex information.

1. Discuss what students know about the harmful effects of the sun.
2. Read the directions as a class.
3. Have students work in pairs to summarize the information in the reading by completing the statements.
4. Have them compare answers with another pair.
5. Review answers as a class. See answers on LP page 388.

 For more practice, use *Grammar Dimensions 4* Workbook page 191, Exercise 2.

EXPANSION 1 [20 minutes]

This expansion activity gives students more practice with summarizing the information in Exercise 2.

1. Have students work in pairs. Ask them to underline the abstract nouns in the sentences in Exercise 2.
2. Ask them to look at the two kinds of abstract nouns in Focus 1. (*abstract nouns + **that** clauses; abstract nouns + infinitives*)
3. Using the underlined nouns from Exercise 2, have students write a sentence for each underlined abstract noun to demonstrate the two types of noun complements.
4. Ask pairs to exchange papers with another pair and discuss their sentences.
5. Ask several volunteers to share a sentence or two with the class.

EXPANSION 2 [30 minutes/homework]

1. For homework, ask students to choose another reading on the health effects of some other aspect of the environment, such as water or air pollution.
2. Have them write at least five sentences summarizing the information using the two types of noun complement structures.
3. During the next class, have students share their sentences in small groups, and discuss.

EXERCISE 3 [20 minutes]

In Exercise 3 students return to the questions in the Opening Task and answer them using a *that*-clause in object position.

1. Read the directions as a class. Ask a volunteer to read the example aloud.
2. Have students work independently to answer the questions in the Opening Task.
3. Have students compare answers with a partner.
4. Ask volunteers to share an answer for each sentence. See answers on LP page 388.

EXPANSION [90 minutes/homework]

Activity 2 (reading/writing) on SB page 396 is a good homework assignment following Exercise 3. In it students research the facts behind a natural phenomenon and then write a short report using at least three noun complements.

LESSON PLAN 2

FOCUS 2 [15 minutes]

Focus 2 explores the forms and uses of adjective complements in subject and predicate position, highlighting how their function determines their location in a sentence.

1. **Lead-in:** If possible, make an overhead transparency of this focus chart and use the "uncover technique" to explain the difference between a *that*-clause noun complement and a restrictive relative clause. Present just one set of examples at a time.
2. After students have given their explanations, uncover the explanation and read it aloud.
3. Repeat this procedure with the second section of the chart.
4. Answer any questions students may have.

EXERCISE 4 [20 minutes]

In Exercise 4 students indicate which sentences contain noun complements, following the principles explored in Focus 2.

1. Read the directions and examples as a class. Ask students to say what kind of clause (b) contains. (*a restrictive relative clause*)
2. Have students work independently to circle their choices.
3. Have them work in pairs to compare their answers. Then, ask them to take turns deleting the abstract noun and then reading the sentence aloud. Does the sentence still make sense?
4. Ask volunteers to share their answers with the class. See answers on LP page 388.

 For more practice, use *Grammar Dimensions 4* Workbook page 191, Exercise 3.

EXPANSION [90 minutes/homework]

In Activity 5 (research on the web) on SB page 397 students research an environmental problem on the Internet, and then discuss the reasons for it with their classmates. Encourage students to use noun complements. The first part of the activity can be assigned as homework following the work students do in Exercise 4, with discussion taking place during the next class.

FOCUS 3 | That Clause Noun Complements in Subject Position

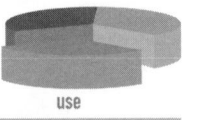

use

EXAMPLES	EXPLANATIONS
(a) Harry had to write many papers in college. He never learned how to type. **The idea that Harry graduated from college without knowing how to type** astonishes me. (b) When Teresa was diagnosed with cancer, everyone thought that she would not survive. Then, after several months of chemotherapy, the doctor said he could see no trace of the disease. **The fact that she was cured** is a miracle.	*That* clause noun complements in subject position contain known or implied information. The predicate comments upon the facts or ideas contained in *that* clauses following *the fact/idea/news*, etc.).

■ EXERCISE 5

The following paragraphs describe amazing facts about famous people. Make observations about each set of facts using a *that* clause following *the fact/idea/news*, etc.

Example: When Beethoven was 28 years old, he became deaf. In spite of this, he was still able to compose music.

The fact that Beethoven composed music while he was deaf is amazing.

1. Marie Antoinette and Louis XVI ate very well, while their Parisian subjects could not afford bread. When hearing of this, the unsympathetic queen is reported to have said, "Why, then, let them eat cake."

2. United States President Richard Nixon resigned from office in 1974 after a very serious governmental scandal. Republican associates who were interested in having him re-elected had installed wiretaps at the headquarters of the Democratic National Committee at the Watergate Hotel. Rather than being honest, Nixon tried to cover up the scandal, and this led to his downfall.

3. In 1919, Rudolph Valentino, a famous American movie star, married Jean Acker. In his silent films, he played the part of the great lover. But, on the wedding day, Acker ran away and Valentino never consummated his marriage with her.

4. For years, athletes did the high jump by jumping sideways or straddling over the bar. Then, Dick Fosbury discovered that he could break world records by going over head first, flat on his back. The technique is now called the Fosbury Flop.

5. The Japanese had long revered their emperor as divine. However, Emperor Hirohito destroyed this image by announcing to his people in 1946 that it was a false conception that he was descended from God. In fact, even at the early age of 14, Hirohito had doubted his own divinity.

FOCUS 4 | The Fact That . . .

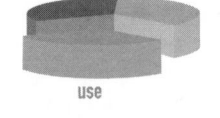

use

EXAMPLES	EXPLANATIONS
(a) **Less formal:** The fact that she refused the money showed her sense of pride. (b) **Formal:** That she refused the money showed her sense of pride. (c) **Less formal:** People generally acknowledge the fact that Japan must find alternate ways to use its space. (d) **Formal:** People generally acknowledge that Japan must find alternate ways to use its space.	*The fact + that* clause noun complements in (a) and (c) are similar in meaning to the *that* clauses in (b) and (d); however, we generally consider them less formal.
(e) **Wordy:** He believed the fact that his daughter had been kidnapped, and he understood the fact that he would need to pay a ransom. (f) **Concise:** He believed that his daughter had been kidnapped, and he understood that he would need to pay a ransom.	In writing, overuse of *that* clauses in object position with *the fact* can lead to wordiness. In most cases, it is better to use the simple *that* clause.
(g) The detectives concealed **the fact that** they had searched the room. (h) The soldiers accepted **the fact that** they had been defeated. (i) The police officers disregarded **the fact that** they needed a search warrant. (j) NOT: The police officers disregarded that they needed a search warrant.	Certain verbs (such as *accept, conceal, discuss, dispute, disregard, hide, overlook, support*) require the use of *the fact that* clauses in object position, however.

ANSWER KEY

Exercise 5 Answers will vary. Possible answers are: 1. The fact that Marie Antoinette was very unsympathetic toward her subjects was despicable. 2. The news that Nixon was aware of the wiretaps at the Democratic National Committee headquarters but tried to cover up this knowledge was the beginning of the end of his presidential career. 3. The idea that Rudolph Valentino's marriage with Jean Acker was never consummated contradicts the idea that he was a great lover. 4. The proposal that athletes could break world records by going over the high-jump bar head first came as a big surprise. 5. The theory that Japanese emperors are descended from God was doubted by Emperor Hirohito at the early age of 14.

FOCUS 3 [10 minutes]

1. **Lead-in:** Ask a volunteer to read the first example. Ask students to identify what position the noun complement is in the example. (*subject position*)
2. Ask another volunteer to read the second example, and again ask students to say what position the noun complement is in.
3. Have a third volunteer read the explanation aloud.
4. Ask several volunteers to create sentences with a *that*-clause noun complement in subject position.
5. Answer any questions students may have.

METHODOLOGY NOTE

In other units, students have been introduced to the concept of new and old information management within texts. Note that this is another example of new information (the comment) being saved for last and old information being placed in subject position. Ask students to watch for this as they read for other classes or for pleasure. Assign them to find at least one example to share with the class by the end of the unit.

EXERCISE 5 [20 minutes]

In Exercise 5, students comment on a series of facts using a *that*-clause in subject position.

1. Read the directions and example as a class. Ask a volunteer to give another example using the information about Beethoven and a noun complement in subject position.
2. Ask students to work in pairs to comment on each set of facts using a *that*-clause in subject position. Tell them to try to use different phrases, such as *the fact that, the idea that,* and *the news that* in their sentences.

3. Have pairs get together with another pair and take turns sharing their sentences.
4. Ask various volunteers to share a sentence with the class, and discuss these. See possible answers on LP page 390.

For more practice, use *Grammar Dimensions 4* Workbook page 192, Exercise 4.

EXPANSION [20 minutes]

This activity will give students additional practice in creating sentences with a *that*-clause noun complement in subject position.

1. Have students work in pairs. Ask them to write down at least two facts that may be new or surprising to their partner. For example, *I have a pet snake that I keep in my room.*
2. Have students take turns reading their facts and commenting on what they hear using a noun complement structure in subject position. For example, *The fact that you have a pet snake in your room is very surprising.*
3. Have pairs work with another pair and take turns reading and commenting on their facts.
4. Ask several volunteers to share their reactions with the class to some of the most interesting, funny, or outrageous facts.

FOCUS 4 [15 minutes]

Focus 4 explores how *the fact + that*-clauses are used in formal and informal writing and speech, and cautions against the overuse of such clauses.

1. **Lead-in:** If possible, make an overhead transparency of this focus chart and use the "uncover technique" to present one set of examples at a time and elicit their explanations. After each set, ask a volunteer to read the explanation in the chart, and discuss.
2. For the second set, ask volunteers to create other examples of wordy, repetitive sentences. Encourage them to offer ridiculous examples.
3. Answer any question students may have.

METHODOLOGY NOTE

This information will be especially helpful to students who are doing expository writing. Remind them to apply these principles when they edit their compositions in other classes.

EXERCISE 6

Read the following passage and write a short paragraph explaining the facts about ice. Exchange your paragraph with a classmate and check each other's paragraphs for excessive use of *the fact + that* clauses.

Example: Several facts about ice can be explained quite easily. For example, ~~the fact~~ that skaters appear to glide as they skate as if they are on water can be accounted for by ice melting underneath a skater's blade. . . .

National Geographic World, Dec 1998 i280 p4(1)

Why in the world? Scientific Facts About the Properties of Ice by *Judith E. Rinard*.

Abstract: Ice has certain properties that make it ideal for sports such as ice skating. Icebergs usually have the larger part submerged and leaving the smaller peak visible. The International Iceberg Patrol leaves warning signs for the safety of ships in polar waters.

Full Text: COPYRIGHT 1998 National Geographic Society

Brrrr! These ICY questions may make you shiver.

WHY DO ICE SKATES GLIDE?
Ice-skaters seem to slide along in a fluid motion. In fact they really do slide on fluid! The fluid is water. Under pressure, ice melts. A skater's whole body weight is concentrated on the blades. The pressure of the blades melts the ice. This forms a thick film of water. Once the skater moves on, the ice immediately refreezes.

WHY DOES ICE STICK TO ME?
When the warm, moist surface of your wet hand meets the freezing cold surface of an ice cube, heat gets transferred. The warmth of your hand heats the ice enough to melt the outside. But the ice quickly cools your skin. The surface of your skin may get so cold that the melted ice freezes again and—ouch! You're stuck. Only ice that's in or just removed from the freezer is cold enough to stick to you. A word of advice: Don't pop an ice cube straight from the freezer into your mouth.

WHY ARE ICEBERGS DANGEROUS?
The R.M.S. *Titanic* is a good example of how a collision with an iceberg can quickly sink a ship. Icebergs are huge chunks of ice floating in the sea. The most dangerous thing about them is that most of their bulk is hidden underwater, and only the tip of an iceberg may be visible. People on a ship may not spot the berg until the ship has slammed into the submerged part. The sharp, deadly ice can rip a hole in a ship. Today the International Iceberg Patrol provides ships with early warnings of icebergs.

WHY SHOULDN'T I TOUCH DRY ICE?
Most ice is frozen water. But dry ice is solid carbon dioxide and much colder than ordinary ice. When heated, it doesn't melt into a liquid. It turns into a smoky-looking gas. Handling dry ice is dangerous because of its super-cold temperature—lower than minus 100 [degrees] F. Touching it can cause frostbite in the fingers. For safety, people wear heavy gloves when handling dry ice.

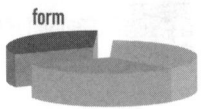

form

FOCUS 5   *That* Clause Noun Complements Following Transitive Adjectives and Phrasal Verbs

EXAMPLES	EXPLANATION
(a) He is tired of **the fact that she refuses to see him.**	When *that* clause noun complements follow transitive adjectives (adjective taking a preposition + a noun phrase) or phrasal verbs (verb + preposition), they must be *that* clauses using *the fact/news/idea/theory*, etc. rather than simple *that* clauses.
(b) NOT: He is tired of that she refuses to see him.	
(c) He played down **the news that his team won.**	
(d) NOT: He played down that his team won.	

Examples of Transitive Adjectives	Examples of Phrasal Verbs
disappointed in	*play down*
worried about	*make up*
proud of	*give in*
sick of	*face up to*
tired of	*put up with*

EXERCISE 7

Imagine that a very wealthy entrepreneur has just lost his fortune. Comment upon the circumstances of his condition using the words below and *the fact/idea/news*, etc. *that* clauses.

Examples: businessman (face up to)
The businessman had to face up to the fact that he had lost his millions.

1. his mother (worried about)
2. his dynamic personality (not make up)
3. his creditors (wary of)
4. his employees (indignant at)
5. his wife (put up with)
6. the lawyers (proud of)

ANSWER KEY

Exercise 6 Answers will vary.

Exercise 7 Answers will vary. Possible answers are: 1. His mother was worried about the fact that her son had not eaten for days.   2. His dynamic personality did not make up for the fact that he had made some poor business decisions.   3. His creditors were wary of the fact that the man did not repay his debts.   4. His employees were indignant at the news that they would have to find new jobs immediately.   5. His wife could no longer put up with the fact that she rarely saw her husband anymore.   6. The lawyers were proud of the fact that they could recover much of the man's fortune.

EXERCISE 6 [25 minutes]

In Exercise 6 students read a series of fascinating facts about ice, and then write a short summary using *the fact + that*-clauses.

1. Ask students if they have ever gotten "stuck" to a piece of ice. What happened? Do they know why it happened?
2. Read the directions and example as a class.
3. Ask students to work independently to write a short paragraph summarizing the facts they have just read. Tell them to include *the fact + that* clauses in their writings.
4. Have students exchange papers with a partner and review and discuss them.
5. Ask one or two volunteers to read their paragraphs to the class.

 For more practice, use *Grammar Dimensions 4* Workbook page 193, Exercise 5.

EXPANSION [90 minutes/homework]

In Activity 4 (listening/speaking) on SB page 397 students watch a mystery or detective program or movie and then analyze what facts were concealed and which led to the crime being solved, using noun complements. The first part of the activity can be assigned as homework following Exercise 6, with discussion taking place during the next class.

LESSON PLAN 3

FOCUS 5 [15 minutes]

Focus 5 explains how, when *that*-clause noun complements follow transitive adjectives and phrasal verbs, they must include *the fact/idea/news/theory*, etc.

1. **Lead-in:** Ask two volunteers to take turns reading the examples. Read the explanation to the class.
2. Point out that the preposition in the transitive adjective and the phrasal verb dictates the need for a *that*-clause noun complement.
3. Ask another volunteer to read the two lists of transitive adjectives and phrasal verbs.
4. Elicit other examples that use the transitive adjectives and phrasal verbs from the lists in the focus chart. For example, *The teacher was worried about the fact that no one had done the homework.*
5. Answer any questions students may have.

EXERCISE 7 [15 minutes]

In Exercise 7 students comment on a series of circumstances using *the fact/idea/news*, etc. *that*-clauses, putting into practice what they have just learned in Focus 5.

1. Read the directions as a class. Ask a volunteer to read the example. Ask students whether the

that-clause noun complement follows a transitive adjective or phrasal verb. (phrasal verb: *face up to*)

2. Have students work small groups. Ask them to take turns commenting on the conditions using *the fact/idea/news,* etc. *that*-clauses.
3. Ask different students to share their sentences with the class, and discuss. See possible answers on LP page 394.

 For more practice, use *Grammar Dimensions 4* Workbook pages 193–194, Exercise 6.

EXERCISE 8

Suppose you saw people doing the following strange actions. What facts would you bring up in order to help clear up their confusion? Write a sentence about what you would say.

Examples: reading a book upside down
I would bring up the fact that it is easier to read a book right side up.

1. washing the dishes with laundry detergent
2. making lasagna without cheese
3. playing soccer with a baseball
4. going to the beach without sunglasses
5. having the radio on with the sound turned all the way down
6. writing the word *fake* with *ph* before *a* instead of *f*.

EXERCISE 9

The following sentences review the structures learned in this unit. Correct those that contain errors or are too wordy according to formal writing rules. Write OK next to those that are correct.

Examples: The teacher overlooked the fact that Hung had not done his homework. OK
The fact that she made a confession untrue.
                                                 was

1. Tom believes the fact that light travels faster than sound.
2. The request for her to stop smoking was ignored.
3. The fact that the automobile increased the distance a person could travel made it possible for a person to live and work in different places.
4. She is tired of that she always has to wash the dishes.
5. We are concerned about that there will be no more food.
6. I am grateful for the fact that the doctor assisted me in my decision.
7. Did the glasses help to conceal the fact that he had a scar on his left eyelid?
8. The fact that Mary finished her homework.
9. The fact that twenty million Russians died during World War II is tragic.
10. The request that we ignore the crime was considered unacceptable.

11. Do you agree the statement that blondes have more fun?
12. That Jerome passed the bar examination made it possible for him to practice law.

EXERCISE 10

What world changes will occur during the rest of the third millennium? In a book called *Megatrends 2000* (New York: Morrow, 1990) John Naisbett and Patricia Aburdene describe what they believe will transform the world, or, in some cases, American culture over the next 1000 years. Here are some of their predictions:

1. The English language will become the world's first truly universal language.
2. Nations, especially the "superpower" countries, will regard war as an obsolete way of solving problems.
3. Even as peoples of the world communicate more closely, individual cultures will increasingly find their unique qualities important and seek to preserve racial, linguistic, national, and religious traditions.
4. The arts will replace sports as American society's dominant leisure activity; Americans will consider alternatives to attending sports events such as football and baseball.
5. The trend of the future in the global economy is "downsizing": producing and using smaller, lighter, and more sophisticated products (for example, smaller computers, lighter building materials, electronic impulses used for financial transactions instead of paper).
6. In the first decade of the third millennium, we will think it quaint that women in the late twentieth century were excluded from the top levels of business and politics.
7. The world's nations will increasingly cooperate to address global environmental problems.

Which of these hypotheses do you consider almost a certainty by the end of the twenty-first century? Which do you think probable? Which do you find unlikely developments? Fill in the following blanks with your opinions.

Examples: I agree with the idea that <u>the arts will become popular, but I do not believe that Americans will lose their love of football</u>.
The prediction that <u>English will be the world's universal language is already true</u>.

1. I am skeptical of the notion that <u>nations will regard war as obsolete</u>
2. The tendency for <u>people to preserve their racial, linguistic, national, and religious traditions will make it hard for all nations to communicate closely</u>
3. I believe the statement that <u>the trend of the future in the global economy is "downsizing"</u>
4. The suggestion that <u>the arts will replace sports seems absurd</u>
5. I doubt the possibility that <u>the nations will cooperate to address global environmental problems</u>

ANSWER KEY

Exercise 8 Answers will vary. Possible answers are: I would remind them of/bring up/mention the fact that... 1. the dishes should be washed with dishwashing detergent. 2. lasagna requires cheese. 3. to play soccer, a person needs a soccer ball. 4. they need to bring sunglasses to the beach as it is bright today. 5. they need to turn up the sound. 6. the f sound is spelled with an f for this word and not ph.

Exercise 9 1. Tom believes that light travels... 2. The request that she stop... 3. OK 4. She is tired of the fact that she always... 5. We are concerned that there... 6. I am grateful that the doctor... 7. OK 8. The fact that Mary finished her homework impressed us. 9. That twenty million Russians died... 10. OK 11. Do you agree with the statement that blondes... 12. OK

EXPANSION [30 minutes]

In Activity 1 (listening/speaking) on SB page 396 students listen to an interview between a university admissions officer and several high school seniors, and then describe interesting facts to a partner using noun complements. This activity is a good follow-up to Exercise 7.

EXERCISE 8 [20 minutes]

In this entertaining exercise students explain a series of strange actions using *the fact/idea/news*, etc. *that*-clauses.

1. Read the directions as a class. Ask a volunteer to read the example.
2. Have students work in small groups. Ask them to write down their explanations, and then take turns sharing them with the group.
3. Ask a representative of several groups to share some of the best explanations with the class. See possible answers on LP page 394.

 For more practice, use *Grammar Dimensions 4* Workbook page 194, Exercise 7.

EXPANSION [20 minutes]

This activity gives students more practice in using *the fact/idea/news*, etc. *that*-clauses.

1. Ask each student to write another strange action on a slip of paper. Encourage them to be as silly or outrageous as possible.
2. Put these into a bag or box and ask each student to withdraw one slip (not his or her own), read it, and tell the class what he/she would do to explain the situation.

EXERCISE 9 [20 minutes]

In Exercise 9 students edit incorrect or overly wordy sentences, combining the skills they learned in Focus 4 and Focus 5. This exercise could also be used as a diagnostic or testing exercise.

1. Read the directions as a class. Ask a volunteer to read the examples. Ask students to locate the explanation for the use of the verb *overlook* in either Focus 4 or 5. (*Focus 4*) Ask a volunteer to read the explanation aloud.
2. Have students work independently to edit the sentences that are too wordy or that contain errors.
3. Have them work in pairs, exchange papers, and review each other's work.
4. Ask different students to share their answers for each sentence with the class, and discuss. See answers on LP page 394.

 For more practice, use *Grammar Dimensions 4* Workbook pages 195–196, Exercise 8.

EXPANSION [30 minutes]

In Activity 6 (reflection) on SB page 397 students express their judgments about oral or written presentations their classmates have made using a *that*-clause noun complement. It is a good follow-up to the work students do in Exercise 9, either as a homework assignment or as an in-class activity.

EXERCISE 10 [25 minutes]

In Exercise 10 students read a series of predictions about life in the third millennium, and then give their opinions of these, using noun complements.

1. Read the directions as a class. Then read the directions after the series of sentences, and ask a volunteer to read the examples aloud.

2. Divide the class into small groups of no more than five and ask students to discuss the ideas, make connections to other things they have read or heard, and express their opinions about the ideas.
3. Have each member of the group fill in one of the blanks, summarizing his or her opinion.
4. Ask the group members to share their completed sentences with each other while you circulate around the room.
5. Ask different students to share a sentence with the class, and discuss. See possible answers on LP page 394.

EXPANSION [40 minutes/homework]

In Activity 3 (reading/writing) on SB page 396 students read several editorials or opinion essays on one topic and write about their own views about the ideas and topics expressed, using noun complements. It is a good homework assignment for students after Exercise 10.

UNIT GOAL REVIEW [10 minutes]

Ask students to look at the goals on the opening page of the unit again. Refer to the pages of the unit where information on each goal can be found.

 For a grammar quiz review of Units 19–21, refer students to pages 197–199 in the *Grammar Dimensions 4* Workbook.

 For assessment of Unit 21, use *Grammar Dimensions 4* *ExamView*®.

Use Your English

ACTIVITY  1 listening/speaking

CD2 Track 18

■ **STEP 1** Listen to the audio. It is a recording of an interview between a university admissions officer and several interested high school seniors. Take note of any interesting facts you hear.

■ **STEP 2** Describe the interesting facts you learned to a classmate. Use as many noun complements as you can.

Example: *The fact that the admissions officer mainly looks at GPA and college entrance examination scores surprises me.*

ACTIVITY 2 reading/writing

Have you ever wondered what causes static electricity? Or why geese fly in a "V"? Or why the ocean is blue? Research one of these questions or one of the issues mentioned in the Opening Task (meteorites, rainbows, oases, etc.). Write a short report explaining what facts give natural phenomena their unusual properties. Use at least three noun complements in your report.

Example: *Some people say that lightning never strikes the same place twice. However, the fact that we cannot scientifically predict when or where lightning will strike makes it difficult to refute this idea . . . .*

ACTIVITY  3 reading/writing

Editorials and opinion essays can be found in newspapers, magazines, and online. Read several editorials or opinion essays. Then write your own view of the ideas in the essays by using noun complements.

Example: *The idea that terrorist cells will ever be abolished completely seems unlikely.*

ACTIVITY  4  listening/speaking

■ **STEP 1** Watch a mystery or detective program on TV or at the movies with your classmates. Discuss why the central characters were not able to solve the mystery or crime sooner than they did. What facts were concealed, disregarded, or overlooked? What facts finally led to the solution of the mystery?

Example: *The mother concealed the fact that Tony had a twin brother. The fact that Tony had a twin brother made the police finally realize that it was Tony's twin, Jimmy, who had stolen the valuable painting.*

■ **STEP 2** Watch a sports event such as soccer or baseball on TV. Discuss the facts that explain causes or effects of key events during the game.

Example: *The fact that the Giants hit three home runs in the first inning of the game gave them a clear advantage against the Dodgers. The news that Keiji Omura had sprained his ankle while sliding into third base didn't help the situation.*

ACTIVITY 5 research on the web

On the Internet, research an environmental problem such as pollution of cities, extinction of animals, or toxic waste. Then, discuss with your classmates the specific reasons behind the problem.

Example: *The fact that people have continued to drive gasoline engines has created a huge pollution problem in cities.*

ACTIVITY 6 reflection

Reflect on the oral or written presentations of your classmates from the past week. What theories, axioms, facts, hypotheses, ideas, proposals, statements, or theses were presented? Summarize your classmates' ideas and then make judgments about them using a *that* clause noun complement.

Example: *My classmate made a presentation on the theory that aliens from outer space visited the earth in 1955. I don't agree with the idea that extraterrestrial beings have ever visited the earth.*

USE YOUR ENGLISH

ACTIVITY 1 listening/speaking
[30 minutes]

Note that the former CD track number (35) is
incorrectly listed in the student book.

CD2 Track
18

■ **STEP 1**

1. Have students listen to the audio once.
2. Ask students to listen again and take notes on
   any facts that interest them.

■ **STEP 2**

1. Have students work in pairs, taking turns to
   describe the facts using as many noun complements
   as possible. Ask volunteers to share their answers
   with the class.
2. Ask several volunteers to describe an interesting
   fact to the class.

ACTIVITY 2 reading/writing
[90 minutes/homework]

1. Ask students to name natural phenomena that
   they do not understand but would like to learn
   more about, such as what happens to bears while
   they hibernate during the winter.
2. Have students choose a topic and research the
   facts that explain it. They could choose one of the
   topics mentioned in the activity, in the Opening
   Task, or any topic of their choice.
3. Ask students to write a short summary describing
   the phenomena and the facts behind it.
4. During the next class, have students work in pairs
   and exchange papers and discuss their findings.
5. Ask several volunteers to share their writings with
   the class, and discuss.

ACTIVITY 3 reading/writing
[40 minutes/homework]

1. Have students choose one or two editorials or
   opinion essays from a newspaper, magazine, the
   library, or the Internet.
2. Ask them to write their view of the ideas using at
   least one noun complement.
3. Ask students to bring in the editorial. Have them
   share with a partner the main points of the essay
   and the sentences they have created to express
   their opinion.
4. Ask several volunteers to read their writings
   to the class, and discuss.

ACTIVITY 4 listening/speaking
[90 minutes/homework]

■ **STEP 1**

1. Discuss mystery or detective programs and movies
   students have seen.
2. Read the directions as a class. Ask a volunteer to
   read the example aloud.
3. Ask students to watch a mystery or detective
   program or movie at home. Have them take notes
   on the facts: which were concealed, which turned
   out not to be important, which led to the solution
   of the crime.
4. During the next class, have students work in pairs
   and take turns describing the story and giving
   their analysis of the facts.

■ **STEP 2**

1. Arrange in advance to discuss a sports event that
   they will be able to see or bring a newspaper
   article describing a sports event to class.

2. Discuss which events had effects or caused a
   change in the game.
3. If students haven't watched the same game, have
   them read a newspaper article describing a recent
   local game.
4. Have students try to come up with the order of
   events that led to an important score in the game.
   One student should record the events on the board
   or overhead projector.

ACTIVITY 5 research on the web
[90 minutes]

1. Ask students to name environmental problems
   that concern them, and write these on the board.
2. Have students research an environmental problem
   and what causes it on the Internet. Ask them to
   take notes and write a short summary of the
   problem and the reasons it exists.
3. During the next class, have students work in
   small groups and take turns presenting their
   reports to the group.
4. Ask several volunteers to share their reports with
   the class, and debate the reasons behind the
   problems if there is disagreement.

ACTIVITY 6 reflection
[30 minutes]

1. Have students think about presentations their
   classmates have made during the past week.
   Then, ask them to write a paragraph in which
   they summarize several of those ideas and express
   their judgments of them. Remind them to use
   that-clause noun complements in their writing.
2. Have students work in pairs and take turns
   sharing their writings.
3. Ask different volunteers to read their paragraphs
   aloud, and discuss.

SUBJUNCTIVE VERBS IN *THAT* CLAUSES

- Use subjunctive verbs in *that* clause complements with verbs of advice and urging

- Use subjunctive verbs in noun complements that refer to nouns of advice or urging

- Use subjunctive verbs in adjective complements

OPENING TASK
Solving Problems

It is not uncommon for two different people or groups of people to disagree about the rightness of an issue or the solution to a problem. Often another person who does not favor either side will be called in to serve as an *arbitrator*.

For this task, one or more classmates should role-play each side of one or more of the following issues. One other person, as the arbitrator, should listen, ask questions, and give recommendations to the two parties (for example, *I suggest that _____; I recommend that _____; I propose that _____*).

■ CASE 1

A young woman would like to attend an all-male college. The president of the advisory board of the college wants to maintain the one-hundred-year tradition of an all-male campus.

■ CASE 2

A man was in a serious car accident one year ago. He has been in a coma ever since and is not expected to recover. The man's parents want to keep him alive. The man's wife sees that there is no hope for his recovery and would like to remove him from the life-support system.

■ CASE 3

A father keeps his children at home rather than sending them to school because he feels children are being taught ideas against his religion. The school board feels it is unlawful to prevent children from getting a well-rounded education.

■ CASE 4

A supervisor fires a worker because the supervisor believes she is often late, undependable, and disrespectful. The worker denies these charges and claims that she is overworked and called names by her supervisor.

UNIT OVERVIEW

Unit 22 builds on the knowledge and skills acquired in Unit 21, in which students worked with noun complements taking *that*-clauses. This unit explores the forms and uses of subjunctive verbs in *that*-clause complements and in noun complements with verbs of urging and advice. It also explains the forms of subjunctive verbs in adjective complements.

GRAMMAR NOTE

The *that*-clauses containing subjunctive verbs are superficially similar to other types of *that*-complements students have studied. The difference—and this must be impressed upon students—is that the form of the verb in the embedded clause does not vary, regardless of the number (singular or plural) of the subject, and regardless of the time of occurrence.

UNIT GOALS

Some instructors may want to review the goals listed on Student Book (SB) page 398 after completing the Opening Task so that students understand what they should know by the end of the unit. These goals can also be reviewed at the end of the unit when students are more familiar with the grammar terminology.

OPENING TASK [30 minutes]

The purpose of the Opening Task is to create a context in which students will need to use subjunctive verbs in *that*-clauses as they role-play situations in which a dispute between people is settled by an arbitrator. The problem-solving format is designed to show the teacher how well the students can produce the target structures implicitly and spontaneously when they are engaged in a communicative task. For a more complete discussion of the purpose of the Opening Task, see To the Teacher, Lesson Planner (LP) page xxii.

Setting Up the Task

Discuss TV shows that feature an arbitrator, such as *Judge Judy* or another court TV show, such as *Divorce Court*. Discuss how the judge or arbitrator handles disputes.

Conducting the Task

1. Read the directions as a class. Point out that the three verbs used in the example sentences are verbs of urging or advice.
2. Have students work in groups of three. Ask each group to solve the four problems, switching the following roles with each new case: someone in favor of the issue, someone against the issue, and the arbitrator. The arbitrator will more than likely supply the largest number of target structures in this role play (subjunctive verbs in *that*-clauses). Therefore, it is imperative that as many students as possible role-play the arbitrator.
3. While students are working, you can circulate around the room noting correct and incorrect uses of the target structure.

Closing the Task

1. Ask representatives of several groups to report on what their group thought about several of the disputes and how they were settled.
2. Don't worry about accuracy at this point, though you may want to take notes of errors in meaning, form, or use in order to focus on those problems later.

GRAMMAR NOTE

Typical student errors (form)

- In *that*-clauses with *should* + base form, adding *be*: —e.g., * *They proposed that we should be eat at 9 o'clock.* (See Focus 1.)
- Using a form other than the subjunctive in adjective complements: —e.g., * *That he types is essential.* (See Focus 3.)

Typical student errors (use)

- Using a tense other than the present tense in *that*-clause complements of verbs of advice or urging: —e.g., * *The customer demanded that the store returned his money.* (See Focus 1.)
- Adding *do* to subjunctive verbs in *that*-clauses: —e.g., * *We insist that he does not make that telephone call.* (See Focus 1.)

LANGUAGE NOTE

Unit 22 adds the subjunctive complement to those complements already presented in the previous unit. The subjunctive complement is similar to the other forms, except for the fact that the verb in the embedded clause is tenseless. These complements occur after verbs of advice or urging or nouns derived from these verbs and when advice adjectives are in the main clause. Point out to students that the subjunctive is a formal structure that native speakers sometimes neglect to use in informal speaking and writing.

It is important that students understand the difference between the use of the subjunctive with verbs of influence and the use of *should* + base form. Point out that in situations in which the subject is a person or persons of considerable social power and status—such as *a boss, a doctor*, or *a parent*—their actions would not be softened by the use of *should*. For example, *The general ordered that his troops go to the front.* NOT: * *The general ordered that his troops should go to the front.*

FOCUS 1 — Subjunctive Verbs in *That* Clauses

form / use

EXAMPLES	EXPLANATIONS
(a) The arbitrator recommends that Susan not **be fired**. (b) It was stipulated that he **abandon** the plans.	*That* clause complements of verbs of advice and urging must contain a present subjunctive verb.
(c) Her father demanded that they **be back** by 12:00. (d) The committee stipulated that Mary **follow** all of the instructions.	The subjunctive verb is the base form of the verb: *be, go, take*, etc. We use the base form for all singular and plural subjects.
(e) **Formal:** The president insisted that the meeting **begin** on time. (f) **Informal:** Jody suggested that we **should eat** at 6:00.	For a similar yet less formal effect, use *should* + base form instead of the subjunctive.

Verbs of advice and urging that require subjunctive verbs in *that* clauses:

advise	*insist*	*prefer*	*stipulate*
beg	*move*	*propose*	*suggest*
command	*order*	*recommend*	
demand	*pledge*	*request*	
determine	*pray*	*require*	

EXERCISE 1

Use the following sentence model to make comments about each of the numbered items. Fill in the first blank with the correct form of the verb in parentheses and the second blank with a subjunctive verb or *should* + base form, whichever is more appropriate.

Base sentence: She (or he) _____ that he (or she) _____ .

Example: A boss to her employee (recommend)
She <u>recommends</u> that he <u>call her tomorrow</u>.

1. A friend who wants to give another friend some information (insist)
2. An actor to a director who may offer him a part in a play (suggest)
3. A doctor to a patient who might have a deadly disease (require)
4. A neighbor to another neighbor who is too busy to talk (propose)
5. A father to an unsuitable companion for his daughter (forbid)
6. A salesperson to a customer (advise)

EXERCISE 2

During the role-play portion of the Opening Task on pages 398 and 399, what were some of the recommendations that the arbitrator made to the conflicting parties?

Example: *He suggested that the president of the advisory board reconsider the all-male policy.*

FOCUS 2 — Subjunctive Verbs in Noun Complements

form

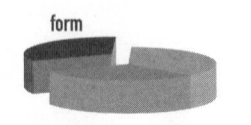

EXAMPLES	EXPLANATIONS
(a) *Suggest:* **The suggestion that he be fired** was met with resistance. (b) *Request:* She didn't listen to **his request that she file a complaint**. (c) *Advise:* **His advice that the criminals be set free** was premature.	Nouns that come from verbs of advice and urging may also take a *that* clause with a subjunctive verb. Some of these nouns are *advice, command, decision, demand, order, pronouncement, recommendation, request,* and *suggestion*.

EXERCISE 3

Imagine that you live in an apartment complex surrounded by some very disagreeable neighbors in apartments 4A through 4D. Answer the following questions, using the prompts provided and a subjunctive verb in a noun complement.

Example: What did the man in 4A do when you told him his music was too loud? ignore/suggestion.
He ignored my suggestion that he turn down the stereo.

1. What did the person in 4B do when you asked her to return your watering can? (not heed/proposal)
2. What did the man in 4C do when you wanted him to stop being a Peeping Tom? (laugh at/demand)
3. What did the woman in 4D do when you told her to stop stomping around? (not listen to/demand)

ANSWER KEY

Exercise 1 Answers will vary. Possible answers are: 1. He insists that she should email him tonight. 2. The actor suggests that the director call his cell phone tomorrow. 3. She requires that he call her office in the morning. 4. She proposes that they meet for coffee at her convenience. 5. He forbids that he ever see her again alone. 6. He advises that she bring her receipt with her for a full refund.

Exercise 2 Answers will vary. Possible answers are: Case 2. The arbitrator advised that the doctor consider the quality of life of the patient in his present state. Case 3. The arbitrator recommended that the school board review the curriculum proposed by the parent. Case 4. The arbitrator suggested that the worker bring in tangible evidence to support her case.

Exercise 3 1. She did not heed my proposal that she return the . . . 2. He laughed at my demand that his ... 3. She didn't listen to my demand that she not stomp ...

FOCUS 1 [25 minutes]

1. **Lead-in:** Write the following three words on the board: *demand, recommend,* and *insist.* Ask students to order these three words according to how strongly the speaker or writer feels about something. (*Recommend* is the weakest, *insist* is stronger, and *demand* is the strongest.)

2. Give students an example using all three verbs: *I recommend that you brush your teeth every day. I insist that you wear your seatbelt. I demand that you stop calling me.* Emphasize that these verbs are used with subjects that are bringing some force or opinion to bear on certain people. Tell students that these are only three examples of such verbs, and direct their attention to the longer list of verbs in the box that follows the focus chart.

3. Ask a volunteer to read the first two examples in the focus chart aloud. Ask students to identify the verbs of advice and urging (*recommends, stipulated*) and the tense of each (*present, past*). Ask them to identify the subjunctive verbs (*be, abandon*) and the tense of each (*present*).

4. Ask students to identify the rule governing the tense of subjunctive verbs in *that*-clauses (*it must be in the present tense*). Then ask a volunteer to read the explanation.

5. Ask a volunteer to read the next two examples aloud. Ask students to identify the verbs of advice and urging (*demanded, stipulated*), the subjunctive verbs (*be, follow*) and the form of the subjunctive verbs (*the base form*).

6. Ask if this base form is used for both singular and plural subjects (*yes*). Ask a volunteer to read the second explanation.

7. Ask a volunteer to read the third set of examples aloud. Ask students to identify the verbs of advice and urging (*insisted, suggested*) and the subjunctive verbs (*begin, should eat*). Ask them which verb seems to express a stronger suggestion (*insisted*).

8. Ask two volunteers to read the verbs in the list. Then have several volunteers create sentences using one of those verbs and a subjunctive verbs in a *that*-clause.

EXERCISE 1 [25 minutes]

1. Read the directions as a class. Ask a volunteer to read the example.

2. Have students work independently to complete the sentences.

3. Have them compare answers with a partner.

4. Ask volunteers to share their answers with the class. See possible answers on LP page 400.

EXERCISE 2 [20 minutes]

1. Read the directions and example as a class.

2. Have students work in pairs and make a list of as many of the arbitrator's recommendations as they can remember.

3. Have each pair compare their list with another pair. Tell them to use complete sentences with subjunctive verbs in *that*-clauses to describe each suggestion.

4. Ask representatives of several groups to share some of their sentences with the class. See possible answers on LP page 400.

 For more practice, use *Grammar Dimensions 4* Workbook page 200, Exercise 1.

EXPANSION [30 minutes/homework]

In Activity 1 (listening/writing) on SB page 404 students listen to a radio broadcaster give advice to a man and a woman about relationships using subjunctive verbs. This activity is a good follow-up to Focus 1 and Exercise 2, either for in-class work or as homework.

LESSON PLAN 2

FOCUS 2 [10 minutes]

1. **Lead-in:** Ask one volunteer to read the three examples, and ask another to read the explanation aloud to the class.

2. Remind students that noun complements are not the same as relative clauses (see Unit 21) but are restatements of the nouns that precede them.

3. Ask volunteers to refer to the list of verbs in Focus 1 and create other sentences with noun complements and subjunctive verbs.

EXERCISE 3 [20 minutes]

1. Ask students if they have ever had troublesome neighbors and have them share their experiences. Inform them that this exercise discusses four problematic neighbors in one apartment complex.

2. Read the directions as a class. Ask a volunteer to read the example aloud.

3. Have students work in pairs to complete the sentences using the prompts and the information provided.

4. Ask students to work in small groups to compare their answers and then read them to the class.

5. Discuss whether anyone has experienced a similar situation. Ask them to describe what they did.

 For more practice, use *Grammar Dimensions 4* Workbook page 201, Exercise 2.

Imagine that an arbitrator listened to two sides of a case and made the following decisions. What is your opinion of the arbitrator's advice?

Example: Mr. Jones built a work shed that interfered with his neighbor's, Mr. Rodriguez's, view of the city. Mr. Jones provided the city maps that showed the shed was built on his property. The arbitrator demanded that Mr. Jones tear the shed down. *The demand that Mr. Jones tear down his shed is unfair considering he had legally built the shed on his own property.*

1. Ms. Nguyen went to an emergency room to deliver her baby. The hospital stated that Ms. Nguyen was not insured and would have to pay for the delivery. The arbitrator decided that the hospital would have to cover the costs of the delivery.

2. Celia Velez was going to get married in December but now she has changed her mind. She had bought a wedding dress at a sale for $3000. She tried to return the dress three days later but the salesperson in the store told her that all sale items were final. The arbitrator recommended that the store take back the dress and charge a 10 percent stocking fee but return the remainder of the money to Celia.

3. Todd Simpson got a poor grade in a class. He claimed that the professor was absent during five weeks of the semester and did not properly mark his assignments. The arbitrator demanded that Todd be given a passing grade because it was determined that he had been given a lower grade than deserved.

4. Mr. and Mrs. Scott paid $5000 for a luxury cruise to the Greek Isles. Mrs. Scott's sister got deathly ill and so Mr. and Mrs. Scott cancelled their cruise in order to assist her. Ms. Nakamura, the cruise line sales manager, refused to refund their ticket because the cancellation had taken place too late. The arbitrator requested that the Scotts be given a full-price ticket on a future cruise.

5. Mr. Liu's dog barks all night long. Mr. Hesterman asked Mr. Liu to quiet his dog on three separate occasions but then called the police to remedy the situation. The police confiscated the dog and charged Mr. Liu a $500 fine for disturbing the peace. The arbitrator ordered that Mr. Liu pay the fine and get rid of the dog.

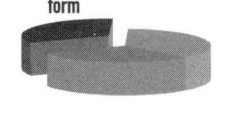

FOCUS 3 | **Subjunctive Verbs in Adjective Complements**

form

EXAMPLES	EXPLANATIONS
(a) **That he type** is essential. (b) It is essential **that he type.** (c) **That she be punctual** is important. (d) It is important **that she be punctual.**	Adjective complements sometimes take subjunctive verbs. This is true when advice adjectives like *advisable, desirable, essential, imperative, important, mandatory, necessary, urgent,* and *vital* are in the main clause.

STEP 1 Using the information from the following job advertisements, fill in the following statements with *that* clauses containing subjunctive verbs.

Example: It is important <u>that the accounting applicant be bilingual in Chinese and English.</u> (accountant)

1. _____ is essential. (chemist)   4. It is imperative _____. (manager)

2. It is mandatory _____. (shuttle driver)   5. It is necessary _____. (nurse)

3. _____ is desirable. (file clerk)

STEP 2 Create five more of your own sentences with information from the ads.

236 Employment

Accountant ★
Accounting firm seeks individual w/ min 2 yr exp. Good communication skills & ability to assist clients. Biling Chinese required. Previous exp in CPA firm a plus. Call Mr. Tang 213-555-1409

Accountant Executive
Local firm has a fabulous opportunity for a tax accountant. Two + years tax or accounting experience, a strong client service mentality, and a team oriented approach required. Position can be full time. Send in resume 555 East King, Big City, PA 34543

Chemist ★
Stable, fast-growing company seeks chemist for formulation of industrial products. Must have BS degree chemistry & min. 5 yrs. exp. Nonsmoker preferred. Excellent benefits. Redex Co. 714-555-2221

Customer Service lot of work full-time. Fax resume to 234-555-4567

236 Employment

Customer Service
30 Jobs Temp to Perm WANTED! People with good Customer Service skills that can work 3:30pm to 12am 5pm-9pm. If you can, we need you ASAP Call! 458-555-6666

Drivers-Shuttle ★
AIRWAY Shuttle needs outstanding drivers for day and eve shifts. Must be clean-cut, highly ethical, energetic. Great benefits and friendly environment.
AIRWAY 818-555-8156

Education:
Elementary Principal Twelve month position available on or before January 1, 2001. Elementary teaching experience and elementary certification required. Knowledge certification required.

236 Employment

File Clerk
Min. 1 yr exp in law file rm. Knowledge of ofc equipment. Ability to work without supervision. Good command of English for switchboard relief. Mrs. Jacobsen 310-555-6662

Grocery
Fox's market has immediate! openings for part-time or full-time meat cutters. Vacation, Life insurance, Medical insurance, Profit sharing. Call 333-555-4444

Manager ★
10 new Asst. Managers for marketing & sales needed. No exp. necessary. We will train. Must be 18 & older. Must have car. Work in a wild & crazy office.
Super's 818-555-8234

Nurse ★
Opportunity for career-minded RN. Participate in clinical trials & oversee needs for patients on daily basis. Need good track record of exp. be able to learn fast, self-starter. If interested, call Westside Hospital 213-555-6210

Exercise 4 Answers will vary. Possible answers are: 1. The decision that the hospital pay the delivery costs seems to be the only humane choice because Mrs. Nguyen was in a desperate situation. 2. The recommendation that Celia at least pay a stocking fee is fair because it is clear she did not read the signs in the store that all sale items were final. 3. The demand that Todd be given a passing grade is the only acceptable solution for irresponsible teaching. 4. The request that the Scotts receive a reservation on a future cruise is fair since the circumstances of the cancellation on the first cruise were very unpredictable. 5. The order that Mr. Liu pay a fine is

Exercise 5 Step 1: Answers will vary. Possible answers are: 1. That the chemist have a BS degree in chemistry ... 2. ... that the shuttle driver be clean-cut, highly ethical, and energetic. 3. That the file clerk have at least one year of experience in a law firm ... 4. ... that the manager be 18 years old or older. 5. ... that the nurse be experienced, a fast learner, and a self-starter.
Step 2: Answers will vary.

EXERCISE 4 [40 minutes]

In Exercise 4 students read about a series of situations and the arbitrator's decision in each. They then express their opinions about those decisions using subjunctive verbs in noun complements.

1. Read the directions and examples as a class.
2. Have students work independently to write their opinions about the arbitrator's decisions.
3. Have them work in small groups and take turns expressing their opinions and discussing these.
4. Ask representatives of several groups to report on how their group judged a situation. See possible answers on LP page 402.

 For more practice, use *Grammar Dimensions 4* Workbook page 202, Exercise 3.

EXPANSION [45 minutes/homework]

In Activity 3 (research on the web) on SB page 405 students research a political, environmental, or civic problem on the Internet and then write a letter to the editor. This activity makes a good homework assignment following Focus 2 and Exercise 4.

FOCUS 3 [15 minutes]

Focus 3 explores how adjective complements can sometimes take subjunctive verbs.

1. **Lead-in:** Review adjective complements from Unit 20 (SB pages 374, 376, 377). Give students additional examples of adjective complements, related to your class or an academic context, and show how they can take subjunctive verbs: *It is necessary that you attend class regularly. That you attend class regularly is necessary.*
2. Read the explanation, and then ask a volunteer to read the examples.

3. Ask volunteers to create other sentences with subjunctive verbs and *advisable, essential, necessary,* and *vital.*
4. Answer any questions students may have.

EXERCISE 5 [20 minutes]

In Exercise 5 students read classified job ads and then complete sentences with *that*-clauses containing subjunctive verbs, practicing what they have just learned in Focus 3.

STEP 1

1. Read the directions and the ad about the accountant's position aloud. Ask a volunteer to read the example aloud. Ask different volunteers to read the other ads aloud.
2. Have students work with partners to complete sentences with *that*-clauses containing subjunctive verbs.
3. Have students take turns reading and comparing their sentences in small groups.
4. Ask representatives of several pairs to share sentences with the class. See possible answers on LP page 402.

STEP 2

1. Have students work individually to create five more sentences.
2. Ask students to volunteer their original sentences aloud. They should say "*job applicant*" in place of the profession.
3. Have the class listen and guess the profession that the description is about.
4. Listen carefully for word order and proper vocabulary use.

 For more practice, use *Grammar Dimensions 4* Workbook page 202, Exercise 4 and page 204, Exercise 5.

EXPANSION 1 [25 minutes]

This activity gives students additional practice with adjective complements that take subjunctive verbs.

1. Have students work in pairs. Ask them to imagine that they are the personnel directors at companies who are recruiting employees. Have them write a list of statements about three jobs they have available and the qualifications applicants should have, such as: *I am looking for an accountant. It is essential that he or she have at least two years of experience . . .* etc.
2. Have pairs get together with other pairs and take turns reading their lists.
3. Ask representatives of various groups to share a job description with the class. Does anyone in class feel that they qualify for that position?

EXPANSION 2 [45 minutes]

In Activity 4 (reflection) on SB page 405 students offer advice to a relative or a good friend who is having difficulty getting good grades in school. It is a good wrap-up activity for students at the end of this unit.

UNIT GOAL REVIEW [5 minutes]

Ask students to look at the goals on the opening page of the unit again. Refer to the pages of the unit where information on each goal can be found.

 For assessment of Unit 22, use *Grammar Dimensions 4 ExamView®*.

 **ACTIVITY 1** listening/writing

 Listen to the audio of a radio broadcaster who gives people advice about relationships.

CD2 Track 19

■ **STEP 1** Jot down notes about each of the problems and the advice given.

	Problem	Advice
a. Female Caller:		
b. Male Caller:		

■ **STEP 2** Now write a short paragraph summarizing your opinion of the broadcaster's advice to these two callers. Use at least two subjunctive complements in your writing.

ACTIVITY 2 reading/writing

Read at least five advice letters and responses in the newspaper from advice columnists such as "Ann Landers," "Dear Abby," or "Miss Manners." Summarize the problems and the advice given to persons requesting the advice.

Example: *A man had attempted many times to quit smoking. Counseling, nicotine chewing gum, and "cold turkey" were all ineffective. Abby suggested that he try acupuncture.*

 **ACTIVITY 3** research on the web

 Select a political, environmental, or civic problem and research the problem on the Internet using a search engine such as Google® or Yahoo®, or a Web site you may know of. Then write a letter to the editor of a newspaper. Include the following parts in your letter and at least two subjunctive complements.

- summary of the issue
- statement of your own opinion
- list solutions to the problem or suggestions for improvement

ACTIVITY 4 reflection

Imagine that your favorite relative or a good friend is having difficulty getting good grades in school. What is some advice that you could give him/her to improve his/her time management, study skills, interaction with professors, etc.?

Example: *I would suggest that he make a schedule with class time, study time, and meal time clearly delineated.*

USE YOUR ENGLISH

The Use Your English activities at the end of the unit contain situations that should naturally elicit the structures covered in the unit. For a more complete discussion of how to use the Use Your English activities, see To the Teacher, LP page xxvi. While students are doing these activities in class, you can circulate and listen to see if they are using the structures accurately. Errors can be corrected after the activity has finished.

ACTIVITY 1 — listening/writing
[30 minutes/homework]

In Activity 1 students listen to a radio broadcaster give advice to a man and a woman about relationships using subjunctive verbs. This activity is a good follow-up to Exercise 2 on SB page 401, either for in-class work or as homework. Note that the former CD track number (36) is incorrectly listed in the student book.

CD2 Track 19

Discuss what radio talk shows students have heard in which people get advice about health. Read the directions and example as a class.

▪ STEP 1

1. Have students listen to the audio once.
2. Ask students to listen again and take notes in the grid. Provide a sentence stem if students are having difficulty: *The doctor suggested that the woman _____.*
3. Have students work in small groups to compare their responses.
4. Ask volunteers to share their answers with the class.

▪ STEP 2
Have students individually write a short paragraph summarizing their opinions of the advice to the two callers. This is a good homework assignment. Review in next class.

ACTIVITY 2 — reading/writing
[60 minutes/homework]

In this activity students read advice letters and responses from newspaper columns and summarize those problems and the advice given using the subjunctive in *that*-clauses. This activity is a good homework assignment following Exercise 1 on SB page 400. During the next class, students can work in small groups to share the most interesting problems and pieces of advice.

1. Discuss any advice columns students are familiar with, such as *Dear Abby, Ann Landers,* or *Miss Manners.*
2. Read the directions and example as a class.
3. Ask students to read at least five letters and the advice given in a newspaper, magazine or online.
4. Ask them to write a summary of the problems and the advice given using the subjunctive in *that*-clauses.
5. During the next class, have students work in small groups and share their reports.
6. Ask several volunteers to share their reports with the class, and discuss.

ACTIVITY 3 — research on the web
[45 minutes/homework]

In this activity students research a political, environmental, or civic problem on the Internet and then write a letter to the editor. This activity makes a good homework assignment following Exercise 4 on SB page 402.

1. Read the directions as a class.
2. Have students research a political, environmental, or civic problem on the Internet.

3. Ask them to write a letter to the editor in which they give a summary of the issue, state their opinion, and list solutions to the problem or suggestions for improvement. Remind them to use verbs of urging and advice and the subjunctive in their writing.
4. During the next class, have students work in small groups and take turns reading their letters and discussing them.
5. Ask several volunteers to share their letters with the class, and discuss.

ACTIVITY 4 — reflection
[45 minutes/homework]

In this activity students offer advice to a relative or a good friend who is having difficulty getting good grades in school. It is a good wrap-up activity for students at the end of this unit, after they have completed Exercise 5 on SB page 403.

1. Discuss whether students have had experiences with friends or relatives who are having difficulties getting good grades in school. What were the problems? What advice did students offer?
2. Read the directions as a class. Ask a volunteer to read the example. Ask volunteers to suggest other solutions.
3. Have students work in small groups to describe the problems of several friends or relatives and list their suggestions.
4. Ask representatives of various groups to share their profiles and suggestions with the class, and discuss.

EMPHATIC STRUCTURES
Emphatic *Do, No* versus *Not*

OPENING TASK
Looking at Consumer Needs

Advertising agencies spend a lot of time and money finding out what consumers like and dislike. VALS™ (Values and Lifestyles) typology* is a system for describing different types of consumers. Imagine that you work for an advertising agency and that you are trying to identify the likes and dislikes of potential consumers. Use the VALS™ typology to help you make your decision.

■ STEP 1

Read the VALS™ (for Values and Lifestyles) descriptions. List items or services that you think the eight groups of consumers would and would not want to purchase.

*VALS™ typology, originally developed by SRI International, is now owned by SRI Consulting Business Intelligence (SRIC-BI). Source: SRI Consulting Business Intelligence (SRIC-BI); www.sric-bi.com/VALS (retrieved on February 12, 2007)

VALS™ TYPOLOGY CONSUMER TYPES	CONSUMER ITEMS OR SERVICES THAT WOULD OR WOULD NOT APPEAL TO GROUP
1. **Survivors:** Have few resources, think the past is better than the future, try to meet basic needs rather than fulfill desires, live lives with a narrow focus. Cautious consumers who may purchase favorite brands at a discount.	NEED: *good medical care* DON'T NEED: *luxuries (expensive fur coats, etc.)*
2. **Makers:** Motivated by self-expression, doers, practical, self-sufficient, suspicious of new ideas, resent government intrusion on individual rights, live within context of family, practical work, and physical recreation. Practical consumers who buy basic products at a good value.	
3. **Strivers:** Trendy, fun-loving, stylish, have jobs but not serious careers, desire more money to meet needs. Active consumers who sometimes make impulsive purchases to demonstrate their ability to buy.	
4. **Believers:** Conservative, conventional, traditional values established by family, religion, community and the nation, follow established routines. Predictable consumers who buy familiar products and established brands but sometimes feel victimized.	
5. **Experiencers:** motivated by self-expression, young, enthusiastic, impulsive, seek variety, excitement, risk. Avid consumers of products relating to fashion, entertainment, and social life.	
6. **Achievers:** motivated by achievement, goal-oriented, deep commitment to career and family, politically conservative, respect authority, value predictability and stability. Image-conscious consumers who want many products and services to demonstrate prestige to peers.	
7. **Thinkers:** motivated by ideals, conservative, mature, wealthy, well educated, active decision-makers, well informed about the world, open to new ideas. Conservative consumers who value durability, functionality, and good value.	
8. **Innovators:** receptive to new ideas, high self-esteem, sophisticated, wealthy, image is important for self-expression rather than power, leaders, lives are varied. Active consumers with upscale tastes.	

■ STEP 2

Conduct a mock advertising agency meeting where you convince members of your team of the needs of each type of consumer.

Example: *Survivors really do need medical care!*   *Survivors will have no money for luxuries.*

Survivors won't buy any expensive fur coats, but they will buy practical warm woolen ones!

UNIT OVERVIEW

Unit 23 reviews the ways in which *do, no*, and *not* structures are used for emphasis in discourse. Please note that due to its length, this unit has been divided into three lesson plans. To review this unit more quickly, review focus charts and have students complete the first exercise after each chart to observe students' grasp of the grammar topics.

GRAMMAR NOTE

The focus charts and exercises on *no* and *not* structures may provide a particularly useful review of standard English rules for students whose native languages use double negation.

UNIT GOALS

Some instructors may want to review the goals listed on Student Book (SB) page 406 after completing the Opening Task so that students understand what they should know by the end of the unit. These goals can also be reviewed at the end of the unit when students are more familiar with the grammar terminology.

OPENING TASK [50 minutes]

The purpose of the Opening Task is to create a context in which students will need to use emphatic structures as they consider the consumer needs of several different segments of the population from an advertiser's point of view. The problem-solving format is designed to show the teacher how well the students can produce the target structures implicitly and spontaneously when they are engaged in a communicative task. For a more complete discussion of the purpose of the Opening Task, see Lesson Planner (LP) page xxii.

Setting Up the Task

1. Ask students what they know about the consumer needs of teenagers in the United States or their home countries. The students may be young enough themselves to know this information first-hand, or they may be parents or brothers and sisters of teenagers and be able to suggest certain current fads (e.g., punk music, skateboards, ballet flats, video games, etc.).
2. Discuss ways in which advertisers target this population and appeal to them.

Conducting the Task

■ STEP 1

1. Read the opening text and discuss the pictures as a class. Read the directions for Step 1 aloud.
2. Divide the class into small groups. Ask each group to read the definitions of each consumer type and brainstorm consumer items or services that would appeal to each group based on the descriptions.

■ STEP 2

1. Ask students to imagine they are at a mock advertising agency meeting in which they must emphasize the actual needs of each group to other members of the agency. Encourage students to be persuasive and forceful in their presentations. They should make it very clear when they agree with others' suggestions and when they don't. This culminating "meeting" can be done using whole class, half class, or quarter class groupings. In any case, make note of the words that students use to make points strongly.
2. While students are working, you can circulate around the room noting ways students emphasize their points and how successful they are.

Closing the Task

1. Discuss the mock ad agency meeting as a class. Which arguments were most convincing? Why?
2. Don't worry about accuracy at this point, though you may want to take notes of errors in meaning, form, or use in order to focus on those problems later.

GRAMMAR NOTE

Typical student errors (form)

- Using *do* + infinitive in emphatic structures: —e.g., * *They really do to enjoy going to the beach.* (See Focus 1.)
- In negative sentences with *not* after the first auxiliary verb or *be*, using *no* rather than *any* for the second negative component: —e.g., * *The candidate won't get no votes that way.* (See Focus 3.)

Typical student errors (use)

- Using *not* and *nothing* in emphatic statements: —e.g., * *The boy insisted that he didn't do nothing wrong.* (See Focus 4.)
- Using *no person(s)* rather than *nobody* or *no one* in emphatic structures: —e.g., * *There was no person in the house when we arrived.* (See Focus 4.)
- Using *nobody* or *no one* rather than *anybody* or *anyone* with *not*: —e.g., * *We didn't ask nobody for help.* (See Focus 4.)

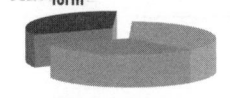

form

EXAMPLES	EXPLANATIONS
(a) I **will** write you a letter as soon as I arrive. (b) He **is** going to Mexico during the winter break. (c) Sally **has** finished her homework. (d) Todd **is** a world-class swimmer.	We can add emphasis to a sentence by orally stressing the auxiliary verb or the *be* verb.
(e) I **do** believe in miracles. (f) Professor Dean **did** get her conference paper accepted.	In sentences where there is no auxiliary or *be* verb, we can add *do* and stress it for emphasis.
(g) Juan **really does** know the answer to the question. (h) They **certainly did** see us at the exposition.	We often add extra emphasis with an emphatic adverb like *really* or *certainly* and a strongly stressed *do*.

EXERCISE 1

Imagine that you are a salesperson. What will you say to each type of consumer listed in the Opening Task in order to persuade them to buy a product? On a separate piece of paper, write two sentences per item using a variety of emphatic structures. Underline each emphatic structure.

Example: Survivor: *I do understand that you need to be careful with your money. But you really must buy this basic black dress for all occasions.*

1. Survivor	3. Striver	5. Experiencer	7. Thinker
2. Maker	4. Believer	6. Achiever	8. Innovator

use

EXAMPLES	EXPLANATIONS
	Emphatic *do* can:
(a) A: You have a good thesis. B: Really? A: Yes, you really **do** have a good thesis.	• add emphasis to a whole sentence.
(b) **Do** come in! (c) **Please do** give him my best regards!	• add emphasis to an imperative. This use of emphatic *do* softens a command and shows polite encouragement.
(d) A: You didn't lock the back door. B: You're wrong. I **did** lock it.	• contradict a negative statement. This use of emphatic *do* is very common in arguments. In such situations, the *do* verb generally refers back to a previous statement.
(e) A: Bob didn't cheat on the test. B: Then, what **did** happen? OR Who **did** cheat? OR What **did** he cheat on?	• be used to ask a clarification question about a previously mentioned negative statement.
(f) It was no surprise to me. He seldom **did** complete his homework. (g) To make a long story short, she always **does** get her own way.	• add emphasis to a verb used in connection with an adverb of frequency such as *never, rarely, seldom, often,* or *always.*
(h) I'm relieved that he **does** have his credit card (because I thought he might have forgotten it).	• emphasize a positive result regarding something that had been unknown or in doubt.
(i) Even though I do not usually enjoy fiction, I **did** enjoy John King's latest novel.	• indicate strong concession bordering on contrast.

EXERCISE 2

Circulate around the room and give at least ten compliments to other students using the auxiliary, *be,* or emphatic *do* verbs.

Examples: *You **have** done your hair very nicely.*
*You certainly **are** wearing a beautiful necklace.*
*That certainly **is** a nice shirt.*
*I really **do** like your loafers.*

ANSWER KEY

Exercise 1 Answers will vary. Sample answers are: 2. (Maker) I do understand this is your choice. This coat certainly is the best value as it will last for years. 3. (Striver) This dress does suit you so well. You must buy it. Your sense of style is fabulous. 4. (Believer) It is a name you trust. It will go with everything you own. 5. (Experiencer) All the Hollywood starlets are wearing this to the awards show. It is so right now! 6. (Achiever) This does say "I am in charge" and "I know I look good in the board room."

7. (Thinker) This has a guarantee and it will be a great value. You are going to find that it is really good for the environment as well. 8. (Innovator) This is certainly what you want to complement an already excellent wardrobe. It is new, it is chic with a European influence.
Exercise 2 Answers will vary.

FOCUS 1 [25 minutes]

Focus 1 introduces students to the forms and meanings of different emphatic structures.

1. **Lead-in:** For a change of pace, ask students to close their books, and dictate the focus chart explanations to them. First, read all three sentences at normal speed. Then, read the sentences, pausing after the following thought groups (indicated by slashes): *1. We can add emphasis / to a sentence / by stressing the auxiliary or the* be *verb. / 2. In sentences where there is no auxiliary or* be *verb / we can add* do / *and stress it for emphasis. / 3. We often add extra emphasis with an emphatic adverb / like* really *or* certainly / *and a strongly stressed* do.

2. Read the sentences a third time at normal speed and ask students to proofread their own dictation results.

3. Ask students to write example sentences for each rule.

4. Ask students to check the accuracy of their dictation as well as their sample sentences by reading the focus chart.

5. Answer any questions students might have.

EXERCISE 1 [35 minutes]

In Exercise 1 students return to the work they did in the Opening Task and write statements a salesperson might make to get each type of consumer to purchase a product, using emphatic structures.

1. Read the directions and example as a class.

2. Have students work independently to write two sentences for each consumer type. They could use the products they thought of in the Opening Task, or think up new ones. Tell them they can be overly dramatic or silly if they like—but they must use an emphatic structure in each sentence.

3. Have students work in small groups and share their sentences.

4. Ask representatives of several groups to share some of their sentences with the class. See possible answers on LP page 408.

For more practice, use *Grammar Dimensions 4* Workbook page 205, Exercise 1 and Exercise 2.

EXPANSION [45 minutes/homework]

Activity 1 (listening/writing/speaking) on SB page 416 is a good follow-up to Exercise 1, either for in-class work or as homework. Students listen to a lecture about how to create a good advertisement, write a summary of the lecture, then revise it to make it more emphatic. Finally, they read their paragraph aloud, using proper stress and intonation.

LESSON PLAN 2

FOCUS 2 [20 minutes]

Focus 2 explains the various uses of *do* to add emphasis. This is a good reference tool for students.

1. **Lead-in:** Write the first example on the board. Ask a volunteer to read the explanation. Explain that, in this example, one person is trying to convince another by using *do*.

2. Ask a pair of students to act out a short dialogue in which one person makes a statement about the other, the second person expresses doubt, and the first rephrases the original statement using the emphatic *do*.

3. Ask two volunteers to read examples (b–g), and a third to read the explanations.

4. Read the final two examples and explanations as a class.

5. Ask students to give other examples for (h) and (i).

6. Answer any questions students may have.

EXERCISE 2 [20 minutes]

This exercise should promote a "party-like" atmosphere as students move around the room and compliment each other using the auxiliary, *be*, or emphatic *do* verbs. This gives them the opportunity to apply what they have just learned in Focus 2.

1. Read the directions as a class. Ask a volunteer to read the examples.

2. Have students walk around the room and give at least ten compliments to their classmates using emphatic structures. Set a time limit, such as 15 minutes, for this portion of the exercise.

3. Ask volunteers to share the best compliment they gave and the best one they received with the class.

EXPANSION [50 minutes]

Activity 4 (reflection) on SB page 417 is a good follow-up to Exercise 2. In this activity students review the consumer types from the Opening Task, decide which type they are most similar to, and then write and talk about their consumer temptations and their academic goals. Encourage students to use emphatic structures such as *do*, *really*, and *certainly*.

Use *do* structures to make the following invitations, requests, or suggestions.

Example: suggestion to sit down
Do sit down.

1. invitation to put a friend's bags in your room
2. request to come early to the party
3. suggestion to tell the children to quiet down
4. invitation to have some more punch
5. request to put the money in a safe place
6. suggestion to turn off the lights when you leave the conference room
7. invitation to have a bite to eat
8. request to let relatives know you'll be late for your visit

■ **EXERCISE 4**

Bruce and Gary are brothers, but they often have arguments. Read the following argument and cross through all the places where you think it is possible to use emphatic *do*. Rewrite those sentences with an appropriate form of the *do* verb. The first one has been done for you.

Bruce: Did you take my flashlight? I can't find it anywhere.

Gary: Well, I haven't got it. I always return the stuff I borrow.

Bruce: No, you don't.

Gary: That's not true! ~~I return the things I borrow!~~ *I do return the things I borrow!* It's probably on your desk. I bet you didn't look for it there.

Bruce: No, ~~I looked on my desk,~~ and it's not there.

Gary: Well, don't blame me. You can't find it because you never clean your room.

Bruce: ~~I clean~~ my room!

Gary: Oh, no you don't!

Bruce: ~~I certainly clean~~ it up! I cleaned it up last night as a matter of fact.

Gary: You didn't.

Bruce: ~~I really cleaned~~ it up last night. Hey, there's my flashlight under your bed.

Gary: Well, I didn't put it here.

Bruce: I bet you put it there. Anyhow, that proves it: ~~You take my stuff~~ and you don't return it.

Gary: I told you before: ~~I return everything~~ I borrow. You just don't look after your things properly.

Bruce: ~~I look after~~ my things. Anyway, from now on, I'm going to lock my door and keep you out.

Gary: You can't. That door doesn't have a key.

Bruce: That's where you're wrong. ~~It has a key~~ and I'm going to lock you out!

Gary: Oh, be quiet!

Bruce: Do you know something? You make me sick. ~~You really make me~~ sick.

Gary: You make me sick too!

Get together with another student and take the parts of Gary and Bruce. Read the dialogue, paying particular attention to the stress patterns of emphatic *do*. If possible, record yourselves and listen to how emphatic you sound.

ANSWER KEY

Exercise 3 1. Do put your bags . . . 2. Do come early . . . 3. Do be quiet. 4. Do have some . . .
5. Do put the money . . . 6. Do turn off the . . . 7. Do have a bite . . . 8. Do let them know . . .

Exercise 4 Answers will vary. Possible answers are:

Bruce: No, I did look on my desk. . .

Bruce: I do clean . . .

Bruce: I certainly do clean . . .

Bruce: I really did clean . . .

Bruce: I bet you did put it . . . You do take my stuff...

Gary: I do return everything . . .

Bruce: I do look after my . . .

Bruce: It does have a key . . .

Bruce: You really do make me . . .

EXERCISE 3 [20 minutes]

In Exercise 3 students use emphatic *do* structures to make a series of suggestions, requests, and invitations.

1. Read the directions as a class. Ask a volunteer to read the example aloud.

2. Have students work in pairs and take turns creating sentences using the information provided.

3. Ask volunteers to share sentences with the class. See answers on LP page 410.

EXPANSION [10 minutes]

Ask pairs to take turns making four more original suggestions to each other.

EXERCISE 4 [40 minutes]

In Exercise 4 students rewrite an argument between two brothers using emphatic *do* structures.

1. Read the directions as a class. Ask students to comment on the boys in the picture: Do they look as though they might argue a lot? Ask two volunteers to read the first four lines of the dialogue.

2. Have students work independently to rewrite the argument using emphatic *do* structures. Remind students to look for instances of the simple verb (without an auxiliary element), for example, *return* in the fourth line, and then add a form of *do*. They should also be attentive to the tense of the verb in order to choose the correct form, in this case, *do* not *did*.

3. Have students work in small groups and compare their answers.

Suggestion: Select one pair of students to model how the dialogue might be spoken. Serving as coach, make corrections if the appropriate word or the appropriate stress has not been used.

 For more practice, use *Grammar Dimensions 4* Workbook page 206, Exercise 3.

EXPANSION [50 minutes/homework]

For additional practice with emphatic *do* structures, assign this activity as homework, then have students act out the dialogues during the next class.

1. Have students write an argument between two people for homework. They can be two brothers, as in Exercise 4, a couple, a parent and child—any combination they like. Tell them to use emphatic *do* structures in their dialogues. Ask them to make a copy of their argument to bring to class.

2. During the next class, have students work in groups of four. Ask students in each group to exchange copies of their dialogues with the other students of the group.

3. Have students perform dialogues that they did not write. Discuss the experience with the class.

FOCUS 3   *Not* versus *No*

form

EXAMPLES	EXPLANATIONS
(a) They do not have any suggestions for the project. They have **no** suggestions for the project. (b) Norwegian tourists did not come to Miami this year. **No** Norwegian tourists came to Miami this year.	To emphasize a negative statement, we can use *no* + noun in place of *not/-n't* + verb.
(c) I have **no** fear of flying. (d) She is taking the bus because she has **no** car today. (e) He has **no** chairs in his apartment.	We use *no* with noncount nouns, singular count nouns, and plural count nouns.
(f) They are indebted to **no one**. (g) I saw **nobody** by the river. (h) He managed **nothing** well. (i) That business decision led him **nowhere**.	We can combine *no* with other words to make compounds. *no* + *one* = *no one* *no* + *body* = *nobody* *no* + *thing* = *nothing* *no* + *where* = *nowhere*
(j) Mike doesn't have **any** money. (k) We haven't seen **any** pelicans all day. (l) NOT: She won't earn no money.	In standard English, a negative sentence (with *not* after the first auxiliary verb or *be*) with a second negative component uses *not . . . any*.

EXERCISE 5

STEP 1   Fiona went to a party last night. To fill in what happened after that, match the first part of the sentence in column A with something from column B that makes sense and is grammatical. The first one has been done for you.

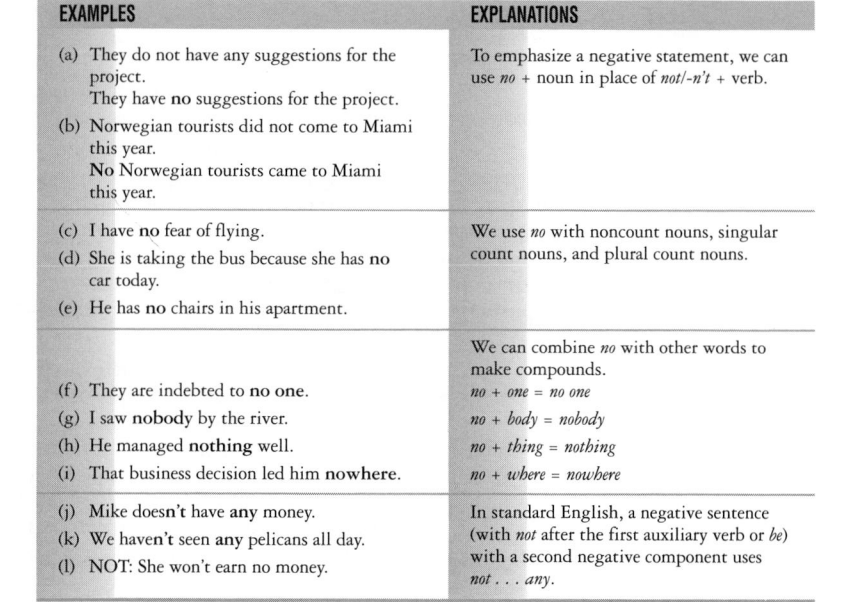

A	B
1. She had hoped to make some new friends, but she didn't meet	a. any food left.
2. She had to drive home, so she didn't drink	b. anyone to dance with.
3. She was very hungry, but when she arrived there wasn't	c. any more parties.
4. She talked to a few people, but she didn't have	d. anyone interesting.
5. Some people were dancing, but Fiona didn't have	e. any fun!"
6. She wanted to sit down, but there weren't	f. any alcohol.
7. Finally, she said to herself: "This party isn't	g. anything to say to them
8. So she went home early and decided not to go to	h. any chairs.

STEP 2   Rewrite each sentence of Step 1 using *no* or an appropriate *no* + compound. Change the verbs as necessary. The first one has been done for you.

She had hoped to make some new friends, but she met nobody interesting.

EXERCISE 6

Edit the following speech for errors with negative constructions. When you are finished, read it aloud to a partner and see if there are any more changes you want to make. The first sentence has been edited as an example.

(1) The year 2025 ~~no is~~ *is not* as far away as it might seem. (2) Today we don't have ~~no~~ *any* direction. (3) If we ~~don't get any~~ *have no* direction, our dream for our nation is sure to explode. (4) No children will have the things we had. (5) There isn't ~~nobody~~ *anybody* who cannot benefit from the few principles I will share with you today. (6) Please listen carefully. (7) If you don't listen to ~~anything~~ *nothing* I say, the consequences will be fatal.

(Continued on next page)

ANSWER KEY

Exercise 5   **Step 1:** 2 f, 3 a, 4 g, 5 b, 6 h, 7 e, 8 c

Step 2: 2. She had to drive home, so she drank no alcohol.   3. She was very hungry, but there was no food left.   4. She talked to a few people, but she had nothing to say to them.   5. Some people were dancing, but Fiona had no one to dance with.   6. She wanted to sit down, but there were no chairs.   7. Finally, she said to herself: "This party is no fun!"   8. So she went home early and decided to go to no more parties.

FOCUS 3 [15 minutes]

1. **Lead-in:** Write on the board: *I don't have any time to relax. We don't have any complaints about our car.* Ask volunteers to restate the sentences using *no* rather than *any*.
2. Read the first two explanations, and ask a volunteer to read the examples.
3. Read the third explanation and examples. Elicit that these sentences do not contain *not*.
4. Point out that it would be incorrect to use both negatives in a sentence.
5. Read the last explanation, and ask a volunteer to read the examples.
6. Answer any questions students may have.

METHODOLOGY NOTE

Students should find this explanation very straightforward and will likely have little difficulty with these concepts. If the information appears too easy, feel free to skip this focus. Note that (l) is a double negative and is not considered grammatical in standard American English.

EXERCISE 5 [30 minutes]

In Exercise 5 apply the principles of Focus 3, combining sentence parts.

STEP 1

1. Read the directions and example for Step 1 as a class.
2. Have students work independently to match the phrases in column A with those in column B.

STEP 2

1. Read the directions and example for Step 2 as a class.
2. Have students work independently to rewrite the sentences using *no* or an appropriate *no +* compound.
3. Have them work in pairs and take turns reading and comparing their sentences.
4. Review answers with the class. See answers on LP page 412.

EXERCISE 6 [30 minutes]

In Exercise 6 students edit a speech for errors with negative constructions, practicing what they have learned in Focus 3. This exercise is continued on SB page 414.

1. Read the directions and example as a class.
2. Have students work independently to edit the speech. Tell them to refer to Focus 3 for ideas.
3. Have them work in pairs and take turns reading and comparing their sentences.
4. Circulate while students are reading the speech aloud.
5. Ask for one or two volunteers to read the speech in front of the classroom with good pronunciation, stress, and phrasing. See answers on LP pages 412 and 414.

 For more practice, use *Grammar Dimensions 4* Workbook page 207, Exercise 4.

EXPANSION [60 minutes/homework]

In Activity 3 (research on the web/writing/speaking) on SB page 417 students research, write, and give a speech about someone whom they admire. This activity makes a good homework assignment following Exercise 6, with students giving their speeches during the next class.

(8) First, it isn't good for ~~nobody~~ [anybody] to feel that they deserve everything when they don't put any sweat and struggle in getting it. (9) Even more, this nation can't tell ~~nobody nowhere~~ [anybody anywhere] that it is entitled to world leadership just because they had it in the past. (10) You can never take ~~nothing~~ [anything] for granted in this country. (11) I hope you will work hard to achieve your dream.

(12) Next, I believe that no ~~people~~ [one] should set goals and then do ~~anything not~~ [nothing] to achieve them. (13) If you set a goal, work hard and humbly to accomplish it. (14) Even if you don't get ~~no~~ [any] credit, it is important to keep trying because you and your maker know what you accomplished.

(15) Another important piece of advice is not to work just for money. (16) Money alone can't strengthen ~~nobody's~~ [anybody's] family nor help ~~nobody~~ [anybody] sleep at night. (17) Don't let ~~nobody~~ [anybody] tell you that wealth or fame is the same as character. (18) It is not O.K. to use drugs even if everyone is doing it. (19) It is not O.K. to cheat or lie even if every public official does.

(20) Finally, no ~~person~~ [one] should be afraid of taking ~~no~~ risks. (21) ~~No anybody~~ [Nobody] should be afraid of failing. (22) It shouldn't matter to ~~nobody~~ [anyone] anywhere how many times you fall down. (23) What matters is how many times you get up.

(24) Let's not spend ~~no~~ [any] more time talking. We are all responsible for building a decent nation to live in! Let's not let ~~no~~ [one] more ~~minutes~~ [minute] pass.

FOCUS 4   When to Use *No* for Emphasis

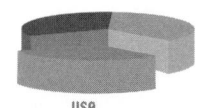

use

EXAMPLES	EXPLANATIONS
(a) I didn't have any friends when I was a child. (b) I had **no** friends when I was a child.	Statements using *no* as the negative word instead of *not* emphasize what is missing or lacking. In speaking, we often stress the word *no* for extra emphasis.
(c) **Neutral:** I didn't meet anybody interesting at the party. (d) **Emphatic:** I met **nobody** interesting at the party. (e) **Neutral:** I didn't learn anything new at the conference. (f) **Emphatic:** I learned **nothing** new at the conference.	*No* + compound also emphasizes what is missing or lacking. Sentence (c) sounds neutral, a statement of fact. Sentence (d) sounds more emotional, emphasizing the lack of interesting people.

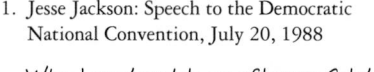

Fiona is describing the party (in Exercise 5) to her best friend and is telling her what a miserable time she had. Imagine you are Fiona and try describing the party from her point of view, emphasizing all the negative aspects of the evening. If possible, record yourself and listen to see how emphatic you sound.

EXERCISE 8

Emphatic language is very common in public speeches. Read aloud the extracts from speeches below and notice the different ways each speaker uses language to emphasize his message. Underline any examples that you can find of the emphatic language discussed in this unit. Do you notice any other techniques the speakers use to get their points across?

1. Jesse Jackson: Speech to the Democratic National Convention, July 20, 1988

   When I was born late one afternoon, October 8, in Greenville, South Carolina, <u>no</u> writers asked my mother her name. <u>Nobody</u> chose to write down our address. My mama was <u>not</u> supposed to make it. You see, I was born to a teenage mother who was born to a teenage mother. I understand. I know abandonment and people being mean to you, and saying you're <u>nothing</u> and <u>nobody</u>, and can never be anything. I understand . . . I understand when <u>nobody</u> knows your name. I understand when you have <u>no</u> name . . . I really do understand.

2. Donald Kagan: Address to the Class of 1994 of Yale College, September 1, 1990

   We now have the mechanisms that <u>do</u> permit the storage of data in staggering amounts and their retrieval upon demand. And one of the by-products <u>is</u> the approaching end of the age of specialization. The doom of the specialist draws closer every time someone punches the keys on a word processor. Of course, we <u>will</u> still need doctors, lawyers, plumbers, and electricians. But <u>will</u> there still be a brisk market for all the specialties we have fostered in the economic and social fields? I doubt it. The future <u>will</u> belong to those who know how to handle the combinations of information that come out of the computer, what we used to call the "generalist." The day of the generalist <u>is</u> just over the horizon and we <u>had better</u> be ready for it.

Repetition is also used for emphasis: 1. teenage mother/I (really) understand   2. and/still

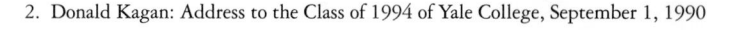

ANSWER KEY

Exercise 7 Answers will vary. Possible answer is: Fiona had a miserable time at the party. She met no friends, had no alcohol, ate no food, had nothing to say to anyone, had no partner to dance with, could find no chairs, had no fun, and decided to go to no more parties.

FOCUS 4 [15 minutes]

1. **Lead-in:** If possible, make an overhead transparency of the focus chart. Use the "uncover technique" to discuss examples (a) and (b) and then examples (c), (d), (e), and (f), uncovering each section of the grid as you go along. If you do not have access to an overhead projector, students can do this in their books.

2. Ask volunteers to create other sentences with *no* for emphasis.

3. Answer any questions students may have.

EXERCISE 7 (OPTIONAL) [25 minutes]

In Exercise 7 students revisit the material in Exercise 5, retelling Fiona's experiences at the party. They practice the principles governing negative emphasis they have studied in Focus 3 and Focus 4.

1. Read the directions as a class.

2. Have students work in pairs and take turns describing what a miserable time they had at the party, referring to the sentences in Exercise 5. See possible answers on LP page 414.

   Suggestion: Once everyone has had a chance to practice, ask for a volunteer who is willing to be critiqued for an audio recording. Record the student.

3. Ask the other students to give positive comments about the student's performance. Then ask students to give one or two suggestions for improvement.

4. Encourage others to record themselves at home for extra practice.

 For more practice, use *Grammar Dimensions 4* Workbook page 208, Exercise 5.

EXERCISE 8 [20 minutes]

In Exercise 8 students analyze the use of emphatic structures and other techniques used in two different public speeches.

1. Read the directions as a class.

2. Have students work independently to underline any examples they can find of emphatic language in the two speeches.

3. Have them work in small groups, share their findings, and discuss the similarities and differences in the techniques the two speakers use.

4. Discuss these techniques with the class. Elicit that both speeches use emphatic language, but the first one also uses the repetition of *I* to emphasize the speaker's identification with someone who is illegitimate by birth and who feels anonymous and disrespected in the society. See answers on LP page 414.

EXPANSION 1 [45 minutes/homework]

1. For homework, ask students to find examples of two other public speeches, researching these in the library or on the Internet.

2. Ask them to print them out, underline the emphatic forms, and then compare the styles of the two speeches.

3. During the next class, have students work in pairs and share their findings.

EXPANSION 2 [60–90 minutes]

Activity 2 (writing/speaking/listening) on SB page 416 is an excellent culminating activity after Exercise 8. Students work in groups to create a new political party, make posters, and prepare and deliver campaign speeches.

UNIT GOAL REVIEW [5 minutes]

Ask students to look at the goals on the opening page of the unit again. Refer to the pages of the unit where information on each goal can be found.

 For assessment of Unit 23, use *Grammar Dimensions ExamView*®.

Use Your English

ACTIVITY 1 listening/writing/speaking

CD2 Track 20

■ **STEP 1** Listen to the audio, a lecture on how to create a good advertisement. Take notes and pay special attention to the suggestions given.

■ **STEP 2** Summarize the speaker's advice in a short paragraph.

Example: *A good ad should have three main ingredients.*
The ad should include information about the product and its unique advantage. . . .

■ **STEP 3** Now revise your paragraph so that it sounds more emphatic. Use some of the techniques you have learned in this chapter.

■ **STEP 4** Now read your paragraph aloud to a classmate, stressing words appropriately.

ACTIVITY 2 writing/speaking/listening

■ **STEP 1** Organize a political campaign in class. Divide into groups. Each group represents a new political party. With your group, create a name and draw up a list of all the things you stand for and all the things you will do if you are elected.

■ **STEP 2** Make a poster representing your beliefs and prepare a short speech to persuade people to vote for you. Each member of your group should be prepared to speak on a different aspect of your party's platform.

■ **STEP 3** Give your speeches to the rest of the class and decide who has the most persuasive approach. If possible, record your speech and afterward listen to what you said, taking note of any emphatic structures you used and how you said them.

ACTIVITY 3 research on the web/writing/speaking

■ **STEP 1** Think of someone famous whom you truly admire because of his or her ideas. This person could be an important figure in any field, such as:

Communications	Katie Couric, Rush Limbaugh, Oprah Winfrey
Politics	Hillary Clinton, Kofi Annan, Hugo Chavez
Business	Bill Gates, Martha Stewart, Rupert Murdoch
Entertainment	Tom Cruise, Angelina Jolie, Stephen Spielberg
Sports	Sanmy Sosa, Lance Armstrong, Anna Kournikova

■ **STEP 2** Go on to *InfoTrac® College Edition* or the Internet to do research about the person you have selected.

■ **STEP 3** Write a short essay describing what traits, activities, or ideas of this person impress you the most.

■ **STEP 4** Give a speech to your classmates convincing them of the admirable traits, activities, ideas, or accomplishments of this person. Use as many emphatic structures from this unit as you can.

Examples: *Even though some people think Rush Limbaugh is an egotistical talk show host, his commentaries do contain some informative news.*

Despite Martha Stewart being a convicted felon, she does continue to be a powerful businesswoman influencing style and homekeeping trends.

There is no Hollywood movie star as controversial as Angelina Jolie.

ACTIVITY 4 reflection

Students often find themselves distracted from their studies. A little grocery shopping or a quick trip to the mall may be a good way for a change of pace. However, certain individuals sometimes end up wasting a lot of time or, even worse, a lot of money shopping when they should be studying. Look at the consumer types in the Opening Task on page 407 and select the type of consumer you are. Then, write a short paragraph describing the shopping temptations you might have at college and how you might overcome these temptations so that you can complete your academic goals. Finally, discuss these ideas with a partner, using emphatic structures from the unit.

Example: *I am an Experiencer. Because of this, I really **might** have the temptation to overspend while I am at college. For this reason, I **do** need to create a budget. . . .*

The Use Your English activities at the end of the unit contain situations that should naturally elicit the structures covered in the unit. For a more complete discussion of how to use the Use Your English activities, see To the Teacher, LP page xxvi.

CD2 Track 20

ACTIVITY 1 listening/writing/speaking [45 minutes/homework]

This activity is a good follow-up to Exercise 1 on SB page 408. Note that the former CD track number (37) is incorrectly listed in the student book.

STEP 1

1. Discuss what students think makes a good advertisement.
2. Read the directions for Step 1 as a class.
3. Have students listen to the audio once.
4. Ask students to listen again and take notes, paying particular attention to any suggestions the speaker makes.

STEP 2

1. Read the directions and example for Step 2.
2. Have students work independently to write their summaries of the speaker's advice. Possibly assign this section as homework.

STEP 3

1. Read the directions for Step 3 as a class.
2. Have students revise their summaries to make them more emphatic. Encourage them to look back on the focus charts in this unit for ideas.

STEP 4

1. Have students work in pairs and take turns reading their summaries aloud, using proper stress and intonation.
2. Ask a volunteer to share a summary with the class.

ACTIVITY 2 writing/speaking/listening [90 minutes/homework]

This is an excellent culminating activity after Exercise 8 on SB page 415.

STEP 1

1. Read the directions for Step 1 as a class.
2. Divide students into larger groups of at least six and have them think of a name for their new party and list what they believe in and what they will do if elected.

STEP 2

1. Read the directions for Steps 2 and 3 as a class.
2. Have the groups create their campaign poster. Ask them to draw up a list of topics that each will address in a speech.

STEP 3

1. You could ask the students to prepare their speeches as homework.
2. Have students give their speeches to the class. If possible, ask students to record their own speeches.
3. Ask the class to vote on who was the most persuasive speaker. Why? What techniques were used?
4. Ask students to listen to their recordings (in class, or at home) and critique them.

ACTIVITY 3 research on the web/ writing/speaking [60 minutes/homework]

This activity makes a good homework assignment following Exercise 6 on SB pages 413–414, with students giving their speeches during the next class.

STEP 1 Read the directions for all four steps as a class.

STEP 2 Have students use the Internet or InfoTrac® to research someone whom they admire.

STEP 3 Ask students to write a short essay describing the traits, activities, and ideas of this person that most impress them.

STEP 4

1. During the next class, have students work in groups of 4–6. Have them take turns giving speeches about the person they researched. They should try to convince their listeners of the admirable traits, activities, ideas, or accomplishments of this person. Encourage them to use as many emphatic structures from this unit as possible.
2. Ask several volunteers to give their speeches to the whole class, and analyze the language and delivery of each.

ACTIVITY 4 reflection [50 minutes]

Activity 4 is a good follow-up to Exercise 2 on SB page 409.

1. Ask students to re-read the descriptions of the various consumer types from the Opening task.
2. Ask them to choose the one they are most similar to.
3. Ask a volunteer to read the directions aloud.
4. Have students work independently to write a paragraph in which they describe shopping temptations and how they might overcome them in order to reach their academic goals.
5. Have students work in pairs and take turns talking about what they have concluded. Encourage them to use as many of the emphatic structures from this unit as possible.
6. Ask volunteers to share their paragraphs with the class, and discuss.

UNIT 24

FRONTING STRUCTURES FOR EMPHASIS AND FOCUS

UNIT GOALS

- Know what kinds of structures can be moved to the front of sentences for emphasis
- Know when to change the subject/verb order for fronted structures
- Use fronted negative forms for emphasis
- Use fronted structures to point out contrasts and focus on unexpected information

OPENING TASK

Film Scenarios

When someone mentions the film industry, we usually think first of actors and directors. When film awards are handed out, however, we are reminded that behind all good movies stand creative scriptwriters.

■ STEP 1

Form groups or teams of scriptwriters. Imagine that you are being considered for a film company contract based on your imaginative ideas.

■ STEP 2

Choose one of the following film scenarios, and complete the last line of dialogue or description. Then add a few sentences to further the plot or the description.

■ STEP 3

When the groups have finished, take turns reading the scenarios along with the completions.

Film 1: Science Fiction

SCENARIO: For weeks the townspeople of Spooner, a small lake resort town, have observed signs that something dreadful has invaded their community. Trees, shrubs, and even the flowers have begun to die. Dogs howl at night and cats are afraid to go out. One sultry summer Saturday night, many of the townsfolk are, as usual, celebrating the end of the week at the local dance hall. Suddenly, they become aware of an eerie, green glow outside. They peek out of the windows to see what it is. In front of them, moving slowly toward them across a field . . .

Film 2: Ghost Story

SCENARIO: Ten men and women have agreed to spend a week in a large and very old mansion on the edge of town. Strange sounds and sights have been observed in this house over the past few years, and the people assembled this evening want to find out if there is truth to rumors that the house has been cursed. They are all seated at the dining room table, with their leader, Madame Montague, at the head.

Madame Montague: *My friends, you all know why we are here. Before we spend another hour in this house, there is one thing that I must demand of all of you. Under no circumstances . . .*

Film 3: Romance

SCENARIO: Brad and Lindsay met about a month ago in a city park when Brad was walking his faithful terrier, Sam, and Lindsay was with her golden retriever, Stella. Ever since then, they have run into each other frequently in the park during their dog walks and have carried on long conversations, but only as friends. Brad, however, is interested in a relationship beyond just a friendship. He wants to let Lindsay know how he feels. One evening, they are sitting on the grass while Sam and Stella romp with each other. Brad looks longingly at Lindsay, and says . . .

Film 4: Mystery

SCENARIO: Detective Hendershot has been asked to investigate the disappearance of Daisy O'Connor, a very wealthy elderly woman, who was last seen at home when one of her friends came for tea. Hendershot has wandered through the house, making numerous observations in his notebook but sees nothing that would give him any leads. Finally, he makes his way out to the garage, which is separated from the house by a narrow walkway. With a key he has found in the kitchen, he slowly opens the garage door. There on the floor of the garage . . .

Film 5: Adventure Story

SCENARIO: After three days of wandering aimlessly in the heart of the Brazilian rain forest, a group of scientists have to admit that they are hopelessly lost. The head of the expedition, Professor Winbigler, feels it is time to warn the others of a great danger to them that she has encountered while separated from the group.

Professor Winbigler: *My fellow scientists, I didn't want to tell you this, but now I fear we may not get out of here for a while. I believe you should be alerted. Far more threatening to our survival than the poisonous snakes and spiders . . .*

UNIT OVERVIEW

Unit 24 covers fronting structures, moving them to the beginning of a sentence, for emphasis, contrast, or focus. It also explains how fronted structures can be repeated as a stylistic device to create cohesion in discourse. Please note that due to its length, this unit has been divided into four lesson plans. To review this unit more quickly, review focus charts and have students complete the first exercise after each chart to observe students' grasp of the grammar topics.

GRAMMAR NOTE

The topic of fronting structures for emphasis and focus will be a new one for many students, even the most advanced. This unit concentrates on the syntactic means of expressing emphasis and focus, and offers students ample opportunities to practice these concepts.

UNIT GOALS

Some instructors may want to review the goals listed on Student Book (SB) page 418 after completing the Opening Task so that students understand what they should know by the end of the unit. These goals can also be reviewed at the end of the unit when students are more familiar with the grammar terminology.

OPENING TASK [30 minutes]

The purpose of the Opening Task is to create a context in which students will need to use fronting structures as they write a scenario and then read it for the rest of the class. The last sentence of each scenario (the one that will need completion) starts with a fronted structure. The problem-solving format is designed to show the teacher how well the students can produce the target structures implicitly and spontaneously when they are engaged in a communicative task. For a more complete discussion of the purpose of the Opening Task, see page To the Teacher, Lesson Planner (LP) page xxii.

Setting Up the Task

Ask students to name some of their favorite films, and then ask them who wrote each. Elicit the names of any scriptwriters students know. Discuss the role a scriptwriter plays in the production of a movie and its final quality.

Conducting the Task

■ STEP 1

1. Divide the class into groups of four or five and have each group select one of the scenarios after scanning, not reading, through the scenarios.
2. Tell them that they are going to act as a team of scriptwriters. Their work will be judged by a film company and, if it is good, they could receive a film contract.
3. Ask students to describe some film plots they've enjoyed in the past.

■ STEP 2

Ask the groups to read their assigned scenarios and work together to complete the last line of dialogue or description for each. Suggest that each group brainstorm a number of possibilities and then choose the best one. Set a time limit for brainstorming and selection (e.g., 10 minutes). If time allows, have them add further sentences to the plot or description.

Suggestion: If students need more direction or motivation, do the first scenario with the class as a whole (without correcting any ungrammatical structures offered for the time being). Brainstorm a list of possible endings.

Closing the Task

■ STEP 3

1. Have groups take turns reading the scenarios and the completions they have written. Because all of the scenarios are meant to be entertaining, encourage the students who read them aloud to do so dramatically.
2. Have students save their work, which they will revisit when they study Focus 1.
3. Don't worry about accuracy at this point, though you may want to take notes of errors in meaning, form, or use in order to focus on those problems later.

GRAMMAR NOTE

Typical student errors (form)

- Deleting the locative adverbial in a fronted structure: —e.g., * *Sitting was our good friend.* (See Focus 2.)
- Inverting the subject and verb inappropriately following fronted adverbials of time or manner: —e.g., * *During the day works she at the office.* * *With great effort moved he the dresser.* (See Focus 2.)
- Not inverting the subject and *be* when there are no auxiliaries: —e.g., * *Very rarely the president is in his office.* (See Focus 3.)

Typical student errors (use)

- In sentences with a fronted structure requiring inversions and a simple subject, omitting *do*: —e.g., * *Never we see such a beautiful sight.* (See Focus 3.)
- In sentences using fronted structures for contrast, not using a parallel construction in both sentences: —e.g., *On the third day we visited the museum.* * *On the fourth day she went shopping.* (See Focus 6.)

FOCUS 1   Fronted Structures

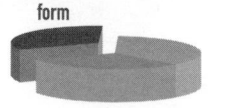

EXAMPLES		EXPLANATIONS
Not Fronted	**Fronted**	In English, you can place special emphasis on some ideas by moving words or phrases from their usual place in a sentence to the front of the sentence. This process is called "fronting," and the resulting structures are known as "fronted structures."
(a) The townspeople went outside **because they were curious.**	(b) **Because they were curious,** the townspeople went outside.	
(c) I would **not** leave this town **for anything.**	(d) **Not for anything** would I leave this town.	
(e) **The storm was so terrible that** many people lost their homes.	(f) **So terrible was the storm that** many people lost their homes.	**Subject-Verb and Subject-Auxiliary Order** When you front some structures, the word order in the rest of the sentence changes. The order of the subject and verb or the subject and the auxiliary is reversed (inverted). The verb or the auxiliary comes before the subject instead of after it. These structures will be shown in Focus 3 and Focus 4.

EXERCISE 1

In the dialogue script on the next page, five friends who have just been backpacking in the mountains are telling some of their classmates about their trip. Each numbered clause contains a fronted structure. For these sentences, underline the subject and circle the main verb and any auxiliaries. If the subject and the verb (or the subject and an auxiliary) have been inverted, write "I" at the end of each sentence.

Example: Not once (did) we (see) a wild animal. I

Judy: Well, to begin with, we had to hike straight uphill for six miles. I couldn't believe how steep it was! Let me tell you, (1) never (have) I (been) so tired in my whole life! I

Toshi: Really! Listen, next time all the food will be freeze-dried. (2) Not for anything (would) I (carry) a 20-pound pack uphill again! I

Phan: (3) At dusk we finally (got up) to our campsite; it was gorgeous! We were on the shores of a pristine mountain lake, surrounded by pine trees. (4) Nowhere (could) we (see) a single person—other than ourselves, that is.

Kent: (5) However, no sooner (had) we (dropped) all our stuff on the ground than the storm clouds rolled in. (6) So, in a big hurry we (unpacked) everything we had.

Mario: (7) Yeah, and not until then (did) I (discover) that I hadn't packed my rain poncho. I

Judy: (8) Neither (had) the rest of us. I

Toshi: We tried to pitch the tents as fast as we could but it wasn't fast enough. (9) With every stake we (pounded) in, it seemed to rain harder. (10) Not only (did) we (get soaked,) but some of our food got wet too.

Phan: But fortunately the storm ended almost as quickly as it had started. (11) And on the other side of the lake the most beautiful rainbow suddenly (appeared.)

Mario: All in all, even though it was a hard climb getting there, it was worth it. (12) You know, seldom (do) you (realize) how peaceful life can be until you get away from civilization!

FOCUS 1 [15 minutes]

This focus introduces fronted structures and explains how, for some of these structures, the order of subject and verb or subject and auxiliary will need to be reversed.

1. **Lead-in:** As an introduction to later focus charts (which will cover the types of fronted structure in detail), discuss the subject-verb word order of the sentences students wrote to complete the scenes in the Opening Task. All of these sentences had an inverted order.

2. Ask students to write an example for each of the five scenarios on the board.

3. Elicit and label the subject, the verb and, for Film Scenarios 2 and 3, the inverted auxiliaries.

4. Ask two volunteers to read the examples and another to read the explanations in the focus chart.

5. Answer any questions students might have.

EXERCISE 1 [20 minutes]

In Exercise 1 students become more familiar with fronted structures and note ones that require subject-verb (or auxiliary) inversion, applying what they have just learned in Focus 1.

1. Read the directions as a class. Ask five volunteers to read the dialogue aloud.

2. Have students work in pairs to underline the subject and circle the main verb and any auxiliaries. Ask them to write "I" next to any sentence in which the subject and verb, or subject and auxiliary, have been inverted.

3. Have pairs work with another pair to compare answers.

4. Review answers as a class. See answers on LP page 420.

For more practice, use *Grammar Dimensions 4* Workbook page 210, Exercise 1.

Order of Subjects and Auxiliaries

form

Chart 1: Fronted Structures That Do Not Require Inversion

When some types of adverbials are fronted, the order of the subject and the verb or the subject and the first auxiliary do not change.

ADVERBIAL NOT FRONTED	FRONTED ADVERBIAL	TYPE OF ADVERBIAL
(a) Lindsay sometimes walks her dog **during the evenings**.	(b) **During the evenings** Lindsay sometimes walks her dog.	Time
(c) Detective Hendershot sorted the evidence **with great care**.	(d) **With great care,** Detective Hendershot sorted the evidence.	Manner
(e) Something strange must be happening **if the dogs are howling**.	(f) **If the dogs are howling,** something strange must be happening.	Condition
(g) Brad showered Lindsay with compliments **in order to win her heart**.	(h) **In order to win her heart,** Brad showered Lindsay with compliments.	Purpose
(i) The townspeople left **because they were afraid**.	(j) **Because they were afraid,** the townspeople left.	Reason
(k) The group would meet in the living room of the old mansion **every night**.	(l) **Every night** the group would meet in the living room of the old mansion.	Frequency (after verbs)

Chart 2: Fronted Structures That Require Inversion

In other types of adverbial fronting, the verb or the first auxiliary must come before the subject.

NOT FRONTED	FRONTED WITH INVERSION	STRUCTURE
(a) The townspeople *were* **so afraid** that they hardly ventured out of their neighborhoods.	(b) **So afraid** *were* the townspeople that they hardly ventured out of their neighborhoods.	Adverbials of extent or degree (*so* + adjective/ adverb + *that*)
(c) A small boy *was* **in the library**.	(d) **In the library** *was* a small boy.	Adverbials of position when the main verb is *be*
(e) We *have* **never** *seen* such a strange sight.	(f) **Never** *have we seen* such a strange sight.	Negative adverbials of frequency that come before the main verb (*never, rarely, seldom*)
(g) Brad *would* **not leave** Lindsay **for anything**.	(h) **Not for anything** *would* Brad *leave* Lindsay.	Other negated structures
(i) A beam of light *was* **moving toward them**.	(j) **Moving toward them** *was* a beam of light.	Present participle + modifiers
(k) A note *was* **stuck in a branch of the willow tree**.	(l) **Stuck in a branch of the** **willow tree** *was* a note.	Past participles + modifiers
(m) The cinematography of this movie *is* **more interesting than** the plot.	(n) **More interesting than** the plot of this movie is the cinematography.*	Comparative structures
(o) (Paraphrase: The soldiers *did not know* that the enemy was just over the hill.)	(p) **Little** *did* the soldiers *know* that the enemy was just over the hill.	Implied negation (Because the negation is implied rather than explicit, there is no nonfronted form with *little*.)

*Note in (n) that the phrase *of this movie* has also been moved to the front to give the reader more information at the beginning of the sentence.

FOCUS 2 [30 minutes/homework]

This focus chart divides fronted structures into three types: those that do not require that the subject and verb or auxiliary be inverted, those that do, and those that may be optionally inverted. Chart 1 appears on SB page 422. Chart 2 appears on SB page 423. Chart 3 appears on SB page 424.

1. **Lead-in:** Give students an overview of what the three parts of the charts cover. If you have gone over examples of inversion for Focus 1 as suggested, students will be familiar with the concept.

2. Ask students to read the examples and the descriptions of the types and structures for homework so they have a general idea of the content.

3. During the next class, explain that most of these fronted structures are more common in written and formal spoken English than in informal English. They are often used in literature as stylistic devices to create special emphasis and focus.

4. Ask various volunteers to read some of the examples aloud, as in a dramatic reading. This will enable students to hear the emphasis put on the fronted structures in an oral context and to get a sense of the rhythm and flow of the sentences. For example, in the fronted form of (p), one would probably increase the vowel sound of *know*, use rising-falling intonation, and pause after it longer than in the not-fronted version.

5. Tell students that these focus charts are an excellent reference tool, as are the other focus charts in this unit.

6. Encourage students to ask questions about anything they do not understand.

Chart 3: Optional Inversion with Fronted Structures

ADVERBIAL NOT FRONTED	FRONTED ADVERBIAL	TYPE OF ADVERBIAL
(a) A leopard appeared from the western hills.	(b) **From the western hills** a leopard *appeared*. (No inversion)	Direction
	(c) **From the western hills** *appeared* a leopard. (Optional inversion)	
(d) An old woman sits **on the park bench.**	(e) **On the park bench** an old woman *sits*. (No inversion)	Position, when the main verb is not *be*
	(f) **On the park bench** *sits* an old woman. (Optional inversion)	

EXERCISE 2

Use the cues in parentheses to add adverbial phrases or clauses to the end of each sentence. Then to emphasize the description you added, move it to the front of a new sentence. You will need to write two sentences for part a. and two for part b. If you wish, you can add other descriptive words or phrases. Be creative; try to use new vocabulary!

Examples: The odd creatures were standing in front of them. (a. manner b. time)
    a. *The odd creatures were standing in front of them with hungry looks on their angular faces.*
    Fronted: *With hungry looks on their angular faces, the odd creatures were standing boldly in front of them.*

    b. *The odd creatures were standing in front of them shortly before midnight.*
    Fronted: *Shortly before midnight, the odd creatures were standing in front of them.*

1. The townspeople were absolutely terrified. (a. time b. frequency)
2. Detective Hendershot will find out what happened to the elderly woman. (a. condition b. manner)
3. The group explored the nooks and crannies of the old house. (a. time b. purpose)
4. The scientists wandered. (a. direction b. purpose)
5. Professor Winbigler faithfully writes in her journal. (a. position b. condition)

ANSWER KEY

Exercise 2 Answers will vary. Possible answers are: 1. a. Not fronted: The townspeople were absolutely terrified on a moonless night. Fronted: On a moonless night, the townspeople were absolutely terrified. b. Not fronted: The townspeople were absolutely terrified every foggy evening. Fronted: Every foggy evening, the townspeople were absolutely terrified. 2. a. Not fronted: Detective Hendershot will find out what happened to the elderly woman if he remains determined.

Fronted: If he remains determined, Det. Hendershot will find out what happened to the elderly woman. b. Not fronted: Det. Hendershot will find out what happened to the elderly woman with his usual cleverness. Fronted: With his usual cleverness, Det. Hendershot will find out what happened to the elderly woman. 3. a. Not fronted: The group explored the nooks and crannies of the old house the first day they were there. Fronted: The first day they were there, the group explored the nooks and crannies of the old house. b. Not fronted: The group explored the nooks and crannies of the old house as they wanted to know if there were really any ghosts. Fronted: As they wanted to know if there were really any ghosts, the group explored the nooks and crannies of the old house. 4. a. Not

EXERCISE 3

Use an appropriate word or phrase from the list below to complete the blanks with fronted structures.

little did I know	peeking out from under a snowdrift
not for anything	stuffed into the toe
never	so embarrassed
sitting at the bottom of the hill	worse than the beginning of my excursion
coming toward me from the right	

I'm not sure if I ever want to go skiing again. (1) _____Never_____ have I felt so frustrated trying to have fun! First, I had trouble just getting on the boots and skis I had rented. One of the boots wouldn't fit; then I discovered that (2) __stuffed into the toe__ was an old sock. I was so nervous that I hadn't realized what it was. Next I discovered that getting to the top of the hill on the chair lift was no small feat. (3) __Little did I know__ that one could fall numerous times before even getting started. Once I made it to the top, I couldn't believe how small everything looked down below. (4) __Sitting at the bottom of the hill__ was a tiny building that I recognized as the chalet. My first thought was: (5) __Not for anything__ am I going to go down this slope. As it turned out, my first thought was probably better than my second, which was to give it a try. (6) __Worse than the beginning of my excursion__ was the end of it. As I raced uncontrollably down the slope terrified, I suddenly saw that (7) __coming toward me from the right__ was another skier. We collided just seconds later. (8) __Peeking out from under a snowdrift__, I muttered an apology. That was it for me for the day. (9) __So embarrassed__ did I feel that I spent the rest of the afternoon finding out how to enroll in a beginning ski class.

fronted: The scientists wandered toward what they thought was civilization. Fronted: Toward what they thought was civilization, the scientists wandered. b. Not fronted: The scientists wandered exhausted to see if they could find a route out of the jungle. Fronted: To see if they could find a route out of the jungle, the scientists wandered exhausted. 5. a. Not fronted: Prof. Winbigler faithfully writes in her journal in front of the Aztec pyramid. Fronted: In front of the Aztec pyramid, Prof. Winbigler faithfully writes in her journal. b. Not fronted: Prof. Winbigler faithfully writes in her journal if she is not too tired from a day of digging Aztec artifacts. Fronted: If she is not too tired from a day of digging Aztec artifacts, Prof. Winbigler faithfully writes in her journal.

EXERCISE 2 [25 minutes]

In Exercise 2 students add adverbial phrases or clauses to the end of each sentence, and then move them to the front of a new sentence for emphasis.

1. Read the directions as a class. Ask two volunteers to read the two examples aloud.
2. Have students work in pairs. Have one student add the adverbial phrase or clause for (a), and the other write a new sentence beginning with that phrase or clause. Then, have them switch roles for (b).
3. Have students work in small groups to compare their answers.
4. Ask several volunteers to share their sentences with the class. See possible answers on LP page 424.

 For more practice, use *Grammar Dimensions 4* Workbook page 211, Exercise 2.

LESSON PLAN 2

EXERCISE 3 (OPTIONAL) [20 minutes/ homework]

In Exercise 3 students complete fronted structures in a passage, continuing their practice of the forms explored in Focus 2. This exercise would make a good review of Focus 2 before beginning Lesson Plan 2.

1. Read the directions as a class.
2. Have students work independently to complete the sentences with an appropriate word or phrase from the list.
3. Ask students to compare their answers with a partner.
4. Review answers with the class. See answers on LP page 424.

 For more practice, use *Grammar Dimensions 4* Workbook page 212, Exercise 3.

EXPANSION [30 minutes/homework]

In Activity 4 (writing) on SB page 438 students write a descriptive paragraph using fronted adverbials of position for contrast or emphasis. It is a good homework assignment following the work students do in Exercise 3.

FOCUS 3 | Patterns of Inversion with Fronted Structures

EXAMPLES		EXPLANATIONS
Not Fronted	**Fronted**	**Pattern 1: Simple Verbs**
(a) I never **said** such a thing!	(b) Never **did I say** such a thing!	When you front a structure requiring inversion and the sentence has only a simple verb, add *do* except when the main verb is a form of *be*.
(c) **He searched** the house so carefully that it took him two hours to complete the task.	(d) So carefully **did he search** the house that it took him two hours to complete the task.	
(e) **The group could** never have guessed what was in the mansion.	(f) Never **could the group** have guessed what was in the mansion.	**Pattern 2: Complex Verbs** Complex verbs have a main verb and one or more auxiliaries. In sentences with complex verbs, invert the first auxiliary and the subject.
(g) **They would** not stay in that house for anything.	(h) Not for anything **would they** stay in that house.	
(i) **The director is** seldom here on time.	(j) Seldom **is the director** here on time.	**Pattern 3: *Be* Verbs** When the verb is *be* with no auxiliaries, invert the subject and *be*.
(k) **The speaker was** so boring that many in the audience fell asleep.	(l) So boring **was the speaker** that many in the audience fell asleep.	
(m) **There has** never been been so much excitement in this town.	(n) Never in this town **has there** been so much excitement.	**Pattern 4: *Be* + Auxiliary Verbs** In sentences with fronted adverbials, invert the first auxiliary and the subject.
(o) **The dust has been** more annoying than the noise during the remodeling of the library.	(p) More annoying than the noise **has been the dust** during the remodeling of the library.	In sentences with fronted comparatives, put both the auxiliary and *be* before the subject.

EXERCISE 4

After each of the following phrases, add a main clause that expresses your opinions or provides information. If the fronted part is a position adverbial, use a *be* verb to follow it.

Examples: Near the school
Near the school is a small coffee shop.
So puzzling . . . that
So puzzling was the homework assignment that most of us didn't finish it.

1. Seldom during the past few years
2. More fascinating than my English class
3. Rarely during my lifetime
4. In my bedroom
5. More important to me than anything
6. Seldom in the history of the world
7. More of a world problem than air pollution
8. So interesting . . . that
9. Stored in my memory, never to be forgotten,
10. Waiting for me in the future
11. In the front of my English textbook
12. Better than ice cream for dessert
13. Loved and respected by many admirers
14. So terrible . . . that

EXERCISE 5

Make up a sentence in response to each of the following. Use a fronted structure for emphasis.

Example: Describe what is in some area of your classroom.
In the back of our classroom are posters of many countries of the world and a large map of the world.

1. State how exciting something is to you by comparing it in degree to something else. (Start with "More exciting . . .")
2. Tell how infrequently you have done something.
3. Describe how angry you were in a certain circumstance. (Start with "So angry . . .")
4. Describe how happy you were in another circumstance.

ANSWER KEY

Exercise 4 Answers will vary. Possible answers are: 1. have I left town. 2. is my history class. 3. has it snowed in my hometown. 4. is a portrait of my family. 5. is my family. 6. have so many governments collapsed at once. 7. is overpopulation. 8. was the new mystery . . . I bought that I read the whole book in one evening. 9. is the memory of the first trip we took to Europe. 10. is, I'm sure, a happy life. 11. is the table of contents. 12. is chocolate mousse. 13. is "the Saint of

Exercise 5 Answers will vary. Possible answers are: 1. More exciting than taking a short trip would be taking a trip around the world. 2. Seldom have I stayed up all night. 3. So angry was I when I found out I failed the exam that I threw it away. 4. So happy was I when my brother came to visit me that I told everyone I knew.

FOCUS 3 [25 minutes]

Focus 3 explores four different patterns of inversion with fronted structures using different types of verbs: simple, complex, *be* verbs, and *be*+ auxiliary verbs.

1. **Lead-in:** Read the explanations, and ask two volunteers to read the examples aloud.
2. For example pairs (e)/(f), (g)/(h), and (m)/(n), ask students to identify the auxiliaries and main verbs that follow the subject *(have guessed, stay,* and *been,* respectively). These verbs have not been boldfaced so that the subject-auxiliary inversion in the fronted versions would be more apparent.
3. Take special note of the comparative form in (p), in which both auxiliary and *be* are fronted. *Annoying* here is a participle adjective and not part of a progressive verb. Students can use the *very* test to identify participle adjectives: *The dust is very annoying* (adjective). NOT: * *My little brother is very annoying me constantly.* (*annoying* = main verb).
4. Answer any questions students may have.

EXERCISE 4 [25 minutes]

In this exercise students complete phrases with fronted structures, applying the principles of Focus 2 and 3.

1. Read the directions and examples as a class. Ask students to identify the type of adverbial in the first example (one of position) and the second (adverbial of extent or degree).
2. Have students work independently to add a main clause expressing their opinions or providing information to each phrase. Remind them that if the fronted structure contains a position adverbial, they should use *be* after it.
3. Have students share their answers with a partner.
4. Review answers as a class. See possible answers on LP page 426.

 work book For more practice, use *Grammar Dimensions 4* Workbook page 213, Exercise 4.

EXPANSION [20 minutes]

This activity will give students additional practice with these patterns of inversion.

1. Ask students to choose one of the sentences they completed in Exercise 4 and write a paragraph developing it. Encourage them to include several different patterns of inversion in their paragraphs.
2. Have them work in pairs and share their paragraphs.
3. Ask a volunteer to read his or her paragraph to the class, and discuss it.

EXERCISE 5 [25 minutes]

In this exercise students create sentences using their own information and fronted structure, applying the principles of Focus 3.

1. Read the directions and example as a class. Ask a volunteer to give another example, describing something in the classroom.
2. Have students work in small groups and take turns talking about themselves, using the prompts.
3. Ask volunteers to give one example of a response to each item. See possible answers on LP page 426.

EXPANSION [40 minutes]

In Activity 3 (writing/speaking) on SB page 438 students work with a partner to write an advertisement using fronted structures for emphasis. If time allows, this could possibly be an extended project with students creating finished advertisements, either on the computer or audio/video recording. Projects might be shared with other classes. This is a good follow-up to the structures practiced in Exercise 5.

FOCUS 4 — Fronted Negative Forms: Adverbials

For all of these fronted negative adverbials below, you must invert the subject and auxiliary or the subject and the simple verb.

Adverbs and Adverb Phrases

WORD/PHRASE	NOT FRONTED	FRONTED
never	(a) The townspeople had **never** witnessed such a strange sight.	(b) **Never** had the townspeople witnessed such a strange sight.
not once	(c) I have **not** missed my Portuguese class **once** this semester.	(d) **Not once** have I missed my Portuguese class this semester.
not for + (noun)	(e) I would **not** commute four hours a day **for all the money in the world!**	(f) **Not for all the money in the world** would I commute four hours a day!
not until + (noun)	(g) She did **not** realize the ring was missing **until the morning.**	(h) **Not until the morning** did she realize the ring was missing.
not since + (noun)	(i) We have **not** had so much rain **since April.**	(j) **Not since April** have we had so much rain.
under no circumstances	(k) You will **not** be allowed to leave **under any circumstances.**	(l) **Under no circumstances** will you be allowed to leave. (*not any → no*)*
in no case	(m) We can **not** make an exception **in any case.**	(n) **In no case** can we make an exception.
in no way	(o) This will **not** affect your grade **in any way.**	(p) **In no way** will this affect your grade.
no way (informal)	(q) I am **not** going to miss that concert **for any reason!**	(r) **No way** am I going to miss that concert.
nowhere	(s) I have **not** been **anywhere** that is as peaceful as this place.	(t) **Nowhere** have I been that is as peaceful as this place.

* Note: Refer to Unit 23, Focus 3 page 412 for a review of double negatives.

Adverb Time Clauses

CLAUSE	NOT FRONTED	FRONTED
not until + clause	(u) I will **not** believe it **until I see it!**	(v) **Not until I see it** will I believe it!
not since + clause	(w) I have **not** had so much spare time **since I started high school.**	(x) **Not since I started high school** have I had so much spare time.

EXERCISE 6

Add the negative fronted structure in parentheses to the following sentences for emphasis. Make any other changes that are necessary.

Example: I hadn't ever been so upset. (never)
Never had I been so upset.

1. We can't let you retake the examination. (under no circumstances)
2. I haven't missed an episode of my favorite program. (not once)
3. My parents won't miss graduation. (not for anything)
4. This didn't change my attitude about you. (in no way)
5. I won't tell you my secret. (not until + a time phrase)
6. She hasn't allowed any changes in the procedures. (in no case)
7. You may not have access to the files. (under no conditions)
8. I wouldn't trade places with him. (not for a million dollars)

EXERCISE 7

Complete the following with a statement based on your experience or opinions.

1. Not since I was a child . . .
2. Not until I am old and gray . . .
3. Not until many years from now . . .
4. Not since I started . . .
5. Nowhere . . .
6. Not for anything . . .

Exercise 6 1. Under no circumstances can we let . . . 2. Not once have I missed . . . 3. Not for anything will my parents miss . . . 4. In no way did this change my . . . 5. Not until the end of the week will I tell . . . 6. In no case has she allowed . . . 7. Under no conditions may you have . . . 8. Not for a million dollars would I trade . . .

Exercise 7 Answers will vary. Possible answers are: 1. have I played that game. 2. will I stop jogging in the park. 3. will I be able to graduate. 4. learning English have I felt so positive about my progress. 5. are there restaurants like they have in Hong Kong. 6. would I drop out of school.

FOCUS 4 [30 minutes]

Focus 4 explains the inversion of subject and verb or subject and auxiliary in fronted negative adverbials.

1. **Lead-in:** To introduce the topic of subject-verb and subject-auxiliary inversion, write some examples of noninverted sentences on slips of paper. Examples: *I have never been so upset about a mistake; I have not missed a day of work this year; You shouldn't drive while drinking under any circumstances; I have not been anywhere that has so many restaurants on one block as this city does.*

2. Have students work with a partner. Give each pair one strip of paper with a sentence to rewrite with a fronted structure. They can use the charts for reference. Have them read the original and the fronted version to the rest of the class (with dramatic emphasis!).

3. Have students work in pairs. One student should read the word/phrase and the first example. The other student should close his or her book, and restate the example using a fronted structure. After six examples, have them switch roles.

4. Answer any questions students might have.

EXERCISE 6 [15 minutes]

In Exercise 6 students add negative fronted structures to sentences for emphasis, practicing the forms they learned in Focus 4.

1. Read the directions and example as a class.
2. Have students work independently to write the sentences.
3. Have them work in pairs, exchange papers, and review each other's work.
4. Ask different students to share their sentences with the class, and discuss. See answers on LP page 428.

work book For more practice, use *Grammar Dimensions 4* Workbook page 214, Exercise 5.

EXPANSION 1 [15 minutes]

For additional practice with fronted negative forms:

1. Have students work independently to create a "warning" that they could put on their bedroom (or dorm room) door using *Under no circumstances should . . .* or *Under no conditions should. . . .*

2. Have them work in small groups to compare their warnings.

EXPANSION 2 [10 minutes/homework]

In Activity 5 (speaking) on SB page 439 students describe a situation or event to which they had a strong reaction using fronted structures for emphasis and contrast. This activity is a good sequel to Exercise 6.

1. Have students first discuss the topic with a partner.
2. Then, assign the topic as homework or as an in-class writing assignment to give students an opportunity to think of what they want to say and how they might include fronted structures in their stories.
3. Have students discuss their stories in small groups or with a partner during the next class.

EXERCISE 7 [25 minutes]

In Exercise 7 students complete sentences with fronted negative forms using their own information.

1. Read the directions as a class. Ask a volunteer to complete the first phrase as an example.
2. Have students work independently to complete the sentences using their own information.
3. Have them work in small groups and take turns sharing their information.
4. Ask different students to share their sentences with the class, and discuss.

EXPANSION [50 minutes]

In Activity 2 (writing/speaking) on SB page 437 students write and discuss things they would never do, and then write a summary of their discussion. This activity is a good follow-up to Exercise 7. You could assign the writing portions as homework before and after the group discussion.

FOCUS 5 — Fronted Negative Forms: Objects and Conjunctions

As with the negative adverbials in Focus 4, these fronted structures require subject-auxiliary or subject-verb inversion.

Noun Phrase Objects

PHRASE	NOT FRONTED	FRONTED
not + singular noun*	(a) The sky was brilliant; he could **not see one cloud** in any direction.	(b) The sky was brilliant; **not one cloud** could he see in any direction.
	(c) We will **not** spend **another penny** on repairing our DVD player.	(d) **Not another penny** will we spend on repairing our DVD player.

*A plural form is possible with *no* (*no clouds could he see*), but the emphasis would not be as strong as with the singular form.

Conjunctions

WORD/PHRASE	NOT FRONTED	FRONTED
neither, nor	(e) I had no idea how the mystery would end.	
	(f) My mother **didn't either.**	(g) **Neither** did my mother.
	(h) My sister **didn't either.**	(i) **Nor** did my sister.
	(j) **No one** else did **either.**	(k) **Neither** did anyone else.
not only (. . . but also)	(l) That movie does **not only** have amazing visual effects, **but** it **also** has a great soundtrack.	(m) **Not only** does that movie have amazing visual effects, **but** it **also** has a great soundtrack.
no sooner (. . . than)	(n) The movie had **no sooner** started **than** the power went out.	(o) **No sooner** had the movie started **than** the power went out.

After each of the following statements, add a sentence using the fronted negative in parentheses.

Example: The German swimmers did not win any medals at the Olympics. (Nor)
Nor did any swimmers from France or the United States.

1. I tried to do the homework but I couldn't understand the assignment. (neither)
2. I've been working on this math assignment almost the entire night. (not one more minute)
3. The main star of the film could not get along with the director. (nor)
4. I just love to visit big cities. (not only)
5. Look how skinny that model is! (not one ounce of fat)
6. We do not want to buy products from companies who use dishonest advertising. (not another dollar)
7. Leon was sorry he had decided to go sailing yesterday. (no sooner)
8. Our art history professor will not accept late papers. (neither)
9. Learning Greek could help you in several ways. (not only)
10. That new romantic comedy was a little disappointing. It did not have a very original plot. (nor)

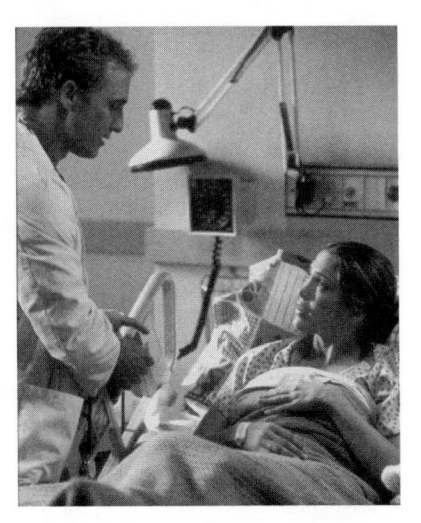

Exercise 8 Answers will vary. Possible answers are: 1. Neither could any of my friends who are in the class.   2. Not one more minute am I going to spend on it.   3. Nor could some of the other actors.   4. Not only are there lots of things to do but also interesting people to watch.   5. Not one ounce of fat does she have anywhere.   6. Not another dollar will be spent on these products. 7. No sooner had he left the harbor when a storm arose.   8. Neither will he let anyone make up quizzes they miss.   9. Not only would you be able to read Greek classics in the original, but it could help you learn the meanings of English words that have Greek roots, prefixes, and suffixes. 10. Nor was the acting very good.

FOCUS 5 [25 minutes]

Focus 5 concentrates on two other fronted negative forms: **objects** and **conjunctions**.

1. **Lead-in:** Ask two volunteers to read the four examples in the first part of the chart (a–d). Elicit the inversion of the subject and the negative form of the verb/auxiliary in the fronted examples.

2. Dedicate more time to the conjunctions in the second part of the chart, as these are more commonly used than fronted noun phrase objects.

3. Read examples (e–i).

4. Then, make statements such as the one in (e) and have students respond using *neither* and *nor.* For example, say: *I don't have time to finish my paper tonight.* Elicit from Student A: *Neither does Johan.* Elicit from student B: *Nor does Kai.* Use past as well as present tenses (e.g., *I didn't watch the news last night. Neither did A. Nor did B.*) Tell students that the *nor* form is not common in informal American English speech.

5. If students seem to catch on easily, ask them to make up negative statements like the one in (e) for others to respond to.

6. For practice of the inverted forms in *not only . . . but also . . .* write examples on the board for students to transform. Write a topic on the board (e.g., *this English class*). Ask students to give you two reasons, two qualities, two conditions, etc.— whatever would fit the topic (e.g., two reasons this English class is helpful). Write the two phrases or sentences on the board.

7. Ask students to write on a piece of paper a *Not only . . . but also* sentence modeled after (m). Ask for a volunteer to write the sentence on the board. Discuss any variations.

LANGUAGE NOTE

The forms *neither* and *not only (. . . but also)* are ones students may find particularly useful in their writing.

EXERCISE 8 [20 minutes/homework]

In Exercise 8 students create sentences using fronted negative structures. Assigning this exercise for homework will give you an opportunity to assess individual progress.

1. Read the directions and example as a class.

2. Have students work in pairs and take turns adding a statement using the fronted negatives in parentheses.

   Suggestion: Point out to the students that these are not complete sentences, but rather partial statements in response to the initial sentence. Write out what the complete sentence would look like, but mention that, in conversation, the speaker would never repeat the whole statement again as the main clause would be *understood* by both the speaker and the listener. Example: *Nor did any swimmers from France or the United States win any medals at the Olympics.*

3. Have them share their statements with another pair.

4. Review answers with the class. See possible answers on LP page 430.

 For more practice, use *Grammar Dimensions 4* Workbook page 215, Exercise 6.

EXPANSION [20 minutes]

For additional practice with fronted negatives, have students do this activity.

1. Have students work in pairs.

2. Ask them to role-play a job interview. They should first decide what the job is. Ask them to take turns as the interviewee answering the question: *Why should I hire you?* using a fronted negative. Give them an example (*Not only am I responsible but also I am very creative.*).

3. Ask several volunteers to share their best sentences with the class.

Fronted Structures: Emphasizing, Contrasting, and Focusing on Unexpected Information

use

Adverb Phrases

Reasons for fronting:

Emphasis

(a) **In the evenings** she writes. It is a time when the house is quiet and peaceful and she can concentrate.

- to emphasize information
- to point out contrasts

Contrast

(b) In the evenings she writes. **The mornings** are devoted to gardening and the **afternoons** to her job at a publishing company.

For adverbials of time, place, or frequency, the context determines whether contrast or some other kind of emphasis is intended.

Emphasis

(c) **On the first floor of the store** are men's clothes. This floor also has luggage.

Contrast

(d) **On the first floor of the store** are men's clothes. **On the second floor** are women's clothes and linens.

The fronting of contrast phrases emphasizes parallel structures. Parallelism of this kind is a stylistic device used to stress ideas and create rhythm.

Participle Phrases and Comparatives

Reason for fronting:

- to emphasize a subject that contains new or unexpected information by moving it to the end of the sentence.

(e) Who could be at Sara's door at this late hour? Sara squinted through the peephole to see who the mystery caller was.

Participle   **Focus on Subject**
Staring back at her was her long-lost brother.

Comparative

(f) **More important to me than anything**
        Focus on Subject
else is my family.

Negative Structures

Reasons for fronting:[*]

(g) **Never** have I seen such a display of bravery!

(h) **Not until the last votes were counted** would the senator admit defeat.

(i) **Under no circumstances** may you enter this building after midnight.

(j) **Not a single promise** did he make that wasn't eventually broken.

- to emphasize unusual or unexpected actions or events.
- to stress particular aspects of events or actions.
- to create strong commands that prohibit actions.
- to emphasize the "negativeness" of things, events, or actions.

[*]These uses often overlap; a fronted negative may emphasize in several different ways.

FOCUS 6 [15 minutes]

Focus 6, unlike the previous focuses, concentrates on the **use** of fronted structures—to emphasize, contrast, and to focus on unexpected information.

1. **Lead-in:** Tell students that the forms here are used mostly in formal English, including literature, to emphasize or show contrasts.

2. Read the examples aloud so that students can hear the rhythms of the sentences. Ask a volunteer to read the explanations.

3. Discuss the differences between the pairs (a)/(b) and (c)/(d) in the use of fronted structures. The first sentences in each pair are identical, but the boldfaced fronted structures have different uses (one for emphasis, the other for contrast) depending on what information is given in the sentences following them.

4. Answer any questions students might have.

EXERCISE 9

State what you think is the main reason for fronting each of the underlined structures. Do you think it is primarily for (1) emphasis of the fronted structure, (2) contrast of the structure, or (3) focus on a delayed subject that contains new or unexpected information? More than one reason may apply. Be prepared to explain your choice.

1. <u>Only when Marta drives</u> does she get nervous. At other times she's quite calm.

2. The phone rang. Howard was sure it was his best friend Miguel calling. Picking up the phone, he shouted, "Yo!" <u>Responding to his greeting</u> was his biology professor.

3. <u>Not since I was in elementary school</u> have I been to the circus. Believe me, that was a long time ago!

4. Welcome to the Little River Inn. We hope you will enjoy your stay here. <u>To your right</u> is a cooler with ice and the soft-drink machines. <u>To your left and around the corner</u> is the swimming pool and jacuzzi.

5. <u>To start this lawnmower</u>, you need to pull the cord very hard and quickly. To keep it going, you should set the lever in the middle.

6. Minh heard a noise coming from underneath his parked car. Getting down on his knees, he looked under the front of it. <u>There, crouched on the right front tire</u> was a tiny kitten.

7. <u>Not until I hear from you</u> will I leave. I promise I'll stay here until then.

8. <u>During the long winters</u> Bonnie does a lot of reading. She loves to lounge by the fire with a good book.

9. The crowd was waiting excitedly to see who would win this year's Boston marathon. <u>A few minutes later, across the finish line</u> came a runner from Kenya.

10. <u>Had I known the movie was so long</u>, I doubt I would have gone to see it. I had no idea that it would last for five hours!

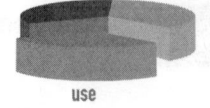

FOCUS 7	Fronted Structures: Creating Cohesion in Discourse

use

EXAMPLES	EXPLANATIONS
	Fronted structures are also used to create cohesion with ideas that have been previously expressed, especially in written English and more formal spoken English. Such structures often express comparisons between ideas across sentences.
(a) *Star Wars* was one of the most successful films ever in terms of box office sales. **Even more successful** was *Titanic,* the highest grossing film of the twentieth century.	In (a), *even more successful* implies *"than Star Wars."* Thus it creates a cohesive link to the previous sentence. Note that we could not understand the second sentence without reference to the first one.
(b) When you write a film script, it is essential that you tell your story so that the reader can "see" it. **Equally important** is making your directing descriptions concise.	In (b), *equally important* is also a comparison, implying *"as important as telling your story so that the reader can see it."*

EXERCISE 10

The following passage offers information and advice about how to be a scriptwriter for films. Underline each fronted structure that is used to create cohesion. The first has been done as an example.

(1) A film script is a document that outlines all of the elements needed to tell a story in a film. (2) <u>Included in these elements</u> are the setting and character descriptions, dialogue, behavioral cues, and sound. (3) It is crucial to keep in mind that since film is a visual medium, you must *show,* not tell your audience what is going on. (4) <u>Equally critical</u> is to be passionate about the characters you create so your audience will share your feelings about them. (5) <u>And certainly as important as creating characters that the audience will care about</u> is developing an engaging conflict or obstacle that the characters have to deal with. (6) The conflict could be something personal, such as a romantic obstacle, or for the good of all people, such as the freedom of a country. (7) <u>Not only</u> do you need to develop some kind of obstacle or conflict but you need a good "hook," that is, an interesting plot idea with an original twist that will captivate your audience and make them want to read on. (8) <u>By creating a hook</u>, you will set your script apart from the many others that agents receive. (9) Finally, be sure to read up on all of the conventions and formatting for scriptwriting so that you meet the expectations of your audience. (10) <u>So important</u> is this last point that if you ignore it and decide to do things your own way, your script will probably end up in the wastebasket.

ANSWER KEY

Exercise 9   *Some answers may vary because uses sometimes overlap. Possible answers are:*   1. (2)
2. (3)   3. (1)   4. (2)   5. (1)   6. (3)   7. (1)   8. (1)   9. (3)   10. (1)

EXERCISE 9 [25 minutes]

In Exercise 9 students analyze a variety of fronted structures in terms of their uses, applying the principles of Focus 6.

1. Read the directions as a class. Read the first sentence, and ask students to identify the reason for using the fronted structure (*to emphasize and contrast information*).
2. Have students work in pairs and analyze the use of each fronted structure.
3. Have them discuss their analyses in small groups.
4. Check to see if the groups agree on reasons, and discuss any differences. See possible answers on LP page 434.

 For more practice, use *Grammar Dimensions 4* Workbook page 215, Exercise 7 and page 216, Exercise 8.

EXPANSION [30 minutes]

In Activity 1 (listening) on SB page 437 students listen to two descriptions of long-admired American movies. Students must listen carefully and select the correct paraphrase. This activity is a good follow-up to Exercise 9 on SB page 434 because of the fronted structures in the audio descriptions. Ask students if any of them have seen either of the two films. If so, ask if they could provide brief oral summaries before beginning the listening task.

FOCUS 7 [10 minutes]

Focus 7 explains how fronted structures are used to create cohesion, mainly in writing and formal spoken English.

1. **Lead-in:** Write the second sentence from the first example on the board before asking the class to look at the focus chart: *Even more successful was "Titanic", the highest grossing film of the twentieth century.*
2. Ask a volunteer to read the sentence aloud. Ask students if the sentence makes sense to them.
3. Explain that fronted structures are used to link ideas across sentences. Explain that this usually occurs in writing, although it can also occur in formal speech.
4. Have one volunteer read (a), and another read the explanation aloud. Then, ask them to read the second example and explanation.
5. Answer any questions students might have.

EXERCISE 10 [15 minutes]

In Exercise 10 students identify fronted structures that are used to create cohesion in a passage about how to become a film scriptwriter.

1. Read the directions as a class. Ask a volunteer to read the first two sentences aloud. Ask students to identify what *included in these elements* refers to. (*The elements needed to tell a story in a film in the first sentence.*)

2. Have students work independently to underline the fronted structures.
3. Have them work in pairs to compare their answers.
4. Review answers with the class. See answers on LP page 434.

 For more practice, use *Grammar Dimensions 4* Workbook page 217, Exercise 9.

EXPANSION [60 minutes/homework]

In Activity 6 (research on the web) on SB page 439 students research movie reviews online and find examples of fronted structures. They then write their own review of a movie or TV program using fronted structures. This activity makes an excellent homework assignment following Exercise 10.

EXERCISE 11

Correct the errors in word order in the following sentences.

1. So great the visual effects were in *The Matrix Reloaded* that I saw the movie twice.

2. Why some people didn't like the sequels to *The Matrix* never I could understand.

3. When putting together a film script to send to an agent, you should not create a fancy title page but keep the page simple. Neither you should put in any illustrations in your script, no matter how nice you think they may be.

4. For any media script you write, be sure to proofread very carefully when you are done. Under no circumstances your script should have any misspellings or grammar mistakes.

Use Your English

ACTIVITY 1 listening

CD2 Tracks 21, 22

In a recent survey, a number of well-known Americans, including authors, media specialists, politicians, and artists, were asked to name movies that they felt defined the American character. Listen to the audio; you will hear descriptions of two of these films. After you have listened to each description, choose the statement which accurately paraphrases an idea in the description.

Pollyanna
a. Americans have never hated or envied the rich.
b. Americans have never hated the rich, just envied them.

Mr. Smith Goes to Washington
a. Political corruption in Washington continues until an innocent man from a small town arrives.
b. Political corruption in Washington stops before an innocent man from a small town arrives.

ACTIVITY 2 writing/speaking

Make a list of some things you believe you would **never** do under any circumstances. Then share your list with one or more classmates to see if they also would never do the things on your list, and have them discuss their lists with you. Finally, write a summary of your discussion, pointing out your similarities and differences.

Examples: *Under no circumstances would I take an advanced course in physics.*
No way would I ever eat squid. (informal usage)

ANSWER KEY

Exercise 11 1. So great were the visual effects in The Matrix Reloaded that I saw the movie twice.
2. Why some people didn't like the sequels to The Matrix I could never understand. 3. Neither should you put in any illustrations in your script, no matter how nice you think they may be.
4. Under no circumstances should your script have any misspellings or grammar mistakes.

Activity 1 *Pollyana* (b) *Mr. Smith Goes to Washington* (a)

EXERCISE 11 [15 minutes]

In this final exercise students review the rules governing sentence word order in fronted structures that they have studied in this unit, and correct any errors.

1. Read the directions as a class.
2. Ask students to work independently to correct any errors they find.
3. Have students share and compare answers with a partner.
4. Ask random students to share their answers. See answers on LP page 436.

EXPANSION [45 minutes/homework]

In Activity 7 (reflection) on SB page 439 students reflect and write about how they can develop three strategies they are already using to improve their writing skills. This activity makes a good final homework assignment following Exercise 11.

UNIT GOAL REVIEW [10 minutes]

Ask students to look at the goals on the opening page of the unit again. Refer to the pages of the unit where information on each goal can be found.

ExamView Test Generator — For assessment of Unit 24, use *Grammar Dimensions 4 ExamView®*.

USE YOUR ENGLISH

The Use Your English activities at the end of the unit contain situations that should naturally elicit the structures covered in the unit. For a more complete discussion of how to use the Use Your English activities, see To the Teacher, LP page xxvi. While students are doing these activities in class, you can circulate and listen to see if they are using the structures accurately. Errors can be corrected after the activity has finished.

ACTIVITY 1 listening [30 minutes]

In Activity 1 students listen to two descriptions of long-admired American movies. Students must listen carefully and select the correct paraphrase. This activity is a good follow-up to Exercise 9 on SB page 434. Ask students if any of them have seen either of the two films. If so, ask if they could provide brief oral summaries before beginning the listening task. Note that the former CD track numbers (38, 39) are incorrectly listed in the student book.

CD2 Tracks 21, 22

1. Discuss briefly the notion of a film defining a country's character.
2. Read the directions as a class.
3. Have students listen to the audio once.
4. Ask students to listen again and choose the statement that best paraphrases an idea in the description.
5. Have students work in pairs to compare their answers.
6. Review answers with the class.

ACTIVITY 2 writing/speaking [50 minutes/homework]

In this activity students write and discuss things they would never do. Then they write a summary of their discussion. This activity is a good follow-up to Exercise 7 on SB page 429. You could assign the writing portions as homework before and after the group discussion.

1. Read the directions as a class. Ask a volunteer to read the examples. Ask several other students to say something they would never do.
2. Have students make a list of at least four things they would never, under any circumstances, do. Tell them to begin their sentences with a negative word or phrase.
3. Have students work in groups of four and share their lists. Ask them to make notes on what people say.
4. Have students write a summary of their group discussion, noting similarities and differences in what everyone said.
5. Ask several volunteers to read their summaries to the class, and discuss.

ACTIVITY **3** writing/speaking

Advertisements and commercials often use strong claims to sell products. Team up with a classmate and imagine you are copywriters for an ad agency. With your partner, choose a product (one that already exists or make one up) to sell; write an advertisement for either print media (magazine, newspaper), radio, or television. Present your ad/commercial to the class, and give them a chance to discuss your claims.

ACTIVITY **4** writing

Write a paragraph in which you describe one of the following:

- the contents of a room as someone might see the room upon entering it.
- a machine or appliance with a number of parts.

Examples: *As you come into the living room, there is a large chintz sofa. In front of the sofa is a maple coffee table. To the left of it is an end table that matches the coffee table, and to the right stands a bookcase. On top of the bookcase sits my favorite vase. It's a deep turquoise blue.*

The parts of my computer include the monitor, the printer, the computer itself, and the control panel. On the control panel are four switches. To the far left is the switch for the computer. Next to it is the switch for the monitor. To the right of the monitor switch is the one for the printer.

ACTIVITY **5** speaking

With a partner or in a small group, describe an event that affected you strongly; for example, a time when you were especially happy, excited, angry, frightened, surprised, etc.

ACTIVITY **6** research on the web

Look up some film reviews of movies you have seen or would like to see on one of the many Web sites dedicated to this purpose (for example, http://www.mrqe. com/lookup has thousands of reviews). Skim the reviews and try to find four to five examples of fronted structures.

Example: *With her crested gray mane, laser glare and perfectly modulated stealth missile sarcasm, Miranda Priestly, the editor-in-chief of the fictional Vogue clone, Runway, is still a monster.* (Carina Chocano, *LA Times,* June 30, 2006).

Then write your own review of a movie or television show that you especially liked or disliked.

ACTIVITY **7** reflection

Think of three things you currently do to improve your writing. Write three statements that represent ways you will try to take each of these things one step beyond what you are currently doing.

Example: *Activity: Proofreading my papers when I have finished writing them*
Not only will I try to be more careful in proofreading my papers in general, but I will check especially for my two most common errors, which are subject-verb agreement and the -s plural on nouns.

USE YOUR ENGLISH

 **ACTIVITY 3** writing/speaking [40 minutes]

This is a good activity for students after Exercise 5 on SB page 427.

1. Read the directions as a class.
2. Have students work in pairs and choose an existing product—or one they think up—to sell.
3. Have them write an ad for the product in which they use at least two fronted structures to emphasize something about the product. Tell students that the ad can be for print, TV, or radio.
4. Have students present their ad to the class, and discuss why people should buy the product.

ACTIVITY 4 writing [30 minutes/homework]

This activity is a good homework assignment following the work students do in Exercise 3 on SB page 425.

1. Read the directions as a class. Ask two volunteers to read the two examples aloud.
2. Have students chose one of the two topics and write a descriptive paragraph using fronted adverbials of position for contrast or emphasis.
3. Have students exchange papers with a partner and read and discuss their work.
4. Ask a volunteer to read a paragraph about the two subjects to the class.
5. Have students work in small groups and take turns reading their descriptions to classmates. The group should try to guess each place.

VARIATION

This activity could be constructed as a guessing game. Have students write a brief description of a place (a room, a building, a park, part of the campus, an area of a city, etc.) using fronted adverbials. The place should be one that they think everyone knows. In their description they should not state what the place is. For example, they could start: *As you walk into this building/If you are on this street/When you get to this part of the campus*, etc.

 **ACTIVITY 5** speaking [30 minutes/homework]

This activity is a good sequel to Exercise 6 on SB page 429.

1. Read the directions as a class. Give students an example of one or two phrases that might precede fronted negatives in informal contexts so that they will sound more natural. Some examples: *Listen, I'll tell you, never have I been so surprised as when I walked into the house and all my friends were there for my birthday! Let me tell you, never was I so frightened as when I saw that movie **Body Count**.*
2. Have students work with a partner or in small groups of four and take turns describing situations which affected them strongly. Remind them to use fronted structures whenever possible for emphasis and contrast.
   Variation: Assign this as a homework or in-class writing assignment.
3. Ask a few representatives of groups to report on one of the stories someone in their group shared.

 ACTIVITY 6 research on the web [60 minutes/homework]

This activity makes an excellent homework assignment following Exercise 10 on SB page 435.

1. Discuss what movie reviewers students like. Do they prefer watching reviewers speak on TV, hearing them on the radio, or reading reviews in print or online? What do they particularly like or dislike about certain reviewers?
2. Read the directions as a class. Ask a volunteer to read the example aloud.
3. Ask students to research online reviews of movies that interest them. Have them find and write down four or five examples of fronted structures used in the reviews. Then, have them write their own review of a movie or TV program using fronted structures.
4. Have students work in small groups during the next class and exchange papers and discuss the reviews.
5. Ask a few volunteers to read their reviews to the class, and discuss.

ACTIVITY 7 reflection [45 minutes/homework]

This activity makes a good final homework assignment following Exercise 11 on SB page 436.

1. Ask students to name some things they already do to improve their writing, such as check spelling or proofread their papers.
2. Read the directions as a class. Ask a volunteer to read the examples.
3. Have students think of three things they already do to improve their writing, and then write at least three statements saying how they might further develop these strategies. Encourage them to use fronted structures.
4. Have students give you their papers for review and comment.
5. Ask volunteers to share any particularly effective strategies they have discovered with the class.

FOCUSING AND EMPHASIZING STRUCTURES
It-Clefts and *Wh*-Clefts

- Use *it*-cleft sentences to put special emphasis on information

- Know what parts of a sentence can be used for focus in *it*-clefts

- Know how to use other kinds of cleft sentences for questions and statements

- Use *wh*-clefts to put focus on information at the end of sentences

OPENING TASK

Does Birth Order Influence Personality?

You may have at times judged someone's behavior according to that individual's position in a family as the oldest, youngest, middle, or only child. For example, you might have considered a friend's "take charge" attitude as characteristic of an oldest child. As for youngest children in a family, people often assume they are the ones who will be the most pampered and spoiled. If you are an only child, you may have heard the generalization that only children are very confident. While controversy continues about whether birth order actually affects adult personalities, it remains a very popular topic in psychology and issues about parenting.

STEP 1

On the next page, read the observations about personality traits that have commonly been associated with particular birth orders: oldest, middle, youngest, and only child.

PERSONALITY TRAITS ASSOCIATED WITH BIRTH ORDER

a. tends to be a high achiever and goal-oriented
b. is often the most secretive
c. is usually very comfortable with older people
d. tends to be skilled at defending himself or herself
e. often acts as a negotiator or mediator
f. may find it harder than other children to learn to share
g. often feels most obligated to follow the parents' rules
h. are often creative and open to exploring new ideas
i. tends to be the most conservative
j. is typically self-sufficient
k. may be confused about self-image as a result of being both welcomed and at the same time disliked by siblings
l. tends to be independent because of greatest freedom from parental attention

STEP 2

Based on your knowledge of your family members' personalities (including yours) or the personalities of friends whose birth order you know, guess which order each trait characterizes: the only child, the oldest child, the middle child, or the youngest child. Here are answers to *a* and *b*:

a. *It's the oldest child who tends to be a high achiever.*
b. *It's the middle child who is the most secretive.*

STEP 3

After you have guessed a birth order for each trait, briefly discuss your choices in small groups.

STEP 4

Check the answers to this task on page A-16. Comment on ones that surprised you the most.

Example: *What surprised me the most is that the middle child is often secretive. My brother's girlfriend is a middle child, and she tells everyone about everything!*

UNIT OVERVIEW

This unit covers two types of structures that are used to emphasize information in English. The focus charts for these units begin with a focus on the forms, followed by the contexts for use. Please note that due to its length, this unit has been divided into four lesson plans. To review this unit more quickly, review focus charts and have students complete the first exercise after each chart to observe students' grasp of the grammar topics.

GRAMMAR NOTE

This unit explores two important focus constructions: *It-* and *Wh-*clefts. These structures are used to place grammatical focus on specific portions of a sentence and the information contained in those portions.

It-clefts are most often used in writing and formal speech situations, though they also occur in less formal speech. *Wh*-clefts are more common in speech, both informal and formal.

UNIT GOALS

Some instructors may want to review the goals listed on Student Book (SB) page 440 after completing the Opening Task so that students understand what they should know by the end of the unit. These goals can also be reviewed at the end of the unit when students are more familiar with the grammar terminology.

OPENING TASK [30 minutes]

The purpose of the Opening Task is to create a context in which students will need to use focusing and emphasizing structures as they match statements about personality traits with particular birth orders: oldest, middle, youngest, or only child. *It*-cleft structures are prompted in the sample answers, given in Step 2. For a more complete discussion of the

purpose of the Opening Task, see To the Teacher, Lesson Planner (LP) page xxii.

Setting Up the Task

1. Take a quick class poll to find out how the class members fall into the various birth orders.
2. Discuss how students think birth order affects personality.

Conducting the Task

1. Read the introductory text as a class.
2. Have students work in small groups. If you found out your students' birth orders before beginning the task, use this information to group them for these steps. Having a range of the different birth orders in each group will enliven the discussion.

■ STEP 1

Ask students to read the directions and personality traits on SB page 441.

■ STEP 2

Have students read the directions and examples. Then ask them to each write their answers to Step 2, matching the personality traits in Step 1 with a birth order.

■ STEP 3

Students should take turns sharing their responses and reasons for choosing as they did.

■ STEP 4

Have students check their answers and discuss those that most surprised them. This last step prompts statements using *Wh*-clefts.

Suggestion: To prompt *Wh*-clefts with other phrases besides the one in the example, start with one of your own observations: *What I thought was the most*

surprising was. . . . You could also ask students if there were any statements that they wondered about, prompting statements beginning with: *What I wondered about was. . . .* Again, offer an example of your own: *What I wondered about was why the middle child would feel like a "fifth wheel."*

Closing the Task

Ask representatives of several groups to share what their group found most surprising.

Don't worry about accuracy at this point, though you may want to take notes of errors in meaning, form, or use in order to focus on those problems later.

GRAMMAR NOTE

Typical student errors (form)

- After *It*, using a phrasal modal, a perfective, or a progressive form rather than *be*: —e.g., * *It is able to study that I am in the library.* * *It's have read these books that she has done.* * *It's writing the paper that John was doing.* (See Focus 1.)
- Transposing elements of a cleft sentence incorrectly, resulting in an incomplete or awkward construction: —e.g., * *It was that they painted the room an awful shade of orange.* (See Focus 2.)
- Not inverting *it* and *be* in *Wh*-questions: —e.g., * *Who it was that called you earlier?* (See Focus 5.)

Typical student errors (use)

- In *It*-cleft sentences emphasizing time, place, and characters, placing the *It*-cleft structure at the end, rather than the beginning, of a sentence: —e.g., * *She was ready to compete in the games when it was early spring.* (See Focus 4.)
- In *Wh*-clefts, not placing the information to be focused on at the end of a sentence: —e.g., * *A great swimmer is what John was.* (See Focus 6.)

Structure of *It*-Cleft Sentences

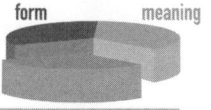

EXAMPLES		EXPLANATION
(a) **No Special Emphasis**: My brother is conservative, not me.		"Cleft" means to divide. *It*-cleft sentences put special emphasis on one part of a sentence.
(b) **Emphasis**: It is my brother who is conservative, not me!		The part that is emphasized is introduced by *it* and a form of *be*.
Focus Element	**Clause**	The cleft sentence divides a sentence into two parts: (1) a focus element and (2) a clause beginning with *that, who, when,* or *where.*
(c) It is the youngest child	who is often both a rebel and a charmer.	
Singular **Plural**		
(d) It **is** oldest children and only children	who tend to be the most assertive.	The verb is singular even when the focus element is plural.
Future		
(e) It **will be** on a Saturday	that we leave, not a Sunday.	The *be* verb is usually present tense. However, we also use other tenses.
Past		
(f) It **used to be** my mother	who did all the cooking, but now we all help.	
(g) It **must** be red wine	that stained this carpet.	We can use modal verbs in cleft sentences to express degrees of probability.
(h) It **can't** be the youngest child	who is the most conservative.	

EXERCISE 1

Complete each blank below with a word or phrase that fits the context. Use a singular or plural form of noun as appropriate for agreement. The first has been done as an example.

1. It couldn't be ___only children___ who are confused about self-image because they don't have any siblings.

2. I think it must be _the youngest child_ who often has the self-image problem because the older ones might have mixed feelings about the baby of the family.

3. It might be ___the only child___ who is generally self-sufficient because as a child he or she might have had to do a lot of things alone.

4. Some psychologists claim that, of all birth order positions, ___it is___ the middle child who is apt to be the most popular among other people.

5. It is _the youngest child_ who may be fearless and have a strong sense of exploration because that child often feels protected by older siblings.

6. Experts on parenting have observed that _it is only children_ who tend to have difficulty dealing with interruptions from others because they did not have brothers or sisters who interrupted them.

FOCUS 1 [15 minutes]

1. **Lead-in:** To practice the form of *It*-cleft sentences, review the personality traits and birth orders from the Opening Task. Tell students that you are going to make some statements about the traits associated with birth orders. Ask them to correct you if you make any statements that are untrue according to the psychologists' observations. Start with a "true" statement, such as *The youngest child may be confused about self-image.*

2. Then give a series of "false" statements and have students correct them. Elicit *It*-cleft sentences and write these on the board to express "true" statements. Example: *The oldest child tends to be the most secretive.* (*Not true*) Correction: *It is the middle child who tends to be the most secretive.*

3. Ask one volunteer to read each explanation, and then have another volunteer read the corresponding example(s).

4. Answer any questions students might have.

LANGUAGE NOTE

Students will most likely be familiar with the form of *It*-clefts but may not use them productively or may use them with a limited range of focus elements. Encourage use of this type of cleft by modeling the structure as you speak with proper emphasis and intonation.

EXERCISE 1 [15 minutes]

In Exercise 1 students complete *It*-cleft sentences using the topic from the Opening Task (birth order), applying what they have just learned in Focus 1.

1. Read the directions as a class. Do the first sentence with the class as an example. Ask students to say what kind of verb is used in the *It*-clause. (*modal*)

2. Have students work independently to complete the sentences.

3. Have them work in pairs to compare answers.

4. Review answers as a class. See answers on LP page 442.

For more practice, use *Grammar Dimensions 4* Workbook page 218, Exercise 1 and page 219, Exercise 2.

EXPANSION [45 minutes]

Activity 2 (writing/speaking) on SB page 455 is an excellent follow-up to Exercise 1. In this entertaining activity students write descriptions of their classmates and then others guess who is being described, using cleft sentences.

FOCUS 2   Focus Elements in Cleft Sentences

form

We can focus on various parts of a sentence in the focus element of cleft sentences.

ORIGINAL SENTENCE	CLEFT SENTENCE	FOCUS
The students are organizing an English book club.	(a) It is **the students who** are organizing an English book club.	Subject
	(b) It is **an English book club that** the students are organizing.	Direct object
We wish to speak to the President of the university about this issue.	(c) It is **the President of the university** to whom we wish to speak about this issue. (formal)	Object of preposition
	(d) It is **the President of the university** who we want to speak to about this issue. (less formal)	
They painted the dormitory recreation room an awful shade of yellow.	(e) It was **an awful shade of yellow** that they painted the dormitory recreation room.	Complement (noun)
They painted it greenish yellow.	(f) It was **greenish yellow** that they painted it.	Complement (adjective)
The President resigned due to illness.	(g) It was **due to illness** that the President resigned.	Prepositional phrase
The baby boom began in the United States after World War II ended.	(h) It was **after World War II ended** that the baby boom began in the United States.	Dependent clause
An amendment to the U.S. Constitution was passed in 1920 to ensure the right of women to vote.	(i) It was **to ensure the right of women to vote** that an amendment to the U.S. Constitution was passed in 1920.	Infinitive or Infinitive clause

EXERCISE 2

Restate the following sentences about the United States civil rights movement of the 1950s and 1960s to emphasize the information indicated in parentheses. Change any other wording as necessary and check to make sure the *be* verb tense is appropriate for the meaning.

Example: Americans honor the famous civil rights leader Martin Luther King Jr. with a national holiday in January. (Emphasize the month).

It is in January that Americans honor the famous civil rights leader Martin Luther King Jr. with a national holiday.

1. Rosa Parks is known as "the mother of the civil rights movement" in the United States. (Emphasize the person's name.)

2. Parks challenged the South's policy of segregating races on buses in 1955 by refusing to get up and give her bus seat to a white passenger. (Emphasize the date.)

3. White and black civil rights workers sat together in "white only" sections of restaurants and other public places in 1960 to protest segregation in the South. (Emphasize the purpose.)

4. In 1962, President John Kennedy sent United States marshals to protect James H. Meredith, the first black student at the University of Mississippi. (Emphasize the place.)

5. The civil rights movement reached a climax in 1963 with the march on Washington. (Emphasize the event.)

6. Martin Luther King Jr. delivered his famous "I Have a Dream" speech during the march on Washington. (Emphasize the speech.)

7. King led civil rights marches in Selma and Montgomery, Alabama in 1965. (Emphasize the places.)

EXERCISE 3

Imagine that each of the situations below is true. Provide an explanation, either serious or humorous, emphasizing the reason.

Example: You were late to class yesterday.

It was because the bus didn't come that I was late to class.

1. You didn't have an assignment done that was due.

2. You missed a medical appointment.

3. You forgot a relative's birthday. (You choose the relative.)

4. You didn't eat anything for two days.

5. You fell asleep in your one of your classes.

ANSWER KEY

Exercise 2   1. It is Rosa Parks that is known as . . .   2. It was in 1955 that Parks challenged . . .   3. It was to protest segregation that . . .   4. It was to the University of Mississippi that . . .   5. It was with the march on Washington that . . .   6. It was the famous "I Have a Dream" speech that Martin Luther King Jr. . . .   7. It was in Selma and Montgomery, Alabama that Martin Luther King Jr. . . .

Exercise 3   Answers will vary. Possible answers are: 1. It was because someone stole my notebook that I don't have my assignment.   2. It was because I overslept that I missed . . .   3. It was because I was so busy that I forgot . . .   4. It was because I was ill that I didn't . . .   5. It was because I stayed up all night that I fell asleep . . .

FOCUS 2 [35 minutes/homework]

Focus 2 explains how the focus element of cleft sentences can focus on various parts of a sentence. You could ask students to read through this chart for homework before you cover it in class.

1. **Lead-in:** Give students an overview of what the three columns of the chart cover. Go over examples of inversion (focus elements followed by clauses) for Focus 1.

2. Explain that most of these fronted structures are more common in written and formal spoken English than in informal English. They are often used in literature as stylistic devices to create special emphasis and focus.

3. Ask various volunteers to read some of the examples aloud, as in a dramatic reading. This will enable students to hear the emphasis put on the fronted structures in an oral context and to get a sense of the rhythm and flow of the sentences. In (a) students should use rising-falling intonation for the word *stu'-dents*. In the fronted form of (b), one could emphasize either *English*, *book*, or *club* depending on the focus of the speaker's intent.

4. Tell students that this focus chart is an excellent reference tool, as are the other focuses in this unit.

5. Encourage students to ask questions about anything they do not understand.

METHODOLOGY NOTE

Although students do not have to remember the grammatical labels for the various structures, they should get a feeling for the different ways we can focus information by fronting with introductory *It*. They should also be aware that these structures create special focus on information and are not just arbitrary restructurings of sentences to achieve "sentence variety."

EXERCISE 2 [20 minutes]

In Exercise 2 students restate information in sentences using *It*-clefts to focus on different types of information, putting into practice what they have just studied in Focus 2.

1. Read the directions as a class. Ask a volunteer to read the examples aloud. Then ask another volunteer to restate the sentence focusing on the object of the preposition.

2. Have students work in pairs and take turns restating the sentences using the information in parentheses.

3. Ask volunteers to give the answers and verify these with the class. See answers on LP page 444.

 For more practice, use *Grammar Dimensions 4* Workbook page 220, Exercise 3.

EXERCISE 3 (OPTIONAL) [20 minutes]

In Exercise 3 students explain a series of situations using *It*-clefts to emphasize the reason for each, continuing their practice of the forms explored in Focus 2.

1. Read the directions and example as a class.

2. Provide more models before students work on this exercise by asking the class to brainstorm more responses for the example (either serious or humorous).

3. Have students do this exercise orally in small groups, with each group brainstorming two or three examples for each item.

4. Ask representatives of various groups to share some of their sentences with the class. See possible answers on LP page 444.

FOCUS 3 — It-Clefts in Spoken and Written Communication

meaning

EXAMPLES	EXPLANATIONS
(a) **It is the middle child** who is most secretive. (The middle child is distinguished from the eldest and youngest children.)	**Distinguish Member of a Group** *It*-cleft sentences can distinguish one member of a group as having certain qualities.
(b) **It is only love** that can bring world peace. (Love is the only thing that can bring world peace.)	In some cases the "group" may include all other things or people. We use *only* before the focus element to convey this meaning.
(c) **It is only my best friend** who can cheer me up when I'm down. (My best friend is the only person who can cheer me up.)	
(d) A: I think the youngest child is the one who tends to be secretive. B: I don't agree. **It's the middle child,** I think, who is most secretive.	**Express Contrast** We sometimes use cleft sentences to point out a contrast or to note something that is commonly believed but not true.
(e) What color paint is this? **It was** *blue* that I ordered, not green!	In spoken English, the contrasting word or phrase receives extra stress. In (e), *blue* is stressed because it contrasts with *green*.
(f) **It was out of concern** that we called our neighbor to see if she was all right.	**Emphasize Purpose or Cause** *It*-clefts can also emphasize the purpose or cause of something. These often include prepositional phrases beginning with *out of* or *for*.
(g) **It was for a general education requirement** that I took art history.	

EXERCISE 4

Which person in your family or circle of friends best matches the following descriptions? In your response, use a cleft sentence beginning with *it is* (or *it's*). Also, try to paraphrase (put in your own words) each description instead of just repeating it, as shown in the example.

Example: would be most likely to complain about young people's behavior

It's my grandmother who would be most likely to say that young people don't act the way they should.

1. tends to watch the most TV

2. has the best sense of humor

3. would be most likely to park a car and forget where it was

4. has the most trouble getting up in the morning

5. is the most artistic

6. would be most likely to stop and help if he or she saw someone in trouble

7. most often tries to get out of doing housework

8. most enjoys shopping

EXERCISE 5

Complete each blank by choosing a word from the list below for a focus element and creating a cleft sentence. The first has been done as an example.

anger	faith	pride
curiosity	music	a sense of humor

1. _____It was anger_____ that made God banish Adam and Eve from the Garden of Eden, according to the Judeo-Christian Bible.

2. _____It is pride_____ that often keeps us from admitting our mistakes.

3. _____It was curiosity_____ that caused Pandora's downfall in the Greek myth; she had to find out what was in the box.

4. _____It is music_____ that has been called the language of the soul.

5. _It is a sense of humor_ that keeps most of us from taking ourselves too seriously and helps us to deal with the ups and downs of life.

6. _____It is faith_____ that has helped many people withstand religious persecution.

ANSWER KEY

Exercise 4 Answers will vary. Possible answers are: 1. It's my sister who tends to be a couch potato. 2. It is my friend Juan who is the funniest. 3. It's I (or me, informally) who would be most likely to forget where I parked. 4. It's my brother Nima who is always tired in the morning. 5. It's my mother who has talent in art. 6. It's my friend Sophia who would be a Good Samaritan. 7. It's my dad who most often makes excuses so he doesn't have to do housework. 8. It's my aunt who loves to shop until she drops.

FOCUS 3 [20 minutes]

1. **Lead-in:** Ask three volunteers to read the first three examples, and then read the explanations for them as a class.

2. To explain further the use of *only* with a focus element, write a few global or local problems on the board, such as *poverty* or *violent crime*. Give an example of a necessary step to address the problem: *It is only education that can make a big difference in the poverty level.* Ask students to identify key solutions to other problems.

3. Ask volunteers to read the last four examples, read the explanations for them as a class.

4. To form *It*-cleft purpose statements, ask students to give you reasons for choices they have made: *Leo, why did you decide to major in computer science?* Purpose statements can be expressed with prepositional phrases as in (f) and (g), with infinitive clauses (*It was to prepare myself for a good job that I majored in computer science*) or with *because*-clauses (*It was because I have always loved to work with computers . . .*). Call students' attention to the *that*-clause structures after the introductory element.

5. Answer any questions students may have.

EXERCISE 4 [20 minutes/homework]

In this exercise students describe members of their families using *It*-cleft sentences, applying the principles of Focus 3.

1. Read the directions and examples as a class.

2. Conduct this as a whole class exercise. Ask one student a question for the first item (*Nicholas, which of your family members or friends tends to watch the most TV?*). Write the question on the board if you think students need it to model the phrasing of the first part. After the student has responded with a cleft sentence, have him or her call on another student. Repeat the procedure with the second student calling on a third, etc. See possible answers on LP page 446.

3. If you want students to focus on skills in paraphrasing information (restating part of the original phrase in their own words), ask them to write their answers as homework. Model one or two more items in class, focusing on paraphrasing (e.g., *tends to watch the most TV → usually spends a lot of time watching TV/is the biggest "couch potato"; has the best sense of humor → is the funniest person I know*).

For more practice, use *Grammar Dimensions 4* Workbook page 221, Exercise 4 and page 222, Exercise 5.

EXPANSION [60 minutes/homework]

In Activity 4 (research on the web) on SB page 456 students research additional information about birth order and personality on the Internet. They then write about their findings, using *It*-cleft structures to introduce their statements. This activity is a good homework assignment following Exercise 4.

EXERCISE 5 [15 minutes]

In this exercise students chose words from a list and complete sentences with *It*-clefts.

1. Read the directions and example as a class. If needed, briefly explain the cultural references in this exercise (Adam and Eve, Garden of Eden, Bible, Pandora).

2. Have students work independently to complete the sentences.

3. Have them review their work in pairs.

4. Ask volunteers to give the answers. See answers on LP page 446.

For more practice, use *Grammar Dimensions 4* Workbook page 223, Exercise 6.

Imagine you have been asked to edit a reference book for errors. Each of the facts below has one incorrect part. Identify the incorrect part. Then write a sentence indicating what needs to be corrected, using a cleft sentence to highlight that element.

Example: Shakespeare wrote *Hamster*, one of his most famous plays, at the beginning of the seventeenth century.

Correction: *It was **Hamlet** that Shakespeare wrote.*

1. Mexico borders the United States to the north.
2. The 2004 Olympics were held in Athens, Italy.
3. One of the most famous tragedies of all time, *Romeo and Juliet,* was written by Molière in 1595.
4. Christopher Columbus sailed to India in 1492.
5. United States astronauts first landed on Mars in 1969.
6. In 1260 Kublai Khan founded the Yuan dynasty in Japan.
7. Leonardo da Vinci painted the famous *Moaning Lisa* around 1500.
8. The brain, the spinal cord, and the nerves are parts of the body's digestive system.
9. Nefertiti ruled India along with her husband King Akhenaton during the fourteenth century BC.

EXERCISE 7

STEP 1 Make lists of your four favorite foods, your four favorite movies (or TV programs), and your four favorite school subjects.

STEP 2 To indicate which item ranks highest in each of the three lists, fill in the blanks of the sentences below. Share one of your responses with classmates.

1. I love to eat _____, _____, and _____. But it is _____ that I would choose if I had to eat only one food for a week.

2. I could watch _____, _____, and _____ quite a few times, but it is _____ that _____.

3. I enjoy _____, I like to study _____, and I also like _____. However, if _____, it is _____ that I would choose.

STEP 3 Make up another list of four favorite things of some other category (e.g., books, sports). Then write a sentence using the pattern in Step 2.

FOCUS 4   *It*-Clefts: Emphasizing Time, Place, and Characters

meaning

EXAMPLES	EXPLANATION
(a) It was **in the early spring** that Sylvia finally felt well enough to make the trip to Budapest.	In narratives such as stories or historical accounts, we may use cleft sentences to emphasize the time, place, characters (or real people) in the narrative.
(b) It was **on a cold day in February, 1860,** that Abraham Lincoln delivered his eloquent Cooper Union speech against slavery.	
(c) It was **in Barbizon** that Rousseau founded the modern school of French landscape painting.	
(d) It was **Shakespeare** who inspired Beethoven's creation of his String Quartet opus 18, number 1.	

ANSWER KEY

Exercise 6   1. It is Canada that borders the United States to the north./It is to the south that Mexico . . .   2. It was in Athens, Greece, that . . .   3. It was Shakespeare who wrote *Romeo and Juliet.*   4. It was America to which Columbus sailed in 1492./It was America that Christopher Columbus sailed to in 1492.   5. It was on the moon that the United States astronauts first landed . . .   6. It was in China that Kublai Khan founded the Yuan dynasty . . .   7. It was the famous *Mona Lisa* that Leonardo da Vinci painted . . .   8. It is the body's nervous system that these are parts of.   9. It was Egypt that Nefertiti ruled . . .

Exercise 7   Step 2: Answers will vary. Sample answers are: 1. fried rice, pizza, chocolate ice cream; lobster   2. *Lost in Translation; Amélie; Crouching Tiger Hidden Dragon; Lord of the Rings;* I would watch if I had only one choice   3. art; English; history; I had to pick my favorite subject; music

EXERCISE 6 [25 minutes]

In Exercise 6 students rewrite sentences with errors, using cleft sentences to highlight the corrected information.

1. Read the directions and example as a class.
2. This content-based exercise requires some cultural knowledge. If you find students who may not be familiar with some of the facts, consider: (1) eliminating those items that could be problematic (e.g., #2); (2) highlighting the part that is false as a clue (e.g., *north* in #1); (3) having students work in groups; (4) having students use reference books or the Internet to research the information.
3. Ask different students to share their sentences with the class, and discuss. See answers on LP page 448.

For more practice, use *Grammar Dimensions 4* Workbook page 223, Exercise 7.

EXPANSION [30 minutes]

In Activity 1 (listening/speaking) on SB page 455 the class is divided into teams and compete in a game show, answering questions posed by the moderator on the audio and using cleft sentences. This activity is a good follow-up to Exercise 6 or Exercise 7.

EXERCISE 7 [25 minutes]

In Exercise 7 students list some favorite foods, movies, and school subjects, and then complete and share cleft sentences describing them.

STEP 1

1. Read the directions for Step 1 as a class.
2. Have students work independently to create their lists of favorite foods, movies, and school subjects.

STEP 2

1. Review Step 2 directions and have a few students recite their own sentence (one student for each topic and sentence style). Have students work independently to complete the sentences using their own information.
2. Have them work in small groups and share their responses.

STEP 3

1. Read the directions as a class.
2. Have students work independently to create another list of favorites and to write a sentence following the pattern in Step 2.
3. Have them share their lists and sentences with a partner.

VARIATION 1

For Step 3 students could create a sentence with blanks modeled after those in Step 2 (but with new verbs: *hate, often* _____, *I rarely* _____, etc.) and give to a classmate to complete.

VARIATION 2

If time permits, you might like to ask a volunteer to conduct a class poll on one of the subjects, such as movies, to see what similarities and differences there are among students.

LESSON PLAN 3

FOCUS 4 [15 minutes]

1. **Lead-in:** Write several well-known dramatic phrases on the board, such as: *It was on a dark and stormy night that . . .; It was in wild jungles of the Amazon that . . .; It was the king himself who . . .*
2. Ask students to identify the focus of each phrase. (*time, place, person*)
3. Read the explanation as a class. Then ask four different volunteers to read the four examples aloud.
4. Ask volunteers to create at least one example of each focus.
5. Answer any questions students might have.

LANGUAGE NOTE

The emphases shown here are most commonly used as stylistic devices in writing and formal speech for both fiction and nonfiction contexts.

EXERCISE 8

Choose one feature to highlight in the following historical facts and write an introductory sentence for a historical narrative about each.

Examples: *It was Cheops who started building the pyramids in Egypt around 2700 BC.*
(Emphasizes person)

It was around 2700 BC that Cheops began building the pyramids in Egypt.
(Emphasizes date)

PERSON	DATE	PLACE	EVENT
Cheops (king)	around 2700 BC	Egypt	started building the Pyramids
Machiavelli (statesman)	1513	Florence, Italy	accused of conspiracy
Chikamatsu Monzaemon (playwright)	1703	Kyoto, Japan	wrote *The Love Suicides at Sonezaki*
John James Audubon (artist)	April 26, 1785	Cayes, Santo Domingo	born
Joaquium Machado de Assis (writer)	1869	Rio de Janeiro, Brazil	married Portuguese aristocrat, Carolina de Novaes
Jean Sibelius (composer)	1892	Helsinki, Finland	wrote the symphonic poem "Kullervo"
Aung San Suu Kyi	1991	Myanmar	received word that she had won the Nobel Prize

EXERCISE 9

Write five autobiographical sentences about yourself, using introductory *it*-cleft structures to highlight places, dates, or events, as in Exercise 8.

Examples: *It was in the spring of 1985 that I was born.*
It was learning to play the piano that made me want to become a musician.

FOCUS 5 — Other Forms of Cleft Sentences

form   meaning

EXAMPLES	EXPLANATIONS
(a) **Who was it** that gave you that information? (b) **Why was it** (that) they decided to move? (c) **When was it** (that) you left Shanghai?	**Wh-Cleft Question** In *Wh*-questions, *it* and *be* are inverted, changing the order to *be* + *it* after the question word (question word + *be* + *it*). In examples (b) and (c), *that* is in parentheses because it is optional.
(d) **Was it out of pity** (that) he let the old man move into his house? (e) **Is it Spanish 3** (that) you're taking this quarter?	**Yes-No Cleft Questions** We must also invert *it* and *be* in yes-no questions.
(f) **What a nice essay it was** (that) you wrote about your father!	**What a + Noun Phrase** This type of cleft sentence (*What a* + noun phrase + *it* + *be*) expresses wonder, delight, admiration, or surprise.
(g) I told you before **(that) it was Marsha who called you**, not Marianne. (h) The President announced **(that) it was because he was ill that he would not be seeking re-election.**	**That Clauses** As you have seen in some exercises in this unit, focus elements may be *that* clauses in reported speech.

ANSWER KEY

Exercise 8   Answers will vary. Possible answers are:
- It was in 1513 that Machiavelli was accused of conspiracy in Florence, Italy.
- It was in Kyoto, Japan, that Chikamatsu Monzaemon wrote *The Love Suicides at Sonezaki*.
- It was on April 26, 1785, that John James Audubon was born in Cayes, Santo Domingo.
- It was Carolina de Novaes whom Joaquium Machado de Assis married in Rio de Janeiro in 1869.
- It was in Helsinki, Finland, that Jean Sibelius wrote the symphonic poem "Kullervo" in 1892.
- It was in 1991 that Aung San Suu Kyi received word that she had won the Nobel Prize.

Exercise 9   Answers will vary.

EXERCISE 8 [20 minutes]

In Exercise 8 students write sentences about historical facts using *It*-clefts, practicing what they have just studied in Focus 4.

1. Read the directions and two examples as a class. Ask a volunteer to restate the example focusing on the place. (*It was in Egypt that . . .*)

2. Have students work in groups of three. Have them take turns creating three different versions of each sentence, each with a different focus. Then, have them choose a different focus for the next sentence.

3. Ask several groups to share their three variations of a sentence with the class. See possible answers on LP page 450.

 For more practice, use *Grammar Dimensions 4* Workbook page 224, Exercise 8 and page 225, Exercise 9.

EXERCISE 9 [20 minutes/homework]

In Exercise 9 students write autobiographical sentences about themselves, using *It*-cleft structures to focus on places, dates, or events. This exercise is a good homework assignment following Exercise 8 and Focus 4.

1. Read the directions and examples as a class.

2. Have students work independently to write at least five sentences about their own lives. Tell them to begin each sentence with an *It*-cleft structure that focuses on time, place, an event or person.

3. Have them share their sentences with a partner.

4. Ask several volunteers to share one or two sentences with the class.

 For more practice, use *Grammar Dimensions 4* Workbook page 226, Exercise 10.

EXPANSION [60 minutes/homework]

Activity 5 (reflection) on SB page 456 is an excellent homework assignment following Exercise 9. In this activity students reflect on and write about goals they have and what they have done or plan to do to accomplish them using cleft sentences.

FOCUS 5 [25 minutes]

Focus 5 concentrates on other forms and meanings of cleft sentences that have not yet been covered in this unit.

1. **Lead-in:** Elicit the nonemphatic forms for (a), (b), and (c), so students can see how these forms differ and how they are constructed. (*Who gave you that information? Why did they decide to move? When did you leave Shanghai?*)

2. Ask a volunteer to read the first three examples. Then, elicit that *it* and *be* are inverted after the *Wh*-question word. Then, read the explanation aloud.

3. Read the two examples and explanation for the second section aloud. Ask students questions to elicit *yes/no* answers like those in the second section: *Tanya, is it in 2010 that you'll be finishing your degree?*

5. Ask a volunteer to read the two examples and explanation for the third section aloud. Ask volunteers to create several other examples of *that*-clauses in reported speech.

6. Answer any questions students might have.

EXERCISE 10

Make up a cleft sentence or question for each situation that follows to emphasize some piece of information.

Example: You told a friend that *The Lord of the Rings* was going to be on TV on Monday night. He thought you said Tuesday and missed seeing it. Tell him what you said.

I told you it was on Monday night that it was going to be on, not Tuesday!

1. You're not sure why a customer service representative at a bank wanted to know your place of birth for a checking account application you were filling out. Ask him.

2. You want to compliment a classmate on a great speech that she gave in class the day before.

3. You've been listening to a history lecture about China and missed hearing the date when the Chinese revolution ended the Manchu dynasty. Politely ask your instructor to tell you the date again.

4. You and your family are watching the news. The newscaster has just announced the cause of a major plane crash to have been an engine failure. A member of your family was distracted and didn't hear this information. Tell him or her what the newscaster said.

5. You have been trying to call a close friend for three hours, but the line has been busy. You wonder who she could be on the line with. When you finally get through, you ask her.

FOCUS 6   Wh-Clefts

EXAMPLES	EXPLANATIONS
(a) **What the world needs** is **peace and justice**. (b) **What we want** is **a woman in the White House**.	Unlike *it*-clefts, *wh*-clefts put focus on information at the end of the sentence.
Starting Point **Be Focus** (c) **Where he goes** is a mystery to me. (d) **What Fay Tomas offers** is honesty and compassion. (e) What she is is a brilliant politician.	The starting point (what we already know or understand) is introduced by a *wh*-word. The focus adds new information. A form of *be* links the two parts of the sentence. When the sentence has two *be* verbs, the second *be* links the two parts. In spoken English, the first *be* verb would be stressed and followed by a pause. (What she *is* is . . .)

EXERCISE 11

Match the phrases in column A with the appropriate word or phrase from column B. Write the letter on the line. Connect them with an appropriate form of *be* and write complete sentences. The first has been done as an example.

Example: 1. *What a lepidopterist specializes in **is** the study of moths and butterflies.*

	A		B
_d_	1. What a lepidopterist specializes in	a.	turkey
_i_	2. What Florida produces	b.	Seoul
_j_	3. What Alexander Graham Bell invented	c.	Portuguese
_g_	4. What Martin Luther King Jr. believed in	d.	the study of moths and butterflies
_h_	5. Where the United States President lives	e.	in Egypt
_b_	6. Where the capital of South Korea is	f.	the 42nd President
_k_	7. What "mph" means	g.	racial equality
_e_	8. Where the Pyramids are located	h.	in the White House
_c_	9. What Brazilians speak	i.	citrus fruit
_a_	10. What most Americans eat at Thanksgiving	j.	the telephone
_f_	11. What Bill Clinton was	k.	miles per hour

ANSWER KEY

Exercise 10 Answers will vary. Possible answers are: 1. I'm not sure why it is that you want to know where I was born.   2. What a great speech it was that you gave the other day!   3. Could you please tell me again when it was that the Manchu Dynasty ended?   4. They said it was because the engine failed that the plane crashed.   5. Who was it that you were on the phone with so long?

EXERCISE 10 [20 minutes]

In Exercise 10 students create cleft sentences to describe a series of realistic situations.

1. Read the directions as a class. Ask a volunteer to read the example aloud.
2. Have students work in pairs. Have one student create a cleft sentence emphasizing some bit of information in the situation. Then, ask the other students to create another sentence focusing on another aspect of the situation.
3. Ask volunteers to share some of their best sentences with the class. See possible answers on LP page 452.

 For more practice, use *Grammar Dimensions 4* Workbook page 226, Exercise 11.

EXPANSION [15 minutes]

To give students additional practice with these other forms and uses of cleft sentences, ask them to role-play one of the situations for the class.

LESSON PLAN 4

FOCUS 6 [20 minutes]

Focus 6 and Focus 7 explore a different kind of cleft: *Wh*-clefts, and how they are used.

1. **Lead-in:** Ask a volunteer to read the first two examples aloud. Elicit a contrast with *It*-clefts: Is the information that is emphasized at the beginning, middle, or end of the sentence? (*the end*)
2. Read the explanation aloud.

3. Read the examples and explanation for the second section aloud.
4. Write several other noncleft statements on the board and have students transform them into *Wh*-clefts: *We want a fair minimum wage for everyone. We need more places for students to study quietly on our campus. We know that global warming may become a serious problem.*
5. Write two categories on the board: *What we want* and *What we need*. Ask students to help you make up sentences to express changes that they would like to see or that they think are needed in your school, in their communities, or in the world in general. Point out that the *be* verb must agree in number with what follows.
6. Answer any questions students might have.

LANGUAGE NOTE

The important distinction here in comparison to *It*-clefts is that these structures focus on information at the end of sentences. The *It*-cleft constructions did the opposite, moving information to the front of sentences for emphasis.

EXERCISE 11 [25 minutes]

In this exercise students apply what they have just learned about *Wh*-clefts by matching and connecting parts of sentences with *Wh*-clefts.

1. Read the directions and example as a class. Ask students to say how many verbs there are in the example sentence (*two*), and which verb links the two parts of the sentences (*be*).
2. Ask students to work independently to match the two columns of phrases and then write complete sentences, connecting the parts with *be*.

3. Have students share and compare answers with a partner.
4. Ask random students to share their answers. See answers on LP page 452.

For more practice, use *Grammar Dimensions 4* Workbook page 227, Exercise 12.

EXPANSION [30 minutes]

In Activity 3 (speaking) on SB page 456 students describe various things that make them happy or sad, using *Wh*-cleft sentences. This activity gives students the opportunity to practice using *Wh*-clefts in communicative contexts following Focus 6 and Exercise 11.

FOCUS 7 | Using *Wh*-Clefts for Emphasis

use

EXAMPLES	EXPLANATION
(a) A: How much money does the director earn? B: **What she earns** is none of your business!	*Wh*-clefts are more common in spoken English than in written English. The *Wh*-phrase often refers to a statement or idea that has been previously expessed.
(b) A: Mozart wrote plays. B: Actually, **what Mozart wrote** was music. Perhaps you mean Moliere.	

EXERCISE 12

Rewrite the underlined words using a *Wh*-cleft. Then act out the conversations with a partner, using appropriate emphasis. The first has been done as an example, with the emphasis in bold italics.

1. **Matt:** Henry drives a Porsche.
   David: Are you kidding? <u>He drives a Ford</u>.
   Matt: Really? He told me it was a Porsche.

   Example: *What he drives is a **Ford**.*

2. **Frank:** Margo tells me you're a painter.
   Duane: That's right.
   Frank: Do you sell many of your paintings?
   Duane: Well, actually, <u>I paint houses</u>.

3. **Nick:** I'm tired. I think I'm going to take a nap.
   Lisa: Nick, <u>you need some exercise</u>. That will make you feel much better than a nap, I think.

4. **Teacher:** Do you have any suggestions about how we can improve this class?
   Fusako: <u>We'd like less homework</u>.
   Ricardo: And <u>we'd prefer a test every week</u>.
   Soraya: And <u>I need more grammar to pass my writing exam</u>.
   Bernadine: And <u>I'd like a different textbook</u>. This one isn't very challenging.

5. **Howard:** Do you know Barry? He writes novels.
   Tessa: I don't think that's true. <u>He writes instruction manuals for computer programs</u>.

6. **Lia:** What are you getting Carol and Bart for their wedding?
   Shelley: <u>They'd really like a microwave</u>, but I can't afford it, so I'm getting them a coffee grinder.

Use Your English

ACTIVITY 1 listening/speaking

CD2 Track 23

Divide into two or three teams for a quiz show competition. Listen to the audio. You will hear questions followed by a choice of three answers. After each question and possible answers, the teacher will stop the audio. Teams will take turns giving answers, which must be in the form of a cleft sentence. For each correct answer, a team will receive two points. Both the answer and the form must be correct to be awarded the points.

Example: Who was president before Bill Clinton?
a. Jimmy Carter b. George Bush c. Ronald Reagan
Correct answer: *It was George Bush who was president before Clinton.*

What does a baseball player get when he or she hits a ball out of the park?
a. an out b. a triple c. a home run
Correct answer: *What the player gets is a home run.*

ACTIVITY 2 writing/speaking

Make up five descriptions that could be used for members of your class. Write your descriptions as verb phrases, similar to Exercise 1. (Be careful not to write any descriptions that would offend anyone or hurt someone's feelings!) Write down who you think best fits the description. Take turns reading your descriptions and have classmates say whom they think matches each, using a cleft sentence. Then tell them whether you agree or disagree. Here is an example to get you started.

Example: A: *tells the funniest stories*
B: *I think it's Josef who does that.*
A: *I agree.*

Exercise 12 2. What I paint is houses. 3. What you need is some exercise. 4. What we'd like is less homework. What we'd prefer is a test every week. What I need is more grammar to pass my writing exam. What I'd like is a different textbook. 5. What he writes are instruction manuals for computer programs. 6. What they'd really like is a microwave.

Activity 1 1. c. It is green that you get when you mix yellow and blue. 2. c. It is in an ocean where you would find sharks. 3. b. It was Beethoven who wrote that symphony. 4. a. It is Seattle that is most known for its rainy weather. 5. c. It is the diaphragm that separates the chest from the

people. 8. b. It is acrophobia that describes an excessive fear of high places. 9. c. It is mass that "m" stands for in physics. 10. c. It was Thomas Edison who invented the light bulb. 11. c. It is the heart that the term cardio refers to. 12. a. It is the Star-Spangled Banner that is being played. 13. b. It is intelligence quotient that I.Q. stands for. 14. a. It is the beginning of the play that you read. 15. b. It is in the game Monopoly that you buy those things. 16. c. It is a clarinet that is being played. 17. b. It is geology that you would study to learn about sedimentology. 18. c. It is in South America that you would find the Amazon Basin.

FOCUS 7 [20 minutes]

Focus 7 illustrates how *Wh*-clefts are often used to make a connection to something another speaker has said.

1. **Lead-in:** Read the explanation aloud first, and then ask two volunteers to read the two examples aloud.

2. Make up a number of false statements on slips of paper such as the one in example (b) (*Mozart wrote plays*). Make up ones that students can easily correct (for example, *We are now learning about gerunds and infinitives.*) Put the slips in a box and have individual students or groups draw them one-by-one and respond with a *Wh*-cleft correction modeled after the answer in (b).

3. Answer any questions students might have.

EXERCISE 12 [25 minutes]

In this final exercise students review the rules governing sentence word order in fronted structures that they have studied in this unit, and correct any errors.

1. Read the directions as a class. Ask two volunteers to read the dialogue in #1 aloud. Then, ask them to reread the dialogue using the *Wh*-cleft.

2. Have students work in pairs to read and revise the dialogues, using *Wh*-clefts.

3. After students have had a chance to read their dialogues with a partner, call on various pairs to act out their dialogues for the rest of the class. Pairs are needed for all but #4, which has 5 speakers. Offer correction of intonation as needed. See answers on LP page 454.

For more practice, use *Grammar Dimensions 4* Workbook page 228, Exercise 13.

UNIT GOAL REVIEW [10 minutes]

Ask students to look at the goals on the opening page of the unit again. Refer to the pages of the unit where information on each goal can be found.

For a grammar quiz review of Units 22–25, refer students to pages 229–231 in the *Grammar Dimensions 4* Workbook.

 For assessment of Unit 25, use *Grammar Dimensions 4* ExamView®.

USE YOUR ENGLISH

The Use Your English activities at the end of the unit contain situations that should naturally elicit the structures covered in the unit. For a more complete discussion of how to use the Use Your English activities, see To the Teacher, LP page xxvi. While students are doing these activities in class, you can circulate and listen to see if they are using the structures accurately. Errors can be corrected after the activity has finished.

ACTIVITY 1 listening/speaking [30 minutes/homework]

CD2 Track 23

In Activity 1 the class is divided into teams and compete in a game show, answering questions posed by the moderator on the audio and using cleft sentences. This activity is a good follow-up to Exercise 6 or Exercise 7 on SB page 448, either for in-class work or as homework. Note that the former CD track number (40) is incorrectly listed in the student book.

1. Discuss what game shows students enjoy watching on TV. Does anyone watch knowledge games such as *Jeopardy*?

2. Read the directions as a class. Ask two volunteers to read the two examples aloud.

3. Divide the class into two teams. Ask a volunteer to be the record keeper, and write down exactly how each team responds to the questions.

4. Have students listen to the first question on the audio. Stop the program, and give each team a chance to respond. Remind them that they must use cleft sentences in their responses.

5. Continue, stopping the audio after each question, and having both teams respond.

6. Review answers with the class, and announce the winner. See answers on LP page 454.

VARIATION

If you prefer not to have a team game, have students write answers individually on a separate piece of paper.

ACTIVITY 2 writing/speaking [45 minutes]

In this entertaining activity students write descriptions of their classmates and then others guess who is being described, using cleft sentences. This activity is a good follow-up to Exercise 1 on SB pages 442–443.

1. Read the directions as a class. Ask two volunteers to read the sample dialogue aloud. Ask two volunteers to give a verb phrase describing someone in class, and have others guess who that person is, using cleft sentences.

2. Have students work in pairs to create ten descriptions (five each) of their classmates using verb phrases such as they used in Exercise 1.

3. Have students work in groups of six and take turns reading their descriptions aloud. The others should then guess, and also say whether they agree or disagree with the description.

4. Ask several volunteers to read their best descriptions to the class, and have the whole class guess.

What makes you happy? Sad? Angry? Annoyed? Puzzled or confused? With a partner, interview each other to find out the answers to these questions. If you wish, make up additional ones. Report a few of your findings to the class.

Examples: *What really makes Julie annoyed is when people throw litter on the beach.*
What makes John happy is having lots of time to pursue his hobby of photography.

 **ACTIVITY** **4** research on the web

 Find out more about how people believe birth order influences personality. Using the keywords "birth order" and "personality" on an Internet search engine such as Google® or Yahoo®, find two or three articles on the topic. Summarize your findings by writing a list of the characteristics you find in addition to ones given in this unit. Use *it*-cleft structures to introduce your statements as was done in the Opening Task.

 **ACTIVITY** **5** reflection

Reflect on five goals that you have for any area of your life. Then state what you have either done or plan to do in the future for the purpose of achieving these goals. In the chart below, state the goal in the left-hand column. State what you are doing or will do to achieve the goal in the right-hand column, using an *it*-cleft structure expression that emphasizes cause or purpose. Two examples are given.

Goal	Activity to Attain Goal
I want to go to law school after graduation.	*It is for this reason* that I am majoring in history.
I would like to improve my tennis game.	*It is for this purpose* that I plan to run at least two miles three times a week.

USE YOUR ENGLISH

ACTIVITY 3 speaking
[30 minutes]

In this activity students describe various things that make them happy or sad, using *Wh*-cleft sentences. It is a good activity for students after Exercise 11 on SB page 453.

1. Read the directions and examples as a class.
2. Have students choose a person—themselves, or a family member—who exhibits some of the personality traits associated with birth order that are outlined in the Opening Task. Ask them to write a paragraph about the topic using cleft sentences.
3. Collect the papers during the next class and give students feedback on their writing.

ACTIVITY 4 research on the web
[60 minutes/homework]

In this activity students research additional information about birth order and personality on the Internet. They then write about their findings, using *It*-cleft structures to introduce their statements. This activity is a good homework assignment following Exercise 4 on SB page 447.

1. Read the directions as a class.
2. Have students search the Internet for additional information about birth order and personality. Ask them to reread the information contained in the Opening Task, and make sure they find new information on the Internet.
3. Ask them to summarize their findings by creating a list of the additional characteristics using *It*-cleft structures to introduce their statements.
4. During the next class, ask a few volunteers to share their finding with the class, and discuss.

ACTIVITY 5 reflection
[60 minutes/homework]

In Activity 5 students reflect on and write about goals they have and what they have done or plan to do to accomplish them, using cleft sentences. This is an excellent homework assignment following Exercise 9 on SB page 450.

1. Read the directions as a class. Ask a volunteer to read the two examples aloud.
2. Ask students to think about at least five goals they have for themselves in any area—or in several different areas—of their lives. Ask them to write down what they have done or plan to do to accomplish them using cleft sentences.
3. Have students work in small groups during the next class and take turns talking about their goals, their achievements toward realizing them, and what they plan to do in the future to reach them.
4. Ask a few volunteers to share some goals with the class, and discuss.

APPENDICES

Appendix 1A   Present Time Frame

FORM	EXAMPLE	USE	MEANING
SIMPLE PRESENT base form of verb or base form of verb + -s	Many plants require a lot of sun to thrive.	timeless truths	now
	Luis works every day except Sunday.	habitual actions	
	We think you should come with us.	mental perceptions and emotions	
	Veronica owns the house she lives in.	possession	
PRESENT PROGRESSIVE am/is/are + present participle (verb + -ing)	They are just finishing the race.	actions in progress	in progress now
	She is picking straw-berries this morning.	duration	
	Someone is pounding nails next door.	repetition	
	My friend is living in Nova Scotia for six months.	temporary activities	
	I am changing the oil in my car right now.	uncompleted actions	
PRESENT PERFECT have/has + past participle (verb + -ed or irregular verbs)	She has attended the university for four years; she will graduate in June.	situations that began in the past, continue to the present	in the past but related to now in some way
	I have read that book too. Did you like it?	actions completed in the past but related to the present	
	The movie has just ended.	actions recently completed	

(Continued)

Appendix 1A

FORM	EXAMPLE	USE	MEANING
PRESENT PERFECT PROGRESSIVE *have/has* + present participle (verb + *-ing*)	I have been dialing the airline's number for hours it seems. I can't believe it's still busy.	repeated or continuous actions that are incomplete	up until and including now
	This weekend Michelle has been participating in a job fair which ends on Sunday afternoon.		

Appendix 1B   Past Time Frame

FORM	EXAMPLE	USE	MEANING
SIMPLE PRESENT	So yesterday he tells me he just thought of another way to get rich quick.	past event in informal narrative	at a certain time in the past
SIMPLE PAST verb + *-ed* or irregular past form	We planted the vegetable garden last weekend.	events that took place at a definite time in the past	at a certain time in the past
	Pei-Mi taught for five years in Costa Rica.	events that lasted for a time in the past	
	I studied English every year when I was in high school.	habitual or repeated actions in the past	
	We thought we were heading in the wrong direction.	past mental perceptions and emotions	
	Jose had a piano when he lived in New York.	past possessions	
PAST PROGRESSIVE *was/were* + present participle (verb + *-ing*)	When I talked with him last night, Sam was getting ready for a trip.	events in progress at a specific time in the past	in progress at a time in the past

(Continued)

Appendix 1B

FORM	EXAMPLE	USE	MEANING
PAST PERFECT *had* + past participle (verb + *-ed* or irregular form)	My parents **had lived** in Hungary before they moved to France.	actions or states that took place before another time in the past	before a certain time in the past
PAST PERFECT PROGRESSIVE *had* + *been* + present participle (verb + *-ing*)	We **had been hurrying** to get to the top of the mountain when the rain started.	incomplete events taking place before other past events	before a certain time in the past
	I **had been working** on the last math problem when the teacher instructed us to turn in our exams.	incomplete events interrupted by other past events	up until a certain time in the past

Appendix 1C   Future Time Frame

FORM	EXAMPLE	USE	MEANING
SIMPLE PRESENT	Takiko **graduates** next week.	definite future plans or schedules	already planned or expected in the future
	When Guangping **completes** her graduate program, she will look for a research job in Taiwan.	events with future time adverbials (*before, after, when*) in dependent clauses	already planned or expected in the future
PRESENT PROGRESSIVE	I **am finishing** my paper tomorrow night	future intentions	already planned or expected in the future
	Amit **is taking** biochemistry for two quarters next year.	scheduled events that last for a period of time	already planned or expected in the future

(Continued)

FORM	MEANING	USE	EXAMPLE
BE GOING TO FUTURE *am/is/are going to* + base verb	The train is **going to** arrive any minute.	probable and immediate future events	at a certain time in the future
	I am **going to** succeed no matter what it takes!	strong intentions	
	Tomorrow you're **going to** be glad that you are already packed for your trip.	predictions about future situations	
	We are **going to** have a barbecue on Sunday night.	future plans	
SIMPLE FUTURE *will* + base verb	It **will** probably **snow** tomorrow.	probable future events	
	I **will give** you a hand with that package; it looks heavy.	willingness/promises	
	Tomorrow **will be** a better day.	predictions about future situations	
FUTURE PROGRESSIVE *will* + *be* + present participle (verb + *-ing*)	I **will be interviewing** for the bank job in the morning.	events that will be in progress at a time in the future	in progress at a certain time in the future
	Mohammed **will be studying** law for the next three years.	future events that will last for a period of time	
FUTURE PERFECT *will* + *have* + past participle (verb + *-ed* or irregular verb)	He **will have finished** his degree before his sister starts hers in 2001.	before a certain time in the future	future events happening before other future events
FUTURE PERFECT PROGRESSIVE *will* + *have* + *been* + present participle (verb + *-ing*)	By the year 2000, my family **will have been living** in the U.S. for ten years.	up until a certain time in the future	continuous and/or repeated actions continuing into the future

All passive verbs are formed with *be* + or *get* + past participle.

SIMPLE PRESENT *am/is/are* (or *get*) + past participle	That movie **is reviewed** in today's newspaper. The garbage **gets picked** up once a week.
PRESENT PROGRESSIVE *am/is/are* + *being* (or *getting*) + past participle	The possibility of life on Mars **is being explored.** We **are getting asked** to do too much!
SIMPLE PAST *was/were* (or *got*) + past participle	The butterflies **were observed** for five days. Many homes **got destroyed** during the fire.
PAST PROGRESSIVE *was/were* + *being* (or *getting*) + past participle	The Olympics **were being broadcast** worldwide. She **was getting beaten** in the final trials.
PRESENT PERFECT *has/have* + *been* (or *gotten*) + past participle	The information **has been sent.** Did you hear he's **gotten fired** from his job?
PRESENT PERFECT PROGRESSIVE *has* + *been* + *being* (or *getting*) + past participle	This store **has been being remodeled** for six months now! I wonder if they'll ever finish. It looks as though the tires on my car **have been getting worn** by these bad road conditions.
PAST PERFECT *had* + *been* (or *gotten*) + past participle	The National Anthem **had** already **been sung** when we entered the baseball stadium. He was disappointed to learn that the project hadn't **gotten completed** in his absence.
FUTURE *will* + *be* (or *get*) + past participle *be going to* + past participle	The horse races **will be finished** in an hour. The rest of the corn **will get harvested** this week. The election results **are going to be announced** in a few minutes.
FUTURE PERFECT *will* + *have* + *been* (or *gotten*) + past participle	I bet most of the food **will have been eaten** by the time we get to the party. The unsold magazines **will have gotten sent** back to the publishers by now.
FUTURE PERFECT PROGRESSIVE *will* + *have* + *been* + *being* (or *getting*) + past participle	Our laundry **will have been getting dried** for over an hour by the time we come back. I'm sure it will be ready to take out then. NOTE: The *be* form of this passive tense is quite rare. Even the *get* form is not very common.

(Continued)

PRESENT MODAL VERBS
modal (*can, may, should,* etc.) + be (or *get*) + past participle

| A different chemical could be substituted in this experiment.
| Don't stay outside too long. You may get burned by the blazing afternoon sun.

PAST MODAL VERBS
modal (*can, may, should,* etc.) + *have* + been (or *gotten*) + past participle

| All of our rock specimens should have been identified since the lab report is due.
| The file might have gotten erased through a computer error.

APPENDIX 3   Sentence Connectors

MEANING	CONNECTORS
Addition Simple addition Emphatic addition Intensifying addition	also, in addition, furthermore, moreover, what is more (what's more), as well, besides in fact, as a matter of fact, actually
Alternative	on the other hand, alternatively
Exemplifying	for example, e.g., for instance, especially, in particular, to illustrate, as an example
Identifying	namely, specifically
Clarifying	that is, i.e., in other words, I mean
Similarity	similarly, likewise, in the same way
Contrast	however, in contrast, on the other hand, in fact
Concession	even so, however, nevertheless, nonetheless, despite (+ *noun phrase*), in spite of (+ *noun phrase*), on the other hand
Effects/Results	accordingly, as a result, as a result of (+ *noun phrase*), because of (+ *noun phrase*), due to (+ *noun phrase*), consequently, therefore, thus, hence
Purpose	in order to (+ *verb*), with this in mind, for this purpose

Appendix 4A Overview of Gerunds and Infinitives

Examples	Explanations
	Infinitives (to + verb) or gerunds (verb + ing) can have various functions in a sentence:
(a) **To know** many languages would thrill me. (b) **Speaking English** is fun.	• subject
(c) His dream was **to sail around the world**. (d) Her hobby is **weaving baskets**.	• subject complement
(e) Paco hopes **to see the play**. (f) Carol remembered **mailing the package**.	• object
(g) By **studying hard**, you can enter a good school. (h) Thank you for **helping me**.	• object of preposition (gerunds)
(i) I don't understand the need **to take a ten-minute break**.	• noun complement (infinitives)
(j) The instruction **to wear safety goggles** has saved many people's eyes.	
(k) I am sorry **to inform you** of the delay. (l) They were pleased **to meet you**.	• adjective complement (infinitives following adjectives)

Appendix 4B Verbs Followed by Infinitives and Gerunds

to + verb

EXAMPLE: Julia hates to be late.

List A

As mentioned in Unit 18, Focus 4, some of the verbs in List A may also take gerund if an actual, vivid or fulfilled action is intended. (Example: Julia hates being late.)

VERBS OF EMOTION

care	loathe	agree	plan
desire	love	choose	prefer
hale	regret	decide	prepare
like	yearn	deserve	propose
		expect	refuse
		hope	want
		intend	wish
		need	

VERBS OF CHOICE OR INTENTION

VERBS OF INITIATION, COMPLETION, AND INCOMPLETION

begin	manage	demand	swear
cease	neglect	offer	threaten
commence	start	promise	vow
fail	try		
get	undertake		
hesitate			

VERBS OF REQUEST AND THEIR RESPONSES

VERBS OF MENTAL ACTIVITY

forget	learn	appear	seem
know how	remember	happen	tend

INTRANSITIVE VERBS

OTHER VERBS

afford (can't afford)	continue	
arrange	pretend	
claim	wait	

List B

Subject + *to* + verb

EXAMPLE: She reminded us to be quiet.

VERBS OF COMMUNICATION

advise	permit		
ask*	persuade		
beg*	promise*		
challenge	remind		
command	require		
convince	tell		
forbid	warn		
invite	urge		
order			

OTHER VERBS

expect*	prepare*
trust	want*

* Can follow pattern A also.

VERBS OF INSTRUCTION

encourage	teach
help	train
instruct	

VERBS OF CAUSATION

allow	get
cause	hire
force	

List C

Verb + *-ing*

EXAMPLE: Trinh enjoys playing tennis.

Note that when the subject of the gerund is stated, it is in possessive form.

We enjoyed his telling us about his adventures.

VERBS OF INITIATION, COMPLETION AND INCOMPLETION

avoid	give up
begin	postpone
cease	quit
complete	risk
delay	start
finish	stop
get through	try

VERBS OF COMMUNICATION

admit	mention
advise	recommend
deny	suggest
discuss	urge
encourage	

(Continued)

VERBS OF MENTAL ACTIVITY

anticipate	recall
consider	remember
forget	see (can't see)
imagine	understand
miss	resent
prefer	resist
regret	tolerate
can't stand	

VERBS OF ONGOING ACTIVITY

continue
can't help
practice
keep
keep on

VERBS OF EMOTION

appreciate
dislike
enjoy
hate
like
love
mind (don't mind)

APPENDIX 5   Preposition Clusters

in + noun + of

in case of
in charge of
in place of
in lieu of
in favor of

on + noun + of

on account of
on behalf of
on top of
on grounds of

in + the + noun + of

in the course of
in the event of
in the habit of
in the name of
in the process of

on + the + noun + of

on the advice of
on the basis of
on the part of
on the strength of
on the face of

Other Combinations

in by means of
with respect to

in return for
in addition to

at odds with
for the sake of

with the exception of

Appendix 6A General Types of Relative Clauses

Example:

   S   S

(a) The contract that was signed
yesterday is now valid.

   S   O

(b) The contract that he signed
yesterday is now valid.

   O   S

(c) I have not read the contract that was
signed yesterday.

   O   O

(d) I have not read the contract that he
signed yesterday.

Noun Phrase in Main Clause	Relative Pronoun in Relative Clause
Subject	Subject
Subject	Object
Object	Subject
Object	Object

Appendix 6B Relative Clauses Modifying Subjects

Example:

(a) A person who/that sells
houses is a realtor.

(b) The secretary whom/that
she hired is very experienced.

(c) The employees to whom
she denied a pay raise have
gone on strike.

(d) Clerks whose paychecks
were withheld must go to
the payroll office.

(e) The mansions that/which
were sold last week were
expensive.

(f) The computer that/which
they purchased operated
very efficiently.

(g) The division whose sales
reach the million-dollar
point will win a bonus.

Types of Noun in Main Clause	Relative Pronouns	Function of Relative Pronoun
person	who/that	subject
	whom/that	object of verb
	whom	object of preposition
	whose (relative determiner)	possessive determiner
thing or animal	that/which	subject
	that/which	object of verb
	whose (relative determiner)	possessive determiner

Appendix 6C   Patterns of Relative Adverbial Clauses

RELATIVE ADVERBS WITH HEAD NOUNS

HEAD NOUN	RELATIVE ADVERB	CLAUSE
a place	where	you can relax
a time	when	I can call you
a reason	why	you should attend

RELATIVE ADVERBS WITHOUT HEAD NOUNS

RELATIVE ADVERB	CLAUSE
Where	he lives
When	the term starts
Why	I called
How	she knows

HEAD NOUNS WITHOUT RELATIVE ADVERBS

HEAD NOUN	CLAUSE
the place	we moved to
the time	I start school
the reason	they left
the way	you do this

Appendix 7A Verb Complements

that	for ... to	's gerund	Type
(a) **That** Tom spent the whole day shopping surprised us.	(b) **For** Tom **to** spend the whole day shopping surprised us.	(c) Tom's **spending** the whole day shopping surprised us.	SUBJECT basic order
(d) It surprised us **that** Tom spent the whole day shopping.	(e) It would surprise us **for** Tom **to** spend the whole day shopping.	(f) It surprised us— Tom's **spending** the whole day shopping. (When this structure occurs, there is a pause between the main clause and the complement.)	complement after *it* + verb
(g) We hope **that** the children take the bus.	(h) We hope **for** the children **to** take the bus.	(i) not applicable	OBJECT indicative form
(j) Ms. Sanchez suggests **that** he wait in the lobby.	(k) not applicable	(l) not applicable	subjunctive form

Appendix 7B Adjective Complements

that	for ... to	's gerund	Type
(a) **That** Lisa went to the meeting was important.	(b) **For** Lisa to go to the meeting was important.	(c) Lisa's **going** to the meeting was important.	SUBJECT basic order
(d) It was important **that** Lisa went to the meeting.	(e) It was important **for** Lisa to go to the meeting.	(f) It was important— Lisa's **going** to the meeting. (When this structure occurs there is a pause between the main clause and the complement.)	complement after *it* + verb

(Continued)

Appendix 7B   Adjective Complements

that	*for . . . to*	*'s gerund*	*Type*
(g) Mr. Walker is happy that she works at the company.	(h) Mr. Walker is happy for her to work at the company. (This structure only occurs with a subset of adjectives like *ready, anxious, happy, eager,* etc.)	(i) not applicable	PREDICATE indicative form
(j) Chong demands that she be on time.	(k) not applicable	(l) not applicable	subjunctive form

Base Form	Simple Past	Past Participle
arise	arose	arisen
awake	awoke	awoken
beat	beat	beaten
become	became	become
begin	began	begun
bite	bit	bitten
bleed	bled	bled
blow	blew	blown
break	broke	broken
bring	brought	brought
build	built	built
buy	bought	bought
catch	caught	caught
choose	chose	chosen
come	came	come
cost	cost	cost
cut	cut	cut
do	did	done
draw	drew	drawn
dream	dreamt/dreamed	dreamt/dreamed
drink	drank	drunk
drive	drove	driven
eat	ate	eaten
fall	fell	Fallen
feel	felt	felt
fight	fought	fought
find	found	found
fly	flew	flown
forget	forgot	forgotten
forgive	forgave	forgiven
freeze	froze	frozen
get	got	gotten
give	gave	given
go	went	gone
grow	grew	grown
hang	hung	hung
hear	heard	heard
hide	hid	hidden
hit	hit	hit
hold	held	held
hurt	hurt	hurt
keep	kept	kept
know	knew	known
lay	laid	laid
lead	led	led

Base Form	Simple Past	Past Participle
leave	left	left
let	let	let
lie	lay	lain
lose	lost	lost
make	made	made
mean	meant	meant
meet	met	met
pay	paid	paid
put	put	put
read	read	read
ride	rode	ridden
ring	rang	rung
rise	rose	risen
run	ran	run
say	said	said
see	saw	seen
sell	sold	sold
send	sent	sent
set	set	set
shake	shook	shaken
shine	shone/shined	shone/shined
shut	shut	shut
sing	sang	sung
sink	sank	sunk
sit	sat	sat
sleep	slept	slept
speak	spoke	spoken
spend	spent	spent
stand	stood	stood
steal	stole	stolen
strike	struck	struck
swing	swung	swung
swim	swam	swum
take	took	taken
teach	taught	taught
tear	tore	torn
tell	told	told
think	thought	thought
throw	threw	thrown
understand	understood	understood
wake	woke	woken
wear	wore	worn
win	won	won
wind	wound	wound
write	wrote	written

ANSWER KEY
(for puzzles and problems only)

UNIT 6

Opening Task Answer Key, page 108

Answers and Explanations

Match each answer with one of the eight statements in Step 1 on page 109.

___ a. The statement about the extent to which speakers look at their partners is true. Women do look at their partners more than men do. One reason for this may be that women often listen more.

___ b. This statement is true. Women generally display more animated behavior. Such behavior may include facial expressions, intensity of eye contact and gestures.

___ c. Most studies indicate that women are more likely to reveal personal information about themselves, so this statement is true . However, in work situations, a subordinate may reveal more information to a superior than the superior reveals to a subordinate; in these situations, the pattern may be reversed.

___ d. The popular belief that women talk more than men is actually not true, so this statement is false. In classrooms, offices, group discussions and two-person conversations, men talk more than women do. The tendency for men to talk more has been revealed in experimental research studies.

___ e. This is another false statement as men are more likely than women to answer questions that were not asked of them.

___ f. The distributions of interruptions are even when women talk with women and when men talk with men. However, when men talk with women, research shows that men tend to interrupt much more than women do, so this claim can be considered true.

___ g. If you guessed false, you are correct! Research indicates that women are much more likely to smile in many different social situations than men. This does not mean women are happier in such situations, but they return smiles more frequently when people smile at them.

___ h. Research at a hospital and in manufacturing firms showed that female and male managers did not differ in their friendliness to subordinates. In these contexts, women managers were not more emotionally open, so the statement is false.

UNIT 25

Answers of Opening Task (page 440)

a) oldest, b) middle, c) only, d) youngest, e) middle, f) only, g) oldest, h) youngest, i) oldest, j) only, k) youngest, l) middle

EXERCISES (second parts)

List of Words for Short-Term Memory Experiment (page 61)

book, hand, street, tree, sand, rose, box, face, pencil, nail, pan, dog, door, school, shoe, cloud, watch, lamp, stair, glue, bottle, card, movie, match, hammer, dance, hill, basket, house, river

Definition of the Serial Position Effect (page 61)

If a person is asked to recall a list of words in any order immediately after the list is presented, recall of words at the beginning and end of the list is usually best; words in the middle of a list are not retained as well. This observation is based on a model of learning that assumes the first words are remembered well because they are rehearsed and because short term memory at that point is relatively empty. The last words are remembered well because they are still in the short-term memory' if the person tries to recall immediately.

Opening Task (page 134)

Student B

Guess the Correct Answer:

1. (a) seahorse, (b) boa constrictor, (c) Canada goose
2. (a) *War and Peace* by Leo Tolstoy, (b) *The Great Gatsby* by F. Scott Fitzgerald, (c) *Pride and Prejudice* by Jane Austen
3. (a) Thomas Edison, (b) Alexander Graham Bell, (c) Robert Fulton
4. (a) mucker, (b) hooker inspector, (c) belly builder

Create a Definition: (* indicates the correct answer)

5. a fly
   It is actually classified as a beetle.
   (a) dragonfly, (b) flycatcher, *(c) firefly
6. a person
   He or she pretends to be someone else.
   (a) cornball, *(b) imposter, (c) daytripper

(Continued)

7. a jar

Ancient Greeks and Romans used it to carry wine.

*(a) amphora, (b) amulet, (c) aspartame

8. a piece of clothing

It is composed of loose trousers gathered about the ankles,

(a) bodice, (b) causerie, *(c) bloomers

UNIT 8

Opening Task (page 148)

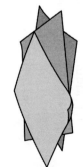

Paper
About A.D. 105

Magnetic Compas
1100s

Television
1920s

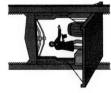

Safety Elevator
1853

Typewriter
1867

Laser
1960

Telephone
1876

Gasoline Automobile
1885

Airplane
1903

CREDITS

Photo Credits

page 267: © Jenny Matthews/Alamy
page 277: © Design Pics Inc./Alamy
page 280: (Top to Bottom) © Hulton-Deutsch Collection/CORBIS, © Fritz Fischer/dpa/Corbis
page 281: © Bettmann/CORBIS
page 288: © Gabe Palmer/Alamy
page 289: © Dirk v. Mallinckrodt/Alamy
page 295: (Top Left) © Photos.com/RF, (Top Right) © Photos.com/RF, (Bottom) © Randy Wells/Stone/Getty
page 301: © Nancy G Photography/Alamy
page 310: © Thomas Kitchin & Victoria Hurst/First Light/Getty
page 314: (Top) © AP Photo/Gregory Bull, (Bottom) © AP Photo/Peter Dejong
page 317: © Brand X Pictures/Alamy
page 323: © AP Photo/IMF, Stephen Jaffe, HO
page 330: © Philip Scalia/Alamy
page 341: © POPPERFOTO/Alamy
page 348: © AP photo
page 352: (Top to Bottom) © POPPERFOTO/Alamy, © North Wind Picture Archives/Alamy, © Photo Japan/Alamy
page 360: © John Mottershaw/Alamy
page 369: © Yellow Dog Productions/The Image Bank/Getty
page 372: (Top) © BananaStock/Alamy/RF, (Bottom) © Kevin Schafer/Alamy
page 388: © Andrew Linscott/Alamy
page 390: © Pictorial Press Ltd/Alamy
page 398: © Thinkstock/Alamy/RF
page 406: (Left) © Jennie Hart/Alamy, (Right) © altrendo images/Altrendo/Getty
page 411: © PhotoAlto/Alamy/RF
page 415: © AP Photo/Scott Audette
page 418: (Top) © Hulton Archive/Getty, (Bottom) © RON PHILLIPS/Stringer/AFP/Getty Images
page 421: © Scottish Viewpoint/Alamy
page 431: © Content Mine International/Alamy
page 436: © Pictorial Press Ltd/Alamy
page 440: © Stockdisc Classic/Alamy/RF
page 443: © Christina Kennedy/Alamy
page 449: © Visual Arts Library (London)/Alamy
page 452: © Sarma Ozols/Stone/Getty

Fine Art Credits

Unit 8
page 162: Illustration on page 162, "Eviction" is reprinted by permission of the artist Diedre Luzwick.

Text Credits

Unit 1
page 5: From Studs Terkel (1988). *The Great Divide.* New York: Pantheon Books.
page 10 (Audio): From Rigoberta Menchu (1994). *I, Rigoberta: An Indian Woman in Guatemala,* Elisabeth Burgos-Debray (Ed.), New York: Verso.

Unit 2

page 12: From Farah Ahmedi with Tamim Ansary (2005), *The Story of My Life: An Afghan Girl on the Other Side of the Sky*. New York: Simon & Schuster.

page 13: From Mike Rose (2005). *Lives on the Boundary*. New York: Penguin Books.

page 16: (Top) From James McBride (2006). *The Color of Water: A Black Man's Tribute to His White Mother*. New York: Penguin, 2006, pp. 80-81.

page 16: (Bottom) From Mitch Albom (1997). *Tuesdays with Morrie: An Old Man, A Young Man and Life's Greatest Lesson*. New York: Doubleday, p. 80.

page 19: From Annie Dillard(1974). *Pilgrim at Tinker Creek*. New York: Bantam.

page 22: From James Thurber (1955). *Thurber's Dogs, A Collection of the Master's Dogs, Written and Drawn, Real and Imaginary, Living and Long Ago*. New York: Simon and Schuster.

page 23: Reprinted with permission from J. Michael Kennedy, "It's the Hottest Little Ol' Race in Texas," *Los Angeles Times*, September 2, 1991.

page 30: Reprinted by permission of the U.F.S. Inc.

page 31: From Edith Hamilton, *Mythology*. Copyright 1942 by Edith Hamilton. Copyright renewed 1969 by Dorian Fielding Reid and Doris Fielding Reid. By permission of Little, Brown and Company.

page 35 (Audio): From Oliver Sacks (1987). *The Man Who Mistook his Wife for a Hat and Other Clinical Tales*. New York: Harper and Row.

Unit 3

page 39: From *Gallup News Service*, June 3, 2005.

page 43: From *Gallup News Service*, June 3, 2005 and July 21, 1999. www.gallup.com; *The Bookseller*, April 11, 2003 p. 27(3).

page 44: Adapted from Kate Allen and John Ingulsrud, "Manga Literacy: Popular Culture and the Reading Habits of Japanese College Students," *Journal of Adolescent & Adult Literacy*, May 2003, v46, p. 674 (10).

page 52: Information from *Gallup News Service*, June 3, 2005 and July 21, 1999. www.gallup.com.

page 53: Adapted from *Reading At Risk: A Survey of Literary Reading in America*. June 2004. National Endowment for the Arts.

Unit 4

page 67: Reprinted with permission from Rosie Mestel, "Swallowing a Lie May Aid in Weight Loss, Research Suggests," *Los Angeles Times*, August 2, 2005.

page 70: Adapted from Marianne Szedgedy-Maszak, "For True Fulfillment, Seek Satisfaction, Not Happiness," *Los Angeles Times*, September 5, 2005.

page 75: From http://www.guinnessworldrecord.com/ (Accessed June, 15, 2006).

page 77: Adapted from "Decoding of Microbe's Genes Sheds Light on Odd Form of Life," *Los Angeles Times*, August 8, 1996.

Unit 5

page 84: Adapted from P. Master (1996). *Systems in English Grammar*. Englewood Cliffs, New Jersey: Prentice-Hall Regents.

page 95: Adapted from P. Master. "Teahing the English Article System, Part II: Generic Versus Specific." *English Teaching Forum*. July 1988.

page 103: (Top) Adapted from J. Mann (1991). "Global AIDS: Revolution, Paradigm, Solidarity." In O. Peterson, (ed.), *Representative American Speeches*. New York: The H.W. Wilson Co.

page 103: (Bottom) Adapted from S. Hall (1987). *Invisible Frontiers*. New York: The Atlantic Monthly Press.

page 104: Adapted from "Monterey Pine Struggles to Survive." In *UC MexUS News*, University of California Institute for Mexico and the United States (UC MEXUS), UC Riverside, Number 43, Spring 2006, p. 19.

Unit 6

page 109: Adapted from Gender Communications Quiz, Georgia Department of Education, http://www.glc.k12.ga.us/pandp/guidance/schoices/sc-f20.htm. (Retrieved December 15, 2005)

page 112: From Deborah Tannen (1990). *You Just Don't Understand: Women and Men in Conversation*, Harper Collins Publishers.

page 124: Reprinted by permission. © NAS North America Syndicate.

Unit 7

page 138: From Charles Keller (1979). *The Best of Rube Goldberg*. Rube Goldberg™ and © Rube Goldberg Inc. Distributed by United Media.

Unit 9

page 169: The Specialty Travel Index, http://www.specialtytravel.com/ (Accessed January 4, 2005).

page 176 (Audio): Serrano, M.L. (1972) *El Escorial*. Madrid: Editorial Patrimonio Nacional.

Unit 12

page 211: (Top) Adapted from Maria Leach (1956). *The Beginning: Creation Myths around the World*, New York: Funk & Wagnalls.

page 211: (Bottom) Adapted from "Oceania/Polynesia Creation Myths," *Encyclopedia Mythica*, www.pantheon.org/articles/o/oceania_polynesia_creation_myths.html.

page 236 (Audio-version 1): Adapted from Edith Hamilton (1969) *Mythology*. New York, Little, Brown & Co.

page 236 (Audio-version 2): Adapted from H.A. Guerber (1992). *Greece and Rome (Myths and Legends Series)*. London: Brackenbooks.

Unit 13

page 245: From John Naisbitt and Patricia Aburdene. Megatrends 2000 Copyright © 1990 By Megatrends LTD.

page 249: From Stephen Hawking (1990). *A Brief History of Time: From the Big Bang to Black Holes*, New York: Bantam.

page 255: From "Long Bets: Accountable Predictions," www.longbets.org (Retrieved June 25, 2006).

page 270: From Colin Woodward (2005). Warming up the seas, Earth Action Network, Inc.

page 276: From Fei Ji (2004). "A Suffering Musician," in Kaplan/*Newsweek* "My Turn" Essay Competition.

page 276: Adapted from Michelle Ng (2004). "My Hands," in Kaplan/*Newsweek* "My Turn" Essay Competition.

pages 276–277: From Isaac Asimov (1974) *Earth: Our Crowded Spaceship*, Greenwich, CT: Fawcett.

Unit 17

page 321: Adapted from U.S. Immigration and Naturalization Service and Bureau of U.S. Citizenship and Immigration Service sources, (2006).

Unit 18

page 348: Adapted from D. Stewart, "The Floating World at Zero G," *Air and Space* (August/September 1991) p. 38.

Unit 20

page 382: From Michael W. Fox, "Inhuman Society: The American Way of Exploiting Animals" (1990). New York: St. Martin's Press, p. 46.

Unit 23

pages 406–407: Reprinted by permission. VALS™ SRI Consulting Business Intelligence (SRIC-BI), http://www.sric-bi.com/VALS (Accessed on June, 22, 2006).

Unit 24

page 435: Adapted from http://www.screenwriting.info/01.php

CREDITS

INDEX

WORKBOOK ANSWER KEY

Unit 1

Verb Tenses in Written and Spoken Communication

EXERCISE 1 [page 1]

(1) arrived   (2) had never been   (3) is studying
(4) expects; will be working   (5) doesn't work out;
'll go   (6) has been living/has lived   (7) has; closes/is
closed; has   (8) have ever been; was; invited   (9) Have
you ever thought   (10) 'll go   (11) had spoken;
had been trying   (12) has given up   (13) will have
known

EXERCISE 2 [page 2]

The explanation for any discrepancy will vary.
Discrepancies will probably occur in regard to aspect
rather than time frame.

EXERCISE 3 [page 3]

Answers will vary. Possible answers are:
1. . . . I thought I could do anything.   2. . . . there
will be a colony established on the moon.   3. . . . a fire
broke out at the Mayfair restaurant.   4. . . . she has
lost a lot of weight.   5. . . . my parents are flying to
Brazil.   6. . . . there was peace and prosperity throughout
China.   7. . . . the cure for many diseases will be found.
8. . . . I heard a noise outside the door.   9. . . . I'll
be taking some time off to travel.   10. . . . the seas
rose several inches.   11. . . . our family has been
operating a small manufacturing business.   12. . . . the
Normans invaded England.   13. . . . I will have left
the country.   14. . . . we have studied more than a
hundred idioms.   15. . . . I will probably be interviewing
someone for my research project.

EXERCISE 4 [page 3]

1. (d) ~~will be~~ is   2. (c) ~~wasn't~~ isn't   3. (d) ~~orbited~~
orbit   4. (c) ~~will take~~ takes   5. (b) ~~have paid~~ pay

EXERCISE 5 [page 4]

1. (c) arrived (c) lived (b) haven't seen (c) was
2. (b) will go (c) will take (c) will do (a) has (c) will
buy (c) was getting (c) swiched (a) get (b) has helped
(b) was going
3. (c) looked (c) looked (c) felt (c) wanted (c) asked
(b) give (b) become (b) is not
4. (c) have been writing (c) have probably never read
(b) wrote (c) is (c) have also learned (b) have hunted
and roamed (a) do
5. (c) have lived (b) isn't (b) gets (b) covered
(b) know (b) ended (d) had done (a) issued
6. (a) has never been painted (b) knows (c) was
planted (c) wanted (c) expanded (c) gelled and
formulated (b) is becoming (c) felt (a) am not
sitting
6. (a) ~~retained~~ retain   7. (d) ~~tells~~ told   8. (a) ~~see~~ saw
9. (c) ~~will have enjoyed~~ will enjoy   10. (b) ~~create~~ created

EXERCISE 6 [page 6]

A student is taking an exam . . . At the end of the
period, the professor announces that time is up and the
students have to turn . . . All the students come to the
front and put their exams . . . one student who
remains. . . . When the student comes to the front . . .
professor tells him that his grade will be lowered for . . .
student stiffens and indignantly asks . . . professor
replies . . . student replies . . . lifts the huge pile of
papers and places . . .

EXERCISE 7 [page 7]

Answers will vary.

Unit 2

Verbs: Aspect and Time Frames

EXERCISE 1 [page 8]

1. had 2. will contact 3. makes 4. decorated 5. will own 6. thought/saw 7. reveal 8. will spend 9. gives 10. will believe

EXERCISE 2 [page 8]

2. past, a 3. past, a/c 4. past, b 5. present, a/c 6. past, a/c 7. past, a/c 8. past, b

EXERCISE 3 [page 9]

1. (a) wonder (b) are looking for (c) have (d) look (e) ask (f) understand (g) work (h) believes (i) feels (j) gives (k) is currently writing (l) provides (m) helps (n) is also looking
2. (a) were talking (b) wanted (c) noticed (d) seemed (e) asked (f) told (g) had (h) went (i) was running (j) had
3. (a) is studying (b) hopes (c) is (d) feels (e) has (f) are constantly doing (g) mails (h) is always telling (e) is
4. (a) has (b) is working (c) improves (d) works (e) is (f) takes (g) is cooking (h) eats (i) goes (j) realizes (k) is taking (l) needs

EXERCISE 4 [page 10]

1. have believed
2. suffer
3. is
4. is
5. lies
6. involves
7. have been
8. have placed
9. possess
10. learned/has earned
11. are
12. have looked/look
13. accepted/accept
14. come
15. understand
16. don't have
17. had
18. were
19. have learned/learn
20. have given
21. had not considered
22. tend
23. had not published
24. have found/find
25. believe
26. is
27. learn
28. have scored
29. feel
30. have collected

EXERCISE 5 [page 12]

1. (A) b (B) b; c (C) b; b
2. (A) a (B) a (C) a
3. (A) a (B) a (C) c (D) b (E) b; b

EXERCISE 6 [page 12]

(1) will be (2) will have gone (3) will have spent (4) will have (5) Will I be (6) will have changed (7) will not have (8) will have spent (9) will be

EXERCISE 7 [page 13]

(1) have been (2) moved (3) took (4) got (5) used (6) was (7) found (8) has been working/has worked (9) have been trying (10) have gone/have been going (11) had been looking/had looked (12) have been talking (13) had planned/had been planning

EXERCISE 8 [page 14]

ACROSS 2. working 3. plays 6. are waiting 9. has run 11. stimulates 12. since
DOWN 1. finished 3. present 4. not 5. have been 7. is taking 8. occurs 10. past

EXERCISE 9 [page 15]

(1) feels (2) are (3) has been (4) are (5) are studying (6) are studying (7) are going (8) keep/have kept/have been keeping (9) complains (10) is calling/calls (11) is trying (12) have come (13) are still living/still live (14) has supported/has been supporting (15) sends (16) mails (17) has visited (18) looks forward

EXERCISE 10 [page 15]

(1) think (2) hear (3) are (4) was trying (5) exploded (6) appeared (7) had been (8) have heard (9) sounded (10) have heard (11) have hosted (12) deal (13) is (14) commits (15) concern (16) invented (17) is (18) appear (19) had been drinking (20) woke (21) had been (22) concerns (23) buys (24) had run (25) wrote (26) have acquired (27) has been looking/has looked (28) concerned/concerns (29) was dying (30) needed (31) has come

EXERCISE 11 [page 17]

ACROSS 2. running 7. progressive 9. will be 10. am going
DOWN 1. will have 3. have spent 4. comes 5. working 6. leaves 8. is flying

Unit 3
Subject-Verb Agreement

EXERCISE 1 [page 18]

Note: The head noun is listed first; the verb, second.

(1) survey is
(2) Americans believe
(3) One is
(4) subscribers receive
(5) piece is
(6) studies have
(7) success comes

(8) writers have
(9) reading is
(10) Neil Postman has
(11) reading remains
(12) look leaves
(13) book is
(14) books have

EXERCISE 2 [page 19]

Head Noun/Modifying Phrase/Verb

(1) kind of fiction [that each person likes to read] is
(2) four most popular writers [in the survey] write
(3) One thing [that most of the favorite books have in common] is
(4) This designation [which is made frequently by book sellers and reviewers] is
(5) book [that is unpopular with literary critics] is
(6) this kind of book [compared to books typically taught in college literature courses] is
(7) review [of books considered popular over the years] shows
(8) Charles Dickens [along with a number of other Victorian writers] was
(9) Shakespeare's plays [widely considered the paradigm of thoughtful literature in English] were
(10) people find
(11) eyeglasses [as opposed to contact lenses] help
(12) desire [not any innate abilities] makes

EXERCISE 3 [page 20]

(1) write   (2) their   (3) has written   (4) are
(5) major writers   (6) have   (7) appeal   (8) interests
(9) Has   (10) tell   (11) Do   (12) is   (13) a good choice   (14) appeals   (15) are   (16) good choices
(17) find   (18) their   (19) books

EXERCISE 4 [page 21]

(2) it   (3) is using   (4) is   (5) is   (6) are writing
(7) their   (8) is   (9) like   (10) comes   (11) helps
(12) like   (13) is   (14) has   (15) doesn't favor
(16) interests   (17) is   (18) tend   (19) do

EXERCISE 5 [page 21]

1. is   2. is   3. is   4. was   5. is   6. have been   7. is
8. are   9. is   10. is   11. are   12. were   13. is
14. is   15. was   16. is   17. are

EXERCISE 6 [page 22]

(1) were   (2) is   (3) deals   (4) were   (5) has
(6) knows   (7) seems   (8) has   (9) has   (10) are
(11) continues   (12) was   (13) was   (14) had
(15) were

EXERCISE 7 [page 23]

(1) has   (2) have   (3) are   (4) reveal   (5) feels
(6) face   (7) own   (8) insists   (9) say   (10) go

EXERCISE 8 [page 24]

(2) is   (3) is   (4) is   (5) are   (6) are   (7) are   (8) is
(9) are   (10) am   (11) am

TEST PREP • UNITS 1–3 [page 25]

1. b	9. c
2. a	10. b
3. c	11. c
4. c	12. a
5. b	13. b
6. a	14. b
7. d	15. d
8. a	16. c

17. c	25. c
18. d	26. c
19. c	27. c
20. d	28. c
21. c	29. b
22. d	30. b
23. d	
24. c	

Unit 4
Passive Verbs

EXERCISE 1 [page 28]

1. was passed (B)   2. have been neglected (D)
3. was rejected (A)   4. were cracked (A)   5. are being
taken (C)   6. can be found (A)   7. are damaged (C)
8. is driven (A)   9. will not be returned (B)   10. was
moved (A)

EXERCISE 2 [page 28]

1. Diving events were added in 1904.   2. Swimming
pools are clearly marked in competitive swimming.
3. Antiturbulence lane lines are used to separate the
swimmers and keep the water calm.   4. In fencing,
the sword tips are connected to lights by a long wire

that passes underneath each fencer's jacket.　5. A bulb flashes when a hit is made.　6. Fungi, once thought of as plants, are now classified as a separate kingdom.　7. The status of women has been advanced by legislation.8.　Stocks are being bought and sold in a frenzy of activity today on Wall Street.　9. Thousands of photographs of the Great Red Spot will be transmitted by the next Jupiter space probe.
10. The old Barlow mansion on the hill was slowly being devoured by termites.

EXERCISE 3 [page 29]

Part A
Paragraph 1: were manufactured; are bought; is found
Paragraph 2: are made; are devoted; are manufactured; are exported; are imported
Paragraph 3: are killed; are listed; are lost
Paragraph 4: was caused; are required; are found; are outfitted; have been passed
Paragraph 5: is related

Part B
Stative Passive
is found; are devoted; are listed; are lost; are found; are outfitted; is related

Dynamic Passive
were produced; were manufactured; are bought; are made; are manufactured; are exported; are imported; are killed; was caused; are required; have been passed

EXERCISE 4 [page 31]

1. is made/D　2. are measured/C.　3. is known/H
4. is covered/B　5. are connected/(is) termed/F/H
6. is surrounded/H　7. (is) found/is considered/A/G
8. are used/E　9. are designed/E　10. are . . . termed/are found/H/A/

EXERCISE 5 [page 31]

(6) is reputed . . . (7) is claimed . . . (8) is said . . . (10) is considered . . . (11) is known . . . was believed (13) is said . . . (14) is conjectured . . . (16) was recently reported . . . was seen (17) is said . . . (20) is supposed . . . (21) were thought . . . (24) must be admitted

EXERCISE 6 [page 33]

1. a　2. b　3. a　4. b

EXERCISE 7 [page 33]

1. (d) It was believed that if a toad crossed your path, you would have good luck./A toad crossing your path was believed to be a sign of good luck.　2. (h) It was believed that if a cat sneezed, it would rain./A cat sneezing was believed to be a sign that it would rain.
3. (g) It was believed that if a lizard crossed the path of a bridal procession, the marriage would have

problems./A lizard crossing the path of a bridal procession was believed to be a sign that the marriage would have problems.　4. (a) It was believed that if you saw a golden butterfly at a funeral, you would have a long life./Seeing a golden butterfly at a funeral was believed to be a sign that you would have a long life.
5. (c) It was believed that if a weasel squealed, a death was imminent./A weasel squealing was believed to be a sign that a death was imminent.　6. (b) It was believed that if a beetle crawled out of your shoe, bad luck would come to you./A beetle crawling out of your shoe was believed to be a sign that bad luck would come to you.　7. (e) It was believed that if a spider fell on you from the ceiling of a house a legacy would come your way./A spider falling on you from the ceiling of a house was believed to be a sign that a legacy would come your way.　8. (f) It was believed that if you fed horsehair to your children, they would do well in school./Feeding horsehair to your children was believed to help them do well in school.

EXERCISE 8 [page 34]

1. It is expected that he will run in the primary elections./He is expected to run in the primary elections.　2. It is rumored that he is undergoing treatment in a clinic in Arizona./He is rumored to be undergoing treatment in a clinic in Arizona.　3. It is believed that the results of the lab tests were misinterpreted./The results of the lab tests are believed to have been misinterpreted.　4. The case is assumed to have been settled out of court./It is assumed that the case was settled out of court.　5. It is alleged that it was the work of arsonists./It is alleged to have been the work of arsonists.　6. A major reshuffling of the White House staff is expected to be announced shortly./It is expected that a major reshuffling of the White House staff will be announced shortly.

EXERCISE 9 [page 35]

1. It is thought that there are approximately 75,000 edible plants found in nature./Approximately 75,000 edible plants are thought to be found in nature.　2. It is estimated that the number of birds that are killed in collisions with TV broadcast towers each year is 1,250,000./The number of birds that are killed in collisions with TV broadcast towers each year is estimated to be 1,250,000.　3. It is believed that the highest mountain in South America is Aconcagua in Argentina./ The highest mountain in South America is known to be Aconcagua in Argentina.　4. It is believed that the estimated number of unsolicited phone calls made by U.S. tetemarketers each second is 200./The estimated number of unsolicited phone calls made by U.S. telemarketers each second is believed to be 200.　5. It is speculated that the amount of time required to set the table for a banquet at London's Buckingham Palace is three days./The amount of time required to set the table for a banquet at London's Buckingham Palace is speculated to be three days.
6. It is reported that the maximum fine for parking

illegally overnight in Tokyo is $1,400./The maximum fine for parking illegally overnight in Tokyo is reported to be $1,400.   7. It is believed that earth's population around 8000 B.C., when farmers began harvesting domesticated plants, was 4 million./Earth's population around 8000 B.C., when farmers began harvesting domesticated plants, is believed to have been 4 million.   8. It is said that the number of people born every 10 days in 1991 was 4 million./The number of people born every 10 days in 1991 is said to have been 4 million.

EXERCISE 10 [page 36]

Note: Underlined words below indicate verbs that should be circled in the student books.

1. could be seen . . . were taken outside/Passive is used to maintain focus on subject—iguanas—and to create cohesion in the passage.   2. has been estimated/Passive is used to maintain focus on subject—English words borrowed by the Japanese—and to create cohesion in the passage.   3. can be read . . . is spoken/Passive is

used to maintain focus on subject—Chinese writing first and then dialect—and to create cohesion in the passage.   4. had been thought up . . . had been sold/Passive is used to maintain focus on subject—the crossword first and then the number of puzzles—and to create cohesion in the passage.

EXERCISE 11 [page 37]

1. Before Harvey's work was published in 1628, the role of the heart in circulation was not recognized.   2. Lipids are built of carbon, hydrogen, and oxygen.   3. The polar caps of Mars are made up not of water but of frozen carbon dioxide.   4. Since that time, however, almost all of the early craters have been destroyed by the forces of erosion and weathering.   5. These organisms are referred to loosely as "blue-green algae." They are believed to have been the first living things on Earth.   6. This field is thought to reverse itself every 11 years.

Unit 5
Article Usage

EXERCISE 1 [page 38]

(1) The   (2) the   (3) a   (4) the   (5) The   (6) the   (7) a   (8) ÿ   (9) the   (10) an   (11) ÿ   (12) ÿ   (13) The   (14) a   (15) a   (16) the   (17) a   (18) ÿ   (19) the   (20) the   (21) ÿ   (22) a   (23) the   (24) the   (25) ÿ   (26) ÿ   (27) A   (28) a   (29) the   (30) the   (31) a

EXERCISE 2 [page 39]

1. a (C)   2. The (I); the (I); ÿ (C)   3. The (I)   4. ÿ (C); ÿ (C); the (I); the (I)   5. ÿ (C)   6. The (I); ÿ (C)   7. ÿ (C)   8. The (I); the (I); ÿ   (10) a (C); the (I)

EXERCISE 3 [page 39]

Answers will vary. Possible answers are:
1. a cat   2. the articles   3. thrillers   4. the spelling checkers on the word processors   5. the long hours

EXERCISE 4 [page 40]

1. the second item/C; the auction/J   2. the subway/H; ÿ friends/K   3. The end/F; the play/J   4. The moon/A; the trail/J   5. the candidates/E; the rich/G   6. The most challenging assignment/B; a physics project/K   7. the mall/I   8. the in-basket/J; the pile/J; the window/J; the fiftieth time/C   9. The function/F; the

EXERCISE 5 [page 40]

1. . . . for a heart-to-a heart talk   2. . . . meal is a breakfast.   3. . . . by the phone.   4. The time is the . . .   5. . . . during the day   6. . . . on the arrival   7. . . . take the heed   8. . . . mouth-to-the mouth   9. . . . on a horseback.   10. . . . to the church

EXERCISE 6 [page 41]

1. a   2. b   3. a   4. b   5. a   6. a   7. a   8. b   9. a   10. a

EXERCISE 7 [page 42]

1. Cheese is a noncount noun./Correction: Cheese is made from milk.   4. Left-handed people is a plural noun./Correction: Generally, left-handed people die earlier than others.   5. Diamond is a simple inanimate object./Correction: A diamond is the hardest stone./Diamonds are the hardest stones.   6. Hydrogen is a noncount noun./Correction: Hydrogen is the first element on the atomic table.   8. Tie is a simple inanimate object./Correction: A tie is worn . . ./Ties are worn . . .   9. Arabian horses is a plural noun./Correction: Arabian horses are prized for their speed and beauty.

the machine/J   10. the population/E   11. The main reason/D; the lecture/J; the most famous living poet/B   12. the ignorant/G; the state of bliss/F

EXERCISE 8 [page 42]

2. The Swiss are noted for their banks and their mountain scenery. (h) 3. Backpackers value lightweight equipment./The backpacker values lightweight equipment. (k) 4. Smokers believe they are being discriminated against today. (f) 5. (The) Hindus believe in reincarnation. (c) 6. The British had a vast empire in the nineteenth century. (a) 7. Marathon runners tend to be thin and wiry. (e) 8. (The) socialists advocate free universal medical coverage. (j) 9. (The) Navajos live in the Four Corners region of the United States. (d) 10. Jazz musicians like to improvise./The jazz musician likes to improvise. (l) 11. (The) beetles are the largest group of insects. (g) 12. Computer programmers must possess excellent mathematical skills. (i)

EXERCISE 9 [page 43]

1. The cheetah   3. The photovoltaic cell   4. The compact disc   7. The liver   8. The potato   10. The stomach

EXERCISE 10 [page 44]

1. The heart pumps   2. (The) skin covers/Hair covers   3. The kidneys filter   4. The ears are   5. The tongue is/The mouth is   6. The scalp is   7. (The) muscles are   8. The brain enables   9. The lungs are/The nose is   10. The nose is

EXERCISE 11 [page 44]

1. A/The zebra   2. Telescopes   3. A/The hammer   4. Dentists   5. Baseball   6. A/The butterfly   7. Ice   8. Chewing gum   9. A/The broom   10. Glasses

EXERCISE 12 [page 45]

1. Rabies is   2. A cold is   3. The flu is   4. AIDS is   5. A heart attack is   6. An ulcer is   7. Cholera is   8. The mumps is   9. Leprosy is   10. A fracture is

Unit 6
Reference Words and Phrases

(b) them/the plays   7. the silk melons findings/These findings (or discoveries)   8. Their foods   10. it/this (crazy) story   9. they/these

EXERCISE 1 [page 46]

ACROSS 1. it   3. country   5. these   7. this
DOWN 2. those   4. them   5. they   6. such   7. that

EXERCISE 2 [page 47]

Answers may vary. Possible answers are:
1. these differences   2. This abasement   3. Men's names   4. This diminutive suffix   5. This suffix   6. This practice   7. Words with a negative connotation   8. Words   9. This problem   10. these rules

EXERCISE 3 [page 48]

Answers may vary. Possible answers are:
1. This characteristic makes a person a giver.   2. These listening skills, some insist, are even more important than speaking skills   3. It goes on to examine the area of morale within organizations.   4. Or do these emotions and urges depend on egotistical instincts?   5. Much of this redefinition will have to examine who our role models are.

EXERCISE 4 [page 48]

1. it   2. it   3. These desires/these issues   4. the Bulls/the Suns   5. the cars/them   6. (a) the words;

EXERCISE 5 [page 49]

Answers may vary. Possible answers are:
1. (a) this (b) that   2. those   3. That   4. these   5. That   6. These   7. This   8. those   9. That   10. This/That

EXERCISE 6 [page 50]

Answers will vary. Possible answers are:
1. This feature   2. These promises   3. these tendencies   4. these phrases   5. These habits   6. These paintings   7. This practice   8. These conditions   9. These precautions   10. these excuses

EXERCISE 7 [page 51]

Answers may vary. Possible answers are:
1. this/this game   2. it   3. This   4. this/that   5. it   6. that   7. This   8. it   9. that   10. this/this fine

EXERCISE 8 [page 51]

Answers may vary. Possible answers are:
Paragraph 1: them, the question Paragraph 2: it;

EXERCISE 9 [page 52]

Answers may vary. Possible answers are:
1. Such measures   2. Such expenses   3. such diseases
4. such a move   5. such a thing   6. Such actions
7. Two such birds (the only correct answer possible)
8. Such symptoms   9. no such person   10. Such
dedication   11. Such people   12. Such actions

EXERCISE 10 [page 53]

Answers will vary. Possible answers are:
1. . . . such senses   2. Such a . . .   3. It . . .   4. . . . .

EXERCISE 1 [page 57]

1. that/Nauru   2. that/Nauru   3. that/Nauru
4. that/Nauru   5. whose currency/Liechtenstein
6. that/San Marino   7. that/San Marino
8. that/Nauru   9. that/the Nazis/San Marino

EXERCISE 2 [page 58]

1. . . . to which I gave money turned out to be a
fraud./ . . . that I gave money to . . .   2. . . . that I
bought last week is now on sale.   3. . . . whose
employees are on strike is probably going to be sold.
4. . . . that I rescued from a tree has been hanging
around our house.   5. . . . who tend to get sick often
may have poor diets.   6. . . . who you saw in the hall
with the dean is actually working on a doctorate in
mathematics.   7. . . . whose works were featured in
last week's *Time* magazine just got another grant.
8. . . . to whom you gave your seat used to work with
your mother./ . . . whom you gave . . .   9. . . . whose
employees are always complaining should take an
honest look at itself.

EXERCISE 3 [page 59]

Answers will vary. Possible answers are:
1. The man who is dressed in a shirt and tie and who
is talking on the phone is a businessman.   2. The
students who are listening to a lecture are all honor
students.   3. That man who is on a treadmill tries to
work out every day.   4. The woman who is repairing
the harness on her horse is a park police officer.

Unit 7
Relative Clauses Modifying Subjects

TEST PREP • UNITS 4–6 [page 54]

1. c	9. b	17. a	25. d
2. a	10. a	18. a	26. c
3. d	11. c	19. d	27. a
4. b	12. c	20. d	28. c
5. d	13. b	21. a	29. a
6. a	14. d	22. b	30. a
7. b	15. c	23. d	
8. c	16. c	24. a	

EXERCISE 4 [page 59]

Answers will vary. Possible answers are:
1. A spouse who is patient and devoted is necessary for
a long and happy life.   2. Housing that is uncrowded
and clean is necessary for a long and happy life.
3. Children who are healthy and respectful are
necessary for a long and happy life.   4. Friends who
are there when you need them are necessary for a long
and happy life.   5. Leisure time that is relaxing and
satisfying is necessary for a long and happy life.
6. A hobby that is absorbing and educational is
necessary for a long and happy life.   7. An education
that is broadening and ongoing is necessary for a long
and happy life.   8. A boss who is courteous and
trusting is necessary for a long and happy life.
9. A neighborhood that is clean, friendly, and free
of crime is necessary for a long and happy life.

EXERCISE 5 [page 60]

Answers will vary. Possible answers are:
1. The man [who is] dressed . . . [who is] talking . . .
2. The students [who are] listening . . .   3. That man
[who is] on a treadmill . . .   4. The woman [who is]
repairing the harness . . .

EXERCISE 6 [page 61]

1. The manager we met was very polite.   2. The
computer at the end of the row is out of order.
3. The crowd cheered the runner trying to regain
the lead.   4. Dedicated students can be found in the
library on Saturday nights.   5. No change.   6. The
paintings we saw at the museum were impressive.

7. The president elected in November saw his popularity decline in March. 8. The parking place near the entrance is reserved for the employee of the month. 9. Angry workers confronted the union leader about the new contract. 10. Programmers experienced with UNIX systems will be given first consideration.

Unit 8

Relative Clauses Modifying Objects

EXERCISE 1 [page 63]

ACROSS 1. whose 2. with 3. whom 4. about 6. to
DOWN 1. which 3. who 4. at 5. that

EXERCISE 2 [page 64]

1. . . singer *whom* . . . 2. . . . neighbors *with whom* we left our dog. 3. . . . the mountain from *whose* summit . . . 4. . . . my keys, *which* I thought I had put in . . . 5. . . . dolphin *that* she had thrown some fish to./ . . . the dolphin *to which* she had thrown some fish.

EXERCISE 3 [page 65]

2. A computer is a device that performs calculations. 3. Irrigation is a process by which water is artificially conducted to soil to promote growth. 4. A seismograph is an instrument that is used to detect and record seismic waves caused by earthquakes. 5. The Nobel Prize is an award that is given to individuals from all over the world who have made outstanding contributions in their fields. 6. Cobras are poisonous snakes whose necks can be spread to form a hood when alarmed. 7. Entomology is a science that is devoted to the study of insects. 8. The tundra is a treeless plain in the Arctic Circle whose soil is a thin coating over permafrost. 9. Margarine is a spread that is prepared from vegetable fats. 10. The Kentucky Derby is a horserace in which 3-year-old horses run over a one-and-one-quarter-mile course at Churchill Downs in Louisville, Kentucky.

EXERCISE 4 [page 66]

Answers will vary. Possible answers are:
1. People were frightened of griffins which were part eagle and part lion and destroyed anyone who strayed into their territory. 2. The most frightening of the three Gorgon sisters was Medusa, whose head was a mass of coiling snakes and whose glance could turn a person into stone. 3. The gates to the underworld were guarded by Cerberus, which was a three-headed dog that threatened anyone who came too close. 4. As one of their tortures, the gods used the Harpies, which were

vultures with the heads of women and whose claws tore at their unfortunate victims. 5. The monster that lay in wait for travelers on the road to Thebes was the Sphinx, which had the body of a lion and the head of a woman and dared those it stopped to solve a riddle or die. 6. Ulysses killed the Cyclops, who was a one-eyed giant who lived in a cave above the shore and ate sheep and men. 7. Ulysses was fortunate to escape from Circe, who was a beautiful witch whose pleasure was to turn men into swine. 8. Ships were often wrecked because of the sirens, who were beautiful nymphs who lived on treacherous rocks and whose irresistible song lured sailors to their doom. 9. Perseus was the hero who killed the Chimera, which was a fire-breathing monster that had both a lion's and a goat's head and the body of a dragon, with a snake for a tail. 10. For the ancient Greeks, the only monsters that were essentially good were the Centaurs, which were half man and half horse and became rude and uncontrollable only when they became intoxicated with wine.

EXERCISE 5 [page 69]

1. I am often disappointed in movies made from books I have enjoyed. 2. We rented the same house our friends had lived in last year. 3. Look at the deer hiding in the shadows! 4. No deletion possible. 5. I felt overwhelmed by the papers scattered all over my room. 6. The trekkers walked down a narrow trail with a terrifying drop. 7. So far we haven't found a candidate competent enough to get the job. 8. Doris forgot to thank the woman she had received a gift from. 9. No deletion possible. 10. I went to the restaurant you recommended.

EXERCISE 6 [page 70]

1. No deletion possible. 2. No deletion possible. 3. No deletion possible. 4. A seismograph is an instrument used to detect and record seismic waves caused by earthquakes. 5. The Nobel Prize is an award given to individuals from all over the world who have made outstanding contributions in their fields. 6. No deletion possible. 7. Entomology is a science devoted to the study of insects. 8. No deletion possible. 9. Margarine is a spread prepared from vegetable fats. 10. No deletion possible.

EXERCISE 7 [page 62]

1. You can't teach an old dog new tricks. 2. A bird in the hand is worth two in the bush. 3. A bad workman blames his tools. 4. People in glass houses shouldn't throw stones. 5. A rolling stone gathers no moss. 6. A watched pot never boils.

EXERCISE 7 [page 70]

1. The Arabs have a culture of which they are justifiably proud.   2. It's a tiny office out of which they work.   3. I don't think there are any to whom we can award it.   4. This is a seminar in which we shall discuss nineteenth-century colonialism.   5. No change possible.   6. That's because she was a girl to whom nothing was ever denied.   7. Darwin was a scientist to whom we all owe a debt.   8. Apparently he was a recluse about whom nothing is known.   9. Of course, they are all magazines to which I subscribe.   10. They are a family whom we just cannot put up.

EXERCISE 1 [page 73]

Answers will vary. Possible answers are:
1. (a) that I bought last week (b) which are pervasive in many countries   2. (a) that is in the library (b) which is a very useful tool   3. (a) that is near the campus (b) which was founded by Ray Kroc   4. (a) that lives in the house next door (b) which is very commonly called "man's best friend"   5. (a) that form on the ground (b) which she imagines are giants, castles, and other fabulous things   6. (a) that I wrote about the Nobel Peace Prize (b) which took me two weeks to write   7. (a) that you ordered (b) which was originally a Greek concept   8. (a) that have large hard drives and expanded memory (b) which are becoming less expensive   9. (a) that is on the first floor of the office building (b) which is a marvelous invention that can transmit both words and images over telephone lines   10. (a) that won last year's Kentucky Derby (b) which has very keen senses

EXERCISE 2 [page 74]

Answers will vary. The following phrases are suggestions: which has an enrollment of five thousand; who come from all over the world; all of which make for some stimulating discussion; which so far has been challenging and quite interesting; with whom I had a nice talk today at lunch; which is a place I've always wanted to visit; whose courses, I understand, are very popular; which is a pleasant community; which has four rooms in addition to a living room, kitchen, and bathroom; all of whom are students; which I check every day.

EXERCISE 3 [page 75]

Answers will vary. Possible answers are:
1. A stethoscope, which is an instrument for listening to sounds produced within the body, is used by doctors and nurses.   2. A hammer, which is a hand tool

EXERCISE 8 [page 71]

1. . . . I hope you will rise to.   2. . . . group your parents dislike.   3. . . . we have been warned about.   4. . . . man he owed some money to.   5. . . . everyone is talking about.   6. . . . letter she tried to hide.   7. . . . students the teachers failed.   8. . . . many Greek warriors sacrificed their lives for.   9. . . . no intelligent person can subscribe to.   10. . . . passage you are speaking about.   11. . . . man the children were staring at.

Unit 9
Nonrestrictive Relative Clauses

consisting of a handle with an attached head made of a relatively heavy, rigid material, is used by carpenters.   3. A spatula, which is a small kitchen implement with a handle and a broad, flat, flexible blade, is used by cooks to lift food from hot pans and grills.   4. A hoe, which is a tool with a flat blade attached at a right angle to a long handle, is used for gardening.   5. Handcuffs, which consist of a pair of strong, connected hoops that can be tightened and locked about the wrists of a prisoner, are used by the police.   6. A compass, which is a device with a magnetic needle that is aligned with the magnetic field of Earth, is used by explorers, sailors, and hikers to determine geographic direction.   7. A tripod, which is an instrument with three legs that supports a camera, is used by photographers and filmmakers.   8. The periodic table, which is an arrangement of the elements according to their atomic numbers in columns indicating similar properties, is used in chemistry.   9. A wrench, which is a hand tool with a fixed or adjustable jaw for gripping, turning, or twisting objects such as nuts, bolts, or pipes, is used by mechanics, repair people, and plumbers.   10. A scalpel, which is a small, straight knife with a thin, sharp blade, is used in surgery and dissection.

EXERCISE 4 [page 77]

Answers will vary. Possible answers are:
(1) which was wise   (2) which was unfortunate   (3) which was foolish   (4) which was very distressing   (5) which was unbelievable   (6) which was really stupid thinking on her part   (7) which was very precious to me   (8) which annoyed me   (9) which I really appreciated   (10) which was inconvenient   (11) which was a relief

EXERCISE 5 [page 78]

Answers will vary. Possible answers are:
(1) one of which   (2) none of which; all of which

(3) one of which (4) many of whom (5) two of whom (6) both of which (7) one of which (8) one of whom (9) a pair of whom

EXERCISE 6 [page 79]

ACROSS 2. all 3. whom 6. both 7. of 8. neither
DOWN 1. each 3. which 4. none 5. some

Unit 10

Relative Adverb Clauses

EXERCISE 1 [page 83]

ACROSS 1. way 2. which 5. reason 6. during
DOWN 1. where 2. when 3. how 4. from

EXERCISE 2 [page 84]

1. The day *when* Christmas . . . 2. . . . reasons *why* December 25 . . . 3. . . . about *how* Zoroastrians . . . 4. . . . that *how* they overlapped after 5. . . . Middle Ages, *when* it became . . . 6. . . . disliked *how* it was . . . 7. No change possible. 8. . . . December 6, *when* someone . . . 9. . . . reasons *why* the two . . . 10. . . . account for *how* December . . .

EXERCISE 3 [page 85]

Part A: 1. Ramadan is the period when Muslims . . . 2. Asian Lunar New Year is the holiday when most Asians . . . 3. The nineteenth century was the time when Queen . . . 4. 1969 was the year when Neil . . . 5. From noon to one o'clock is the hour when many . . . 6. 1945 was the year when World . . . 7. Winter is the season when people . . . 8. The Meiji Restoration is the period when the first . . .
Part B: 1. Downstairs is the place where a house is coolest. 2. Mecca is the city where every Muslim . . . 3. North is the direction where a compass needle points. 4. Saudi Arabia is the country where about one-third of all the world's oil is located. 5. The capitol is the building where a government meets. 6. A cemetery is the place where people are buried. 7. Argentina is the country where the 1978 and 1986 World Cup champions are from.
Part C: 1. A chance . . . is the reason why people immigrate. 2. . . . mileage is one reason why people buy compact cars. 3. . . . spelling is one reason why written English can be difficult. 4. . . . productivity is one reason why businesses use machines. 5. . . . behavior are the reasons why sharks have no natural predators. 6. . . . fluorocarbons is the reason why the ozone layer is healing. 7. . . . humor is the reason why people like Charlie Chaplin.

TEST PREP • UNITS 7–9 [page 80]

1. b 9. a 17. b 25. b
2. a 10. d 18. a 26. d
3. c 11. a 19. d 27. d
4. a 12. a 20. c 28. b
5. c 13. a 21. d 29. d
6. d 14. c 22. c 30. d
7. b 15. d 23. b
8. a 16. c 24. a

Part D: 1. . . . training is how athletes build strength. 2. . . . seed is the way you get coriander. 3. . . . conference is the way politicians disseminate information. 4. . . . minutes is how basketball games tied at the end are decided. 5. . . . details is one way projects fail. 6. . . . service is how clients are kept. 7. . . . fuels is one way the atmosphere will remain clean.

EXERCISE 4 [page 88]

Answers will vary considerably.
1. To get a better job is why 2. why there is so much aggression in the world. 3. 1947 was when 4. why English has so many complicated rules. 5. Around eleven is when 6. Cairo is where

EXERCISE 5 [page 88]

1. 1990 was when the Berlin . . . 2. Italy is where Ferrari . . . 3. . . . and 4 to 6 P.M. are when rush hour . . . 4. February 14 is when Valentine's . . . 5. . . . February 19 is when Asian . . . 6. Evening is when people eat . . . 7. Nepal is where the world's . . .

EXERCISE 6 [page 89]

Part A: The best answers are from the following:
(from Exercise 3, Part A) 3. The nineteenth century is the time Queen . . . 4. 1969 was the year Neil . . . 5. From noon to one o'clock is the hour many . . . 6. 1945 was the year world . . . 7. Winter is the season people . . .
(from Exercise 3, Part B) 1. Downstairs is the place a house is coolest. 2. . . . Muslim must make a pilgrimage to. 4. . . . the country about one-third of all the world's oil is located in. 5. . . . the building a government meets in. 6. . . . place people are buried in. 7. . . . country the 1978 and 1986 World Cup champions are from.
(from Exercise 3, Part C) 1. A chance . . . is the reason people immigrate. 2. . . . mileage is one reason

people buy . . . 3. . . . spelling is one reason written
English . . . 4. . . . productivity is one reason
businesses . . . 5. . . . behavior are the reasons
sharks . . . 6. . . . fluorocarbons is the reason the
ozone . . . 7. . . . humor is the reason people like . . .
Part B: (from Exercise 5) 2. . . . country Ferrari . . .
are made in. 3. . . . and 4 to 6 P.M. are the times
rush . . . 4. . . . day Valentine's. 5. . . . the time
Asian Lunar . . . 6. . . . time people eat dinner.
7. . . . country the world's . . . found in.

8. (b) the cemetery where/b
9. (b) How/g
10. (a) when/f

EXERCISE 7 [page 90]

1. (a) at time when/a
2. (a) the manner in which you have behaved/c
3. (a) when/g
4. (b) when/f
5. (a) why/g
6. (a) a second-hand store where/b
7. (a) A place where/d

EXERCISE 8 [page 91]

Answers will vary. Possible answers are:
1. a time in which 2. where 3. a year in which 4. a time when 5. a place where

EXERCISE 9 [page 91]

Answers will vary. Possible answers are:
1. a place known for its vastness and relentless dryness. 2. a century in which the Black Death raged. 3. a mountain on which many had died. 4. a time in which a huge population will have to deal with shrinking resources. 5. a place where many strange deeds had been done.

Unit 11
Correlative Conjunctions

Wilmington Campus. 2. You can take either anthropology or economics. 3. You can take both English composition and linguistics. 4. We offer not only philosophy but also anthropology on Tuesday nights. 5. We offer technical writing both during the daytime and in the evening. 6. You can take it on either Thursday or Friday. 7. You can take it on either the Wilmington or the Philadelphia campus. 8. Neither astronomy nor physics is offered at times convenient for you. 9. You can take either linguistics or philosophy at the Philadelphia campus. 10. You can take either astronomy or physics at night.

EXERCISE 4 [page 96]

Answers will vary. Possible answers are:
1. . . . become a more responsible and independent person. 2. In the fall, I will take not only . . . 3. . . . hard at both my job and school. 4. You can either come with us now or come with Lisa later. 5. Not only Imelda but also Nelson got into the honors program. 6. OK. 7. OK. 8. Marcus told me that he would either take his children . . . 9. You will need to present either a driver's license or major credit card . . . 10. OK. 11. In Britain and Australia, trucks are known as lorries and utes, respectively.

EXERCISE 5 [page 97]

ACROSS 1. to 3. in 4. where 6. place 8. way
9. during
DOWN 1. time 2. on 4. when 5. reason 7. at

EXERCISE 1 [page 92]

Answers will vary. Possible answers are:
1. Neither Andy nor Emily smokes. 2. Both Andy and his wife, Emily, work. 3. Neither their son nor their daughter lives with them at present. 4. The Morgans will buy either a Dodge or a Toyota within the coming year. 5. The Morgans subscribe not only to *Newsweek* and *The Atlantic Monthly* but also to *National Geographic* and *Home*. 6. They are going to spend their next vacation in either Mexico or Brazil. 7. Both snorkeling and walking are things they like to do on vacation.

EXERCISE 2 [page 93]

1. No, neither Tony Perez nor Laura Park has . . .
2. Yes, both Tony Perez and Emma Singh can work in . . . 3. You could hire either Tony Perez or Laura Park, both of whom have training in microcomputer repair. 4. Yes, both Emma Singh and Laura Park have more . . . 5. She has not only a B.S. in electrical engineering but also an M.B.A. 6. Yes, both Tony Perez and Emma Singh are proficient in Pascal. 7. She is proficient in both Pascal and C. 8. Yes, both Tony Perez and Emma Singh can . . . 9. No, neither Laura Park nor Emma Singh has experience with . . . 10. No, neither Laura Park nor Emma Singh has applied to this company before.

EXERCISE 3 [page 94]

Answers will vary. Possible answers are:
1. You can take both linguistics and philosophy at the

Unit 12
Sentence Connectors

EXERCISE 1 [page 98]

ACROSS   2. although   6. example   8. consequently
10. furthermore   11. yet
DOWN   1. matter   3. however   4. fact   5. hand
7. before   9. whereas

EXERCISE 2 [page 99]

1. an added idea   2. a contrast   3. a similarity
4. an example   5. a result   6. a contrast

EXERCISE 3 [page 99]

1. *Furthermore*, she has a grasp . . . (Other possible connectors: all simple addition and emphatic addition connectors)   2. . . . painkiller *as well*. (Other possible connectors: all simple addition and emphatic addition connectors)   3. *In fact*, I've even . . . (Other possible connectors: all intensifying additive connectors)
4. *As a matter of fact*, when she's not . . . (Other possible connectors: all intensifying additive connectors)   5. *In addition*, the incidence . . . (Other possible connectors: all simple addition and emphatic addition connectors)
6. *What is more*, you have to . . . (Other possible connectors: all simple addition and emphatic addition connectors)   7. We could *also* listen . . . (Other possible connectors: all simple addition and emphatic addition connectors)   8. *Besides that*, I could . . . (Other possible connectors: all simple addition and emphatic addition connectors)   9. *Actually*, I can't even . . . (Other possible connectors: all simple addition and emphatic addition connectors)
10. *Moreover*, some patients tried . . . (Other possible connectors: all simple addition and emphatic addition connectors)

EXERCISE 4 [page 100]

2. Bob and Sheila are thinking about . . . Alternatively,/On the other hand, they might . . .   (h)
3. You already . . . On the other hand,/Alternatively, why don't you ask . . .   (a) 4. The new Fords . . . On the other hand, the Toyotas . . .   (i) 5. The city council . . . Alternatively,/On the other hand, they could have . . .   (b) 6. We might put up a . . . Alternatively,/On the other hand, we could plant . . .   (e) 7. The critics praised . . . On the other hand, they found . . .   (c) 8. To keep the insects . . . On the other hand,/Alternatively, consider using . . .   (g) 9. I guess I should . . . On the other hand,/Alternatively, maybe I . . .   (j) 10. Let's get a newspaper . . . On the other hand,/Alternatively, let's call . . .   (f)

EXERCISE 5 [page 101]

Answers will vary. Possible answers are:
1. (a) To illustrate (b) for instance   2. in other words   3. in particular   4. namely   5. for example
6. that is   7. Specifically

EXERCISE 6 [page 102]

Answers will vary. Possible answers are:
1. Likewise, the Greeks feel that ties to land are permanent.   2. In the same way, eating with your left hand is incorrect in India.   3. Similarly, Suraiya demonstrates her environmental awareness by recycling paper products and by composting organic matter instead of just throwing things in the trash.
4. Similarly, B-cells manufacture antibodies to help keep the body healthy.   5. Likewise, in autumn you can find a breathtaking waterfowl concentration in California's Klamath Basin.

EXERCISE 7 [page 103]

Answers will vary. Possible answers are:
1. Dandelion relieves rheumatic pain. Cayenne helps in the same way.   2. One of the properties of echinachea is that it is a blood purifier. Likewise, one action of cayenne is that it purifies the blood.   3. Dandelion is prepared by putting a few teaspoons of root into one cup of water, bringing it to a boil, and letting it simmer for ten to fifteen minutes. Echinachea is prepared in a similar way.   4. Chamomile has a positive effect upon the stomach. Ginger likewise has a positive effect.   5. To prepare ginger, pour a cup of boiling water onto one teaspoon of the fresh root and let infuse for five minutes. In the same way, cayenne can be prepared by pouring a cup of boiling water onto one half to one teaspoon of powder and letting it stand for ten minutes.

EXERCISE 8 [page 105]

Answers will vary. Possible answers are:
1. Dandelion relieves congestion of the liver and gallbladder. Cayenne, however, relieves colds and headaches.   2. The flowers of the chamomile herb are used. In contrast, it is the roots of echinachea, ginger, and dandelion that we use.   3. Echinachea is prepared by boiling the root with water and letting it simmer. Ginger, on the other hand, is prepared by putting boiling water onto the root and letting it infuse.
4. Chamomile is taken as a drink. Dandelion leaves may be eaten raw in salad, though.   5. Dandelion

affects the liver, kidneys, gallbladder, and pancreas. Echinachea, however, affects the blood and lymph system.

EXERCISE 9 [page 105]

1. . . . so well, however/on the other hand/though
2. On the other hand/however/nevertheless/nonetheless
3. In fact/however 4. OK 5. Despite this/Nonetheless/Nevertheless/However/Even so 6. OK

EXERCISE 10 [page 106]

Answers will vary. Possible answers are:
1. The expedition encountered blizzards . . . . Even so, they reached . . . 2. He lost his parents . . . Despite this, he became . . . 3. For many years he was addicted. . . . With a lot of persistence and help from friends, however, he managed to kick the habits and actually became . . . 4. . . . community is often very challenging. In spite of the difficulties involved, there are the benefits of new . . . 5. Our car broke down in Colorado. . . . We got across the country nonetheless.

EXERCISE 11 [page 107]

Answers will vary. Possible answers are:
Chart A: 1. Ariadne . . . gave Theseus . . . Thus, he was able to find his way . . . 2. King Henry . . . wanted. . . . Therefore, he divorced . . . 3. Adam . . . are the forbidden fruit. As a result of this, they were . . .

Unit 13
Modal Perfect Verbs

EXERCISE 1 [page 113]

Part A (1) could have been (2) may have spent (3) shouldn't have expected (4) shouldn't have hung up (5) could have done
Part B (6) could have been handled (7) should have been told (8) might not have been have been said (10) could have been avoided
Part C (11) must have been thinking (12) could have been hoping for (13) should have been paying

EXERCISE 2 [page 114]

Meaning-word clue/Modal
(1) annoyed/should/could/might have accepted (2) It was well within her abilities/could have done
(3) thoughtless/could have worked (4) regretted / should have been (5) angry/could/might have called
(6) rude/could/might/should have had (7) was perfectly able/could have helped (8) strongly criticized/could/might/should have told
(9) reproached/should/could/might have remembered
(10) thoughtless/could/might/should have thought

4. Tristan . . . drank the . . . Consequently, they fell. . . .
5. Inanna . . . descended into . . . Because of this, she brought her beloved . . . .
Chart B: 1. The Aztecs were anxious to keep the sun in the sky and increase their crops. To do these things they believed they had to sacrifice prisoners of war. To survive, he had his men plug their ears and had himself tied securely to the mast of his ship. 2. Ulysses wanted to hear the song of the sirens. To survive, he had his men plug their ears and had himself tied securely to the mast of his ship. 3. James Bond felt he had a duty to save the world from megalomaniacs, with this in mind, he was ready to risk his life. 4. Johnny Appleseed wanted to spread apple trees around the United States. For this purpose, he sowed seeds wherever he went.

EXERCISE 12 [page 108]

1. Similarly, 2. remains, in fact, 4. considerable; however, 5. exploration, though 6. For example,
8. plants, for instance,

TEST PREP • UNITS 10-12 [page 110]

1. a
2. b
3. d
4. b
5. a
6. d
7. b
8. b

9. c
10. c
11. b
12. d
13. c
14. a
15. b
16. d

17. b
18. c
19. d
20. a
21. c
22. c
23. c
24. c

25. b
26. c
27. a
28. d
29. d
30. b

EXERCISE 3 [page 115]

(1) are to have (2) were supposed to have (3) were to have been (4) are we supposed to have (5) are to have (6) were we supposed to have (7) are to have
(8) are supposed to

EXERCISE 4 [page 116]

Part A 1. must have 2. should/would have
3. must have 4. can't have 5. would have
6. must have
Part B 7. should have 8. must have 9. can't have
10. can't have 11. wouldn't have

EXERCISE 5 [page 116]

Answers may vary. Possible answers are:
(1) Could/might it have someone else who looks like my client? (2) Could/might it have been someone else who looks like my client? (3) Could/might he have gone in the door of another room? (4) Could/might you have remembered it incorrectly? (5) Could/might it have

been later?   (6) Could/might you have been drinking?   (7) Could/might it have been a lot?
(8) Could/might you be an alcoholic?
(9) Could/might you have been drunk?

EXERCISE 6 [page 118]

Answers will vary. Possible answers are:
1. You may not have switched on the external drive first.
2. That could/may/might have been another cat.
3. You could/may/might have left it on another table.
4. You could/may/might have put on some weight.
5. That could/may/might be someone else's care he's driving.
6. They may/might not have sent cards to anyone this year.

EXERCISE 7 [page 118]

(3) would have   (4) might/could have   (5) would have   (6) may/could have   (7) would have

(8) might/could have   (9) might/could have
(10) would have   (11) might/could have
(12) might/could have   (13) might/could have

EXERCISE 8 [page 119]

1. By 8:00 P.M. I will have been working for 12 hours.
2. By 2020, the Anderson family will have owned their farm for 120 years.   3. By June, Jason will have lost 60 pounds.   4. Two years from now, our club will have elected its second president.   5. By 2027, Hong Kong will have been part of China for 30 years.   6. By 2011, Lisa will have completed her bachelor's degree.

EXERCISE 9 [page 120]

ACROSS   1. could   3. would   4. to have
5. have walked   6. may have   7. regret
9. irritation   10. supposed
DOWN   1. contrary   2. must have   6. might
8. should

Unit 14
Discourse Organizers

EXERCISE 1 [page 122]

ACROSS   2. Next   5. rhetorical   7. summary
9. sequence
DOWN   1. introduce   3. So far   4. First   6. There are   8. finally

EXERCISE 2 [page 123]

1. a   2. b.   3. (A) a (B) a   4. b   5. a   6. b   7. b

EXERCISE 3 [page 123]

Answers will vary. Possible answers are:
1. *To start with*, I always need more than I have.   2. *To begin with*, you have to draw up the plans.   3. *First of all*, I had to sweep the porch and the stairs.   4. *First*, boil some water.   5. *First of all*, get a good grammar book.   6. *In the first place*, you have to be attentive day and night.   7. *One of its causes* is overcrowding.

EXERCISE 4 [page 124]

Answers will vary. Possible answers are:
1. To begin with, you have to choose an interesting topic. Next, you have to narrow the topic down. Then, you have to compile a list of books and journals to read. Lastly, you have to put your ideas and findings down on paper.   2. To begin with, the weather is usually fine. Then, the days are long. Finally, it's when

I get my vacation.   3. To start with, you have to set aside a part of every day for exercise. Then, you have to exercise no matter what the weather is or no matter how you're feeling. Lastly, you have to be careful about what you eat.   4. First, I check the oil every week. Then, I check the other fluids. Finally, I have the oil changed every 3,000 miles.   5. To begin with, you encounter new words. Then, you often find new idioms. Finally, you see how grammatical structures are used.   6. To start with, you totally relax. Then, you dream. Finally, your body gets reenergized.   7. First of all, he/(she) is considerate. Next, he/(she) is caring. Finally, he/(she) has a good sense of humor.

EXERCISE 5 [page 125]

Answers may vary. Possible answers are:
1. There are; types; The first; The others   2. There are; kinds; One; The second; The last   3. There are; ways; To start with; Second; Next; Lastly   4. There are; theories; The first one; A second; Finally; there are 5. There are; properties; The first; Second; Third; Finally

EXERCISE 6 [page 126]

Answers will vary. Possible answers are:
1. Briefly, I will survey different communities around the world and show how the warming of the atmosphere has led to some alarming changes   2. In short, my client is innocent of the charges that have been brought against him.   3. All in all, there was a

lot more going on in the fifties than we normally think
4. As has been previously mentioned, the link between
the smoking of tobacco products and lung cancer is
well documented. 5. In summary, only in the
preservation of diversity lies a healthy future for us all.
6. Overall, we've never been in a stronger position
7. In summary, pay particularly careful attention to the
purity of your water and fresh food. 8. Briefly, plastic
plays a vital role in our contemporary world.

EXERCISE 7 [page 127]

Answers will vary. Actual topics and sources of
questions:
1. The text is about the diversity and development of
animal life around the planet. (David Attenborough,
The Trials of Life, 1990, Boston: Little, Brown)
2. The text is about the typical clutter that prevents us
from being as efficient as we can be, and it makes
suggestions about how we can become better organized.
(Stephanie Winston, *Getting Organized*, 1978, New
York: Warner Books) 3. The text is about a charitable
foundation that is concerned with culture and the
environment. (Cottonwood Foundation, by Genevieve
Austin, *Buzzworm*, May/June 1993) 4. The text is about a
guide to computers that offer integrated features
designed to satisfy the needs of all members of a family.
(from *Home*, September 1993) 5. The text is a protest
against overdevelopment in a community. (from a letter
to the editor, *Newport Chronicle*, June 17, 1996)

EXERCISE 8 [page 128]

Implications: 1. It's time you treated yourself to what
you really deserve. 2. No one needs all that sugar.
3. Gadgets do not deliver the sound that you want.
4. There is no liberty. There is no peace. 5. This is
exactly what you've been waiting for.

EXERCISE 9 [page 129]

Answers will vary. Possible answers are:
1. Shouldn't all young children be vaccinated? (They
should.)/Isn't it our obligation to have all young children
vaccinated? (It is.)/Don't we want to eradicate disease in
the very young? (We do.) 2. Shouldn't the sales of
powerful herbs be regulated? (They should.)/Isn't it time
we did something about controlling the sales of
powerful herbs? (It is.) 3. Don't we waste too much
money on needless paperwork in our medical system?
(We do.)/Don't we need to cut the high costs of medical
care? (We do.)/Can't we save money by cutting wasteful
administrative practices? (We can.) 4. Isn't winter a
great time for a vacation? (It is.)/Don't you need a break
from the cold weather? (You do.) 5. Isn't it better to
be safe than sorry? (It is.)/Shouldn't you be safe? (You
should.)/Doesn't it make sense to be safe rather than
sorry? (It does.)

Unit 15
Conditionals: *If, Only If, Unless, Even Though, Even If*

EXERCISE 1 [page 130]

1. were . . . would . . . say 2. had taken . . . had
studied/studied . . . could have had/would have had
3. look . . . will see/should see 4. had trained . . .
would be 5. takes . . . is 6. smoke and eat . . . run
7. were . . . would not allow . . . 8. want . . . have
to/will have to 9. had asked . . . would have helped.
10. had bought . . . would have been able 11. did not
eat . . . did not get 12. had studied . . . would not
have felt 13. graduate . . . will buy

EXERCISE 2 [page 131]

1. . . . will qualify . . . only if . . . 2. . . . will lose . . . only
if . 3. You should take . . . only if . . . 4. People were
invited . . . only if they . . . 5. We got . . . only if . . .

EXERCISE 3 [page 132]

1. Only if/Not unless you change . . . will your engine
run smoothly. 2. Only if/Not unless you keep . . .

will the tread of your tires . . . 3. Only if/Not unless
you live . . . do you need to add . . . 4. When . . .
only if/not unless . . . will you obtain an accurate . . .
5. Only if/Not unless it was built before 1980 will
your vehicle be . . .

EXERCISE 4 [page 132]

Sentences can begin with either *Only if* or *Not unless*
1. Only if I am totally exhausted can (e) 2. Only if
you are a serious photographer should you (a) 3. Only if
if I exercise every day do I! (d) 5. Only if the book is
overdue do will (h) 6. Only if the danger of frost has
passed will (i) 7. Only if they are freezing do (f)
8. Only if you ask and receive permission should
you (c) 9. Only if I washed it and cleaned it was I (b)

EXERCISE 5 [page 133]

1. unless she knew word processing, she would have to
spend a lot of time rewriting. 2. unless we stop the
timber industry/unless the timber industry is stopped,

virgin forest will be destroyed. 3. if she hadn't been so frank and outspoken, she might have gotten the job she wanted. 4. if he hadn't found someone to practice French with, he wouldn't feel so confident. 5. if we had not spoken only English, I would have understood more about my grandparents. 6. If she were not such a great music lover, she would not have so many tapes and CDs. 7. if it were harder to get a gun, the number of murders would decrease. 8. If he had had health insurance, he would have gone to see the doctor by now. 9. unless it rains soon, their crops will be ruined.

EXERCISE 6 [page 134]

1. Even though 2. even if 3. even though 4. even though 5. even though 6. even if 7. Even though 8. even though 9. even though 10. even if

EXERCISE 7 [page 135]

(1) unless (2) even if (3) Only if (4) only if (5) If (6) even if (7) only if (8) unless (9) if (10) only if (11) unless

EXERCISE 8 [page 136]

1. Don't get on the tube in rush hour unless (d)
2. Take the riverboat up the Thames to Hampton

Court if (h) 3. Don't rent a car unless (a) 4. Go to visit the crown jewels on a weekend only if (j) 5. Check to see that the flag is flying over Buckingham Palace if (i) 6. Expect to pay 15% VAT (value added text) when you purchase anything except food or books even if (b) 7. Be sure to visit the London Museum at the Barbican if (e) 8. Be prepared to encounter accents and dialects that will perplex you even though (g) 9. Always say Sorry when you bump into someone even if (f) 10. Take a stroll on Hampstead Heath, London's largest park, if (c)

EXERCISE 9 [page 137]

ACROSS 3. despite 4. even 5. emphasis 8. contrary 11. though 12. Not DOWN 1. unless 2. were 6. might 7. hadn't 9. Only 10. Don't

TEST PREP • UNITS 13–15 [page 138]

1. d
2. c
3. c
4. c
5. b
6. d
7. b
8. c
9. a
10. c
11. d
12. b
13. b
14. c
15. a
16. a
17. a
18. c
19. d
20. b
21. b
22. c
23. b
24. c
25. c
26. c
27. c
28. c
29. a
30. d

Unit 16

Reducing Adverb Clauses

EXERCISE 1 [page 141]

While I am waiting for a helicopter to arrive/While waiting . . . After we spend a couple of days in Kathmandu/After spending / Having spent . . . When we started out/When starting out . . . After we had trekked for a week/After having . . . Before we climbed the high pass/Before climbing . . . while I was huffing and puffing my way to the top of the pass/while huffing and puffing . . . While he was scrambling over loose rock/While scrambling . . . Before I left the U.S./Before leaving . . . .

EXERCISE 2 [page 142]

Answers will vary. Possible answers are:
1. Before signing up for a class . . . 2. After having received your syllabus/After receiving . . . 3. While listening to lectures . . . 4. When hearing something you don't understand 5. While taking part in discussions 6. After finishing class 7. After having finished your homework/After finishing . . . .

EXERCISE 3 [page 142]

Note being very rich, Truhana had to go . . . Having a long way to go, Truhana had . . . Daydreaming, she began . . . getting a good price for the honey, I will buy . . . "Loving Lamb so much everybody will, . . . And making so much money, I'll soon . . . And being rich and respected, I'll marry . . . Taking so much pleasure in her fantasy, Truhana began . . . Seeing clearly now the ruin of her dreams, Truhana . . .

EXERCISE 4 [page 143]

Answers will vary. Possible answers are:
1. Alerted by Dr. Watson 2. Being experienced as a detective 3. Having noticed the curtains fluttering 4. Determined that evidence lay outside 5. Startled by a sudden noise 6. Scared out of his wits 7. Attempting to calm him 8. Wanting to get to the bottom of the matter 9. Realizing there was no way out 10. Having discovered that the boy had simply been trying to test him

EXERCISE 5 [page 144]

Answers will vary. Possible answers are:
2. clutching a plank from the ship   3. Pulled by the currents   4. laughing and praying   5. Looking around   6. hoping to find food   7. After picking some fruit   8. while looking through the debris on the shore   9. using branches and the tools he had found.   10. startled to find footprints in the sand

EXERCISE 6 [page 144]

The ending of the story will vary.

EXERCISE 7 [page 145]

1. d   2. f   3. g   4. a   5. h   6. b   7. c   8. e

EXERCISE 8 [page 147]

ACROSS   1. frightened   4. shocking   6. pleasing   7. Embarrassed   9. amused   10. Puzzling   11. Boring

DOWN   1. frustrated   2. irritated   3. confused   5. Intrigued   8. Annoying

EXERCISE 9 [page 148]

Answers will vary. Possible answers are:
1. While cleaning the yard, Sam spotted an opossum sniffing under the hedge.   3. After hiking all day long, I found the thought of a tent and a sleeping bag very attractive.   5. Having planted bulbs in the fall, we enjoyed many flowers in the spring.   6. Being late, Robert found the highway very long as he raced to work.   8. Frustrated by overly complicated questions, the students found the test infuriating.   9. After hoisting it up to the fifth floor with a heavy rope, the movers brought the piano in through the window.   10. After putting on sunglasses, he realized that the glare wasn't so bad.

Unit 17
Preposition Clusters

EXERCISE 1 [page 150]

1. count on   2. pay for   3. commented on   4. consented to   5. decided on   6. rely on   7. think about   8. approve of   9. complain about   10. believes in

EXERCISE 2 [page 151]

ACROSS 1. scowled   4. stare   5. winking   7. glanced   8. frowned   9. grinned
DOWN 2. looking   3. gazed   4. smiled   6. sneered

EXERCISE 3 [page 152]

Answers will vary. Possible answers are:
1. My parents did not let me associate with troublemakers because they wanted me to succeed. (a)   2. The police dealt with the suspect harshly to get him to confess. (d)   3. Community members joined with each other to celebrate the end of the flood. (e)   4. The administration consulted with the teachers about a change in the degree requirements. (c)   5. I united with my neighbors in protesting the proposal to widen our street. (g)   6. The minority political party would not cooperate with the majority to find a solution to the welfare problem. (b)   7. My great uncle sided with the rebels during the Civil War. (f)

EXERCISE 4 [page 152]

1. (a) differ from (b) retires from (c) withdraw from (d) detached from
2. (a) escape from (b) Fleeing from
3. (a) dissented from (b) separate from
4. (a) deviated from (b) shrank from (c) recoiling from (d) abstained from

EXERCISE 5 [page 154]

1. prays for   2. asked for   3. thirsts for/longs for/yearns for   4. is yearning for/is longing for   5. years for/long for   6. hope for/ask for   7. longing for/yearning for [infinitive forms also OK—to long for, etc.]   8. wish for

EXERCISE 6 [page 154]

1. afraid of   2. safe from   3. sorry for   4. ignorant of   5. unhappy about   6. homesick for   7. proficient in   8. enthusiastic about

EXERCISE 7 [page 155]

Answers will vary. Possible answers are:
1. The World Wildlife Fund is interested in (b)   2. MADD is committed to helping reduce (e)   3. The

National Trust for Historic Preservation is dedicated to (d) 4. CARE is dedicated to (g) 5. The Sierra Club is accustomed to (f) 6. The March of Dimes is concerned about (a) 7. The International Eye Foundation is dedicated to (c)

EXERCISE 8 [page 156]

1. On the   2. on   3. in   4. In the   5. in   6. in the
7. On the   8. On   9. in

EXERCISE 9 [page 156]

1. On account of   2. In the course of   3. With the exception of   4. On the strength of   5. at odds with

EXERCISE 1 [page 158]

(1) growing/object of preposition   (2) to grow and to adapt/object   (3) maintaining/object of preposition; to think/subject complement; to keep/object; getting/object of preposition   (4) improving/object of preposition
(5) memory training/object of preposition   (6) to draw/object   (7) to mentally file/noun complement
(8) memory training/object of preposition
(9) showing/object; asking/object; to recall/object
(10) to establish/object   (11) to associate/object
(12) to exaggerate/object; to superimpose/object
(13) To find/subject; calling/object of preposition

EXERCISE 2 [page 159]

ACROSS 1. producing   2. Being   3. to stop
7. having been   10. received
DOWN 1. published   4. to find   5. having seen
6. been fired   8. Getting   9. to have

EXERCISE 3 [page 160]

Answers may vary. Possible answers are:
2. To change/Changing old habits (d)   3. Climbing mountains is (a)   4. To get caught cheating would be (j) 5. Saving lives is (c)   6. Paying the bills on time is (e) 7. Before doing anything inside a computer (b)
8. To make a chocolate cake (i)   9. To succeed in school was (g) 10. To stay in good shape (k)
11. Trying too hard (f)

EXERCISE 4 [page 161]

2. Genghis Khan's desire was to   (c) 3. What Abraham Lincoln is remembered for was emancipating (g) 4. My personal dream is to   (a) 5. The goal of the

---

6. in return for/in the process of   7. By means of
8. In the name of

EXERCISE 10 [page 157]

Answers will vary. Possible answers are:
1. According to statistics   2. With respect to the computer   3. According to a recent poll   4. Based on the witnesses' testimonies   5. Relating to your insurance policy   6. According to several scientists
7. With respect to my grandparents   8. Based on what I have discovered this year   9. Speaking of basketball
10. Pertaining to viruses

Unit 18
Gerunds and Infinitives

Peace Corps is to   (d) 6. One of the things Henry VIII is remembered for is beheading   (b) 7. The ambition of every rock group is to   (e) 8. One reason to become a doctor is to   (j) 9. What a workaholic enjoys is working   (f) 10. What everyone loves is receiving/to receive (h)

EXERCISE 5 [page 162]

Answers will vary. Possible answers are:
1. to get well   2. to relax   3. to let go   4. to keep up
5. to persist   6. to set aside   7. to create/to expand
8. to do/to try to accomplish

EXERCISE 6 [page 162]

Answers will vary. Possible answers are:
(2) to reach   (3) to get   (4) to make it   (5) to see
(6) to discover   (7) to find   (8) to turn back   (9) to stay   (10) to cross   (11) to be caught   (12) to have found the cave   (13) to set off again   (14) to have brought   (15) to be back   (16) to be alive

EXERCISE 7 [page 163]

1. I couldn't stop watching it.   5. I used to hate eating meat   8. Her lawyer advised her to drop the case.   9. I really appreciate your mentioning that 11. Would you hesitate to help   14. Gauguin hated living in France and yearned to paint   16. I don't deny visiting   17. She appears to be having trouble 18. he expected us to put in

EXERCISE 8 [page 164]

Part A (2) to see   (3) to concentrate, to leave
(4) tutoring, reading   (5) hawking   (7) to operate

(8) to use (9) to invent (11) manufacturing (13) experimenting, inventing (14) to invent (15) advancing (16) making, making (17) Moving, taking out (19) to record (22) perfecting, to replace (23) to see (24) passing (25) to make and distribute, to design (26) doing (28) to flow, to pursue

Part B (3) be unable + to concentrate; be forced + to leave (4) begin + tutoring (7) learn + to operate (8) neglect + to use (9) start + to invent (11) begin + manufacturing (13) devote (one's life to) + experimenting (14) want + to invent (15) care little about + advancing (16) become absorbed in + making (17) begin + taking out (19) test (a way) + to record (22) turn (one's attention to) + perfecting (23) try (materials) + to make; go on + to design (24) try + passing (25) exist + to make; go on + to design

EXERCISE 9 [page 166]

Answers may vary. Possible answers are:
1. to teach 2. to do/doing 3. to catch 4. experimenting; blowing up 5. to invent 6. to make/making 7. to work 8. to carry 9. inventing, advancing 10. to record 11. to replace 12. producing 13. to use

EXERCISE 10 [page 166]

1. Bob's 2. Maria's 3. the pool's 4. For a brand new car 5. Our candidate's 6. Eve's ... for her family 7. The timber company's 8. Pieter's 9. the high school's

EXERCISE 11 [page 167]

1. Democracies insist on holding free elections on a regular basis. 2. Some democracies call for the people to vote whenever they want to determine the level of popular confidence in the present government. 3. The candidates argue about spending money for projects and programs. 4. The voters hope for their elected officials to do what they promised during their campaigns. 5. The people consent to accept the

Unit 19
Perfective Infinitives

EXERCISE 1 [page 174]

1. to have been 2. to have acted 3. To have wasted 4. to have made 5. (a) to have joined (b) to have gone 6. (a) To have dared (b) to have done 7. (a) to have invited (b) To have prepared (c) to have stayed 8. (a) to have eaten (b) To have resisted (c) to have put in

EXERCISE 2 [page 175]

Answers will vary. Possible answers are:
1. to have finished all my research 2. for us to have undertaken 3. have shaken the hand of President Kennedy 4. to have learned how to use the computer 5. to have been one of the richest men who ever lived 6. to have seen the All-star game this year 7. to have

verdict of the majority. 6. People complain about elected officials forgetting their promises. 7. Elected officials often think about getting reelected.

EXERCISE 12 [page 168]

Answers will vary. Possible answers are:
1. I had to put off going there until I could finish my work. 2. I can't put up with taking any more abuse from the new manager. 3. I'm looking forward to walking around Paris and sitting in cafés. 4. She did, but she decided to go through with having it again because her condition seemed to be getting worse. 5. I've given up drinking. 6. We've taken up reading and playing chess again. 7. Not much. I carried on studying till nearly dawn.

EXERCISE 13 [page 169]

Answers will vary. Possible answers are:
1. James Watt was a Scottish engineer who is celebrated for inventing ... 2. Robert Fulton was an American inventor who was successful in improving ... 3. Samuel Colt was an American inventor and industrialist who was successful in pioneering ... 4. Joseph Henry was an American physicist and educator who was proficient at guiding others in research that led to ... 5. Enrico Fermi was an Italian physicist who was famous for building the ... 6. Count Ferdinand von Zeppelin was a German aeronautical engineer who was celebrated for perfecting ... 7. George Eastman was an American inventor and manufacturer who was famous for inventing ...

TEST PREP • UNITS 16–18 [page 171]

1. a	17. a
2. b	18. a
3. d	19. d
4. b	20. a
5. b	21. d
6. c	22. c
7. c	23. d
8. a	24. d
9. d	25. b
10. d	26. b
11. d	27. a
12. a/c	28. d
13. d	29. c
14. c	30. c
15. a	
16. c	

attended my graduation   8. have attended grad school
9. us to have skate-boarded down that steep hill

EXERCISE 3 [page 175]

1. to have been/relative to the past   2. to have experienced/relative to the past   3. to have finished/relative to the past   4. to have been/relative to the past   5. to have written; to have changed/relative to the past   6. to have begun/relative to the present   7. to have made/relative to the future

EXERCISE 4 [page 176]

1. To have seen what is right and not to have done it is cowardice.   2. To have died for an idea is to have placed a pretty high price upon conjecture.   3. There are two tragedies in life. One is not to have gotten your heart's desire. The other is to have gotten it.   4. To have interpreted is to have impoverished.   5. The easiest person to have deceived is one's self.

EXERCISE 5 [page 177]

1. . . . consider America to have been discovered . . .
2. . . . not to have been . . .   3. . . . reported the high government official to have been selling . . .
4. . . . found all the jewels to have been stolen.
5. . . . people claim the Nazca lines in Peru to have been . . .   6. . . . low enough for them to have been accorded . . .   7. They promised all the work to have been done . . .   8. . . . expects their papers to have been checked . . .   9. She was thrilled to have been chosen . . .   10. The guerrillas claimed to have been educating . . .

EXERCISE 6 [page 178]

1. . . . not to have tried . . .   2. . . . never to have heard . . .   3. . . . never to have given . . .   4. . . . not to have had . . .   5. . . . not to have investigated . . .

EXERCISE 7 [page 178]

Answers will vary. Possible answers are:
1. I would love to have had more . . .   2. I would hate to have been discovered . . .   3. I would prefer to have been given . . .   4. I would like to have spent more time . . .   5. I would hate to have come . . .   6. I would prefer to have been able . . .   7. I would like to have known . . . .
8. I would love to have been served . . .   9. I would like to have done even . . .   10. I would hate to have come . . .

EXERCISE 8 [page 179]

Answers will vary. Possible answers are:
1. It was nothing less than a miracle for them to have escaped the burning wreckage alive.   2. It was really

---

sweet of your mother to have sent a cake and gift for our anniversary.   3. We were shocked to have read about the latest international banking scandal that involved so many prominent figures.   4. It is generous of you to have spent so much of your free time doing volunteer work in the community.   5. It would have been totally unacceptable for anyone to have come to this gala event in ragged old clothes.   6. It must be thrilling to have gone hang gliding in the Alps.   7. It would have been tedious to have worked sixty hours a week on an assembly line, doing the same thing over and over again.   8. For the whole family to have gotten together at Thanksgiving would have been marvelous.   9. It was incredibly annoying to have gotten caught in a ten-mile-long traffic jam on the freeway this afternoon.

EXERCISE 9 [page 180]

Answers will vary. Possible answers are:
1. I seem to have left my wallet with my license at home.   2. The lead singer seems to have had too much to drink.   3. The waiter appears to have forgotten us.
4. The printer ribbon (or ink cartridge) seems to have been quite low on ink. 5. There appears to have been a mistake. I believe I asked for a nonsmoking room.

EXERCISE 10 [page 181]

Answers will vary. Possible answers are:
1. By June, I expect to have finished all the courses I am presently taking—that is, Advanced English, English Composition, Accounting, Computer Science, and Calculus.   2. By the time I graduate, I plan to have played on the soccer team and contributed a few pieces to the College Review.   3. Before I make a job commitment, I plan to have visited Hewlett-Packard and possibly Claris.   4. Once I was supposed to have helped my father paint the house but I injured my leg playing football.   5. Within the next five years, I hope to have gotten married and to have finished all my degree work and to have found a job I like.

EXERCISE 11 [page 182]

Answers will vary. Possible answers are:
1. I drank enough coffee to have kept me awake twenty-four hours.   2. That horror movie was scary enough to have given me a heart attack.   3. The slide show of their last trip was boring enough to have put anyone to sleep.   4. The storm was snowy enough to have buried all the cars on the street   5. After exam week, I was tired enough to have slept for days.
6. The salesman was convincing enough for me to have wanted to buy the stereo system right away.

EXERCISE 12 [page 182]

1. Derek's too serious to have gone to see . . .
2. Dr. Mayer's far too dedicated a teacher to have

returned . . .   3. The border's too well guarded for them to have . . .   4. That lawyer's arguments were

3. The border's too well guarded for them to have . . .   4. That lawyer's arguments were too convincing for him to have . . .   5. His excuses were somehow too contrived to have been believed.

Unit 20
Adjective Complements in Subject and Predicate Position

EXERCISE 1 [page 184]

Answers will vary. Possible answers are:
1. to have carried someone on its back for such a length of time   2. giving its life to save a human being   3. an elephant could be so careful   4. the chickens are treated this way   5. to have found his way such a distance   6. camouflaging themselves in such intelligent ways

EXERCISE 2 [page 185]

Answers will vary. Possible answers are:
1. I would be ready to take my first step.   2. I would be happy to be taken to a playground.   3. I would be eager to go to school.   4. I would be anxious for my friends to call me.   5. I would be eager to try something new.   6. I would be ready for a challenge to motivate me.

EXERCISE 3 [page 185]

Answers will vary. Possible answers are:
1. It is insensitive   2. It seems odd/is unfortunate   3. is sad   4. It is fascinating/is disturbing   5. will be helpful   6. It is compulsory   7. is wonderful   8. It is certain/is foolish   9. It appears likely/will be difficult.   10. is regrettable

EXERCISE 4 [page 186]

Answers will vary. Possible answers are:
1. That Bokassa could be so self-indulgent is terrible.   2. That someone could have so many credit cards and such a wallet is quite amusing.   3. That someone could have lost so much money so fast is hard to imagine.   4. That someone could be so mean and callous is pathetic.   5. That such a disaster occurred is terribly tragic.

EXERCISE 5 [page 187]

Answers will vary. Possible answers are:
1. It's frightening that two highly dangerous submarines could collide.   2. It's fortunate that the submarines that collided didn't explode.   3. It's unfortunate that a man died on the ship in the North Sea.   4. It's encouraging that more habitats are being set aside for threatened species.   5. It's shocking that so many people may have AIDS.   6. It's good that some of Iraq's deadly weapons have been destroyed.

EXERCISE 6 [page 188]

Answers will vary. Possible answers are:
1. For carpenters to take no measurements would be unusual.   2. For scuba divers to dive without first checking their oxygen supply would be unusual.   3. For critics to write only positive things would be unusual. 4. For vegetarians to order hamburgers at a restaurant would be unexpected.   5. For Buddhist monks to go hunting would be unexpected.   6. For ballerinas to play football would be unexpected.   7. For computer programmers not to like math would be unusual.

EXERCISE 7 [page 189]

1. factual   2. potential   3. potential   4. factual   5. factual   6. potential   7. factual   8. factual   9. potential   10. factual

Unit 21
Noun Complements Taking *That* Clauses

EXERCISE 1 [page 190]

ACROSS   1. plan   2. to   3. for   4. motivation
9. reason
DOWN   1. permission   2. that   5. theory
6. news   7. fact   8. to say

EXERCISE 2 [page 191]

1. rain on barren hills   2. indigenous people are forced to relocate   3. water supplies may dry up during dry seasons   4. the World Bank and other aid organizations have contributed to the destruction of fragile mountain habitats

EXERCISE 3 [page 191]

1. a   2. a   3. a   4. b   5. b

EXERCISE 4 [page 192]

Answers will vary. Possible answers are:
1. The fact that Edison could spare only an hour for his marriage was proof of his complete devotion to his work.   2. The news that a polio vaccine had been discovered reduced the terror that people felt at the approach of summer.   3. The idea that a celebrity like Alexander Graham Bell could really be ill at ease in public belies the idea that all celebrities enjoy basking in the limelight.   4. The idea that Haydn had to resort to a devious method to communicate to his employer his need for a vacation is highly amusing.   5. The belief that the mind was controlled by reason was brought into question by Sigmund Freud.

EXERCISE 5 [page 193]

2. the fact   5. ~~the fact~~   7. ~~the fact~~   9. ~~the fact~~   11. ~~the fact~~   13. the fact

EXERCISE 6 [page 193]

Answers will vary. Possible answers are:
1. Carlos and Teresa are accustomed to the fact that their house is small.   2. Jorge is excited about the news that he has received two scholarship offers.   3. Jorge has had to put up with the fact that his little brother is noisy and messy.   4. Gloria is jealous of the fact that Jorge seems to get all the attention.   5. Julio is thrilled about the idea that the bedroom will soon be all his.   6. Guadalupe is concerned about the notion that her older sister is attracted to potentially dangerous situations.   7. Gloria is annoyed with the fact that her younger sister talks on the phone a lot.

EXERCISE 7 [page 194]

Answers will vary. Possible answers are:
1. I would remind them of the fact that they should always thank someone who has done them a courtesy.   2. I would remind them of the fact that they shouldn't smoke in a nonsmoking area.   3. I would remind them of the fact that the windshield fluid is a completely different substance from the radiator fluid, which would only smear their windshield.   4. I would remind them of the fact that "enjoy" is followed by a gerund.   5. I would remind them of the fact that it is polite to say "excuse me" to anyone they bump into.   6. I would remind them of the fact that it is cold outside.   7. I would remind them of the fact that the speed limit is 30 mph or less.

EXERCISE 8 [page 195]

1. OK   2. What explains the fact that in some cases . . .   3. . . . was bizarre.   4. OK   5. She was conscious of the fact that . . .   6. OK   7. . . . about the fact that he has . . .   8. OK   9. . . . the notion that we . . .   10. OK   11. . . . supported the fact that the . . .   12. OK

TEST PREP • UNITS 19–21 [page 197]

1. b
2. a
3. a
4. c
5. b
6. b
7. a
8. c
9. d
10. b
11. c
12. a
13. c
14. b
15. d
16. b
17. b
18. d
19. c
20. b
21. a
22. b
23. b
24. b
25. a
26. c
27. b
28. c
29. b
30. b

Unit 22

Subjunctive Verbs In *That* Clauses

EXERCISE 1 [page 200]

1. John recommends that Bill (should) see an eye doctor.   2. They demand that the chief assign more police to . . .   3. They insisted that she get . . .   4. The memo stipulates that all personnel (should) wear formal . . .   5. Betty suggests that he/she try the house special.   6. The town planner proposes that they ban . . .   7. The teacher advises that he/she should check his/her figures again.   8. The librarian requested that we lower . . .   9. The president of the union insists they not lose hope.   10. She begs that he/she not send . . .

EXERCISE 2 [page 201]

1. He laughed at my suggestion that he ban students from chewing gum . . .   2. He/She smiled at my demand that the shops be closed . . .   3. He/She disregarded my request that he/she not print any . . .   4. She did not listen to my advice that she forbid . . .

EXERCISE 3 [page 202]

Answers will vary. Possible answers are:
1. Kurt's suggestion that he poison the dog was

immoral.   2. Sally's proposal that he talk to the dog's owners again was worth a try.   3. Lisa's recommendation that he make friends with the dog might or might not work.   4. Rod's suggestion that he release the dog from its chain was somewhat risky.   5. Scot's advice that he buy earplugs was a good temporary solution.   6. Kate's suggestion that he get other neighbors to sign a petition was a good idea.

EXERCISE 4 [page 202]

Answers will vary. Possible answers are:
PART A 1. That Matthew L. be hospitalized immediately.   2. that Peter S. stop smoking   3. That Louise M. have a pregnancy test   4. that Greg A. apply a cold pack to his knees.   5. that Ronnie P. drink less coffee.
PART B Students' original responses will vary.

EXERCISE 5 [page 204]

ACROSS 1. build   3. vital   6. mandatory
7. stipulates   9. suggested   10. decision
DOWN 2. desirable   4. that   5. take   7. should
8. be

Unit 23
Emphatic Structures: Emphatic *Do, No* Versus *Not*

EXERCISE 1 [page 205]

no doubt; Africa does; no sight; no small; no sense; do need; do need; Do that; no package; . . . no lazy; no other; Do make

EXERCISE 2 [page 205]

1. They did like   2. I will fix   3. They have made   4. I certainly do have   5. They really are going   6. I did notice   7. The senate will allow   8. Judy has learned   9. I certainly do understand   10. I really have seen

EXERCISE 3 [page 206]

1. **Meg:** Yes, I did remember.   2. **Nita:** Oh, then who did take the money?   3. **Ole:** Have you heard that Robert did manage to pass the chemistry exam? **Tuan:** I'm glad he did pass. Now he won't . . .   4. **Paula:** It does seem that everyone in Darren's family has a major problem. **Rod:** Yes, he does have a dysfunctional family.   5. **Aziz:** No, he never does send cards.   6. **Hilda:** Not bad. Even though I don't usually like spicy food, I did find the flavors intriguing.   7. **Sarala:** Of course. It's a bit wet after the rain. Do watch out for the puddles.   8. **Taylor:** That's ridiculous. I did pay it. I do like watching golf on TV. **Nick:** No, I really do enjoy the suspense and the skill that you see.   9. **Nick:**   10. **Carla:** Did you hear that the Bonington expedition did make it safely to the top of Nanga Parbat? **Al:** That's great news! When I heard there were storms, I did doubt they would make it.

EXERCISE 4 [page 207]

had no time; had no comforts; had no warm room or soft bed; with no food, home, money, or job; had no way out; with no friends; had no dress or ride; will have no husband; want no husband; is no princess

EXERCISE 5 [page 208]

Answers will vary. Possible answers are:
There are no windows in our room. We have no water in our room. We have no clean towels. We have no air conditioning. There is no water in the swimming pool. The restaurant has nothing that we like. There is no private beach. There is no one around to help us. There is no taxi available to take us around. There is no grocery store within easy walking distance. There is nothing for the children to do.

Unit 24
Fronting Structures for Emphasis and Focus

EXERCISE 1 [page 210]

Fronted structure is underlined; inverted subject/verb is in **bold**.   1. With great excitement/Fronted structure.   2. Seldom **do we eat**/Fronted structure/Inversion.   3. Because we wanted to have a good view of the stage/Fronted structure   4. No fronted structure.   5. Rarely **did my parents allow**/Fronted structure/Inversion   6. To cut down on cholesterol/Fronted structure   7. No fronted structure.   8. Nowhere in the town **could I find**/Fronted structure/Inversion   9. No fronted structure.   10. Rain or shine/Fronted structure

EXERCISE 2 [page 211]

Answers will vary. Possible answers are:
1. a. Just after sunset b. With their arms waving
2. a. To find a lead b. In the living room 3. a. As the clock was striking twelve b. Because they wanted to know what was inside 4. a. In the valley below b. To their utter amazement 5. a. To find out how she's doing b. Twice a week

EXERCISE 3 [page 212]

(1) Little did I realize (2) Fluttering through the air
(3) In the center of the village (4) Not for anything
(5) Almost never (6) So weak (7) Around me (8) Not quite as bad as everyone feared (9) Never (10) Never Little did we suspect (11) No sooner

EXERCISE 4 [page 213]

1. (c) 2. (j) 3. (g) 4. (a) 5. (k) 6. (e) 7. (f)
8. (i) 9. (b) 10. (d) 11. (h)

EXERCISE 5 [page 214]

1. Under no conditions does that restaurant permit smoking. 2. Not once has he ever said he was sorry.
3. Not for anything would I take that drug.
4. Never had she felt so insulted. 5. Under no circumstances will the theater allow children to see that movie. 6. Not until recently did I realize the complexity of the health care dilemma. 7. In no way does this alter my opinion. 8. In no case can they leave the children unattended at home. 9. Not since I left home have I felt this way. 10. Nowhere have I seen such fascinating architecture as in India.

EXERCISE 6 [page 215]

ACROSS 3. Not only 4. Neither 6. Nor 8. anyone
DOWN 1. will 2. sooner 5. either 6. Not
7. could

EXERCISE 7 [page 215]

1. contrast of the structure 2. focus on the delayed subject 3. emphasis 4. emphasis 5. focus on the delayed subject 6. contrast of the structure
7. emphasis 8. focus on the delayed subject
9. emphasis 10. contrast of the structure

EXERCISE 8 [page 216]

1. *Nowhere have I heard of such high prices.* (form)
2. Fronted negative not appropriate for this context; *scarcely* should not be emphasized. (use) 3. Fronted negative not appropriate for this context; *little* . . .
should not be emphasized. (use) 4. *Never have I been in such pain before.* (form) 5. No way = informal register.
Inappropriate for context. (use) 6. *Under no circumstances can I take cortisone.* (form)

EXERCISE 9 [page 217]

1. c
2. e
3. g
4. b
5. h
6. a
7. f
8. d

Unit 25

Focusing and Emphasizing Structures: *It*-Clefts and *Wh*-Clefts

EXERCISE 1 [page 218]

1. It is/was Carl Jung who (e) 2. It is in Dubai where (i) 3. It is/was Florence that (g) 4. It is/was Marco Polo who (a) 5. It is/was at Versailles where (h)
6. It is/was the Wright Brothers who (b) 7. It is/was in China where (d) 8. It is/was the Black Death that (j) 9. It is Wyoming that (f) 10. It is the Haj that (c)

EXERCISE 2 [page 219]

1. It was Thoreau, not Emerson, who lived . . . 2. It is the students who have the . . . 3. It was in Toledo that . . . 4. It is his thoughts of his children that . . .
5. It wasn't our cat who killed . . . 6. It is Marjorie who will . . . 7. It is Ivor who must have taken . . .
8. It is my aunt who has . . . 9. It's the number three bus that you need to catch. 10. It was shrimp, not steak, that I ordered.

EXERCISE 3 [page 220]

2. It was the German scientists Otto Hahn and Fritz Strassman who demonstrated the process of nuclear fission in the winter of 1938. 3. It was to inform him about recent discoveries concerning uranium and also about the possibility of constructing a powerful bomb that Albert Einstein wrote a letter to President Roosevelt in 1939. 4. It was to develop an explosive devise based on nuclear fission that the top-secret Manhattan project was established in August 1942. 5. It was in a squash court beneath the stands of an abandoned football field at the University of Chicago on December 2, 1942, that Enrico Fermi and his colleagues produced the first controlled nuclear reaction. 6. It was J. Robert Oppenheimer who the Army chose in 1943 to direct the lab in Los Alamos, New Mexico, where the atomic bombs would be designed and assembled. 7. It was in huge reactors and separator plants in Washington and Tennessee where the uranium and plutonium for the bombs were produced. 8. It was on July 16, 1945, that the first atomic bomb was detonated near Alamogordo, New Mexico.

EXERCISE 4 [page 221]

Answers will vary. Possible answers are:
2. It's because they got buried under a heap of papers that I forgot to renew them. 3. It's because the test was too hard that I didn't get the grade I wanted. 4. It's because I was in a great hurry this morning and wasn't paying attention to what I put on that I am wearing two different socks. 5. It's because I have some family obligations that I can't make it to class today. 6. It's because I was late to my sister's wedding that I was caught speeding.

EXERCISE 5 [page 222]

Answers will vary. Possible answers are:
1. It's my cousin Erik who is . . . 2. It's my friend Cheryl who tends . . . 3. It's my nephew Alex who tends . . . 4. It is my father who has traveled . . . 5. It's my mother-in-law who would be . . . 6. It's my friend Mike who tends . . . 7. It's my friend Beth who . . . 8. It's my cousin Galen who is . . .

EXERCISE 6 [page 223]

2. It is stamina 3. It is memory 4. It was stagefright 5. It is inspiration 6. It was a drought

EXERCISE 7 [page 223]

2. It was out of a sense of honor 3. It is out of generosity 4. It was out of malice 5. It was for his country 6. It was out of frustration

EXERCISE 8 [page 224]

1. It was Sean Connery who starred . . . 2. It is Botswana that is directly . . . 3. It was Abraham Lincoln who was elected President in 1860. 4. It is the brain that is divided . . . 5. It is *Frankenstein* that is the name of Mary Shelley's novel. 6. It was Hernando Cortés who . . . 7. It is a vaccine that makes a person . . . 8. It was the Bible that Gutenberg published in 1445. 9. It is the game of chess that ends . . .

EXERCISE 9 [page 225]

Answers will vary. Possible answers are:
1. It was the prophet Mohammed who fled Mecca for Medina, Arabia, in 622. 2. It was in Armenia that Ashot I founded the Bagratide dynasty in 859. 3. It was in 1298 that Marco Polo began dictating his memoirs in a Genoan jail. 4. It was in 1581 that Francis Drake returned to England after a voyage of circumnavigation. 5. It was in Vienna that Beethoven became Haydn's pupil in 1792. 6. It was Frank Whittle who built the first jet engine in England in 1937.

EXERCISE 10 [page 226]

1. It is just after midnight in Istanbul when the famous writer John LeCarré's plane lands. 2. It is in the Red Sea that oceanographer Jacques Cousteau prepares to dive at dawn. 3. It is during an avalanche on Mt. Makalu in the Himalayas that the mountaineer Peter Hillary finds himself wondering whether he should retire. 4. It is Colin Bragg, the gangster, who suddenly disappears in Nassau one day in February. 5. It is at the end of a long and intense week at the Sloan Institute that medical researcher Tsering Paldum first notices some rapid changes in a fungal culture.

EXERCISE 11 [page 226]

Answers will vary. Possible answers are:
2. Would you please tell me again how it is that gamma globulin types differ? 3. I told you yesterday that it was on the fifteenth, not the sixteenth. 4. Who was it that could have been calling so late last night? 5. He said it was because of a low pressure front coming in from the south that it was going to rain. 6. I don't understand what it is that I should fill out on this form.

EXERCISE 12 [page 227]

1. What Kennedy said was (e)   2. What made . . . was . . . (i)   3. Where Tristan da Cunha . . . is (k)   4. . . . planet is (h)   5. . . . was crowned . . . (j)   6. . . . revision easier is (b)   7. . . . characteristics is (c)   8. . . . iron mask was/is (d)   9. What athletes have to do is . . . (f)   10. . . . Hamlet believed is (a)   11. . . . noted for is (g)

EXERCISE 13 [page 228]

1. What follows the verb *forget* is an infinitive.
2. What Muslims cannot eat is pork.   3. What the Confederate army wore was gray.   4. Where the Olympic Games started was in Greece.   5. What all children need is love.   6. What *must* indicates is obligation.   7. What our galaxy is called is the Milky Way.   8. What Vincent van Gogh did was paint pictures.

TEST PREP • UNITS 22–25 [page 229]

1. d	9. a	17. a	25. b
2. b	10. c	18. d	26. a
3. c	11. d	19. b	27. a
4. a	12. d	20. d	28. c
5. c	13. c	21. a	29. a
6. b	14. d	22. b	30. b
7. c	15. b	23. c	
8. c	16. a	24. d	

AUDIO SCRIPT

(CD1 Tracks 1, 2) Unit 1, Page 10, Activity 1

(CD1 Track 1) Passage 1

From when I was very tiny, my mother used to take me down to the *finca*, wrapped in a shawl on her back. She told me that when I was about 2, I had to be carried screaming onto the lorry because I didn't want to go. I was so frightened I didn't stop crying until we were about halfway there. The lorry holds about 40 people.

But in with the people go the animals (dog, cats, chickens), which the people from the Altiplano take with them while they are in the *finca*. It sometimes took two nights and a day from my village to the coast. By the end of the journey, the smell—the filth of people and animals—was unbearable.

(CD1 Track 2) Passage 2

Any tree will do to make a house, but (I think this is part of our culture) only if it's cut at full moon. We say the wood lasts longer if it's cut when the moon is young. When we build a house, we make the roof from a sort of palm tree found near the foot of the mountains. We call it *pamac*. For us, the most elegant houses are made with cane leaves, because you have to go a long way to get them. You have to have men to go and get them to make the house. We were poor and had neither money to buy cane leaves nor anyone to go and get them. They're only found down on the *fincas* on the coast and they're very expensive. The landowners charge by the bunch . . . and it takes 50 bunches for a house.

(CD1 Track 3) Unit 2, Page 35, Activity 1

Dr. M. was a distinguished musician. For many years he had been a singer; later he became a teacher at the local school of music. It was at this school that others began to observe Dr. M.'s strange problem. Sometimes Dr. M. did not recognize the faces of people he had known for a long time. Sometimes he saw faces where there were none: on a water hydrant, for example, or on the carved knobs of furniture. When Dr. M. finally went to Dr. Oliver Sacks's clinic, these events had been going on for years.

At the clinic, it was while Dr. Sacks was examining Dr. M.'s reflexes that the first bizarre experience occurred. Dr. Sacks had taken off Dr. M.'s left shoe to test his reflexes. He later left Dr. M. for a few minutes, assuming Dr. M. would put the shoe back on. When Dr. Sacks returned to his examining room, Dr. M. had not put the shoe on. Dr. Sacks asked Dr. M. if he could help, and Dr. M. said that he had forgotten to put the shoe on. Finally Dr. M. looked down at his foot and asked if his foot was his shoe. When Dr. Sacks pointed to Dr. M.'s shoe nearby, Dr. M. told him that he thought the shoe was his foot!

Later, as Dr. M. was getting ready to leave, he started to look for his hat. He reached for his wife's head and tried to put it on. Poor Dr. M. had mistaken his wife for a hat!

(CD1 Track 4) Unit 3, Page 57, Activity 1

For many years, the Gallup organization has been asking Americans what their attitudes are about child raising. We will be summarizing some of this information in response to three questions asked on this topic. The polls we will mention were taken during the following years: 1947, 1973, 1980, 1990, and 1996.

The first question is: What do you think is the ideal number of children for a family to have? Comparing four polls between 1973 and 1996, over 50% agree in all four polls that the ideal number is two. The next most popular number of children is three. There is a slight increase, however, in the number of people who think that three, rather than two children, is ideal in 1996 compared to those polled in 1990. In 1990, almost two-thirds, or 67%, say that two is the ideal number, with 18% saying that three is ideal. In 1996, only 57% think two is ideal and 21% believe three is ideal. One of the biggest differences between 1973 and 1996 is the percentage of people who think four or five children are ideal. For example, in 1973, 20% of the respondents fell into these categories compared to only 11% in 1996.

The second question is: Which do you, yourself, think is easier to raise—a boy or a girl?

Those polled had four choices to answer this question: a boy, or girl, no difference, or no opinion. The responses reveal that more Americans today than in 1947 feel there is a difference in raising boys and girls. In 1947, 24%, or almost one of every four persons asked, say there is no difference. In 1996, only 12% feel there is no difference. More people in 1947 also had no opinion: 11% compared to 8% in 1996. More people in both time periods agree that boys are more difficult to raise than girls. In 1996, over half, 51%, say that boys are more difficult compared to 42% in 1947. During both time periods, fewer than one-third think that girls are more difficult to raise.

The final question is: Do you think children are better off if their mother is home and doesn't hold a job or are the children just as well off if the mother works?

A comparison between polls in 1990 and 1996 indicate that fewer Americans than before believe children are better off if the mother is at home. In 1990, 73% respond that they are better off if the mother is at home; in 1996 64% feel this way; 31% of the respondents in 1996 say that the children are just as well off if the mother works, compared to 24% in 1990.

Now you will hear seven statements. Listen carefully to each statement and decide whether it is true or false based on the notes you have taken.

1. Most Americans think the ideal number of children for a family is three.

2. In the 1973 poll, more Americans think that four or five is an ideal number of children than do respondents in the 1996 poll.

3. In the 1996 poll, the majority of respondents believe that there is a difference between raising boys and raising girls.

4. Almost three-fourths of the respondents in 1996 say that boys are the most difficult to raise.

5. The majority of respondents to the 1990 and 1996 polls say that children are better off if the mother is at home.

6. If we compare the 1990 and 1996 polls, the percentage of respondents who believe that children are just as well off if the mother works increases.

7. In 1996 almost half of the respondents indicate that children are just as well off if the mother works.

(CD1 Track 5) Unit 4, Page 79, Activity 1

When psychologists conduct experimental research with human subjects, they often don't tell the subjects the true purpose of the experiment because that knowledge may change the way the subjects behave. In the Milgram experiment, the real purpose was to see if people will obey an authority figure who tells them to do something that goes against their moral code. However, what the researchers told the subjects was that they would be participating in an experiment to see how punishing affects learning. More than 1,000 people participated in the experiment at various universities.

For this experiment the researcher told subjects that they would be in the role of "teacher." They introduced a man as a "fellow volunteer" who would be in the role of learner. However, the "learner" was actually someone who knew the true purpose of the experiment. The researchers seated the subject in front of a machine that they said would deliver electric shocks when the subject pulled down a lever. They strapped the learner in a chair in an adjoining room where the subjects could see him. The researchers told the subject that the task of the "learner" was to recite

a list of word pairs that he had memorized. They instructed the subject to give the learner an electric shock whenever he made a mistake. The shock levels as marked on the shock machine ranged from "Slight shock" to "Danger—severe shock" to "XXX," the most severe level. As the experiment progressed, the researchers told the subject to administer increasingly higher voltages. The learner-victim did not actually receive any shocks, but he acted as if he did whenever the subject pulled a lever. At certain levels, the victim shouted to the subject to stop or demanded to be set free. The results of the multiple experiments revealed that almost two-thirds of the subjects obeyed the researchers to the fullest, regardless of how much the learner-victim shouted or how much pain he seemed to be experiencing. Most subjects delivered what they thought were dangerous amounts of shocks to another person. Although most people protested to the researchers and sometimes implored them to stop the experiment, most of them did not disobey when the researchers ordered them to continue.

Today, I will be talking about computers. First I will provide a little background information. Then I will tell you about how they work and their various sizes.

Historically, the earliest computing device was the abacus used by the ancient Greeks and Romans and, interestingly, this device is still in use in the East today. There are mechanical devices using sliding scales, similar to the slide rule, which date back almost two millennia. These were used for performing various kinds of calculation, usually as an aid to navigation.

In 1642, the French philosopher-mathematician Blaise Pascal built a mechanical adding machine, and in 1671, a German philosopher-mathematician, Gottfried Leibniz, built a machine to perform multiplication. In 1835, the British mathematician Charles Babbage designed the first mechanical computer, the analytical engine. The work of another British mathematician, Alan Turing, in the 1930s, marked the next major milestone. He developed the mathematical theory of computation and, in particular, showed how a machine could be conceived which could perform any computation (the so-called Turing Machine). The digital computer is the direct descendant of these ideas. In the 1940s, American mathematician John van Neumann developed the basic design for today's electronic computers. Finally, with the development of the transistor in 1952 and the subsequent microelectronics revolution, the Computer Age was started.

Now, how does a computer work exactly? A computer is a collection of various components. At the heart is the CPU (central processing unit) which performs all the computations. This is supported by memory, which holds the current program and data, and "logic arrays," which help move information around the system. A main power supply is needed and, in the case of a mini- or mainframe computer, a cooling system. The computer's "device driver" circuits control the peripheral devices, or add-ons, which can be attached. These will normally be keyboards and (visual display unit) VDU screens for user input and output, disc drive units for mass memory storage, and printers for printed output.

Sometimes more intelligence has been attributed to computers than should be. A computer can only carry out tasks as commanded by the programmer, who translates instructions written in everyday language into a program that is a coded form matching the electronic coding within the computer's internal machinery. The program and data to be manipulated—that is, text, figures, images, or sounds—are input into the computer which then processes the data and outputs the results. The results can be printed out or displayed on a VDU, or stored in a memory unit for subsequent manipulation. Whatever the task, a computer can function in only one of four ways: input-output operations, arithmetical operations (addition, subtraction, multiplication, and division), logic and comparison operations (for example, is the value of A equal to, less than, or greater than B), and movement of data to, from, and within the central memory of the machine. The programmer's role is to devise a set of instructions, an algorithm, that utilizes these four functions in a combination appropriate to the job in question.

(CD 1 Track 7) Dialogue 1—A couple on their way to a party

Woman: I hate to say this, Mark, but I think we're lost.

Man: Lost? Nah, we're not lost. What makes you think that?

Woman: Well, I don't know how you define lost, but we've just driven by this corner three times now. Let's stop at the next gas station and get directions.

Man: Oh, we don't need to do that. I can figure this out. We'll just keep going straight for a while instead of turning again.

Woman: But I don't see how that's going to help. Why don't you slow down and I'll ask that woman coming down the street if she knows where Banks Avenue is.

Man: Hey, don't you trust me? I'll get us there. Don't worry. We don't need to ask anyone for directions.

(CD1 Track 8) Dialogue 2—A couple at home

Woman: Hi, dear. You're home early!

Man: Yeah, I finished meeting with all my clients at 3, so I thought I'd beat the rush hour traffic. So how was your day? You were at the university all day weren't you?

Woman: Yeah, I had a really busy day! I had conferences with students all morning. Then I had to attend that seminar I told you about and two committee meetings in the afternoon. I thought the last one would never end!

Man: Huh. . . .

Woman: And in between I was working on my presentation for the trip to Montreal next month. And guess what? I got a phone call from our old friend Rebecca. She's got a job now at a college in New Jersey. Remember her?

Man: Yeah.

Woman: So how about you? How was your day?

Man: Oh, fine.

Woman: Well, did you have a busy day too?

Man: Yeah.

Woman: So . . . what did you do?

Man: Oh, nothing important.

(CD1 Track 9) Unit 7, Page 145, Activity 1

In the United States there are a number of ways to leave property to those you want to have it after your death. Fortunately, there are safe and understandable methods you can use that will save time and money when your property is passed on. A few terms are necessary in understanding the nitty-gritty details of "estate planning."

Estate planning is one of the more jargon-ridden areas of law. However, there are some legal terms that anyone who wants to learn about the subject must know. Some are euphemisms. For example, a dead person is referred to as a *decedent*. Others are technical terms like the following:

Testate means to die leaving a will or other valid property-transfer device.

Intestate means to die without having left a will or any plan to transfer property.

Realty property is real estate, or in other words, the land and the buildings on it.

Personal property is every kind of property, from stocks to cash to furniture to wedding rings to your pet canary and your old magazines.

Gifts means property you transfer freely—that is, not by sale or trade—to a person or institution.

Finally, *estate* means all the property you own, minus anything you owe.

(CD1 Track 10) Unit 8, Page 161, Activity 1

Second Chance

Kimi Tamura and Fred Escobar were born in the same year but in different cities in the U.S. When they were 12 years old, their families both moved to Los Angeles. The Tamuras and the Escobars moved to the same neighborhood near downtown Los Angeles. Coincidentally, the Tamuras lived on the third floor and the Escobars lived on the fourth floor of the same apartment building.

Kimi and Fred met each other for the first time in school. Kimi will never forget that day. She had long, beautiful braids which hung down her back. During the first hour, Fred had managed to tie her braids in a knot around the back of her chair. When Kimi got up to write an answer on the blackboard, her head tugged back and she screamed in pain. The whole class laughed at the joke, except the teacher who made Fred stay after school and wash the blackboards.

After this experience, Fred knew that "It was love at first sight." He was glad he lived in the same building as Kimi. Fred continually thought of all kinds of excuses to knock on her door. "Could she loan him a newspaper?", "Did she have any paper he could borrow?", "Did she want to walk to school with him?", and so on. He did everything he could to see her as often as possible.

When Kimi and Fred turned 16, they started to go steady. They also gave each other special birthday gifts. Fred gave Kimi a ring which had the engraving "My true love forever." Kimi gave Fred a bright red model car. On the hood, she had painted the words "My heart races for you."

Kimi and Fred were sweethearts during the rest of high school. They were even the king and the queen of the high school prom. This did not get in the way of their studies. They wanted to get married some day, but not then. They both had important career plans and wanted to wait a while. Kimi wanted to be a writer. She had dreams of writing The Great American Novel. Fred wanted to be an engineer. He had dreams of designing a

famous bridge some day. Unfortunately, their preferred colleges were on different coasts (Fred in California and Kimi in New York) and for one reason or another, the two friends lost track of each other.

Fred ended up marrying a nurse he had met in one of his college classes. Kimi ended up marrying an artist she had met at her church. The years went by; both Fred and Kimi raised wonderful families. Unfortunately, when they were in their 50s, they became widowed. On his 60th birthday, Fred began thinking of his old sweetheart Kimi whom he had not seen for more than 40 years. He decided to try to locate her. He dialed an L. Tamura in the directory and fortunately reached Kimi's sister. She told him that Kimi was now living only a few miles from Kimi's original apartment in Los Angeles.

When he found this out, he nervously dialed her number and asked if he could meet her the next Saturday evening at 6:00 in the lobby of a Los Angeles hotel in which they had had their high school senior prom. Kimi was delighted to hear from him and immediately accepted his invitation. Not knowing whether they would recognize each other after so many years, they both agreed to wear carnations on the lapels of their coats.

On Saturday, Kimi arrived early to the hotel but realized that she had forgotten one thing—the carnation. She knew of a florist shop just around the corner, so she decided to make a phone call to see if by chance it was still open. As she sat in the phone booth making her call, she looked towards the front door and saw a large man with a red carnation walk in. Kimi could not believe her eyes—this could not be "her Fred." He was very unattractive: he was smoking a cigar and had a scruffy beard. His clothes looked filthy and he had gained a lot of weight. Kimi turned her back toward the door of the phone booth and started to dial.

(CD1 Tracks 11, 12, 13) Unit 9, Page 176, Activity 1

(CD1 Track 11) Number 1

We will begin our tour this morning with a bus ride past several interesting sites in Hong Kong. Flagstaff House, which contains a Museum of Tea Drinking—it's one of the finest surviving colonial buildings in Hong Kong. The House, which is open daily from 10 A.M. to 5 P.M., is on the east side of Cotton Tree Drive. As you can see, Cotton Tree Drive, which is a major highway, has very little in the way of pedestrian facilities. As we head up Cotton Tree Drive, on our right is the Victoria Peak Tram Terminus. The Peak Tram, whose construction we owe to a Scottish railway engineer, goes up a 45-degree incline to the top. Just ahead of us is on Garden Road are the Botanical and Zoological Gardens, which you may want to walk through when you have more time. These gardens contain many tropical varieties of plants, some of which are over 100 years old.

(CD1 Track 12) Number 2

Before entering the grounds of El Escorial, I would like to explain a few features, some of which may surprise you. The Monastery of San Lorenzo de El Escorial is a gigantic parallelogram which has four towers of 55 meters at each corner. It is covered by slate columns, on top of which are large metal globes with a weather vane and a cross. On the eastern side of the building, in the center, protrudes the upper part of the temple and the rooms of Philip the II's Palace. Also projecting above the building are the twin bell towers and the

magnificent dome of the temple, which reaches a height of 92 meters. In the building, the greater part of which is of Doric style and fashioned in granite, 9 towers rise up, and there are 15 cloisters, 16 patios, 88 fountains, 86 staircases, more than 1200 doors, and 2600 windows, all of which produce a dramatic display.

(CD1 Track 13) Number 3

Welcome to the Getty Center, which is lodged in the beautiful foothills of the Santa Monica Mountains! Today we will explore this scenic place designed by Richard Meier, who is famous for his contributions to architectural Modernism. All of you have just ridden up the hill on the tram, which was designed to make visitors feel "elevated out of their day-to-day experience." I hope you feel this way as we walk up toward the museum entrance on the travertine beneath your feet, a stone which was mined and transported from Italy. We will then take some time looking at the varied displays of paintings, sculptures, and artifacts within the museum itself. From here we will move on to the Museum Courtyard, which features a beautiful 120-foot fountain and then on to the Central Garden, which gradually circles downward to a magnificent round pool. Finally, the view to the south is a favorite for visitors, some of whom will see the panoramic view of Los Angeles for the first time. I hope you will give yourself some time to take pictures from this sight at the end of the tour. Well, let's get started!

(CD1 Track 14) Unit 10, Page 193, Activity 1

1. the state to which you would go if you wanted to vacation at Yellowstone National park

2. the date on which sweethearts give each other valentines in the U.S.

3. the California city in which the Golden Gate Bridge is located

4. one of the months during which people born under the zodiac sign of Capricorn celebrate their birthday

5. the reason for which Americans celebrate Memorial Day

6. the way in which you would spell the last name of the first President of the United States

7. the reason you would buy a jack to put in your car

8. the way in which you pronounce the state that the city of Chicago is in

9. the kind of store to which you would go to get a prescription filled

10. a reason for which you would call a hotline

11. the century in which Alexander Graham Bell invented the telephone

12. a country in which there are a lot of kangaroos and koala bears

13. the state in which you would find the Pittsburgh Pirates baseball team in their home stadium

14. the reason for which some roads have a double yellow line down the center

15. the day on which American children go trick or treating

16. the way in which you would get help from a telephone operator if you needed it while making a phone call

17. the country to which you would go to visit the Giza Pyramids

18. the month during which most U.S. schools have their graduation ceremonies

19. the reason for which you would multiply $\frac{1}{2}$ the base times the perpendicular height of a triangle

20. the way in which you would spell the abbreviation for the National Organization for Women

(CD1 Track 15) Unit 11, Page 206, Activity 1

Advisor: Welcome to New World Alternative College. My name is Ms. Sims and I'll be your college advisor for the next two years.

Student: It's nice to meet you. I've been looking forward to getting into this school for many years. I guess it would be a good idea to know how to get out of the school as well! (*Chuckle*)

Advisor: To begin, I'd like you to look at the required and elective courses listed at the top of your Student Information Sheet. As we discuss your choices, I will write them down on your study plan. Is that all right?

Student: Sounds great to me!

Advisor: I would like to schedule you for four classes each semester so that you can complete your degree in two years. In order to take any humanities or environmental studies courses, you must take an English composition prerequisite and a life science prerequisite, respectively. I always like to have students do this during their first semester. Which English course would you like to take? It can be either Expository Writing or Technical Writing. For life sciences, you can take either Psychology or Biology.

Student: I'd like to take Expository Writing and Psychology during my first semester.

Advisor: Good. Now you have several choices for your two other courses during the first semester. I think it is good to get a firm grounding in math early on. Not only General Mathematics but also Computer Science is offered during fall semester only. Why not take one of these?

Student: OK. I took both algebra and trigonometry in high school. I would prefer taking Computer Science because I will learn something new.

Advisor: Great idea! Well, this semester seems to be a little heavy. Why not take one of your electives? Neither U.S. History nor World History is offered in the fall, so your only option is either Chinese or French.

Student: I guess I'd like to try French.

Advisor: Good, we are moving along nicely. Let's go on to spring semester. Not only World History but also U.S. History is offered in the spring. Would you like to take one of these?

Student: Yes, I would. I'd like to take World History. I'd also like to take both of my social science requirements in the spring.

Advisor: Oh, I'm sorry to tell you that neither Economics nor Geography is offered in the spring; however, both Anthropology and Communication Studies are.

Student: OK. Let's go for those. I guess I can choose one more class for this semester. What would you suggest?

Advisor: Why not take one of your environmental studies courses? Either the Greenhouse Effect or Air Pollution is a good course to begin with in this area.

Student: I think I'll choose the Greenhouse Effect.

Advisor: Great! Well, we have completed your plan for Year 1. Let's move on to your second year. You have completed not only your prerequisite English and life science courses but also your social science and other mathematics requirements. Why not take both of your humanities requirements for a change of pace?

Student: Is Linguistics one of the options?

Advisor: Yes, either Linguistics, Philosophy, or Religious Studies.

Student: I am not very interested in religion, so I guess I'll take both Linguistics and Philosophy.

Advisor: OK. Now, let's see. You still need to choose two physical science courses. Either Astronomy or Physics is offered every semester, but Geology is offered in the spring only.

Student: Oh, I'd like to take both Astronomy and Geology. Please put me down for Astronomy in the fall and Geology in the spring.

Advisor: For the fall term, you still need to select one of your environmental studies courses. I would highly recommend either

Air Pollution or Endangered Wildlife.

Student: Air pollution it will be!

Advisor: Now for the spring we already have you down for Geology. You must take Biology, your last life sciences requirement, and two of the following courses: Garbage Disposal, Hazardous Waste, or Acid Rain.

Student: I would like to take Acid Rain and either Garbage Disposal or Hazardous Waste. What can you tell me about these two courses?

Advisor: Garbage Disposal and Hazardous Waste, respectively, take local and global perspectives on the whole garbage problem. Are you more interested in the concerns of your own community or across the world?

Student: I guess for now, I'm more interested in the problems at home and will take Garbage Disposal. Thanks for that advice!

Advisor: Well, it looks as if we are finished with your study plan. I've enjoyed speaking with you today. Don't forget to stop by sometime either to visit or to discuss questions or problems.

Student: Thank you, Ms. Sims. I will!

(CD1 Tracks 16, 17) Unit 12, Page 236, Activity 1

(CD1 Track 16) Version 1

There once was a young man named Narcissus who was so handsome that all of the beautiful nymphs in the forest wanted to be with him from the moment they saw him. But Narcissus rejected all of them, breaking their hearts. Even the fairest of the nymphs, whose name was Echo, could not win Narcissus' heart. Echo was a favorite of Artemis, the goddess of the hunt. However, it happened that Echo made Hera, the queen of the goddesses, very angry one day and Hera punished her by never allowing her to use speech again except to repeat what was said to her. And so Echo followed Narcissus, unable to speak to him except to echo his words. One day Narcissus was calling to his friends and said "Is anyone here?" Echo called back "Here, here!" Narcissus then yelled "Come" and Echo, repeating him, responded "Come" and jumped out from her hiding place with her arms outstretched. But when he saw her, he proclaimed, "No, I will die before I give you power over me" and went on his cruel way. Echo retreated to a cave in shame, where she wasted away in sorrow until only her voice was left. But shortly after his meeting with Echo, another maiden who had been scorned by Narcissus made this prayer to the gods: "May he who loves not others love only himself." Nemesis, who was the god of righteous anger, heard this prayer and determined to bring about the request. And so one afternoon, when Narcissus bent over a pool of water to get a drink, he saw his own reflection and fell in love with it. He realized why everyone else was so in love with him, and he burned with a love for himself. But Narcissus knew he could never reach the beauty that he saw, because it was himself, and that only death would set him free. So he pined away at the edge of the pool gazing at his reflection until he died. Echo was there but she could only repeat Narcissus' words to himself: "Farewell, farewell," as he died. Although Narcissus had scorned all of the nymphs, they were kind to him in death and went looking for his body for burial. But in the place where he had lain gazing at himself a new and beautiful flower was blooming, so they named it Narcissus.

(CD1 Track 17) Version 2

The lovely nymph Echo lived a carefree life until one day she saw the handsome Narcissus as he was hunting in the forest. She immediately fell deeply in love with him and, when he did not return her love, she became very upset. In her despair, she implored Venus, the goddess of love, to punish Narcissus by making him suffer the pain of love that is not returned. Then Echo wandered off to the mountains where she pined away until nothing was left but her voice. The gods, seeing this, were displeased with Echo's lack of pride. To punish her, they condemned her to haunt rocks and solitary places, and, as a warning to other maidens, to repeat the last sounds which fell on her ear. Only Venus remembered poor Echo's last prayer and waited for a chance to punish the scornful Narcissus. One afternoon, after hunting, Narcissus hurried to a lonely pool to get a drink. When he knelt over the pool to quench his thirst, he suddenly paused. Near the bottom of the pool he saw a face so fair that he immediately lost his heart, for he thought it belonged to a water nymph who was gazing up at him. With great passion, he reached toward the vision, but the moment he touched the water the lovely face disappeared. When the agitated waters became mirrorlike again, the beautiful face, with curly locks, ruby lips, and anxious eyes staring up at him, reappeared. As Narcissus addressed what he thought was a water nymph, she appeared to be answering, but he could hear no sound. Again he tried to reach through the water to her and again she disappeared. Hopelessly in love, Narcissus repeated his attempts to reach the nymph, who continued to gaze back with intense longing but who could never be touched. And so Narcissus lingered day after day at the pool, without eating and drinking, until he died, never suspecting that the nymph was himself reflected in the water. Thus, Echo was avenged. But the gods took pity on the beautiful corpse by the side of the pool and changed it into a flower bearing his name. Since that time the narcissus flower has flourished near quiet pools.

(CD2 Tracks 1, 2) Unit 13, Page 258, Activity 1

(CD2 Track 1) Conversation 1

A: Hello.
B: Hello, Mei? This is Lin calling. Do you have a minute?
A: Sure. What's up?
B: Well, I'm kinda upset. I got my first essay back from my composition instructor this morning and I got a D.
A: Oh no!
B: Yeah, I had no idea my paper was that bad! So at the end of class, when I was walking out, the instructor must have noticed I was upset 'cause she asked me if anything was wrong. And I said Oh it's nothing 'cause I couldn't think of what to say. I mean, it was a final grade for the paper so I can't change it and it would've sounded pretty silly to tell her I was bummed out about my grade. So what was I supposed to say?

(CD2 Track 2) Conversation 2

E: Good afternoon. Consolidated Airlines Customer Service, this is Mario Perez speaking. How may I help you?
C: Mr. Perez, I'm calling about a problem I had with your airline on a vacation I took last week. I was flying from Dallas to Miami and I didn't want to check my luggage so I brought it with me to the gate.
E: Uh huh . . . .

C: Well, when I tried to board the plane, they told me that my luggage was too big to store in the overhead bins and that it would need to be checked separately. As it turned out, they checked the luggage on a later flight than the one I came in on. When I got to Miami I had no idea that the luggage wouldn't be on my plane so I wasted my time at the baggage claim.

E: Oh, I'm sorry. . . . The policy for . . .

C: Then when I found out it was on another plane, I couldn't wait for it, so I had to drive 15 miles back to the airport the next day just to get my luggage.

(CD2 Track 3) Unit 14, Page 278, Activity 1

Who has not wished at some time for a photographic memory? It seems that this would be a great asset for recalling all the things we've worked so hard to learn in school as well as remembering our past experiences. In fact, however, a perfect memory is not the wonderful thing we might suppose. All in all, as I will explain, some things are better forgotten.

In the late 1960s, the Soviet psychologist Alexander Luria described a journalist (we'll call him "S" as Dr. Luria did) who had an amazing ability to remember giant grids of numbers and long lists of words after seeing them for just a few seconds. If you tried any of the short-term memory experiments in Unit 4 of *Grammar Dimensions 4*, you know how difficult this is to do. Even after a passage of 15 years, this man could reproduce the number grids and word lists both forwards and backwards. This ability did not come naturally, though. S. developed a variety of memory tricks to accomplish his feats; many of them involved forming visual images to recall the information. At first, this helped to impress other people with his recall abilities. Later, however, he could not forget. The images kept coming into his mind and

distracting him. It made him unable in some cases to carry on a conversation; in fact, Luria described him as "rather dull-witted." Finally, images began to interfere so much with S's ability to concentrate that he had to quit his profession; he supported himself by traveling from place to place as a performer, demonstrating his unusual recall abilities.

If you think about it, there are a number of problems that could result from a perfect memory. First of all, every time you remembered the past, you would not only remember all the good things, but also the negative aspects that you'd probably just as soon forget. We all have relationships that are probably better off because we have selectively forgotten some negative experiences. Would you really want to remember every painful experience, every angry argument, every embarrassing episode? Secondly, the act itself of remembering might take hours instead of minutes. A third problem might be the difficulty you'd have to organize all the information in your mind. Think of the clutter!

In short, a certain amount of forgetting is beneficial to our survival and our sanity.

(CD2 Tracks 4, 5) Unit 15, Page 297, Activity 1

(CD2 Track 4) Passage 1: How to Prevent Insomnia

Have you ever had trouble trying to get to sleep? The inability to sleep when you are tired is called insomnia. Some people have chronic insomnia—that is, they often find themselves unable to sleep. Other people experience insomnia once in a while due to changes in lifestyle, illness, or other stressful situations. If you are temporarily troubled by insomnia, here are a few tips to help you: First, if you didn't get much sleep during the previous night, don't try to oversleep the next night to make up for it. It is important to get up at the same time each morning so that your body's inner clock is set for a regular time to get up. Another thing you might try is a light snack before you go to bed. People on a diet often have trouble getting to sleep because they are

hungry. They would probably benefit greatly from a nighttime treat, according to Dr. Michael Stevenson, director of an insomnia clinic. A third way to combat insomnia is to stop worrying about getting enough sleep. You don't necessarily need eight hours of sleep to feel good the next day.

Now you will hear three statements. Choose the one that accurately paraphrases information from Passage 1:

a. Don't oversleep even if you didn't get enough sleep the night before.

b. Eat a light snack at bedtime only if you are not dieting.

c. You should worry about getting enough sleep only if you don't get eight hours every night.

(CD2 Track 5) Passage 2: How to Prevent Sports Injuries

In one recent year, American hospitals recorded almost three million injuries that could be attributed to sports and recreation. Many sports injuries can be prevented with a little care and common sense. One important rule for preventing injury is to pay attention to pain messages. If your body starts to hurt, it is telling you to stop. But there are some measures you can take to prevent pain and injury in the first place. Warming up before you participate in sports, even if it is only for ten minutes, is one way to reduce injuries. Warming up can consist of a brisk walk followed by stretching. Conditioning is also important for sports. This consists of building muscle strength and flexibility. Many athletic trainers recommend weight training for all sports as it helps to develop good movement ability. In addition to warming up, cooling down is a crucial part of exercising.

Especially after you have finished a strenuous activity, you need to return to a resting state gradually with moderate movement such as walking. It is dangerous to sit down or stand still directly after vigorous exercise, according to Steve Farrell, a research scientist. Farrell says that a failure to cool down after such exercise could result in a heart attack or even death in some cases.

Now you will hear three statements. Choose the one that accurately paraphrases information from Passage 2:

a. You should warm up for a sport only if it is strenuous exercise.

b. Unless you want to develop large muscles, weight training is not usually recommended for conditioning.

c. Even if you are very tired, you should always keep moving for a short time after vigorous exercise rather than stopping.

(CD2 Track 6) Unit 16, Page 311, Activity 1

Example for Steps 1 and 2: Swish, zoom, zoom. The propeller turning and engine roaring, the plane is ready for takeoff. The pilot radios the control tower for permission to move toward the runway. You are going for your first ride in a small plane. Your heart pounds as the wheels leave the ground, and you clutch your seat more tightly. Ascending higher and higher, you see nothing but white fog in every direction. Finally, the fog clears and you are astounded at the sight below.

1. Hiking for hours, you feel exhausted. Your mouth is dry and sweat is running down your forehead. You thought for sure you would be there by now. Hadn't they said to take the trail up to Conrad's peak and then head eastward for two miles? Shouldn't you be there by now? Sitting down, you lean back on a dusty rock and take a swig of water from your canteen. You close your eyes momentarily, but you are awakened by a sound off to your right.

2. You have awakened suddenly. Looking at your clock on your nightstand, you see that it is 3:25 A.M. The air is cool and you hear a soft rustling below your bedroom window. Could someone be trying to get into your house? Or is it just the large leaves and twigs falling

loudly to the pavement below in the dead of night? Feeling too afraid to sleep, you decide to get up to investigate.

3. Everything is almost ready. Decorated with banners and signs, the auditorium looks welcoming. Volunteers have already put out more than 200 seats, arranged neatly in rows. The microphone stands ready for the heavy use it will receive. The noise level grows louder and louder. Suddenly, a woman appears on stage.

4. Having heard about the disaster, you were not sure what to expect. Piling supplies in the back of your van, you thought about the problems ahead. Would you be able to get there in time? Would you have the skills and knowledge to be of help? Being a professional, you knew your limitations. You stepped on the gas pedal and drove for hours it seemed. Finally, you reached what you had been looking for.

5. The village is awake and bustling. Standing on the corner, a woman tries to sell handmade baskets of various sizes. Calling for customers, an artist points to his three latest landscapes. An intellectual-looking man sits on his front porch reading a newspaper. Holding a baby in her arms, a woman crosses the street. But what captures your attention is the two children.

(CD2 Track 7) Unit 17, Page 328, Activity 1

Contributions of John F. Kennedy on Policies in the U.S. and Abroad

In 1960 John F. Kennedy of Massachusetts was elected President of the United States. Kennedy's administration was **known for** promoting programs which would protect human rights in the U.S. and

abroad. In the U.S., he **united with** Americans of all colors and religions by issuing an executive order which would allow all people equal access to government employment. Also a minimum wage bill was adopted which resulted in a raise of $.25 per hour (from $1.00 to $1.25) for interstate commerce workers. The elderly were happy about the Social Security Act of 1961 which increased old-age benefits and permitted the retirement age to be 62.

Regarding school segregation, it was during Kennedy's administration that the first university, the University of Mississippi, was forced to admit the first black student. Kennedy's administration made many attempts to develop international cooperation for peace. Many men and women enlisted in the Peace Corps to serve the world's underdeveloped countries. Volunteers cooperated with local technicians to build roads in Tanganyika, Africa. The U.S. also joined with Canada and 18 European nations to form the Organization for Economic Cooperation and Development. Latin Americans were enthusiastic about the Latin American Aid Bill of $600 million which became effective in 1962. On the strength of the space programs of the U.S. and Russia, the two nations consulted with each other and decided to establish a cooperative program of space exploration.

John F. Kennedy contributed to many positive causes. It is difficult to know how many other good things he would have succeeded in doing if he had not been assassinated on November 22, 1963.

(CD2 Track 8) Unit 18, Page 349, Activity 1

One of the longest and most expensive murder trials in Texas history involved the multimillionaire T. Cullen Davis. Cullen Davis was the son of Kenneth W. Davis, known as "Stinky Davis," who made his millions in the oil boom of the 1920s. Cullen inherited much of this money after his father died.

As a young man, Cullen was not very conspicuous in public life. He had no accomplishments in high school, he dressed and acted conservatively, and he did not converse easily. This all changed when he met his second wife, Priscilla Wilborn.

Priscilla was a handsomely figured platinum blond. She had been married twice and had born three children before she met Cullen. She was not from a well-off family and did not even graduate from high school. But, she did have a lively personality and wore racy clothing: cowboy boots, skin-tight hot pants, and bikini tops.

As a monument to their new life together, Cullen built a $6 million house on a 181-acre estate that Cullen's father had bought 30 years before. All seemed fairly well until Priscilla claimed that Cullen's violence had caused him to break her collarbone. He also beat her teenage daughter Dee and hurled her daughter's kitten against the kitchen floor and killed it.

Priscilla and Cullen were separated in July 1974. Priscilla stayed in the mansion while Cullen moved out. While waiting for the divorce, she entertained various characters at the mansion, from motorcycle bikers, construction workers, and alleged drug peddlers, some with criminal records. She claimed that she only did this to rehabilitate them. On the afternoon of August 2nd, a hearing on the divorce ended in the judge granting Priscilla an increase in support payments and $42,000 from Cullen to pay for her attorney fees.

That same evening a horrible tragedy followed. Priscilla and a boyfriend returned from a party and discovered Priscilla's 12-year-old daughter murdered. Her story revealed that her former husband, Cullen, dressed all in black and wearing a woman's wig stepped out and had both of his hands covered in a plastic garbage bag. In his hands he carried a revolver. She then claimed that he said "hi" to her and then shot her in the chest. Following this, he shot her boyfriend from behind a door and killed him. When Priscilla tried to run and escape outside the house, Beverly Bass and her friend "Bubba" Gavel were driving up the driveway. When they came to her aid, Cullen is reported to have turned and shot Bubba with a shot that ultimately paralyzed him.

The next day the police located Cullen at home and found four handguns in his car. However, none of the handguns matched the murder weapon. Cullen was charged with murder and trespassing and spent a year in jail before the case was decided. Because he had a lot of money, he hired the best criminal lawyer in Texas—Richard "Racehorse" Haynes. Much money was spent in pretrial investigations. Haynes tried to discredit all of the witnesses in the crime, especially Priscilla who had been known to associate with some "undesirable" people. Money was also spent in investigating potential jurors for the case.

In the closing argument of the trial, "Racehorse" Haynes tried to argue that Priscilla's reputation discredited her as a witness. Prosecutors for the case pleaded that Priscilla's character had nothing to do with the question of whether Cullen had committed murder or not. In the end, the jury deliberated just over four hours before arriving at the verdict of not guilty. After the trial, jurors admitted that they did not necessarily believe that Cullen was innocent, but they could not pronounce him guilty beyond a reasonable doubt.

(CD2 Tracks 9, 10, 11, 12) Unit 19, Page 370, Activity 1

(CD2 Track 9) Message 1

Hi, this is Patricia O'Connell calling. I'm having a party to celebrate the end of summer session and I hope you can come. It'll be on Saturday, the 25th of July, starting around seven at my house. Let me know if you can make it. You can reach me at 555-8533.

(CD2 Track 10) Message 2

Hi, it's Ray. I can't remember when you said you were getting back from your trip. Just calling to see if you got the birthday present I sent in the mail last week. Hope you like it. Anyway, give me a call when you get a chance.

(CD2 Track 11) Message 3

Hi, it's Immouna. I just wanted to let you know that I did find the books you needed for your project when

I was at the library a few days ago, so I checked them out and brought them home with me. You can pick them up at my house whenever you want. If I'm not going to be here, I could leave them on the porch. Give me a call when you get back from your vacation. Hope you had a great time.

(CD2 Track 12) Message 4

Hello, this is Mr. Liu at the Student Services office. We've just finished reviewing our applications and interviews for the part-time administrative assistant position, and you were the top candidate. We would like to offer you the position. It would start on August 15th. Please let us know as soon as possible if you are interested in accepting our offer. You can leave me a message at 555-7269 any time.

(CD2 Tracks 13, 14, 15, 16, 17) Unit 20, Page 381, Activity 1

(CD2 Track 13) 1. (*Conversation between friends*)

Student 1: Did you know that crazy guy, Tom Barker, will be going to Harvard next year?
Student 2: No, how can he afford it?
Student 1: He got a $50,000 scholarship from one of the local service clubs.

(CD2 Track 14) 2. (*Lecturette*)

Human beings and animals have existed side by side since the dawn of history. More often than not, however, human beings have dominated animals. This does not mean that they have not admired or even revered animals for their intelligence, beauty, loyalty, and strength. But it does mean that they have generally been willing to kill animals in order to feed or clothe themselves.

(CD2 Track 15) 3. (*Interview*)

Student Professor, tell us how Los Angeles ranks against the rest of the nation in terms of charity.
Professor Well, the prognosis is not good. Los Angeles ranks near the bottom of all U.S. cities in

per-capita giving. The hard facts are that half of all private giving goes to churches and synagogues for basic upkeep. Little to none transfers from the rich to the needy. By 2015, starvation, homelessness, illness, and death in Los Angeles County could resemble the conditions during the Great Depression.

(CD2 Track 16) 4. (*Newscast*)

Breaking News. A unique fossil was discovered last week in the sands of Mongolia's Gobi Desert. Scientists discovered a fossilized rock of a carnivorous dinosaur nesting on its eggs like a bird. This is the first time anyone has learned anything about how the Earth's most fearsome parent may have tenderly cared for its young.

(CD2, Track 17) 5. (*Conversation*)

Student 1: I just bought a new laptop.
Student 2: That's great. I wish I could afford one. Does it have Wi-Fi and Bluetooth capabilities?
Student 1: It sure does. It also has a gigabyte of RAM and can burn DVDs.

(CD2 Track 18) Unit 21, Page 396, Activity 1

Student 1: Thank you for allowing us to interview you today. We are seniors at May Valley High School and would like to know how students are actually admitted to the university.

Admissions Officer: Well, I'm happy to inform you about this. Now's the time to ask these questions—before you graduate from high school. In selecting students we look at two main things, your college entrance test scores and your GPA, or grade point average.

Student 2: My parents were immigrants to this country and I didn't have the best schools in my neighborhood. How can I pass the exams? How can I go to the university?

Admissions Officer: Well, that reminds me of another important point. Students who are economically disadvantaged can sometimes be admitted with a lower GPA or college entrance exam score than the other candidates. The reason for this, I think, is many of these students not only have had to work hard at their studies, but also they have had heavy family responsibilities, like babysitting, caring for the sick, translating maybe for loved ones, or taking on extra jobs. Special federal and state programs have been set aside to help these students get admitted to the university and pay their tuition.

Student 1: Does it make any difference how you get a high GPA?

Admissions Officer: Good question. If you have a high GPA only because you have done well in nonacademic subjects like PE, woodshop, auto mechanics, etc., then that could hurt you. We normally throw those courses out from the start and look carefully at your college prep English, math, and science class.

Student 1: Are those the only things you consider—how about a student's involvement in student organizations on campus. For example, I am the editor of the school newspaper. Will that help?

Admissions Officer: It can only help in a split decision about a candidate. If a student's test scores and GPA are borderline, then supplementary criteria might be considered like involvement in clubs, athletic teams, debate teams, and that kind of thing.

Student 2: Are you the only one who makes the decision about future students?

Admissions Officer: No, I am only one of a 15-member team who considers all of the evidence in order to make a decision. As you can see, the decision is always made very carefully.

Student 2: And fairly, it seems. Thank you very much for your time.

Student 1: Yes, thanks very much.

Admissions Officer: You're welcome. Thank you. I hope to see your applications coming through anytime now. Good luck in your studies!

(CD2 Track 19) Unit 22, Page 404, Activity 1

Dr. Laura: OK, we're ready for our first caller. What's you name, and what's your problem?

Caller 1: Uh, hi, my name is Sally. Um you know, my husband just lost his job and we're really strapped for money. Um, but the worst part is that (*breath*), you know, he's . . . he's home all the time. He's really getting on my nerves and I don't know what . . .

Dr. Laura: Uh, listen, Sally. You married your husband—for better, for worse, it doesn't matter if he's getting on your nerves. You should stay with him and help him.

Caller 1: Well, wha . . . how? I mean, should I take another job? Uh well . . .

Dr. Laura: Well, that might help him, but I think most of all you should encourage him, help him get through the tough times.

Caller 1: But he's a pain in the neck!

Dr. Laura: OK. Thank you very much Sally. Next caller.

Caller 2 Hi, this is David. Um, this is really embarrassing. I'm supposed to get married in three weeks and I'm . . . I'm not getting cold feet—.

Dr. Laura: That's embarrassing?

Caller 2: No, that's not the embarrassing part. Um, it's not that I'm getting cold feet, it's just that I'm suddenly realizing that my fiancé and I have nothing in common. She—

Dr. Laura: Uh, do you love your fiancé?

Caller 2: Well, yeah. I wouldn't . . . I wouldn't have proposed to her if I didn't love her.

Dr. Laura: I see, but you have nothing in common.

Caller 2: No, it's scary—

Dr. Laura: I think you've got a conflict here and I think you should take some time. I think you need to think things over.

Caller 2: You think I should postpone?

Dr. Laura: Yes, I do.

Caller 2: That so embarrassing, all of the invitations are out—

Dr. Laura: I think you need to get . . . I think you need to get to know your girlfriend a little bit better before you propose. I don't think you've taken enough time to think about this.

Caller 2: OK. Thank you.

Dr. Laura: You're welcome.

(CD2 Track 20) Unit 23, Page 416, Activity 1

How to Create a Good Advertisement

Today I'd like to give some helpful hints about creating a good advertisement for your own company or store.

Every good advertisement needs just three main ingredients. First, the ad should include information about the product and its unique advantage. Next, don't razzle-dazzle your prospective customers but do give a clear statement of the information. Do respect your audience by giving a straight and simple message. Finally, do give a unique presentation. The first two ingredients make an ad good. The third one makes it great.

Now let's discuss three important features of an ad. First, do pay attention to the headline that you give to your ad. Always present features in terms of reader benefits. You do want to induce reader interest and stimulate further reading of the advertisement. Believe it or not, simplicity always wins. Don't be tricky. I recommend that you include no teasers, rhymes, double meanings, coined words, or humor because this really can confuse the customer.

The next consideration is the illustrations. Your illustration does need to capture the attention of the prospect. It does need to create a favorable impression of the product and clearly identify the subject being sold. Do make sure that the picture, drawing, or photo emphasizes any unique characteristics of the product in a positive light.

Finally, we turn to the body copy. The words in the body copy are very important because they are used to interest, inform, involve, help, convince, persuade, and induce a response from your audience. And we all know what that response does need to be: BUY, BUY, BUY, of course.

(CD2 Tracks 21, 22) Unit 24, Page 437, Activity 1

(CD2 Track 21) Passage 1: *Pollyanna*

This movie, based on a novel, tells the story of a young girl named Pollyanna during the first decade of the twentieth century. Since Pollyanna's parents have died, leaving her an orphan, she goes to live with her Aunt Polly, a wealthy woman in a small town. The town is filled with pessimistic people who tend to see the negative side of everything. Pollyanna, on the other hand, sees the good in every situation. Because of Pollyanna's charm, the townspeople are eventually won over by her cheerful optimism, and they, too, try to look for the positive in events that occur, even when unfortunate things happen. According to Yale law professor Stephen L. Carter, the film *Pollyanna* defines the American character because it "captures the American belief in the future as good and the individual as important." He also notes the values of American capitalism it embraces. Pollyanna's rich aunt, who owns everything in town, gets to keep all her property but learns the social obligations that accompany great wealth. Never have Americans hated the rich, claims Carter, but only envied them and wanted them to be nice.

(CD2 Track 22) Passage 2: *Mr. Smith Goes to Washington*

Another film that reflects America's belief that one person can make a difference is *Mr. Smith Goes to Washington*. The theme of this movie, made in 1939, is that evil will triumph unless good people take action, and that the American political system works because, in fact, good people will not let it fail. In this film, not until an innocent young man arrives in Washington does political corruption stop. That man, Mr. Jefferson Smith, has been selected by the corrupt politicians to replace a deceased senator. They think he will unknowingly go along with a dishonest scheme that will put money in their pockets. When Mr. Smith goes to Washington, he believes that all politicians have the same unselfish goals that he has to help the American people. He comes to see that his idealistic views of the system are unrealistic, and he then sets out to expose the corrupt politicians who are trying to destroy the integrity of the government. Mr. Smith succeeds in his goal and the system is saved.

(CD2 Track 23) Unit 25, Page 455, Activity 1

1. What color do you get when you mix the colors yellow and blue? (c.)

   Is it . . . a. purple? b. brown? c. green?

2. In what body of water would you find sharks? (c.)

   Would it be . . . a. in a lake? b. in a river? c. in an ocean?

3. Who wrote the following symphony? (b.)

   Was it . . . a. Bach? b. Beethoven? c. Brahms?

4. Which of the following American cities is most known for its rainy weather? (a.)

   Is it . . . a. Seattle? b. Miami? c. Minneapolis?

5. What part of the body separates the chest from the lower part of the torso? (c.)

   Is it . . . a. the stomach? b. the trachea? c. the diaphragm?

6. In what sport is a puck used? (b.)

   Is it . . . a. in football? b. in hockey? c. in soccer?

7. Which of the following is a bone disease that afflicts elderly people? (c.)

   Is it . . . a. halitosis? b. thrombosis? c. osteoporosis?

8. Which word describes an excessive or illogical fear of high places? (b.)

   Is it . . . a. photophobia? b. acrophobia? c. claustrophobia?

9. What does the *m* in the physics formula mc² stand for? (c.)

   Is it . . . a. molecule? b. matter? c. mass?

10. Who invented the light bulb? (c.)

    Was it . . . a. George Westinghouse? b. Rudolph Diesel? c. Thomas Edison?

11. What body part does the medical prefix *cardio* refer to? (c.)

    Is it . . . a. the lungs? b. the stomach? c. the heart?

12. Listen to the following song. What is being played? (a.)

    a. "The Star-Spangled Banner"
    b. "America the Beautiful"
    c. "Hymn to America"

13. What does the abbreviation I.Q. stand for? (b.)

    a. Intelligent question?
    b. Intelligence quotient?
    c. Intellectual quota?

14. If you have just read the prologue of a play, which part did you read? (a.)

    a. The beginning? b. The middle? c. The end?

15. In what popular board game do you buy hotels, railroads and utility companies? (b.)

    Is it . . . a. Risk? b. Monopoly? c. Go?

16. Listen to the following music. What musical instrument is being played? (c.)

    Is it . . . a. a saxophone? b. a violin? c. a clarinet?

17. In what field would you study if you wanted to learn about sedimentology? (b.)

    Would you study . . . a. physics? b. geology? c. linguistics?

18. In what continent would you find the Amazon basin? (c.)

    Is it . . . a. Asia? b. North America? c. South America?

GRAMMAR DIMENSIONS 4 LESSON PLANNER

S-14